'Solitary and Wild'

Frederick MacNeice
and the Salvation of Ireland

... A square black figure whom the horizon understood –
My father. Who for all his responsibly compiled
Account books of a devout, precise routine
Kept something in him solitary and wild ...

from 'The Strand' (1945) by Louis MacNeice

'Solitary and Wild'

Frederick MacNeice
and the Salvation of Ireland

DAVID FITZPATRICK

THE LILLIPUT PRESS
DUBLIN

First published 2012 by
THE LILLIPUT PRESS
62–63 Sitric Road, Arbour Hill
Dublin 7, Ireland
www.lilliputpress.ie

ISBN 978 1 84351 194 6

1 3 5 7 9 10 8 6 4 2

A CIP record for this title is available
from The British Library.

Set in 10.5 pt on 14.5 pt Caslon by Marsha Swan
Printed in England by MPG Books Ltd, Cornwall

Contents

Illustrations

SOURCES

Engravings from the *Banner* and ICM, *Reports*: ICM Office, Dublin; engravings of Ballyconree: *The Story of the Connemara Orphans' Nursery from its Commencement to the Year 1876* (Glasgow, Campbell and Tudhope, 1877), BLL; engravings by Denis O'D. Hanna: George A. Mitchell, Rector, *A Guide to Saint Nicholas' Church, Carrickfergus* (Carrickfergus, 1962), author's collection. Family photographs: CMMC; photograph of effigy of FM: Jane Leonard.

1. His Son's Father

I

'Just another bourgeois liberal, I would have said. Although he was a great Home Ruler, in his day.' Nick laughed. 'Not a popular position for a Protestant clergyman, surely?' 'Carson hated him. Tried to stop him being made bishop.' 'There you are: a fighter.'[1]

This exchange appears in John Banville's melodrama *The Untouchable* (1997), where Victor Maskell (Anthony Blunt's world-weary double agent, incongruously grafted on to Louis MacNeice's Irish roots) discusses his father with Nick, another hybrid figure who turns out to be the Fifth or Sixth Man. Banville's account, though a travesty of what scholars have written about Frederick MacNeice, demonstrates the pervasiveness of his posthumous reputation as an heroic outsider within the 'Black North'. Critics and biographers concur that Louis MacNeice's attitudes towards religion, morality, politics, and above all Ireland, were profoundly influenced by those of his clergyman father. Louis was both attracted and repelled by the unity and humanity of his father's world view, sustained by his serene faith in Christ as peacemaker and reconciler. The rector (later bishop) is almost universally portrayed as a tolerant if puritanical southerner, courageously opposing all forms of sectarianism and violence, abhorring both revolutionary republicanism and Ulster unionism, and supporting Home Rule.[2] Admittedly, Frederick MacNeice's early association with the Society for Irish Church Missions to the Roman Catholics, notorious for its 'aggressive' campaign of proselytism in both Connemara and

Dublin, casts some doubt upon his liberal and non-sectarian credentials. However, it has been surmised that his parents' bruising experience of sectarian conflict while missionary teachers on Omey Island, culminating in the family's fabled flight in 1879, left Frederick (then thirteen years old) with a lifelong detestation of sectarian confrontation and intolerance.[3] His mental world as an adult was that of a liberal Protestant nationalist, fundamentally at odds with the political outlook of his congregations and neighbours in Belfast and Carrickfergus.

Louis MacNeice's supposed childhood experience of alienation within Protestant Ulster is often cited in explaining his youthful repudiation of its values and symbols, his romantic identification with the West of Ireland, and his sympathy with non-violent nationalist and anti-imperialist movements. By this account, while rejecting his father's religion and morality, Louis paradoxically embraced much of his outlook on Ireland and Irish politics. The rector's presumed support for Home Rule is crucial to this widely held analysis of the poet's Irishness and political vision. Yet the supporting evidence is remarkably threadbare, being restricted to assertions by Louis himself, ambiguous utterances by his father in later life, and academic inferences based on possibly misleading extracts from published sermons and addresses. This book will assess the credibility of such interpretations, present fresh evidence indicating a very different political viewpoint, suggest reasons for the subsequent disregard of such evidence, and assess the consequences for our understanding of the poet's Irishness and for our reading of some of his most celebrated works.

The most authoritative testimony to Frederick's nationalism is that of his son, whose imaginative and finely embroidered autobiographical writings have been so widely accepted at face value as a reliable factual source: 'My father was one of the very few Church of Ireland clergymen to be a Home Ruler. This was another reason for despising Co. Antrim and regarding myself as a displaced person. Sometimes this feeling caused an inner conflict in me.'[4] Another passage implies that Frederick's reputation as a Home Ruler was established before 1917, when his second wife was thought 'very daring' for having gone 'so far afield as my father – especially as he was a Home Ruler'.[5] These recollections were written in 1940, two decades after Home Rule had ceased to be a practical option (except for six counties of Ulster), and they reflect the 33-year-old poet's renewed respect for his father and for many aspects of both southern Ireland and Ulster.

It is notable that Louis's numerous evocations of his boyhood give no particular illustrations of his father's nationalism, and that (according to Stallworthy) 'neither his letters home [from preparatory school] nor his parents' letters to him mention the worsening situation in Ireland'.[6] When at home, he appears to have paid little attention to political conversations, for his older sister Elizabeth recalled that 'there was so much talk in the house about Carson and the covenant that he must have heard it though he never in later years seemed to have memory of doing so. Of course, he heard the history of it later on.' In his autobiography, Louis vaguely recalled having 'heard political arguments' before the Great War, which 'were all about Orangemen and Home Rulers'. Elizabeth's punctilious recollections of her parents and brother stop short of attributing nationalism to Frederick, while stating that 'his political opinions differed widely' from those of 'the Northern people whom he served'.[7] Louis was surely a less reliable witness to his father's views. As a child and youth, he was strikingly incurious about most aspects of his father's career and background. At the age of nineteen, when seeking a passport, he knew so little that he had to ask his stepmother (not, significantly, his father) for 'the *date* and *locality* of Daddie's birth'.[8] It is difficult to avoid the conclusion that Louis's account of his father's supposed nationalism was based on adult surmise rather than childhood observation.

It is a curious fact that Frederick MacNeice himself never advocated or endorsed Home Rule in his many published booklets and sermons. As Fauske has guardedly averred, 'MacNeice had gone to Carrickfergus with a reputation as a Home Ruler, a reputation bolstered by his stance against the Covenant, but of his politics he actually said nothing in public throughout his life.'[9] Though not strictly accurate, as we shall show, this assessment highlights the difficulty of defining the political stance of one whose politics were avowedly non-partisan. The only text that has been cited as a direct affirmation of nationalism, as distinct from a disavowal of party politics, is Frederick's historical sketch of Carrickfergus (1928). In retrospect, he considered that 'the extension of the franchise in 1884 made inevitable some form of Home Rule for Ireland', and that subsequent elections 'surely' constituted 'a writing on the wall'. MacNeice went on to dismiss Carson's initial confidence that resistance in Ulster 'could defeat, and not simply delay, the whole Home Rule policy', and to deplore the growing acceptance of partition as the Ulster leaders themselves 'began to think along Nationalist lines'.[10] On the face of it, this analysis demonstrates that Frederick was not merely an opponent of partition, but a pragmatist who accepted, however reluctantly, the necessity for Home Rule. We shall return to the question of whether as a younger man he had indeed, like the prophet Daniel, accurately divined the ominous writing on the wall of Belshazzar's palace, *'mene, mene, tekel, upharsin'*: 'MENE; God hath numbered thy kingdom, and brought it to an end. TEKEL; thou art weighed in the balances, and art found wanting. PERES; thy kingdom is divided, and given to the Medes and the Persians' (Dan. 5: 25–8).

The practical proof of Frederick's nationalism, liberalism and non-sectarianism, as expounded by a distinguished procession of MacNeicians, relates mainly to four episodes: his public repudiation of the Ulster Covenant in September 1912, his espousal of an ecumenical 'League of Prayer for Ireland' between 1920 and 1924, his initiation of a similar campaign in 1935–6 in response to renewed sectarian conflict in Belfast, and his successful resistance in the same period to the government's proposal that the union flag should officiate perpetually over Carson's tomb in St Anne's Cathedral.[11] In each case, scholars have drawn inferences from Frederick's words and actions that are by no means self-evident. Opposition to the Ulster Covenant implied rejection of the threat of violence as a political tool, but not approval of any particular political programme. Collaboration with other Protestant clergymen, in two ecumenical and non-partisan campaigns for reconciliation, was likewise consistent with unionism as well as nationalism. Finally, Frederick's refusal to sanctify Carson's legacy in the form of a flag raises the issue of which aspect of Carson's political career gave offence to his fellow southerner. In order to test the implications of these episodes for our understanding of Frederick MacNeice's politics, we must first re-examine the historical record.

II

The chapters that follow reveal a more complex, equivocal, and formidable figure than the father evoked by his son's writings, and hence by the scholars whom those writings have influenced. In his life's journey from a remote schoolhouse in Connemara to a bishop's mansion on Belfast's Malone Road, Frederick MacNeice faced and overcame many challenges. These included chronic poverty, expulsion from his childhood home, social inferiority as an undergraduate, overwork as a novice clergyman in Belfast, initial hostility from two of his congregations, the fearful suffering and early death of his first wife, the mental incapacity and lifelong dependency of his elder son, the nihilistic rebelliousness of his younger son, resistance in the Church to his daring schemes for regeneration, recurrent public controversy, and the destruction of much of his life's work in the Blitz. Undaunted, he showed remarkable fortitude, patience, political skill, and measured eloquence in negotiating pitfalls and disarming opponents. When confronted by hostile congregations in Belfast and Carrickfergus, he relied on indirect methods to win support. Instead of trying to browbeat sullen loyalists into becoming tolerant, broad-minded evangelicals like himself, he joined Orange and Masonic lodges, accepted office in unionist organizations, and so won the trust of his brethren. Likewise, within the Church of Ireland, his success in redirecting its resources towards working-class Belfast was achieved through cultivating influential Orangemen rather than his liberal but less influential natural allies. At his peak, he seemed an 'awe-inspiring' figure,[12] one of the few clergymen temperamentally and intellectually equipped to confront and conceivably even stem the inexorable tide of secularism. His mission was nothing less than the salvation of Ireland.

Though Frederick's basic precepts remained unshaken by these challenges, his analysis of political and sectarian issues was profoundly modified by the eruption of Ulster militancy in 1912 and, most of all, by the Great War. His magnificent and justly renowned pursuit of internationalism, tolerance and peace made it expedient to obscure his previous immersion in opposition to Home Rule and Rome Rule. Yet even in later life, he remained devoted to the British monarchy, empire and constitution, and hostile to many aspects of Roman Catholicism and Irish nationalism. Without actual falsification of the record, he persuaded many observers, not to mention posterity, that he was and always had been liberal, ecumenical and nationalist in his outlook, and therefore an heroic outsider in Ulster. Louis played a major part in propagating this attractive but deceptive image during the last five years of his father's life and for decades thereafter. By recovering some of the complexities of Frederick's career, Louis's upbringing, and their troubled relationship, it is possible to detect additional layers of meaning in many of Louis's writings. Since this is a biography not merely of a great missionary but also of the father of a celebrated poet, it concludes with a reassessment of Louis MacNeice's multifaceted debt to his father, and new readings of eight poems illuminating his ambivalent family relationships.

In preparing this study, I have had to rely largely on external sources, whether published or in archives. Though a few personal letters, diaries, draft writings and other useful documents survive in several collections of family papers in Oxford and Carrickfergus, these provide only intermittent insight into Frederick's personality or daily life, leaving his first forty years almost undocumented. In reconstructing his career, I have therefore been heavily dependent on the records of institutions such as the Society for Irish Church Missions, Trinity College, Dublin, the parishes and dioceses with which he was connected, and organizations (some of them secretive) to which he belonged. Since his sermons and addresses from 1908 onwards were widely reported in the daily, provincial, and clerical press, I have used this material systematically to amplify the threadbare record provided by his published books and pamphlets. In order to avoid contamination from the very source that I seek to deconstruct, I have been quite abstemious in quoting the many biographical references that appear in Louis MacNeice's published writings. Instead, in the last two chapters, I treat some of these writings as texts rather than sources, setting Louis's accounts against my reading of the historical record. If this exercise contributes something fresh to the study of one of Ulster's foremost writers, my sometimes pedantic burrowings will have been justified.

My first purpose, however, is to reconstruct and contextualize the life of a man remarkable in his own right, whose character and thought were shaped and reshaped by the contrasting influences of a turbulent childhood in Connemara, struggling youth in Dublin and Belfast, and prosperous middle age in Carrickfergus. By the time that he became a bishop at the age of sixty-five, Frederick MacNeice was outwardly unrecognizable as a rough-hewn product of the Irish Church Missions. Yet behind his mask of diffident urbanity and orderly self-control, as his son observed in 'The Strand' (1945), there remained 'something in him solitary and wild'.[13] It is this submerged life force which sets his life apart from that of a conventional Man of God, and which poses the greatest challenge to his biographer. This book, above all, pays tribute to a major, misunderstood figure in the political and spiritual history of Ireland. Only by taking salvation seriously, sinners though we may be, can historians hope to make sense of yesterday's Ulster, Ireland or world.

III

Excerpts from poems by Louis MacNeice are taken from the most recent edition of his *Collected Poems*. Biblical quotations usually follow the Revised Version (1885), that preferred by Frederick. Names of places normally follow the Ordnance Survey, while personal names are regularized according to the most authentic contemporary sources, such as signatures on official documents or letters (variant forms are retained within quotations). The names of the families central to this book raise peculiar complications, variant spellings of surnames being compounded by regular changes in the order of forenames. Frederick McNeice and therefore his children became MacNeice in 1914 (with occasional earlier occurrences). Both spellings are used in this book, according to context. Frederick (Fred, Derrick) began as John and alternated between Frederick J. and John F. on three significant occasions; Eliza became Elizabeth (Lily) in later life, having been known in youth as Margaret; Frederick Louis (Freddie) dropped the patronymic as an adolescent; Caroline Elizabeth (Elsie) seems never to have used her first name, a practice shared with her stepmother Georgina Beatrice (Bea). To reduce the consequent confusion, these characters are normally named, in turn, as Frederick, Lily, Louis, Elizabeth and Beatrice.

Unless otherwise stated, biographical information is derived from a host of works of reference, not normally specified in footnotes. Persons of public standing have been documented through appropriate editions of *Burke's Peerage* and *Landed Gentry*, *Walford's County Families*, *Who's Who*, *Who's Who in Northern Ireland*, *Thom's Irish Who's Who*, *Kelly's Handbook*, *The Oxford Dictionary of National Biography*, and similar compendia. Less prominent figures have been traced through annual issues of *Thom's Directory*, the *Belfast and Province of Ulster Directory*, and family schedules of the Census of Ireland for 1901 and 1911. Material on clergymen of the Church of Ireland is taken from Canon J. B. Leslie's manuscript succession lists in the Representative Church Body Library, many of which have now been revised, extended and published. Details of office-holders in the Orange Order are derived from confidential printed reports of the Grand Orange Lodge of Ireland and the various County Grand Lodges. Information on Masonic careers is taken from the annual *Irish Freemasons' Calendar and Directory* and registers in Freemasons' Hall, Dublin. Trinity College careers have been tracked from the annual *Dublin University Calendars*, published lists of graduates, Burtchaell's and Sadleir's *Alumni Dublinenses*, and manuscript registers in the College Muniments. Biographical footnotes are intended to be suggestive rather than comprehensive. Uncertain dates of birth (usually inferred from subsequent records of age) and death (based on disappearance from registers or directories) are given in italics.

Essential help and access to records were provided by officers and archivists at many institutions, especially Norman Weatherall and Dean Houston McKelvey at St Anne's Cathedral, and David Hume, Jonathan Mattison and David Scott at Schomberg House (Belfast); Barry Lyons and Rebecca Hayes at Freemason's Hall, Andrew Whiteside at St Patrick's Hospital and the Revd Eddie Coulter at the Office of the Society for Irish Church Missions (Dublin); and Judith Priestman at the Bodleian Library (Oxford). Pauline Murphy made available records of the Irish Association. Ian Beggs and James Woodside were kind enough to allow me to consult and cite material in private archives. Further documentary material was consulted at the following institutions: General Register Office, Gilbert Library, National Archives, National Library, Representative Church Body Library and Office, Trinity College Library and Valuation Office (Dublin); Central Library, Linen Hall Library and Public Record Office of Northern Ireland (Belfast); and British Library (London). The writing of this book has been facilitated by a period of leave from many duties at Trinity College, Dublin, by the tolerance of my colleagues in the Department of History, by generous assistance from the Arts and Social Sciences Benefaction Fund and the TCD Association and Trust, and by a grant from the Grace Lawless Lee Fund to allow reproduction of poems by Louis MacNeice. The published work of Louis MacNeice and unpublished papers of the

MacNeice family are cited and quoted by kind permission of David Higham Associates, on behalf of Corinna MacNeice, literary executor of the MacNeice estate.

For advice and guidance in the early stages of preparation, I am deeply grateful to participants in the centennial celebration of Louis MacNeice held at the Queen's University of Belfast in September 2007, especially Jonathan Allison, Terence Brown, Christopher Fauske, Edna Longley, Michael Longley, Canon J. R. B. McDonald, Peter McDonald and Jon Stallworthy. It was this memorable event that induced me to suspend work on a history of the Loyal Orange Institution in order to unravel the career of a reputed 'Protestant Home Ruler' whose name I had long since noted as the chaplain of several Orange districts in Belfast. As a newcomer to the field, I was privileged not only to hear the views of some outstanding scholars, but also to benefit from their generous and open-minded responses to my somewhat iconoclastic conference paper. That paper, portions of which reappear here, was speedily published in *Field Day Review*, 4 (2008), through the kindness of Breandán Mac Suibhne. Sections of the final chapter appeared in *Irish Pages*, v, I (2009).

Valuable advice by letter has since been offered by many others, including John Kerrigan, Miriam Moffitt, Fred Rankin, Corinna MacNeice and Dan MacNeice, who sadly died before I had the opportunity to meet him. Helen Rankin, who recently retired as curator of the Carrickfergus Museum, was exceptionally generous in giving me unrestricted access to the museum's rapidly expanding MacNeice Collection, permitting me to copy and reproduce photographs and documents in that collection, and sharing her extensive knowledge of Carrickfergus and its history. I am particularly grateful to Jonathan Allison for allowing me to consult his magnificent edition of *Selected Letters of Louis MacNeice* (London, Faber, 2010) in advance of publication, and for his encouragement and advice throughout. Edna and Michael Longley, both learned champions of Louis MacNeice as a great Irish and Ulster poet, convinced me that a full-scale biography of his father was worthwhile, and offered inspiration and wisdom as well as practical assistance. Antony Farrell of The Lilliput Press was remarkable for his patience and wry good humour, no matter how many self-imposed deadlines were missed or word-limits exceeded. Fiona Dunne indulged some of my whims without unduly compromising her work as copy-editor.

My deepest debt is to Jane Leonard, who first induced me to study Frederick MacNeice's career and supplied innumerable documents, references, and often arcane information on topics ranging from rugby to war service and beyond. Her factual contribution is so multitudinous that I have been obliged to abbreviate my gratitude by adding the symbols '[JL]' to many of the resultant citations. She also meticulously criticized numerous drafts, excising purple and grey passages alike, and endured two years of relentlessly ecclesiastical and literary talk. In partial recompense for the consequent loss of 'family time', our daughters Julia and Hannah have enjoyed a steady flow of waste paper on which to draw designs more exhilarating than any sermon or critical commentary.

'Reading the Irish Bible to Roman Catholics': ICM, *Report* (1880).

2. Child of the Missions

OMEY, 1866–1879

I

On 18 August 1930, the archdeacon of Connor took his second wife and elder son on a fortnight's motoring holiday in the Irish Free State. As usual, he kept a detailed and methodical diary of the tour.[1] Reaching Maynooth on the second day, he visited the 'R. C. College' but 'did not care for the decoration of the church', finding it 'too florid'. Having dutifully inspected various ancient monuments in the midlands, admired postcard attractions such as the Cliffs of Moher, and observed the slightly improved condition of the Clare peasantry ('few of the people are without shoes or boots'), he reached Clifden in Connemara on the ninth day. There, in the course of lunch at the Railway Hotel, the MacNeices discovered that provision for tourists in the West of Ireland had improved little since Thackeray's devastating account, in *The Irish Sketch Book*, of his visit to Ballinasloe.[2] There were two waiters in tail coats, 'but such a pair of hopeless men I have hardly ever seen'. The menu promised lobster as the sole alternative to soup before the main course of mutton, but after half an hour there was no sign of the local delicacy that his wife Beatrice had innocently ordered: 'We did our best to catch the eye of either waiter. Now and again one of them approached and then returned and had a conversation with his colleague. There were whispers and wise looks and nudges.' The lobster never came; the mutton, when delivered, 'did not look very tempting' and 'was not specially well cooked'; the bill, shockingly, came to six shillings each.

When they eventually found accommodation outside the town, 'everything felt damp: the bedroom was very damp, the walls dripping. However we pulled the bed out as far as possible from the walls and also used our rug under the sheet.' The food, at least, was 'tolerably good'. After further exploration of Connemara, they drove to one of the western extremities of Ireland's Atlantic coast: 'At Streamstown we turned west through Claddaghduff with very fine views of Streamstown Bay and the islands.' Then they turned back, without leaving the mainland.

On the eleventh day, after buying some tweed for his daughter, Frederick MacNeice got his feet wet at last:

> Set out for Omey through Streamstown and Claddaghduff. At Claddaghduff, Bea and I crossed Omey strand, carrying our footwear. It was a wonderful day. We went to the west of the island where there is a very small island which is sometimes accessible by land [Illaunakeegher]. It has most glorious rocks. We had some refreshments. Sheep were being put into a boat for the island of – [?Cruagh]. It was very interesting. Bea tried to get some photographs. ... We drove from Claddaghduff across a road over the bog and west of Sellerna Church. Sellerna Church is a ruin.

Between these sober lines recorded by an Ulster clergyman in his sixty-fifth year, one hears the muffled voice of the boy who had been reared among those rocks and regularly crossed that strand to worship with his family at the Emmanuel Church in Sellerna (from the Irish *Sailearna*, place of sallows or willow beds). The voice of the boy was echoed by his son in 'The Strand', which pictures him, on another island, 'carrying his boots and paddling like a child'.[3]

This was not Frederick MacNeice's first pilgrimage to the island of his birth, which he had explored with Louis three years earlier. That visit is commemorated by a celebrated passage in *The Strings are False*:

> Omey was home-coming too. It is a small roadless island covered with crisp grass and when the tide is out you reach it across the sands. ... My father was trying to make out where his house had been, had discovered a few stones on a knoll exposed to the Atlantic, when a bare-footed weatherbeaten woman came over to him, gripping the rocks with her toes, and said to him, 'Which of them would you be?' The brogue she spoke in was as rich as a pint of stout and she reeled off a list of Christian names. My father told her which he was. Sure she knew he must be one of them, she said, the way he knew the lie of the ground. When the MacNeices went away, she went on (my father had been then about nine), the potatoes had stopped growing on the island and everyone had gone to America.

Louis's account dramatizes his father's emotional responses, so well concealed in Frederick's own more humdrum prose. Thus he cries out 'The sea!' upon first catching sight of the Atlantic, driving the young classicist to a frenzy of temporary empathy. Once on the island, 'his nostalgia would make him walk fast, swinging his stick, and then break off impatiently. "Terribly backward," he would say, "terribly backward".'⁴ To make sense of Frederick MacNeice's nostalgia for Omey Island, we must first examine the meaning and consequences of that backwardness for those, like his parents, who had set out to rectify it.

II

The island of Omey (perhaps from the Irish *Iomaith*, meaning bed) occupies about one square mile, much of it under water, six miles north-west of Clifden. The islanders scratched a living among loose sandy soil, drifting sands, and rocky knolls, dependent for subsistence on small patches of arable and rough grass.⁵ Asenath Nicholson, an American evangelist who walked about the island in May 1845, observed stone huts, mud huts, and 'habitations dug in the sand, as rabbits burrow', without windows or furnishings.⁶ Just after the Famine, most of the remaining islanders still lived in 'huts' that were 'nothing more than holes sunk in the sand', containing no hardware except 'an iron pot for boiling sea-weed collected on the shore, which, with small shell-fish, is their chief, if not only food'.⁷ There were only two houses worthy of description in 1853, one slated but old, the other thatched, deteriorated by age, and in poor repair.⁸ These belonged to the island's two 'lords' or middlemen, the Maddens and the Bodkins, whose genteel pretensions were mocked by the presence of 'calves, pigs, hens, and ducks' in the floorless living quarters.⁹ The middlemen had originally leased their lands from Connemara's two great proprietors, the Martins of Ballinahinch Castle and the D'Arcys of Clifden Castle. Both estates had fallen so heavily into debt that they were auctioned immediately after the Famine by the Court of Incumbered Estates, being for the most part purchased, respectively, by the Law Life Assurance Company and the brothers Eyre from Bath. The auctioneers of the D'Arcy estate assured potential buyers that Omey Island, despite the minuscule current rental, would be a sound investment:

> The Royalties are of considerable value, as much derelict timber is thrown on shore every year; it is also in the immediate vicinity of good fishing ground; and if the inhabitants had only the means, they might make this place valuable as a depôt for curing and drying fish, the island affording shelter to boats from all the prevailing winds.¹⁰

Yet the new owners failed to build roads or piers, and forty years later an inspector for the Congested Districts Board indicated that Omey was not among the islands involved in fishing, fish-curing, or kelp-production. Farming and housing remained primitive throughout the Clifden region. The spade held sway, 'the surface being too rocky and uneven for ploughs and harrows'; seaweed rather than dung was the principal manure; the local cows and sheep badly needed impregnation by Galloway bulls and Scotch black-faced rams; the swine were 'most inferior, great bony long legged beasts, and very difficult to fatten'. In the Sellerna division, including Omey Island, barter was still 'extensively practised; eggs and fish being exchanged for tea, sugar, and tobacco'. The dietary was simple if nutritious, consisting of 'tea and home-made flour bread', along with 'potatoes and fish or eggs' for dinner. The most obvious tokens of poverty, however, were the buildings:

> The houses with walls about six feet high, and roofed with straw or rough sedge, are very small. In many there is only one apartment, but generally the buildings consist of a kitchen and one room. They have no chimney, the fire being laid on the hearth, and a hole made in the roof to allow the smoke to escape. Livestock are always kept in the kitchen during the winter months.[11]

The island itself remained a by-word for backwardness within this backward region. A journalist from the London *Daily News*, who visited it in November 1880, 'had heard wild stories of Omey Island, of troglodytes, hungry dwellers in rocky seaside caves, and rabbit-people burrowing in the sand'. He found no cave-dwellers, but identified a large uninhabited tract of sandbank where people had once 'clung to their stone cabins till the sand finally covered them', whereupon they migrated to neighbouring townlands. Housing remained primitive, even in the case of the 'bettermost' cabins occupied by the middlemen. He found that one of the 'ladies' had acquired an unplayed 'cabinet pianoforte' as 'mute evidence of solvency'; yet her parlour was still overrun by 'chickens, ducks, and geese'. Over in the kitchen, 'the girls were running about with bare feet and dirty faces, and the neighbouring gossips, also bare-footed and dirty beyond all imagination, were hanging round the fire, talking amongst themselves about the stranger'.[12]

In 1841, the island's 62 dwellings contained 397 inhabitants fairly evenly spread between the island's 5 townlands. The immediate demographic effect of the Famine was unusually severe, and only 205 people remained in 35 houses by 1851. The two southern townlands were virtually depopulated, whereas the more accessible northern region proved more resilient. As in much of the impoverished Atlantic fringe, Omey's population recovered somewhat over the next two decades while that of Ireland as a whole inexorably declined. By 1871, the island had 49 occupied houses with 281 inhabitants, after which it too succumbed belatedly to continuous depopulation, sustained by heavy emigration and fuelled by rising economic expectations. Three decades later, the population of Omey's 3 remaining settled townlands, now thoroughly reorganized into separate holdings, had declined to 28 families with 114 members.[13] These changes masked significant local shifts of population, leading to wild fluctuations in every townland except Sturrakeen, home of the Bodkins. The southern townland of Gooreenatinny, seat of the Maddens, was spectacularly repopulated after the Famine, so that 91 people lived there by 1871 compared with 7 in 1851. Cartoorbeg lost almost its entire population in the 1850s yet reversed that trend over the following decade. By contrast, the north-western townland of Gooreen, which had lost little of its population between 1841 and 1861, was utterly empty by 1881. This was probably the abandoned 'sandbank' observed by the correspondent of the *Daily News*. Gooreen's decline is graphically confirmed by the two Ordnance Survey maps prepared in 1839 and 1898. The initial survey recorded a clachan (cluster) of thirteen buildings around the ruined church of Templefehen. By 1898, every building in the townland had disappeared from the map, along with the ruins themselves.[14]

Omey's population was overwhelmingly Irish-speaking, though by 1901 every head of household but one was bilingual. No less than 18 of the 28 householders were illiterate, while 2 others could read but not write. Though only two houses were of the lowest (fourth) class, most had only one or two rooms with a single front window. Virtually every householder claimed to be a farmer, occasionally doubling as a fisherman or carpenter.[15] Since no census schedules survive for the nineteenth century, the islanders' characteristics must be inferred from census tabulations for larger districts. In the surrounding barony of Ballynahinch, which embraced the western portion of Connemara, Irish remained prevalent in 1881, when 15 per cent of the population spoke Irish alone while 62 per cent were bilingual. The proportion ignorant of the language had risen somewhat from 15 per cent in 1851 to 23 cent in 1881, but the most notable change was the decline in Irish monolingualism, one-third of the population having spoken Irish alone in 1851. Knowledge of Irish was more widespread among females than males, while children were far less likely than adults to speak the language.[16] These patterns were not specific to west Connemara, reflecting the general advance of formal education and the growing perception that fluency and literacy in English were essential for success, especially among prospective emigrants. Educational progress was also evident in the slowly declining proportion of illiterates, who comprised 71 per cent of west Connemara's population in 1861 and 48 per cent in 1891. Illiteracy in English, like ignorance of spoken English, was commoner among women; but the gap closed steadily as girls took particular advantage of easier access to primary education.[17] These changes reflected a vigorous competition for the minds, and also the souls, of young people born into a bubble of Irish speech and culture, within a wider Irish world dominated by English and American speech and culture.

III

For certain evangelical visionaries, Connemara seemed ideal terrain for resuscitating the moribund 'Second Reformation', which had aroused so much excitement and rancour in the 1820s. Its population, though overwhelmingly Catholic in name, was relatively untouched by formal religion as well as education. Under the extraordinarily complacent leadership of the 'Lion of Judah', Archbishop John MacHale, the entire ecclesiastical province of Tuam had been unusually slow to introduce devotional reforms and abnormally resistant to the state's attempt to diffuse primary education through the National system introduced in 1831. To Protestant optimists, the illiterate, Irish-speaking, impoverished people of Connemara, not yet effectively disciplined either by their clergy or by nationalist organizers, seemed highly susceptible to a campaign by missionaries conversant with Irish and willing to carry their tracts and gospel message into the wilderness. Such hopes inspired the formation of the Connaught Home Mission Society in 1830 and the appointment in 1841 of the first Presbyterian 'Irish missionary', whose campaign opened in Clifden's only schoolhouse, made available to him by Hyacinth D'Arcy of Clifden Castle.[18] Both the D'Arcys and the Martins took up the cause of proselytism as well as Protestant 'colonization', but such campaigns soon faltered and the few pre-Famine converts relapsed.[19]

The most sustained attempt to challenge popery in Connemara was an astonishing crusade conducted by the Society for Irish Church Missions to the Roman Catholics (ICM), under the charismatic command of Alexander Dallas, rector of Wonston in Hampshire. An intrepid veteran of Waterloo, he organized his missionary campaigns with military precision and thoroughness.[20] Founded in London in 1849, the organization was dominated by British sponsors who regarded Ireland, and Connemara in particular, as a missionary field akin to India or China. Nearly £90,000 was raised in the first five years, of which only £6000 was collected in Ireland.[21] The Open Bible, disseminated by Irish manpower and British money, was still widely expected to rout the archaic and inefficient faith by which the aboriginal inhabitants were currently deluded. Of all the 'home' missionary organizations, the ICM was the most ambitious and professedly 'aggressive' in its pursuit of Irish souls. Its primary object was 'to strive, by all holy means, to dispel the darkness and ignorance from the minds of Irish Roman Catholics; and to seek to communicate to as many of them as possible the saving truth of the Gospel'.[22] Dallas aimed not only to save souls, but to demonstrate the indissoluble link between acceptance of Protestant truth and access to employment, education in English and attachment to the union with Britain. His message was promulgated through massive mailshots,[23] religious handbills exposing the errors of popery and distributed by the million,[24] interminable sermons and 'controversial' lectures on Transubstantiation or the Blessed Virgin, an impressive network of schools, and some orphanages catering initially for children bereaved or deserted during the Famine.

This extravagantly expensive campaign was conducted by a highly disciplined and rapidly expanding army of missionary clergymen (all ordained in the Established Church but often converts from Rome), lay scripture readers, school teachers and assistants. The Society's agents all received monthly salaries on an incremental scale, along with housing rented or owned by the Society. This cadre of salaried 'agents' was supplemented by a multitude of senior pupils employed as 'Irish teachers' to visit homes where the agents might not have been welcome, in order to spread the gospel by reading or reciting passages in Irish. Though not necessarily declared converts, the Irish teachers were expected to display an 'inquiring mind'.[25] Regular meetings, services and classes were arranged in each parish to co-ordinate the work of the agents and Irish teachers; while solidarity with the wider missionary movement was fostered through frequent tours of inspection by Dallas, his staff, and a steady stream of inquisitive clergymen and well-wishers. Like tourists on a pilgrim package, such visitors were shepherded around Connemara by approved agents, carmen and boatmen from one safe house to another, and in due course supplied with a neatly devised guidebook with maps and pictorial posters.[26] Copious reports of ICM enterprises throughout Ireland were provided, primarily for the benefit of British sponsors, in the Society's annual reports and in Dallas's brilliantly designed bulletin, *The Banner of the Truth in Ireland*.[27] Morale was boosted by statistical reports giving the number of confirmations in mission churches and attendance at mission schools. The barrage of apparently factual detail was leavened by heartening stories of peasants embracing Christ in the teeth of communal opposition or intimidation, and of dialogues between amazingly articulate converts and bullying, inept priests (sometimes personified as Archbishop MacHale),[28] who were invariably confounded by the biblical and theological expertise of the 'Jumpers'.

The Banner of the Truth in Ireland (1879–81).

'A Holy Well': *Banner* (1880).

'Roman Catholics Going to a "Station"': ICM, *Report* (1880).

The principal engine of salvation was the Society's network of free day schools, in which children of all ages received basic instruction in reading, writing and arithmetic in addition to immersion in the catechism, selected scriptures and religious history.[29] Outside school hours, many pupils (and adults) were also taught to read or memorize scriptural texts in Irish by the 'Irish teachers', who were paid a few pence monthly for each successful 'Irish scholar'.[30] Though never restricted to converts and their children, the primary purpose of the schools was to open young minds to the word of God rather than to provide a rounded general education. As with most ICM enterprises, the spiritual agenda could only be accomplished, if at all, by offering temporal inducements. These included provision of milk, food and clothing, all commodities in short supply in Connemara during the Famine and for many decades afterwards. As a result, the Society was widely denounced, by liberal Protestants as well as the Catholic clergy and press, for practising 'Souperism'.

In order to reassure sponsors of its sincere determination to save rather than buy souls, Dallas ensured that separate committees paid for provisions distributed in schools, the upkeep of orphans, and relief for 'persecuted converts' (through the Society for Protecting the Rights of Conscience in Ireland and the Priests' Protection Society). These committees, often composed of kindly ladies, had no formal association with the ICM. Such payments were construed not as bribery but as philanthropy, directed towards those already within the Society's care. Dallas was equally careful to dissociate his mission from party politics, while lauding the consequential effects of proselytism in leading converts towards acceptance of the union with Protestant Britain. Agents were instructed 'to separate the spiritual department from the political' and to avoid 'giving the occasion for the excitement of political feelings in Romanists', thereby obstructing 'their access to the hearts of the Roman Catholic population'. The resignation of a few scripture readers who were active Orangemen was a small price to pay for asserting the uncontaminated spirituality of the missions.[31]

A year or so before the formal creation of the Society in March 1849, Dallas had arranged to reopen several disused schools near Clifden, in order to exploit the British Association's scheme for distributing Famine relief through existing schools. Among the earliest mission schools were those in Sellerna and Bally-conree, where the first orphanage was established after Dallas had rescued an infant from a dunghill where it was about to be mauled by a hungry pig.[32] The subsequent explosion of missionary activity in Connemara was made possible by the enthusiastic involvement of Thomas Plunket, bishop of Tuam, who carved out several new districts from the existing parish unions to be manned by missionary curates.[33] These livings were perpetuated through the zeal of Plunket's chaplain and nephew, who pursued the great cause of 'church extension' by initiating the West Galway Endowment Fund in 1857.[34] Dallas's closest collaborator was Hyacinth D'Arcy, the one-legged former proprietor of Clifden Castle, who had recently bounced back as rector of Omey (Clifden). As the Earl of Roden observed when visiting D'Arcy in 1851, he was 'one of the most interesting chastened Christian men I ever met', having responded to the loss of his estate by moving into 'a very small house in the town' and immersing himself in missionary activity.[35]

'Clifden, Connemara': ICM, *Report* (1880).

In the early years, about half of the Society's ample revenue was poured into building churches, renting schoolhouses and missionary accommodation, and enrolling agents for service in Connemara. By 1 August 1850, the missions in Connemara embraced seventeen stations in six districts, with four clergymen, seventeen readers, two 'lay agents', sixteen schoolmasters, six mistresses, twelve weekday services and nine Sunday services in Irish. A school offering a weekday service in Irish was already operating in Omey Island, a station in the Sellerna district.[36] An early visitor to the new island school was Dallas himself, whose text when addressing 105 worshippers, 'almost all' former Romanists, was 'Ye are the light of the world' (Matt. 5: 14). The evangelist almost perished on the moonlit return journey to Ballyconree, when his enthusiastic but unco-ordinated orphan rowers struck a rock and turned the boat on its side. But for an order from Dallas to stop rowing, a moment earlier, the boat would have capsized. 'That's the hand of God', cried one of the oarsmen.[37]

In Sellerna, the missionary John Conerney and his staff soon encountered local opposition. They were 'assailed with stones by Priest Magee's labourers', threatened and abused by 'Priest Flannelly, and a mob of about 100 men', waylaid by a whiskey-fuelled gang on the high road to Clifden, and pursued by 'a mob' from Cleggan who 'continued hooting and pelting stones' over a mile of road.[38] A month or so after these incidents, Mrs Conerney reported that she had visited all four schools in the district, including Omey. The children were 'cursed by the Priests every Sunday, for coming to learn God's precious Word in our Schools. Could you but see their emaciated forms and naked bodies, you would not cease begging clothing for them.' The scripture readers had been relatively 'well received' in Omey and Cleggan, and a man who had 'lately struck one of the Readers with a spade, expressed the sorrow he felt for the unjust way in which he had treated him'.[39] Those who chose to spread God's word in places such as Omey Island could scarcely expect to escape insults, threats, cuts and bruises, with the recurrent risk of being shunned, expelled or even murdered.

IV

John McNeice was born on Omey Island on 20 March 1866. His forename Frederick (which did not appear in the register of births) was a favourite among loyalists and royalty, Queen Victoria's three eldest daughters having married Fredericks between 1858 and 1866. Frederick John was the fifth among ten children of William Lindsay McNeice and his wife Alice Jane, who jointly conducted the ICM's island school. William was already a schoolmaster in Moyrus when he married Alice Jane Howell (from nearby Bunowen) in Clifden on 22 March 1851.[40] He is said to have attended the Connaught Missionary College in Ballinasloe, a small boarding school established in 1846 by the first Professor of Irish at Trinity College.[41] Though not associated with the ICM, it had close links with a similar body that had opened a mission in Ballinasloe, the Irish Society for Promoting the Scriptural Education of the Native Irish through the Medium of Their Own Language. While its 'primary object' was to train 'eligible persons, for Missionary work among the Roman Catholic population of Ireland', the College also aimed to provide 'a suitable education for Pupils intended for other professions', one-third of the pupils being charged less than half the cost of their upkeep. Apart from 'gratuitous instruction in the Irish language', William McNeice would have been regularly examined on the scriptures read at daily prayer, prepared for possible entry to Trinity College, and put through a regular routine of 'athletic games and exercises'.[42] With this preparation, he eventually became a teacher at the newly established ICM school at Moyrus.[43] Before long, the McNeices moved on to Omey Island, where the first child (Caroline Elizabeth) was born in late 1852. William became known locally as 'Croisín' (the little cross or crutch), reputedly because he seemed 'a little martyr of a man'.[44]

Unlike many ICM agents, Frederick's father was an 'original Protestant', from Lugawarry near Stonehall in the coastal parish of Ballysadare, five or six miles south of Sligo town. Born about 1826, William was a younger son of Ferguson McNeice, one of the district's many Protestant farmers.[45] About one-fifth of the parish population were Protestant Episcopalians, a proportion that scarcely varied between 1834 and 1901. They were much better educated than the Catholic majority, with few illiterates of either sex.[46] According to Louis's sister Elizabeth, who made local enquiries about her Sligo background in the 1950s, William's grandfather Anthony had allegedly been baptized and named by a Catholic priest, though his parents and children were Protestants. From Elizabeth's literary perspective, Anthony's family conformed to Maria Edgeworth's stereotypical 'squireen'. 'They were hard-riding, hard-drinking, hard-gambling men very much given to litigation' who, in Frederick's opinion, 'were a feckless lot'. Anthony was reputedly an agent to the O'Hara estate, one of the largest in Sligo, and was said to have eloped with a daughter of the gentry named Peggy Duke who had attracted his attention on the hunting field.[47] Anthony's rise was reflected in his supposed acquisition of Stonehall House and of extensive lands for which he acted as middleman. Despite their 'feckless' ways and resultant loss of property and spells of penury, Elizabeth concluded that none of the McNeices 'lived as peasants'. Instead, they kept up appearances by procuring watercolour portraits of the daughters and sending them to church on horseback to be handed down by their 'beaux'.[48] Such was the colourful Sligo heritage of the McNeices, as depicted in family lore.

A more prosaic record emerges from the voluminous papers of the O'Haras of Annaghmore, one of the few Gaelic families 'to have maintained its former standing in county and national affairs into the eighteenth century and beyond'.[49] Through a canny sequence of apostasies, favourable matches, and managerial improvements, the O'Haras managed to avoid bankruptcy and retrieve much of the wealth dissipated through confiscations, 'derisory' rentals and extravagant expenditure.[50] The first reference to Frederick's ancestors in the parish of Ballysadare occurs in a 'List of Graziers of Lisduff' compiled in 1758, indicating that Thomas 'McNees'[51] was in possession of fourteen Irish acres with an annual rent of about £8 (Irish currency), as well as grazing rights worth £5 10s. His flock was decidedly modest, amounting to '7 sum' (the equivalent of seven mature cattle in sundry livestock).[52] In the same year, as part of Charles O'Hara's attempt to regularize management of the estate, he was granted a lease of these lands, at an annual rent of about £10, for the term of three lives including those of his sons, Anthony and Ferguson. Dreadful penalties were to be imposed if he failed to send his 'corn malt or grain' for grinding to O'Hara's own mill at Coolany.[53] By 1785, the market value had almost doubled, and the family was inhabiting an 'exceeding good Sleated house Garden and good Offices'.[54] No McNeice, however, seems ever to have occupied the big house at Stonehall,[55] sublet land to inferior tenants (so far as is recorded), or acted as an agent or official for the O'Haras. The Lisduff farm passed on to Anthony and then his son Thomas, who shared a new lease signed in 1811. This lease was to expire after twenty years or else the life of the Duke of Clarence, a fortunate gamble since King William IV survived until 1837.[56] Though not returned as a titheable occupier in Lisduff in 1825, Thomas had regained possession at a much higher rent by 1846.[57]

Meanwhile, in the 1770s, Thomas the elder and Anthony had acquired leasehold in neighbouring Lugawarry, which Anthony briefly augmented after his father's death before settling back into the condition of a comfortable farmer rather than a 'squireen'.[58] Lugawarry later became a place of settlement for Catholic refugees from the sectarian conflagration centred in Armagh, but there is no hint of strife among the McNeices and their neighbours.[59] By 1822, the Lugawarry farm had been divided between Anthony's sons Thomas and Ferguson, whose slightly smaller share amounted to eleven Irish acres (nineteen statute acres) at an annual rent of about eight guineas.[60] Ferguson, the eldest son, must have relished his new-found independence, having married Margaret Lyndesey by licence in 1803 and doubtless produced a family long before the arrival of William Lindsay in about 1826.[61] By contrast with the aridity of Omey Island, Lugawarry had substantial areas of 'arable gravelly clay', while Lisduff was yet more blessed with plenty of 'good strong gravelly clay'.[62] The McNeices thus seem to have been relatively 'snug' farmers, as Thomas's descendants remained until quite recent times.[63]

Like most of Charles King O'Hara's tenants, however, the McNeices were severely shaken by the potato blight and privations of the later 1840s. Thomas had already fallen into arrears before November 1846, when Ferguson followed suit, though their debt at that early stage was relatively small.[64] Thomas was better placed than his brother to cope with the sudden loss of farm income, as his combined holdings were worth four times as much as Ferguson's share of Lugawarry.[65] While several neighbours were willing to surrender their holdings in return for assistance in emigrating to America, members of the McNeice family remained in possession when Griffith's Primary Valuation of Ballysadare was published in 1858.[66] By then, however, all three farms in Lisduff and Lugawarry were occupied by Thomas's sons, whereas Ferguson and his line had disappeared from view.[67] It seems likely that the richer branch had secured possession as a result of Ferguson's death or insolvency. In any case, by 1851, Ferguson's son William Lindsay had abandoned Ballysadare for Connemara, a region still more afflicted by famine, to serve the Irish Church Missions.

Sixteen-year-old Alice Jane Howell, whom he married in Clifden on 22 March 1851, was a daughter of John Howell (a Welsh coastguard) and his first wife (reputedly an Eccles from west Cork).[68] Though administered by the Board of Customs between 1822 and 1856, the coastguards were in practice an auxiliary of the Royal Navy, their officers and men being drawn exclusively from naval personnel and constituting a naval reserve. Like John Howell, most of those stationed in Ireland were natives of Britain. In addition to detecting invaders and saving lives, Her Majesty's Coastguard Service still had the unpopular duty of patrolling the coast in revenue cruisers in order to intercept smuggled goods, much prized by Connemara consumers. During the Famine, however, they had recovered public esteem by transporting and distributing essential relief along the west coast.[69] Coastguards and their children formed an important element of the small (though expanding) Protestant marriage market in Connemara, with less than 200 Episcopalians in Omey parish in 1834 and half that number in William's parish of residence, Moyrus.[70] Two of Alice Jane's sisters also married into the missions, so providing an essential network of support for the McNeices in their otherwise isolated life on Omey Island. Michael Couhill, who married Ellen Martha Howell in 1861, was a scripture reader who worked on the island from 1864 to 1866; Michael McNamara, who married his fellow teacher Mary Anne Howell in 1864, soon became a scripture reader in Claddaghduff, the village through which islanders walked to and from the mainland at low tide.[71] The opening of mission churches in Connemara had helped to reverse the tendency of the coastguards to 'forget religion altogether' while 'their little ones went over to the Church of Rome', as one coastguard in the Sellerna district recalled in 1865.[72] The coastguards and missionaries of Connemara had become not only mainstays of Protestantism but staunch upholders of Queen and Constitution, always conscious of their vulnerability as a tiny minority in a fiercely Catholic and increasingly nationalist environment. Such was the frontier stock from which Frederick MacNeice emerged.

V

For William McNeice and his family, Omey was not a temporary station but a long-term home. William spent twenty-seven years on the island, rising to the dignity of reader in his final year. By 1856, Alice Jane was also employed by the

ICM as a teacher at the island's only school, somehow combining that post with bearing and rearing her ten children until the family's departure from Omey in 1879.[73] While her husband's monthly salary gradually rose from £2 in 1856 to £4 15s. in 1879, Alice Jane's remained unchanged at £1 10s. for most of her career. However, her reproductive efforts were often indirectly rewarded through salary increments of 5s. for William, Alice's childless stretch between 1860 and 1866 also being a period of static income. In 1869, the family's monthly earnings were briefly augmented by 10s. while Caroline acted as an assistant teacher, before progressing to the ICM training college in Dublin.[74] Though better paid than teachers in the rival network of 'National' schools, the McNeices earned little more than a family of farm labourers. Along with their income, the quality of the schoolhouse in which they lived also improved somewhat over the years. The earliest known building, in the north-eastern townland of Cartoorbeg, was rented by the ICM for 8s. monthly yet valued at only 10s. per annum.[75] In 1858 this was replaced by a 'handsome school-house, built in an ecclesiastical style' and licensed for divine worship, valued at £3 10s.[76] Fourteen years later this building became a National school, superior premises worth £5 15s. having been acquired in Sturrakeen, about 300 yards south-west of the previous schools. There, in relative comfort, the McNeices spent their last few years in Omey.[77]

Scattered missionary reports indicate that the number of pupils on the roll declined from ninety-three in 1851 to seventy in 1868, while 'average attendance' on weekdays fell from seventy-nine in 1851 to forty in 1866. Attendance at the island's Sunday school was slightly higher.[78] These figures may have been inflated in order to impress sponsors, for only twelve pupils were 'actually present' when government inspectors visited Omey Island on 25 June 1868 (others may have been helping out on the farm or attending the Clifden fair). Several ICM schools in Galway were even smaller, and attendance on that day varied between a solitary pupil and sixty-five.[79] Four-fifths of those attending were Protestant Episcopalians, a proportion that surpassed three-quarters in 1871 and rose subsequently to nine-tenths or more.[80] When the schools came under close scrutiny by a Royal Commission in 1868, the ICM's mission secretary testified that almost half of its pupils throughout Ireland were of Catholic parentage and a quarter were 'original Protestants', while one-tenth came from mixed marriages and almost one-sixth were the offspring of converts. The teachers were submitted to quite a rigorous course of training: 'It embraces a thoroughly good knowledge of Scripture. They must learn grammar thoroughly, arithmetic, up to fractions for instance, and mental arithmetic thoroughly well. They learn to sing, and sing by note. The girls learn needlework and English history, and an outline of history generally.' The pupils, typically aged between three and fourteen years, were given food only when 'extremely poor', where it was 'the custom of the country', and in seasons of dearth such as the prelude to the potato harvest. Such relief was invariably provided by 'local friends' rather than by the ICM itself. Though the Irish language was widely taught, as parents generally wished, this was done 'as a separate thing' outside school hours.[81]

The assistant commissioner for West Connaught, a decidedly sceptical witness, depicted the schools as a formidable weapon in the 'warfare' between purported 'religious truth' and 'error'. While thanking Hyacinth D'Arcy and his missionary colleagues for their assistance, he noted that advance notice of his inspections appeared to have resulted in 'packing'. In West Connaught, over three-fifths of those inspected came from Catholic families, with far fewer 'original Protestants' and children of 'mixed marriages' than elsewhere. The assistant commissioner observed that 'the walls are generally covered with placards containing texts of Scripture', that the children sang only hymns, that the copybooks had short texts as headlines, and that memorized texts were invariably hymns or commandments. As for relief, he found that children in Connemara generally received at least half a pound of Indian meal daily between January and June, with one suit of clothes annually. None was charged for tuition or equipment, and attendance was usually rewarded by payments to parents. Since the majority of these pupils were neither converts nor children of converts, though most voluntarily attended both church and Sunday school, the relief did not strictly amount to 'Souperism'. The assistant commissioner noted that the ICM schools achieved 'rather higher' pass rates than the National schools, while the income of their schoolmasters was 'very much better'.[82] These reports, both sympathetic and hostile, suggest that the mission schools were functioning fairly effectively in secular instruction, and serving a much broader market than the shrinking population of converts. Their effectiveness as an instrument of salvation was another matter.

One test of success for the McNeices was their success in competing with the rival National school, established under Catholic patronage. Despite MacHale's aversion to that system, the parish priest of Clifden eventually sought state aid to support the first National school on the island in 1862. The schoolhouse was a converted dwelling of two rooms (one for the school, the other for the teacher), thatched, with an earthen floor, a grateless open fire and imperfect plastering; the nominated teacher, though of 'good' character, had displayed an 'inferior method of conducting' the school where he had previously taught. Nevertheless, the district inspector of National schools pointed out that the islanders had hitherto 'been obliged to send their children across to the mainland, or allow them to attend the

Mission School, of the Irish Church, or let them grow up in ignorance'.

Despite objection from the missionary at Sellerna, who cheekily claimed that the new school 'was got up for "proselytizing" purposes', he grudgingly endorsed the application because of the urgent need for instructing children 'without interference with their religious principles'. Master Michael Conroy was therefore allowed an initial annual payment of £15 (one-third of William McNeice's salary), being retained until 1869 despite two severe reprimands and one temporary withdrawal of salary for 'incompetency'. Pupils presumably learned little from a teacher noted for his 'bad spelling and penmanship, & generally defective preparation'. Along with three lay instructors, Conroy conducted prayers and training in the Catholic catechism at 3.30 each afternoon and for two hours on Saturday mornings. After Conroy's dismissal and the reopening of the school four years later, the inspectors remained unimpressed by the state of the new schoolhouse and the competence of the teachers, and the school was again intermittently closed before being struck off the list in 1883.[83] Average daily attendance declined from forty-one in 1862 to twenty in 1869 and seventeen in 1874, the last year for which such returns were published. In that year, less than one-quarter of pupils on the roll bothered to attend.[84] It is clear that the mission school, with the help of sponsorship far more generous than that available in the National system, more than held its own in the battle to instruct the island's children. The same applied throughout the Clifden district, where ICM schools accounted for one-third of all children in attendance in 1871 and comfortably outnumbered their 'National' rivals.[85]

Outwardly, the organization of the mission in Connemara changed little over the McNeices' twenty-seven years on the island. In 1858, the island's first church service was held in the new schoolhouse with 102 people present, of whom 32 took Holy Communion. Thereafter, the Sellerna missionary regularly visited Omey to perform a Sunday evening service.[86] In the same year, William and Alice secured the help of a monitor named Stephen Coursey, who within a few years had become a reader with a salary similar to the master's. Between 1864 and 1866, Omey had the luxury of a second reader, the post briefly occupied by Alice's brother-in-law, Michael Couhill. After Michael's departure, Coursey and the McNeices worked as a threesome until William himself was promoted to reader in 1878, allowing the appointment of an extra schoolmaster. They were assisted by a band of 'Irish teachers' numbering a dozen in 1868, six being enrolled in the school and six others being otherwise connected with it. The number of agents in the Sellerna district remained fairly stable, fluctuating between ten and fourteen over the period 1856–79. The only major change was in the number of Irish teachers, which fell from twenty-eight to twenty between 1867 and 1880. The entire Connemara mission hovered around sixty (excluding paid assistants and Irish teachers), peaking in 1859 when Connemara had seven ordained missionaries, twenty-two readers, and forty-four schoolteachers.[87] Protestant ministers actually outnumbered Catholic priests in west Connemara in most years, though the gap was closing. By 1874 there were ten clergymen of each denomination, but the priests had to cater for a population seventeen times as large.[88]

The McNeices served under two missionary clergymen. The Irish-speaking convert John Conerney was the Sellerna missionary until 1855, returning to the parish in 1874 upon the departure of George Shea. Shea was presumably a convert, for his brother Henry (another Connemara missionary) had deserted Rome in his seventeenth year. In his final report, George Shea reflected on the improvement in Sellerna over the past quarter-century: 'In days gone by Sellerna was a dark place, none darker in Ireland; wholly given to idolatory, the priests having full control, no schools, the children brought up in ignorance – taught to look to the priest for a place in heaven thereafter. … Your missionary can say, not only once, but thrice was I stoned.' Yet his ministry had ended triumphantly with a week of nightly meetings attended by over 200 devotees, while 'Roman Catholics were at the doors and windows', marvelling at the scene. Sellerna was 'no longer the dark place'.[89]

How justified was the buoyant optimism exuded by the missionaries and organizers when addressing potential sponsors through *The Banner of the Truth* and the Society's annual reports? Despite heroic attempts to suggest a ceaseless torrent of conversions from idolatory, the confirmation returns published after successive episcopal visitations to the Clifden district reveal slow but inexorable decline after the excitement of the early 1850s. Over 900 confirmations were performed in west Connemara between 1851 and 1855, but only about 200 were confirmed at each of the (roughly triennial) visitations between 1860 and 1874. After a six-year gap, the bishop confirmed 255 people in Clifden in 1880, with much smaller numbers recorded in 1883 and 1890. After adjustment for defective returns, it appears that about 2500 confirmations were performed in west Connemara between 1849 and 1880, involving at least 2200 converts.[90] Most of these confirmations were presumably of children who had recently passed through the mission schools, though statistics compiled in 1851 indicate that adults accounted for almost one-quarter of those confirmed.[91] Few attempts were made after the early 1850s to enumerate the population of converts actually adhering to the missions, or the number who had 'lapsed' after confirmation, though frequent reference was made to losses through emigration.

The decision to ascertain religious affiliation in the census of 1861 aroused 'fears and cautions' in the ICM, though repeated attempts were made to portray its results as 'gratifying' and to emphasize the expansion of Protestant numbers since 1834.[92] The census for Omey civil parish confirmed the dramatic multiplication of Episcopalians, from 191 in 1834 to 827 (13 per cent of the population) in 1861. Later counts, however, revealed a gradual but steady decline. The Protestant minority was much smaller elsewhere in west Connemara. Throughout the region, the total number of Episcopalians rose from 454 in 1834 to 1668 (7 per cent) in 1861.[93] Since the estimated number of confirmations between 1849 and 1860 exceeded 1500, a substantial proportion of those received into the Church must already have relapsed or emigrated. Before any returns for 1861 had been published, the *Banner* claimed to have ascertained that Omey alone had about seventy adherents of the Established Church, nearly one-third of the island's population in 1851.[94] Such extravagant estimates were subsequently avoided, and in 1869 Dallas lamented that many of his missionaries were no longer pursuing the 'conversion of souls' but accepting the more comfortable rôle of country clergymen catering for a small, settled minority.[95]

The true profile of post-Famine Protestantism in Connemara is best docu-mented by the census returns of literacy and occupation, and the surviving regis-ters of the parishes of Sellerna and Omey. A rough test of the Society's success in converting and retaining adult 'peasants' is provided by the proportion of Epis-copalians who could neither read nor write. Though far lower than the figure for Catholics, 26 per cent of Episcopalians in west Connemara were illiterate in 1861, falling to 11 per cent by 1881. On the assumption that no 'original Protestants' or Protestant children were illiterate, these returns indicate that about 360 illiterate adult converts had been retained up to 1861 and 130 up to 1881.[96] The occupational returns for County Galway also suggest that the missionary campaign had left a limited but lasting demographic imprint. The census of 1881 indicates that almost half of all Episcopalian occupied men were engaged in government and defence and nearly one-tenth in the professions, far more than their share of the total popu-lation (one in thirty). They were also over-represented in services and commerce but very seldom found in unskilled sectors such as general labour. Though also under-represented in farming, the fact that a quarter of Galway's Protestant males had agricultural occupations suggests that a fair number of 'peasant' converts had not yet relapsed.[97]

The absence of such returns for Connemara is partly remedied by the parish registers, which reflect the declining importance of converts and the growing dominance of officials such as coastguards and policemen. In Omey parish, the number of marriages rose from twenty-seven in the Famine period (1846–50) to fifty-six in the following quinquennium, thereafter falling steadily to only eleven in the 1870s. The proportion of illiterate spouses peaked during the later 1850s, when three brides in four and nearly half of the grooms were unable to sign the register. The frequency of baptisms predictably reached its maximum somewhat later than that of marriages (in the period 1858–63), before likewise shrinking to a trickle.[98] Far fewer marriages were celebrated in Sellerna church, with up to two annually between 1857 and 1870 and only occasional weddings thereafter. Of the twelve grooms returned between 1857 and 1868, five were labourers, four ICM agents, and one a farmer. One-third of the newly weds were unable to sign the register, and most had local surnames. By contrast, all but one of the eight grooms married between 1869 and 1889 were either policemen or coastguards, and every spouse was able to write.[99] The eventual predominance of missionary agents and officials is further demonstrated by the registers of Sellerna's vestrymen in the 1870s. Among the twenty-eight vestrymen for whom occupations could be ascertained, there were eleven ICM workers (including William McNeice), three coastguards, one policeman, two 'esquires' with property qualifications, six farmers, four labourers and one tailor.[100] Some converts stood fast and reared their children through the missions, and the Society itself provided employment for a substantial proportion of those converts who kept the faith. Yet behind the heartening public messages of missionary enthusiasm hovered the chastening realization that, by the 1870s, few new converts were being secured. Furthermore, the missions had lost most of the illiterate farmers and labourers who had swarmed into their churches and schools in the immediate aftermath of the Great Famine. Dallas's dream of saving the native Irish from 'fatal error' had shrivelled into a mere marketing device for subsidizing uneconomic western parishes.

VI

How was the gradual retreat from crusade to conservation reflected in the experience of the Omey Island mission station? Though the McNeices were never mentioned by name in the Society's publications before 1879, frequent accounts were given of the challenges faced by its agents on the island and their reiterated triumph over the forces of ignorance and evil. Central to the missionary experience, at least as narrated for the benefit of sponsors, was the contrast between the eager curiosity of ordinary Catholics and the vindictive hostility of the priests who misled them. This contrast implied that if only they could be weaned from their mentors, Irish Catholics would readily embrace the advantages of Protestantism and the British connection. Throughout the McNeices' sojourn on Omey, euphoric reports of enlightenment alternated with chilling examples of persecution, sometimes affecting the island itself. The Omey school was frequently praised in missionary publications and portrayed as a model. In July 1851, Conerney believed that 'every child in the island is attending. I don't know any where more intelligent children than they are.' Next summer, when two English clergymen visited the island, 'the school-house was very much crowded with adults and scholars, and the answering was excellent'.[101]

The precariousness of mission life was revealed during Bishop Plunket's visit in August 1853, which included a tea party that went madly wrong. After consecration of the new church at Sellerna, according to a visitor from London:

> A large party proceeded in cars about two miles, to Omey Island, where we had assembled the children of Turbot Island, to partake of a treat provided by the three Ladies B. and our party. *En route* walls of stone had been speedily built to impede such a party of Jumpers as the inhabitants of those Western Isles had never before beheld; and the clergyman had again and again to remove those stones as we drove along. Here and there boys and women were concealed behind hedges, and let fly volleys of stones as the cars passed. Mr. McCarthy [a Dublin missionary] was at length struck by a large granite stone, and his head cut severely. The converts and children of Omey received us with warm greetings, and we distributed our cake and tea among many happy faces; when again our peace was molested, and a fight ensued! Many of the ladies were much alarmed, and the convert women and girls were too much frightened to enjoy their meal.

Eventually a second party, including Alexander Dallas, fought its way through another hostile crowd on its journey from Cleggan school, 'though one Scripture reader had a very narrow escape, and an orphan girl was struck'. Spirits were revived by evening visits to a 'dark and smoky' cabin, in which a nonagenarian 'living skeleton', reclining on straw and rags, assured Mr Conerney that she was happy: 'Oh, yes; I am going *home*! Jesus is my all.' The party then crept into an underground mud hovel to visit 'a mother and her twin babes on a heap of rags. Not a single article of furniture had they; but they were contented.' The visitors were delighted with the McNeices' school, crowded with children and also their parents, 'listening with intense joy to the really wonderful knowledge of their children'.[102]

By another account, the trouble at the tea party was stirred up by 'bigoted Roman Catholics, who had come to the island, some from a distance, evidently bent on mischief', following inflammatory 'altar harangues' on the previous day. One outsider, enraged by a flag 'erected by the people of the island as a mark of their gratitude to the friends of the mission', had torn it down and snapped the pole. It was this gesture that provoked two or three islanders, though not yet converts, to take on the invaders: 'sticks were brandished in the air, the men leaping from the ground with loud yells'. When clergymen and readers tried to stop the fighting, a lay agent was 'knocked down and severely kicked'. The writer deemed the scene 'truly characteristic of Ireland: the men screaming, eager for the fighting; the women, some trying to make peace, others howling piteously, calling for revenge; the children crying and terrified'. When Dallas eventually joined the party with Hyacinth D'Arcy, after 'quelling a similar riot on the opposite shore', the combined influence of the Waterloo veteran, the former landlord, and the divine will served to chasten the combatants and restore calm. The visitors departed 'thankful that God had overruled an occurrence which seemed likely to prove so serious'. This widely circulated narrative affirmed not merely the resilience of the missionaries and the vindictiveness of their 'bigoted' adversaries, but also the divisions within the Catholic community that the missions had brought to light.[103]

In the following year, the Society was assured that 'the converts of Omey Island are much improved in their manners, habits, and intelligence': 'Nothing, save the spirit of a martyr, will enable the converts to stay firm, as more than half the island has already passed into the hands of a Roman Catholic landlord [Thomas Eyre], who is trying to possess himself of the whole island, banish the converts, and abolish the school.'[104] An orphan who had been offered a situation on the island, provided that he attended chapel rather than church, contemptuously informed his prospective mistress: 'I would not bow down to the wafer for all you are worth!'[105] The island was by now a major attraction on the pilgrim trail, and so excited some lady visitors in 1855 that they dedicated any profits arising from the resultant travelogue to the erection of a new schoolhouse on Omey:[106]

> We then went on, in torrents of rain, to Omey Island. 'Omey' (the Irish of which signifies *'forlorn, forsaken'*)[107] is situated off the coast of Sellerna. As we were walking across the strand, the tide being out, we saw numbers of women and children running to and fro, suddenly disappearing and appearing again out of their cabins, which, indeed, are ... nothing more than holes sunk in the sand, covered with sod. With instinctive Irish politeness, they were carrying chairs, or whatever they could find. ... On reaching the school, we found the small cabin in which it is held crowded to excess with boys, girls, and adults, amongst whom there was not one original Protestant. While Mr. B[urke] examined them, their bright grey eyes beamed with gratitude; their mouths were wide open.

They proceeded to entertain the ladies with 'The Omey Islander's Hymn', fondly modelled on Hawker's celebrated 'Song of the Western Men'.[108] The hymn was itself to become a minor evangelical classic.[109] Having promised that 'never more shall priest of Rome | Beguile us with a lie', the children of the mission reached their climax:

> For every Omey islander
>   Can tell the reason why.
> Then we'll not shut the Book of Life,
>   But will their threats defy,
> Since every Omey islander
>   Knows well the reason why.

By then the tide was in, 'and we were obliged to return in the Mission boat. Some of the school boys rowed us; the schoolmaster steered. One of the boys remarked, "This is the Gospel ship"; another replied, "And Christ is our captain".' Thus William McNeice farewelled his visitors and awaited his reward.

Omey remained a fortress against priestly aggression, and in 1856 'the priests ... sent a young man to Omey Island to open a school there, but this attempt proved futile, for only one child left the Mission school in consequence'. The new school was closed after three weeks, and two similar experiments reportedly failed over the next year or so.[110] In 1857, Shea reported that a newly appointed priest had gone from house to house in the island, in pursuit of his 'ungodly design' to prevent children from attending school. The scripture reader followed the priest's steps and secured unusually matter-of-fact accounts of five of the discussions that had occurred. One example probably refers to Thomas Toole of Sturrakeen, a small farmer with several children appearing in parish records:

> Visited T.T. The priest visited this man, and asked him: 'Have you any going to the Jumpers' school?' R.C. I have three. P. Do you go to Mass. R.C. Sometimes. P. Why don't you take your children from that cursed place? R.C. I don't know; I see more children going to it, and they are learning very fast in it too. ... P. I will give you a week's time, and if you don't take them out of it before that, I will excommunicate you, and will not give you absolution. R.C. You may do that if you like, but God will give me absolution. P. Ha! ha! I suppose you are a Jumper yourself; I will excommunicate you. He then left him.

Having failing to persuade a mother to remove her daughter (an Irish teacher) from 'that cursed place', the priest signified his disgust by shaking 'the dust of his feet on the threshold' (a recurrent trope in mission dialogues). Another islander rebutted the charge of Souperism by declaring: 'Whatever I am the Jumpers saved me, and you would not have many but for them; they kept the country alive when ye would let them die.' After exclaiming, 'Oh! I think ye are all corrupted in this island,' the priest 'went away, and said no more'.[111]

The relative success of the Omey mission was clearly an irritant for Patrick McManus, parish priest of Omey, and his ever-changing company of curates.

During 1858, all those associated with the ICM were 'denounced from the altar of Claddaghduff Chapel', and the parishioners exhorted to shun those who attended Protestant services or allowed members of their households to do so. Twice, the missionary and converts were assaulted at Claddaghduff, after Mass, as they made their way to Omey church. George Shea viewed with contempt the priest's attempt to apply his own methods in reverse: 'The houses of the children were visited by the priest and National schoolmaster, and money, food, and clothes *offered*, but NOT GIVEN!'[112] Over the next two decades, however, there is no record of violence erupting on the island, now firmly established in mission folklore as a citadel for resolute converts who had outfaced their enemies against fearful odds.

A 'flying visit' from Alexander Dallas himself had the effect of 'putting a match to a train of gun-powder', so Hyacinth D'Arcy claimed in 1860. From Sellerna, the two architects of the ICM went on to Omey:[113] 'The rain began; but we reached Omey in the carriage, and found the school-house quite full. Text, John xvii.3.[114] Then a baptism. Walked round to the south side of the island, and got well wet. A boat met us here from Ballyconree. It blew and rained pretty fresh; so we did not reach Ballyconree till half-past seven.' When the island was threatened with the withdrawal of the reader in 1863, George Shea managed to reverse this cost-cutting measure by alleging that over forty Romanists had expressed their regret, exclaiming, 'What were we, and what will we be now, but like cows and horses!'[115] The island continued to be portrayed in ICM propaganda as a model mission station. According to an English visitor in 1865:

> In the afternoon I went to the Island of Omey. There I preached in the large room to a most attentive congregation of converts, and afterwards administered the Lord's Supper to about thirty communicants. Poor creatures were there, barefooted and bare-legged, with their long hair flowing wildly down their backs, and with only one or two garments on them! Yet with what attention, with what earnestness, with what a solemn spirit and manner it was entered into! How audible the responses![116]

The year 1866, that of Frederick McNeice's birth, was reportedly one of particular spiritual advance in Omey, with the closure of 'the priest's school', the opening of every door to the readers, several marriages and baptisms, an admission by the Catholic landlord that the converts 'were the best men on his land', and the island's first Protestant burial service – for 'a gentleman' who had converted in his sixty-second year. Despite pressure from relatives to call a priest, he declared that 'he would wish to pass into his Saviour's, and into no other hands', so enabling the missionary to perform 'the beautiful burial service, and in a Roman Catholic cemetery – to a congregation of over 300 persons, very nearly all Romanists'. As Shea modestly remarked: 'To God be the glory. His work in the soul will teach us all to love Him, to love the Queen and her laws, and to love one another.'[117]

As the flow of public conversions dried up, missionary reports concentrated on the interest exhibited by Catholics in the mission's schools and Irish classes, so offering a half-promise of future salvation. In 1868, twenty or more 'Romanists' were attending class meetings in Omey on Thursday evenings, including a man who, six years earlier, had stoned Shea 'by order of the priest, and left [him] on the field as dead'. During a bout of sickness he expressed a desire to see the missionary, who was reassured by the man's wife that 'he will not now take a stone to you, *for he knows better*'. Another Catholic, on his deathbed, allegedly told the reader (Stephen Coursey) that 'in your schools the children are taught well, and know more about religion than any of us. Tell the Minister to take charge of my poor children, and to bring them up as Protestants.' The fidelity of emigrant converts was also emphasized, as in the report of a letter from America to an islander on the verge of emigration, urging the latter to 'take to him Irish Testaments and Irish books, as he never could forget the Word of God which he learned when in Omey Island from an Irish teacher'. Such anecdotes served to mitigate the underlying failure of the mission to supplant the Catholic faith, though on Anniversary Day, each 17 January, Dallas's dream was regularly invoked. In 1876, 'the church in Omey Island was crowded with worshippers, who fervently united in prayer for the extension of the good work of conversion'. Two years later, however, John Conerney dwelt on past achievements rather than future prospects: 'In every branch of Missionary labour the good work is carried on with much success in the interesting island of Omey. The adult converts are zealous, faithful, and exemplary, standing fast in the liberty wherewith Christ hath made them free.'[118] William and Alice McNeice might justifiably have felt that they had not lived in vain.

3. *Outcast*

OMEY, 1879

I

By the end of 1878, the McNeice family was in transition. William and Alice, now about 52 and 45 respectively, had seven children still at home, ranging from Charlotte (20) and William (18) to Herbert, a mere toddler. But on 10 October, their eldest child Caroline Matilda (26) had married John Henry Frizzell, a strapping sub-constable of the Royal Irish Constabulary stationed in Connemara. Caroline and John were married by licence in St Joseph's church, Spiddal, by her old mentor George Shea, but William McNeice was not present to give her away.[1] This event renewed the family's connection with Sligo, since John's father (a retired constable himself) had left his native Louth to serve the Constabulary and marry in the county. Soon after the wedding, Caroline resigned from the ICM after nearly nine years' service. She had left home in 1869 to attend the female training school in Dublin, subsequently teaching in Dublin and in various Galway stations.[2] A few months before the wedding, the family had also lost Lindsay, stricken by brain fever in his fifth year.

Of the seven children living in the schoolhouse, only Charlotte had so far achieved any independence. She had spent a few months assisting her elder sister as a monitress in Spiddal before returning to the island in January 1876. Twelve-year-old Frederick was the eldest of the middle group. There are no contemporary accounts of his boyhood experiences as an islander, though he seems to have become a keen rower and to have amused himself with some form of hurling on the sandbanks.[3] Frederick presumably shared the responsibility for rearing Ferguson (10), Alice (8) and Margery (7). It cannot have been easy to maintain such a family on a combined monthly salary of £6 15*s*., and William's recent promotion to reader had brought no additional income apart from a small gratuity in February 1878. Living conditions were further threatened by agricultural recession and a succession of poor potato crops, soon to cause distress in the Clifden district on a scale unknown since the Famine.

A few weeks before Caroline's marriage, William McNeice's temper was ruffled by an ominous event recalling the painful confrontations of his early years on the island:

> Three priests lately paid an unexpected visit to the Irish Church Missions school in the island of Omey, and asked each child his or her religion, telling them they would not allow them to attend that school in future, and getting violent and abusive. The teacher told them to keep quiet and behave as gentlemen, or else to leave the place. The reply made was that they were sworn to exterminate all heretics and Jumpers, and they were quite determined to do so.

They had then visited an 'aged convert' who cannily described himself as a 'Catholic' but not as 'a *Roman* Catholic, I belong to the Catholic Apostolic Church'; whereupon 'one of the priests then seized and shook him, and said he would throw him out of doors'. 'Old John' further outwitted and enraged the priest by asking his daughter to attend Mass, as demanded, which she firmly refused to do. After more threats, a second priest had defused the confrontation by saying: 'Come away, the man is sincere in his belief.'[4]

Sectarian animosity in west Connemara was further heightened in late November, when a young curate named William Rhatigan 'forcibly entered the school' at Belleek to demand two children claimed by their grandmother. When Mrs Ellen Young, the teacher, objected to their removal, Rhatigan 'terrified both her and the children' by describing her as a 'rap' and 'an unfortunate wretch'. A subsequent court action for trespass and assault was dropped when Rhatigan apologized for using 'offensive epithets in a moment of excitement', apparently inflamed by the recitation of passages from the Bible on Mrs Young's instructions.[5] Three months later, the house and schoolroom were 'set on fire over [the] heads' of Mrs Young and her husband, a blind coastguard pensioner, and burnt to the ground.[6] Rhatigan, who spent fifteen peripatetic years as a curate in the archdiocese of Tuam without securing his own parish, was soon to win praise from a 'special commissioner' for the *Daily News* as a 'zealous and hard-working young minister of the gospel'.[7]

On 27 February 1879, William Rhatigan returned to the island. According to Charlotte's account, published in the next issue of the *Banner*:

> The priest visited the school on Thursday last, and beat my dear father with a heavy stick he brought with him. My father then turned him out, and a crowd gathered. The priest went on waving his stick to the mob to come to help him, but did not find where he was going, until he fell over a rock outside the school door and hurt his head. So then they said father beat him and cut his head, but, indeed, that is not true.

Her mother was hit by stones but 'not much hurt', while the reader Stephen Coursey received 'several blows'. All of the school windows were broken but not the door, beyond which the family durst not venture even on the following Sabbath. Police protection was provided for the first two or three nights, after which the McNeices were left alone under siege, the windows blocked 'with stones, and everything we can think of'. They were sustained only by a bag of flour and a cow, which would soon die unless she could be let out of the house 'somewhere by night'. When the missionary and his daughter tried to visit the McNeices on the Saturday, they were beaten and repulsed at Claddaghduff, with further attacks on Monday including the breaking of grandmother Howell's windows. The family feared worse to come, having heard 'that our house is to be thrown down' and that houses of two island converts were to be burnt. Charlotte's letter depicts an unprepared and irresolute father, who 'does not know what to do or how to manage'.[8]

Though no police were on hand to supply a less partisan account, several were present at Claddaghduff chapel on the following Sunday, 2 March, when Rhatigan referred to the incident in his sermon. Though speaking mostly in Irish, he pointedly began in English in order to convey his version to the police. The priest informed them that 'he went very near being murdered' when 'he went into the school-house at Omey to look after some Roman Catholic children'. He named his six assailants as McNeice, his wife, his daughter ('a big woman', clearly Charlotte), his son (William), the teacher Michael Davies, and one of the Courseys. Rhatigan urged the congregation, 'if ever insulted by Jumpers to resent it to the last', and remarked 'that if it occurred in Tipperary they would not allow their Priest to be beaten'.[9]

Official inquiries into the 'scuffle' were sceptical of both versions of the battle of Omey. Having reported the destruction of 116 panes of glass worth £3, and supplied the names of 26 rioters to the police, William McNeice had not followed up the sub-inspector's invitation to lodge an information against the priest and initiate a private action. A resident magistrate reported that no information was likely to be lodged, as the ICM 'intended to proceed against the Revd. Mr

Rhatigan in the Superior Courts, if so advised'. McNeice himself attributed his inaction to the unavailability of police to escort him to the house of a magistrate. Galway's Crown Solicitor advised against any public prosecution, having 'come to the conclusion that neither parties [*sic.*] are free from blame for their connection with the transaction and they seem to share that opinion themselves'. The Solicitor General concurred, dismissing the incident as 'a private quarrel'.[10]

William Rhatigan's words deeply stirred his congregation at Claddaghduff, who soon showed that Tipperary had little to teach the men and women of Connemara. Police witnesses reported that a crowd of up to 200 people had assembled after the sermon, three cheers being raised for the priest. The mob had 'hooted and shouted' at the house of Stephen Coursey's brother Pat before moving on to his own, where stones were thrown and a window broken. Both men were 'what is called a Connemara Jumper'. Rhatigan, having intervened to secure the release of a boy arrested for stone-throwing, had exhibited his authority by instructing the crowd to disperse.[11] Two days later, a policeman accompanying another schoolmaster was told by a man emerging from a field that Master Booth had nothing to fear: 'that it was Macniece the Man in the Island that the people were on for Murdering on account of his striking the Priest and they would have blood for blood. ... He said the People could not help it from the way the Priest was abused and that they would murder him if he came from the Island.' Next day, William McNeice nevertheless left the island and had an unpleasant experience when passing through Claddaghduff at noon. Hearing a cry for protection, Sub-Constable Thomas Hanlon observed a man running away from three women (Honor Gorham, Celia Gordon, and Mary Davis) who, he claimed, were 'going to take his life'. As Hanlon escorted McNeice to the reader's house, spectators gathered and said 'that was the one beat the Priest and that they would have blood for blood'. Thus encouraged, Honor 'threw a large sod of turf at him', Celia 'brandished a short bit of stick', and Mary threw a stone that broke another of Stephen Coursey's panes. Honor protested that the teacher 'had called her a whore', and Martin King indicated that belligerence was not restricted to women by announcing that 'he would have Macneece's life'. The policeman, having eventually persuaded the crowd to disperse, 'conducted Macneece onto Omey Island and left him near his own house'.[12]

As sectarian attacks multiplied elsewhere in the Clifden district, demands multiplied for reinforcement of the police and for prosecutions against those responsible. The unionist press throughout Ireland paid close attention to the outbreak of 'religious intolerance in Connemara'.[13] The *Banner* looked forward with grim exultation to the possible benefits of persecution: 'The blood of the martyrs has ever been the seed of the Church, and will, we do not doubt, prove to be so again'.[14] On 12 March, ten missionary clergymen addressed a memorial to the Lord Lieutenant, calling for an enquiry and 'adequate security for life and property', while expressing reluctance 'as Clergymen to have recourse to litigation in the local Courts, where it might be difficult for us, or for humbler agents, to obtain protection in the present excited state of Public feeling'.[15] Eight additional policemen had already been sent to Clifden and Cleggan two days earlier; but the memorial drew a sharp direction for an enquiry from the Duke of Marlborough, which contributed to a flurry of investigations by the police, resident magistrates and Crown Solicitor.[16] Meanwhile, McNeice remained with his family on the island, 'practically a prisoner in his own house'.[17]

'Persecution of the Convert Boatmen': ICM, *Report* (1880).

II

On Saturday, 22 March, Sub-Constables Thomas Sheehan and John Dumphy were sent on protection duty to Omey Island, where they stayed overnight with the McNeices. As Sheehan deposed: 'On the following morning William Macneece told me that as he was so long from Prayers and as he had protection that he would go to Church on that day to Sel[l]erna.' Frederick and the younger children stayed at home with Alice. Fearful of trouble, the policemen loaded their rifles and placed them at half-cock, before leaving the house with Charlotte and the two Williams. When the party approached the chapel at Claddaghduff, on the only road to Sellerna, it was attacked by stones and turf thrown by a score of men and women, who boasted that 'they had caught him, they would have his life'. As Sheehan backed towards the house of Michael Lynch, fending off the crowd while William dashed for safety, he was warned to 'leave until they would get in to Macneice to have his life as satisfaction for beating the Priest'. After a half-hour stand-off at Lynch's front door, Sheehan temporarily lost his rifle after vainly firing when an assailant jerked his shoulder. Though knocked down and beaten, he retrieved his rifle and cap, returned to the house, and found the door broken in and Dumphy defending those within. Sheehan, a Catholic, begged one of Rhatigan's fellow curates (Thomas J. Flannery) to intervene before McNeice was murdered, and after surrendering his empty cartridge and accepting responsibility for any injury inflicted by the shot, he secured Flannery's assistance in ejecting a man as he climbed through a window. He then 'saw William Macneece inside the House with his head uncovered and his face and the back of his head covered with blood and I saw blood flowing down the back of his Coat'.

Despite police reinforcements and Flannery's appeals, the mob still pressed for vengeance: 'The women shouted to the men in Irish "Take that black devil out of that and kill him [Sheehan] as it was he killed the Woman".' Though nobody had been seriously hurt by Sheehan's wild shot, he was once again knocked down, kicked, and deprived of his rifle, which he again recovered only to find it broken. Back in the house, he observed that McNeice's 'son appeared to have received injuries, and the daughter had a cut on her head from which the blood was flowing. McNeece had several cuts on his head and was bleeding.' At this point Constable Michael Murphy arrived, and ordered Sheehan and others to take the McNeices 'as quick as possible to the Barracks at Cleggan'. This they did while the rest of the party created a diversion near the chapel, though on the way to Cleggan a woman, who had heard rumours about the shooting, remarked pleasantly 'that the Policeman ought to be killed and the eyes picked out of him'. Sub-Constable Fitzpatrick also sang Father Flannery's praises, reporting that he had driven back the crowd and held two men bound for the house of refuge until 'they shook themselves out of him, the Bell then rang and he succeeded in getting them all in to Mass'. Fearful of further attacks, Murphy arranged for William to be removed from Cleggan by a senior police officer and a resident magistrate, while young William and Charlotte were kept overnight at the barracks. With the teacher Michael Davies, they returned to the island next morning under police escort. Meanwhile, Fitzpatrick and Dumphy had been despatched to Omey 'as a protection for Macniece's wife and his other Children'. So ended the siege of Claddaghduff.

These events naturally aroused curiosity on the island, where up to twenty men and women gathered near the school on Monday, 24 March. Fitzpatrick reported animated discussion as to whether a stone that had struck him in the back had been flung by a girl in the crowd, whether Sheehan's shot had actually caused injury (the victim's son stating that the doctor had found 'nothing the Matter with her'), and 'how we were to be fed in the Island'. According to Dumphy, the police were informed 'that only for the Revd. Father Flannery interfered they would have beaten McNiece better, that they were sorry they allowed Davis the Teacher to leave the Island but that they would not do so again'. Rumours that the police were to erect a protection hut aroused further anger. A neighbour had visited the family 'in the Ordinary way' to warn them 'that the people of Claddaghduff and the surrounding locality were determined to resist with force the putting up of the hut and would not allow any Parties to be arrested by the Police and that they would arm themselves with Forks and other Weapons'.[18]

Passions were further aroused on Tuesday by another sermon from Father Rhatigan at Claddaghduff, when his targets were no longer the McNeices but the magistracy and the whole missionary movement. Rhatigan reportedly described the local unpaid magistrates as 'a low mean despicable lot', while praising the resident (stipendiary) magistrate as a restraining influence, but for whom 'Connemara would be now glittering with the Bayonets of the Soldiers & Police'. Announcing a public meeting to condemn the magistracy, he warned that if they did not receive the same protection 'as the soupers, … we will endeavour to protect ourselves, and I promise You that You will always have the Priests at the front'. He then gave detailed instructions on how to deal with mission agents:

> Now I warn you not to allow those mean soupers into your houses not to speak to them, and not allow them walk on your lands, and if you find that they are going about distributing tracts and insulting your religion I would not strike them with a snowball that would whiten them but some other substance that would blacken them.[19]

Later that week, the Crown Solicitor visited Clifden to assemble police evidence about the disturbances for preliminary proceedings at petty sessions. Though reporting on 31 March that 'things appeared to have quieted down since the removal of Mr. Macneece' on the evening of the siege, he recommended that summonses (for riot, affray and unlawful assembly) be issued against those alleg-edly involved in several riots, including seventeen names supplied by McNeice himself. Though implying that the case against William Rhatigan was weak, he cannily suggested summonsing the priest, in the belief that he would confront his accusers in court and that 'they will all go into the same Boat with him' instead of absconding. After a meticulous appraisal by the Solicitor General, the government decided to press ahead.[20] In preparation for further conflict as the court hearing approached, one hundred extra police were sent to Clifden along with eight members of the Reserve Force from Dublin. The *Galway Express* reported that the hut destined for the island would accommodate five men in a space twelve feet square, 'composed of 16 pieces, each loopholed, and … lined inside with iron plates, the whole weighing four and a half tons'. The 'peasantry' at Omey had optimistically declared that 'they will throw it into the sea'. In the event, the police deployment was sufficient to allow the hut to be transported as far as Claddagh-duff and assembled there.[21] The crisis in Connemara was by now widely covered in both Irish and English newspapers, and the Chief Secretary had faced several questions in the House of Commons.[22] On 5 April, the nationalist *Galway Vindicator* looked forward gleefully to 'the expected disturbances in Connemara' should William McNeice ever return home, and noted the presence of several Dublin journalists in Clifden.[23]

III

On Easter Monday (14 April), the vestrymen of Omey Parish expressed their 'very deep regret that this usually tranquil portion of Her Majesty's dominions should have recently been the scene of so many violent outrages, the offspring of religious bigotry, which are calculated to imperil the whole district of Connemara'.[24] That same evening, William McNeice and his police escort reached Clifden from Dublin, leading to nothing worse than some hooting from 'a boy named Brown', who was arrested.[25] Next morning, the courthouse was 'thronged for an hour or two before the proceedings commenced', in the presence of five justices of the peace, two resident magistrates, the Crown Solicitor as prosecutor, and eight priests. In all, twenty-five men and four women were charged with respect to three separate incidents, most prominently the riot at Claddaghduff on 23 March. Collation of their surnames with ICM and parish records suggests how deeply proselytism had cut through kinship networks in Connemara: no fewer than thirteen of the eighteen surnames of alleged offenders were shared by agents or Protestant parishioners in the district.[26] The cross-examination of police witnesses by W. ffrench Henderson produced some lively theatre but failed to shake their carefully co-ordinated testimony. He also met his match in Stephen Coursey, the reader, who was greeted with 'subdued groans'. He admitted to being 'baptized by a Roman Catholic priest, I suppose', but could not remember attending Mass ('derisive laughter') before becoming a Protestant in about 1853. Asked if being a scripture reader were 'a calling in life', he replied, 'Not in this life.' When Henderson sneered that 'I suppose in Claddaghduff it is not easy to live on locusts and wild honey', Coursey testified that he received £4 5s. monthly from the ICM for teaching 'the people that each man who reads Holy Scripture can take his own interpretation therefrom'. He considered himself 'a sober, proper, honest man'.[27]

When the hearing resumed on Friday morning (the fourth day), it was William McNeice's turn to speak after reaching the courthouse without incident. After declaring that he had always been a Protestant, he described his welcome at Claddaghduff on 23 March. The three Furies who had assailed him three weeks earlier were waiting:

> When we arrived there a crowd of people standing near the chapel made a rush at us and many of them threw stones. I know those who struck me with stones – Celia Gordon, Ellen King, and Mary Davis (identified). Honor Gorham threw a stone, but I cannot say it struck me. I and my children ran. Old Tom Coursey, of Claddaghduff, ran across the road and thought to trip me.

Once inside the house of Michael Lynch, he was again threatened (with a mug) by Ellen King, who had climbed through a window. In the kitchen, she and Celia Gordon resorted to stones ('so many stones were thrown at me that many of them did me little harm'), after which their menfolk set about kicking him. When McNeice declined to kneel before the priest, he was allegedly struck by part of the broken door. He declined to join in the chorus of praise for Father Flannery, who had demanded an 'apology' (presumably for the alleged attack on Rhatigan), asked McNeice to accompany him to chapel, and falsely suggested that he was a Jumper. Under insistent questioning, however, McNeice admitted that 'had it not been for his interference I might have got worse treatment than I did'. Flannery himself was embarrassed and irritated by the compliments showered upon him by the prosecution, which gravely imperilled his popularity in the parish.

After a stormy cross-examination, in the course of which the defence attorney temporarily retired from the case, William was replaced in the witness box by Charlotte and then by his son William Lindsay, who declared that he had been kicked 'in the legs and every part (laughter in the gallery)'. Soon afterwards, the magistrates returned the sixteen remaining defendants for trial at the next quarter sessions (several having already been released on bail and three, including Father Rhatigan, discharged). This decision, from a unionist perspective, 'appeared to surprise the accused and their friends, who had been treating the whole affair as a good joke'. Three were allowed bail and the rest removed to the bridewell under a strong police escort. According to the *Vindicator*, a collision between the police and a hostile crowd was averted only by the exertions of Fathers Rhatigan and Flannery. The 49-mile journey to Galway jail, next morning, took twice the usual time because of bad weather and 'frequent stops for changes of horses and for the purpose of enabling the prisoners and the escort to obtain refreshments'. William McNeice was escorted separately to Galway, with a lengthy break at Moycullen Barracks, and on to Dublin by the 4 o'clock train.[28] His family remained on the island, 'their house being guarded day and night by five policemen'.[29]

The protracted legal proceedings entailed heavy expenses. Just after the hearing at petty sessions, Archbishop MacHale himself contributed £5 'in defence of the sacred interests of religion and of holy faith'.[30] An appeal for the 'Connemara Anti-Jumper Defence Fund' was launched by Fathers Rhatigan and Flannery, as honorary secretaries, on 12 May. Having pondered whether aggrieved Catholics were 'to restrain their feelings and not to wreak vengeance on the murderers' heads', the curates advised against vengeance and in favour of 'that which just laws would permit'.[31] For its part, the ICM had allocated £16 13s. to pursuing the Rhatigan case in February.[32] Involuntary levies were also applied to local rate-payers who bore the cost of the additional police, amounting to more than seventy men by 24 April, including those manning a special station at Claddaghduff and the protection post at Omey.[33] In preparation for the trial, both parties generated a barrage of propaganda. MacHale organized a census of 'so-called converts' in the Clifden district, which (in the opinion of H. C. Cory, Hyacinth D'Arcy's successor as rector of Clifden) grossly understated the true number.[34] Defence lawyers persuaded two judges of the Queen's Bench Division to release the prisoners on bail, after the MacDermot, QC, had facetiously offered 'the undertaking that we will not wreck any more schoolhouses or kill any more policemen until after the trial (laughter)'.[35] Following a meeting called by Father Rhatigan, the released prisoners were welcomed in Clifden by a procession of 300 people escorted by a band, but no disturbance resulted.[36]

Further parliamentary questions resulted in a heated debate on Souperism and the distribution of offensive tracts by ICM agents.[37] For its part, the ICM published a booklet entitled *Romish Persecutions in Ireland*, and warned its sponsors, at the annual meeting on 13 May, that the campaign in Connemara reflected Rome's conviction that 'English rule in Ireland' was weakening.[38] Conerney's report from Sellerna alternated between exultation and despair. He exulted that 'J— S— of Omey Island, our oldest convert', had remained 'faithful unto death', being 'feared by his enemies, and held in great esteem for his blameless and consistent life'. After recounting the recent 'repetition of the violence that characterized the early days of the Mission', he concluded: 'We have suffered much, but we have great reason to thank God and take courage. The poor converts have been waylaid and beaten, their lives threatened, their houses broken. A reign of terror now prevails. We look to the Lord for deliverance.'[39]

In the schoolhouse on Omey, Alice McNeice and her children remained under siege, despite their police guards. Though still employed as a teacher, Alice was scarcely in a position to hold classes. On 22 May, she wrote to William in Dublin that Mary Stuffle (an Irish teacher) had come 'upstairs to me crying for protection', closely followed by two men who, when she 'ordered them off', vowed to deliver her to the waiting priest and her uncle William. Mary had defiantly declared that she would tell the priest that she was a baptized Protestant and 'of age, therefore no person has any claim on me'. After Alice had promised to 'protect her until death', the priest had sent word 'that if she was not at confession on Saturday, 24th, he would drag her downstairs by the head'. At her own request, Mary was then sent off overnight to a 'place of safety', while Alice waited up all night in case of an attack: 'We dare not venture out of the house.'[40] Associates of the McNeices were also at risk, including the postmaster at Cleggan (Robert William King), a convert who had continued to supply the family in Omey 'in face of the decree sent forth'. It was reported that his children were being beaten and stoned by boys at the local National school.[41]

On 10 June, Alice ventured as far as Clifden with three police escorts, only to find the road obstructed on the return journey by 25 large stones. In this case, 'no injury resulted. The Constable saw her safely home & they were not further molested. ... The motive was manifestly sectarian.'[42] About a week later, a second memorial of protest was addressed to the Lord Lieutenant by the Connemara clergy, alleging 'a violent and systematic persecution', eliciting renewed assurances of police protection and appeals for abstention from inflammatory language from Lowther, the Chief Secretary.[43] The McNeice family's isolation was interrupted by a surprise visit on 14 July from Canon Cory, whose party arrived, with two policemen, 'in a large boat manned by convert boatmen'. Having been warned not to land by 'a number of the natives', the intruders were obliged 'to walk by the longest possible course, skirting the shore until they reached the school-house'. Their interview with the McNeices and some visiting converts 'was affecting in the extreme', revealing that attempts had been made to deprive the family of water and their cattle of pasture. When retrieving their anchored boat, Cory's party was again abused: ' "May the curse of God rest on you all, ye devils," was the mildest phrase.'[44]

IV

The legal contest resumed on 30 July, when six of those indicted for the riot on 23 March were tried at the Galway Summer Assizes. Originally scheduled for quarter sessions, the trial had been transferred in view of 'the seriousness of the offence preferred against the Clifden rioters'.[45] In such a case, the prospect of convictions by a Galway jury was remote, however damning the evidence might seem. From the Catholic and nationalist perspective, the true defendants were not those in the dock but the ICM. Father Rhatigan, already exonerated at petty sessions, reinforced this interpretation by authenticating and circulating a sensational document, just before the trial and in the courthouse itself. This was a collection of twelve personal statements attributed to former Jumpers and Irish teachers or their relatives, the intended effect of which was 'to prove BRIBERY, CORRUPTION, AND HYPOCRISY on the part of those who are agents of that gigantic humbug called the "Irish Church Missions to Roman Catholics in Ireland".'[46] If true, these declarations suggested that Connemara's supposed converts and activists had been motivated by greed rather than conviction. No fewer than seven islanders were prepared to flaunt their deceitfulness, perhaps in return for further rewards.

John Conneely admitted that he had sent several of his children 'naked' to 'the jumpers school', in exchange for which they received 'suits of clothes three or four times in the year'. He claimed that McNeice had promised clothes for those attending, and that Coursey had offered his eldest boy 5s. monthly as an Irish teacher if he went to church. The teacher had also 'advised us to care no more about the Blessed Virgin than any other woman', that 'the priests had no power from God to forgive sins, and if they knew the truth they would not be Catholics'. Patt Faherty, three years a Jumper until March 1879, made similar claims and admitted that 'it was not religion I wanted but money'. Martin Walsh stated that McNeice had offered him clothes for his niece if she attended his school, and promised to pay him as an Irish teacher if he went to church, though he 'could read no Irish' (a story echoed by John King). Michael Davis likewise claimed that his mother had sent him to the school 'for the purpose of getting clothes'.[47] Anne Stuffle, six years a Jumper until late 1878 and a former Irish teacher, corroborated these accusations, adding that 'McNeice used to be mocking the Blessed Sacrament, and say that the priest said it was God, &c., &c.'

The most poignant testimony came from Mary Stuffle, presumably the girl who had sought protection from Alice McNeice only two months earlier:[48]

> I was brought up a Protestant by my father. My mother and brothers were Catholics. My father would not let me be a Catholic. My father was receiving

ten shillings a month for being a jumper. My father when he was dying, said he would have neither priest nor minister. They were giving us clothes, &c. I was sent to Dublin to the Bird's Nest.[49] I had to walk all the way from Galway here to Omey.

These statements were immediately dismissed by Canon Cory as the work of unreliable hypocrites: 'What will your readers think of the honesty of such men, or of the value of their testimony?' If they had once sold their souls for money or clothes, he implied, they could do so twice. No handbills abusing the Mother of God or Holy Communion had been issued, and Cory considered that 'the Blessed Virgin is a holy and happy saint, highly privileged and honoured'. As for the provision of relief: 'This is called bribery; I call it Christian charity.'[50] Though probably authentic, it is impossible to judge whether these accounts reflected motives at the time of conversion, or retrospective rationalizations composed after recantation and under powerful communal and clerical pressures. The testimony of disillusioned converts, as of former communists vilifying 'the God that failed', cannot be accepted at face value. In the atmosphere of Clifden in 1879, however, it had a devastating impact.

Three Queen's Counsel conducted the prosecution under instruction from the Crown Solicitor, with the MacDermot, QC, leading a more modest team for the defence. The irascible Henderson again acted as defence solicitor. Little additional evidence was presented, but some illuminating statements emerged under cross-examination. William McNeice claimed ignorance of events since 23 March (ignoring his appearance at petty sessions): 'He had since been conveyed to Dublin, and had not been in Connemara since. (Laughter.) He did not know anything about his school being opened or closed, except what he heard about it from his wife by letter.' When assailed by a barrage of leading questions about proselytism from the MacDermot, based on extraneous documents such as Father Rhatigan's dossier rather than any evidence before the court, McNeice stoutly denied giving 'any provocation to the people of Connemara':

> I swear I never said a word to any of the prisoners about their religion, or ever gave any of them a tract of any sort. I never said their religion was a colossal lie, or spoke a word about religion to them in my life. I never said it was a gigantic fraud, or that the Blessed Sacrament was a mere wafer. I never scattered tracts at all or gave them to anyone. *Did you ever say the priests were leading their flocks to hell?* Never, or anything of the sort. I never offered money to man, woman, or child to change their religion in any way.

If William McNeice had indeed avoided disparaging the Catholic faith throughout his career as a teacher and reader for the ICM, he was surely unique;

yet, in denying that the teaching of Holy Scripture had any sectarian implications, he merely echoed the rhetoric of Dallas and his fellow proselytizers.

Charlotte again corroborated her father's evidence, adding that she had been struck on the head by a stone while 'stooping over her father' in Michael Lynch's kitchen; but William the younger was not called as a witness. After further evidence on the second day, the defence concluded its case with a general assault on the character of the ICM and the veracity of William McNeice. It was for the jury to assess his sworn denial that he had described Holy Communion as 'nothing but a wafer':

> He had denied that he had used to the prisoner John Davis the blasphemous expression 'every time you go to Communion you have the devil in your carcase.' Davis had shouted from the dock that McNeice had used the words. It was for the jury to say if they would believe the unsworn testimony of the Connemara peasant or the oath of the Bible reader.

Lord Justice Deasy objected to this line of defence and other histrionic digressions, just as he had deplored an outburst of applause from the prisoners following the MacDermot's opening speech, declaring 'that he would not allow his court to be turned into a theatre'. Equally wishful was his appeal to the jury to 'dismiss from their minds all the inflammatory matter which had been presented to them' and concentrate only on the substance of the indictments. After an hour and a half, the jury acquitted two of the six defendants, but could not agree on the remaining cases. After a second inconclusive retirement, and overnight discussions, the prosecution decided to suspend the case and 'let the prisoners stand out on the same bail' until the next assizes. The judge remarked approvingly that 'you are exercising a wise discretion; besides, you see at this period of assize, it would be difficult to find a jury'. Since the trial had dealt with only one of the three riots, eleven other persons under indictment were also remanded on bail.[51] As in most such cases, the Crown displayed further discretion by making no subsequent attempt to round up the accused or risk another inconclusive trial.[52]

The collapse of the trial was a major setback for both the government and the Protestant interest. The Crown witnesses were 'hooted and yelled at' by a 'disorderly mob' and an attempt was made to run them down at the car-office; the reader Stephen Coursey was stoned under police escort as he travelled back to Claddaghduff.[53] By contrast, the defendants were greeted with 'great excitement' on their journey home, being met by a temperance band in Moycullen, an evening bonfire attended by over 2000 sympathizers in Oughterard, and an address to an assembly of 'frieze-coated peasants' in Errismore, delivered from the step of a car by the priest 'in charge of the accused'.[54] The chief protagonist of the crusade against the Irish Church Missions was lauded as a national hero. As the *Vindicator* reported when Father Rhatigan returned to Clifden on 6 August:

> The people turned out in their hundreds in procession order, to meet him, headed by their brass band, bearing green banners and playing national airs suitable to the occasion. He was met by the great throng some miles outside Clifden. A special car was sent to meet him, and a large bonfire was lighted to honour his return after his great Galway triumph.

After a short address, he 'ordered them to disperse quietly to their houses'.[55]

V

Father Rhatigan's incontestable 'triumph' did not immediately lead to the extinction of the missions in Omey or elsewhere in Connemara. Alice McNeice's employment on the island ended in August or September, when she and her children presumably rejoined William in Dublin. The island school was revived by William King and his wife, and Stephen Coursey remained as reader. John Conerney reassured the Society in May 1880 that normal operations had resumed and that morale had been restored after the 'dismay' caused by the 'reign of terror' in Sellerna. Pupils were 'now flocking into our Schools'; a large afternoon prayer meeting had been held at Omey on anniversary day with 'our enemies at peace, no insults of any kind'; and on 28 February, one year after the wrecking of 'our beautiful church', he and Canon Cory had found the building 'well filled' and had enjoyed 'stirring addresses' from 'our Clifden friends'. All was now 'peace on the Island, and all around'. Yet 1880 turned out to be 'the most trying year I have remembered in all my experience since our Society was called into existence', with distribution of official relief through the rival National schools, widespread intimidation against those associated with the Society and its schools, and further emigration of persecuted converts. In Omey, however, the school was 'well attended' and the oldest remaining convert had 'had a happy triumph over death a few months since'. Next year, intimidation had returned to the island, with wreckage of the mission's 'ferry boat' and 'fiery trials' for the Irish teachers in Omey, who 'still suffer hardships in the battle-field'. This was followed by a gradual 'passing away' of the 'reign of terror', friendlier relations with the islanders, and enrolment of pupils withdrawn from the National schools.[56]

These fluctuating reports could not conceal the declining vitality of the entire Connemara mission, highlighted by a drastic reorganization arising from Canon

Cory's resignation from the Society following claims by the London committee that the work 'had become, in some parishes, more pastoral than missionary'.[57] In Sellerna, the number of agents declined from fourteen in 1878 to five throughout the period 1885–91. The number of Irish (and English) teachers fell even more rapidly, from twenty in 1880–1 to 10 in 1882–4, and eventually only five in 1891.[58] The Society's decline reflected that of the Protestant population as a whole. In the civil parish of Omey the Episcopalian component fell from 10 per cent in 1881 to 7 per cent in 1891 and 6 per cent in 1901, when only 689 Episcopalians remained in the whole of west Connemara.[59] Protestant marriages virtually ceased in both Clifden and Sellerna, and fifteen of the twenty children baptized in Sellerna between 1897 and 1913 were children of coastguards. Not a single non-Catholic remained on Omey Island in 1901.[60] By 1906, the disused mission schoolhouse at Sturrakeen was reportedly 'down'.[61] The collapse of the community sustained by the missions was attributable to many factors other than the battle of Omey and the siege of Claddaghduff. It was accelerated by agricultural recession and distress later in 1879, social polarization attributable to the ensuing 'Land War' in Connemara, and mass emigration of families from west Connemara with assistance from J. H. Tuke's scheme. Yet, if Father William Rhatigan had not stumbled over a rock in Sturrakeen, Connemara's bizarre community of Soupers and Jumpers might have lingered on for another generation. Or, from another viewpoint, the 'marvellous light' might yet have glowed in the West.

4. *Apprentice*

DUBLIN AND BEYOND, 1879–1898

I

What loyalties, resentments, precepts, and skills might thirteen-year-old Frederick have carried with him when he escaped from the island? Until 1878, his childhood had been largely untroubled by the sectarian confrontations associated with the 1850s, and through his father's schools he would have known most of the island's children, Catholic as well as Protestant. With them, he would have walked, rowed, hurled, played and fought. Though surely aware that he belonged to a separate caste defined by its spiritual mission, he would not have imagined that this caste was at risk of imminent extermination. He would have witnessed extreme poverty among his neighbours, and himself lived plainly without waste or luxury. He would have been well versed in the scriptures and liturgy, soundly trained in the basic skills (now so rare) of calligraphy, recitation and mental arithmetic. He was presumably familiar with the Irish language.[1] If he had been allowed to grow up on Omey until he was ready to seek further education or employment elsewhere, his island upbringing might well have receded into the amalgam of nostalgia and contempt expressed by so many of his emigrant contemporaries.

How should we comprehend the impact on such an adolescent of his family's horrific experience during those six months under siege in their own home? Once-friendly neighbours became accusers; initiates into the mysteries of the caste relapsed and became its bitter enemies; shopkeepers, tradesmen and boatmen withdrew their services; members and friends of the family were abused and assaulted, and their property damaged. Such conflicts, deeply hurtful in personal terms, were also finely woven into a Manichean melodrama, in which each conversation or dispute became part of the perpetual struggle between God and Satan. The missionaries demonized the priests, the priests demonized the missionaries, and those who attacked the McNeices and their associates no longer treated them as slightly quirky neighbours but, in moments of passion, as dehumanized agents of darkness. In the volatile mind of an adolescent, so grotesque and protracted an ordeal might have produced contrary and competing reactions: heightened loyalty to the evangelical cause; loathing and distrust of Catholics as well as Catholicism; abhorrence for all forms of sectarianism and passionate longing for peace; rejection of the spiritual life and pursuit of material comfort; or, for one of practical bent, the realization that discretion and diplomacy are essential in times of crisis. In coping with the trauma associated with ostracism and uprooting, each of these responses might have played a therapeutic part. Since Frederick was never to record his reactions, they must be inferred from episodes in his subsequent career. In Stallworthy's opinion, the outcome is unambiguous: 'The flight from Omey left some of his brothers and sisters with a fear and bitterness that led them to reject Connemara, but for John [Frederick] it was the prelude to a long life largely devoted to spreading the Christian gospel of love and reconciliation between all classes and creeds in Ireland.'[2]

Another disturbing consequence of the last phase of Frederick's life on Omey has not hitherto been noticed, because of the mistaken assumption that the entire family left the island together. The accepted narrative is that originated by Elizabeth Nicholson, on the basis of a conversation with 'the sister of one of the men who organised their escape': 'The following night [24 March 1879], friends of the MacNeices brought a coach to the mainland side of Omey strand, and William, Alice, and their eight children were driven the sixty miles to Galway and put onto the Dublin train.' Unlike 'some of the others … Fred was very brave'.[3] By this account, the Omey ordeal lasted for less than a month and involved the entire family, whose solidarity should have been reinforced by shared suffering. In fact, it clearly refers to an event occurring five or six months later, after a family nightmare that William, already safe in Dublin, had not shared. During that period, William made only two brief visits to the county in order to testify in court. In the time of crisis, it was not William but Alice who had to fight off hostile priests, negotiate for food and fuel, shelter terrified Protestant girls, tend to her own seven children, maintain the semblance of neighbourly relations, and run the school (if operative). Alice's predicament was worsened by the absence of her adult children. Caroline's husband, Sub-Constable Frizzell, had been transferred from Galway (West Riding) to Mayo on 1 February 1879.[4] In August, William the younger briefly became a probationer at the ICM's training school in Dublin, which accounts for his failure to join Charlotte and his father in the witness box at the Assizes.[5] This suggests that he missed the family's final weeks on the island, leaving Frederick as the eldest boy at home. While Frederick doubtless accepted the need for his father's absence, this experience must have left an imprint on his relationship with both parents and on his assumptions about parenthood, marriage and gender. Once again, we must rely on inference rather than personal testimony, seeking clues in his own performance as a husband and parent.

II

At the end of September 1879, both Alice and William formally terminated their service with the Connemara mission. Alice retired, but William redirected his evangelical zeal to the expanding Dublin enterprise, which had already replaced Connemara as the major focus of missionary endeavour. William was retained as a reader at the improved monthly salary of £6 10s., a post that he kept with one further increment until his retirement as a septuagenarian in March 1905. Until January 1883 he was on the 'Dublin Supplementary' list, indicating that he had responsibility for no fixed district. As such, he may have been temporarily sent to Athlone, as recorded by his grand-daughter.[6] For much of this period, the family lived at 5 Sydney Terrace, a stylish tradesman's house valued at £21 per annum off Avoca Avenue in Blackrock.[7] The contrast between the rigours of Omey and the suburban comforts of south County Dublin must have startled the new arrivals. From 1883 onwards, William's work was no longer supplementary, and the family seems to have moved to the headquarters of the ICM at 135 Townsend Street.[8] There they may have remained until 1893, when the McNeices moved to a house at Clonsilla, eight miles outside the city.

As a mission field, Dublin was utterly unlike Connemara. In Connemara, the missions offered a path out of backwardness, ignorance and presumed brutishness; in Dublin, they promised redemption from unspoken sins and vices scarcely imaginable on Omey. In Connemara, the scripture reader's attempts to win over individual Catholics were constantly thwarted by the social dominance of the priesthood and the tightness of communal and kinship bonds. In Dublin, as in most cities, the Catholic Church had been far less successful in exerting social control and inducing nominal Catholics to perform their religious duties. The opportunities for conversion by stealth, through clandestine visits and personal influence,

' "Bird's Nest", Kingstown': ICM, *Report* (1882).

therefore seemed at least as favourable as in the west. In May 1883, the Dublin superintendent noted the relative absence of 'persecution' in the city, apart from sporadic outbreaks of window-smashing in mission schools.[9] The ICM had developed several clusters of schools and homes in the Coombe, behind the Four Courts, and in Kingstown (Dún Laoghaire). But the hub was in Townsend Street, a squalid thoroughfare running slightly to the north of Trinity College where the Society had located its mission church, training schools, major day schools, and homes for girls and older lads. The training schools were a nucleus for the mission community, providing quarters for unmarried teachers and agents as well as students.[10]

From these vantage points, a small army of workers pursued the work of salvation through twenty-one 'branches' of mission work. The agents were far less isolated than in the scattered stations of Connemara, where even twice-weekly meetings with colleagues were problematic. As the superintendent reported in May 1882:

> The first, and most important branch is *The House-to-House Visiting of Roman Catholics*. It must be confessed that at all times this is a work attended with

considerable difficulties, and requiring on the part of the workers a much larger amount of self-denial, wisdom, judgement, and zeal in the Master's cause, than any other form of Mission work. It is comparatively easy to conduct a service, to address a meeting, or to teach a class, but to go patiently, steadily, and daily to the dens of wickedness and vice in such a city as this, requires the spirit of a true Missionary and a martyr. ... Each morning they assemble for prayer, and having committed themselves to the care and guidance of the great Head of the Church for the day's work, they go forth to their respective districts. ... It is a cause of regret that the number of these city agents is so few. We never before had so few.[11]

Such, we may surmise, was William McNeice's daily routine after his return to the city. There is no record of his particular triumphs and setbacks, but stray documents

'Children Attending Lurgan Street Schools': ICM, *Report* (1880).

from the early twentieth century, such as a register of converts and a scripture reader's journal, testify to the intensity and longevity of this forgotten urban crusade.

On 6 September 1882, sixteen-year-old Frederick became the senior child at home when Charlotte was married in Booterstown parish church. On this occasion, William did turn up as a witness. Charlotte, like Caroline, chose a Protestant policeman from her father's native county.[12] Sub-Constable James Kavanagh, a farmer's son living in Clonfert near Ballinasloe, may well have been one of the police protectors who had virtually monopolized the family's social life during the crisis of 1879. After eight years stationed in Galway, Kavanagh was transferred in 1884 to Meath, where he retired on pension as a sergeant in 1905. Whereas Sub-Constable Frizzell's police record was exemplary, Kavanagh's early career was tarnished by punishments including a forty-shilling fine three months after the wedding.[13] This was to be the last family marriage until 1902, and the two younger daughters and Herbert were still living with their parents in 1901. In August 1889, however, the family was shaken by the death of William the younger, who had been wasting away for two and a half years from consumption (pulmonary tuberculosis). It is noteworthy that Frederick, rather than his father, undertook the responsibility of registering William's death, purchasing the perpetual right to a burial plot in Mount Jerome Cemetery, and acting as attestant.[14] As in the island crisis of 1879, William the elder proved unable to perform his conventional paternal duties.

Nothing is known of Frederick's adolescence in Dublin, though it seems likely that he attended the Society's male school in Townsend Street. The inspector's report for the year 1888–9 recorded the range of subjects then available. Pupils could progress from 'alphabet' to 'intelligent reading', from mere writing to transcription 'from dictation', and from arithmetic to 'compound rules' and 'proportion'. History, geography and abundant religious instruction were provided, but no languages ancient or modern.[15] Despite the inadequacy of this curriculum, I have found no evidence that Frederick attended any 'superior' school or college until 1887, when he was twenty-one. His name does not appear in the published lists of successful candidates in the recently introduced state examinations for 'Intermediate' students.[16] It has been stated that he 'finished his schooling at a Dublin day-school where, at the age of seventeen, he won a medal for oratory, encouraging his father's hope that he might become a barrister'.[17] Yet the only such prize on record is a neatly engraved silver-gilt medal inscribed thus: 'The Harden Memorial Medal Awarded to F. J. McNeice for Oratory 1886–87'.[18] This was not awarded by a school but by the Church of Ireland Young Men's Christian Association, as a prize 'for the best Speaker at the Tuesday Evening Meetings' of the Junior Branch.[19]

This society, quite distinct from the ancestor of today's YMCA,[20] had been founded in Dublin in 1860 and held regular meetings in the Gregg Memorial Hall at 8 Dawson Street. Its patron was the Duke of Abercorn; its president was Lord Plunket, archbishop of Dublin and a key supporter of the ICM; and its secretary until his death in 1884 had been William Hackett Harden. On 14 October 1887, 'Mr J F McNeice' received not only the medal but another prize for the best essay, though he fell short in elocution.[21] The Association aimed 'to promote the Spiritual, Intellectual and Social Improvement of the Young Men of Dublin', supplying an informal substitute for those who could not afford regular higher education. It was open to 'All Young Men' producing a satisfactory 'certificate of character' from a clergyman or an approved layman. Members paid six shillings annually to attend services, public lectures by prominent clergy and laymen, 'Scripture, Prayer, and Conversion meetings', and educational classes (including lectures on political economy sponsored by the Barrington Trust). Members could also use the central lending library, an essential amenity for self-improvers in an era when Dublin had no public provision for borrowers.[22] Through the Association, Frederick would have met other earnest young men of modest means and evangelical bent, sharing their temperate amusements and worthy aspirations.

Dublin in the 1880s provided ample informal opportunities for even a penniless young man to broaden his mind and sharpen his wits. Passion and contests of principle had been temporarily restored to political debate through Gladstone's attempts to tame Irish landlords and enact a measure of self-government. Election rallies, normally the occasion for dreary recitations of empty promises, took on added interest in a period when parliamentarians were being jailed, when long-standing parties were fragmenting and realigning, and when Ireland's constitutional future suddenly seemed negotiable. Frederick may have been remembering episodes of political theatre, such as the general election of 1885 that transformed both nationalist and unionist representation, when looking back over half a century in 1931: 'As a youth I had, in Dublin, many opportunities of hearing distinguished men. I heard Edward Gibson, Thomas Sexton, Timothy Healy, Lord Justice Fitzgibbon, and that most graceful orator, David Plunket.'[23] This was an eclectic list, including two notable Catholic Home Rulers and 'Obstructionists' as well as three celebrated unionist lawyer-politicians.[24] Both Gibson and Plunket (the archbishop's younger brother) represented Dublin University, but Frederick made no reference to the oratorical skills of Edward Carson, Plunket's colleague between 1892 and 1895.

His probable exposure to the public debates of this volatile period did not, however, deter him from the evangelical cause that had inspired his parents and siblings. A few weeks before collecting his prizes from the YMCA, Frederick had entered the male training school for ICM teachers, where he spent less than four months before becoming a probationer on the Dublin Supplementary list in December 1887. He was one of thirteen students, with two lay instructors, including a teacher of music. In November 1888, he secured a post as 'Assistant Master Outdoor' at the Townsend Street male school, sharing the work with four other teachers and a monitor. By now he was self-supporting, with a monthly salary of £4 and a ten-shilling increment in July 1889. Four months later, having buried his brother William, Frederick returned to Connemara.[25]

His new appointment was at Ballyconree (Kingstown), the village four miles north-west of Clifden where a boys' orphanage had been founded in 1849. This had originally catered for Famine victims from Galway and Mayo, housed in a former glebe-house whose remote location by a 'quiet little bay' had been chosen by a former rector, so it was said, to facilitate discreet delivery of contraband. The orphans were offered 'a judicious mixture of industrial training with mental culture', gardening, and carpentry taught by a Catholic instructor.[26] By 1874, the supply of locally accessible orphans having failed, the 'Connemara Orphans' Nursery' was 'open to the whole of Ireland'. Admission was restricted to 'entire orphans' (lacking both parents), under twelve at the time of admission, who were to be 'trained in the principles of the Protestant Church of Ireland and carefully taught the Holy Scriptures'. Incorporating the Glenowen girls' orphanage at Clifden, its funding came from 'a Committee of Ladies (mostly English)' rather than from the ICM itself, anxious as ever to deny charges of Souperism.[27] In 1885, the obligatory pilgrimage to Ballyconree still required a trek 'over rough ground', but the well-tended farm offered a 'pleasing contrast with the adjoining land'.[28] These mainly immigrant orphans supplied an increasing proportion of confirmations in Clifden, masking the decline in local conversions. The orphan population was also in long-term decline by November 1889, when Frederick arrived as teacher.[29]

Nevertheless, the orphanage was one of Connemara's last instruments of salvation to expire, the end coming in spectacular fashion on 29 June 1922. During the bombardment of the Four Courts in Dublin, which precipitated civil war, Clifden republicans expressed their rejection of the Irish Free State by burning down the orphanage, reportedly 'as reprisal for inmates' loyalty'. After evacuation by destroyer to Queenstown and thence England, most of the remaining boys were fortunate enough to be rehoused in the more agreeable surroundings of Parramatta, west of Sydney.[30]

'Orphans Waiting for Admission': *The Story of the Connemara Orphans' Nursery* (1877).

III

In March 1891, a new teacher took over the Society's female school at Ballyconree. Her name was Eliza Margaret Christina Clesham (formerly Clisham).[31] 'Lily', like Frederick, was a product of the missions, having spent ten months as a monitress in Clifden before moving from Connemara to Dublin in September 1884. After almost a year at the female training school (with just seven fellow students), followed by twenty months as a probationer on the Supplementary list, she had spent four years as a schoolmistress for the Society in Grand Canal Street. She was to remain at Ballyconree for two decades on a monthly salary of £4 (increased by £1 in 1898), also acting as a contributor and collector for the Society's Clifden Auxiliary. Though her salary was modest, Eliza had the run of a large school building, with seven rooms, four front windows, and a cow-house. In 1902, she received an unusually generous gratuity of £10 upon her retirement from the missions.[32] The occasion was her marriage to Frederick McNeice.

Though it has been surmised that Lily and Frederick had met in Dublin before becoming engaged in about 1892, it seems likely that the friendship flourished (even if it did not begin) in the wilder terrain of west Connemara.[33] Unlike Frederick, Lily was the daughter of a 'Jumper', whose extended family had been bitterly divided by religion. She was born in Killymongaun, a townland two miles east of Clifden on the road to Galway, on 18 October 1866, and baptized by Hyacinth D'Arcy on 11 November. Lily's parents were Martin Clisham, the son of a mason and farmer who had died in December 1863, and his wife Rose (otherwise Chrystyner Rosetta), a servant in Clifden whose father was a ship carpenter named John Bush.[34] Both parents were of recent British origin, William Clisham having reportedly helped build the town of Clifden for Hyacinth D'Arcy's father, while Rose had been brought over from London to work in the Clifden orphanage.[35] After William's death, Martin had taken over his farm of 32 acres, of land so rough and rocky that the annual valuation was scarcely £3.[36] Even so, William had enjoyed the relative security of leasehold, having taken out a lease for three lives in 1831.[37] With Martin's father dead and possession of the farm assured, Rose and he were married by Hyacinth D'Arcy in December 1865, Martin being unable to sign his name on the register. Lily was their first and probably only child. She was to lose her mother while still a toddler, for Rose was buried in Clifden churchyard in July 1869, in her thirty-sixth year.[38] Martin did not remarry, and eventually moved into the schoolhouse with his daughter.[39]

'The Old House at Ballyconree': *The Story of the Connemara Orphans' Nursery* (1877).

Martin Clisham had already 'embraced Protestantism' before his father William's demise (aged seventy-eight) in 1863, an event that provoked an unseemly struggle for the old man's soul between D'Arcy and his Catholic rivals. Though hitherto 'an ardent persecutor' of his convert son, the dying man had reputedly been won over, even before reiterated visits from D'Arcy in the last three weeks of his life. Despite vehement declarations by Martin and his mother that William would see no priest, a priest arrived at the house with 'a gang of the most ruthless of the baser sort' and anointed the 'half-lifeless body', amidst shouts of 'exultation'. The coffin and Martin the convert were borne to Ardbear on a jaunting car, followed by several D'Arcys, a Catholic curate (Patrick Walsh), and 'a large mob' who wrongly anticipated that the Protestant burial service would be performed. After the ceremony, three cheers were raised for the Pope, and, amidst 'hooting and yelling', a man standing beside Hyacinth D'Arcy was felled by 'a tremendous blow'.[40] A similar struggle may have erupted in April 1865, when Michael Clisham of Aughrusmore was listed in the Protestant Burial Register with a cryptic note: 'Buried by his R.C. relatives in Ardbeer'.[41]

This melodrama eerily re-enacted an earlier episode, in which Martin himself had fallen dangerously ill and been anointed by a priest, before offering a 'dying confession' of the Protestant faith and undergoing 'an almost miraculous recovery'. In 1875, he told his story to a visiting clergyman from Liverpool, who was investigating accusations against the ICM by an ex-Protestant priest in that city. Holding his interviewer 'in breathless suspense' for an hour or more, Martin explained that his conversion had resulted in 'bitter persecution at the hands of his father' until he, like Martin's mother, had also seen the light: 'Martin Clisham then declared to me, that if a mountain of gold was heaped on one side of him, and the flames of Smithfield on the other, and his choice given him, he would deliberately (God assisting him) choose the latter, rather than return to his former superstition and soul-destroying faith.'[42] Similar zeal was displayed by Timothy Clesham, a farmer's son from Mannin near Clifden who spent fifteen years with the Irish Church Missions before enrolling at Trinity College, taking Holy Orders, and becoming a missionary in Mayo.[43] After his father's death during the Great Famine, he and his mother had lived in her brother's house until Timothy's expulsion as a result of his attendance at Derrygimla school and conversion.[44] If Frederick and his family had been grievously abused as 'Soupers', his future wife sprang from a background peopled by persecuted 'Jumpers' and vengeful Catholic kinsmen. In selecting each other, and choosing to pursue missionary careers long after reaching maturity, they both gave every sign of holding fast to the evangelical dream for which their fathers had suffered.

IV

On 26 January 1892, Frederick John McNeice raised his sights by taking the entrance examination for Trinity College, Dublin, so preparing the way for a career in the Church of Ireland. At twenty-five, he was an unusually mature entrant from a relatively humble background. When asked to name his schoolmaster, he ignored both Townsend Street and his father in favour of 'private study'.[45] Like nine-tenths of the 1200 or so students, he was a 'Pensioner', whose fees in the first year amounted to £31 16s. For many Trinity men, this was a modest burden; but for Frederick, it represented more than half of his former annual salary with the ICM.[46] Years of preparation had been required to save for his fees and to pass the entrance examination. This he accomplished with ease, with particularly strong marks in Greek and Mathematics. Entrants were faced with fairly straightforward arithmetic challenges, such as: 'Reduce 1.85 of 3s. 4d. to the decimal of a guinea.' Frederick's weakest paper was in History and Geography, where he would have tackled such topics as 'On what occasions were laws enacted by the British Parliament dealing with religious questions?'[47]

In those days, all non-professional students took a wide range of lectures and examinations in 'Arts', which embraced both Sciences and Classics as well as Catecheticals. All subjects were compulsory in the two 'Freshman' years, but some options were available to Junior and Senior 'Sophisters'. Most of those preparing for Holy Orders started taking additional courses in the Divinity School as Junior Sophisters, with the prospect of securing a Testimonium in Divinity soon after becoming a Bachelor in Arts (about fifty Testimonia were awarded annually). So qualified, they could look forward to ordination in a church that still relied overwhelmingly on Trinity men for its personnel. By comparison with today's relentless schedule, students had considerable freedom in determining when to take examinations, which terms to take off, and whether to prolong or compress the normal period of four years for the course in Arts. Apart from requiring fees for four years and credit for eight of the twelve terms, the College was remarkably indulgent in its treatment of students, particularly non-residents like Frederick. Since credit for four terms could be secured either by attending lectures or by eventually taking an examination, it was theoretically permissible to miss as many as six terms, which in any case were agreeably short. Students were, however, subjected to two general examinations at the end of their Freshman and Sophister periods, the first of which was nicknamed 'Little-Go'.

Students were not required to reside in College, which entailed renting a shared room, attending and paying for nightly 'Commons' (dinner), appearing at daily services in Chapel, and enduring strict moral policing by the Junior Dean.

The cost of residence normally exceeded the fees for tuition.[48] Those lacking sufficient means were free to live with their parents or work for wages. Frederick probably belonged to both categories. He paid no rental to the 'Registrar of Chambers' and appears to have incurred no 'Buttery' charges, implying that he never attended Commons or purchased any supplies.[49] Even as a senior Divinity student, he took no reported part in the weekly debates of the College Theological Society, where so many of his future clerical colleagues and rivals attempted to make their mark as orators, thinkers or organizers.[50] In short, he was one of the invisible majority of Trinity students whose only recorded impact was on class lists and examination returns.

During his third (Junior Sophister) year in College, Frederick subsidized his studies by becoming resident master at Elm Park, Ranelagh, where new buildings had recently been completed for boarders at Rathmines School.[51] This appointment offered accommodation within easy walking distance of College, excellent opportunities for clerical and professional networking, and presumably a stipend. Charles William Benson's celebrated nursery of bishops catered especially for the sons of clergymen, merchants, officials and bankers.[52] In June 1894, Frederick accompanied Benson and a party of masters and senior boys on the annual excursion to Holyhead, 'the great event of the year' when the headmaster, in jocose mood, would tell sufferers from seasickness 'how conducive to health it was for them to "cast up their accounts".'[53] On this occasion, an unexpected thrill interrupted the familiar routine:

> After visiting the old Church at St. Cibi [Cybi] the party proceeded to the South Stack lighthouse, where, as usual, they admired the bridge steps, birds, &c. ... On the return journey in the *Shamrock* the boys were delighted to find the famous Dr. W. G. Grace and the other members of the Gloucestershire XI on board. The Doctor and J. J. Ferris good-naturedly gave their autographs until their pencils were well-nigh worn out.

By the end of 1895, another master had taken charge of the boarders, Frederick having disappeared without further trace in the school magazine.[54]

Frederick's record as a student was solid but unspectacular. He won no exhibitions or prizes (apart from two small catechetical premia), did not compete for Scholarship, and chose not to prepare for the Honor examination in any field. Frederick's performance was much stronger in Classics than Sciences, but his aggregate scores in Little-Go and the final Degree examination were both sufficient, by the practice of the time, to merit a First-Class Honor.[55] He would have faced questions such as 'Why is revenge unlawful?' in Ethics, 'How is the latitude of a ship at sea determined?' in Astronomy, and 'Ought an University to be a place of professional education?' in English Composition. Short passages from Aristophanes and Horace had to be translated into English, while a dozen lines in English would have been the basis for his Latin Composition.[56] Since those securing Firsts for the 'Ordinary' degree were rewarded by the honorific 'Respondent', Frederick's name appeared in the roll of 'Graduates in Honors' below those who had successfully taken the more demanding Moderatorship papers. On 28 June 1895, Frederick John McNeice duly graduated as a Bachelor in Arts, Respondent. In a peer group keenly aware of such nice distinctions, Frederick's achievement would have seemed, at best, worthy.

Frederick's performance was less consistent in the Divinity School, which he entered in late 1893 after showing sufficient acquaintance with Stewart's *Outlines of Moral Philosophy* and Locke's *Essay on the Human Understanding*. His mark (45 per cent) in the entrance examination was exceeded by twenty of the forty-nine candidates.[57] In the final Divinity examination, which he eventually sat in December 1896, he came seventh among the 29 candidates and secured a Testimonium in Divinity, Second Class. The Divinity examinations tested mastery of various theological textbooks and lecture courses, with Frederick excelling in the study of the New Testament in Greek and of both Testaments in the Authorized Version. His weakness was Hebrew, a compulsory element of the programme for which he received no marks at all. His attendance was exemplary at the lectures of John Gwynn (Regius Professor of Divinity) and John Henry Bernard (Archbishop King's Lecturer in Divinity), a future archbishop of Dublin and authority on the mysterious relationship between Swift and Stella.[58] According to Frederick's contemporary Thomas Drury, Bernard's lectures were 'models of clear thinking, interesting, well delivered, with an introduction to each'; whereas Gwynn, though 'the most versatile scholar of all his family', lacked 'the knack of getting his teaching "across".'[59] What Frederick made of their performances is unknown.

The seriousness with which Frederick approached New Testament studies is attested by his notes defacing a Greek and English New Testament that he acquired in 1894. The margins are crammed with at least ten thousand minuscule annotations in both languages, including translations of Greek words at variance with the Authorized or Revised Versions, and numerous cross-references.[60] The word 'Covenant' was subjected to particularly minute exegesis.[61] The diverse calligraphy suggests that Frederick continued to annotate his Testament long after leaving College. It is therefore slightly surprising that he scarcely ever quoted Greek phrases in his available sermons or diaries, with a single exception: κγριε βονθει μοι ('God help me'). This would become his mantra whenever crisis loomed.[62] He retained sufficient interest in Latin to try teaching it to his children in 1917, though Louis's sensuous engagement with Latin declensions aroused his 'impatience' and disapproval: 'Sure no language . . . could be composed on those principles'.[63] Frederick's undergraduate years at Trinity had given him a solid grounding in the Greek and Latin languages, in biblical exegesis and history, and in the doctrine of the Church of Ireland (with extensive treatment of early heresies, doctrinal controversies, and the Reformation). Though neither 'high' nor liberal in its prevalent ritual and theology, by contemporary English standards, Trinity's Divinity School was sufficiently broad in outlook to be deeply distrusted by many Low-Church evangelicals, especially in Ulster. Since its members were appointed without formal reference to the Bench of Bishops or the general synod, the tenor of the Divinity School was often at odds with that of the clergy and laity beyond College walls. For someone raised with the Irish Church Missions, five years at Trinity should have exercised a mildly liberalizing influence.

While Frederick was still a Freshman, his parents and siblings had moved into a small house in Clonsilla, a village by the railway about eight miles to the west of Dublin. The house was set in pasture by the bank of the Royal Canal, in a holding shared by a 'meeting house' and schoolhouse that may have been used by the ICM.[64] The McNeices occupied three rooms with two front windows, and had a fowl-house in the yard.[65] Clearly, evangelical service had not made them rich. Frederick's example doubtless influenced his younger brother Herbert, who was still living in the family home in 1904. Though nearly a decade younger, Herbert followed Frederick to College in October 1896, on the basis of 'private tuition', having twice unsuccessfully taken the Sizarship examination in Hebrew. Sizars were exempt from annual fees and Commons charges, but candidates were required to humiliate themselves in advance by 'proving that they are persons of limited means and entitled to compete for admission on the ground of poverty'. Having done so, Herbert's self-esteem was further dented by abject failure in 1894 and a mediocre if improved performance in 1895.[66] Despite this unpromising start, Herbert eventually surpassed his brother's academic achievements, taking Honor courses leading in 1900 to a silver medal ('Junior Moderatorship') in History and Political Science. Having not attempted the undergraduate Divinity course, and prudently abandoned his quest for a BD, he was neverthless ordained in 1904 and went on to serve the Church in England for nearly half a century.[67]

V

Soon after graduating in Arts, and more than a year before securing his Testimonium in Divinity, John Frederick McNeice had been ordained as 'Curate assistant' in the union of Cappoquin and diocese of Lismore. In a characteristic token of this *rite de passage*, he reversed his Trinity forenames by promoting the biblical 'John' over the secular 'Frederick'.[68] With his university degree and clerkship in Holy Orders, he was now in effect the head of the family, taking central position beside his mother in the only surviving family photograph.[69] Arranged in front of a rough-hewn stone wall, presumably at Clonsilla, the McNeices mingle with other solemn figures, perhaps agents or students of the ICM. William, with his white hair, pointed beard and maddish eyes, sits awkwardly in the front row jostling Margery's knee and avoiding that of Ferguson. From September 1895, Frederick was licensed 'to preach the *Word of God* to perform the office of *Deacon* and to discharge such Divine Offices as belong to the Order of Deacon'. His annual salary of £120, paid out of diocesan funds, was more than double his meagre income as a teacher for the ICM.[70] A few days later, the novice curate preached his first sermon.[71] The curate-in-charge, soon to formally assume the incumbency as befitted the son of a former diocesan chancellor, was Robert Burkitt.[72]

Frederick's Waterford appointment introduced him to a Protestant community equally unlike those of Connemara and Dublin. He was entering the decaying world of the former Ascendancy, which over the next few years would lose most of its remaining property and political influence. The parish was still dotted with ruined castles, handsome houses and elegant demesnes overlooking the Blackwater, a picturesque river springing from the Galtees and meandering through Cork and west Waterford down to Youghal. Episcopalians were even thinner on the ground than in Connemara, accounting for less than 5 per cent of the local population in 1901.[73] Throughout County Waterford, the occupational distribution of Episcopalians was not unlike that in Galway, with heavy over-representation in defence, commerce, the professions, government and service, and relatively few in agriculture and general labour.[74] This superficial resemblance masked the fact that in Cappoquin, devoid of the 'Soupers' and 'Jumpers' who set the parochial tone in Sellerna or Omey, parish life was dominated by the gentry. In 1897, all but two of those elected to parish offices at the Easter vestry belonged to landed families. Of the fourteen parish leaders, ten were magistrates or higher county dignitaries, six were military ex-officers, at least five were major landed proprietors, and all but four appear in the standard directories of the gentry and aristocracy.[75]

As a curate, Frederick therefore had to master the manners, language and attitudes of an unfamiliar social caste. His upbringing would have allowed few opportunities for meeting gentlemen of 'quality', and even at Trinity his class-mates were mainly of professional or mercantile origin. How did he cope with local grandees in the vestry such as Major Henry Philip Chearnley of Salterbridge, Sir Richard John Musgrave, 5th Bt, of Tourin and Mount Rivers, and Major Henry Charles Windsor Villiers-Stuart of Dromana, three of the eight greatest land-owners in the county? It may have been easier for a man fresh from College to mix with parish intellectuals such as Richard John Ussher of Cappagh, the great ornithologist, Dr Richard William Forsayeth of Whitechurch House, an amateur archaeologist, or Sir John Keane, 5th Bt, of Cappoquin House, later a notably enlightened member of Seanad Éireann. Frederick should also have felt at ease with District Inspector George B. Heard, RIC, and the former factory manager John Stanley, who devoted much of his life to the Cappoquin Rowing Club. Even so, Cappoquin presented a daunting social challenge to a curate without wealth, pedigree or local connections. This experience was essential preparation for the relatively exalted social milieu that Frederick was to enter, through his second wife, in 1917.

Cappoquin's pastoral demands were less daunting. The 'Church population' of the parish was only about 200, virtually all of whom regularly attended Sunday services. The majority of adult male parishioners were registered as parochial elec-tors (vestrymen), who numbered thirty-five in 1909. The number of communicants averaged thirty-three in 1891, rising to about seventy-five at Christmas and Easter, confirming the high level of religious observance among Cappoquin's Protestant minority. Thirty-two pupils were enrolled in both Sunday and day schools in 1891, but numbers were slowly falling. Most worrying was the infrequency of baptisms, with four in 1899 and three in 1909. The parish was not yet in terminal decline, and the offertory almost doubled between 1899 and 1909.[76] Yet, for an energetic curate imbued with evangelical ideals, Cappoquin was a most inappropriate posting. Frederick would have had ample spare time to establish his claim to some more challenging parish, save towards the marriage that he had promised Lily Clesham when still a Freshman, and pursue his studies. In July 1896, his probation ended when Robert Burkitt, now the incumbent of Cappoquin, nominated him for ordi-nation as a priest. He was thereupon licensed 'to preach the *word of God* to admin-ister the Sacraments and to perform all other Divine offices therein'.[77]

Over the next five years, Frederick set about strengthening his academic credentials by working towards the degree of Bachelor in Divinity. This entailed taking further examinations in six subjects and eventually submitting a thesis to the Regius Professor. Like most candidates who had already secured curacies, Fred-erick staggered his studies over several years, returning to College on six occasions between December 1897 and June 1901 to sit a single paper. As always, his perfor-mance was steady but unremarkable.[78] At the end of 1898, when he was halfway through, Frederick decided to abandon his relatively sybaritic life in Cappoquin to take on a more demanding assignment. As he reflected on New Year's Eve, 1938: '40 years ago today I left Dublin at about 5.30 for Belfast, to take up work as Curate of Trinity Church under Rev. R. J. Clarke. They have been strenuous years, with much of interest, and much also of sorrow. I went that night to 19, Brookhill Ave. There I lodged for over two years.'[79] His new lodgings were in an avenue of neat semi-detached two-storied houses behind the Belfast Royal Academy, off the Antrim Road in Cliftonville.[80] His most valuable baggage was perhaps his surname, which misleadingly suggested an Antrim background. What would Frederick McNeice make of Ulster? What would Protestant Ulster make out of him?

5. *Orangeman*

BELFAST, 1898–1908

I

Why did Frederick McNeice abandon his comfortable perch in Cappoquin to take a curacy in one of the poorest and roughest parishes of inner Belfast? He had no close Ulster connections. He had not been pushed out of Cappoquin, whose parishioners betokened their approval with a purse of sovereigns.[1] Urban grime replaced the rural idyll of the Blackwater basin; the work was more demanding; the curate's stipend was probably slightly smaller.[2] There was nothing superficially attractive about the Church of the Holy and Undivided Trinity, one of a cluster of parishes jostling for the attention of inner-city Protestants. The days were long gone when worshippers could look out from the church porch across green fields stretching as far as the Antrim Road.[3] By 1899, the massive 56-year-old building was hemmed in by a warren of tiny streets and cramped mill-workers' terraces. Though the parish was only about half a mile square, the population of nominal Episcopalians vastly exceeded that in sleepy Cappoquin. Instead of three or four baptisms each year, as in Cappoquin, there were 300 or more at Trinity church. Yet few of those who were baptized, married or buried there would ever have attended an ordinary service. With 79 registered vestrymen in 1902, 126 communicants on Easter Sunday and 160 on Christmas Day in 1905, the number of parish activists was only about double that in Cappoquin. The margin was even smaller at ordinary Holy Communion services.[4]

Despite appearances, Belfast had two powerful attractions for an earnest but ambitious curate handicapped by his relatively late ordination. First, it offered exhilarating opportunities to join the pan-Christian crusade, then at its height, against urban secularism and religious indifference. The multitude of non-practising Protestants was both an affront and a challenge to the missionary spirit. Second, the city was one of the few places where the Church of Ireland was investing in new buildings and livings, despite systematic discrimination against the diocese in the allocation of central funds.[5] Between 1892 and 1904, when Thomas Welland was bishop,[6] fifteen new churches and ten new parishes were inaugurated in the city. This signified 'church extension' on a scale unknown since the 1870s and unmatched until a burst of church-building in the early 1930s.[7] For a not-so-young clergyman in a hurry, with boundless energy but without powerful patrons, no locality offered better prospects of securing an incumbency after minimal probation.

Many Trinity-trained 'southerners', entering what they regarded as 'the Black North', were initially taken aback by the prevalence of Low-Church evangelical precepts and their political embodiment in the Orange Order. As Trinity's Divinity students had been informed by a College magazine in 1896:

> What has happened to a former well-known member of the School may serve as a warning to those whose thoughts are at present turned towards northern curacies. This reverend gentleman has, he assured me, been practically compelled to join the local Orange Lodge; in fact, his parishioners did not appear to realise that such a thing as his not becoming an Orange brother could be possible. Probably next '12th' we shall see him arranged in all the glories of an Orange-coloured sash, heading a mighty procession.[8]

Incoming clergymen had three options: to alienate their parishioners by remaining aloof; to follow the precedent of many unionist politicians by becoming token members; or to try to use Orangeism as an instrument of moral regeneration. This last was the strategy adopted by many of Frederick's close associates among the clergy of Belfast.

But Frederick McNeice was far better prepared than most southern clergymen for his first Ulster parish. Inexplicable though this might appear to his later apologists, he was already a seasoned Orangeman. In Dublin, he had witnessed the 'most impressive' oratory of Richard Kane, the clerical Grand Master of Belfast and Gaelic Leaguer, who had died a few weeks before Frederick's arrival.[9] He admired Kane's 'fine voice', 'commanding presence', and 'entire absence of bitterness'. Writing in the 1930s, he distanced himself from Kane's immersion in unionist party politics, but praised his commitment to 'religious freedom', his refusal to demand privileges for his own people, his 'warm Irish heart', his love for Ireland, and his pride in being an O'Cahan. 'As a young man' he had found 'something very attractive about Dr. Kane', whose record proved that zealous Orangeism was perfectly compatible with Irishness and personal tolerance.[10]

Perhaps inspired by Kane's example, the curate at Cappoquin became chaplain to one of Dublin's oldest and largest lodges, Cumberland LOL 440. This office entitled him to election as a District chaplain with the right to attend any lodge meeting in the city's District no. 3. The earliest available returns show that he was already chaplain of his lodge by October 1898, being elected for the District a year later. Last returned as a lodge chaplain in November 1901, he relinquished his District office only in 1903, after almost five years in Belfast.[11] Though presumably an infrequent attender except when visiting his family in Clonsilla or taking College examinations, he thus gained access to a Protestant community spectacularly unlike his parishioners in Waterford (a county devoid of Orange lodges). With 62 brethren in 1899, Cumberland was one of nine lodges in a District catering for 368 members, one-third or more of the City's total Orange population. Dublin's Orangemen were mainly tradesmen or manual workers, with only a smattering of merchants and professionals. Even those who laboriously compiled lodge minutes and returns were sometimes barely literate. On 7 October 1898, for example, the District secretary artlessly recorded a resolution urging the 'exclusion of elitrate voters' from the new Local Government franchise.[12]

Frederick was one of a small and fluctuating band of evangelical clergymen who carried their mission into the lodges that met monthly at the Order's headquarters in Rutland Square. Cumberland itself had had no less than six chaplains in 1875, but turnover was rapid and by 1899 six sufficed for the entire District. The District's most prominent lay brethren were Frank Donaldson and Robert Lindsay Crawford, who led a vituperative campaign against 'Ritualism' in the Church of Ireland and even within the Orange chaplaincy. Donaldson, an agent from Armagh, served as Grand Secretary for Dublin City from 1899 to 1921. He secured posthumous notoriety as people's churchwarden in the parish of St Barnabas, where his High-Church adversaries included the new incumbent, Edward Morgan Griffin, and Griffin's raw protégé Johnny Casey. Sean O'Casey's first autobiography conjured up the 'pale, pitiless face' of 'a man to whom any speck of colour on a church wall or in a window meant popery and auto-da-fés of burning protestants every morning in Rutland Square'.[13] Donaldson, a member of Frederick's lodge, was succeeded as District Master in October 1900 by Robert Lindsay Crawford, later renowned for his political idiosyncrasy. Having helped establish an Independent Orange Institution, Crawford successively embraced Home Rule and republicanism before becoming a trade representative in New York for the Irish Free State.[14]

Crawford and Donaldson pursued their evangelical crusade against Romanism and Ritualism through the *Irish Protestant*, the Dublin Protestant Thousand, public demonstrations, and private denunciations of erring clerical brethren. Their targets included three Orange bishops associated with that 'notoriously Ritualistic' and 'Romanizing society', the Society for the Propagation of the Gospel in Foreign Parts. Their insistence on the religious foundation of the Institution carried an important political implication, which anticipated Frederick's later objection to the link between Orangeism and unionism. In September 1898, for example, Donaldson and Crawford induced a bare majority of the District lodge to denounce Salisbury's government and urge the 'formation of an independant Orange Protestant Parliamentry Party' (as the secretary spelt it), pledged to put down Ritualism.[15] Dublin's Orange and evangelical underworld provided invaluable preparation for the people and precepts awaiting Frederick McNeice in Belfast.

The pathway from proselytism to Orangeism was less straightforward than might be assumed. Though the Order was avowedly evangelical and sponsored missionary work at home and abroad, its version of sectarianism differed fundamentally from that of Dallas's ICM. Whereas William McNeice and his comrades exulted in conversion and welcomed every Jumper as a brother, the Orange Order was profoundly suspicious of converts and of the children or spouses of Roman Catholics. Those contaminated by Catholic connections were admissible only by special dispensation of the Grand Orange Lodge of Ireland, and liable to expulsion upon discovery of such associations. The ICM aimed to entice Catholics across the denominational border, while the Orange Order (like the Catholic hierarchy) did its best to reinforce and patrol that border. Whereas overt advocacy of unionist party politics was abhorred by the ICM as an impediment to proselytism, the Orange and unionist causes were often indistinguishable. Such tensions had led to lingering mutual distrust following an acrimonious dispute between the ICM and the Grand Orange Lodge in 1855. By 1900, however, the decline of proselytism and the political fragmentation of Orangeism had helped reconcile these two evangelical crusades. The ICM's organising superintendent joined Frederick's former lodge in 1904, and three candidates for admission to the Order in January 1902 gave their address as the Mission House in Townsend Street.[16] Nevertheless, Frederick's espousal of Orangeism should not be attributed primarily to his sectarian upbringing. Rather, it was a rational response to the formidable social and religious challenges facing an outsider aspiring to become a missionary in Protestant Belfast.

For an evangelical clergyman seeking to promote sobriety and morality among working-class Protestants, active involvement in fraternities, friendly societies, and youth groups was an essential adjunct to the work of parochial organizations. These lodges and societies offered access to workers in other parishes and other denominations, along with those unattached to any church. Once trusted by the brethren, an astute clergyman could use lodge meetings and informal mutual networks to inculcate moral precepts and discourage anti-social behaviour. In order to win the necessary trust, it was sometimes necessary to endorse political or social demands which might seem at odds with conventional religion and morality. This applied particularly to the Orange Order, at once the most powerful and the most controversial of fraternities catering for tradesmen and workers. Clergymen wishing to mobilize Orangemen as a force for good, in essence a 'religious' rather than a 'political' institution, could not always avoid embroilment in sectarianism and unionist politics.

Though Orangeism was always stronger in rural Ulster than in Belfast, membership had kept pace with the city's industrial expansion, rising from 6,000 in the early 1890s to over 10,000 in 1902–3. After a brief setback attributable to poor organization and defections to an 'Independent' splinter group, it recovered to 13,000 by the outbreak of the Great War and surpassed 20,000 in 1920.[17] As Belfast Orangeism blossomed around the turn of the century, clergymen flocked into the Order, taking advantage of their privileged access to District lodges to visit any number of private lodges and gain higher offices at county or national level. The number of Deputy Grand Chaplains trebled from six or seven in 1898–1901 to twenty-one in 1902, peaking at twenty-six in 1909 before a purge of absentee chaplains culled the group to only three or four after 1910. Though the Church of Ireland still contributed most of these chaplains, Methodist and Presbyterian clergymen were becoming increasingly active and prominent in Orange government. In November 1907, for example, the clergymen elected to county office in Belfast included six Presbyterians, two Methodists, and a Congregationalist.[18] For Protestant ministers seeking allies outside their own communions, the Orange Order was becoming increasingly attractive. Clerical influence was most obvious in the multiplication of 'Temperance' lodges (which met without the lure of alcoholic refreshment) and 'Total Abstinence' lodges (which required members to take a personal pledge). By 1910, Belfast had 60 Temperance and 29 Total Abstinence lodges with 4,408 members, accounting for almost half of the city's Orangemen.[19] Despite the Order's unsavoury reputation for drunken and disorderly behaviour, especially around 'the Twelfth', the conduct of many lodges had vastly improved since the 1880s. Orangeism now seemed a genuinely useful instrument for moral-ists and philanthropists aiming to instruct and discipline the masses.

The new curate of Holy Trinity had much in common with the incumbent who recruited him. A decade older, Richard Clarke had also graduated from Trinity College as a Respondent and secured a second-class Testimonium in Divinity. He too was a stranger to industrial Ulster, being the son of a schoolmaster in Virginia, County Cavan.[20] By the turn of the century, he was prominent among the Belfast brethren, delivering sermons in the Ulster Hall for the main July anni-versary service in both 1899 and 1900. These events were organized by Armagh True Blues LOL 154, the flourishing inner-city lodge to which Clarke belonged. His commemorative rhetoric, though conventional enough in its historical refer-ences and phrasing, emphatically reminded Orangemen of their solemn obliga-tion to obey the civil magistrate. In 1899, he quoted Macaulay's dictum that 'we can never advance the kingdom by violating the laws of the kingdom', citing King James II as a case in point. Next year, he drew an implicit parallel between the 'true heroism, the glory of martyrdom' exhibited in 1641, 1688, and 1689, and that displayed in South Africa, where 'our life-blood has been poured out' without loss of morale. He recounted the story of a wounded soldier whose first words as he recovered were: 'Did we win?'[21] Such performances were rewarded by his election as a Deputy Grand Chaplain for Belfast, an office that he retained for several years after moving northwards to Carnmoney, midway between Belfast and Carrick-fergus.[22] Despite subsequent claims that he and his family were 'Protestant Home Rulers',[23] he went on to sign the Ulster Covenant and accept office in the East Antrim Unionist Association.[24] In outward appearance at least, this gracious and liberal-minded minister had become an utterly conventional unionist Orangeman.

Frederick McNeice lost little time in following Clarke's example, becoming a member of St Thomas's Total Abstinence LOL 410, whose sixty-odd members met on the first Thursday of each month in the parochial hall on the Lisburn Road.[25] At first sight, a south Belfast lodge was a surprising choice for a cler-gyman based in central (and briefly in east) Belfast. The explanation probably lies in Frederick's unsuccessful candidacy for a new parish about to be 'carved out' of St Thomas's. Since 1899, William Dowse (the rector) had assigned one of his curates to take services in a schoolhouse further down the Lisburn Road, pending the consecration of St Nicholas's church in 1901. According to Frederick's recollection published in 1931, Dowse had 'hesitated a little' between the curate (Samuel Mitchell) and himself.[26] He chose Mitchell, whereupon the magnani-mous Frederick 'gave it as my decided opinion that he was the man for the place'.[27]

Though neither Dowse nor Mitchell belonged to LOL 410, it teemed with Deputy Grand Chaplains, including three curates of the parish as well as a Congregational minister.[28] It is tempting to infer that Frederick was the 'Orange' candidate for St Thomas's. We may surmise that the lodge provided Frederick with a ready audience of regenerate working men, a springboard into the inner circles of Orangeism, and a discreet venue for cultivating or canvassing both lay and clerical allies.

Immediately upon reaching Belfast on New Year's Eve, Frederick had plunged into parish work, delivering his first sermon next evening. A fortnight later he was administering Holy Communion, several weeks before his formal appointment to the curacy on 3 February. By the end of 1899 Frederick had taken no less than forty-six services, not far short of Clarke's contribution.[29] He expressed his evangelical bent by attending the annual meeting of the Church of Ireland YMCA in January 1899, and a conference of the Church Missionary Society in October 1900.[30] Frederick clearly impressed his chief during the two years he spent as curate at Holy Trinity. In April 1899, Clarke assured the Easter vestry meeting that 'Mr. McNeice's heart was fully in his work, and he was devoting all his gifts most earnestly to the Church work of their parish, and proving himself a real help and power for good'. In an oblique foretaste of things to come, the same meeting reminded the world, including Frederick, of the menace of High-Church 'Ritualism': 'We deplore the attempts which have been made in various quarters to introduce practices which are contrary to the principles of the Church of Ireland, and pledge ourselves to oppose every such invention.'[31] Clarke again lauded his curate, almost in the same words, in the following year.[32] On 13 January 1901, however, Frederick took his last service as curate of the parish,[33] and prepared to vacate his lodgings in Brookhill Avenue. On 6 March, he was licensed to the curacy of St Clement's on the outskirts of Ballymacarrett, perhaps the most testing appointment then available in Belfast. Far from resenting the brevity of his tenure, the parishioners farewelled him with a handsome gold pocket watch and chain in a black leather case, lined with episcopal purple velvet. The presentation appeal was so well supported that 8s. remained for deposit in the social fund.[34]

II

The recently erected iron church of St Clement, on the Beersbridge Road in east Belfast, had become a notorious focus for conflict over Ritualism since the installation of its first incumbent in June 1897. William Peoples, a farmer's son from County Londonderry, had been entrusted with the task of inaugurating a new parish while a curate in Ballymacarrett.[35] Though a trenchant advocate of 'the uncatholic nature of the Roman claims' on issues such as papal infallibility, he himself was accused of Romish tendencies.[36] As Frederick tactfully observed in 1931:

> Mr. Peoples was an able and a devoted man. Very soon after the opening of the church there were difficulties between him and his congregation, not really of a very serious character. ... Sympathisers, who added fuel to the fire, came on the scene from outside. On Sundays crowds gathered round the church and in the church. There were unseemly scenes. It was thought wise to close the church for a time.[37]

In March 1899, the diocesan council had suspended the church for a year, in view of Peoples's refusal 'to act on the advice and direction of the Lord Bishop in respect of certain points which have caused so much excitement in Belfast'. The council also over-ruled his objections to many of the 190 applicants for registration as vestrymen, clearing the way for the Easter vestry to repudiate its minister.[38] Peoples suffered the further embarrassment of being defended in the House of Commons by the anti-Parnellite leader John Dillon, who referred to an 'organised system of persecution', including rallies at the steps of the Custom House where 'Father Peoples' was excoriated for his 'Ritualistic practices'. The Chief Secretary for Ireland (Gerald Balfour) responded that, ever since the opening of the church, Peoples had been opposed by the entire congregation of '700', apart from one churchwarden and about twenty parishioners.[39]

On the appointed day (Easter Monday), neither Peoples nor his church-warden was present, leaving 150 vestrymen to conduct an 'open-air meeting' in front of the locked hall. One of the newly elected select vestrymen observed that Peoples had done his best 'in carrying out the Ritualistic programme': 'But they (the men of Ballymacarrett and of St. Clement's) were not the jellyfish Rev. Mr. Peoples thought them to be. ... But what was the first thing he did? He put a cross on the cloth of the communion table, and five crosses under it; he turned to the east in the service; and introduced flowers about the altar.' After an appeal to parishioners to 'agitate and agitate' for the bishop to be given power to 'treat any traitor to the Church as that traitor deserved', his resolution of condemnation was adopted with 'applause'.[40] The continuing agitation by Low-Church evangelicals and Orangemen was eventually successful. In order to outmanoeuvre Peoples and restore order, St Clement's was temporarily united with another new parish (St Donard's), while a smaller iron church was erected on the opposite side of Beersbridge Road. Peoples then resigned and departed for England, never again to be entrusted with a parish.[41]

The united parishes were placed in the safer hands of William Lee,[42] a prominent Orangeman who, when a curate in Carrickfergus, had been elected as the first

Worshipful Master of Total Abstinence LOL 1537.[43] Lee was an enthusiastic frat-ernizer, becoming a Knight Templar and a Prince Mason as well as a long-serving member of the Grand Orange Lodge of Ireland. According to Frederick, Lee gath-ered together 'a strong band of loyal, hard-working people', as well as 'some cranks, and some who had Ritualism on the brain'. He recalled attending 'a social meeting in St. Donard's in the early days of Mr. Lee's ministry', at which the views of the future curate were placed under intense scrutiny. One parishioner informed him that 'Yon man who took the service on Sunday morning was a Puseyite. It is easy to know a Puseyite. There are three special marks, and he had all three.' Most tell-ingly, like Frederick, 'he was clean-shaven – that is one of the most certain marks of a Puseyite'. Honours were even in the debate that followed: ' "You all remember," I said, "Dr. Kane, the Grand Master of the Belfast Orangemen; he was clean-shaven: surely he was not a Puseyite." "He was clean-shaven," replied our instructor, "and that was the chief fault that was in him. If he had lived a little longer a deputation would have waited on him concerning that very thing." '[44] Frederick's problem in St Clement's was not so much doctrinal ignorance, or religious indifference, as the dangerous amalgam of a little knowledge with a surfeit of zeal.

For sixteen months, Frederick and William Lee maintained a slightly awkward division of responsibilities within the not-so-united parishes. In later years, Fred-erick emphasized that his appointment as curate of St Clement's had been made by Bishop Welland with Lee's consent: 'We interchanged a good deal. I visited, as a rule, in St. Clement's district, and occasionally in St. Donard's, and I took the services and preached, for a time, in both places. I remember distinctly the committee meetings in the little vestry room of St. Donard's iron church. The patience of Mr. Lee was, indeed, wonderful.'[45]

Their amicable collaboration was publicized in July 1901, when Frederick was listed among the clergy attending the Orange anniversary service for District no. 6. After proceeeding in regalia from Ballymacarrett Orange hall to St Clement's, the brethren heard William Lee's appeal to render unto Caesar that which was Caesar's. Failure to observe this dictum 'was the cause of many or all of the political troubles that existed in civilised countries, and especially in our own. As regarded the Orange Institution, he thought it was not right for Orangemen to look upon it as a political organisation.' As members of a religious institution, Orangemen should stand by 'their brethren in the South and West of Ireland [who] were being persecuted for their faith', and should protest against 'any truckling on the part of their legislators to please their hereditary enemy – the Romish Church'.[46] Lee's Orange zeal was again evident in March 1902, when he revisited Carrickfergus to celebrate the opening of a new Orange Hall in Lancasterian Street. Having listened to the rector (George Chamberlain) and another uninitiated clergyman extolling the virtues of Orangeism, he mocked those who, 'while always sympathising with the Order, never thought of joining it. (Laughter.)'[47] In east Belfast, his clerical targets would have been few indeed.

The parishioners of St Clement's, and probably Frederick himself, remained anxious to assert their autonomy. The iron church was again uprooted and reassembled on Templemore Avenue, after an interval in which 'we had services in a tent, and very enjoyable they were'.[48] Despite his intimidating workload, Frederick found time to visit Dublin in June 1901 in order to take his final examination and become, at long last, a Bachelor in Divinity. He returned seven months later to conduct the marriage of his sister Alice to Thomas Magee, a Galway farmer's son who had become a clergyman in the Scottish Episcopal Church at Gartcosh, near Glasgow. As so often on important family occasions, William McNeice played no recorded part, though his youngest daughter Margery witnessed the union.[49] The parishioners of St Clement's remained restive, seething with indignation at the 1902 Easter vestry about the 'unsatisfactory state of affairs in connection with the Divinity school in Trinity College, Dublin, as the Church at present has no control over it'.[50] A few months later, the two parishes were formally separated, Lee keeping St Donard's while Frederick became the third incumbent of St Clement's. As he ruefully recalled in 1931, he thereby took on a parochial debt of £1,000 in return for an annual stipend of £150 without a house.[51] Once again, he marked an important change in status by changing the form of his name, reverting to Frederick John (as in College days) on the occasion of his promotion from curate to incumbent.[52]

III

Shortly before installation as incumbent on 25 July 1902, Frederick undertook two further *rites de passage*. Exactly one month earlier, he completed a test of patience that had outlasted even his quest for a degree in Divinity. After a decade of long-distance engagement, about which nothing is known, he made the long journey to Clifden to wed Eliza Clesham, the schoolmistress at Ballyconree. They were married by Thomas Nee, the rector of Omey, who had taught Eliza at the ICM's female training school in 1884. Their immediate prospects were not bright, especially as Eliza's aged father Martin, the convert, soon came to live with them in Belfast. At the time of marriage, Frederick was boarding in a substantial house at 410 Upper Beersbridge Road called Sweet Home Villa, a witty reference to its owner's surname. He shared its nine rooms and small garden with the wife and seven children of a retired coastguard, all members of the Church of Ireland and presumably of his congregation.[53] The McNeices subsequently moved to a doctor's house at 211 Albertbridge Road, a far less salubrious environment on the city side of Ballymacarrett. According to Elizabeth Nicholson, her mother 'developed a frank dislike of the North of Ireland which she retained for the rest of her life', possibly as a result of coming 'straight up against the more dour and bigoted inhabitants of the city'.[54] The fact that she almost immediately became pregnant with Elizabeth, who was born just before the McNeices' departure from Ballymacarrett, may have intensified her sense of displacement and alienation.

After a short holiday in the Lake District, Frederick made his only reported appearance 'on or near the platform' on 12 July, when he attended the annual demonstration of Belfast Orangemen, on the Downshire estate at Castlereagh. He therefore witnessed a celebrated confrontation that eventually led to the creation of an Independent Loyal Orange Institution repudiating the Order's long-standing alliance with the Irish Unionist Party. An introductory address from the unionist leader, Colonel Edward Saunderson, was rudely interrupted by Thomas Henry Sloan, an obstreperous Worshipful Master prominent in the Belfast Protestant Association. Two speeches reaffirming Orange principles, the first by William Lee of St Donard's, were drowned out by the 'clamourous calls' of Sloan's supporters. When 'hoisted up on the platform amid cheers', ostensibly to restore order, Sloan falsely accused Saunderson of voting against the mandatory official inspection of convent laundries, a key test of evangelical steadfastness at that period. Since Saunderson was Grand Master of Belfast as well as party leader, Sloan's assault was doubly an affront to his authority. This embarrassing altercation exposed the depth of division between those regarding Orangeism as a 'religious' and as a 'political' institution. The platform party included Frederick's anti-Ritualist companions in Dublin's District lodge no. 3: Frank Donaldson (who remained faithful to the leadership while excoriating the unionist government) and Robert Lindsay Crawford (who became Grand Master of the Independents in 1904).[55] Most Orange clergymen and brethren stayed with the original body, yet Sloan's wider concerns about political manipulation of the Order were shared by many leading officers (indeed, the argument is not yet at an end). In later years at least, these concerns were undoubtedly shared by Frederick McNeice.

Faced with the daunting challenge of balancing the books of St Clement's, the new incumbent tried out his skill as a publicist. As so often in later life, he relied on the goodwill of the Protestant press to provide a free forum. On the very day of his institution as incumbent, he sent an appeal for funds to the editor of the *Belfast News-Letter*. Having detailed the ever worsening deficit, which could not be fully paid off by his mainly proletarian parishioners, he addressed the conscience of 'the outside Christian public':

> On every side opportunities for mission work offer, but we are not free to face them. The parish is without endowment, without school-house, without parochial hall, without minister's residence. The only structure we possess is an old iron church. But the work is for 'God's poor,' and we have promise of help from Him.[56]

By April 1903, he could assure the Easter vestry that the parish debt had fallen from over £1,000 to £400, thanks to a successful bazaar and strong public response to his appeals, reinforced by the belief 'that the congregation of St Clement's Church was composed of peaceable, law-abiding, loyal members of the Church of Ireland'. Yet the parish remained in a condition 'without parallel in Ireland', devoid of all the necessary amenities.[57]

During his short incumbency, Frederick showed far greater skill than William Peoples in handling a restive and opinionated congregation. He was helped by the fact that virtually none of the leading rebels against Ritualism remained active in the parish: only one select vestryman or parish officer elected in 1899 still held office three years later.[58] His congregation would have been reassured by his active support for the ICM through sermons and collections, an association recognized by his subsequent election to the executive committee of the Society's Belfast Auxiliary.[59] Yet Frederick, despite his Orange and ICM credentials, was not immune from suspicion. Just before Christmas, he received a resolution signed by almost the entire select vestry: 'After having considerelling [*sic.*] the Past History of St Clement's Church & what it has cost our Church & Protestantism, we Protest against Your Having Early communion on Christmas day, or at any other time.'

The people's churchwarden, a plumber named Job Cherry, explained the problem to his 'Dear Friend & Pastor':

> It is not in any Hostile Spirit to you, But as a Matter of Duty – For until the fact can be Explained away that Our Lord Instituted the Holy Communion after Supper time, no man has any right to hold it before Morning Service. As far as I have heard it Explained Properly from Scripture – their [*sic.*] is Scripture for Communion once a Week But not Early Communion. Sorry if I Have given you any Pain. But you cannot be more Pained than I am. My Good wife & Family Holds my views Man Changes but God never Yours for the Master Job Cherry. Compliments of the Season To you & your Partner.[60]

This quaint missive indicates the magnitude of the challenge facing Frederick at St Clement's. Churchwarden Cherry was a man of weight in the parish, a 'Registered

Plumber, Gasfitter, and Sanitary Engineer' with three addresses, and a Poor Law Guardian for Court ward. His letterhead was decorated with tasteful drawings of modern bath-tubs and water-closets, and his envelope carried the armorial crest of Belfast with the city's motto, dervied from Psalm 116: 12 ('Pro tanto quid retribuamus'). He lived outside the parish in County Down, in a superior house with seven front windows and eight rooms.[61] Yet Cherry, barely literate though he was, was so literal in his reading of the Bible that no clergyman, however Low, would have passed all his tests for orthodoxy.

While at St Clement's, Frederick never lost contact with his old parish. He returned to preach at Holy Trinity Church in April 1901 and again in June 1902, when the morning collection was devoted to St Clement's parish.[62] In early 1903, he managed to abandon a posting that had become unbearably onerous if, in some masochistic sense, enjoyable: 'I shall never forget my time in St. Clement's as Curate and Rector. I enjoyed it greatly. I was on the verge of a physical break down when, in May 1903, I returned to Trinity Church as successor to Canon Clarke.'[63] Relief, coupled with pride in his achievement, was obvious in Frederick's first and last address to the Easter vestry on 15 April: 'He regretted that his successor would have so many difficulties to face, but he (Mr. McNeice) in starting had many more to face.' He had come to the parish as 'a stranger among strangers, and left it, having gained many friends'.[64] His successor, the hymnographer William Ralph, lasted less than three years before escaping to England, a course also followed by Francis Doherty after his seven years as incumbent.[65] Frederick revisited St Clement's in April 1906 to welcome Doherty, who was aware that he was about to enter a minefield. While complimenting St Clement's as 'the most loyal parish in the North of Ireland', Doherty noted ruefully that it 'had had a history in the past' and 'had a little bit of history, he thought, in the present'.[66]

IV

On 16 April 1903, Frederick attended his second Easter vestry at Holy Trinity, where Richard Clarke extolled the man who was about to succeed him as incumbent: 'Mr. McNeice had worked in the parish; he was known to them all; he had ability, energy, and a sympathetic mind.' Foremost among those welcoming him was Louis Plunkett, the parish treasurer, who offered his 'hearty congratulations . . . on behalf of the congregation' to a minister who had been 'unanimously chosen' by the trustees of the parish. Frederick replied that, having 'left against some of their wishes to take up the work of St. Clement's parish', he now returned as 'an older and he hoped a wiser man'.[67] Frederick John McNeice was instituted as incumbent on 17 April, on a substantially increased stipend, and delivered his first sermon on 3 May.[68] Meanwhile, his life had been further complicated by another happy yet taxing event. On 24 April, while still enduring the gloomy environment of Albertbridge Road, Lily had borne her first child. Caroline Elizabeth was named after Frederick's eldest sister, who had died in 1895, but she was usually called Elizabeth or 'Elsie' after her mother. The baby had to wait five weeks before being baptized by her father on Whitsun, at a special afternoon ceremony.[69] The move to Holy Trinity had brought no relief to the indefatigable Frederick, who, in the temporary absence of a curate, took almost every service between May and August. As at St Clement's, the parochial work proved exhausting and stressful, as Lily observed in September 1906: 'Fred is better. He started off this morning at 9.30 for a clerical meeting and returned *this evening* at 7 and remained about half an hour and flew off once more. It is now 10 p.m. and he is still out!! That is the sort of life he leads – no wonder he is *thin*.'[70] A curacy in Cappoquin, with its wealthy parishioners, sparsely populated pews, and lazy afternoons, must sometimes have seemed enviable in retrospect.

The surviving parish records enable us to look more closely at the people to whom Frederick ministered between 1903 and 1908. As in St Clement's, few of the parishioners were people of means or 'weight'. No less than 49% of the fathers of those baptized in 1903–4 were mere 'labourers', while 35% were tradesmen or skilled workers. Only 9% claimed the slightly higher status of shopkeepers, whitish-collar workers, or members of the civil and military services, while there were but three professional men (a surgeon, an assistant dentist, and Frederick himself). The profile of those actively involved in parochial affairs was conspicuously different. Those who registered as vestrymen were mainly white-collar workers (28%), members of the services (26%), skilled workers (24%), and shopkeepers or merchants (14%), with two professional men (a doctor and a civil engineer). Virtually no unskilled workers were registered, confirming that most of the families who baptized their children in Trinity church were merely nominal parishioners.[71] The identikit (median) vestryman was a 47-year-old, typically heading a household of five members in a six-roomed house.[72] Two-thirds were natives of Belfast, Antrim, or Down, while most of the remainder came from the broader Ulster hinterland of industrial Belfast.[73]

Perhaps as a result of the dispersion of workers previously employed in local mills, the vestrymen were scattered through every city ward and occasionally farther afield. Very few resided in the immediate vicinity of the church, while two-fifths lived more than one kilometre away. Almost two-thirds lived in the north-westerly sector, stretching out along the Antrim Road with its more substantial, suburban housing.[74] Following his return to Holy Trinity, which lacked a rectory, Frederick himself rented a succession of houses in the vicinity of the Belfast Royal Academy, all within a mile of the church. After three years at 38 Cliftonville Avenue, the McNeices spent a year across the street at no. 25 before moving a block eastwards to 1 Brookhill Avenue (a few doors away from Frederick's lodgings between 1899 and 1901).[75] Renting six different houses in less than a decade must have added further stress to Frederick's unsettled life in Belfast.

While incumbent of Holy Trinity, Frederick formed a close alliance and friendship with Louis Plunkett, a wealthy marine insurance broker who contrived, as treasurer and subscriber, to keep the parish virtually free from debt.[76] At every Easter vestry, Frederick took care to compliment 'their good friend' and 'worthy and highly respected treasurer', 'to whom they were under fresh obligations year after year', 'who had helped them by his name, and far too generously by his purse', a man admired 'for all the help he gave, and for the example he set' – in short, 'their best friend'.[77] He was remembered in the parish as 'a man of gracious and striking personality, humble and generous'; and in the *Belfast News-Letter* as 'a man of outstanding business ability, sincere, and of a very kindly disposition … whilst in social circles in the city he enjoyed a signal measure of popularity'.[78] In a parish virtually devoid of wealthy philanthropists, whether gentry or businessmen, Plunkett was a precious asset. Though he had long since deserted Cliftonpark Avenue for a succession of mansions in south Belfast, he long remained a Trinity pew-holder and parish officer, eventually representing the diocese in the general synod.[79] Plunkett was also a zealous Freemason, rising from Entered Apprentice in 1877 to the dizzy heights of Prince Mason, Grand Inspector, Inquisitor, and Commander (31°), and eventually Prince of the Royal Secret (32°). As a Prince Mason, he shared a chapter (lodge) with prominent churchmen such as John Baptist Crozier and William Shaw Kerr, both important figures in Frederick's career.[80] Plunkett's goodwill and extensive connections were to prove invaluable to Frederick McNeice long after his departure from Belfast.

During his incumbency, Frederick became ever more entangled in the inner circles of the Orange Order. Though avoiding public appearances on the Twelfth or at anniversary services, he was regularly re-elected as a Deputy Grand Chaplain for Belfast. This was admittedly a purely titular office, and he attended only one monthly meeting of the Belfast Grand Lodge during his entire career. This record was unexceptional, as most of his fellow chaplains missed every meeting in most years.[81] Even Bishop Crozier attended only one meeting during his tenure as Grand Chaplain of Belfast.[82] The practical activity of Orange clergymen was typically conducted in private and district lodges, to which those with county office had unrestricted access. Frederick served as a District chaplain in no fewer than four of Belfast's ten Districts, retaining his connection with Ballymacarrett (District no. 6) right up to his departure from Belfast. The territory of these districts ranged over much of north, east, and south Belfast. Frederick's Orange connections were further extended by his membership of at least three private lodges. After several years in St Thomas's Total Abstinence LOL 410 (District no. 5), he spent a year in King and Constitution LOL 638 (District no. 3), before transferring or affiliating to Roe Memorial Total Abstinence LOL 938 (District no. 6) in 1906.[83] These lodges had no obvious link with Holy Trinity, instead offering access to Orange networks extending far beyond his own parish. In the absence of records for his lodges (all now defunct), we can only conjecture how assiduously Frederick attended meetings, or how effectively he exploited his Orange associations in Belfast. Even so, his multiple and ever-changing lodge affiliations suggest that the Order offered benefits more substantial than a cup of tea or a peculiar handshake.

While Frederick built up his reputation as an industrious pastor and a zealous Orangeman, his family was multiplying. Two years after Caroline Elizabeth's arrival, Lily bore her first son, who suffered from Down's Syndrome or 'Mongolism', as it was then termed. William Lindsay Bushe McNeice was born on 31 March 1905, at 38 Cliftonville Avenue. As with Caroline Elizabeth, the boy's names paid tribute to both families, recalling Lily's English mother as well as Frederick's father and his long-dead eldest brother. He was baptized by Edward Moore, a curate in Ballynafeigh who had overlapped with Frederick as a Divinity student at Trinity College.[84] When promoted to an incumbency in north Down later in 1905, he was 'preached in' at his first evening service by Frederick.[85] In 1912, Moore too would risk parochial hostility by declining to sign the Ulster Covenant, unionist though he was.[86]

The last child followed on 12 September 1907, when Frederick Louis McNeice was born in the corner house at 1 Brookhill Avenue. Like Caroline, he was baptized in Holy Trinity Church by his father.[87] His names had a distinctly royal ring, both Frederick and Louis (or Lewis) being recurrent names in the House of Hanover. But the name Louis was primarily a tribute to his Godfather, Louis Plunkett, whose great-uncle had been a prominent clerical schoolmaster of French origin.[88] Freddie's arrival was marked by an intricate silver christening mug in a black leather case with gold lettering and borders, a superior example of Belfast workmanship.[89] Plunkett may have been the inspiration for Louis's whimsical 'Godfather', celebrating a man who signed 'huge cheques without thinking, never is overdrawn', and was adept 'at all surprises, disguises'. If so, he continued to inhabit the poet's dream-life long after Plunkett's death in 1918, for 'The air raids

| Found him lying alone on his back and blowing | Carefree | Smoke-rings – a pipe-dream over the burning city'.[90]

The arrival of the next generation coincided with the loss, in rapid succession, of all three remaining grandparents. On 4 March 1904, Alice Jane McNeice succumbed at the age of seventy to heart failure following hepatic ascites, often associated with cirrhosis of the liver. Her daughter Margery witnessed the death in Clonsilla. Alice's husband followed on 13 December 1906, when Herbert witnessed the death from senility of William Lindsay McNeice, aged '77'.[91] William's contribution to the ICM was briefly acknowledged in the annual report for 1906–7, which regretted the loss of a reader 'who laboured for many years on the Society's staff'. He had retired with an annuity less than two years earlier.[92] No hint remains of Frederick's reaction to the loss of his parents, who were duly interred in the family grave at Mount Jerome Cemetery.[93] Meanwhile, on 13 September 1906, Martyn Clesham (described as a 'merchant') had succumbed to hepatitis and cardiac exhaustion at the ago of seventy-five. He died during a family holiday near Millisle, County Down, in the presence of his son-in-law. His burial place at Carrowdore, which had no family associations for either the McNeices or the Cleshams, was to become an unlikely shrine for later generations. Having lived with her father in both Ballyconree and Belfast, Lily was bereft: 'It is very lonely for me now. I had so much to do before that I feel the loss all the more.'[94]

By 1908, with three young children and a relentless workload in his inner-city parish, Frederick McNeice was ready to move on. The invitation, when it came, was even more challenging than his summons to St Clement's in 1901. The inferno that he entered in November was Carrickfergus.

6. Diplomat

CARRICKFERGUS, 1908–1912

I

In November 1908, the normally docile parish of St Nicholas's, Carrickfergus, achieved nationwide notoriety by fiercely resisting the appointment of Frederick McNeice as its rector. The vacancy arose from the terminal illness of George Chamberlain, incumbent since 1886, who was now recumbent and no longer capable of administering a large and busy parish.[1] Chamberlain, a native of Limerick, was the first rector of Carrickfergus to be nominated by a board of parochial and diocesan representatives, rather than by Crown patronage. His own appointment had reportedly been backed by 70 per cent of the parish yet opposed by two of the three parochial representatives, without causing an enduring rift.[2] He was one of the clergymen chided by his former curate, William Lee, for extolling the Orange Order while declining to join it.[3] Chamberlain had acquired his first parish when only twenty-eight, but did not quite fulfil his early promise. As Frederick tactfully remarked in 1933: 'He was a richly-gifted man, and was himself a rich gift to this church and to the people of the neighbourhood. ... In the end it will matter little who was bishop, or archdeacon, or incumbent. Was he faithful where he was? That alone will matter.'[4]

In recent months, the parish had been administered by William Bradley, curate of the parish since August 1907.[5] Unlike most of Chamberlain's curates, Bradley was an Ulsterman, his father having been curate and later rector of Monaghan.[6]

Denis O'D. Hanna, 'St Nicholas' Church': George A. Mitchell, Rector,
A Guide to Saint Nicholas' Church, Carrickfergus (1962).

He already had considerable support in the parish, but was not yet prominent in the Orange Order.[7] When Bishop Crozier convened the board of nominators, comprising three parochial and three diocesan nominators, three candidates were proposed by the parochial representatives.[8] Bradley's claim was pressed by Samuel Close, a prominent civil engineer and architect described 'as a big rugged man who shunned publicity, but who was gentle and kind'.[9] The other two candidates were both southerners with parishes of their own. Oswald Scott, a Dubliner who had administered parishes in Belfast and Down,[10] was put forward by Thomas Gorman, a clerk whose heroically long service in the choir and Sunday school is commemorated by a brass plate on the organ. The third candidate was Lawrence Story,[11] an equally experienced minister from Galway who was proposed by his reputed 'relative', Thomas MacGregor Greer of Sea Park and Tullylagan Manor in Tyrone.[12] The board failed to reach a clear decision, making it necessary to propose an outsider. On 8 November, Frederick was approached by George Ewart on behalf of the board: 'Interviewed re Carrickfergus. Left myself in the hands of Bishop and nominators.' His nomination proved acceptable to the entire board, with the exception of Thomas Gorman. On 10 November, Frederick received notice of the nomination from the adjourned board and 'wrote to Bishop accepting'.[13] The bishop happily endorsed the nomination of his brother Orangeman and colleague in the Belfast Grand Lodge.

The announcement of Frederick's appointment provoked 'an impromptu meeting of the parishioners' in the town hall, which was 'filled to overflowing'. The meeting heard a succession of plaudits for Bradley, indignant denunciations of the two parochial nominators who had backed Frederick, and ringing assertions that the parishioners were democratically entitled to choose their own rector. It was claimed that 'Mr. Bradley had a way with him that had won all their hearts', and that he was 'very popular' as a result of his able administration of the parish. Bradley prudently stayed away from the meeting and dissociated himself from the protest. Another protestor, evidently unfamiliar with Frederick's Low-Church credentials, declared menacingly that 'they were not going to be priest-ridden in St. Nicholas Church'. James McFerran, a prominent Orangeman and Freemason who managed the Barn Spinning Mills, moved a resolution condemning 'the action of two of the three parochial nominators in going against the wishes of the entire parish'. The meeting resolved to present Frederick with a petition urging his withdrawal, and to send the parochial nominators a memorial of protest. This was signed by all but two members of the select vestry and 'almost the entire congregation'.[14]

Next day, Frederick's claim to the parish was further assailed in a bombastic letter sent to the local newspaper by John Heron Lepper of Rhanbuoy, a mansion by the Belfast road just beyond the shipyard. He wrote that Bradley had 'won the approval, esteem, and love not only of his own church people, but of all classes and creeds as well'. He denounced the two parochial nominators who had ignored the petition supported by nine-tenths of parishioners, declaring that 'rule by Rome would be more tolerable, for it at least does not pretend to listen to the popular voice'. Should they 'submit like a pack of schoolboys, and accept an unknown pedagogue without a murmur?'[15] The oxymoron 'unknown pedagogue' hinted that Frederick's background as a schoolmaster was indeed known to Lepper, who had graduated from Trinity College in the same year as Herbert McNeice.[16]

Lepper's attack on episcopal despotism carried considerable weight in Carrickfergus, even though he was not yet a select vestryman. His late father, a wealthy flax-spinner, Freemason and yachtsman, had bequeathed the parish an endowment which, in Bradley's words, 'conferred a great boon on clergy and people alike'.[17] Lepper was a cultivated, indeed remarkable young man, who had left College with a gold medal in Modern Literature, despite a 'grievous lifelong physical handicap – he could not even walk across a room without crutches'. This did not prevent him from yachting, like his father, in Belfast Lough and taking country walks 'in his self-propelled chair'. He was called to the Bar in 1903, but never practised, married an English law graduate, and settled into the life of a gentleman of leisure and writer of historical romances.[18] Shortly after graduation, he was initiated as a Freemason in Louis Plunkett's Belfast lodge (Acacia no. 7), subsequently joining its élite equivalent in the Belfast Orange Order, also no. 7 (Eldon).[19] Lepper soon set aside Orangeism to pursue the more speculative discipline of Freemasonry, belonging to at least six other Irish lodges before moving to London, where he eventually became the librarian at Freemasons' Hall and historian of the Irish order. In Carrickfergus, Lepper belonged successively to Harmonie Lodge 282, St Patrick's Lodge 43, and eventually Lodge 346, founded in 1913 and named after himself (an unusual distinction for a 34-year-old). His eloquent attack on Frederick's appointment was not merely a personal opinion, but an expression of views widely held in the two great fraternities in Carrickfergus.

Four days after the initial protest, an exclusively male affair, a meeting of 'the Ladies of the parish' was chaired by the wife of George Edmonstone Kirk of Thornfield, a wealthy landlord (and son of a former dean of Connor) who was absent in China.[20] Mrs Kirk had herself come from London to add weight to the protest. She praised Bradley for having raised attendance at evening services, while declaring that there was 'absolutely no personal feeling whatever against the gentleman chosen by the nominators'. On the same Saturday, Frederick met a delegation of parishioners without promising withdrawal, while 'several influential personages' were appointed to lobby the bishop in the hope of securing that outcome. Further protest was postponed, and the congregation listened to a sermon from Bradley on 'forbearance', as a means of avoiding 'disappointment'. The drama in Carrickfergus soon became a matter of debate throughout the Church of Ireland, evincing various expressions of support for the blameless target of the protesters. William Lee, Frederick's old colleague at St Donard's, proposed a motion of congratulation on behalf of the Belfast Younger Clergy Union.[21] The *Church of Ireland Gazette* praised Frederick's record at Holy Trinity, where he had 'served with ability and zeal', and regretted 'that after the appointment was made known, a section of the parishioners of Carrickfergus met and expressed their dissatisfaction'. The next issue emphasized 'that there is no objection to Mr. McNeice personally' and anticipated a happy outcome to the dispute: 'His appointment is generally recognized to be an excellent one, and since he neither sought the parish, not desired it, but simply obeyed the call of duty, his numerous friends are confident that he will soon be regarded in Carrickfergus with the same affection and confidence as he has up to this received wherever he has worked.'[22]

Meanwhile, Lepper convened a further meeting on Monday, 23 November, two days before Frederick's institution as rector. The resumption of protest was justified by Bishop Crozier's refusal to meet Mrs Kirk, despite her husband's formidable credentials. Lepper further praised Bradley's record in trebling school attendance, achieving a seven-fold increase in evening congregations, boosting collections, and clearing the debt for church renovations. He also referred to the circulation of 'very ugly rumours', presumably about Bradley: 'slanderers had gone behind their backs with tales to those in authority'. Modulating into Orange oratory, he proclaimed that 'the natives of Carrickfergus had borne themselves like men on many a battlefield', recalled 'the days of King William of Orange, when they raised the standard in Carrickfergus which had never been lowered', and urged his audience to 'stick shoulder to shoulder at the guns'.

Henry Blackburne, the vestry's honorary solicitor, entertained the meeting with a detailed account of the private proceedings of the board of nominators. Blackburne suggested a boycott of parish collections, believing 'that if they stopped the supplies they would soon bring these people to their senses', a proposal greeted by 'Hear, hear, and applause'. Mrs Kirk proposed a pledge 'to support the Select Vestry should they see fit to adopt a line of conduct' affirming the unpopularity of the appointment, adding (perhaps with reference to Bradley's sermon) that 'our forbearance has been ill rewarded'. She also quoted a response to Colonel McCalmont, MP, from Bishop Crozier, enquiring sarcastically 'whether any other rector would be acceptable to us, if the present appointment were rescinded'. Cries of 'Oh' greeted Crozier's parting shot: 'You know me well enough to know that I am not the man to be ruled by mob law.' After a discussion as to whether parishioners should 'stay away' or go to neighbouring parishes, and a playful suggestion that Lepper himself might conduct Sunday meetings in the YMCA mission hall, it was announced that Mrs Kirk was 'prepared to subscribe largely to a fund to provide conveyances for those who are unable to pay for themselves to go to Whitehead or Jordanstown'.[23] Next day, ten members of the select vestry protested that Crozier had ignored 'the spirit of the Constitution', when informing Mrs Kirk that he would not be 'worthy of holding the office of Bishop if I allowed popular clamour to nullify the Laws of the Church'.[24] The stage was set for a campaign of civil disobedience to Church authority, and a disagreeable reception for the new rector of Carrickfergus.

Frederick had stood firm throughout these preliminary sallies, despite Louis Plunkett's reported warning that transfer to a hostile environment might imperil Lily's health.[25] Always punctilious in enjoining obedience to properly constituted authority, whether civil or ecclesiastical, he considered that acceptance of his bishop's invitation was an act of duty. When himself a bishop, he chastised those who attributed moral primacy to the views of parochial representatives in making appointments.[26] Upon reaching Carrickfergus for the institution on 25 November, Lily and he were met by extra police at the entrances to the church and in nearby streets. This was deemed unnecessary by the *Carrickfergus Advertiser*, since 'prominent churchmen in the town' had already taken appropriate precautions.[27] According to Elizabeth's (second-hand) account, however, her parents were greeted by 'jeering crowds' at the railway station, forced to take tea behind locked doors in the vestry room, and insulted by Millies (female mill workers) scrabbling at the windows of the waiting room back at the station. Potential protesters were apparently excluded from the church when the police locked the gates after admission of the official party.[28]

The ceremony attracted a 'large attendance' of clergy, along with visitors and 'a number of members of other denominations', but only a 'meagre sprinkling' of parishioners. Thomas Gorman, the people's churchwarden, temporarily set aside his objections to sign the certificate of institution. Bradley read from the tenth chapter of St John's Gospel, perhaps savouring the implications of the opening verses: 'He that entereth not by the door into the fold of the sheep, but climbeth up some other way, the same is a thief and a robber. But he that entereth in by the door is the shepherd of the sheep.' After remarking defensively that 'it was not a question of every seat in the church being filled', Bishop Crozier stated that the new rector was beloved 'all over the diocese to which he belonged', and that the Church already owed much to him for his work in diocesan synods. Even the *Advertiser*, which had given such sympathetic publicity to the protestors, reported that 'wherever Mr McNeice has worked he has won the esteem and affection of the people' – as measured by his 'purse of gold sovereigns' from Cappoquin, his 'gold watch and chain, books, etc.' on relinquishing the curacy of Holy Trinity, and further 'valuable presentations' from St Clement's.[29] The *Church of Ireland Gazette* expressed relief that the ceremony had 'passed off quietly', and applauded Crozier's innovation in 'conducting the institution of an incumbent in his own parish'.[30]

On the following Sunday (Advent), Frederick delivered two farewell sermons at Holy Trinity on appropriate themes: 'Remember them that have the rule over you, which spake unto you the word of God' (Heb. 13: 7–8, morning) and 'I thank my God upon all my remembrance of you' (Phil. 1: 3, evening). The select vestry duly expressed its 'deep sense of serious loss' at his departure.[31] Meanwhile, at St Nicholas's, Bradley conducted his last service as acting incumbent. Most of the 'very large crowd' exercised 'passive resistance' by declining to contribute to the collection, 'a number of seat-holders' having already 'given up their sittings' and removed their books and cushions. The boycott of collections followed yet another meeting chaired by Lepper, unmoved by a letter from Bradley urging parishioners to accept the appointment as 'binding' and to restore the 'spirit of harmony'. The revelation that the rector's stipend was immune from interference by parishioners 'threw a damper over the proceedings'. They could, however, obstruct the appointment of a curate, who was paid out of the parochial sustentation fund. The meeting rejected the general withholding of pew rents, but resolved (on Henry Blackburne's proposal) to 'discontinue all other parochial contributions'. A committee was established to divide the parish into campaign districts and to place these under supervision.[32] Frederick prepared to face his adversaries by commencing 'the visitation of the parish' over the following week, before conducting his first service on 6 December. Bradley read the lessons, the dean of Belfast called for 'Christian spirit', and in the evening Frederick gave a suitably anodyne sermon quoting 'St. Patrick's Breastplate', one of his favourite hymns:

> Christ in quiet, Christ in danger,
> Christ in hearts of all that love me,
> Christ in mouth of friend and stranger.[33]

The last public exhibition of discontent occurred on 18 December, when a further meeting decided to ask the Midland Railway Company about 'a suitable train' for parishioners travelling to other churches 'in Belfast and neighbourhood'. The *Church of Ireland Gazette* wondered what 'the discontented parishioners expect to achieve' beyond injuring 'the church locally', and reported 'a very fair congregation and quite the average number of communicants' at a recent service.[34] The focus of resistance was removed just before Christmas, when Crozier recommended Bradley's appointment as curate at St Mark's, Dundela. Before he could be transferred, the incumbent of Jordanstown conveniently expired, enabling Bradley to be instituted as his successor on 26 January after a remarkably rapid process of nomination. The *Gazette* declared that, in Carrickfergus, 'the recent trouble is now a thing of the past, and that the parishioners there, with scarcely an exception, are loyally supporting their new rector'.[35] Frederick did not attend the farewell ceremony in the parochial hall, chaired by Lepper, at which Bradley was presented by Mrs Kirk with a solid silver salver and a purse of sovereigns. Instead, it was left to the Independent minister in Carrickfergus to praise Bradley for doing 'what in him lay to keep the old flag flying', whichever flag that might have been.[36] The definitive gesture of reconciliation was delayed until 31 March, when Bradley was married in St Nicholas's to Doris Barbour Pirrie. Her father, managing director of the Barn Mills, was one of the chief protesters.[37] The church was filled to 'utmost capacity', flags and bunting decorated the vicinity of the Barn Mills, and Frederick was among the officiating clergy. He was not, however, credited with any of the multitude of wedding presents enumerated in the *Advertiser*.[38]

Since the drama of Frederick's appointment to Carrickfergus has been recounted elsewhere, it may seem superfluous to probe further into the local circumstances and personal connections of those involved. By his daughter's account, as summarized by Stallworthy: 'The hostility lasted for about a year, but the new rector performed his duties (and those of the curate he could not afford) so well that opposition to him and his family melted away, and in due course he came to be loved and respected as in his previous parishes.'[39] Likewise, Rutherford concludes that 'things settled down very quickly and the parishioners soon discovered the worth, ability, and courage of their new rector'.[40] The happy ending signified the eventual triumph of virtue and goodwill, just as the initial protest, however misjudged, was motivated by goodwill towards another virtuous minister. Though adequate as the plot for an uplifting melodrama, this construction ignores the process of diplomacy by which Frederick eventually disarmed his critics. By looking closely into the background and affiliations of his opponents, we may expose something of the personal tact and political acumen that he applied to seemingly daunting problems. What follows is based on nominal records concerning the protestors and parish officers, which illuminate their place in Carrickfergus society and involvement in various fraternities and societies. Having identified the wider networks represented by the protestors, we may track Frederick's involvement with each network as well as his personal dealings with key opponents. The personality that emerges is patient, subtle, yet in certain respects elusive.

II

The parish that Frederick entered in 1908 covered about twenty-six square miles, stretching from the north shore of Belfast Lough through fertile farmlands into the boggy fringes of Antrim's mountainous interior. Just over half of the parish population lived in the town of Carrickfergus, a minor industrial centre between Belfast and Larne. The town's population had hovered between 4000 and 5000 ever since 1861, and was mainly sustained by a few long-standing enterprises. In 1888, these included 'a flax spinning mill, a weaving factory, bleach works, print works, a ship yard, and several salt works, giving between them employment to over 1,500 people'.[41] The port had fallen into decline and the garrison had shrunk to a small outpost of the Royal Garrison Artillery, though the ancient town walls and

Castle compound recalled the town's strategic importance in the distant past. Easy access by railway to Belfast (only nine miles to the south-west) had also reduced its importance as a regional centre and market town. Carrick remained largely dependant on textiles and mining rather than engineering and shipbuilding, the industries that had recently transformed Belfast into one of the most dynamic industrial cities in the British Isles. In 1911, when almost half of the town's adult males owed their livelihood to industry, less than 8 per cent were engaged in the heavy industrial sector. Textiles and minerals each accounted for 11 per cent, with 9 per cent in building.[42]

Carrick's rather old-fashioned industrial structure was reflected in the town's social institutions, including several charitable foundations, various fraternities, temperance tea-rooms and youth organizations, active congregations of all the major Churches and a range of sporting clubs. Several townsmen were prominent in the East Antrim Unionist Association, and occasional attempts were made to spread the gospel of liberalism as expressed in the *Ulster Guardian*, edited by a native of the town.[43] The town had its own fine newspaper, the *Carrickfergus Advertiser*, owned by James Bell, a Scottish Presbyterian and Freemason of faintly liberal tendencies, who 'never could be induced to enter into public life or go into political or controversial matters'.[44] The borough had lost its parliamentary representation in 1885 and been absorbed into County Antrim in 1898, when Carrickfergus was compensated with an urban district council that regularly failed to satisfy the expectations of the *Advertiser* and social improvers. Despite lax administration, litter-strewn streets, wretched slums, recurrent drunkenness and sporadic vandalism, the Christian ethic suffused pre-war Carrick to a degree unimaginable today.

The 'anglican order' (a term popularized by Louis in 'Carrickfergus')[45] was by no means dominant in the social and economic life of Carrick, much less an 'Ascendancy'. Less than a quarter of the population of the parish in 1911 was Episcopalian (23 per cent), though the proportion was much higher in the town (29 per cent) than the rural hinterland (16 per cent). In the urban district, Presbyterians were the largest denomination (41 per cent), but there were significant groups of Methodists (5 per cent) and Independents (11 per cent), as well as Roman Catholics (15 per cent). The two 'Irish Quarters', immediately south-west of the parish church, were notoriously poor and included some of the worst tenements and courts in the town. Yet, despite their distant association with the expulsion of Catholics from the walled town in 1677, the Irish Quarters by 1901 were dominated by Episcopalians (40 per cent) rather than Catholics (18 per cent). Likewise, the relatively affluent 'Scotch Quarter', originally settled in about 1665 by a colony of Scottish fishermen, was no longer abnormally Presbyterian (40 per cent). It now housed disproportionately large components of Methodists (15 per cent) and Independents (13 per cent). The major Catholic cluster (34 per cent) was in Minorca Place, where the chapel was located, but Catholics were found throughout the town and there was no pronounced residential 'segregation' according to religion. The location of Episcopalians certainly does not suggest a wealthy élite, but rather a community encompassing the full spectrum of occupations and dominated by workers and tradesmen.[46] In Antrim as a whole, Presbyterians and Non-Conformists were far more likely than Episcopalians to have professional and white-collar occupations. Prominent in certain sectors such as defence and government service, Episcopalians were under-represented in law, medicine, teaching and even commerce. They were notably over-represented in cotton and flax, as well as service occupations, and had their fair share of general labourers. Though less disadvantaged than Catholics, Antrim's Episcopalians were mainly plain enough folk.[47]

The select vestry of St Nicholas's, though a social élite within the congregation, was solidly bourgeois rather than smart. Analysis of the occupations of thirty-eight parish officers elected between 1908 and 1912 suggests a governing group intermediate between the grandees of Cappoquin and the tradesmen and white-collar workers of Holy Trinity. Only five were skilled tradesmen, with no unskilled workers, only one carrier and two shopkeepers (both butchers, known as 'fleshers'). There were eleven white-collar workers (including two managers and three clerks), eight professional men (including three lawyers), three magistrates and four members of the civil or military services.[48] The typical (median) parish officer was aged about forty-four in 1911, and lived in a first-class house of eleven rooms with six front windows. Over three-quarters were married men and heads of family, and 43 per cent came from outside the county (mostly from Belfast or Down).[49] Two-thirds of the parish officers were publicly associated with the protest against Frederick's appointment.[50] The most important exceptions were his two supporters among the parochial nominators (Samuel Close and MacGregor Greer); the rector's churchwarden, John Hind, and his son James, both prominent engineers; Joseph McCaughen of Windmill Hill, a landowner and magistrate; Stewart Alexander Woods, a leading Orangeman and Freemason who was Company Sergeant-Major in the Royal Garrison Artillery; and Head-Constable William Young, RIC. Several of these men were to become Frederick's close allies as he gradually consolidated his position in the parish.

Forming alliances with the protestors was more challenging, but essential. A rector could not afford to remain at odds with men of influence such as Heron

Lepper; John Pirrie of the Barn Mills and his manager James McFerran; John and Robert Campbell, who managed the brickworks and gasworks respectively; Samuel Close's son Richard, who became an architect still more eminent than his father; the solicitors Tyndall S. Johns and Henry Blackburne; Henry's son James, Clerk of Petty Sessions; William F. Coates of Glyn Park, magistrate, stockbroker, and future Lord Mayor of Belfast; Isaac Graham, Northern Bank manager; or Ezekiel Caters, a builder responsible for major church renovations earlier in 1908.[51] Apart from their importance as employers or public figures, men such as these performed essential services as contractors or professional advisers to the parish, in addition to contributing heavily to parochial collections.[52]

In order to win their confidence, Frederick needed to penetrate the organizations and networks through which they exercised influence and forged alliances based on friendship and mutual trust. In this respect, the Unionist Association, to which many of the protestors belonged, was less important than ostensibly non-political bodies such as the Freemasons and the town's rugby football club. At least fifteen of the forty protestors have been identified as Freemasons, while sixteen or more belonged at various times to the rugby club.[53] While no comprehensive list of local Orangemen is available, three leading protestors in addition to Heron Lepper were at various times members of Eldon LOL 7, the lodge catering for Belfast's commercial and professional élite.[54]

For the McNeices, the first year in Carrickfergus was something of an ordeal. Chamberlain lingered in the rectory until his death in September 1910, and the McNeices could not move in until the New Year. Meanwhile, they rented a four-storey house beside a coal yard in Governor's Place (or Walk), overlooking the harbour and Castle grounds. With no front garden and an exposed position on the main coast road, it lacked even the suburban privacies of Brookhill Avenue.[55] The move to Carrick brought virtually no increase in stipend, and Frederick's workload was greatly increased by his inability to employ a curate until the parish income returned to normal.[56] There were initially few visitors from the congregation apart from the McCaughens of Windmill Hill, though Frederick's younger sister Margery was an occasional guest, remembered by Louis for hitting his sister with a hairbrush.[57] Neighbours of other denominations were sometimes more sympathetic than his own parishioners. When leaving the parish, Frederick is said to have expressed 'gratitude to the first lady in the town who had extended a welcome and given him hospitality, a Presbyterian lady, Mrs Charles Legg'.[58] A welcome diversion came in March 1909, when Frederick returned with Lily to Holy Trinity to receive 'a handsome solid silver tea and coffee service, a case of silver spoons, and an ornamented drawing-room lamp', along with 'an address in album form'. Louis

Plunkett presided over the tea, followed by a concert, and Richard Clarke averred that 'he had never had a more loyal and energetic co-worker than Mr McNeice'.[59]

A few weeks later, Frederick faced his first Easter vestry, for which he prepared by annotating the printed list of current parish officers according to the degree of their defiance. Of the twelve officers, eight were loftily declared to be 'Contra Ecclesiam Dei'. Three of these had exhibited 'a moderate change', but the remainder had so far 'shown no repentance'. In this examination, Frederick awarded A (presumably for particular obduracy) to Henry Blackburne and Robert Campbell, and an intermediate score of B to three others, including James McFerran. He also listed eight 'Non Vestrymen who took a leading part and are still hostile more or less', including John Pirrie, Heron Lepper, and George Kirk.[60] One could scarcely imagine a more methodical preparation for the next vestry elections.

The outcome was dispiriting. Apart from Samuel Close, all of the fourteen successful candidates had been protestors. Among the five newcomers was Heron Lepper, who became a parochial nominator as well as a select vestryman. Of the eleven successful candidates classified by Frederick in advance of the meeting, only three had escaped his censure. The remainder were equally divided between his four categories (A unrepentant, B unrepentant, still hostile, and moderately changed). His strongest supporters, such as John Hind and MacGregor Greer, were not re-elected. Samuel Close, whose record of proposing Bradley (yet accepting Frederick) gave him a foot in both camps, declined to replace Hind in the key post of rector's churchwarden. He was, however, re-elected as a parochial nominator. Of the six retiring or defeated officers, most were relatively favourable to Frederick, the exception being Thomas Gorman, who had initiated the campaign against his appointment without publicly participating in the protest.[61] The rector could take some comfort from the fact that none of the diehards except Lepper ('still hostile') and McFerran (B unrepentant) were elected to the higher offices, opening up the possibility of practical cohabitation with his churchwardens, nominators, and synodsmen. In his address to the vestry, Frederick took care to placate his opponents and to avoid recrimination. He expressed 'deep sorrow' at the death of George Kirk, adversary though he had been, and lamented the illness of George Chamberlain – 'one of the ablest, saintliest, most unselfish men who ever served in the ministry of the Church of Ireland'. He complimented Thomas Gorman, who retained the important post of honorary treasurer, for proving 'himself a capable Chancellor of the Exchequer' by conjuring a credit balance of £17.[62] But he also lavished praise on the 'bright and winning' example of the aged Sunday school teacher, Miss Maria Johns, who had reportedly broken the boycott of collections in November with her 'crackling five-pound note'.[63]

III

Having failed to secure control of the select vestry, Frederick applied his diplomatic skills to a broader constituency of humbler men. His credentials as a chaplain at District and county level in Belfast allowed easy access to the Orangemen of the Carrickfergus District (Antrim, no. 19). There were only eight lodges operating in the District, of which three met in the town: Bennett's Chosen Few LOL 553, Scotch Quarter Invincibles LOL 947, and Carrickfergus Total Abstinence LOL 1537.[64] The offices of District Master and Chaplain were both held, seemingly in perpetuity, by J. Hamilton Bennett, vicar of Kilroot and also a prominent Blackman and Freemason.[65] Every July, the vicar rekindled the ancient loyalties and antipathies of the brethren in his church and at the field, while the local lodge completed its perambulations by marching round Kilroot House and listening to yet another vicarial address 'from the steps of the porch'.[66] Bennett's eloquence was in some demand, and Frederick had once invited him to Holy Trinity to preach at a Sunday School anniversary service.[67]

On the morning of Sunday, 10 July 1909, Frederick delivered a 'special sermon' for Orangemen at St Nicholas's, on the text, 'Remember the days of old' (Deut. 32: 7). He prepared carefully for this event, announcing it at least five weeks in advance and evidently supplying the *Advertiser* with the text for publication.[68] This was the first of many sermons given generous space by the Bells, who in later years often issued them in pamphlet form in response, presumably, to popular demand. This sermon provides the first elaborated statement of his religious and political views, and his conception of Orangeism. He reminded the brethren of past 'assaults made on the faith' at the behest of 'a foreign bishop', and lauded the memory of early Protestant martyrs who 'felt there could be no reform for the Church and no progress for the State unless they had Home Rule for England in Church and State'. Having jolted his audience with this mischievous formulation, Frederick pointed out that by Wesley's time, religious indifference had displaced the 'danger of Papal usurpation' as the major menace. In a characteristic rhetorical climax, he asked, 'What inheritance is threatened to-day? What special dangers have we to fight against?' There would be 'little use talking about the men of 1689, if the men of 1909 have forgotten how to worship Almighty God'. The worst current dangers were neglect of the Sabbath and intemperance, which Orangemen could counter by campaigning for the closure of public houses on the Twelfth. He took the opportunity to attack both nationalist and unionist MPs for failing to promote the temperance cause, emphasizing that 'the Orange society is not a party society, and was never intended to be such'. It should therefore 'throw the weight of its influence on the side of any party that tried to lessen the temptation to temperance'.

His sermon challenged the very foundation of Orange commemorative culture, in words recalling Sir Horace Plunkett's celebrated aphorism that 'Anglo-Irish history is for Englishmen to remember, for Irishmen to forget':[69]

> Would to God we had the strength and wisdom not only to remember but to forget. Surely there is no true wisdom in recalling year after year the story of the wrongs inflicted on Protestants in 1641, or any other rebellion; and surely at this hour of the day it should be regarded as utter silliness for men on the other side to talk and declaim of the wrongs, real or imaginary, suffered by Ireland during 700 years of British domination.

He admitted that many Irishmen, 'chiefly of our faith', remained insecure in their lives and property, 'aliens and outcasts' when they refused to join immoral 'conspiracies', and subject to lawless intimidation:

> Yet I think we can see the beginning of better days. At all events the old order is changing, old policies are breaking up, and on their ruins, here and there, even in Ireland, groups of men, few in number, but fearless and chivalrous in Spirit are agreeing on a few positive convictions – one that this country, our fathers' country and our own, is worthy of our whole-hearted love, and the other that no one within its borders should be penalised because of his religious or political convictions.

Finally, he called on the brethren 'to unite with others of any creed, on great questions that are not political, for our country's good'; and affected to hear a voice saying, 'Sirs – Not withstanding your differences – ye are brethren.' The congregation offered a 'hearty and liberal response' to the collection, and no expressions of dissent were reported.[70]

The tone of his sermon, though relatively liberal and unsectarian, was perfectly consistent with the widespread view among Orange clergy that the proper function of Orangeism was 'religious' rather than 'political', and that its focus should be on current moral issues rather than past conflicts. What was unusual for an anniversary sermon was his open rejection of the unionist alliance and his abstention from commemorative rhetoric, though he took care to avoid enumerating 1690 among the episodes no longer worthy of commemoration. His sermon was in marked contrast to the official District sermon delivered that evening by Hamilton Bennett. Most of the nine lodges present at St Nicholas's reassembled at St John's, Ballycarry, where Bennett discussed the teaching that 'a house divided against a house falleth' (Luke 11: 17). Having celebrated the Reformation, he urged both political and social unity:

As members of the Orange Institution, and as Conservatives and Unionists, he asked them to allow no dissension to enter their ranks. ... There was a tendency to-day to attack the classes and to say that the man was as good as his master. In one sense he was, but there must always be hewers of wood and drawers of water. It was necessary and essential that degrees and grades should exist.[71]

Pre-war Orangeism was broad enough in outlook to encompass Frederick's liberality and Bennett's old-fashioned intransigence without open collision.

Though Frederick did not attend the East Antrim demonstration on 12 July, the anniversary sermon was soon followed by his admission to Total Abstinence LOL 1537, with no hint of outrage or dismay at his liberal sentiments. After delivering the opening prayer, he was welcomed to the monthly meeting by William O'Neill, WM, a Congregationalist bread-server who eventually became District Master. He offered Frederick 'a hearty welcome to 1537, and hoped that his presence and sympathy would tend to the betterment of Orangeism generally in Carrickfergus'. The rector 'told them to work on and not to be discouraged because their membership was small, as great things had often been done by a very few men. He assured the lodge of his sympathy and assistance whenever called on.' The lodge immediately acted on his repudiation of party politics, by declining to support a protest by the Unionist Association (echoing a resolution presented at the field on the Twelfth) against Lloyd George's budget: 'The members decided not to sign the same, as they could not conscientiously protest against the increased taxation on licences and liquor. A report of the recent sermon which was preached in St. Nicholas Church was given by the secretary. The turnout of members was the largest in Carrickfergus for some years.'[72] The spirited engagement of 'Bro. Rev. F. J. McNeice' with Carrickfergus Orangeism was underway.

Ever since its foundation in September 1896, LOL 1537 had done its best to remain totally abstinent. Under by-laws drawn up by William Lee, then curate of Carrickfergus and founding Master of the lodge, every member had to take 'a pledge to abstain from all intoxicating liquors or beverages, in or out of Lodge, in public or private'. Brethren were required to report violations (or face a fine of 5*s*.), and convicted offenders were suspended from the lodge until they had paid a similar fine and renewed their pledge.[73] The outcome of this moral crusade was discouraging. Nearly one-quarter of those on the roll between 1911 and 1914 were punished for pledge violations, and one-third of offenders repeated the offence and retook the pledge, sometimes two or three times.[74] The atmosphere in the lodge room sometimes resembled that of a confessional box, as contrition was all too easily overwhelmed by renewed temptation. The drink problem intensified in

1911 and 1912, coinciding with rapid recruitment of new members. Membership rose from only 20 at the start of 1909 to 66 in 1913, reaching its peak at 108 in 1922.[75] Frederick's active involvement therefore coincided with moral crisis in the lodge as well as rapid expansion. His arrival may well have intensified the pursuit of drinkers, for the lodge had been without an ordained chaplain since 1903.[76]

The Orangemen whom Frederick tried to guide towards sobriety, tolerance and obedience to the law, were mainly workers with very little education. Between 1909 and 1912, the lodge contained no other professional man, and only a handful of shopkeepers and white-collar workers. Just over one-third were skilled workers, notably in the tailoring and building trades, with substantial groups (six in each) of salt-miners, bread-servers and labourers. The bread-servers formed a particularly effective cabal, providing three Worshipful Masters, serving for a total of fifteen years, between 1898 and 1918. The census returns for members of 1537 contrast sharply with the comfortable world of the select vestry. Hardly any brethren lived in first-class houses, the median house having only about four rooms and three front windows. The typical Orangeman was aged twenty-eight in 1911, more than half were unmarried dependants, and all but 8 per cent were natives of Antrim. Like most Orange lodges, 1537 embraced Protestants of all major denominations.[77] Only one-quarter (19) of the seventy-three identified brethren were Episcopalians, half the number of Presbyterians (38). There were also six Methodists and ten Independents. Involvement in the lodge therefore gave Frederick a forum for influencing evangelical Protestants of all creeds, and working men of all grades in many trades.

Frederick was an intermittent and usually inconspicuous Orangeman in Carrickfergus. He was never listed in the *Advertiser* as a speaker on the Twelfth, and seldom delivered anniversary sermons in July or November.[78] Though twice elected as lodge chaplain, he seems never to have paid dues. The minutes refer to his participation in but four of the monthly meetings between 1909 and 1912, after which his name was only once entered in the roll book.[79] His first public service to the lodge after his introductory sermon in 1909 was to chair the unveiling of a new banner on Easter Monday, 1911. The banner depicted William III landing at Carrickfergus, and Christ with the woman of Samaria at the well, emblazoned with the text: 'Quit ye like men, be strong' (1 Cor. 16: 13). It was unveiled by Mrs Coates, wife of a leading protestor, in whose absence the task would have passed to Mrs Heron Lepper. The McNeices sat with the Coateses and the McCalmonts on the balcony of the YMCA Hall, following a procession through the town invigorated by the town's brass and reed band.[80]

As chairman, Frederick developed his earlier thesis that Orangeism 'was not a party society', even though 'for some twenty-five years or more the Orange Society had been more in alliance with one of the great parties in the state than with the other':

> The Orange Society had learnt by experience not to put its trust in political parties. They remembered that it was the Conservative Party that called Sir Antony McDonnell [*sic*] to Dublin Castle.[81] ... Again, the Orange Society was essentially a democratic society. The vast majority of its members were tradesmen, working men, small farmers. Their sympathies naturally were with proposals that were likely to benefit the struggling classes in the population. They were not blind followers of great landowners or millowners; many of them were Trades Unionists.

Such men 'were just as interested as other Irishmen in the settlement of the land question, or the licensing question. They would welcome as readily as other Irishmen additional powers – properly safeguarded – to enable local authorities to deal with canals, extend railway and tramway lines, and such matters.' Orangemen 'made no claim whatever for any ascendency, for any favoritism from this Government or any Government', and should be punished no less than a 'Fenian' if they broke the law.

As for Home Rule, it should be rejected by Orangemen primarily because of its implications for religious freedom:

> Convince Irish Protestants that Home Rule would really be Home Rule, and the rest of the controversy would be free from bitterness. The financial side of the question was no doubt important, still many Irishmen thought that if they had an Ireland free from Rome's interference, from Rome's demands for the surrender of the individual conscience, and the surrender of so much of the inividual's purse – such an Ireland would be able to pay its own way (Applause). ... The reason why they so resolutely opposed Home Rule was that they believed the rule of Rome would thereby be indefinitely extended, and the liberties of those who had never submitted to the Roman yoke, and who never would submit, be very seriously curtailed.

After a sally against the Nationalist Party for failing to support the inspection of convents and condoning attacks on missionaries and colporteurs in Munster and Connaught, he turned to the *Ne Temere* decree of 1907, which invalidated 'mixed' marriages not conducted by a Catholic priest. This decree had recently become a cause célèbre in Ireland following the persecution of a Belfast Presbyterian, who had defied demands to remarry her Catholic husband in a Catholic church and raise their children as Catholics.[82] The Party's failure to renounce this papal directive had become the chief proof of both Romish aggression and nationalist pusallinimity:

> That Irish Nationalist politician had his 'head in a Roman halter'. He might cry out that it was a most delightful bondage. Their ideals were different. They had learnt from Wiclif [*sic.*] and Tyndale, and others to stand out and to hold out for two great principles – the supremacy of the Bible in the Church, the supremacy of the King in the State. 'Fear God – honour the King.'

Despite his eloquent rejection of intolerance, privilege and partisanship, Frederick's ringing conclusion merely elaborated the conventional (and credible) belief that Home Rule would mean Rome Rule.

If Frederick's jibes against landowners and millowners were designed to assert common cause with the plebeian Orangemen against Antrim's oligarchs, they failed to goad Bro. Colonel McCalmont, MP, until recently the proprietor of vast estates acquired through the international financial speculations of his family firm.[83] The 'only exception' he took to Frederick's speech 'was his reference to Orangemen as poor men. He himself looked upon them as the salt of the earth, the best men in the country (Applause) – the men who were chiefly instrumental in 1886 and in 1893 in upsetting the monstrous diabolical scheme of Mr Gladstone to introduce what he called Home Rule in Ireland.' Frederick secured the last word, explaining that he had not deemed them 'poor in spirit', but 'men who from a worldly standpoint did not possess wealth or influence'.[84] He was duly thanked at the next lodge meeting for his 'kind assistance', and given the honour of presiding at the annual election of officers, including his own as Chaplain.[85]

On 12 November, Frederick delivered another anniversary sermon to a 'good attendance' of Orangemen who had marched in regalia from the Orange Hall in Lancasterian Street to St Nicholas's Church. His text was 'Let us run with patience the race that is set before us, looking unto Jesus' (Heb. 12: 1–2). He warned that in 'a critical period in the history of our country … many who now made loud professions would go over to the other side'. He could scarcely have been thinking of himself. As in 1909, he urged Orangemen to 'remember the days of old', this time concentrating on 'the brave and unflinching stand' of the early Reformers rather than any subsequent retreat of the papal menace. Home Rule, a distant prospect in 1909, was now an imminent threat as a result of Asquith's dependence on nationalist support since 1910, and the abolition of the Lords' veto on legislation passed (in three successive sessions) by the House of Commons. In early speeches, Frederick had seemed remarkably equitable in attributing blame and suffering to Protestants and Catholics. Now, he spoke only of the menace of *Ne Temere* and the persecution of Protestants: 'In the South and also the West of Ireland there were numbers of Protestants who were being ostracised and boycotted, whose cattle were from time to time maimed, and they themselves insulted going to their place of worship, and yet no protest was forthcoming in the name of those who were supposed to speak for Ireland.' The parallel with his own childhood experience in Omey is unmistakable, as also in his final appeal for courage and resilience in the defence of virtue. Orangemen should 'be of good courage and play the man for the people and the cities of their God'. Ominously, the collection was devoted to the Carrickfergus Nursing Society.[86] As Ulster's crisis loomed, Frederick's attitude to Home Rule and the menace of Rome appeared to be hardening.

A few weeks later, the rector chaired a meeting of brethren and associated ladies to prepare for the Carrickfergus Orange bazaar in January 1912. Lily was among the fifteen ladies who 'volunteered their valuable assistance' in setting up the lodge's stall and raising funds to clear the debt on the Orange hall.[87] The bazaar was opened by Heron Lepper in defiant mode:

> No matter what the change might be in the affairs of the empire, they sincerely hoped never to see the day when a lodge of the Molly Maguires would sit there with Joe Devlin in the chair, and a picture of John Redmond on the wall instead of a portrait of the King, while a big green placard, with 'God Save Ireland' on it, adorned the entrance.

Lily presided over the work stall, assisted by Mrs Ezekiel Caters, while the work stalls of other lodges were staffed by other leading protestors such as Mrs James McFerran and Mrs Heron Lepper.[88]

The bazaar was deemed a success, and the lodge subsequently entertained the 'stallholders and assistants' to an 'excellent tea'. Lily, hitherto out of the public eye, was presented with a kettle and stand 'in recognition of her services as president'. Her husband took the opportunity to reiterate his argument that the Orange Order's opposition to Home Rule was based on religious grounds: 'Convince them that Home Rule was not Rome Rule and that it would benefit the country and they would be Home Rulers.' Meanwhile, as *Ne Temere* demonstrated, Home Rule remained 'a danger to their civil and religious liberties'. His Presbyterian colleague at Joymount, John Minford,[89] 'spoke of the increasing popularity in the parish of Mr and Mrs McNeice, and hoped that it would be long continued'. Having witnessed a delightful rendition of 'We Never Will Surrender', Frederick delivered yet another speech and a benediction, whereupon the hall was cleared for 'dancing and games … until well on in the morning'.[90]

His insistence that Orangeism should reinforce law and order was put to the test on Saturday night, 6 July 1912, when several hundred thugs, mainly 'youths and girls', 'paraded the town, smashing windows and maltreating persons in the street'. The purpose of the disturbance, which was 'organised to a certain extent', was to injure 'Roman Catholic residents and their property'. The police were assisted by John Campbell, chairman of the urban council and a member of 1537, and by leading vestrymen such as the Lynns. Though nobody was seriously hurt, attacks were made on thirty-three houses, of which all but four were occupied by Catholics. Six men were eventually convicted and imprisoned for one month, all first offenders of 'good character'. The *Advertiser* attributed the incident to various external factors (the recent attack by Hibernians on a Sunday School party at Castledawson, County Londonderry; disloyal utterances by two servicemen; and imitation of an outbreak of window-smashing in Belfast). On the following morning, the preachers at Orange anniversary services in Carrick and Ballycarry deplored the violence without proposing any practical remedy. Frederick, preaching at an ordinary Sunday service, lamented the 'disgrace' upon a town hitherto noted 'for the kindly feeling that existed among its inhabitants no matter what their differences in religion or politics. ... At the present time, when, for public reasons, the feelings of very many are stirred, let us be more than careful; let us throw the weight of our influence on the side of peace, law and order; let us strive to be reconcilers, to be peacemakers.'

His words were immediately given practical effect at a meeting of Orangemen and members of the unionist club, called 'to consider what steps should be taken in view of Saturday's disturbance, to assist the local authorities in the event of any further outbreak, and at the same time to consider the positions of the loyalist organisations'. As chairman of the meeting, Frederick stated that 'he was credibly informed that there was not an Orangeman amongst those who were engaged in the disturbance'. On the contrary, 'several of the brethren', such as John Campbell, had helped restore order. Since 'it was their duty to assist the local force in the event of assistance being required from whatever source', extra police were unnecessary. The outcome was a remarkable resolution, proposed by Campbell and seconded by another Orangeman: 'That the Carrickfergus Orange Brethren and Unionist Club members enrol themselves as special constables in order to assist the local police authorities in preserving the peace of the town and district by placing themselves each evening in different parts of the town from 7.30 p.m. to 10.30 p.m., or longer if necessary.'[91] There were no further reports of sectarian disturbances in Carrick in 1912, and the town remained singularly untouched a decade later, when civil war threatened to engulf the province.

IV

Orangeism, though an important element in Frederick's social strategy, was one of many instruments by which he consolidated his standing within the parish and beyond. His sociability extended to the town's rugby club, of which he became a 'vice-president or patron' in September 1909. His twenty-five fellow patrons included Heron Lepper and ten other parochial protestors, several leading Presbyterians and Non-Conformists, and the parish priest (Father Francis C. Henry). Never again was Frederick to share such an office with a Catholic clergyman.[92] The club had faltered several times since its reputed foundation in 1865, being 're-established' in both 1898 and 1905, but secured some outstanding results after affiliating with the Irish Rugby Football Union in 1908.[93] Though Frederick seems to have had little if any knowledge of the game,[94] patronage of the club was a useful tool in his search for acceptance in the town.

In campaigning against intemperance, he collaborated with clergymen and laymen of all Protestant denominations. In November 1909, he chaired a meeting in the parochial hall with 'representatives from all the temperance organizations in the town', in the presence of Presbyterian, Methodist and Congregationalist ministers. He expressed the hope 'that in the not too distant future men and women who represented all the churches' would work together to observe the Sabbath, counteract betting and gambling, and pursue temperance. Four months later, Frederick presided at the opening of a 'Catch-My-Pal' club, where working men could 'have a smoke and a game' under the aegis of the town's Total Abstinence Union. Once again, several ministers of other denominations participated.[95] He also attended the annual social meeting of the St Nicholas Working Men's Reading Room in January 1912, admiring the 'fine new billiard table' while Lily and other ladies 'presided at the tea-tables'.[96]

Reconciliation with parish adversaries such as Heron Lepper was no less important than developing the pan-Protestant crusade against vice and intemperance. Shortly before the Easter vestry of 1910, Frederick asked Lepper to chair a pre-St Patrick's Day event in the parochial hall, 'devoted to items of national interest'. Lepper, a member of the St Patrick's Masonic lodge, applauded the saint's 'unparalleled success' in disseminating 'the message of a pure faith', and urged the people of Carrick to emulate him: 'Let them do their best to be brave, unselfish, true to their friends, patient in difficulties but determined to surmount them.' After Lepper's parting 'Cead mile failte!' [*sic.*], a choir trained by his English wife sang melodies by Moore, with help from a harpist. Two Irish-speaking Protestant clergymen named O'Sullivan and O'Connell sang in and talked about the Irish language. Frederick responded that 'he was glad to think that the day had gone past when Irishmen sought to apologise for their nationality', and celebrated 'the new spirit that was abroad' (or so it then seemed). He refrained from uttering any phrases in Irish that might have lingered from his Omey upbringing. His two rebel churchwardens proposed the vote of thanks, which was passed unanimously.[97]

The Easter vestry scarcely disturbed the grip of the former protestors on parish government, but Frederick's ally John Hind was elected as an additional synodsman and other supporters (including his son James) became 'sidesmen'. Hind's post resulted from the long-desired decision to appoint a curate, though Robert Morrison was not licensed until October.[98] Frederick concentrated on safe issues such as temperance, the Sunday school and the Boys' Brigade (under John Hind). He warned darkly that 'there might be times of peculiar difficulty and peril not far off. If such times came they must learn to quit themselves like men, like God's men; they must forget small points of difference, and prepare to unite for the defence of great principles.'[99] At the next Easter vestry, which reaffirmed the status quo, Frederick would have been at one with a resolution proposed by his former adversaries, Henry Blackburne and Heron Lepper: 'That we protest against the publication in Ireland of the Papal decree, "Ne Temere", as an attempted encroachment on the laws of the United Kingdom, and as containing regulations on the marriage question which constitute a menace to the morals of society, the structure of the family, and the peace of life.'[100]

As the crisis loomed, Frederick's political views seemed to have moved closer to those of conventional unionists, who could scarcely have taken exception to his sermon upon the coronation of George V in June:

> May we prove ourselves worthy of our King and of the Empire, worthy of the flag which, generation after generation, has been carried over land and sea by brave, heroic, devoted men; the flag which floats to-day on every continent, and which, wherever it floats, gives to our fellow-subjects the assurance of liberty, just rule, and the possibility of progress.[101]

With every month that passed, the rector's rhetoric fitted more comfortably into the increasingly militant outlook of Protestant Ulster and his own parishioners. At the Easter vestry of 1912, his old supporters recovered some of their former influence, both John Hind and Joseph McCaughen being elected as diocesan synodsmen.[102] His unionist credentials were proclaimed in June 1912, when the East Antrim Constitutional (Unionist) Association elected its usual multitude of vice-presidents. Frederick's name took pride of place among the nine clergymen (including Richard Clarke and Hamilton Bennett), jostling for attention with former antagonists such as Heron Lepper and James McFerran. The Association's secretary was

Henry Blackburne, who had devised the boycott of parochial contributions in 1908. Frederick sent his apologies for missing the momentous occasion.[103]

His reputation as an able and fearless clergyman now stretched far beyond Carrick, through the columns of the Belfast press and the *Church of Ireland Gazette*, and he was gradually penetrating the inner circles of the diocesan synod. While still in Belfast, he had been appointed to a committee on social services, designed 'to arouse the interest of all its members in the problems concerned with our present social system and the needs of the poor'.[104] At his first diocesan synod after transfer to Carrickfergus, Frederick was elected as a 'supplemental' to both the diocesan council and the general synod.[105] Though supplementals were only required to serve if enough elected representatives retired or died during their term of office, these appointments offered the promise of future influence in the central as well as local government of the Church of Ireland.

Within the diocese, his involvement in the Clerical Society was particularly important in extending his circle of influence. In March 1912, he discussed a paper on 'Roman Canon Law and Present-day Problems', doubtless relating to *Ne Temere*, and was elected to the committee.[106] In the same month, he initiated a series of evening sermons entitled 'Themes for the Times', concerning 'the dangers to which our country and our Church and may soon be exposed'. The first sermon, on St Patrick's Day, was delivered by Thomas Chatterton Hammond, rector of St Kevin's in Dublin and a future superintendent of the city's Irish Church Missions. During his ministry, 'more converts had been received out of the Church of Rome at St Kevin's than in any other parish church in Ireland'.[107] Frederick had not forgotten the quest to which his family had contributed so zealously, and at such fearful cost.

In early 1911, the McNeices were at last promoted from Governor's Place to the rectory, when they exchanged houses with George Chamberlain's widow and family. The rectory was a solid Victorian house with thirteen rooms, twenty front windows, an acre of garden, and three out-offices (shed, store and redundant harness-room).[108] Set beside the railway line, it backed on to a cemetery. On the opposite side of the North Road, which led up to the look-out point at Mile Bush and on to the Antrim hills, was a field rented by the rugby club on the Sunnylands estate. The severity of the house, and the magic of the garden, are well known to all readers of and about Louis MacNeice.[109] His elder sister Elsie, who was then seven, recollected the resultant transformation of family life:

We had always before lived in streets. Now suddenly we were in another world with a lawn to play on, trees to climb, and a garden which seemed to be full of apple-blossom. … My mother was very pleased by this move. All her instincts were of the country and she began at once enlarging the henyard, planting rose trees, acquiring cats and dogs and hens and so on.

Lily initially demonstrated that an evangelical upbringing was quite consistent with showing 'a great capacity for the enjoyment of life', especially dance: 'her feet never failed to tap to a dance tune, and she persuaded my father to let me go to dancing classes'.[110] Her life was eased by the arrival of Margaret McCready, a 34-year-old 'mother's help' from Armagh, and Annie Bogue, a 20-year-old servant from Tyrone. There was nothing unusual for a unionist employer in the fact that Margaret was an Episcopalian and Annie a Catholic: the Leppers, for example, had two Catholic servants and one Protestant, while the MacGregor Greers (in their house at Tullylagan in Tyrone) had four Protestants and a Catholic.[111] Louis was later to avenge himself upon his substitute mother by depicting her as a joyless, life-denying, Hell-fixated child-slapper. By contrast, indulgent Annie, 'the only Catholic I knew', was 'a buxom rosy girl from a farm in County Tyrone'. Yet, by Elizabeth's account, Margaret's 'sharp tongue' concealed 'a kind heart', and she gave the children 'many little pleasures'.[112] From Lily's point of view, the acquisition of assistance with her three young children, one of whom needed constant attention and encouragement, was an immeasurable boon.

Lily had her mother's help, the children had a garden, Frederick had his curate, and the vestry was no longer in a state of simmering rebellion. After three years of patient negotiation, the new rector was not an interloper any more but a familiar if occasional presence in the Orange hall, the rugby club and the YMCA balcony. His combination of Christian charity and tolerance with unionist convictions and fear of Romish domination, expressed in simple but powerful addresses, had already made him something of a local celebrity among readers of the *Carrickfergus Advertiser*. By the end of 1911, however, Ulster and unionism were careering towards a crisis that was to unsettle Frederick in his comfortable convictions, and imperil his esteem in the Protestant community. Simultaneously, the family idyll was shattered by Lily's illness, depression and death. Frederick's response to both challenges was courageous but also level-headed.

7. Dissident

CARRICKFERGUS, 1912–1914

I

On 28 September 1912, 'Ulster Day', Frederick McNeice once again courted unpopularity by ostentatiously declining to endorse 'Ulster's Solemn League and Covenant'. This document, signed by more than three-quarters of male Protestants in the province,[1] was designed to intimidate Asquith's government into abandoning the Government of Ireland Bill by raising the spectre of civil disobedience and, in the last resort, rebellion. The Covenant eloquently expressed the contradictions inherent in Orangeism and unionism. The King's 'loyal subjects' undertook to use 'all means which may be found necessary' to defeat a measure supported by His Majesty's government. While invoking God as Ulster's defender, they threatened to deploy force. By affirming that 'Home Rule would be disastrous to the material well-being of Ulster as well as of the whole of Ireland', the document hinted that if Ulster were exempted, Home Rule for the remaining provinces might be tolerated despite the potentially devastating consequences for the small Protestant minority outside the province.

For Christian ministers, the Covenant raised particular problems. How could such a pledge be reconciled with the duty of obedience to lawful authority? Was it consistent with liberty of conscience implicitly to bind oneself to obey the political leaders who would determine which particular means were 'necessary'? Was it blasphemous for politicians such as Sir Edward Carson and Captain James Craig to proclaim a new covenant among God's people, 'in sure confidence that God will defend the right'? What would be the impact of partition on the various Churches, all of which were national institutions catering for congregations throughout the island? In forming a judgment, ministers and the public were impeded by the fact that public preparations for Ulster Day preceded publication of the document by several weeks. This shrewd procrastination ensured that many potential dissidents committed themselves in advance, on the basis of rumour and guesswork, to a pledge that they had not read.

Despite these objections and initial doubts, the leaders of the Church of Ireland in Ulster threw their weight behind Carson's strategy. Charles D'Arcy,[2] who had succeeded Crozier as bishop of Down when Crozier was elevated to Armagh in 1911, relished the 'burden of responsibility. Most of the clergy and very many of their people would be guided by my decision.' He also claimed much of the credit for persuading the apprehensive Crozier to endorse the Covenant. D'Arcy, who was not an Orangeman, convinced himself that the document was an instrument of peace, which would ensure 'that no politician, no matter how violent, could dare to use force'.[3] After consultations with leaders of other Protestant churches, but before publication of the text, D'Arcy informed his clergy that services, with 'special prayers and a sermon', would be held in parish churches on Ulster Day. In other districts, ecumenical services might be offered in other churches, if more 'suitable'.[4] As a result, the clergy could scarcely avoid public notice if they chose to abstain. Most of his clergy acquiesced, though some required reassurance about the Covenant's implications before deciding to sign it. The archdeacon of Dromore, for example, secured a personal assurance from Craig 'that the proposed Covenant was only intended to the present situation and to the measure of Home Rule actually before us', leaving open the possibility of accepting some other constitutional settlement in future.[5]

A few clerical correspondents of the *Church of Ireland Gazette* expressed misgivings, including one ('John Presbyter') whose letter bears pronounced affinities with Frederick's opinions and style. Writing in late August, he felt that clergymen in the Belfast district were 'in a very unenviable position' in the absence of a text, when Carson's offsiders were demanding 'unquestioning obedience' to their great leader. Though agreeing 'that Home Rule would be ruinous for Ireland', he was 'not convinced that we should, by speech or by example, counsel resistance to the expressed will of the people of the United Kingdom'. To attend the public meeting or take the pledge 'would be in opposition to all we have ever striven to teach'; though there were other clergymen and laymen who 'will be able, with a clear conscience, to take the pledge'. Carson's threats, 'if translated into action, …

would involve anarchy and civil war'. He hoped that the Church of Ireland might, 'even at this late hour … give a lead', and encourage its members to 'follow the things that make for peace'.[6] Canon Sterling Berry, from the sanctuary of Booterstown, also warned of dangerous consequences when the Church 'intervened in politics and entered the arena of civil strife'; but his appeal had limited impact.[7]

On 2 September 1912, Frederick was re-elected as chaplain of LOL 1537, though in view of his sporadic attendance a lay chaplain was also appointed. At the same meeting, William O'Neill 'gave a report on the Ulster Day Demonstration', and the secretary and he were instructed to represent the lodge on the local organizing committee.[8] Two days later, Hamilton Bennett (the District Master and Chaplain) chaired a meeting to make 'arrangements for the celebration of Ulster Day in Carrickfergus'. Bennett promised to sign the Covenant and 'use his influence to get all he could to sign'; Frederick's curate, Robert Morrison, performed the 'devotional exercises'; and the minister of Loughmorne Presbyterian church offered to put on an Ulster Day service. The committee agreed to invite all ministers in the town to do likewise, and to ask the urban district council to open the town hall for the subsequent ceremony.[9]

When the committee met a fortnight later, Frederick joined his curate in the discussions. The committee also included former protestors such as William Coates, Tyndall Johns and Heron Lepper (as secretary of the Carrickfergus unionist club), officers of Orange lodges, and several stalwarts of the East Antrim Women's Unionist Association. The response of the town's ministers was not encouraging, though the meeting was told that 'the Parish Church had been at their disposal from the first conception of holding religious services on Ulster Day'. John Minford, Presbyterian minister at Joymount, initially argued 'that one service – that previously arranged for in the Parish Church – would be sufficient'. For various reasons, no services would be held in the Congregational (Independent) or North Street Presbyterian churches, though the Methodist minister was 'quite agreeable' to opening his own. It was agreed to hold 'local services' at 3 pm before the town's signing ceremony in the courthouse (adjacent to the town hall). All men and women over sixteen were invited to sign, 'whether or not they were connected with the Orange Order or Unionist clubs'. At this point, Frederick clouded the atmosphere by stating 'that in the absence of the text of the Covenant, and to obviate any misconception, it must be understood that the services were quite distinct, and it did not necessarily follow that those who attended must sign the Covenant'. Undeterred, the Covenanters agreed to arrange for a bonfire to mark Carson's departure for Liverpool at 9.30 pm, as well as illuminations of dwellings and displays of the union flag by 'every Loyalist'.[10]

In the event, two services were held in the town, one in the parish church, the other uniting Presbyterian, Methodist and Congregational ministers in Joymount Presbyterian church. Outside the town, signing ceremonies were arranged in several Orange and parochial halls, with Hamilton Bennett and William Coates officiating at Kilroot. The united service included a guarded address from Alexander Cuthbert, the minister at North Street Presbyterian church, who recalled the cry of 'No Surrender', sought 'divine guidance', promised to 'defend what we believe to be right and true', and protested that 'I would not take part in this meeting did I not believe that this question is not a political question but one pre-eminently religious'. He offered no explicit judgment of the terms of the Covenant.[11]

At St Nicholas's, Morrison conducted the service, Archibald Dobbs of Castle Dobbs read the lessons,[12] and Frederick delivered the sermon – one of the most widely misrepresented documents of the Ulster crisis. In a celebrated peroration, the only portion of his address quoted by Frederick himself in his historical study of Carrickfergus (1928), he outlined four divergent interpretations of the Covenant:

> First there is the view of those who take it to mean a policy of physical force, and who are persuaded that the circumstances justify such a policy. Secondly, there's the view of those who say it does not mean a policy of physical force, and who sign it in the belief that it does not. Thirdly, there's the attitude of those who look at it simply as a resolution against Home Rule, and a demand for an appeal to the nation.

While all those holding such views could sign it 'with a clear conscience', there was a fourth group 'who try to study the Covenant primarily from the Church's standpoint'. These included 'some who think that it means a call to arms, and who also think that as the Church of Christ is in this land to interpret the life of Christ and to exhibit the mind of Christ, she cannot sound that call'. Such men held that the Church's divine mission was 'to publish the Gospel of Peace'; that 'Ireland's greatest interest is in peace, and they shrink from a policy which, as is avowed, in the last resort, means war, and worse still, civil war'. The effect of 'even the avowal of such a policy' might be to 'intensify the bitterness that many of them hoped was fast dying away. This is the attitude of a minority, possibly a small minority. This is my own attitude.' Having desisted from asking 'anyone to adopt my view', he asserted his right to 'hold the opinion I have expressed', and once again hoped that God would help all Irishmen to hear the voice saying: 'Sirs, ye are brethren.'[13]

This was without doubt a brave and powerful address, which may well have shocked and dismayed conventional unionists. It did not dissuade most parishioners from walking over to the courthouse, where Heron Lepper collected the town's first hundred signatures, beginning with Archibald Dobbs and a kinsman, Henry Blackburne, Tyndall Johns, Joseph McCaughen and Lepper himself.[14] As Elizabeth recalled, parishioners such as Tommy Robinson (a flesher on the select vestry) were disappointed by the address: 'That was a grand sermon the Rector gave us. But he spoilt it all at the end by telling us he wasn't going to sign the covenant.' Robinson, however disappointed, was among those who followed his example.[15] Yet nothing in the rector's address, or the flesher's comment, or Elizabeth's account, implies that Frederick took the further step of repudiating unionism. It seems perplexing that almost every student of the lives of Louis MacNeice and his father has nevertheless drawn this inference, without considering the earlier portions of that 'grand sermon'.

Frederick's principal theme was the 'characteristics of the opposition in Ulster and Ireland to the policy of Home Rule'. First, it was 'a democratic opposition … not by any means a movement of landlords, or linen lords, or any other lords'. Working men of various social and political views had 'a common conviction that Home Rule would be a death blow to the industrial life of Ireland', a view in which they were 'joined by the farmers of Ulster, and I may add of Ireland'. Second, it was a 'markedly Nonconformist opposition', in which Presbyterians, though 'still mainly liberal in their sympathies', had come to the 'practically unanimous … conviction that Home Rule would be disastrous to Ulster, to Ireland, and to the Empire'. Third, it united the 'Episcopal and non-Episcopal' community in the fear that a predominantly Roman Catholic parliament 'could not be trusted to do justice to a Protestant minority'. Frederick cited the Church's blessing of governments that had oppressed Protestants in Québec, Italy, France and Spain. Reiterating a favourite metaphor, he asked: 'Is it any wonder that the Irish Roman Catholic has been described as a rebel whose feet are in British fetters and whose head is in a Roman halter? … Are not the Bishops the patrons of the Party? Are not the Priests, almost as a rule, the chairmen of the local branches of the United Irish League?' He remained unconvinced of any 'growing independence on the part of the Roman Catholic laity of Ireland', citing recent abuses arising from the *Ne Temere* decree in Sligo. Leaving no doubt as to his own views, he asked:

> Isn't the fear of the Irish Protestants a reasonable fear? … Our alternative policy is the policy of equal rights for Ireland with England and Scotland. These we have. Ireland has self-government just as England and Scotland have. There may be some grievances here as elsewhere. If there are we do not think they could be redressed by an Irish Parliament, and we think they could be redressed by the Imperial Parliament.

All previous Irish parliaments, Protestant and Catholic, had been 'ghastly failures'.

Frederick had not yet lost hope that the benefits of the union would eventually be acknowledged by nationalists: 'As the masses advance in prosperity and in education the desire for Home Rule and the interest in agitation will die away.' The union could thus be maintained by appealing to reason, making threats of violence superfluous:

> Finally, our ideal for Ireland is an Ireland in which no man shall be molested or insulted because of his political or religious convictions; ... and in which the humblest man in the land shall have the strength of an impartial Government behind him while he keeps within the law. ... Let no word be spoken, let nothing be done to wound the feelings of our Roman Catholic neighbours. ... Let us treat Protestants who may differ from us on this political question in a similar spirit. ... One of the chief reasons we oppose Home Rule is because we believe it would lessen individual liberty. ... And because such are our ideals, therefore, we recognise the rights of others, whether majorities or minorities, to think their own thoughts and be true to their own convictions.

The Irish nation, in all its diversity, should and still could find fulfilment within the United Kingdom.

In a passage deleted from the peroration explaining his rejection of the Covenant, as published in 1928, he reaffirmed his unionist convictions with singular passion:

> I wish you to know why though holding as I do that Home Rule would be a betrayal of those whose only crime has been their loyalty, and would be a wrong to the country, and to every class in the country, yet I am not persuaded by anything I have heard or read that the Church of Christ, because faced with difficulty and danger, should, for the maintenance of her life, resort to weapons which the Founder and her Lord did not use.[16]

II

Frederick's address was lavishly praised by the liberal *Ulster Guardian*, all the more so because it came from a notable unionist:

> Perhaps what strikes us as the best display of moral courage was given by a Church of Ireland rector. ... But Mr. McNeice's Unionism is of too staunch a character and has been too often manifested in his parish for him to risk being dubbed a Home Ruler because he is commended in a Home Rule organ. ... Why then do we praise an opponent whom we have most cause to dread?

Because even a Liberal and a Home Ruler can appreciate a gallant deed, no matter by whom it is done, and no one who knows the history of Carrickfergus and of St. Nicholas' Parish for the past few years will fail to estimate correctly the amount of pluck that was behind the simple confession of the rector on Saturday last.[17]

The *Guardian* seems to have been the only Belfast newspaper to make any reference to the address, which would have spoiled the intimidating display of solidarity conveyed by myriad reports of local ceremonies in the *News-Letter* and other unionist organs.

As Frederick admitted, only a 'minority' of his parishioners and clerical colleagues shared his combination of deeply held unionism with rejection of the threat of violence. Even so, he was by no means alone. If three-quarters of Protestants signed the Covenant or Women's Declaration, one-quarter did not. In Carrickfergus parish, the proportion of non-Covenanters exceeded one-third (36 per cent for men and 41 per cent for women), indicating a much higher level of dissent than in East Antrim as a whole.[18] The non-Covenanters included up to 16 per cent of those elected as officers of the Carrickfergus unionist club in 1914, 23 per cent of brethren in LOL 1537, 28 per cent of parish officers, and 41 per cent of those who went on to join Heron Lepper's Masonic Lodge 346.[19] In Frederick's domestic circle, Margaret McCready (Lily's supposedly bigoted mother's help) did not sign the Women's Declaration; whereas Archie White, the Orangeman so affectionately portrayed by Louis in 'The Gardener', scrawled his mark on a sheet in the courthouse.[20]

Many of the leading ex-protestors were not merely Covenanters but agents responsible for compiling batches of signature lists. These included Henry Blackburne, John Campbell, Tyndall Johns, Heron Lepper and James McFerran. So (in Tyrone) was Frederick's ally, Thomas MacGregor Greer. John Hind's daughter Gertrude, a close friend of the Greers and McNeices, was an agent gathering signatures for the Women's Declaration. Frederick's old mentor Louis Plunkett was also a Covenanter, though not an agent. In short, Frederick's closest friends as well as his former adversaries were, in most cases, enthusiastic supporters of the Covenant. Yet this difference of opinion appears to have caused no open division within the parish and no personal rift with families like the Plunketts, the Hinds or the Greers. In an increasingly militant society, this was a tribute not merely to the balance with which Frederick had presented his case, but also to the strength of the personal and fraternal alliances that he had so painstakingly fostered during almost four years in Carrickfergus.

Carrick's Protestant clergymen were divided in their opinion of the Covenant. Frederick later attested that 'the ministers of religion in Carrickfergus, in permanent charges, did not sign the Covenant'.[21] He chose his words carefully, for the signatories included his own curate (Robert Morrison), the Methodist minister and the two Presbyterian ministers at Woodburn, just outside the town.[22] Nevertheless, Frederick's stance was shared by four ministers, Alexander Cuthbert and John Minford (Presbyterian), James Lyon (Congregational) and John McCleery (Unitarian).[23] They were not among the handful of non-Covenanting ministers named in the *Ulster Guardian*, such as the rector of Tullylish (Gilford) and 'many of the clergy' in Moira, Waringstown and Donaghcloney.[24] Another dissident was Frederick's successor as bishop of Cashel, Thomas Harvey, who is said to have 'made a similar declaration to his congregation and also refused to sign the covenant'. This was indeed a bold act for a rector who had moved to Portrush from Sligo only a few weeks earlier, and who remained in Antrim for but four years before returning permanently to the South.[25] Defiance of both the popular will and the opinion of every bishop in Ulster was a course fraught with peril, for any but the most trusted and respected clergyman. Frederick McNeice had proven himself to be such a minister.

Clerical unease with the implications of the Covenant was revived at the diocesan synod in November 1912, when Lord Dunleath[26] secured leave to introduce a militantly Carsonite motion without the usual notice: 'We approve of the Ulster Covenant, and are prepared to stand by our Unionist members of Parliament and other leaders in their efforts to maintain our civil and religious liberties.' According to the *Church of Ireland Gazette*, 'there was apparently only one dissentient' when D'Arcy put the motion to the synod. The bishop responded that 'I think I may say the resolution has been passed unanimously', a deceit greeted with applause. The Belfast press obediently omitted any reference to the dissentient, who was probably not Frederick McNeice.[27] The only clergyman under D'Arcy's jurisdiction openly hostile to the resolution was Edward Moore, Frederick's old friend who had baptized William at Holy Trinity church in 1905. Moore, who abandoned Glencraig in 1915 for a quieter clerical life in Somerset and Croydon, wrote what Frederick must have felt: 'As one who did not sign the Ulster Covenant, I wish to say that, while not opposed to the general resolution passed at the meeting of the Diocesan Synod against the Home Rule Bill, I do not agree with that part of the resolution which expresses approval of the Covenant.'[28] Other correspondents objected to the resolution on procedural and tactical grounds, but only one anonymous 'lay Synodsman' was prepared to echo Moore's conscientious objection to the Covenant.[29] Frederick's tactful silence was rewarded by further signs of approval from the diocesan élite. Already, in early October, he had been elected president of the Belfast Younger Clergy CMS Union, reading an inaugural paper on 'The Church's Attitude towards Social Questions and War' for which he was 'warmly congratulated'.[30] At the diocesan synod, he was re-elected as a 'supplemental' representative on the general synod and member of the diocesan council, without any loss of voting support.[31]

As the parliamentary confrontation intensified and repeated proposals for compromise faltered, the prospect of civil war became ever more imminent. In October 1912, three months before the official inauguration of the Ulster Volunteer Force, drilling commenced in the Orange hall under the direction of the Carrickfergus unionist club: 'Arrangements were made for the formation of a rifle club, carrying on drills, and route marches. Squads were formed and leaders appointed for different districts.'[32] The chairman of the inaugural meeting was Captain Arthur Dobbs,[33] whose father had read the lessons on Ulster Day and headed the list of signatories at the courthouse. Before long, weekly drilling was also underway in Kilroot Orange hall and the Barn Mills dining hall. The *Advertiser* carried weekly advertisements for Cambridge & Co. Ltd, High Street, which claimed to be the 'Headquarters in Ireland for Explosives, Arms, and Ammunition'. Carrick's gunmen were invited to procure 'Belgian and American Single and Double-Barrel Guns, Rifles, Revolvers, Automatic Pistols, etc.'[34] Robert Cambridge, though not an Orangeman, presided over the annual reunion of LOL 1537 in March 1913, at which the Presbyterian minister of nearby Loughmorne gave an ominous address: 'He hoped when the time came for action, if it did come, that the Protestants would be animated by the actions of the Apprentice boys of Derry.' The severity of his message was sugared by performances of 'Killarney' and 'The Shamrock of Ireland', suggesting that the lodge had not fully succumbed to Ulster provincialism.[35] Frederick was not reportedly present at either the reunion or the 'Twelfth' demonstration in Carrickfergus, where clerical speakers declared that 'constitutional means had failed them, and there was only the alternative of force', and urged all unionists to 'quit themselves like men' in 'the hour of emergency' so that 'Home Rule would be utterly destroyed'.[36]

Frederick observed the gathering constitutional crisis and the popular mood of militarism with apprehension. His diary for 1913 took note of the parliamentary progress of the Government of Ireland Bill, especially the defeat in the New Year of an amendment to exclude Ulster from its scope. Immediately afterwards, he visited Heron Lepper for a 'convtn. on Political situation' – a sign of the easy relationship he had achieved with former adversaries, despite his dissentient view of the Covenant and paramilitarism. His missionary friend Chatterton

Hammond again visited Carrick to preach, receiving £5 for his services in discussing 'Some dangers which confront Irish Protestants and how to meet them'.[37] Frederick's unflagging unionism was obvious in his diary entries for the last two days of January: 'H. R. Bill rejected by Lords. ... Hogg, Home Ruler, in for Derry. Serious blow to Union.'[38] On 11 February, as a vice-president of the East Antrim Constitutional (otherwise Unionist) Association, he attended the meeting that unanimously selected Major Robert McCalmont to succeed his father as unionist candidate for the constituency.[39] In later months, as domestic problems took over most of his time and energy, there were fewer diary references to political or public matters. Yet Frederick's influence is apparent in a remarkable decision taken by LOL 1537 on the eve of its annual reunion: 'In connection with the enlistment forms for the Ulster Volunteer force the members were of the opinion that it was not business for the lodge & it was decided to return them to Unionist Club.'[40]

The first anniversary of Ulster Day was proclaimed by D'Arcy to be a 'day of prayer for Ireland', with four services at St Nicholas's of an almost 'penitential character', inviting participation 'by men and women of goodwill no matter what their political opinions'.[41] At the main morning service, the rector reasserted his Irish nationality: 'Why may not we claim, and rejoice to claim, that we are Irish, no matter what our remote ancestors called themselves, and that while remaining Irish we also can be members of a wider unity, sharers in the strength and glory of the Empire for which our fellow-countrymen have made such splendid sacrifices?' He chose this occasion to declare that 'a great wrong has been done on our side' by those appealing 'to race hatred, and to religious, or rather irreligious bigotry'. He still hoped that the government might withdraw the Home Rule Bill, so preserving the liberty and prosperity of Catholics as well as Protestants and avoiding catastrophe: 'Its passing will be, as we fear, the signal for strife and war – civil war – in which treasure will be squandered and lives lost.' The Bill should be 'submitted to the people' (presumably through a general election), in the hope that it would be rejected. If not, as he obliquely indicated, continued resistance to Home Rule might not be sustainable: 'We shall have to consider afresh our responsibilities, for one thing is certain, that the same Bill or any similar Bill with the strength of the people behind it would make a difference, and a profound difference, for us all.' Meanwhile, as so often, he sought guidance from God. He had also apparently sought guidance from the Greers, having cycled over to Sea Park in early September and 'read over MSS'. The editor of the *Advertiser* received 'a considerable number of enquiries concerning the above address', and decided to publish it as a pamphlet (the first of many).[42]

1. Frederick McNeice *(back row, centre)* with his parents, family and associates, Clonsilla, Co. Dublin, late 1890s.

2. Frederick *(left)* and Ferguson John McNeice, Belfast, early 1900s.

3. Frederick and Lily McNeice, *c.*1902.

4. Lily McNeice with dog and book, Carrickfergus, Co. Antrim, *c.*1910.

5. Elizabeth McNeice, Belfast, *c.*1912.

6. Louis and Elizabeth McNeice, 1910.

7. Frederick McNeice, rectory garden, Carrickfergus, Co. Antrim, *c.*1910.

8. Louis and Beatrice MacNeice, rectory garden, *c.*1917.

9. Archie White, Carrickfergus gardener and Orangeman, *c.*1910.

10. Beatrice MacNeice outside the rectory, Carrickfergus, Co. Antrim, *c.*1920.

11. Frederick MacNeice bidding farewell to wartime troops, Carrickfergus station, *c.*1914.

12. Opening of Hayes Memorial Hall, Dundela, Belfast, 12 Oct. 1929.

13. Wedding party for Elizabeth and John Nicholson, 18 Oct. 1928.

14. Louis MacNeice *(second from left)* with Mary Pilkington *(left)*, Hugh Davies and Barbara Nicholson, at the wedding of Elizabeth and John Nicholson, 18 Oct. 1928 (74 Limestone Rd, Belfast).

15. Frederick MacNeice at Spitzbergen, Norway, July 1928.

16. Frederick MacNeice with islander, Omey Strand, Co. Galway, Aug. 1930.

Occasionally, Frederick observed the leaders of militant unionism in person, reinforcing the dolorous message of the daily press and his own local knowledge. A few days after the Ulster Day service, he witnessed a major UVF rally in Tyrone: 'Motored Cookstown II, started at 9. Demonstration at Cookstown, Carson & F. E. Smith. Afternoon at Mrs MacGregor Greer's. Carrickfergus about 9.'[43] Dorinda MacGregor Greer's diary entry was more illuminating and more enthusiastic. After a detailed account of the morning's drill competition for local UVF companies, she described the afternoon's proceedings:

> Bea & Eva & Mr. McNiece came from Carrick in their car. We gave lunch to the Pall Mall Gazette Correspondent. Sir E. Carson, Mr. F. E. Smith, Gen Sir G. Richardson Col Hackett Pain. Capt. Craig arrived at 1.15. The Review went off well. Mac looked so dignified & nice . . . Sir E. Carson spoke so well & the whole thing could not have gone off better. I had a few words with Sir Edward & he spoke of Papa. After the Leaders had gone to Dungannon – motored to the Fair hill & saw the whole 5th. Batt. U.V.F. march thro' Cookstown, a most impressive sight – lead [*sic.*] by man on horseback. ... Bea & Eva & Mr. McNiece came here to tea.[44]

Through his friendship with the Greers, in particular, Frederick could take the measure of Ulster's leaders at first hand, and find them wanting.

III

As Ulster lurched towards seemingly inevitable disaster, the McNeice family faced its own day of reckoning. In early 1912, Lily began to show alarming symptoms of illness and mental disturbance, though in June she took the children to Portstewart on the usual summer holiday. She was suffering from a uterine fibroid, which she wrongly attributed to 'Louis's difficult birth'. Around Christmas, she again fell ill but seemed to recover.[45] Throughout 1913, Frederick's diary was dominated by Lily's worsening condition. Lily and he were initially unwilling to approve the 'big operation' recommended by the senior surgeon of the Samaritan Hospital for Women on the Lisburn Road in Belfast, Dr John Campbell.[46] After discussion with a local doctor, James Huston of Governor's Place, he decided to seek 'another's opinion – a Dublin opinion'.[47] This was secured from the celebrated gynaecologist Sir William Smyly, former master of the Rotunda and also a Masonic 'Grand Inquisitor' (31°).[48] Louis Plunkett, one the few who shared this distinction, may have acted as intermediary. Smyly concurred with Huston's opinion, strongly advising an operation that 'wouldn't be very serious'; but Frederick prevaricated and cancelled the planned operation in Dublin. Lily remained unwilling to go ahead, as Frederick observed on 24 January: 'In the very early morning or about midnight Lily said she thought she ought to postpone operation & await another attack. I prayed for some clear, unmistakeable guidance. Lily very weak when got up. I did some messages. On my return found she had again become unwell. Is this the guidance?'

He wrote to London for a copy of the *Healer* (a monthly devoted to 'Spiritual Healing'), still 'trusting for a Change which can be through God'.[49] Frederick remained cautiously interested in non-physical remedies for disease, declaring in 1924 that 'I have no wish to belittle what may have been achieved by those who might be classed as Mental or Faith Healers. There are maladies that yield to treatment of that sort. Moreover, there is, I think, the possibility, too, of much advance in medical treatment along psychological lines.'[50]

For nearly two months, the family was in suspense as Lily's condition fluctuated. When not confined to bed, she was encouraged to take the air: 'Early part of day. Drove with Lily & Freddie for her hour.' Finally, on 18 March, the decision was taken to perform a hysterectomy in Belfast.[51] She was probably treated in Dr Campbell's Samaritan Hospital, with its 'roomy and well lighted' wards that were 'open for the treatment of all classes, without distinction of creed':[52] 'Stayed in. Lily tired; didn't sleep through the night. Afternoon, 91st Ps: later on Ps. xvi.[53] Prayer with Lily, Elsie, Freddie. 5.10 started for Bft. in Motor. Private Hospital, stayed over 2 hours. Prayer. Saw Mrs. T. Clesham. 10 train Cfergus.' The widow of Timothy Clesham, the former ICM missionary at Aasleagh, provided a tenuous link with Lily's origins, so remote now that both parents were dead and her kinsfolk alienated by sectarian divisions. Next day, Frederick was back in Belfast for further visits to the hospital, prayer, and a call on the Plunketts. At last, on Good Friday, the operation was successfully completed: '3.30. Saw Lily "God has been very good to us".' A month later, after alternating reports that Lily was 'rather depressed' and 'wonderfully well', she returned to Carrickfergus.[54]

Depression prevailed. For nearly six months, Frederick's diary was peppered with references to Lily's almost unalleviated despondency, her regular drives with Miss Price, the nurse, and his own consolatory visits to the Plunketts in Windsor Park, Belfast, and the Greers in Sea Park. As Elizabeth recalled:

> We were taken to see her in the nursing-home and told she was getting better and would soon be back. She came back but she was still in depression. She was at home all that summer and seemed to be nearly always sad and crying. A nurse came to stay in the house and nearly every afternoon a hired phaeton used to come to take my mother for drives. She and the nurse would sit on the main seat and one child was always taken to sit on the little seat facing them.

Ten-year-old Elsie noticed that her mother 'developed ideas of having committed unforgivable sins and was inclined to talk even to the children about Death and Judgement, Hell and Heaven and kindred subjects. ... My father, who hated hell-fire religion, tried to comfort and reason with his wife.' Elizabeth, herself a psychiatric doctor in later life, attributed Lily's ravings to her background in the ICM, surmising that 'her early education was probably much influenced by Calvinist ideas'.[55] For Frederick, reared in the same ghoulish (though not strictly Calvinist) milieu, her reversion to the primitive terror of divine punishment must have carried particular pathos.

The family misery was slightly lifted on 30 May, when the rector and his wife received 'valuable presentations from present and former members' of the congregation, including another welcome 'purse of sovereigns'. The ceremony, in the rectory, 'was of a private character owing to the illness of Mrs McNeice'. Subscriptions were raised by a sub-committee consisting of Henry Blackburne, Henry Lynn and Isaac Graham (all ex-protestors) and Commander Dawes, RN. An address, signed by the curate, the churchwardens, and the entire select vestry, pointed out that 'your task from the outset was a difficult one', Chamberlain having been 'respected and beloved by all'. This time no reference was made to the qualities of William Bradley: 'By your kindness of heart, unfailing courtesy to old and young alike, charitable disposition, and unremitting attention to your ministerial duties, you have filled your sacred office with characteristic prudence and tact, surpassing all our expectations.' The address, ensconced in a gold frame, depicted the church, town and castle from Fishermen's Pier, along with the ancient corporate seal, Chichester monument, diocesan arms, choir and rectory. 'Frederick MacNeice' responded gracefully with a tribute to the character of his predecessor.[56]

This was almost the first use of the Gaelic form 'Mac', which Frederick was to employ in public, with frequent lapses, for the rest of his life.[57] In signing private letters, however, he normally remained 'Frederick McNeice' until his elevation to the episcopacy. He had already twice altered the form of his name in times of personal transition, upon becoming curate of Cappoquin in 1895 and rector of Holy Trinity in 1903. In Hibernicizing his surname and abandoning the form customary in Antrim, he may have been declaring his primary attachment to Ireland rather than Ulster, as an oblique response to the partitionist thrust of Carsonism.

Further solace was forthcoming on 13 June, when the rector's diary revealed a new fraternal interest: 'Lily & Miss Price drove: Davey: Car. Greenisland. Masonic.' The occasion was Frederick's initiation as an Entered Apprentice in Lodge 346, a 'Temperance' lodge named after its first secretary, John Heron Lepper. He progressed speedily through the higher degrees of 'Blue Masonry'

(Fellow Craftsman and Master Mason), before securing his Grand Lodge certificate in October 1913.[58] Unlike many Freemasons, he was sufficiently interested in the ritualistic and speculative elements of the craft to embrace 'Red Masonry' by entering Royal Arch Chapter 253, Carrickfergus, in October 1914. This catered for members of all Carrickfergus lodges and many farther afield, supplying still wider contacts of potential value.[59] He did not, however, penetrate the more exalted degrees, Prince Masonry and beyond, favoured by wealthy allies such as Archbishop Crozier and Louis Plunkett. Frederick was never a lodge officer, and the registers supply no further record of his Masonic career except the fact of his resignation in 1923. His interest in Freemasonry was primarily local and social, offering camaraderie with a religious flavour, and a route of occasional escape from a troubled and tormented household. This connection is obliquely suggested by a diary entry for 30 July 1913: '8.20. Masonic Lily depressed all day.' With its emphasis on goodwill, benevolence, charity and harmony, the brotherhood offered an additional pathway out of his darkness.

Freemasonry also gave invaluable opportunities for consolidating his acceptance and status in the town and parish. Those who founded Lodge 346 on 31 March 1913 were refugees from other lodges, mainly (like Lepper) from St Patrick's Lodge 43, Carrickfergus. Otherwise, most of the hundred entrants over the next decade were (like Frederick) newcomers to Freemasonry. The lodge soon attracted many key figures in the select vestry, the Orange Order and local politics. Frederick could now fraternize on intimate terms with ex-protestors such as the builder Ezekiel Caters, the banker Isaac Graham, the solicitor Henry Lynn, and Lepper himself; leading Orangemen like Stewart Woods and Councillor John Campbell; and other notables such as David Bell (editor of the *Advertiser*), David Law (town clerk), Law's predecessor James Boyd, and Thomas Cambridge (the explosives merchant). Many of these acted as lodge officers during Frederick's decade as a member.

The lodge register for 1913–16 suggests a social profile intermediate between the élite of the select vestry and the plebeian membership of LOL 1537. The typical Freemason was a 33-year-old (by 1914) living in a house with eight rooms and four front windows. Two-fifths lived in first-class houses, but the majority of Freemasons were still single and not yet heads of household. Episcopalians accounted for fourteen of the thirty-eight identified members (37 per cent), along with sixteen Presbyterians, four Methodists, two Congregationalists, and two Baptists. Over two-fifths of members (sixteen) were skilled workers and artisans, a higher proportion than that for the select vestry or LOL 1537. Otherwise, there were eight white-collar workers, seven dealers (including Tommy Robinson the flesher and his brother William), five professional men and only two unskilled workers.[60]

Initiation into Heron Lepper's lodge consolidated the networks of trust that Frederick had been so assiduously constructing, and gave him further opportunities to work with well-placed Protestants of other congregations.

In the course of Lily's illness, Frederick called with increasing frequency on the hospitality and generous support of the Greers of Sea Park and Tullylagan. Thomas MacGregor Greer (Mac)[61] and his formidable wife Dorinda (Dindie) lived mostly in Tullylagan, near Cookstown, where they were enthusiastic actors in each episode of Ulster's drama (Covenant, Ulster Volunteers, Gun-Running).[62] Thomas's widowed mother and unmarried sisters, Beatrice and Eva, lived alternately in Sea Park (just north of Greenisland) and a London mansion. The delights of Sea Park, with its 'tower with a telescope', 'walled garden with bees', and croquet lawn, were celebrated by Louis in 'Soap Suds', recalling a visit at the age of eight.[63] Margaret Greer had inherited Sea Park from her father John Owden, a linen magnate like her late husband Thomas, the last representative of Carrickfergus in the House of Commons.[64] Thomas, though a pillar of St Nicholas's who had endowed the east window and the clock on the church tower, came from a long line of lapsing Quakers.[65] The entire family was profoundly evangelical and relentlessly puritanical, in a reportedly delightful way. Beatrice's family had numerous landed and military connections, some of them unfortunate: a niece married the surrenderer of Singapore, and a first cousin mothered the insane murderer of Francis Sheehy-Skeffington in 1916.[66] Beatrice and Eva had long since surrendered to contented spinsterhood, Eva forming a lifelong intimacy and partnership with the domineering poetess 'Elizabeth Shane', otherwise Gertrude Hind.[67] Such were the kindly benefactors who helped Lily and her family through the rigours of 1913. On 7 August, as Lily's depression intensified, Frederick noted in his diary: 'Motored with Elsie & the Miss Greers to Antrim. Lunched at Sea Park. Afternoon: Lily at Sea Park.' The Greers, and their splendid home, became a haven for the afflicted.

The Hind family had also became close friends, offering practical help and comfort in these troubled years. Like many Belfast businessmen and manufacturers, John Hind had celebrated his success by moving outside the grimy city, into the former deanery at Carrickfergus.[68] Born in Shropshire, he had bought back the residue of his father's collapsed company and built up a large business as an engineer and machine maker in Great George's Street. In addition to his parish labours as churchwarden, synodsman and organizer of the Boys' Brigade, he was a major contributor to parochial funds.[69] His son James also became an engineer, but other offspring had loftier ambitions. His elder son John became a missionary and eventually bishop in Fukien, partly under the influence of parents who were 'earnest Church people', supporters of the Church Missionary Society, and generous in paying his exotic expenses.[70] None of the daughters married.[71] Adelaide also worked as a missionary in China and Agnes became lady superintendent of two private hospitals in Dublin.[72] Gertrude, long after her departure from Carrickfergus to live with Eva Greer in Bath and later Glasdrumman, County Down, remained a frequent guest and host of the MacNeices. She appears in various snapshots of melancholy groups in the rectory garden.

On 25 August 1913, Elsie and Freddie saw their mother for the last time, leaving painful images and unanswered questions that were to haunt them lifelong. Lily and Frederick were motored by Commander Dawes to Great Victoria Street, where they caught the 2.15 train to Dublin. After leaving Lily at Agnes Hind's Belgrave Private Hospital in Rathmines, Frederick spent two nights at the College Hotel before returning to Belfast. Next evening, he was made a Master Mason at the Masonic hall.[73] For nearly two months, his diary recorded a succession of usually doleful messages from Dublin: 'no cheery news', 'no brighter', 'appallingly doleful letter'. One Sunday in September, he sang '7 Hymns – specially "Art thou weary".' Letters from Lily and Miss Hind inspired his usual lament, 'God help me' in Greek, balanced in the next entry by 'Freddie: birthday – "God bless him".'[74]

Eventually, Lily's condition deteriorated to the point where more drastic treatment was required:

> October 11, Saturday. Letter from Miss Hind rather bright. Later letter v. serious. Saw Dr. Huston, Mr and Mrs Graham, Miss Hind, Mrs Greer 4. oc train to Belfast; 5.45 train to Dublin. Saw Miss Hind at Hospital. I cdn't see Lily.

> October 12, Sunday. Called to Dr. Cope's. Got his judgments. Worse than expected. Saw Dr. Leeper: got Form. St Catherine's Church. Hymn 421.[75] Had dinner alone in College Hotel. Went to St Patrick's. All cold & purposeless. ...

> October 13, Monday. Afternoon: Met Miss Hind: saw Dr. Cope. Signed form. Took it to Hospital. Tea alone in Hotel. In Warren's. Supper alone.

> October 14, Tuesday. Called to Hospital: saw Dr. Leeper: he advised me not to see Lily just yet.

With another sigh in Greek, he returned home that evening to comfort his children.

St Patrick's Hospital for Lunatics and Idiots, established in 1746 in accordance with the will of Jonathan Swift, was a progressive and well-run institution under the medical superintendence of Richard Leeper.[76] Statistics for the later nineteenth century indicate that the majority of the patients were women, four-fifths being Protestants, two-fifths recovering after treatment, and one-third dying in the hospital. Early in his long tenure, Leeper had largely eliminated such indignities as the straitjacket (though padded rooms were used), rid himself of illiterate staff and incurable cases, and opened a second hospital (St Edmundsbury's) for convalescents.[77] In 1909, an inspector of lunatics had reported favourably on the circumstances of the 122 patients in the 2 institutions, tended by 39 staff in daytime and 7 at night:

> There was not very much noise or excitement, and the patients appeared to be judiciously cared for, and were suitably dressed according to their station in life. Various games, both indoor and outdoor, are provided for their amusement; ten gentlemen and twenty-six ladies go out driving, and various excursions have been made of late to the country. Four of the gentlemen amuse themselves by gardening, and twenty-nine ladies pass their time at sewing and housework.[78]

Such was the world that Lily inhabited for the last year of her life.

Lily's documents of application make melancholy reading: a patient of temperate habits and Protestant faith, of no occupation or trade, aged (almost) forty-seven, whose youngest child was aged six, and who suffered from suicidal 'melancholia', probably caused by 'uterine trouble' after her operation. Asked about 'relations affected mentally', Frederick mentioned a niece but not William. Dr George Cope[79] testified to Lily's insanity from personal observation: 'Says she is an Evil Spirit – hears strange voices says every thing is wrong – restless – says she wishes she was dead.' Superintendent Hind had told him 'that patient attempted to get out of the Window – Cries frequently & states that she complains of Evil Spirit'. Another doctor reported that 'she says that the room is full of evil spirits: & that the nurses are some of them, that she herself is possessed with evil spirits'.[80] When examined on admission, Lily's physical condition appeared to be normal. But her appetite and ability to sleep were only 'fair', her reaction to questions was 'bad', and the general prognosis was also 'bad'.[81]

Frederick undertook to pay two guineas weekly for her upkeep, pending a ruling on charges by the governors (including Archbishop Crozier), and named two 'respectable Persons' who could attest to his income. These were John Hind and Isaac Graham, the Northern Bank manager.[82] The hospital charges, in addition to the expenses arising from Lily's illness and care in Belfast and Carrickfergus, stretched Frederick's meagre resources. On 22 October, he raised this delicate subject in a carefully phrased letter to Dr Leeper. Lily had no property 'except a cottage in Co Galway which has been a distinct loss for some years', but her personal bank account contained £70, the 'bigger part of a presentation made to me some months ago'. Part of the balance was due to his quarterly stipend, which he had regularly handed over because Lily had 'kept the household accounts'. He tentatively suggested that Leeper should ask her to sign a blank cheque giving him access to the balance, but recognized the pitfalls of such a course: 'If I am asking an impossible thing then do not hesitate to refuse for I shall understand [word illegible] & I must try to manage somehow. ... P.S. It would be useful to me even in paying hospital fees &c.'[83] In the event, Lily's meagre assets remained untouched until her death.

A few months later, Frederick applied to the governors for relief, explaining that the full fee of two guineas weekly could not be met from his annual stipend of £307, augmented by £15–20 in fees. The balance of the presentation fund had already been exhausted in additional expenses. Children's insurances had to be paid and 'a large house & garden kept up'. He did not ask for any reduction of the normal rate, but proposed that half of the charge be held on account for future repayment. He offered 'his word of honour as a Clergyman' to pay the weekly guinea, and promised Leeper that 'if my poor wife gets better before twelve months I think it would be possible for me, after that time, to pay back gradually the difference'. Should this arrangement be rejected, 'I will simply try & get my friends to assist me for a time.' The governors relented, charging Lily only 25s. weekly for the next six months, even though this was below the cost of her upkeep. Frederick, while offering his 'sincere thanks for the consideration shown to me', still expressed the hope that 'later on I may be able to make up that difference'.[84] This correspondence reveals not only the inadequacy of clerical stipends for those without private means, but also the astuteness and tact with which Frederick negotiated. A less accomplished diplomat might have surrendered his dignity by begging for a rebate, a request unlikely to have been granted. Instead, he proposed an honorable but unworkable compromise, which prompted the governors to adopt a 'better and kinder' option that would not mess up their accounts.

Lily's forty-seventh birthday occurred during her first week in St Patrick's: 'God take care of her'. Frederick's visits to the calm and comfort of Sea Park became even more frequent: 'Walked over to Sea Park. Remained until 10.00'; 'Tea & Dinner Sea Park.'[85] On Sunday, 23 November, after preaching on 'The Breaking of the Golden Bowl' (Ecc. 12: 6),[86] he 'saw the Miss Greers as far as gate'. The next three days were spent in Dublin: 'Called to Hospital: long conversation with Dr. Rutherford.[87] Hopeful report. Saw Dr. Leeper: also hopeful. No visitors to see her for some time.' After tea at the College Restaurant, he went 'to Kingstown for Mail Boat. Saw Mrs Greer & the Misses Greer off at 8.30.' He returned to face a bleak winter and bereft Christmas in Carrickfergus: '8 a.m. H.C. 11.30 a.m. Preached: God to us – son c'd Immanuel. Gave Mrs Millar £1. Elsie help[ed] in

C. [Church?]. Quiet Xmas. Poor Lily in 'Hospital'. Gave Miss John[s] the sacrament of H. Com.'[88] In the absence of Frederick's diary for 1914, few signs remain of his state of mind or personal routine during Lily's final year in confinement. One address, however, suggests that he found some solace in nocturnal rambles up the North Road from the rectory. In an otherwise prosaic speech on the need for rubbish 'receptacles' and better manners, he expatiated upon the delights of a walk that his son was to remember as part of the dreary regimen enforced by the dour Miss McCready.[89] He wondered if 'any of them had ever walked up to the Milebush on a bright starry night':

> He had occasionally done so, and as one looked down towards Belfast Lough, and up to the lights of Belfast, and over to the County Down, or over the hills towards Carnmoney, one felt it was as beautiful a picture as the human eye could rest upon. He often thought there must be a fault somewhere, that prevented people from settling in greater numbers in Carrickfergus.[90]

Glimpses of light amidst the darkness alleviated his long vigil.

Lily's state of mind showed no signs of improvement. Week after week, the hospital's medical journal listed 'Mrs. McNeice Melancholia' among the 110 or so cases under treatment, of whom up to 80 were women. Few untoward incidents were reported in the journal, though in July and August 1914 a 'sleeved jacket' was ordered to be worn at night by a Catholic spinster from Cork, 'to prevent further self mutilation by means of pulling out her hair, beating her face with her fists and attempting to gouge out her eyes'.[91] Lily's 'delusional melancholia' was expressed less dramatically, and she was never subjected to such indignities. Yet her case-notes painfully record the extent of her mental collapse:

> Oct. 19. Mrs McNeice is in a very depressed and delusional state. Cries aloud declaring that we are about to try to destroy her and that she is going to hell, etc. Says it is all her own fault and that she cannot be forgiven … .
>
> Oct. 27. Mrs McNeice continues in a very delusional state. Says she is possessed of an evil spirit and that she will be smothered etc … .
>
> Nov. 5. Mrs McNeice remains very delusional. Says she has all sorts of diseases and that we are about to take away her health from her etc.

Her subsequent condition fluctuated in response to an alternating provision of bromides and thyroid gland tablets: 'now very quiet', 'again somewhat agitated', 'has been very noisy and is on the bromides again', 'hears voices frequently and is often noisy'. The drugs seem to have improved her ability to eat and sleep, but her mental condition remained alarming on 12 June 1914: 'Mrs McNeice is still miserable and delusional. Takes food moderately. Has hallucinations of hearing. Sleeps fairly well.' Not once do her case-notes mention any reference to her absent husband and children.[92] Lily was imprisoned in a private hell from which there was no escape or prospect of redemption.

IV

Throughout this protracted personal agony, Frederick remained engrossed in the problems created by Ulster's ever-worsening crisis. His unionism remained unquestioned, as shown by his election in February 1914 as the first of five clerical vice-presidents of the Carrickfergus unionist club. The multitude of office-holders (fifty-one in all) included twelve parish officers, eight members of the Lepper lodge and four brethren in LOL 1537. Their social profile closely resembled that of the parish officers, except for the heavier concentration of professional men (including five clergymen, three medical practitioners and three lawyers). The twenty-one Episcopalians were slightly outnumbered by Non-Conformists (eighteen Presbyterians, three Congregationalists, and two Methodists). Archibald Dobbs, who was re-elected as president, was said by Robert Cambridge to be 'in close touch with their great leader (Sir E. Carson)'.[93] Three of the lay vice-presidents reappeared three weeks later as company commanders in the 3rd Battalion, Central Antrim Regiment, when 700 Ulster Volunteers assembled at the Barn football ground for a review by General Sir William Adair, KCB. Tea followed in the dining hall of Barn Mills, by the kindness of Mrs Kirk of Thornfield.[94] Frederick evidently missed this entertainment; but later in March he presided over 'a grand social and ball' for the annual reunion of LOL 1537, 'dealing with the present crisis generally' and delivering a 'short prayer' before the dancing began.[95]

Frederick's growing alarm at the militarization of Ulster, and of the Church of Ireland, is reflected in an anonymous letter to the *Guardian* (a clerical magazine), published early in March and preserved in family papers. Responding sharply to the dean of Belfast's defence of Ulster's resistance, 'Pro Pace' (a non-signatory of the Covenant) looked forward to the possibility of an 'honourable compromise' following 'an appeal to the country'. He declared that 'hitherto the Ulster Unionist Party has offered no solution of the Irish Question'. The current effort 'to place a fence round Ulster or part of Ulster and exclude it from any share in the larger life of the country' was 'a poor solution'; the statesman's aim should be 'to heal the wounds of the country; to unite all men in North and South, and to give our land some measure of peace'. The Church of Ireland had until recently 'largely betrayed its trust', having 'exerted instead all its powers in the interests of a class and [given] itself to the support of the worst features of English administration'. Its clergy were now to be seen 'approving of organised resistance to the law of the land, frequenting drill-halls, sometimes acting as recruiting-officers, and as captains of companies, and asking for the blessing of God upon a course admittedly fraught with danger to the whole Empire'.

Dean Grierson had defended the use of force on the ground that Ulster would 'never submit to be ruled by a Government predominantly Roman'. 'Pro Pace' retorted: 'Has the Church of Ireland no way of combating that predominance except by force?' In conclusion, he affirmed the view that 'all Churches must unite against the growing worldliness of the age', and prayed 'that all men in Ireland may unite in the cause of righteousness and justice and upright dealing': 'Moderate men – leaders in business – in Belfast, are looking forward to a wise and just settlement. The Church of Ireland has almost forgotten her high prerogative of peace-maker.'[96] In style and content, the views of 'Pro Pace' are indistinguishable from those of Frederick MacNeice. In public, however, the rector was more oblique in his references to Ulster's political and clerical leaders. On 8 March, he pleaded with parishioners 'to use all their influence, so that there might be no exhibition of a temper that might have most disastrous consequence for the cause dear to them all'. Instead, they should seek, with God's guidance, 'to secure order and maintain peace'.[97]

Intimations of war and possible civil war were intensifying. On the morning after the Orange ball, 2 warships delivered 105 officers and men of the 2nd Battalion, King's Own Yorkshire Light Infantry. The *Advertiser* remarked that 'it seems quite like old times to have the Castle again garrisoned'. Customs officers searched the headquarters of the Carrickfergus Amateur Rowing Club for 'munitions of war ... evidently acting on incorrect information'. Meanwhile, 'the members of the Ulster Volunteer Force have had a busy time during the week, mounting guard at certain centres', and proving 'constantly on the alert' when challenging visiting patrols in nocturnal manoeuvres.[98] Frederick himself recalled the arrival of the Yorkshires on 21 March:

> Some of the women who looked on were almost in tears. Through that day the wildest rumours were in circulation, and were believed. It was stated that the leaders of the Ulster Volunteer Force were to be seized that night, that the warrants for their arrest had come. The writer of these chapters was in the town late that night. Near Joymount he met a youth whose great coat seemed scarcely large enough to cover something he wished to conceal. He had two rifles. He was on his way to act, if necessary, as sentry before the entrance of the house of one of the Ulster Volunteer officers. ... It was a mercy no policeman challenged them, for the answer might have set Ulster on fire.[99]

Next morning, he welcomed the Yorkshires to St Nicholas's with an appeal in keeping with the sentiments of 'Pro Pace'. In case of rebellion, there was an obvious risk that the garrison and the parishioners would find themselves in bloody combat. In the presence of Major McCalmont, MP, and Major Tulloch of the Yorkshires, he declared that if Ireland were 'to be stained with human blood then I say that it will be a black crime, an awful tragedy, and that the consequences will be such as no man living can foresee'. He asked sarcastically if the government's proposals (for temporary exclusion of Ulster counties voting to opt out of Home Rule) were such 'as to justify the shedding of a drop of human blood'. Exclusion for 600 rather than 6 years would be no better, since it would still entail 'the partition of Ulster' within itself, and the intensification of 'the antagonism of Romanist to Protestant and of Protestant to Romanist' within both jurisdictions. Partition of the province would also entail 'a new tragedy', as Protestants in counties not excluded from Home Rule would feel that 'a wrong had been done to them', which 'might justly be counted as a great betrayal'. Speaking as an all-Ireland unionist reared in Galway and Dublin, he invited the congregation to 'go one step further': 'What of the Protestants in Galway, Clare, Limerick, Cork, Dublin? Do they not belong to us? Have they no claim on us? Is it a question of arithmetic, or a question of principle? … To any such arrangement we should, as I hold, say "No," a thousand times "No."' He hoped it could never be truly said 'that at a great crisis in our country's history we deliberately separated ourselves from our scattered brethren in the South and West of Ireland, who, in season and out of season, have been faithful to the principles that they and we hold in common'.

He believed a 'better way' could be found than the bloody combination of 'coercion' and 'active resistance':

> But if it is to be found we on our side must be prepared to go some considerable distance for the sake of a peaceful solution, for things cannot remain as they are. Could not a truce be called, and during the truce could not delegates – not politicians – representing all Irish parties, and representatives of commercial, industrial, and every Irish interest meet together?

If this proposal, anticipating Sir Horace Plunkett's Irish Convention of 1917–18, proved impracticable, there was 'still another course left':

> It is to ask – honestly ask – for an appeal to the people of the United Kingdom, while there is still an United Kingdom, and to agree to accept the verdict of the people whatever that verdict be. Meanwhile our immediate duty, locally, is plain.

It is to do all in our power to maintain order; to put our strength into the things that make for peace. As loyal citizens of the King we shall exhibit no antagonism to the soldiers of the King.

Those of other political and religious opinions must be reassured that 'they have absolutely nothing to fear from us'. No provocation must be offered, no retaliation given in case of provocation: 'Let us do the stronger thing; the most Christ-like thing. Let each of us act as if he were a magistrate, specially responsible for the maintenance of order, for the keeping of the peace.'[100] If a properly mandated government of the United Kingdom imposed Home Rule, the true unionist's duty was to make the best of it. Home Rule, though obnoxious, was less corrosive of liberty than either partition or civil war.

It is characteristic of Frederick's boldness and determination that he reiterated this message at the first church parade of the local UVF, under Captain Arthur Dobbs, at which the Yorkshires were again present under Major Tulloch: 'Seldom has such a large congregation assembled within the walls of the sacred and historic building. Special seats were reserved for the Yorkshires in the Donegall aisle, while the Volunteers occupied the nave and gallery.' Extra seats had to be placed in the aisles. The rector's text was 'Verily, verily, I say unto you, That ye shall weep and lament, but the world shall rejoice' (John 16: 20). He hoped that there were 'forces at work' in both Germany and Britain, which would 'make war between these two great civilized nations impossible and unthinkable'. As for Ireland, there could be no doubt that Britain could 'ultimately crush all the opposition that could be organized against her in this province, as in all the provinces of Ireland'. But this would be a 'ghastly success' creating the 'bitterest antagonisms for generations to come'. Ulster might offer a 'stubborn resistance', but at the end of it 'we should be as far off as ever from a settlement. The province would be poorer, immeasurably poorer, than it is to-day; the divisions between its people would be more profound.' God might intervene yet be unrecognized, perhaps in the form of 'the light to the soul of one man, or a few men, whose altered convictions, at such a time as this, might persuade a great and just people to hesitate before taking a course that might have the most disastrous consequences'. He urged his hearers to 'admit that something may be said for those who view the situation from another point', ending with an affirmation of hope: 'The chapters of our country's story – taking the centuries as chapters – have all been stained with blood. Possibly we are going to witness the opening of a new chapter.' For Ulster, as for himself, there was still hope that the miseries of the present would eventually give place to a positive future. After a hearty rendition of the National Anthem by the congregation, the Volunteers formed up outside and stood to attention as the Yorkshires left for the castle and the courthouse: 'The Yorkshires acknowledged the salute with military precision.'[101]

The Easter vestry on 14 April passed with gracious exchanges of mutual esteem between the rector and the former protestors, with no significant change in the select vestry and no political discussion.[102] Ten nights later, the latent menace of the UVF took alarmingly practical form when 25,000 service rifles, each with a hundred rounds of ammunition, were smuggled into Larne, Bangor and Donaghadee. Some of Frederick's closest allies were implicated in the 'gun-running'. Thomas MacGregor Greer brought a carload of arms overnight from Larne to Tullylagan, where he 'spent the morning packing up ammunition in small bundles to distribute round the companies in case of a raid'.[103] According to Elizabeth Nicholson, Mac also stored weapons in the cellars of Sea Park, whose owner (his mother) 'had been born and brought up a Quaker & was highly indignant when she found that her house had been used for this purpose'. Despite his disapproval of the gun-running, Frederick always remained 'on very good terms' with the extended Greer family.[104] As in the Covenant episode, the alliances that he had built up within and beyond the parish proved powerful enough to withstand merely political disagreements.

On 24 May, Frederick again addressed a church parade of the UVF, with 300 Volunteers from Carrickfergus, Greenisland and Jordanstown who were marched from the Orange hall to the church by Captain Dobbs. The Government of Ireland Bill had completed its third course through the House of Commons, coinciding with a military parade and rumours of naval manoeuvres but 'no demonstration of any kind in the town'. The rector spoke of 'the interdependence of civilised nations', the need to advance 'not through conflict but through co-operation', and the undeniable fact of 'change' in 'our modern world'. He praised Carson's qualities but urged their more productive application: 'You have a leader whom you can trust. He has shown that he possesses great qualities – courage, honesty, unselfishness, judgment. … I would prefer that he and the other Irish leaders should meet and settle the question as best they could, rather than that the hills of Ulster should become armed camps.' Once again, his unaltered unionism was made explicit:

And speaking as a Unionist to Unionists I say – 'We must make it plain, abundantly plain, that while we are opposed to the change of Government now proposed, and with which we are now threatened, we are no less opposed to the thought of a war which would range us against the soldiers of the King, or against our fellow-countrymen.'[105]

Once again, a few weeks later, he headed the list of clergymen elected as vice-presidents of the East Antrim Unionist Association, the second name being that of his old mentor, Richard Clarke.[106]

Frederick no longer confined his appeals to parishioners and fellow ministers. He had begun sending copies of his sermons to public men such as Lord Loreburn, the retired liberal Lord Chancellor. Loreburn responded that 'your opinions are in many respects my own. I do not believe exclusion is a good way of settlement, and only acquiesce in it because it will avert actual fighting.' He hoped that the House of Commons would 'insist' on a peaceful settlement, but admitted that 'the time is now dangerously short'.[107] The rector also sent a copy of his first address to the Yorkshires to William Sanday, the celebrated Oxford theologian, who endorsed his conclusion that Ulster unionists were bound to accept the decision of the electorate and commended him for 'the wise reserve that you are showing'.[108]

Frederick's papers contain several scribbled draft letters to unidentified like minds, venting his frustration at the obduracy of both government and opposition: 'Where is the statesmanship in forcing men, & such men as those in N. E. Ulster, under a particular kind of God? And where either is the statesmanship in such an attitude as that of Mr Bonar Law & his party?' In Ireland, North and South should be brought to see the absurdity of saying: 'I have no need of thee.' In another draft, he explained that 'I am not a Volunteer or Covenanter' and had always thought the Ulster movement 'a blunder': 'I have stood aside fr the Mil movt in Ulst. ever since its inc. & have public counselled toler. & good will. Five or six addresses on these lines.' In a third letter, drafted in the last week of July, he wrote that 'companies of armed men are drilling & parading nightly', with a march through the streets of Carrick on 23 July. They could not prevail against regular soldiers, 'but they cld, in an irreg way, give much trouble, & numbers of them, I am told, are ready to die, to be killed rather than "give in".' Bitterness would intensify, and 'later on too, if things go on as they now are, there will be serious diffic. for t. l. [those like?] myself who cannot identify ourselves with the movement'.[109]

Frederick's all-Ireland unionism and loathing of partition, though unusual in Ulster, was commonplace among 'Southern' Protestants. Its logical implications had been most forcefully developed by Sir Horace Plunkett, the former unionist MP who had devoted his later life to economic and social regeneration driven by reconciliation and co-operation between classes and creeds. Plunkett's usually sensible proposals seldom prevailed, partly because of a condescending manner perfectly encapsulated in the title of an earlier manifesto, *Noblesse Oblige*.[110] In his trenchant pamphlet, *A Better Way*, completed on 20 July 1914, Plunkett proclaimed that partitition would 'proclaim to the world the bankruptcy of British statesmanship in Ireland'. Unlike Frederick, he rejected the option of holding another general election to determine whether or not Home Rule had a popular mandate. Plunkett argued that the only practicable alternative to coercion and civil war was 'for both parties in Ireland to come together and learn by actual experiment, honestly and fairly tried, upon what terms and conditions they can jointly govern it'. This could be done by applying Home Rule to the entire island, while allowing the entire province of Ulster 'after a stated period ... to vote itself out if the majority so desire'. Having persuaded himself that Ulster might accept the proposal (which he discussed with Carson, receiving a courteous rebuttal), Plunkett likened Ireland's salvation to an act of racial seduction: 'Our children's children will read with pride how one of our oldest legends came true – how the man of the North won the woman of the South and a new Ireland was born.'[111]

Within four days of signing the preface, Plunkett had sent Frederick a copy and elicited an enthusiastic response. Frederick indicated, more explicitly than in any public statement, that he had come to accept that some form of all-Ireland Home Rule would be preferable to the stark alternatives:

> A few weeks ago in conversation with a member of the Ulster Unionist Council I said – 'If only the Government could be persuaded to drop both Bills, & the Opposition to accept the principle that Ireland, as a unit, should have self-government then it might be possible to construct a new Bill which would secure to "Ulster" all that Ulster values most, & at the same time to preserve the integrity of Ireland'. He said I should agree to that. But the sad thing is that numbers are not free to say a word, for what they think is the best solution, but must go on debating over what no one, in Ireland, believes in.

For Frederick, so deeply opposed to partition, exclusion would only be tolerable if it applied to the whole province, with provision for a future vote on reinclusion. This would be 'the shortest cut to unity', since the small current majority of unionists would quickly collapse, 'especially if in Dublin a generous spirit were shown'. Plunkett's proposal, based on the same calculation but avoiding exclusion, was 'infinitely better'. He only wished that 'the average Covenanter' could be persuaded to study Plunkett's refutation of 'Ulster's four Chief reasons against a trial'.[112]

Such, then, is the evidence for and against the claim that Frederick MacNeice was a Home Ruler. On the one hand, he feared the consequences of Home Rule, especially for religious liberty, and extolled the virtues of the United Kingdom and the British Empire. On the other, he regarded the partition of Ireland as a worse outcome than all-Ireland Home Rule, and rejected the threat of rebellion as an outrage against lawful authority, which might undermine the United Kingdom more thoroughly than Home Rule itself. By the eve of the Great War, he had (at least in private) accepted the inevitability of some form of Irish self-government. This outcome reflected the rapid elimination of options that he had until recently found more attractive, such as the gradual conversion of lay Catholics to the advantages of the union. Home Rule, like war, was only justifiable as a last resort to avert a greater evil.

8. *Patriot*

CARRICKFERGUS, 1914–1918

I

The outbreak of war in Europe, disastrous though it was, brought a measure of relief to all parties in Ireland including Frederick MacNeice. As unionist and nationalist leaders alike affirmed their support for Britain's cause, the menace of rebellion and civil war evaporated. After six weeks of political manoeuvring, Asquith's government postponed constitutional reform indefinitely by the ingenious expedient of simultaneously enacting and suspending Home Rule, while promising a future amendment act to cater for Ulster on terms yet to be negotiated. With disconcerting speed, yesterday's potential rebels became loyal patriots in the struggle against a common enemy. In Carrickfergus, 102 members of the town's 3 UVF companies had enrolled in 'Lord Kitchener's army' by 17 September, when they began training at Clandeboye camp, County Down. They were headed by Major Robert McCalmont, MP, and their old company commanders, the ex-protestors William Coates, Tyndall Johns and James McFerran.[1] Along with other companies of the Central Antrim Regiment, they were incorporated into the 36th (Ulster) Division as the 12th Battalion, Royal Irish Rifles.

Frederick's Orange and Masonic brethren did not escape the war's impact. Heron Lepper's lodge supplied six of the twenty-seven Carrickfergus Freemasons who reportedly served in the wartime forces. The three brethren who lost their lives included Archie Lemon, treasurer of the Carrickfergus unionist club and an agent on Ulster Day.[2] Nine members of LOL 1537 served, a William Robinson dying at Gallipoli in September 1915 and Alexander Hill going down with the *Princess Alberta* in February 1917.[3] On his way to the Dardanelles, Robinson had written a 'very interesting letter', which was read to the lodge by the 87-year-old lay chaplain, who defied expectation by outliving him.[4] The Orange Order tempered its seasonal enthusiasm in 1915, when the usual 'drumming parties' were silent and 'scarcely a drunken man' was to be seen on the Twelfth in the streets of Carrick.[5] Nor was support for the war effort limited to the town's Protestant organizations. When thanking those who had provided 'presents, puddings and entertainments for our men at Christmas', the Soldiers' Comfort League singled out the hospitality offered by the St Nicholas Catholic Club.[6] Fleetingly, the moral demands of war seemed capable of uniting Ulster's fractured communities. The war's toll on the town was documented in Frederick's history of Carrickfergus, which listed 132 'names of men and boys who went forth from this place and did not return, and who in the Great Tribulation, gave all that they had'. Separate lists named 493 ex-servicemen who had returned to Carrickfergus, suggesting that almost half of the younger men of the parish had served.[7] If accurate, this would imply, by Irish standards, an astonishingly high level of voluntary enlistment in Carrickfergus. In fact, the Roll of Honour was probably inflated by inclusion of natives of the parish who had moved elsewhere before enlistment.

Frederick's long-standing aversion to violence was affronted by the outbreak of hostilities in central Europe in July 1914. In an unsigned article in the parish magazine, evidently written just before Britain's entry, he offered a stark prognosis:

> But now that war has been declared the question may be asked – Who or what will be benefited by it? Will it advance the prosperity, the happiness of a single nation in Europe or elsewhere? Will it promote, in any way, the good of any people, or any cause, anywhere? It cannot do any of these things. The circumstances of our modern world are teaching us that no nation can be enriched by another's poverty, or be strengthened by another's weakness, or profit in any way by another's distress. It is through co-operation and not through conflict that nations can help one another, and advance the civilisation of the world. The war will mean, even for the 'victorious' nation, losses incalculable. And – as always in war – the masses of the people will be the chief losers. It is calculated that millions of men may engage in the war. They will go forth to kill and be killed in a quarrel not of their making. ... Through the influence of England the war may be localised, God grant it.[8]

God did not so grant. Faced with the fact of British mobilization, it would have been reckless for Frederick to have maintained this notably impartial analysis.

Furthermore, after 4 August 1914 the moral issue no longer concerned the legitimacy of war as a means of pursuing national interests, but the relative merits of the protagonists (whether judged according to culpability, war aims or likely consequences of victory and defeat). Throughout Europe, pacifists were becoming patriots as the option of peace disappeared.

Press reports allow us to follow Frederick's own shift from pacifism to patriotism. In the September issue of the parish magazine, readers were offered an enigmatic editorial entitled 'The Cloud', which avoided direct discussion of the war.[9] By early September, he was involved with the local branch of the Prince of Wales's National Relief Fund, and was already mourning two lieutenants of the Yorkshire Light Infantry, killed 'near the French frontier'. Until recently, they 'used to occupy a pew near the pulpit', and he recalled 'many conversations, both religious and political, with them'. Now, they had been 'laid to rest in the soil of France in consequence of the awful conflict'.[10] On 10 September, Frederick and Richard Clarke were among those who discussed a paper on 'the Ethics of War' delivered to the diocesan Clerical Society in Belfast.[11] Frederick was elected president of that society a few months later, remaining an active member for many years.[12]

On 26 September, the rector explained the significance of the union flag to a congregation of children who had processed with flags and badges from the parochial hall to the church: 'Some of them were almost too small to march, they toddled, and all were as proud and happy as they could be.' Ignoring the blue cross of St Andrew, he interpreted the red crosses of St George and St Patrick:

> These colours in their flag had come to mean that in the great Empire to which they belonged there was a great and growing passion for righteousness and justice. The white symbolised these things, and the red meant that a man should be so taught that he would be prepared to lose even life rather than part with purity and goodness – that righteousness was to be secured and retained at any cost, any sacrifice.

Thus uplifted, the children marched back to the parochial hall, stood to attention, sang the National Anthem, and tucked into their tea.[13]

At last, on the following day, Frederick was ready to expound his views on the war, the occasion being the Ulster Day anniversary service attended by a parade of Ulster Volunteers 'equipped with caps, belts, and armlets'. Despite the absence of 'the Clandeboye contingent', the church was 'entirely filled'. The war, in Frederick's opinion, 'was a conflict of ideals. That was the reason why it had excited the enthusiasm of people of all races and creeds all over the world in a way that no previous war in the history of the world had ever done.' Germany was only nominally a Protestant nation, the atheist Nietzsche being 'the most powerful voice in Germany today'. Germans were imbued with 'a great hatred of everything British – British ideals, British character, the British constitution, British people'. The Anglo-French alliance proved that it was possible for a truly Protestant and a 'distinctly Romanist' nation 'to differ in religion and yet be true to one another as comrades and friends'. This example carried hope for Ireland: 'He did verily believe that arising out of this conflict there was the opportunity of doing something to bind Ireland, north and south, Romanist and Protestant, more and more to Britain and the Empire. ... There were indications everywhere in the land of a disposition to forgive and forget.' Addressing the Volunteers, he observed that 'many of them recently were nobly ready to sacrifice much for their country. Let them, face to face with possibly the greatest struggle of the nations in history, learn to sacrifice something for internal peace.' They should demonstrate 'that they might be of different religious faith and politics and yet be at one in their love of the Empire, their loyalty to the King'.[14] Like John Redmond and Sir Edward Grey, he believed that the common experience of war might eventually bring peace to Ireland.

By embracing Britain's cause, Frederick reclaimed his fellowship with parishioners and neighbours from whom he had been somewhat distanced since Ulster Day. Though his social and fraternal connections had proven strong enough to withstand the impact of political dissidence, he had become a tolerated outsider, wistfully observing the resurgence of communal solidarity during Ulster's crisis. As he recollected in 1928:

> In Ulster it was indeed a wonderful time. Every county had its organisation: every town and district had its corps. The young manhood of Ulster enlisted and went into training. Men of all ranks and occupations met together, in the evenings, for drill. There resulted a great comradeship. Barriers of class were broken down or forgotten. Protestant Ulster became a fellowship.[15]

With party politics suspended and the Volunteer spirit redirected to a worthier cause, Frederick no longer needed to be an outsider fearful of his future in Ulster. The effect of war was to reinforce his stake in the parish and the province.

When addressing the Easter vestry in April 1915, the rector gave voice to the heightened patriotism of his parishioners: 'England is acting for us, speaking for us, spending for us; she is going forth in defence of the rights of the weak, as against the aggression of the strong, for freedom as against despotism.'[16] Two months later, he was re-elected as a vice-president of the East Antrim Unionist Association.[17] His undiminished status in the Orange Order was acknowledged in October, when he was invited to address a 'vast concourse' assembled at St John's church, Ballycarry, for the funeral of the long-serving District Master and Chaplain. Hamilton Bennett had taken a prominent part 'in all the stirring events of the last forty years', arguing 'powerfully, passionately, persuasively' against Home Rule, yet never losing 'the regard of those who differed from him in religion or politics'. Perhaps speaking of their difference over the Covenant, he remarked:

> You might differ from him, you might oppose him, you did not lose his friendship. Next time, after the difference, you met him he was as genial as ever. ... What is the secret of such power as he possessed over so many persons whose circumstances differed so greatly? I believe it was his kindliness, his good nature, his sympathy, his tenderness.[18]

When celebrating the power of a clerical politician, in terms reminiscent of his praise for the Orangemen's hero Richard Kane, the rector was also portraying himself.

By early 1916, as the war dragged on without prospect of early peace or victory, the focus of his sermons was shifting from celebration of war ideals to mourning and lamentation. On 11 April, he peered once again into the future, bleaker now:

> In the days to come there will, all through the land, be many memorials of the sacrifices made in this agonising conflict. For a generation or more there will be living memorials – men who have suffered loss in their bodies – an eye, a hand or leg – men who will all their days on earth bear the marks of the terrible struggle in which they had been engaged. And there will be other memorials, too. In oldest castle, in humblest cottage, in every kind of home in town and country there will be material things – a cap, a sword, a scroll, a medal, a something that will have a dearness, a sacredness, because it belonged to the brave dead.

Uncertain about the likely consequences of the war, not yet disillusioned, he predicted that 'the significance of the struggle itself will be better understood ... when the blessings of peace will be once more enjoyed'.[19]

Distant though it might seem in loyal Carrickfergus, the eruption of rebellion in Dublin shattered the political truce in Ireland and resurrected the constitutional debate that had so poisoned pre-war life. In his address to the Easter vestry on the eve of Pearse's surrender, the rector first damned those 'responsible for the government of Ireland', who had 'so completely failed to read the signs of the times'. Next, he damned the 'wicked purpose' of the rebels, who appeared to be 'in a minority, with some elements of strength'. The rebellion could not succeed and lacked popular support:

> The Empire will be equal to the task of restoring order in Ireland, and also taking its full share in winning victory over the unholy combination represented by

Germany, Austria, and Turkey. The insurrectionists aim ultimately at an Ireland, outside the Empire, an Ireland as separate from England as Sweden is from Russia, and during the earlier, preparatory stage an Ireland under German rather than British influence. For neither of these objects would it be possible to-day to find support from more than a very small proportion of the people of Ireland.

The 'real Ireland' found 'its best representation, the representation of its soul, in the hundreds of thousands of Irishmen now fighting' in a Manichean struggle: 'Yes: and in the fight for right against wrong, for light against darkness, for liberty against despotism, every part of Ireland – north, south, east, west – has been represented by the men who, far from the land of their birth, gave up their all for the cause that had appealed to their hearts.' Likewise, those at home should be ready, if required, 'to assist in keeping order in our town and neighbourhood', and to show themselves 'wholeheartedly on the side of the King'. Two days later, in another address issued as a pamphlet, he again deplored the government's 'refusal to govern' and reminded parishioners of their duty as citizens: 'Any outbreak in our end of Ireland would be nothing less than a disaster to the Empire and the Empire's allies. Let our influence and strength be placed unreservedly on the side of the police authorities.'[20]

Frederick's unionism, reinforced by the rebellion, was again affirmed in July when he retained his office in the East Antrim Unionist Association. Unusually, he took the trouble to apologize for his absence from its annual meeting in Ballyclare.[21] On 13 August, he conducted a memorial service for 'Carrick's dead heroes' with musical assistance from the band of the 4th Battalion, Royal Irish Rifles, and a collection for the UVF Patriotic Fund. He reassured the survivors that 'the choice was between war and dishonour', and celebrated the words of a bereft widow: 'Such sacrifices there must be and thank God our boys were not unmanly.' Though avoiding, as always, the invidious rôle of a recruiting agent, he pointedly reminded his listeners of their privileged position: 'For one reason or another – good reasons no doubt – you and I through this war have remained at home. Through all the awful time we have been safe. Yes, but at what a cost!' The price of their survival was 'the blood of our townsmen', which could be justified only by the outcome: 'Henceforth let life be fuller of love and sympathy, let your aims be higher, your interests wider.'[22] He spoke for himself as well as his auditors.

II

During the first few months of war, Lily McNeice still languished in St Patrick's Hospital. No longer concerned with delusions and hallucinations, her case-notes recorded inexorable physical rather than mental deterioration as she developed symptoms of tuberculosis:

> Sept. 1. Mrs McNeice has not been looking well for some time past. Her right lung is suspicious and she has a nasty cough. Takes food fairly well.

> Sept. 13. Mrs McNeice's sputum was examined for tubercle bacilli with a negative result.

> Dec. 16. Mrs McNeice is failing rapidly. The cough is still present and her breath sounds on the right side are deficient. Is taking food badly.

> Dec. 18. Mrs McNeice died this morning. Cause of death: A. Melancholia 2 years 2 months; B. Pulmonary Tuberculosis 5 months.[23]

The total cost of her upkeep in St Patrick's for fourteen months had been £70 13s. 8d.[24]

Just before Christmas, eight years after her father, Lily was buried in the churchyard at Carrowdore. She had left no will, and her estate was administered jointly by Louis Plunkett, John Hind and Frederick. Its gross value was £161 16s., consisting of two small bank balances and an interest worth £45 in a farm of three acres at Tullyvoheen, near Clifden, which she had inherited from one of the Cleshams and let out to a tenant on the Frewen estate.[25] The 'golden bowl' of Frederick's sermon in the previous November had been broken, the silver cord loosed, the pitcher broken at the fountain, the wheel broken at the cistern: 'Vanity of vanities, saith the preacher; all is vanity' (Ecc. 12: 6, 8).[26]

Like the coming of war, Lily's death must have left her husband with a sense of deliverance as well as desolation. The protracted agony was ended, the financial burden was lifted, and planning for an orderly family life became practicable. In the absence of personal correspondence and diaries, we cannot know Frederick's feelings or reactions. His immediate concern was to reassure and comfort three young orphans: Elsie was eleven, William (Willie) nine and Freddie seven. All three children had recently contracted measles and were being kept together with bandaged eyes in a darkened room. In his autobiography, Louis recalled his inability to cry when his father broke the news and the falsity (as it seemed in retrospect) of Frederick's attempt to make Christmas jolly.[27] Lily's death was not marked by a public funeral or elaborate tributes. The brethren of LOL 1537 expressed their sympathy to the rector by standing in silence after William O'Neill had 'dwelt on the valuable services rendered to the lodge by her, and of the esteem and respect in which she was held by the brethren'.[28] At the Easter vestry, Frederick expressed his gratitude for the support shown by parishioners throughout his personal crisis:

When I think, as I often do, of your sympathy, your tenderness, your forbearance, your indulgence – though many things were left undone – because you know the cause, your silence, as well as your words. When I think of the numberless ways in which you helped me and tried to help me through two trying years, I thank God.[29]

The illness and loss of Lily was not the only source of pain and torment to afflict Frederick in the years of war. The recitation of names on the Roll of Honour entered a new register as his own relatives joined the forces, in several cases never to return. A ten-page letter addressed to Beatrice Greer at 9 o'clock on Christmas night, 1915, offers a rare glimpse of his troubled state of mind. The festival had been something of an ordeal: 'Xmas Day is over, & on the whole well over.' Yet it brought one wondrous experience, an unexpected visit from a 25-year-old nephew who had emigrated to Canada five years earlier. Having worked in Winnipeg and as an engineer helping to extend the Hudson Bay Railway, he returned home to enlist. After six months in the Irish Guards and promotion to corporal, he secured a commission in the Royal Field Artillery. Frederick was transfixed by his nephew's youthful splendour:

He is quite a fine looking fellow – 6 ft. 2 ins. in height, well-educated, with all his wits about him, able to do anything. The time in Canada made a man of him. He will be off on Monday night. His mother – my sister – died when he was 5. Is this too detailed a report? I think so. He is almost as much opposed to militarism as I am & is hoping the war will not mean the beginning of militarism in Canada & U.S.A.[30]

Beatrice's piety and patience may have been tested by Frederick's next seven scrawled pages, reproducing his sermon on Christmas morning. Yet his words illuminated an inward struggle to master the emotions associated with love, desire and death. He had dwelt on the corrupting power of love, in the pre-Christian sense of self-gratification, which 'means for someone bitter, scolding tears, agony & it means another agony for Him who died on the Cross'. By contrast, 'when love, God's love, is received, it cleanses, purifies, & in time transforms him who receives it'. As for death, 'it matters of course, in time, to relatives & friends, but Eternally it doesn't, for nothing can separate him who trusts in God from the love of God in Christ Jesus. Because He is God & nothing can separate therefore the soldier in the battlefield, or the sailor watching in the North Sea, is as safe.' He had reflected on the different meanings of Christmas for the young, whose 'hearts beat faster', and for older people: 'They have recollections of things that were, of fair scenes on which the shadows have fallen: they through the Christmas recollect faces they can see no more on earth: & there are memories of voices that for the time they cannot hear.' In a postscript dated 27 December, he promised to 'write a letter tomorrow. This is just a sermon.' Meanwhile, he might 'post this in Larne as I am thinking of going down to see my nephew off. He is splendid: a fine young fellow in every way, physically, intellectually, morally. I do hope poor boy will come through safely.' Louis was also to remember the 'tall blond young man' who 'had trouble at Sunday morning service with his khaki cap in the pew' and who 'hurt my feelings by pinching my arm, telling me I had no muscle'. After passing the test of reading a military manual aloud, Louis 'forgave him because of his smile. Not long afterwards we received a newspaper cutting that he had been killed in action.'[31]

2nd Lieutenant Archibald Frizelle, killed in early May 1916 and buried in Vlamertinghe military cemetery near Ypres, was a younger son of Frederick's eldest sister Caroline, who had died in 1895. He was born just south of Ballycastle, County Mayo, where his father John Henry was stationed with the RIC. Educated at Ranelagh school, Athlone, and Mountjoy school in Dublin, Archie joined Wanderers football club in Dublin, on whose war memorial his name appears.[32] He died after less than a month at the front. A photograph published in *Irish Life* confirms his good looks, only partly shadowed by the low-brimmed cap: clean-shaven, firm-chinned, frank-eyed.[33] Three years later, Archie was followed by his much elder brother William Robert, a lance-corporal in the 2nd Battalion, Irish Guards, killed in Flanders on 13 April 1918 and named on the Ploegsteert memorial.[34] William left a widow in Essex. The two brothers are touchingly commemorated by a plaque outside the door of Ballycastle parish church: 'This path is in memory of the Frizelle boys who lost their lives in the Great War 1914–1918. Fondly remembered in this Parish. The strife is o'er | The battle won.'[35]

Of all the black days that the war brought to Ulster, the most gruesome and the best remembered was 1 July 1916. No fewer than four Antrim McNeices, none related to Frederick, perished with the Ulster Division at Thiepval on the first day of the calamitous battle of the Somme.[36] Another fatality on that day was 2nd Lieutenant Thomas Henry Clesham, eldest son of Lily's relative Timothy, the late missionary rector of Aasleagh. Thomas had attended Trinity College, briefly contemplating a clerical career, before going to 'South Africa to take up an important post in the mining fields'. After service with General Botha's Natal Light Horse at the outbreak of the war, he secured a commission in the Manchester Regiment in July 1915 and also qualified as an aviator. 'Beloved by his comrades', he was killed 'just as he led his men over a parapet' at Mantauban, aged about thirty-four. He lacked Archie's fine features but sported a Chaplinesque moustache.[37] He too played rugby, and his name is commemorated on the war memorials at

Lansdowne football club, Trinity College and Thiepval.[38] As a past member of Lodge 14, Galway, he also appeared on the Masonic roll of honour.[39] We know nothing of Frederick's thoughts as he learned of the deaths of his kinsmen, but his personal losses only brought him closer in spirit to his neighbours and parishioners. On 12 July, in place of the Orange demonstration (cancelled because of restrictions on assembly under martial law), commemorative and interecessionary services were held throughout Ulster. A brief newspaper account of the service at St Nicholas's was followed by more than a column of casualty reports, more sombre than any sermon, naming dead and missing servicemen from Carrickfergus and Larne.[40]

Freemasonry, more than Orangeism, remained a lasting source of comfort and strength for Frederick. This is apparent in his eulogy for the station master at Trooper's Lane, Hugh McAteer, a Past Master of St Patrick's Lodge 43, who had been one of the leading select vestrymen '*contra ecclesiam dei*' in 1908–9. McAteer was killed while trying to close a gate that had swung open at a level-crossing. Fifteen hundred people, two-thirds of them Freemasons, witnessed Frederick's tribute in Glynn church on 1 October 1916. He explained the essence of the Craft to the unititiated minority:

> Freemasonry isn't rules, ritual, regalia, and symbols. These are but outward things. Freemasonry is a spirit, a passion, a temper, a life. Freemasonry is a combined attempt to build human life on two great foundation truths – the fatherhood of God, and the brotherhood of man. Into that great society men of goodwill are admitted as brothers. If always true to its principles, they will never be false to God, to one another, or to their fellow-men.

The 'secret' of Freemasonry was 'easily discovered … in the life and work of such a man as Hugh McAteer'.[41] Its ideals were also those of Frederick MacNeice.

A mature widower with three young children needed other forms of comfort and support, which the charitable brethren assembled in Victoria Street could not supply. Annie Bogue and then Margaret McCready had left the household, and soon 'the handles were falling off the doors and the house was in general disrepair'. Despite a succession of father's helps, servants and governesses, a single rather unpractical parent could scarcely cope with the demands of a large house and garden, two high-spirited youngsters, and one docile but profoundly dependant boy.[42] A letter sent by Freddie to his absent father, probably in the early months of war, suggests that the younger son was doing his best to be or, at least, seem dutiful:

> My Dear Dad, We are all well, and were at church this morning. … I made a flag for Willie on Friday. Miss MacCaughin did not come but she sent Willie a

Union Jack. Willie made a birthday sermon. I am out without a coat now. I read eight chapters of Job and some out of St. Matthew. Miss [Mc]Cready says my writing is very bad. On Saturday I climbed up a tree and got very dirty. I had a bath. ... I read some Genesis. We got apple dumpling for dinner today. ... From Freddie with love.[43]

Even without the additional expenses arising from Lily's illness, money was perennially tight at the rectory. As Frederick wrote to Louis in 1936, when sending a timely cheque for £50: 'We are so sorry you are having so much worry over household matters. I know well what it means: I was through it all years ago. ... In the years between 1914 & 1917 I found it most difficult to make ends meet.'[44] The rector's stipend of about £300, though higher than that in most parishes of Connor, had barely been sufficient to maintain a family and household even in normal times. Wartime inflation, which doubled the cost of living between 1914 and 1918, scarcely affected the real earnings of wage-earners but was ruinous for the clergy. As Primate Crozier remarked at the general synod in June 1916, 'the only sufferers' during the 'period of wonderful financial prosperity', resultant from the Great War, had been 'the great body of the poorer clergy and others who are heavily taxed on small fixed incomes'.[45] Despite increased parochial contributions, the Church of Ireland could not afford any significant increase in stipends, though a small capital sum (£7500, equivalent to about £7 per incumbent) was allocated in 1917 to endow war bonuses for needy ministers.[46]

One of the first to press the issue was William Shaw Kerr, then rector of Seapatrick and a leading Orangeman, who urged the diocesan synod in October 1916 to call for a national 'scheme for increasing clerical stipends'. Even more galling than shortage of money was the resultant loss of status. Kerr contrasted the straitened circumstances of his colleagues with the prosperity of 'skilled tradesmen earning as much as £10 a week', almost twice Frederick's income. He also referred pointedly to 'the splendid business-like movement which their Presbyterian brethren had set going'.[47] Unable to raise central support, D'Arcy and his diocese pressed ahead independently. The laymen of Down and Connor and Dromore were applauded in May 1918 for their munificence in raising £13,000 for a Clerical Income Augmentation Fund, yet even this capital endowment could only marginally improve clerical earnings in a united diocese with almost 250 clergymen.[48] In Carrickfergus, the rector's stipend remained static until 1922. So long as he remained without independent means, Frederick edged ever closer to financial ruin and social humiliation as the war wore on. Deliverance came just in time.

On 19 April 1917, at Trinity church, St Marylebone, Frederick acquired a new wife and, according to his custom on such momentous occasions, a new order of names. In the presence of her married brother and sister and aged mother as witnesses, Georgina Beatrice Greer, a spinster aged forty-four, married 'John Frederick MacNeice', a widower aged fifty-one.[49] For five years or more, the Misses Greer of Sea Park had been his staunchest friends and helpers in adversity. Eva, who was two years younger, was perhaps too deeply in thrall to the formidable Gertrude Hind to devote her middle age to any husband. Though deaf and seemingly settled into a benevolent aunthood, Beatrice Greer had strong qualifications as a rector's wife, as Louis grudgingly admitted: 'Never mixing in social frivolities, never going to the theatre or dances, never learning to ride or to sail or properly to play any games, never (or hardly ever) reading contemporary literature, and never recognizing Darwin, but doing Good Works and following a daily mid-Victorian routine – cold bath in the morning, Family prayers.'[50] She was also jolly and appropriately childish with children, and cosseted her step-children as though they were her own. Before long, 'Madre' (otherwise 'Drina') had been accepted by both Freddie and Elsie as an endearing if bizarre addition to the household.

Beatrice was pious, highly methodical, closely connected with many prominent landed gentry and industrialists, and rich. The death of her mother, a few weeks after attending the wedding, brought a windfall of about £34,000, far exceeding the legacies for Eva and their married sister Helena Lowry. Though a similar bequest as well as Sea Park went to brother 'Mac', Beatrice received the preferential treatment due to a dutiful unmarried daughter.[51] Born and mainly resident at Sea Park, she was equally at ease in London, where the family had a town house, and Dublin, Eva's birthplace. She had all the moral attractions appropriate to the higher form of love extolled by Frederick in his Christmas sermon. She also had the social credentials to shepherd her husband into circles that he, as a teacher's son without wealth or influence, could scarcely have penetrated alone. The rector could begin to imagine himself as a bishop.

Beatrice lost no time in restoring order in the rectory, imposing formal dining, mahogany furniture, family retainers, and other signs of opulence memorably caricatured in her stepson's autobiography. Her wealth also made it feasible to despatch Elsie and then Freddie to boarding schools in Dorsetshire (both associated with Sherborne school).[52] From September 1917 onwards, the MacNeice family no longer lived together except in holiday periods. Though a commonplace arrangement for those born to land or wealth, this was an alarming novelty for children used to close living in a relatively modest home. For Freddie at least, exile to Sherborne and later Marlborough College fuelled resentments that would take almost a lifetime to quell.

In an otherwise articulate and opinionated family, one voice has remained unavoidably silent. William, two years older than Freddie but severely restricted by Down's Syndrome, was also despatched from Carrickfergus to an expensive exile after Beatrice assumed control of the household. Though exceptionally affectionate and patient with William, whom she tended for decades as an adult, Beatrice must have been relieved to find an institution specializing in the education and upbringing of children like William. Freddie, who had found it a crushing burden to be the only member of the family able to interpret William's utterances, approved of his removal and bitterly resented his holiday visits home.[53] William spent about seven years in the Scottish National Institution for the Education of Imbecile Children at Larbert, near Falkirk in Scotland (no such provision was available in Ireland). Opened in 1863, it had been granted royal patronage in 1916. Its medical director from 1893 to 1935 was Durward Clarkson, whose ambition was to offer lifelong care for mentally defective adults as well as children.[54] Clarkson drew a sharp distinction between 'educable cases' and 'idiots', telling a Royal Commission in 1906 that 'once an imbecile always an imbecile, and they require care all their lives'.[55] Pending creation of a 'colony' for adults, the Larbert Institution catered for children with some 'mental weakness or pecularity', who might 'be rendered capable of education and self-guidance and some measure of usefulness', as well as 'cases of more decided imbecility' to be prepared if possible 'for restoration to their own homes'.[56]

Under the Mental Deficiency and Lunacy (Scotland) Act, 1913, Larbert had become one of two institutions in Scotland certified to cater for 'defectives' qualifying for state aid. By 1 January 1917, it housed 197 boys and 129 girls, of whom only 1 in 9 was, like William, a private patient. Larbert received a favourable report after two inspections in 1916: 'The children in this institution were found, with a few exceptions, to be in excellent health and condition. Each pupil is evidently studied individually, and everything is done to develop his or her natural tendencies. The general air of industry, brightness, and contentment which prevailed at the time of our visit was very pleasing.'[57] Nine years later, the number of child inmates had increased to 468, one-sixth of whom were now private patients, and the inspectors were even more complimentary:

> The medical and nursing care are of a high standard and the kindly care and homely comforts afforded to the children are on a scale that places them beyond criticism. ... At one of the visits the patients were seen at dinner, which was a substantial meal served under most admirable circumstances. The tables were furnished with white table-cloths, spotlessly clean. There were decanters of

water and aluminium tumblers for the use of the patients at every table, and the order and quietness that reigned in the dining-hall amongst so many patients were noticeable and indicated the kindly yet strict discipline that is maintained throughout the institution.[58]

Larbert remained William's haven until, having reached adulthood, he could no longer be accommodated in its quiet and orderly precincts.

III

For eighteen months after Frederick's second wedding, the war continued to depopulate and despoil Europe, an attrition that Frederick observed with ever deepening dismay. On 1 July 1917 he gave 'a very fine and impressive address' on the text, 'I am the resurrection, and the life' (John 11: 25). The service commemorated not only 'the glorious deeds accomplished' a year earlier but also the recent deaths of six local servicemen. The names of twenty-three parishioners 'who had fallen in the war were read out from the pulpit, the congregation standing in reverence while listening to the names of the honoured dead'. Music was again provided by the band of the 4th Battalion, Royal Irish Rifles, and the collection was devoted to the UVF Hospital for the Limbless.[59] A week later Frederick delivered an anniversary sermon to local Orangemen, who had marched from the Orange hall under the command of their new District Master, ex-CSM Stewart Woods. He depicted the entry of the United States into the war and the overthrow of the Tsar as signs 'that in the days that are coming the only government that will be tolerated will be government by the people for the people'. Once peace was restored, 'the poor, the workers, the men who toil with their hands must be regarded as entitled to a fuller life than they have known hitherto'. Life at the Front, untroubled by strikes, provided a democratic example, since 'officers and men took equal risks'. The pressure for international co-operation was apparent in demands for a League of Nations and in the 'closer fellowship' now developing in 'the great Commonwealth which men speak of as the British Empire'.

As always, he drew connections between his vision of the zeitgeist, generated by the horrors of war, and his hopes for Ireland. Orangemen should recognize the legitimate grievances of nationalist Ireland and admit that 'there must be some cause for such discontent other than the supposed incorrigible nature of the people governed'. Recalling that Catholics had once observed the July celebrations, in the belief that 'the victories at Derry and the Boyne were victories for freedom', he boldly speculated that 'a time may come when Irish Protestants will take a similar pride in the story of the heroic defence of Limerick'. Further, he urged Ulstermen to promote the cause of 'fellowship – brotherhood in Ireland' by participating in Sir Horace Plunkett's forthcoming Irish Convention, as even Carson had urged in 'conciliatory words'. The notion of a representative convention cutting across party lines had been proposed by Frederick himself in March 1914. Compromise was inevitable, but within limits:

> To all whom it may concern, we declare that the Protestants of Ulster will never consent to the creation of an Irish Republic, or to the separation of Ireland from the free nations which constitute the British Empire. That would be a movement backwards, a movement away from Federation. Our policy in this respect is the policy of Grattan, the policy of Burke, two of the noblest and greatest Irishmen that ever lived, who all through their lives were intensely loyal to the connection with Great Britain.

'Changes of some sort there must be', and the time had 'come for the union of all men of good-will – Protestant and Roman Catholic – who believe that Ireland's greatest interest is peace'. If only the Catholic bishops would publicly appeal for 'loyalty to the King ... then even yet the apostles of revolution and ruin may be defeated on Irish soil by Irishmen'. In welcoming the brethren to 'this house of prayer', he promised that God would commit those who opened their minds to a 'ministry of reconciliation'. His 'thoughtful and practical' exposition reportedly 'commended itself to the congregation', and was published as a pamphlet.[60]

Despite Frederick's brave attempt to claim Carson as a fellow conciliator, his contemplation of a Federal or Dominion future for Ireland set him somewhat apart from most Ulster unionists. Even so, his pamphlet 'aroused great interest as a timely and well-considered contribution', and seemed 'simply splendid' to a correspondent in the *Advertiser*: 'There speaks the true British patriot, the fervid but tolerant Irishman, the charitable Christian, and the honest courageous man. How I have waited and longed for some leader of my fellow-Protestants to voice these noble sentiments.'[61] The spirit of compromise was to some extent shared by General Sir William Adair, who presided over the Twelfth demonstration in Ballycarry (martial law having been lifted). Citing Carson's directive to enter the Convention, he offered his own cautious advice to the brethren: 'If other Irishmen had something to offer which gave them greater personal freedom, a better chance of progress, a more comfortable life, a more prosperous career, and it seemed good to them, they should adopt it.'[62] Frederick's more expansive vision remained that of a pragmatic all-Ireland unionist, closely attuned to the thinking of Plunkett, Lord Dunraven, and the less intransigent wing of the Irish Unionist Alliance led by Viscount Midleton. His deviation from Ulster orthodoxy was insufficient to prevent his re-election as a vice-president of the East Antrim Unionist Association in August 1917, when the possibility remained of agreement at the Convention. He retained this office even in June 1918, shortly after the Convention's undignified demise amidst a flurry of contradictory reports.[63]

In between grave pronouncements on national and international issues, Frederick maintained the normal round of a wartime clergyman. His growing influence in the Church of Ireland was marked by his election in October 1915 as a full clerical representative to the general synod, and likewise to the diocesan council two years later.[64] He was a punctilious attender at the general synod in Dublin, missing only one day's sitting except in 1917, when he departed for London in mid-synod to get married.[65] So far, however, he had taken little part in public ecclesiastical debates, apart from proposing in 1916 that the diocesan Sunday schools might be provided with 'a uniform programme of religious instruction, with simple text-books or notes for teachers'.[66] Frederick's public activity was still mainly at parochial level. In mid July 1917, he braved 'unfavourable' weather to attend a military tournament and sports organised by the 4th Battalion, Royal Irish Rifles, the 'Jumping Competition' being reserved to officers. In early October, he helped organize an 'Our Day' collection for the Red Cross, which raised over £500. He was also warmly thanked by District Master Woods for conducting the anniversary service, which had yielded over £20 for an Orange charity. On 19 October, he participated in dedicating a Roll of Honour with 166 names of 'members connected with the congregation'. He honoured the memory of twenty-five who had died, and spoke of others 'whose bodies have been broken in war, but whose resolution and whose spirit are unbreakable'.[67]

A month later, he tackled other hazards of war when welcoming a detachment of the 6th Battalion, Royal Fusiliers, warmly recalling the Yorkshires' visit four years earlier: 'They were English soldiers; they behaved as English gentlemen'. He hoped the Royal Fusiliers would likewise represent 'England at her best, England strong and just and generous, England with a passion for liberty, England the guardian and champion of weak and oppressed peoples'. The parishioners, in turn, might 'succeed in interpreting Ireland to you; … Ireland with its spiritual instinct and spiritual vision, the Ireland that may do so much in coming days to build up the old waste places, to bind up the broken-hearted, to save the nations from materialism and to preach to them the Gospel of peace and goodwill'. He warned them against 'unwise friends' who might 'drag you down' in the absence of appropriate clubs in the town, declaring that 'they do not represent the real Ireland. Ireland has for long centuries been famed for the bravery of her sons and the chastity of her daughters.' The 'real Ireland' of Frederick's sermon, and his readings from 'St. Patrick's Breastplate', might equally well have been voiced from any Roman Catholic pulpit of the period.[68]

In January 1918, Frederick joined the seven other Protestant ministers (but not the two local priests) in inviting the people of Carrickfergus to respond to the King's 'National Call to Prayer', an act of 'Confession, Supplication, and Thanksgiving'. A few days later, he proposed the vote of thanks to his wife's sister-in-law, Dorinda MacGregor Greer, at an American Tea and Bean-Board for the Royal Fusiliers. Mrs Greer had enumerated the articles despatched by the Carrickfergus Soldiers' Comfort League, including 2000 pairs of socks, 627 mufflers, and 245 pairs of mittens. She observed with disgust that 'in the fighting area they had mud to deal with and live in – mud such as they knew nothing about in this country, mud in which horses could disappear'.[69]

At last, on 11 November, news arrived in the town of an Armistice, which would allow the surviving manhood of Europe to emerge from that morass:

> The church bells joyfully announced the great event, quickly followed by the bells of the 1st Presbyterian Church. The horns, whistles, and sirens of the various public works in and around the town and on the steamers at the harbour were sounded, and the enthusiasm quickly spread to the civilian populace. Flags were flown from almost every house in the town, and even the old church tower and the North gate were bedecked in this way. The vessels in the harbour all hoisted their colours. … When darkness fell bonfires were set ablaze in various parts of the town. A torchlight procession marched through the principal streets, and an effigy of the German monster was consigned to the flames.

'Pyrotechnics' were visible from the military camp at Sunnylands, opposite the rectory; but the public houses closed their doors, tea was served for soldiers in the parochial hall, services of thanksgiving were held, and order prevailed.[70] As peace returned to Europe, Frederick prepared to resume his war on war.

9. *Peacemaker*

CARRICKFERGUS, 1918–1926

I

The return of peace in Europe signalled the renewal of revolution in Ireland, as Sinn Féin set up a rival parliament and prepared for the possibility of 'war' with the forces of the Crown. The voice of moderation was scarcely audible in either nationalist or unionist Ireland; Lloyd George's new coalition government offered no proposals for constitutional change beyond some form of Home Rule, a policy emphatically rejected by Irish voters in December 1918; and the menace of sectarian civil conflict in Ulster had never been greater. The bitterness rekindled by the Easter rebellion and the Conscription struggle of 1918 had extinguished the spirit of reconciliation so widely expressed after August 1914. For a clergyman in Carrickfergus, the immediate threat to peace was not nationalist revolution but unionist reprisals against the Catholic minority. Frederick MacNeice remained implacably opposed to republicanism, and his former advocacy of compromise on the national question had no relevance to the post-war political situation. His only hope of restricting the harm done by the drift towards revolution was to campaign for tolerance and forbearance on the part of Ulster Protestants. In this endeavour, as before, his rôle was that of an enlightened unionist poised near, but not beyond, the boundary of acceptable criticism of Carson's partitionism.

For eighteen months after the Armistice, the revolutionary movement scarcely touched Ulster and attacks on southern Protestants were not sufficiently frequent or systematic to provoke counter-attacks on northern Catholics. Devlin's Ancient Order of Hibernians remained a serious obstacle to republicanism in the province, and the Irish Volunteers (IRA) were weak and generally inactive in Ulster. The legacy of the Great War therefore outweighed civil conflict in the rector's engagement with public affairs. At the end of May, 1919, Beatrice made presentations at the rectory to three female war workers, playfully thanking those who would have subscribed to the presentation fund if so requested. Her husband had been busy broadening the minds of working men by organizing a series of classes on the League of Nations, for which he was presented with an inscribed umbrella.[1] A few weeks later, a meeting of parishioners agreed to erect a bell tower at the east end of St Nicholas's as a war memorial, matching the memorial organ to be placed in the Congregational church.[2] In January 1920, Frederick and three other ministers attended a meeting of 'well-wishers' to select improved accommodation for the Comrades of the Great War, which had supplanted a rival body as the main society for Carrick's ex-servicemen in August 1918.[3] Soon afterwards, he visited the Orange hall to witness the unveiling, by Dorinda MacGregor Greer, of a Roll of Honour naming ninety-two local Orangemen who had served in the war.[4] The rituals of commemoration culminated, on 27 November 1920, in the dedication of the memorial bell tower (costing £3000) and peal of eight bells (with contributions from the Royal Garrison Artillery, Thomas MacGregor Greer and other parish stalwarts). Despite extra seats in the nave, 'many people were unable to get into the church'. After the dedication by Bishop Grierson, Frederick read out a preliminary list of fifty-six names including five not connected with the congregation: 'In time, Mr. MacNeice said, he hoped the tower would contain the names of all the gallant men from Carrickfergus, Protestant and Roman Catholic, who in the great war made the supreme sacrifice.'[5]

In July 1920, disturbances in Londonderry had initiated a cycle of sectarian conflict on a scale unknown in Ulster since 1912. Frederick's first response was a sermon on the eve of the Twelfth, in which he contrasted Christian teaching with the baneful principle of 'an eye for an eye'. His listeners should show their opponents 'absolutely no ill-will', instead longing 'for the chance of showing kindness to them'. They should resist the advocates of sectarian polarization: 'We are waiting for another voice, for someone to say, and in the spirit of Christ: "Some of you in Ireland are called masters and some men; some of you are Protestants and some Roman Catholics; some of you are of one party and some of another; but I say unto all of you, "Ye are brethren".'[6]

This theme was developed in a letter to the press, signed jointly by Frederick and three other Carrickfergus ministers.[7] This celebrated manifesto, widely published in the Dublin and Belfast papers, sought to mobilize Christian principles against the forces of darkness in Ireland:

> The country seems to be moving towards utter anarchy. No concerted effort has, as yet, been made by the Churches for the restoration of order and peace. ... It may be that peace can only come to Ireland through the Churches. ... If the Christian forces were only mobilised in time there would be no serious rioting in Derry or elsewhere. ... Is there place for one League more – a League of Christian Irishmen and Christian Irishwomen who believe in prayer, and who, in prayer, would seek first for justice?

The ministers hoped 'for a united appeal to the people of Ireland in the name of the leaders in the churches – Roman Catholic and Protestant alike'. Pending this unlikely event, readers wishing to 'help in such an effort' were invited to send their names to Carrickfergus.

Denis O'D. Hanna, 'The War Memorial Bell Tower' (replaced original tower, 1962): George A. Mitchell, Rector, *A Guide to Saint Nicholas' Church, Carrickfergus* (1962).

Frederick pursued the theme of reconciliation on 25 July, when he imagined an apostle crying 'Forget, forget that past: don't recall the story of old feuds, old animosities, old triumphs, old humiliations.' Christ himself was inviting them to 'risk something for the possibility of a new beginning in Ireland':

> We are here, in the providence of God, Protestants and Roman Catholics, side by side, in a very small country. Surely it must be that we are here, not to destroy one another but, according to our opportunities, to help one another, and to remember that to us, as disciples of Christ, there has been committed a ministry of reconciliation. Things reach us of horrors perpetrated in different parts of our country, of things done that would have seemed impossible a few years ago. Do not imagine that the knowledge of such cruel wrongs would justify any of you attacking other people who had no responsibility for the deeds that move you to indignation. ... Don't imagine we are thinking of Protestants in Clare or Galway if we imitate in Antrim or Down those injustices of which we complain. ... Our people here are, I believe, a fine people, brave and chivalrous. May they be led to put their strength into the things that make for peace.[8]

The two sermons were published as pamphlets in mid August, initiating an occasional series whose title, *Words for the Times*, provocatively suggested affinities with the Oxford Movement's *Tracts for the Times*. They appeared with a strong recommendation from the *Advertiser*: 'No one who is interested in Ireland and her needs should fail to read and study the lessons drawn and the conclusions arrived at. The pamphlets will be found helpful and hopeful at a time of great sorrow and tension.'[9] Frederick's message appealed particularly to expatriate Irish clergy of liberal views, such as the Manchester curate (and son of a former archdeacon of Clogher) who wrote that Frederick's sermon on 'Orange Sunday' expressed his own 'deep conviction of Ireland's need'.[10] Other kindred spirits forgathered in the newly formed Belfast branch of the Irish Christian Fellowship, an ecumenical and anti-sectarian body initiated by Bolton Waller in 1915.[11] The Fellowship, an offshoot of the Student Christian Movement, formed 'a comradeship of Irish men and women who desire, as followers of Christ, to understand and express His spirit in relation to the whole of life'.[12] On 21 September, the branch decided to invite Frederick to address a public meeting and to join its committee. Though Frederick never attended a committee meeting, he joined the branch and probably encouraged Miss McCaughen of Windmill Hill, the first parishioner to welcome him to Carrickfergus in 1908, to follow suit.[13] The Fellowship was later to provide his crusade with essential organizational support.

The campaign for reconciliation, like Alexander Dallas's proselytism, relied primarily on the belief that men and women of goodwill would respond generously to repeated and well-publicized appeals to reason based on Christian principles. Unlike Dallas, Frederick and his clerical colleagues made no systematic effort to recruit organizers, raise money or lobby politicians. In an individual letter to the press in September 1920, Frederick called for 'a truce in Belfast', denounced reprisals and 'the possession of firearms by civilians', and regaled readers with a stream of biblical quotations reminding them that Christ's disciples were the custodians of 'a ministry of reconciliation'.[14] A 'prayer card' had been circulated in late August for a 'League of Prayer for Ireland', committing signatories to daily prayer 'for goodwill and peace in Ireland' and declaring that 'this pledge will not bind anyone to any political party, or any political opinion, but it will suggest a particular temper or spirit'. According to Frederick's account in 1928, 'numbers of cards' were sent to Britain and the United States, with 'numerous' well-wishers joining the League in Dublin, Wexford, Wicklow and Cork. Three bishops and 'many parochial clergy' participated, some anonymous Roman Catholics and Sinn Féiners were enrolled, and the aged widow of Lord Frederick Cavendish, assassinated in the Phoenix Park in 1882, became 'an enthusiastic member'. Though 'the response from all sorts and conditions of men and women, Unionist and Nationalist, was wonderful', Frederick accepted that the campaign's impact had been small: 'if a similar attempt had been made, on a larger scale, and by more representative men, a new chapter might have been opened in Ireland'.[15] In the absence of membership returns and organizational records, there is no reason to suppose that the League of Prayer ever enrolled many members or exercised significant influence, either within or beyond the Protestant churches. Its contribution was to provide a public forum for a message of hope that few had the courage or conviction to utter, and to show the world that Ulstermen had not altogether abandoned tolerance and liberal views.

On 7 November, the rector again addressed the Orangemen, Orangewomen, Orange juveniles, Blackmen and Apprentice Boys of Carrickfergus. Carson, the Ulster Unionist Council and the Grand Orange Lodge of Ireland had recently negated the rhetoric of half a century by embracing the principle of Home Rule. Under the long-gestated Better Government of Ireland ('Partition') Bill, this was to be granted to two separate parliaments of 'Southern' and 'Northern' Ireland, though the statute proved a dead letter outside Ulster. Frederick selected a typically topical text: 'For he is our peace, who made both one, and brake down the middle wall of partition' (Eph. 2: 14). He denounced those, like Clemenceau, who had dictated 'a peace of vengeance', condemned the imposition of indemnities on Germany, and warned that such measures risked 'a Bolshevist growth and a general social upheaval'. As for the current 'Belfast Boycott', it relied on the 'fallacy' that any consequent impoverishment and suffering 'could be confined to the north'.

'Work boycotts' against religious minorities were 'stupid and criminal'. While southern Protestants 'could, perhaps, be driven altogether from the country, ... the Roman Catholics in and around Belfast constitute so large a minority that it is safe to assert that they could not be expelled': 'Whether men like it or not Protestants and Roman Catholics must live side by side here. Circumstances which we didn't make determine our duty for us. What is it? It is, I believe, to learn to live happily and helpfully together. ... I believe good would result if the two policies of boycott were definitely repudiated.' As for Carrick, 'thank God there has been peace here. Here, where you are strong, no harm has been done to anyone because of religious or political differences. I rejoice in believing that not even an unkind word has been spoken.'[16]

Frederick and his fellow ministers undoubtedly helped to insulate the town from the sectarian frenzy sweeping Belfast and much of the province, which had led to the mass expulsion of Belfast's Catholic workers from their jobs and homes. Though only Protestants signed Frederick's appeals, their work was applauded in December 1920 by George McKay, parish priest of Carrickfergus. When sending the parish's impressive contribution of £182 10s. to the Expelled Workers' Fund in Belfast, McKay confirmed Frederick's rosy account of communal relations in Carrick:

> With one or two exceptions our people have been free from the evils that have arisen out of the recent labour troubles. This fortunate state of affairs may be attributed to two principal causes – The people of Carrickfergus of other denominations appreciate the good qualities of their Catholic fellow-countrymen, with consequent mutual respect and goodwill, and I must also add that the clergymen of the other denominations in the town have for the past four months been assiduously preaching peace and a Christian tolerance of the rights of their neighbours.[17]

Another joint letter to the press expressed the rather vague hope 'that numbers in our own country, in the Churches, and outside the Churches, unitedly or apart, may find it convenient ... to pray specially for the coming of peace in Ireland' on 'Peace Sunday' (19 December 1920).[18] For the time being, as violence, murder, and destruction enveloped Ireland, their prayers were unheeded.

How aberrant was the clerical campaign against reprisals in the volatile context of post-war Ulster unionism? As Frederick had predicted, the end of hostilities was accompanied by signs of plebeian discontent with the unionist hierarchy and support for radical and Labour alternatives. Though the unionist bosses of Carrick, led by Dorinda Greer, had duly supported Robert McCalmont's re-nomination for East Antrim on 30 November 1918, Carson's intervention had been required to avert a challenge from George Hanna as an 'Independent Labour Unionist'. When McCalmont resigned a few months later, having accepted command of the Irish Guards, Mrs Greer's and Carson's support for the 'Official Unionist' candidate failed to prevent Hanna's election as a 'Democratic Unionist'. Charles Legg, a veteran Carrickfergus shipowner and 'liberal' who also claimed unionist and Temperance credentials, lost his deposit.[19] Hanna, a prominent Orangeman, had won significant support from the brethren and sisters in Carrickfergus, suggesting a dangerous fault-line in the unionist consensus. This was rectified by Hanna's adoption in future elections as an official unionist.[20] The East Antrim Unionist Association responded to plebeian pressure by reforming its rules in advance of the first elections for the parliament of Northern Ireland. After a lengthy discussion about the extent of Orange representation on the executive committee, the chairman claimed that 'the rules of the association were the most democratic in Ulster'.[21]

The weakened position of Carrick's grandees was confirmed by the election of John Campbell as president of the town's unionist club in November 1919, greeted by cries that 'The Campbells are comin'.'[22] A few weeks later, he also became chairman of the urban district council. Of the eighteen councillors, thirteen were newcomers and almost half were more or less skilled workers. Only three shopkeepers were elected, along with six councillors of higher social rank.[23] Campbell, a brickworks manager of intermediate social credentials, was an arch-fraternalist (Freemason, Orangeman, Blackman, Good Templar) who eventually became a member of the House of Commons at Stormont.[24] By comparison with his predecessors as club president and council chairman (the late Archibald Dobbs and Charles Legg), Campbell represented the 'democratic' upsurge in post-war unionism. This minor revolution was short-lived: Dobbs's son Arthur had become chairman of the club by August 1920, and Legg retrieved command of the council in 1925.[25]

Though Frederick's social views were well attuned to the mildly radical spirit of the times, he played no recorded part in unionist bodies or Orange lodges after the Armistice. This he had in common with his Presbyterian and Congregational collaborators in the crusade for peace. Yet denunciation of Protestant reprisals was commonplace among unionist spokesmen, whose authority was undermined by illegal acts carried out by shadowy organizations. When opening an Orange bazaar in September 1920, Major Arthur Dobbs warned that even Carrick was threatened by a 'volcano': 'He was entirely against reprisals. (Applause). The man at whom they were aimed was untouched, but misery and suffering were forced on numberless entirely innocent persons.'[26] This speech was heard by Beatrice, Frederick and four of his clerical collaborators.

Frederick's campaign against reprisals, through an appeal addressed to Catholics as well as Protestants, was perfectly consistent with total immersion in the Ulster unionist cause. This was demonstrated by the political career of his Methodist co-signatory, James Ritchie.[27] A few days before signing the first joint appeal for peace (while Frederick was warning parishioners against revenge and ill-will towards Roman Catholics), Ritchie had delivered an Orange anniversary sermon exposing the Roman hierarchy's plot to disrupt the British Empire. Next day, at the Carrickfergus field, he urged 'workers not to allow Rome into their trade unions', asked 'all to abide by decisions of their great leader, Sir Edward Carson', and offered a justification for partition:

> Not since the days of the Inquisition had Rome been so much on the alert as at the present moment. ... In the North they did not know half of what was being done in the other parts of Ireland. There was a reign of terror in the land. Many people did not like the idea of there being two Parliaments in Ireland, but he would rather have their Parliament in Ulster and show that they were capable of governing themselves and managing their own affairs.[28]

The rector and Alexander Cuthbert, minister of the First Presbyterian church, were among those who apologized for missing the demonstration and therefore Ritchie's stirring address.

Ritchie's loyal rhetoric was rewarded in February 1921 by his election as the Carrickfergus unionist club's only vice-chairman, an office that enabled him to participate in the selection of unionist candidates for the first House of Commons of Northern Ireland (which was to include seven Antrim members elected through proportional representation). On 14 March, at a meeting where Dorinda Greer withdrew her own candidacy 'on the counsel of Sir Edward Carson, and also on account of the state of her health', Ritchie 'proceeded to trace the history of Ulster from the plantation, and showed how at all times the Roman Catholic Church had plotted for domination'. They should therefore 'bless the day that Ulster set up its own Parliament'.[29] These sentiments disgusted Charles Legg, who dismissed Ritchie's fears of Rome as groundless, quoting Sir James Craig's recent warning against words 'that would create discord' and Craig's contemplation of a future all-Ireland parliament:

> At a time like this, when all men of goodwill are seeking a way by which peace can be brought to our beloved land, it is nothing less than a crime to speak as was done on that occasion. ... Can this be the Rev. James Ritchie who recently signed, jointly with his colleagues in the town, an appeal to all men to promote by prayer and action the peace of Ireland?[30]

Legg's attack provoked several letters in Ritchie's defence, a resolution of confidence from the unionist club, and a 'strong protest against the unprovoked and vicious attack' from LOL 1537, which considered that his 'speeches have always been characterized by fairness and toleration towards all law-abiding citizens'.[31] When Ritchie left Carrick for his next station in mid 1922, the Lodge organized a farewell presentation of 'a handsome morocco wallet filled with a goodly supply of treasury notes' (£35). The bread-server William O'Neill, now District Master, affectionately recalled Ritchie's arrival in the town in July 1919, revealing in the process that Frederick had avoided public appearances in regalia even when an active Orangeman: 'He [Ritchie] was practically the first man to be on the streets with a sash on. He felt it was like an earthquake in Carrickfergus to see a clergyman doing that.' In response, Ritchie affirmed 'that Ulster to-day was saving the Empire', expressed pride in Craig, and admitted that he had differed with some of his own congregation.[32] The peace crusade was broad enough in outlook to incorporate unrepentant partitionists like Ritchie as well as liberals like Legg. 'The Way to Peace for Ireland' did not signify that Frederick MacNeice had abandoned his lifelong unionism, any more than his refusal to sign the Covenant had shown him to be a Home Ruler.

II

Despite his disapproval of partition, Frederick extolled the King's visit to open the parliament of Northern Ireland on 22 June 1921. The bells of St Nicholas 'rang out a merry peal' as the royal yacht left 'Carrickfergus waters' for Belfast; and the rector rejoiced when the monarch conferred a baronetcy on his churchwarden William Coates, currently Lord Mayor of Belfast, who 'in those dark and dreadful days [had] discharged the duties of his high office with conspicuous wisdom, courage and impartiality'. Frederick, like most peacemakers in Ireland and Britain, warmed to 'His Majesty's fine appeal for a new spirit in Irish politics'. George V looked forward to 'a day in which the Irish people, North and South, under one Parliament or two, as those Parliaments may themselves decide, shall work together in common love for Ireland upon the sure foundations of mutual justice and respect'. His 'appeal to all Irishmen to pause, to stretch out the hand of forbearance and conciliation, to forgive and to forget', closely resembled Frederick's own sermons.[33] Messy and unsatisfactory though the Better Government of Ireland Act might seem, the provisions for a 'Council of Ireland' (never to be implemented) held out hope for an eventual reversal of partition. Furthermore, the speech was obviously part of a broader strategy to reopen the constitutional question and instigate negotiations with republican revolutionaries (which began in earnest in October). Frederick could dream once more of an Irish nation-state within the Commonwealth, if not the United Kingdom, bound together by shared loyalties to the nation and the Crown. Meanwhile, attacks on policemen, soldiers and reputed 'informers' continued with unprecedented ferocity, especially in Munster, while sectarian conflict intensified in Ulster.

Less than a fortnight after the royal visit, the rector delivered his sermon for the fifth Somme anniversary, preceded by the reading of 132 names so far inscribed on the Roll of Honour. At the request of the local Comrades of the Great War, the collection was devoted to St Dunstan's Hostel for Blinded Soldiers in London. Frederick remembered the war as, in one sense, 'a dreadful time, a time of insecurity, when the confidence of ordered civilized life seemed to have collapsed. Some men said it was a war to end war, but no one said that now.' He reflected on the moral justification of the war, asking 'was the war necessary at all?' He offered an equivocal answer. Britain's entry was justified by 'the conditions that existed at the time', which required that covenants, treaties, and contracts be honoured; yet, in a saner world, 'other conditions' might have prevailed. He upheld the belief that the war was a contest of 'ideals', between those who maintained 'that all nations – the smallest with the greatest – should be secure against aggression', and those idealizing force. Like the preceding Ulster campaign, the war had been, in another sense, 'a wonderful time': 'Everybody served, not only those who went out, but those who remained behind – all were serving. There was created a comradeship and brotherhood which had not been known in the country before. ... The war had given a most wonderful revelation of the worth of the ordinary man.' No longer an outsider, Frederick had been able to experience that solidarity in person. Yet, in retrospect, the chief lesson of the war was to teach people how to avoid its renewal:

> They should dedicate themselves afresh to live for the ideals for which their brave men and boys gave their lives – freedom, brotherhood, and equality of opportunity. Don't let them be hypnotised by the newspapers and the politicians. Unless they were on their guard they would be let into another war without any reason given for it until it was upon us.

In future, he maintained that international disputes must be resolved by conference, conciliation and arbitration. He did not, on this occasion, elaborate the implications for Ireland and Ulster.[34]

After the fairly successful imposition of a ceasefire by the Crown and republican forces, on 11 July, Frederick's chief preoccupation was again the worsening civil conflict in Belfast and beyond. On 4 October, he enlisted members of the

Irish Christian Fellowship to post an appeal to all 'Men and Women who in any capacity represent the people' in Belfast, including 'Orange, Sinn Fein, and Labour Leaders'. As before, the appeal offered no machinery for co-ordinating individual attempts 'to work with others, no matter who or what they are, for the restoration and preservation of order in Belfast, so that all her people may be free to live their lives and do their work in peace'.[35] Frederick also expressed his rejection of sectarianism by assisting at the dedication of a Presbyterian memorial tablet to Major W. H. Davey, who as editor of the liberal *Ulster Guardian* had lavished praise upon the rector for his rejection of the Covenant. He heard a Presbyterian minister celebrate Davey as 'a mystic and a visionary' who had 'advocated a closer fellowship and unity in Irish life'.[36] Frederick's world was peopled with such kindred spirits, dead or living, on whom his appeals to common humanity had made a personal impression.

Early in the New Year, Frederick participated in a four-day conference at the Queen's University, sponsored jointly by the Irish Christian Fellowship and the Student Christian Movement. Its purpose was 'to gain the Christian perspective in the troubled times in which we live', through discussion of topics such as 'peace and progress in Ireland' and 'possibilities of fellowship in Ireland'.[37] Frederick chaired an evening meeting in the (Presbyterian) Assembly Hall, and conducted 'an intercession for peace' following an address on 'The Christian Conception of God' from Ernest Davey.[38] Davey was a brilliant young professor at the Assembly's College who, five years later, had to fight off charges of heresy pressed by the Bible Standards League. He too was a champion of plain speech, accessible Christianity, and co-operation with like-minded clergy of other Protestant denominations.[39] Like W. H. Davey, presumably a kinsman, his family origins were in Carrickfergus.

In spring 1922, the escalating conflict in Northern Ireland claimed the life of the rector's nephew and namesake, Sergeant Frederick J. Frizelle, RIC. After a brief taste of civilian employment in a Sligo drapery, Frederick had followed the example of his father and grandfather by joining the police in 1901. He married the daughter of a Belfast publican in 1912, and was transferred to Londonderry in the same year. There he remained through the Great War, in which he lost his brothers Archibald and William as well as his sister's English husband. Unlike so many members of the 'Old RIC', he served throughout the Anglo-Irish conflict, being promoted to sergeant just before the Truce.[40] With covert support from Collins as well as his republican adversaries in southern Ireland, the IRA repeatedly breached the ceasefire in a futile and counter-productive 'Northern campaign', ostensibly designed to defend the Catholic minority. At 10.30 pm on 4 May, Sergeant Frizelle and two special constables were accosted by three undisguised strangers, while on patrol at the Loop, near Moneymore in south Londonderry. According to Frizelle's own dying account to a journalist, they politely said 'Good evening' before 'whipping out revolvers' and firing. In another version from a lady witness, they opened proceedings with 'It's a sharp night', allowing the sergeant to respond 'It is', before firing several shots that killed the two constables instantly and left Frizelle with fatal wounds. He had the presence of mind to summon help with Very Lights, but the district inspector's rescue party was itself ambushed at midnight without further loss of life. The inquest found Frizelle and his men had been murdered by 'members of an unlawful organization'.[41] So ended the bloody sacrifice of the Frizelle family in militant defence of the empire and the union. Though Frederick MacNeice's reaction to his nephew's murder is unknown, it surely strengthened his resolve to fight for peace in Ulster.

The climax of the rector's campaign for reconciliation was his anniversary address to Orangemen on 9 July 1922. This was soon published as a pamphlet, 'dedicated by permission to Lady Frederick Cavendish', the most august supporter of the League of Prayer.[42] In an ecumenical gesture, the lessons were read by his Presbyterian colleagues Cuthbert and Minford. The demoralizing cycle of sectarian atrocities in Ulster was nearing its end, as the police and Ulster Special Constabulary crushed republican resistance and belatedly restrained loyalist paramilitarism. In southern Ireland, an equally brutal civil war had just begun. Frederick spoke of the prevalence of 'anti-Christian' attitudes throughout the country and risk of a 'return to barbarism', wishing that he could forget the recent waves of sectarian boycotts and expulsions. While declining to discuss 'the wisdom or unwisdom' of partition or the Anglo-Irish Treaty, he pointed out that 'the Great War marked the close of an era. ... The Union as men knew it for one hundred and twenty years is gone; the old order whether for good or evil has passed away.' Yet 'men on both sides continue to make plans and to recommend policies that have little or no relevance to the altered circumstances in which we find ourselves. One of the tragedies in Irish politics is that there is such large agreement, North and South, as to the efficacy of physical force.' While the outside world sought 'the elimination of war', whose futility had been demonstrated 'on a gigantic scale' between 1914 and 1918, 'Irishmen are making preparations for a trial of strength in battle'. If 'civil or religious war' were 'allowed to come, it will I believe, postpone, at least for a generation, all chance of reconciliation between North and South, and will involve all parts of the country, and all interests in the country in a common ruin'.

As always, he tried to argue the case against violence from both the nationalist and unionist viewpoints. 'A true patriot' seeking a united Ireland would wait 'until the confidence of Northern Ireland should be won, feeling that Irish unity could only come through the consent of the people themselves, North and South'. He would recognize the ability of 'the people of North-East Ulster ... to meet force with force'; their willingness to 'sacrifice their all in a fight which they considered to be a fight for their homes and hearths, their churches, their liberties'; and the possibility that 'military victory might be theirs'. Yet, whatever the military outcome, unionists too should recognize that 'the political problem which is the real problem, would be as far off as ever from solution'. He pleaded for 'recognition of facts': that both sides appealed to the principle of 'self-determination', that the true dispute centred upon the interpretation of that principle, and that clear acceptance of Ulster's right to withhold its consent from integration was a prerequisite for any future conference between northern and southern representatives. As for the prospect of eventual unification:

> Ireland is a unity geographically. Commercially, too, it is plain that if one part of Ireland is depressed all its parts are affected by the depression. ... If it became clear, as it might, that what was desired was a political unity, within the British Commonwealth, ... then it should be possible, with goodwill on both sides ... to find a way to a final settlement of what has been known as the Irish question. ... However, I have no wish, from this place, to express opinions one way or another on such problems.

After this careful analysis, which resembled Sir James Craig's ruminations during recent negotiations with Michael Collins,[43] Frederick returned to his dream of bringing into 'a common movement people who belong to different churches and different political parties' while agreeing on 'very elementary questions of principle'. These included recognition of basic rights (to life, opinions, work and home), entailing various moral obligations (to seek 'to live happily and helpfully together', to eliminate arms in private hands, and to repudiate reprisals). Furthermore, every minority 'should be able to feel that it has a right to protection by the majority from assault or insult'. The Carrickfergus brethren belonged to 'a very strong majority' that had not hitherto abused its power: 'I thank God, and congratulate you that the weakest of the minority here have had no reason to fear for your strength.' They should shun the terms of insult so often used by politicians, such as 'hereditary enemies', remembering that for Christ an enemy was one who hated the righteous, who 'might, indeed, be a member of your own church or party'.

This address was among the most eloquent and persuasive of Frederick's pronouncements on current affairs, combining cogent applications of moral principle with a keen sense of what was politically practicable. As ever, he had sought

ways to accommodate his own and his congregation's unionist loyalties with legitimate nationalist aspirations, proposing membership of the emerging Commonwealth rather than the dismembered United Kingdom as the basis for any future
Irish unity. Awed, maybe inspired, the brethren contributed liberally to Orange
charities and marched back to the Orange hall.

Frederick's 'Orange Sunday' address, which he sent as usual to influential
well-wishers, attracted some attention. Bolton Waller, the anti-sectarian publicist
and future clergyman who was to publish works such as *Ireland and the League
of Nations* and *Paths to World Peace*, shared Frederick's desire to form 'what I
suggested before, some sort of unofficial body working for conciliation'. Writing
just after the death of Arthur Griffith ('a terrible loss'), he informed Frederick
that Stephen Gwynn (essayist, former nationalist MP, and wartime officer) had
mentioned the address in the *Observer* – but 'he calls you McNeill!'[44] Once again,
there is no evidence that practical effect was given to the laudable but hazy notion
of a 'common movement' of like-minded conciliators. Frederick's worst fear of
an all-Ireland sectarian civil war was not realized. But the faint possibility of
reversing partition steadily receded with the creation of a 26-county Free State
in December 1922, the erection of customs barriers in 1923, continued instability
in the south, and (to the astonishment of many observers) the creation of a viable
state in Northern Ireland. Those, like Craig, who in early 1922 had contemplated
voluntary unification were now implacable defenders of partition, and the Catholic minority in Northern Ireland became even more disengaged from political
decision-making. Though the much smaller Protestant minority in the Free State
exercised a stronger voice in public affairs and suffered little violence or blatant
discrimination after 1923, the aggressive involvement of the Catholic hierarchy in
political issues with 'moral' connotations confirmed Frederick's old anxieties about
'Rome Rule'. No wonder that, in October 1923, Frederick seemed pessimistic
when writing to Rosamond Stephen, an English-born conciliator, lay missionary,
and secretary of the Irish Guild of Witness: 'We know next to nothing of what is
happening in Dublin & the South. Everything seems wrong in Ireland – wrong
temper, wrong words, wrong spirit.'[45]

Frederick became increasingly impatient at the inability of Irishmen and
Ulstermen to face contemporary realities, and their obsession with irrelevant past
disputes. In November 1923, he again addressed the assembled 'loyal orders' on
the anniversary of the Gunpowder Plot: 'What were they to consider that day?
Was it Guy Fawkes? Guy Fawkes had as much to do with the world they were
living in as Jack the Giant Killer or Robinson Crusoe. ... They should not allow
the solemn recollections of the past and the glorying in the great figures of history

blind them to the needs of the present.' Instead, they should confront evils such as intemperance and gambling, and band the brethren and sisters together 'to protect the honour of womanhood'. They should display 'kindness to their neighbours' and practise the Christian virtues that they proclaimed: 'They might have twenty sashes round their necks and know all the signs and countersigns and passwords, but if more frequently they were to be found outside the church than inside the church they were no defenders of the Faith. They were only shams and humbugs.'[46]

As the prospect of political progress disappeared, Frederick paid closer attention to social issues. Ulster's industries had not recovered from the post-war recession, and the economic outlook was as bleak as in the Free State. In January 1924, he spoke of the continued prevalence of unemployment, poverty and disease, exacerbated by 'reckless expenditure' on luxuries. He spoke with striking moderation about drink, stating that he was 'no intemperate advocate of temperance. … Some of the best men I ever knew were moderate drinkers. I am a total abstainer myself, and have been from early boyhood, and would always advise and urge total abstinence.' He attributed intemperance to social rather than personal failings: 'Suppose you had to live in Wilson's Place or in some of the houses in either of the Irish Quarters, or in the courts off them, what then? Would it be very difficult to entice the average man to spend his earnings somewhere else than in a damp, dark, cramped, miserable room?' The solution to intemperance, like disease, was to inspect 'all slum property in Carrickfergus', perhaps putting 'on the gable or wall of each condemned house a large D in red paint'. Citizens should then give their 'support, moral and material, to such local authorities as may pledge themselves to provide the necessary houses'. Owners should be bought out, if necessary, 'at any price', and the open fields surrounding the town should be covered with sanitary dwellings:

> Here we are in a beautiful part of the country surrounded by hills and sea; there are spaces on which many houses might be built, houses which might be homes, houses in which families might be reared in decency, in health, in happiness; and yet on this favoured spot which might be an earthly Paradise there are streets in which human beings are huddled together in darkness, dampness and despair.[47]

His vision has been amply realized, as any visitor to the estates now sprawling around the town will confirm. Sunnylands and the rectory itself were to succumb to development as the town's population multiplied, mainly after the Second World War. Whether Frederick would consider today's Carrickfergus 'an earthly Paradise' is, however, open to doubt.

In September 1924, the ministers of Carrickfergus issued their final joint manifesto to the press, recalling the 'astonishing' response to their League of

Prayer.[48] The prolonged controversy over the Boundary Commission, belatedly convened under the terms of the Anglo-Irish Treaty, had again aroused fears of civil war if Northern Ireland were faced with significant loss of territory. These fears were confirmed when Craig promised to resign as prime minister, in case of an unfavourable decision, and to prepare, 'as their chosen leader, to defend any territory which they might consider had been unfairly transferred'.[49] According to Frederick and his colleagues: 'No political issue in Ireland demands the shedding of a drop of human blood. If the country is allowed to drift into civil war, it will be a proclamation to the world of the bankruptcy of organized Christianity in Ireland; and will, we believe, mean the indefinite postponement of every real hope of reconciliation between North and South.' On this occasion, prayer prevailed in one respect. The Boundary Commission collapsed and the three governments agreed to maintain the current border, arbitrary though it was, while reaching a financial settlement that saved the two Irish states from bankruptcy. The risk of civil war receded; but the prospect of reconciliation remained remote, a dream never to be realized in Frederick MacNeice's lifetime.

III

However elusive elsewhere, brotherhood and goodwill were attainable within the intimate world of the parish. As rector, he spared no pains to maintain parochial harmony, even keeping a record of the ten favourite hymns of each of thirty-one zealous parishioners. These included his wife and daughter, Eva Greer and Gertrude Hind, and one coyly identified as 'No Name', who may have been Frederick himself. If so, his hymnic taste was unremarkable, embracing 'Onward Christian Soldiers' and the Orangeman's favourite, 'O God Our Help in Ages Past'. Beatrice leaned towards the ecstatic ('Holy, Holy, Holy' and 'Praise My Soul'), while Elizabeth's choices overlapped with both lists.[50] The influence of the Greers was further underlined at the Easter vestry in 1924, when Dorinda Greer joined her husband on the select vestry. Women had been eligible for parish offices only since 1920, and Dorinda was not re-elected in the following year.[51]

Frederick's cordial relationship with former opponents was evident in January 1924, when he spoke at the funeral of the solicitor Henry Blackburne, who had plotted the boycott of parochial collections in 1908. He remembered Blackburne as 'a distinguished oarsman' who had excelled all in the town in this 'clean and manly sport'. Equally active in the murkier world of unionist politics as an electoral agent and organizer, Blackburne had been respected by his 'political opponents'. Perhaps thinking of his own case, Frederick remarked: 'I often rejoice that here in

Carrickfergus men can be opponents politically and yet remain good friends'. His final tribute transcended cliché: 'Troubles come to us all. I speak of what I know. … In those days no one was more sympathetic, no one more helpful, than Henry Blackburne. I shall never forget that fact.'[52]

Press reports testify to the relentless round of ecumenical causes that Frederick endorsed in his struggle to rescue the citizenry from religious and moral indifference. In October 1925, the Girl Guides belatedly came to Carrick, prompting Frederick to declare somewhat guardedly that he 'supported the Girl Guides movement when it was under proper discipline and control'. This was presumably the case, since the Divisional Commissioner for East Antrim was the wife of James McFerran, a stalwart of St Nicholas's. But the movement was also supported by a Presbyterian minister, and the Guides' first bazaar was opened by Dorinda Greer in the Independent Hall.[53] In the same building, Frederick chaired a bazaar for the Carrickfergus Amateur Flute Band, whose president was the Presbyterian liberal, Charles Legg.[54] Sectarian boundaries were further breached at the funeral of James Lyon, the Congregational minister who had collaborated with Frederick in his campaign for reconciliation. In addition to a host of Congregational clergy and three Presbyterian ministers, the funeral was attended by George McKay, the parish priest who had so warmly applauded his Protestant counterparts for their campaign against reprisals. It was Frederick who read the lesson asking, 'How are the dead raised? and with what manner of body do they come?' (I Cor. 15: 35), a passage that he discussed at length in a published sermon delivered a few weeks afterwards. In his sixtieth year, he may have pondered how his own 'personality', raised as a 'spiritual' rather than a physical body, would 'share in the unexplored and inexhaustible wealth of the world to come'.[55]

As he grew older, Frederick abandoned some of the affiliations that had helped him to find a secure footing in the parish but eventually became superfluous. He never appeared on the roll of LOL 1537 after 1915, and was no longer termed 'Brother' when addressing gatherings of Orangemen. Nevertheless, he continued to allow Orange services to be held in his church, reading the lessons to an assembly of Loyal Orangewomen in May 1923 at which the collectors included Dorinda Greer of Miriam's Daughters Women's LOL 7, Carrickfergus.[56] Even Freemasonry gradually lost its allure. When members of the Grand Lodge of Free and Accepted Masons of Ireland visited the town in October 1921, it was still 'Bro. the Rev. Canon MacNeice' who conducted them about the church, delivering an 'admirable and succinct account of the building'.[57] In 1923, however, he resigned from the order, playing no part in the elaborate jubilee service held at Joymount Presbyterian church for his own Royal Arch Chapter (no. 253).[58]

One link that he did not sever was that with the Irish Church Missions, which remained active in proselytizing Dubliners under the energetic leadership of his friend Thomas Chatterton Hammond. Between 1909 and 1918, the parish of St Nicholas had made no contributions to the ICM, though Frederick remained on the executive committee of the Belfast Auxiliary until at least 1913. Between 1925 and 1928, and perhaps earlier, the parish offered regular annual contributions in excess of £10.[59] Advocate though he was of toleration and ecumenical harmony, Frederick had clearly not repudiated Dallas's dream of bringing salvation to deluded Romanists through the Open Bible.

In the immediate aftermath of war, however, most ministers were less preoccupied with salvation than with the mundane matter of money. The cost of living had doubled during the crisis, yet most of the clergy (almost alone among Irish workers) were paid at pre-war rates, with a ludicrously low minimum income of £200 per annum for incumbents. Having sacrificed their comforts during the war, clergymen expected to recover them in peacetime. Some were impressed by the stunning post-war success of trades unions in winning higher income and better conditions for classes of workers never before organized, such as shop assistants, clerks, servants and farm labourers. In November 1919, the Representative Church Body established a Committee on Retrenchment and Reform to devise ways of ensuring a 'living wage' and reducing the glaring disparities in workload. After twenty-three meetings spanning six months, it proposed doubling the minimum stipend for both incumbents and curates, empowering bishops to amalgamate small parishes, and reorganizing the Church's financial administration.[60] To make this possible, it was essential to induce the laity to increase its contribution to parochial income. While few bishops or synodsmen disputed the necessity of rationalization, many were fearful of mobilizing the laity in the manner of the Presbyterian and Methodist Churches. Ministers like Frederick, reared in a missionary movement dominated numerically by lay agents and funded by lay sponsors, had no such qualms. For them, the financial crisis supplied an opportunity to eradicate the vestiges of 'Ascendancy' and break down needless barriers between minister and parishioner.

In February 1920, Frederick was elected president of the newly formed diocesan branch of the Church Reform League. Its objects were to promote the reorganization of Church finances, redistribution of manpower, amalgamation of superfluous parishes and dioceses, adaptation of the Church to 'modern needs', and 'adequate representation on the Councils of the Church for the furtherance of such reforms'. William Shaw Kerr, who had broken clerical silence on the issue of income in 1916, presided over the first meeting of twenty clergy and six laymen.[61] The meeting was also addressed by George Chamberlain, incumbent of Clondalkin and son of the late rector of Carrickfergus. As editor of the *Church of Ireland Gazette*, Chamberlain vigorously supported Frederick's various campaigns for peace and reform.[62] Frederick adopted a characteristically moderate tone. While others openly deplored the 'present lack of leadership in the Church' and 'suggested action more on the lines of trades-unionism', he simply 'claimed for the clergy a man's work & a man's wage'.[63]

Under his influence, the League worked strictly within the existing administration, as a lobby rather than a rival authority. He and Kerr gave evidence to the RCB's committee on its behalf and probably influenced the report. In preparation for the general synod in May 1920, the League followed Frederick's advice by affirming its approval for the committee's report, though Kerr advocated even more far-reaching reforms. Two public meetings were arranged in Dublin in the hope of influencing the synod's response. Frederick, while supporting the committee's recommendations at the second meeting, proposed that 'larger contributions to assessment are required from the laity'. No fewer than sixty-seven parishes in the diocese of Connor claimed to be unable to provide the current minimum stipend, and 'they must push and persuade until that situation was altered'. In a speech of 'considerable power', he noted 'a wonderful change' among the clergy, many of whom would no longer accept a parish so small or poor that it could not provide an adequate stipend.[64] Further meetings were held in various towns in the united diocese, though only one local sub-branch seems to have been formed.[65]

The League's campaign appeared to be successful, since the general synod approved the report in principle and, at a special session six months later, acts were passed that incorporated most of the key demands. The reformist *Church of Ireland Gazette* remarked grudgingly that 'the grip of the dead hand has been relaxed', but condemned a 'loophole' allowing poor parishes to avoid paying the minimum stipend, 'a course which would be repudiated by the humblest member of the smallest Trade Union'.[66] Even so, substantial reforms were approved after forceful advocacy from the new primate, Charles D'Arcy, and an effective intervention from Frederick. He assured the synod that, if the Bill were passed, many parishes in Down and Connor and Dromore would rapidly raise the required funds: 'The Bill would be a powerful lever in the hands of Diocesan Councils to bring pressure to bear upon parishes so that they might move.'[67] When Frederick stood down as president of the Belfast branch in December 1920, allowing a layman to lead the campaign and so allay the justified suspicion that the League was a trade union for greedy clergymen, he was congratulated on his 'extremely able' performance of the office and his 'very convincing Public advocacy' of its objects. Yet he was not elected to the new committee and played little part in the League during 1921.[68]

Despite its apparent initial success, the League never became an efficient organization. Though about 120 members from the three north-eastern dioceses joined in the first few months, very few laymen took part. Many members failed to pay their modest annual subscription of 2s. 6d. (later 3s. 6d.), few laymen were enlisted, the roll of members was very casually kept, and the branch never paid its dues to the General Council of the League in Dublin.[69] Nor could League members be persuaded to act as a disciplined faction within the diocesan synod, so as to bolster the representation of reformists in key positions. Despite strenuous objections from leading Churchmen such as Crozier and Kerr, 'canvassing' for diocesan elections had long provided a much needed element of excitement at annual synods.[70] The *Gazette* urged branches of the League to aim 'to capture the Diocesan Councils, and to place on each Council a strong majority determined to make Reform effective'. Though 'anything in the nature of ecclesiastical engineering is distasteful to us', the reformers 'must use the methods we find to hand'.[71] At the Down diocesan synod in November 1920, only two of the six clergymen put forward by the League for membership of the diocesan council were elected.[72] A year later, when a much more ambitious list of nominees was circulated by the League, the outcome was dispiriting: of its forty candidates for various positions, only eleven were elected. Seven names proposed by the executive had been rejected at a general meeting, when 'the debate with reference to the list was the most animated that has ever taken place at any meeting of the League'. Among those dropped from the list were Kerr and Frederick, who was to have been proposed for the key position of diocesan nominator.[73] It is clear that Frederick was an active and contentious combatant in the murky world of clerical politics, conscious that merit alone would not advance either his reformist ideas or his personal career.

The League's failure to control the diocesan elections provoked a motion for its dissolution in view of the 'lack of loyalty on the part of its members'. This was withdrawn after objections from seven speakers, including Kerr and Frederick, who were both elected to the executive committee.[74] Spurred on by the energetic Kerr, the League organized further public meetings involving prominent laymen such as James Milne Barbour (then a junior minister in Craig's first government and a senior Freemason) and Judge Thompson (the Recorder of Belfast). At a meeting in the Clarence Place hall in February 1922, George Chamberlain rather patronizingly urged a liturgy more suitable for 'simple people'. This provoked a sharp retort from Canon Hugh Murphy of St George's, notorious in Low-Church circles for its ritualistic tendency, excellent music, and renting of pews: 'He had been 43 years in Belfast, and knew that the working classes were more conservative in regard to the Prayer Book than much better placed people.'[75] *The Irish Times* continued to mention the League's 'campaign against ecclesiastical abuses' such as patronage, the 'iniquitous' buying and selling of livings, and 'traffic in seats for worshippers'.[76] But the Belfast branch was in terminal decline, and held its last meeting in December 1922. Though Frederick helped frustrate two further motions for dissolution, it was finally agreed to suspend its meetings indefinitely.[77] In the course of three years, the crusade for Church reform had subsided into a tepid aspiration.

In the labyrinthine networks of the Church of Ireland, he began to reap the rewards of hard work, unfailing tact, perceptive public interventions, and the Greer connection. After prolonged probation as a 'supplemental' (since 1909), Frederick had become a diocesan representative on the general synod in 1915 and a member of the diocesan council two years later. From 1919 onwards, he almost invariably headed the list of Connor clergymen elected to that council.[78] In March 1921 he attained the non-stipendiary dignity of precentor of Connor, a ceremonial post subordinate to those of dean and archdeacon in the cathedral hierarchy and carrying the honorific 'Canon'.[79] During that year he was also elected to the board of St Anne's Cathedral and, for the first time, as a supplemental diocesan nominator. In synod debates, he spoke with increasing confidence and authority, his views being closely attuned to those of Primate D'Arcy and his own bishop, Charles Grierson.[80] In May 1924, he firmly opposed a motion by Canon Murphy to prohibit clergymen from denouncing each other's pronouncements from the pulpit. In Frederick's view, 'public opinion was sufficient to deal with such possibilities'. After D'Arcy had denounced the proposal as 'most mischievous', striking at the ordination vow by undermining a rector's responsibility 'for the protection of his people from dangerous error', the general synod dismissed the motion by a large majority.[81]

Murphy's motion arose from a notorious confrontation at St Patrick's, Ballymacarrett, in which the rector had been so incensed by a sermon distinguishing between vice and sin that he instantly emerged from the sanctuary to chastise his own curate before an astonished congregation. Frederick Chesnutt-Chesney, who had been ordained for the parish three years earlier after serving as a wartime officer with the 6th Lancashire Fusiliers,[82] was pitted against the equally gallant rector and wartime chaplain, John Redmond.[83] In a working-class parish where numerous 'sinners' had recently been 'converted' to Christ through an energetic missionary campaign, Chesney had cast doubt on the very notion of conversion and declared that many mere vices were falsely identified as sins. These included 'gambling, drinking, smoking, dancing, and the like', some or all of which (so Chesney implied) were among 'many legitimate practices' wrongly condemned by zealots as sinful. Redmond had responded that all vices were sins, and that these included gambling, drinking, and (according to Chesney's account, which Redmond denied) dancing. Having failed to persuade Bishop Grierson to demand a public apology from Redmond, Chesney petitioned the diocesan court for redress.

The hearing was attended by a large crowd, mainly female supporters of Chesney, who boisterously applauded the curate and his counsel and ate sandwiches in court during the luncheon adjournment. Redmond justified his intervention by declaring that 'so far as these young converts were concerned, they would think that they were free to go back to gambling and drinking, which they had given up'. The court dismissed the petition on legal grounds, condemned Chesney for dragging the case before the public eye, criticized Redmond for reproving his curate before the congregation, approved Grierson's handling of the dispute, and divided costs between the two ministers.[84] Frederick's emphatic rejection of Murphy's motion was at once an endorsement of hierarchical authority, and an expression of fellow feeling for clergymen such as Redmond who were actively working to save souls imperilled by indifference or secularism. Chesney's heartwarming and crowd-pleasing indulgence of 'legitimate' vices was utterly alien to the puritanical tradition in which Frederick had been reared.

In the diocesan synod, Frederick was now a forceful proponent of Church extension, lay mobilization, and administrative reform. In November 1924, he warned parishes which had failed to raise the required minimum stipend that 'they were weakening the influence of the Church' in general: 'The times demanded the best men for the ministry, and the Church should encourage them to put their whole strength, ability, and enthusiasm into fighting the battle of the Lord. (Applause.)' Though certain clergymen lamely protested at the inclusion of their parishes in the diocesan council's 'black list', embarrassed by their own failure to plead for lay support with sufficient pathos, Frederick's aggressive tactics clearly made a strong impact.[85] In the following year, he seconded a proposal, endorsed by Bishop Grierson, for the division of the united dioceses as a prelude to further church extension: 'A speaker in Dublin recently said that Protestantism was a spent force; but to that he replied Protestantism was not a spent force but a virile force in Down and Connor and Dromore. (Applause.)'[86] The *Church of Ireland Gazette* extolled his power and panache as an advocate:

> The Canon has considerably enhanced his reputation in the Synod. He marshalls his facts with rare skill and presents them in an attractive and forceful manner.

His speech in support of the resolutions dealing with the suggested division of the diocese was really a masterpiece. Everything that could possibly be said in favour of the resolutions was put forward by the Canon, and it is mainly due to his speech that the Synod adopted, almost unanimously, the resolution.

Though the resolution had no practical force in the absence of 'acceptable financial proposals' from the general synod, Frederick's 'inspiring speech' suggested that he was not merely a skilled debater, but a potential leader.[87]

The prospect of securing a see brightened on 7 April 1926, when he became archdeacon of Connor.[88] He thus assumed responsibility for examining ordinands and incumbents as well as assisting the bishop in administering the diocese. His reward for undertaking these duties was an annual honorarium of £50 and the title 'Venerable'. His belated appointment as a diocesan nominator, also in spring 1926, gave him considerable influence in future appointments to benefices.[89] The *Carrickfergus Advertiser* noted his 'responsible parish work' and 'prominent place in the councils of the Church as a whole'. In Belfast, he had been 'a cultured preacher and indefatigable worker'; in Carrickfergus, 'many improvements' had been accomplished 'under his leadership, backed up by his great powers of organisation'. Perhaps primed by Frederick himself, the tribute proclaimed that the League of Prayer had penetrated Palestine, China and British Columbia. His publications, mainly distributed by the Bells, had achieved 'very wide circulation' and attracted commendations from various famous people.[90]

As in 1903 and 1913–14, Frederick's tireless labour brought him close to collapse. Between 1910 and 1922, he had been assisted by a succession of curates. Robert Morrison had moved sideways to Hillsborough in 1914, Robert Birney had secured a parish in Cavan in 1918, and Thomas Bloomer had left Ulster in 1922 for England, eventually becoming a bishop.[91] Bloomer, whose memoir was entitled *Notes on a Happy Life*, was presumably the eccentric remembered by Louis in *Zoo*: 'While I was at School at Marlborough my father had a curate who was Anglo-Catholic (an unheard-of thing in our parish) and, also unheard-of, zoo-crazy. He lived in a shack which was really a soldiers' home and built there a huge rabbit house, pasted round with photos of lions.'[92] Four curateless years followed, placing the rector under additional strain. At his first Easter vestry as an archdeacon, he rejoiced in the spirit of 'comradeship' in the parish, 'a spirit that was growing stronger with the years', and welcomed the 'absence of faction and of friction' in parochial committees. He also thanked parishioners for their 'considerateness … during a rather trying year. In 1925 he was threatened with a physical breakdown. One result was that the parish was not worked as a parish should be.' Presumably acting as a trustee, he presented the parish with the title deeds of four houses in St Bride's Street, and £500 on deposit, to provide accommodation for Church organizations. In response, the vestry lauded his 'inherent ability' and 'devoted service', declaring that his promotion had given 'great satisfaction to people of all classes and creeds'.[93] Furthermore, funds were found to appoint assistants for the remainder of Frederick's tenure in Carrickfergus.[94]

IV

Throughout these strenuous years, the rector saw little enough of his children. William remained in Larbert until about 1924; Elizabeth moved on from Sherborne to Oxford, graduating in 1925; and Louis (as he was signing himself by 1925) remained in England as a boarder at Sherborne (1917–21) and then Marlborough College (1921–6). Nineteen-year-old William's return from his children's home in Scotland aroused contrary responses in his siblings. According to Elizabeth: 'He came back to live at the Rectory for good about 1924, I think. Like most Mongols, he had a very kind & affectionate nature & after he went back to live in Carrickfergus after my father's death became very much beloved by everybody there. My stepmother was devoted to him.'[95] Louis's reaction, in a self-pitying letter to his friend John Hilton in 1929, was exasperation:

> Once or twice while I was a little boy my brother was brought from Scotland to stay with us. Each time he seemed to be uglier & more monstrous & on one occasion I had to sleep in the same room for a fortnight; one morning he woke me up by beating me on the face with a shoe. ... When I was 17, however, owing to a (sentimental &, I think, foolish) proposal of my sister, the family reinstated my brother at home. In case you don't know what Mongols are like, they are stunted & very ugly but very goodnatured; my brother, for instance, is talking & laughing all day long; he, of course, talks only very imperfectly. The result of this was that while the rest of the family seemed even to enjoy it (as a Christian burden?) I became in a strange way hollow.[96]

Behind Louis's self-justifying rhetoric lurked envy of the moral strength and generosity of the family whose outlook he was still struggling to escape.

Beatrice, ever jolly and kind, did her best to divert the children when they returned to the rectory during vacations. Shortly after the Armistice, she had a tennis court marked out on the front lawn, where Louis would act as umpire while the girls of the parish competed for boxes of chocolates.[97] Though a keen tennis-player of the daredevil volleying type, Louis was scathing about the sodden courts installed by the Ulster bourgeoisie in futile imitation of their Home Counties models. As he wrote of 'the North' in 1938:

> And each rich family boasts a sagging tennis-net
> On a spongy lawn beside a dripping shrubbery.[98]

The main family reunion, offering some distraction from the tensions and ennui normally associated with vacations at home, was a September holiday. No longer always choosing Ulster seaside resorts such as Portstewart or Ballycastle, the MacNeices had begun to explore the West of Ireland, Wales and Scotland, helped by the acquisition of those emblems of privilege, a motor car with chauffeur. According to Louis's recollection in 1957, his father had ruled southern Ireland out of bounds throughout the 'Troubles': 'How can you mix with people who might be murderers without you knowing it?' A visit to Donegal for his seventeenth birthday, in 1924, aroused mixed feelings in Louis. Though resenting his 'disparagement of southern "lawlessness",' Louis pronounced that Frederick had 'redeemed himself' by mixing easily with the locals and cheerfully accepting their misdirected greeting, 'Good day, Father.'[99] He was disappointed by the relative luxury of their lodgings facing Sheephaven Bay: 'Farragh is not a proper cottage at all. It has an upstairs, a slate roof and a drawing room and a dining-room apart from the kitchen. A redeeming attribute is its lack of a bathroom.'[100] Louis particularly resented the family pilgrimages to Scotland in 1922 and 1925, objecting in retrospect to his father's invidious comparisons between Scottish virtues and 'the defects of the Irish peasantry'. On the second visit: 'I was annoyed when my father compared his own countrymen unfavourably with the hardworking, well-informed, clean and thrifty Scots, and I felt like screaming when my step-mother pointed out the beauties of the scenery.'[101]

Earlier in 1925, Frederick and Beatrice had even ventured beyond the British Isles. As Louis condescendingly observed, his father was 'very untravelled' but well stocked with racial stereotypes, deeming 'the French a disgusting race because they used toothpicks'.[102] Frederick's sententious diary of the cruise to Portugal confirms his low opinion of Catholic peasants.[103] In Lisbon, he noted a 'mixture of races' including 'the Southern Italian type' and the 'negroid type, grissly [*sic.*] hair, & facial characteristics'. There was also 'a demotic type':

> Undoubtedly some of the men and women bore striking resemblances to a type of Southern Irish. Generally the men and women were low sized: the men about 5.4. There are exceptions, and generally they are fat, & look as if they did not take exercise. ... Priests are not in evidence as they are in Ireland but perhaps

they dress differently. ... This morning I visited a R.C. Church not far from this. Service was on. It seemed like play-acting. Men & women came in, sprinkled themselves with water, made genuflexions: one man [went?] on reciting – I suppose prayers – while another occasionally moved about from altar to altar, now lighting Candles, now attending to something else. ... Altogether it gave an unfavourable impression of Portuguese Religion.

By contrast with the human and ecclesiastical environment in Portugal, he had been fascinated by some of his fellow passengers. He was strongly impressed by the moral character of Miss Hunt, an Irish girl who avoided card games and was not beautiful yet 'attractive'.[104] It is a tribute to Frederick MacNeice's self-control that no other recorded utterance, except perhaps his sermon-letter to Beatrice Greer at Christmas 1915, is more charged with repressed eroticism.

10. *Unifier*

CARRICKFERGUS, 1926–1931

I

The mid-Twenties had been a time of transition for the MacNeices. William came home from Larbert; Elizabeth graduated from Oxford; Louis, the rebellious public schoolboy, became an undergraduate dandy at Merton College; the rector rose to archdeacon. Though Beatrice and Frederick were now frequent visitors to Britain, summer holidays remained the main forum for family reunions. For Louis, summer in Carrickfergus had become an embarrassment, at least as depicted in letters to stylish English friends. The family car was 'stupid', the curate with whom he played golf in Portstewart was partial to *Lilac Time*, the family 'think I'm an imbecile', and the neighbours were 'dear, good, patient people' who displayed execrable taste when choosing flowers for the harvest festival.[1]

Holidays away from home were only slightly more interesting. In September 1927, Louis accompanied his father on a motor tour embracing Omey and Ballysadare, imagining that 'all the time my reactions to the West were half my father's'.[2] After this empathetic experience, the next shared holiday was a disappointment. In July 1928, the MacNeices took another scenic and instructive cruise, this time to Norway with Louis aboard. By contrast with the Portuguese, Frederick was delighted by the well-behaved, blond, blue-eyed Lapps, but considered the passengers 'utterly silly'. They were for ever 'singing, playing, dancing': 'All the time we were passing through a wonderful Norwegian fjord! It is hard to understand it. Why do such people come to Norway? They could have Cinemas, & "Three Blind Mice" & café time at home.'³ Louis, tongue-tied and miserable, observed these scenes with condescension and a touch of envy. In 1961, he remembered watching an 'American group of young men and women – the kind my family would have described as "fast" – who spent their days playing "Dance, Dance, Dance, Little Lady" on a portable gramophone'. He blamed his diffidence on upbringing: 'I was far too much throttled by my father's dog-collar to get to know them.' In an earlier version, the revellers were 'middle-aged Americans', 'English spinsters', or 'liverish old men and mammose but crack-voiced women wearing paper caps, blowing whistles'.⁴

Before returning to Oxford for his third year, Louis spent a fortnight in Carrickfergus, summoning his friends John Hilton and Anthony Blunt to alleviate his ennui. As he warned Blunt: 'You will have to go to Church if you come here. However my father is quite an impressive performance.'⁵ Hilton, his fellow student at Marlborough and Oxford, enjoyed visiting the rectory:

> The archdeacon, though an impressive and awe-inspiring figure, had too much warmth and evident humanity to be really frightening. ... His stalwart frame bore a massive head with the long upper lip of the archetypal Irishman and a strong development of muscles beside the mouth, which became more marked in Louis also later on. Louis's stepmother, by contrast, had a sort of sharp-pointed vivacity, with bright darting eyes and quick movement; but her considerable deafness made communication difficult.⁶

Just after leaving Carrickfergus, he told his own parents that 'the MacNassa family were very delightful, especially Mrs. MacNeice, who turns out to be a stepmother, but defies all the traditions of that tribe. In spite of being very deaf she is a great joke especially when fighting or arguing with Louis or prancing after him prancing.'

He was also diverted by dinner 'with a Belfast aunt, lately engaged in gun-running'; and tea 'with another aunt who lives in the most beautiful garden in Ulster with a famous poetess Miss Hine, writing as Elizabeth Shane, who is antipathetic towards Louis'. These exotic creatures were Beatrice's sister-in-law Dorinda and her unmarried sister Eva. Less delightful was a nostalgic ramble with Louis through the 'brambles gorse nettles thistles and broken rocks' of the Knockagh. The high point was his last day in the rectory before departing for Bray on Dublin Bay:

> Mrs. MacNeice threw Nietzsche downstairs this morning and the archdeacon said he was only fit to light candles with, but he is very broad, I should think, on the whole. He can put the weight further than Anthony or Louis and gave me

several solemn warnings about the beautiful girls of Dublin. It is rather nice to get back to electric light.[7]

Hilton's visit to the rectory coincided with elaborate preparations for Elizabeth's wedding to John Nicholson, who had graduated in Natural Sciences at Oxford two years after Elizabeth. Nicholson was altogether a suitable husband: heir to a baronetcy, grandson of a celebrated colonial politician and chancellor of Sydney University, nephew of the recently retired organist of Westminster Abbey, and son of an architect specializing in cathedrals who had married a clergyman's daughter.[8] Among those cathedrals were Down, Connor, Dromore, and St Anne's, since Sir Charles had become consulting diocesan architect in 1924. Nicholson embarked on a busy career as a London surgeon in 1929, and three years later Elizabeth also qualified in medicine, becoming a clinical assistant at the Tavistock Institute of Medical Psychology.[9]

As the wedding approached, Louis sent Hilton a droll account of his evenings in the rectory: 'Every night we play Fantan loo and faro, or sometimes pam for a change, while my father & the bishop sit happily in the corner with their snuff-boxes out and their gouty legs (2 per bishop, 1 per arch deacon) propped up in the commode.' Some diversion was provided by the presence of 'Madame La Comtesse de Pilkington', Elizabeth's schoolfriend and bridesmaid, whose height and 'funny voice' had tantalized Louis when the three travelled together to Liverpool in 1923.[10]

Three days before the wedding in Carrickfergus on 18 October 1928, Elizabeth was presented with 'a very handsome and valuable canteen of stainless cutlery' and other gifts, before tea and songs in the parochial hall. Her well-wishers included the Sunday and Day School teachers, Young People's Union, Women's Fellowship, Mothers' Union, Bell Ringers, and members of Beatrice's Bible Class. Louis might have loosened his Christian roots, but not Elizabeth. The select vestryman who chaired the entertainment admitted that he was not 'long acquainted' with Miss MacNeice, but expressed 'a very sincere affection for her father, their beloved Rector' and her mother. Frederick made an uncharacteristically facetious speech concerning 'recent irregularities' such as the holding of vestry meetings without the rector's knowledge, and acknowledging 'all the kindnesses they had done to himself and his family during those years. All this was rather awkward for it made him firm in the resolution that he would remain in Carrickfergus for the remainder of his life. (Loud applause).' Clearly, other possible outcomes had occurred to him. The speeches of thanks preceding the National Anthem included one from John Campbell of the urban district council, who had recently introduced Carrickfergus to the British Fascist movement.[11]

Frederick himself performed the ceremony, with the assistance of his younger brother Herbert, one of the few MacNeice relations to visit the rectory.[12] Photographs suggest a very Twenties wedding, with copious hats, caps and stoles, though Louis's supercilious expression as he smirks behind the shelter of the towering bridesmaid, Mary Pilkington, reminds one of an episode recounted in his autobiography:

> The wedding reception was given in the Parochial Schools, the blackboards and multiplication tables being removed for the occasion or concealed by flowers and ferns. C–A–T spells Cat. That evening one of the bridesmaids and I took one of Elizabeth's wedding presents, a huge and hideous china jar – the sort of thing you put a palm in – and rolled it downstairs to smash at the feet of my stepmother.[13]

A difficult young man, indeed.

Through the survival of Beatrice's diary for 1929, we may savour the flavour of family life in the year preceding Louis's own marriage. On New Year's Day, Beatrice and Louis attended Holy Communion with about twenty others and took down the church decorations. In the afternoon, she showed how wholeheartedly she had embraced the responsibilities of a stepmother. She treated 24-year-old William precisely as any well-informed parent today would deal with Down's Syndrome in a young child, through constant attention and mental stimulation: 'I took Willie in the Park & along the Scotch Quarter & back thro the Park – fed the swans – ice on the pond – Derrick to Belfast in car at 8.15 p.m. to St Clements Church extension scheme – Party at Thornfield [Mrs Kirk's] at 8 p.m. Louis did not go.' Louis did take tea with William Parr, Frederick's curate and organist, on the eve of his escape to Heysham and London on 8 January. Life in the rectory returned to the normal round of sermons, walks, and letters: 'Derrick preached on "I believe in the Resurrection of the body – the life of the world to come" ... Read Willie some of Pilgrim's Progress in afternoon. Wrote to Louis – & so did Derrick.'[14]

A few weeks later, in a telegram to his father concerning a drunken escapade in Oxford that nearly led to his being sent down from Merton, Louis abruptly broke the news that he was 'engaged to be married gaudeamus love ever writing = Louis'. His explanatory letter, identifying the utterly unsuitable Mary Ezra (Mariette), made 'Derrick very upset'.[15] Mary's mother, though married to an irreproachable Oxford classicist, was theatrically Jewish and exotic. John Hilton did his best to soften the impact of this act of defiance by writing a reassuring letter to Beatrice. Frederick's response is disarming in its sectarian candour:

17. Loading sheep, Illaunakeegher, Co. Galway, 29 Aug. 1930.

18. Loading turf, Omey Island, Co. Galway, Aug. 1930.

19. Domestic staff at Bishopsgrove, including Rebecca Shaw with dog, *c*.1932.

20. Louis and Mary MacNeice and unidentified guests visiting Bishopsgrove, Waterford, *c*.1932.

21. Beatrice, Mary and Louis MacNeice at Bishopsgrove, 25 Aug. 1932.

22. Frederick and Beatrice MacNeice visiting the former episcopal palace, Waterford, 15 May 1931.

23. Sophie Popper, Daniel and Frederick MacNeice with motorcade, near
Cushendun, Co. Antrim, 1939.

24. Beatrice MacNeice with chauffeur, late 1930s.

25. Frederick and Beatrice MacNeice on tour, late 1930s.

26. Daniel and Frederick MacNeice at Cushendall, Co. Antrim, 1937.

27. Frederick MacNeice on the patio at Bishop's House, Malone Rd, Belfast, late 1930s.

28. Beatrice and William MacNeice outside Bishop's House, late 1930s.

29. Louis and Daniel MacNeice at Bishop's House, *c.*1938.

30. Receiving the Duke of Gloucester at St Anne's, Belfast, 1938.

31. Frederick MacNeice with Gladstone bag, date unknown.

32. Frederick MacNeice in regalia, *c.*1938.

33. Effigy of Frederick MacNeice as Bishop of Cashel, St Nicholas's Church, Carrickfergus, Co. Antrim.

It was good of you to write. But how could you think I could approve Louis'
choice? It is a terrible disappointment. It promises to both nothing but misery.
... Altogether I am very much crushed by the news. ... This letter is for yourself.
The thought of an engagement to a Jewess is dreadful. If she is a religious Jewess
it will be awful, & if she is an indifferent one it will be no better.[16]

Undaunted, Frederick and Beatrice soon decided to tackle the enemy on her
home ground. The ensuing melodrama, involving multiple confrontations and
negotiations in Oxford between two pairs of equally disapproving parents, as well
as disapproving tutors, has been well told elsewhere from Hilton's viewpoint.[17]
Beatrice's account casts little light on the negotiations but much on the relentless
succession of meals, including an unappetizing lunch of 'Omelette & Kidney, &
Pudding – cold Cheese Tart', supplied by Hilton. After lunch, the 'Jewess' was
introduced by Louis, the inspection party was reinforced by the Nicholsons, and
'Derrick Elizabeth & I went to see Mrs. Beazeley. Saw her & the Professor &
Mary – Returned to Hotel for dinner – 6 of us – John & Elizabeth caught 9.25
back to London.'[18]

According to Hilton, 'not only was everyone wonderfully reasonable at every
point but they all even liked each other and came to the most concordant and
harmonious conclusions', agreeing that 'it should be called an understanding and
not an engagement'.[19] Next day, Beatrice accompanied Louis to London to inspect
the Nicholsons' flat in Finsbury Park (where there was no water for the tea because
of a burst pipe) and collect the typescript and manuscript of Louis's lost Marlborough novel, *Out of Step*.[20] They were back at Merton by 9 pm: 'Derrick met me
there – He had spent the day in Oxford & seen two of Louis' tutors.'

Louis reported to the hotel for breakfast next morning and dutifully attended
two lectures before parting on good terms: 'Went to Louis' room in Merton at 1
oc. & found John Hilton there & table laid for lunch – Had lunch about 1.30.
Chops & caramel cream – & coffee & cheese – made acquaintance of Storie the
Scout – Walked to Hotel & took Taxi with luggage to Station. Louis & John saw
us off – 3.30.'[21] The visit had been a success; yet, as Hilton discerned: 'If there is real
unhappiness in the situation, I am afraid it is still to come.'[22]

Relations with Louis seemed warm enough when he returned to Carrickfergus on 19 March 1929, for the Easter vacation. Louis had heralded his arrival by
sending his first book of poems, *Blind Fireworks*, which Beatrice dutifully perused:
'I read it all through in the evening.' (One wonders what she made of cheeky pieces
like 'Happy Families', 'The Humorous Atheist Addresses His Humorous Maker',
or 'Cynicism'.) The Liverpool boat was met by David the chauffeur, and that

afternoon Louis himself drove Beatrice and another visitor to Cushendall for tea in the Temperance Hotel. They motored to Glasdrumman on the south Down coast for lunch with Eva Greer and Gertrude Hind on Holy Thursday, and to one of Louis's old haunts on Good Friday: 'Drove in car after tea with Louis, Mrs. Woods & Willie to get "Palm" – & up to monument on Knockagh – Fish lunch.' Twice they drove Frederick to Belfast, and even enjoyed a 'Lively Evening' (by Beatrice's standards) at a tea party. The outcome of this peripatetic jollity was Louis's driving licence, which he secured on 15 April. His appalling subsequent record as a driver suggests that the MacNeices had placed their lives seriously at risk. Beatrice's diary gives no hint of tension, though the atmosphere may have clouded on the Sabbath: 'I had Bible Cl. 14 present. Had talk with Louis after supper.' Otherwise, Louis played a great deal of tennis at the rectory, conducted his daily correspondence with Mary, and endured five weeks at home without recorded rebellion.[23]

The 'understanding' between Louis and Mary was a perennial source of misunderstanding for his father and stepmother. They were back in Oxford on 10 June, having endless teas, lunches and dinners with Louis, Mary and the Beazleys, sometimes in the college garden.[24] During the summer, the tempestuous Marie Beazley found a new weapon for obstructing her daughter's marriage by demanding proof that William's 'mongolism' was not an hereditary disorder. This necessitated further negotiations, and a fortnight's visit to Carrickfergus by Louis. His boat was met by Frederick at 7 a.m. on 13 July, a low point in the Ulster calendar when nothing but emblems, rubbish and the stale smell of spilt liquor remain from the heady festivities of the previous day. A 'Letter from Mrs. Beazley re Willie' arrived a few days later, in response to which Frederick wrote for support to his 'doctor in Larbert'.[25] Since Dr Clarkson believed that nine-tenths of his young 'imbecile' patients had at least one mentally unsound parent, his response may have been unwelcome.[26] Frederick's own view was that 'there were few, if any, diseases that were hereditary', an opinion relevant not only to Down's Syndrome but also to tuberculosis and melancholia, twin causes of Lily's death in 1914.[27] Louis was agitated by a telegram from Mary on 19 July, going 'off for long walk after dinner', and returned to Oxford three days before his ticket was due to expire.[28]

The outcome was a month-long family holiday on Achill Island in Mayo, to which Mary was invited. Frederick reportedly had 'a special love' for Achill, having visited the island alone in 1911.[29] Despite close living with the elder MacNeices and the Nicholsons, Louis and Mary found opportunities to escape and enjoy the exotic local culture: 'The world on the whole was gay.' Beatrice, as always, worked tirelessly to feed her flock, occasionally rueful when left behind to make the tea, or kept waiting for Derrick as he climbed mountains or returned from an island service. Yet, with what Louis termed a 'local peasant girl' to look after the rented former rectory (at Doogort), she had time to give shape, if not voice, to her contentment: 'Made a sketch of Clare Island for Derrick.'[30] Louis stayed in touch throughout the year, perhaps encouraged by her attentive reading of *Blind Fireworks*: 'Long letter from Louis about Oxford Poetry.'[31] When the children were gone, the quiet diversion of 'visiting' remained. Just after receiving Louis's literary letter, she and Derrick spent Saturday afternoon calling vainly at Castle Dobbs and two other local mansions, before finding the McFerrans at home in Oakfield: 'Home to tea at 4.30 – Trimmed brown beaver hat with ostrich feather mount.'[32] She was surely too kindly a soul to resent Frederick's gesture towards his first wife on the fifteenth anniversary of her death, a week before Christmas, when the church was presented with choir and chancel stalls of oak 'with thankfulness for the life and love of Elizabeth Margaret MacNeice'.[33]

When the 'understanding' was retrospectively consummated at the Oxford registry office on 21 June 1930, 'neither the Beazleys nor the MacNeices came to the wedding'.[34] In fact, the latter had not been informed, as 'Madre' protested in a letter to Louis over a month later: 'I am sure Daddie felt it a bit having to be told by a Stranger about his Son's wedding, but he did not say so.'[35] Despite this second blow, and Louis's lingering resentment against his father, the ever-patient Frederick and Beatrice averted an open breach. Louis and Mary quickly settled into a stupor of domestic bliss in Birmingham, where Louis had secured an assistant lectureship in Classics shortly before his triumphant final examination ('Greats').

In February 1931, Frederick and Beatrice made a slightly awkward one-day visit to Birmingham:

> Went out & saw the Cathedral & Burne Jones window – Louis & Mary came to the [Midland] Hotel at 12.45 & we had a good lunch (4/– each) in the French Restaurt. in the Hotel – Took Train to Selly Park Road & had tea at the College – saw all over it & the garden – & back to the town for dinner – Louis & M. left us at 9.30 p.m.

It was clearly a relief to go on next morning to London, where they had a more relaxed time with the Nicholsons. Once again, a motor car helped ease family tensions. On 9 March, Beatrice received 'Letter from Louis & Mary excited about offer of car', whereupon she 'Ordered car for Louis & Mary – £135, Sliding roof, for £114.'[36] By accepting this belated wedding present, they re-entered the family fold.

Beatrice's diaries offer occasional hints of restlessness amidst the record of busy domesticity. One Friday night in January 1931, she 'read aloud after dinner "Diary of a Provincial Woman"'; while three days later the archdeacon conjured up the world outside Carrickfergus with 'a lecture on Ireland illustrated with lantern slides' in support of the Youth Fellowship library.[37] Occasionally, the humdrum routine of the rectory was enlivened by meetings with Ulster's grandees as well as the notables of the parish. When the Duchess of Abercorn visited the town in October 1929, Frederick showed her over the church before joining a throng of 200 for tea at Thornfield, where the Girl Guides formed a guard of honour and a bridge tournament was held to aid the British Sailors' Society. Their host was Lady Coates, president of the Belfast Ladies' Guild, whose husband was once again Lord Mayor of Belfast. Four days later, when the Duke (as Governor of Northern Ireland) received the freedom of the city, Frederick was among 600 gentlemen invited for lunch at City Hall. Though not senior enough to join the bishop of Down, Rabbi Shachter, and other Church leaders at the top table, he topped one of the centre tables.[38]

On 15 March 1931, it was the prime minister's turn to visit Carrickfergus: 'Derrick to Early service – I went to 11.30 & H.C. The Prime Minister & Lady Craigavon in Church – Went to lunch at Thornfield to meet them. 10 at lunch – 2 Coates, 2 Chichesters 2 Moores – ourselves, 2 Craigavons.'[39] 'Ourselves' had secured a niche among Ulster's foremost oligarchs.

II

Even before his appointment as archdeacon of Connor in March 1926, Frederick had become one of the most active, effective and popular members of the diocesan synod. In November 1925, he once again headed the list of Connor clergymen elected to the diocesan council, not to mention the council's finance committee.[40] His dominance was even more conspicuous by November 1927, when he was also the first to be elected to the general synod. In both contests, he easily outscored the deans of Belfast and Connor as well as his old mentor, Canon Clarke. He also topped the poll for the three diocesan nominators who shared responsibility for the selection of parochial clergy.[41] His popularity was undiminished at his last synod as archdeacon in 1930, when he once again outscored the deans of Connor and Belfast on all three fronts.[42]

As a senior clergyman pre-eminent in his own synod, Frederick had ever-expanding opportunities to influence the Church at large. While his views on clerical politics, peace, goodwill and Christian unity were already well known, he made full use of his office to spread them more widely than before. At Christ Church, Lisburn, he reminded parishioners of the new rector's duty to perform 'the ministry of the Word': 'Don't, for the Church's sake, allow him to be dragged into the arena of party politics. There, as a rule, the clergyman is a man in the wrong place – a lost man.'[43] His visit to Dublin for the general synod in May 1929, with Beatrice, was enlivened by teas with the Irish Christian Fellowship and the Provost's wife, browsing in a church bookshop, inspecting Sarah Purser's 'Tower of Light', and discussing 'The Teaching on Personal Religion' at a clerical meeting in Trinity College.[44] Other events, such as an all-Ireland clerical conference in November, also drew him to Dublin, though on that occasion Beatrice stayed in Carrickfergus, where she 'mended bead chains & wore my new red jumper for first time'.[45] Frederick's growing repute in the inner circles of the Church was recognized in 1930, when he became a canon of St Patrick's Cathedral at the behest of the dean and chapter.[46]

Within the diocese, Frederick was more active than ever in the numerous associations seeking to promote co-operation and avoid division among the clergy. Having hitherto avoided notice in the Diocesan Temperance Society, the newly appointed archdeacon was added to the committee organizing a temperance rally at the Ulster Hall in June 1926. His name was put forward by two former army chaplains of otherwise opposed views, Charles Manning and John Redmond.[47] Manning, who had married George Chamberlain's daughter when a curate in Carrickfergus, disapproved of the 'local option' campaign for empowering local authorities to prevent the local sale of alcoholic liquor.[48] He believed that temperance was best promoted by 'educational methods' rather than legislation. This issue threatened to erode support for the official unionist party, headed by the distiller Craigavon. Redmond, later a prominent Orangeman, supported the dissident cause. Manning and Redmond were the main protagonists in a vigorous debate in December, following Craigavon's statement that so long as he remained prime minister, the issue of licensing legislation would remain closed. Redmond believed that 'the Churches had to take the moral & spiritual point of view' while taking care 'to preserve the stability of the Northern State'. Bishop Grierson urged them to 'stick to the Prime Minister (through thick and thin)' and avoid alienating 'the main body of Church people'. Frederick's contribution, though gnomic, showed how formidably his presence could loom in the middle of the road. While dissociating himself from Manning's position, he 'did not see that Temperance was bound up with Local Option' and urged 'renewed vigour' in the broader temperance campaign. Manning's motion was eventually withdrawn following a proposal to procrastinate for a month, after which the matter was left 'in abeyance' at another meeting attended by Frederick. Having helped avert a potentially disastrous political intervention by the clergy, he played no further recorded part in the society as an archdeacon.[49]

Meanwhile, Frederick had embarked on a moral crusade that required collaboration on a wider front. With notable energy and eloquence, he sought to transcend the often bitter divisions among Churchmen and between the Reformed churches, in order to maximize the moral influence of Christianity in an ever more secular environment. As a mere archdeacon, he could scarcely hope to change the face of the Christian world. Instead, he tried to identify and mobilize friends and colleagues who were sympathetic to the cause of 'reunion', through personal influence and participation in various organizations. He was particularly active in the Diocesan Clerical Society, serving on the committee, occasionally acting as chairman, and delivering a paper on 'The New Testament and the Term of Christ' just before his collation as archdeacon. He also responded to papers on theological or topical issues such as 'Renovation in Education' (by the controversial Presbyterian ecumenicist, Ernest Davey), 'The Moral Basis of the League of Nations' and 'The Future of Institutional Christianity'. Another paper, on 'Christian Unity & the Mission Field', was given by the Lord Bishop of Fukien, John Hind from Carrickfergus.[50] In November 1928, Frederick spoke on 'Our Place in Ireland to-day' to the Clerical Society of Ireland, which gathered clergy from every diocese for its annual meeting. Next day, he was elected vice-president of the society.[51] In the following year, he addressed this body on 'Reunion: Prospects and Possibilities', drawing responses from nine colleagues including old associates such as Thomas Drury and Shaw Kerr.[52]

The goal of Protestant unity was omnipresent in Frederick's sermons and writings, culminating in *Reunion: The Open Door*, a booklet published in 1929 and dedicated to the Irish Christian Fellowship. He longed 'for a healing of divisions which have been, and which are a source of weakness to the Reformed Churches in Ireland and a great reproach to all who call themselves by the name of Christ'. He had recently participated in a meeting organized by the Fellowship in Dublin, which urged application in Ireland of calls for Christian unity emanating from the Lambeth conference in 1920 (of bishops from the various Anglican churches) and the Lausanne conference on Faith and Order in 1927 (embracing almost all major Christian denominations except the Church of Rome). The Fellowship had bemoaned the 'great waste of man-power and of money' caused by competition between sects, concluding that 'an attempt to draw together would bring new life to our Churches, especially where our numbers are small'.[53] In contrast with many previous campaigns for Protestant unity, no common antagonist (whether Roman Catholicism or secularism) was explicitly identified. Frederick's booklet received approving reviews in the *Church of Ireland Gazette* and *The Irish Times*, consolidating his reputation as one of Ireland's ablest pan-Protestants.[54] He remained in contact with the Fellowship, dividing visiting lecturers and also, perhaps, sharing its frustration at the difficulty of extending ecumenicism beyond the sphere of liberal Protestantism. As some members of the Belfast branch ruminated in 1931, they 'would like to get into touch with Roman Catholics far more than is done, though they could not see how. Nevertheless they would like the idea to be considered, also the possibility of making contacts with Jews, as is increasingly being done in England.'[55]

Just before the Fellowship's conference, on 10 March, he had revisited Trinity College and stayed with the Provost in the august capacity of Select Preacher. His text was 'Behold, I have set before thee an open door, and no man can shut it' (Rev. 3: 8). His sermon stressed the baneful effects of 'denominational distinctions' in mission fields such as China, India and Persia, and refuted the belief that any organized episcopacy had existed in apostolic times. Though making no direct reference to reunion with the Roman Catholic Church, he quoted approvingly the bishop of Bombay's belief that 'the door leading towards union with Protestants is much more open than the door towards reunion with Rome'.[56] As St John the Divine proclaimed in the less ecumenical ninth verse of Frederick's text: 'Behold, I will make them of the synagogue of Satan, which say they are Jews, and are not, but do lie.' Frederick, for all his unifying zeal, was never to open that second door.

Apart from a few impassioned adherents of the doctrine of apostolic succession, virtually all activists in the Church of Ireland agreed that reunion was desirable but, in the short term, unattainable. Each year, the general synod endorsed a vacuous report from its Home Re-Union committee, reaffirming the principle while stressing the seemingly insurmountable practical impediments. Primate D'Arcy was the most eloquent advocate of the principle, while Archbishop Gregg of Dublin, an unashamed Episcopalian, led the sceptics. Both prelates had initially welcomed the aspirations of the Lambeth and Lausanne conferences; but, by May 1928, Gregg found 'it impossible to see how certain cleavages which became manifest [at Lausanne] will ever be bridged'.[57] In 1929, it was Frederick's turn to second adoption of the latest report:

> He could see no reason why representatives of the Church of Ireland and of the other Churches should not be encouraged ... to face the facts of the situation as it was to-day, such as their divisions in Ireland, how they originated, why they persisted, what reasons were there at the time that seemed to justify those divisions, and finally, to ask themselves if those reasons still justified their divisions. If they could not at once secure Re-union, and it was a very difficult and complicated question, could they not, at all events, have a greater measure of unity than they had at present? ... Could they not declare that they desired

immediately more intimate relations between the Presbyterian Church and the Church of Ireland, while always having before them as their goal the Re-union of the Churches?

His reward was election to the Home Re-Union Committee, and also as a delegate to the United Council of Christian Churches and Religious Communions in Ireland. Significantly, he was not added to the delegation already engaged in tortuous discussions with Presbyterian counterparts.[58] At the next synod, Shaw Kerr still radiated optimism about eventual union with the Presbyterian Church, while Frederick helped secure an expression of rejoicing in the scheme for union adopted by the various Protestant denominations in southern India.[59] Yet no agreement was reached with the Presbyterians on the vexed issues of episcopal authority and ordination, and the indecisive outcome of the next Lambeth conference in 1930 left little hope for practical progress on any front. The campaign for Christian reunion fizzled out, nothing having been achieved.

Equally frustrating, for a proto-feminist like Frederick, was the obstinate refusal of the general synod to admit women, even though they had been eligible for select vestries since 1920. At the general synod in May 1930, Lord Glenavy (former chairman of the Free State's Senate) introduced a petition with over 1500 signatures, which was vehemently supported by Frederick: 'No answer had been given to the question as to why women were excluded. What he objected to was the exclusion of a woman simply because she was a woman. Women would look upon some of the arguments brought forward as relics of the stone age.' The proposal was narrowly defeated on second reading, despite support from a clear majority of the clergy. As usual, the lay representatives on the synod (who outnumbered the clergy by two to one) were more inclined to resist reform, a curious by-product of the democratization of Church government after Disestablishment.[60] In the following year, the *Church of Ireland Gazette* was 'surprised and disappointed' by the failure of a similar proposal to 'secure a majority, either of clergy or laity'. Women remained ineligible until 1949, and a decade later the general synod included only seven women.[61]

Frustrated in his pursuit of reunion and synodswomen, Frederick contributed to one significant victory for reform. In 1911, 39 per cent of the Episcopalian population of Ireland was concentrated in the united dioceses of Down and Connor and Dromore. Fifteen years later, that proportion probably exceeded 47 per cent. A single bishop was therefore responsible for almost half of the national flock. The proportion of Episcopalians in the region had been growing for more than half a century, while the Presbyterian component remained static and that of Roman

Catholics declined.[62] The concentration of Episcopalians in and around Belfast was intensified by steady shrinkage elsewhere in Ulster, in the 'south and west', and (after partition) in the Dublin region. These trends, confirmed by the census of 1926, suggested limitless possibilities for expansion of the Church of Ireland in the north-east, during a period of decline and demoralization in all other regions. If only the Church of Ireland could emulate the entrepreneurial and missionary zeal exhibited by its Presbyterian and Methodist rivals, surely it could stem the tide of secularism and bring salvation to the mass of nominal Episcopalians, four-fifths of whom were typically absent from church on Sunday.[63] For optimists like Frederick, the challenge resembled that facing Alexander Dallas in Connemara, as he sought to reveal the Word of God to the disorganized hordes of nominal Catholics through exposing them to the open Bible. Like Dallas, Frederick and his fellow enthusiasts realized that such missions could only be accomplished at vast expense, requiring unprecedented mobilization of the laity as well as assistance from central funds.

As archdeacon of Connor, Frederick quickly became a key ally of Bishop Grierson in trying to induce the other twelve prelates, and the inflated southern majority in the general synod, to subsidize a Belfast crusade. The united diocese was absurdly under-represented at all levels of Church government, still dominated by bishops with little to lose but their palaces, clergymen with tiny congregations, and lay synodsmen drawn from the learned professions and the vestiges of the landed gentry. For such men, the proper use of any surplus revenue was to subsidize unviable livings and bishoprics, as parish collections dwindled and church property fell into disrepair. Why should a venerable institution in seemingly terminal decline, yet clinging to considerable assets, cast caution aside by establishing new churches and missions to cater for the working classes of Belfast?

Belfast's appeals aroused much resentment and resistance, especially from southern laymen. Even the eminently justified appointment of an extra bishop, originally proposed by the general synod's standing committee in 1925, was thwarted for nearly two decades. The most equitable method of raising the required salary of at least £1500 and providing a suitable mansion would have been to amalgamate two southern sees, a procedure stoutly resisted by their representatives and rejected as 'a dishonour' by Frederick.[64] When the proposal approving division in principle was brought before the diocesan synod in November 1925, he had eloquently seconded its adoption. Next May, at the general synod, he argued that both an extra bishop and additional clergy were required in the Belfast region. Rejecting the cautious view that the Church could afford only one of these innovations, he declared 'that one with a soldier's eye and statesman's brain would single out

Belfast and neighbourhood as the one spot of strategic importance for the Church of Ireland, the one place challenging the Church to advance'.[65] News of Frederick's performance reached Oxford, enabling Louis to tell Beatrice, tongue in cheek, that he had heard 'that Daddie made a stupendous speech at the Synod'.[66] The separation of Connor from Down and Dromore was accepted in principle but repeatedly postponed until the problem of funding could be resolved.[67]

By October 1930, Bishop Grierson and a diocesan committee, including Frederick, were satisfied by the Representative Church Body's proposal to fund an extra episcopal stipend from central revenues, while requiring the diocese to supply a residence. This compromise was vigorously opposed at the diocesan synod, where Canon Richard Clarke's amending motion was approved by a small majority, only to be lost on a technicality. Frederick stoutly defended the committee's recommendation, dismissing another proposed amendment out of hand, declaring that 'we don't want to make debating points, or to think of victory and defeat', and negotiating a compromise whereby further consultations with the RCB would be held in preparation for a special diocesan synod.[68] Frederick reinforced the 'strong committee' appointed to conduct these negotiations, which eventually approved the clarified terms by ten votes to eight.

When brought before the special synod, the majority's recommendation was firmly rejected by both orders, a serious setback to the archdeacon as well as the bishop. Grierson, sensing the synod's hostile mood, had urged delegates to 'consider the question with calmness and with a wide outlook', and forbore from offering the 'guidance' which he had presaged in his introductory remarks. On behalf of members of the liaison committee who had signed a dissentient report, an amendment was put forward to postpone the issue of division (partly on the ground that any available funds should be devoted to impoverished parishes and missions in Belfast). The amendement was supported by several wealthy lay benefactors, including John Milne Barbour (parliamentary secretary to the ministry of Finance); while Sir Robert Kennedy of Cultra Manor (a much bemedalled retired diplomat) tried unavailingly to propose 'a middle course'. Frederick admitted that the RCB's discouraging response since the October synod meant that 'no one imagined now that there was a capital sum' available to endow a second bishopric, but suggested that small contributions would be made 'from time to time towards building up capital'. His advocacy was uncharacteristically feeble, and his remark that 'no doubt they would be responsible for annual sums' provoked 'Laughter and cries of "How much?".'

The outcome was a fiasco, as two-thirds of each order voted against division of the diocese.[69] In his study of the Church in Belfast, published a few months later,

Frederick analysed the diverse grounds on which the scheme had been opposed, rejecting each in turn and hoping that good sense would prevail in future. He was at pains to refute the paramount objection that an extra bishopric would harm the cause of church extension, urging that 'the two hang together'. While believing that 'the door has not been finally closed', he admitted that a systematic estimate of the 'administrative cost' would be needed to reassure doubters.[70] The division of the diocese was eventually accomplished in 1945.[71]

Meanwhile, Frederick had been pursuing the greater goal of church extension with some success. His missionary enthusiasm met with scepticism, as he recalled in 1938:

> The fourth of those Church extension movements was in our own day – in 1927. I remembered quite well talking it over with a Belfast clergyman and telling him that we hoped to provide churches for five districts at least. He said it would be quite impossible, that the money would not be forthcoming, but he did not know as I did the quality of our people.[72]

In May 1927, the general synod agreed to grant £6000 'towards the spiritual needs of the growing Church population of Belfast', of which all but £1635 (allocated in 1926) would be 'held in suspense in case that it should be decided to divide the See'. The message was clear: if church extension in Belfast were to receive substantial support, the demand for an extra bishop must be shelved. Despite this grudging response, the *Church of Ireland Gazette* detected 'a turning-point in policy. For the immediate future the Church of Ireland is likely to concentrate its attention chiefly upon the call from its own people where they are found in greatest concentration.'[73]

This was triumphantly confirmed in 1928, when the general synod approved the provision of up to '£50,000 for Church extension in and around Belfast', in the form of advances for approved projects repayable over thirty-five years. Victory was secured with help from Archbishop Gregg of Dublin (deputizing for Primate D'Arcy, who was ill), and through the tactful tactics of the Belfast representatives: 'The Synod was educated on the subject, and the passage of the Bill was remarkable in that the Belfast Synodsmen, though they must often have felt themselves able to correct or amplify statements made by other speakers, practised self-restraint and left the discussion of the Measure to the rest of the House.'[74] The sum, modest though it might seem today, was extravagant by the standard normally guiding the Representative Church Body, and sufficient to pay for several new churches. Frederick was clearly delighted with the outcome, publishing detailed tabulations of church extension between 1927 and 1932 that documented the vital contribution made by the general synod towards the erection of five churches in outer Belfast.[75]

Without substantial fund-raising from the laity, it would be impossible to make effective use of the new parishes. Clergymen needed houses and incomes; the crusade against secularism needed schools, halls and missions. At the diocesan synod in October 1928, Frederick outlined the scale of the challenge that remained in Connor. While fifty clergymen in thirty parishes and mission districts catered for 60,000 nominal Episcopalians, the remaining 70,000 were served by only 16 ministers in 6 parishes. The Church of Ireland still lagged far behind the Presbyterians, who had about forty missions in Belfast involving thirty laymen, and the Methodists, who had lavished £50,000 on a central hall and were spending £30,000 on another. Despite the munificence of the general synod, far more central and local funding was required in a situation 'presenting their Church with the finest opportunity in all her long history'.[76]

When the diocesan Church Extension Commission reported to the diocesan synod in October 1929, two and a half years after its creation, it pressed for further reforms designed to attract and mobilize the apathetic laity, including weekday opening of churches and abolition of pew rents – an intolerable barrier to the 'missionary work' of church extension. The Church 'must follow her people' into the suburbs and rationalize surplus provision in the inner city. Its chairman was Lord Justice Best, Freemason, Orangeman, and father of Louis's tennis-playing friend at Christ Church, Oxford.[77] Frederick was among the twelve signatories of the final report, whose phrasing strongly suggests that he drafted several key passages.[78] Its evangelical strategy for reinvigorating parochial life aroused controversy, particularly when embodied in proposals for the radical reorganization of poorly performing parishes (including Holy Trinity). The archdeacon showed his steel when assailed by squeals of protest from slighted clergymen and synodsmen, fiercely resisting all attempts to amend the commission's recommendations. While taking note of Canon Cooke's sarcastic enquiry as to whether Christ Church, Belfast, was to become 'a museum or motion picture house, or a place for a dog show',[79] he ensured that the commission's critical comments on that parish would not be referred back for revision. Faced with an attempt to maintain St John's, Laganbank, which commanded a local 'church population of only fifty people', he declared that the congregation should rebuild their church in a suburb such as Dundela or Knock: to stay put would be 'utterly absurd, grotesque, and ludicrous'.[80]

He also stood by the commission's refusal to close or criticize St George's, another parish relying almost entirely on outsiders for its survival. Sustained by wealthy pew-renting suburbanites, St George's was ill-attuned to Frederick's Low-Church and democratic disposition.[81] Yet it was also evangelical in practice, offering weekday services for urban workers and organizing social events. Frederick offered no support to Orange protestors such as Henry O'Connor, who wanted 'to know why St. George's particularly met the needs of English people, as stated in the report. Were these English people of a certain type? Were they the Anglo-Catholics of England?'[82] Frederick's uncompromising defence of the commission's report temporarily alienated some of his supporters, and for once he was outscored by the deans of Belfast and Down in the annual election for the diocesan council. But the report was adopted after enthusiastic endorsement from Bishop Grierson as well as the archdeacon, and the prospects for winning back the Episcopalian souls of Belfast seemed bright.[83] As the report averred, the Church's opportunity in Belfast was, 'perhaps, the most promising she has had in her long history. Here she may yet find compensations for the serious losses sustained elsewhere in recent years.'[84] Such hopes were almost immediately blighted by the consequences of worldwide depression, as unemployment soared and Ulster's industries faced collapse. By 1931, the most that any sane salvationist could hope for was to keep the existing churches open and await economic recovery.

III

Though no longer a practising Orangeman or Freemason, Frederick had not lost his sympathy with these controversial embodiments of the ideal of brotherhood. As a well-disposed former insider, his criticisms carried peculiar force. At a Masonic service in Glenarm in August 1926, he rejected claims that the fraternity was 'a secular organisation', pointing to the presence at lodge meetings of 'the volume of the Sacred Law' and the Freemason's undertaking 'that his trust is in God'. He admitted, however, that its influence could be applied in a manner incompatible 'with the highest Christian ethics':

> Ireland more than most countries had suffered from the fact that the testimonials of political and sectarian organisations weighed more where appointments were being made than professional knowledge and experience or diplomas of universities and it was alleged that Masonry was not guiltless in this respect. All he wished to say was that if any Masons used their influence when making appointments to places of position, in favour of those who were not qualified for the place, it showed that they misinterpreted the spirit and principles of the organisation to which they belong. No man because he is a Mason, is expected to give preference, whether a dispensary doctor or an architect or an engineer or anyone else, to any Mason who does not possess those qualifications possessed by other candidates.[85]

This restricted defence of equality of opportunity, which left open the course of favouring qualified Masons over qualified outsiders, doubtless drew on personal observation of the workings of the Heron Lepper Lodge 346.

When the normal rotation of July anniversary services pointed to St Nicholas's in 1927, Frederick conducted the ceremony but engaged a 'special preacher' to proclaim the unchanging verities of Orangeism ('justice, toleration, loyalty and truth') and its continued value as, so some believed, 'the real source of militant Protestantism which would prevent the encroachment of the enemy' (Rome). The preacher was James Rutherford, then rector of Willowfield in Belfast, who would succeed Frederick as rector of Carrickfergus four years later.[86] In November 1928, Frederick himself addressed another Orange service convened by the local Royal Black Preceptories and the Apprentice Boys of Derry club. Echoing the advice he had offered two decades earlier, he spoke 'not of heroes or traitors of 200 or 250 years ago, but of heroes or traitors of to-day. Who was the man who to-day was undermining the Protestant cause in Ireland? Among such was the intemperate man.' He doubted the effectiveness of either 'local option' or general prohibition (as practised so disastrously in the United States), but urged all Orangemen 'to discourage excessive drinking'. Already, among the 'new villas' of Greenisland and Downshire Park, public fear of property depreciation had prevented the granting of licences through an informal exercise of local option. Eventually, control of the liquor traffic should 'be taken out of private hands'. The 'Orange Society' had already done something 'to discourage intemperance', but should 'work for the ideal that there would be no lodges except total abstinence lodges, and that it would be an unforgiveable offence for a man wearing Orange colours to be seen entering a public house on one of the great days of the Order.'

Orangemen should also resist the encroachment of gambling, 'protect the chastity of women', and help to drive out urban councillors who failed to tackle 'the housing problem in Carrickfergus'. Above all, they should become apostles of peace:

> The day of the blackthorn stick and the revolver and the rifle was over. It was not only a detestable, cruel thing, it was utter futility. It was now absolutely certain that Belfast or any other large city could no longer be defended against attack from the air. They could not be saved from ruin. Put their strength into the things that made for peace, into the movements for brotherhood and reconciliation, and above all be champions of friendly relations between England and America. ... These great nations could preserve the peace of the world.[87]

The prescience of his advice was demonstrated in 1941, when the heart of Belfast, including many prized products of church extension, was destroyed in the Blitz while England prayed helplessly for American intervention.

The death of Stewart Woods, in January 1929, brought a powerful defence of Protestant fraternalism from his 'long-standing friend', the rector. Woods had been 'greatly trusted, greatly honoured' by Freemasons, and 'an acknowledged leader' (as District Master) among Orangemen:

> The Masonic and Orange Societies, in the public mind, are thought of as secret societies, and it is sometimes magined that there is some virtue in signs and passwords and badges. These are but trifles. The real Mason or Orangeman is not the man who can repeat passwords, and make sure of signs and tokens, but he who, day by day, builds his life on a good foundation, and with imperishable materials. Mr. Woods did this. His membership of these societies did not mean antagonism to those who were members of other groups or churches. And he did not make the mistake too often made by others of substituting the Masonic Body or the Orange Society for his Church.

The former artillery officer had been a weekly attender at St Nicholas's and a regular communicant, indeed, a Mr Standfast: 'Having a soldier's faith he did not question the right of his great Captain to command.'[88]

There was another informal brotherhood that Frederick, unlike many denizens of Carrick, did not forget. On Remembrance Sunday, 1929, he preached at the dedication of the St John Memorial Window commemorating members of the Antrim Royal Artillery who had died in the war. The rector read out the 131 names on the town's Roll of Honour, lamenting that many others, 'alas, came back broken men, blinded, maimed, and of those considerable numbers are to-day without the necessaries of life, living in foul slums or in workhouse infirmaries. This is to our discredit as a people.' In retrospect, he celebrated the war years of rationing and sacrifice: 'That was a glorious interval. The spirit of that brief period must be recaptured.' They should dedicate themselves 'to the task of building a new world, a world more just and merciful than that which went down in ruins in the war'.[89] He would return to this theme a year later, when addressing members of the British Legion: 'It is twelve years since the Armistice was signed. The hopes that were then cherished have not been realised.' As 'industrial depression' thickened and the risk of renewed war sharpened, it was essential to recognize the interdependence of nations and seek 'a world unity'.[90]

IV

As befitted a settled country clergyman in his sixties, officially 'Venerable' and presumably approaching retirement, Frederick took up history. By studying the past in Carrickfergus, he could not only pursue the origins of current alliances and antagonisms, but also draw lessons for the enlightenment of his parishioners and neighbours. Between January and June 1928, the *Carrickfergus Advertiser* published weekly instalments of his account of the town from earliest times to the present.[91] Readers were urged to send information and suggestions to David Bell, the editor, especially 'the names of the men, and boys, and women of Carrickfergus who served in the war. ... No denominational distinctions will be made.'[92] Despite the extravagant publicity and opulent presentation of the articles, sometimes using an unusually large and readable fount spread over two columns, only one reader responded with a published letter. When published as a book in Belfast and London as well as Carrickfergus, *Carrickfergus and Its Contacts* attracted two polite notices in the *Belfast News-Letter*, which studiously avoided its more controversial findings.[93] It is in fact a well-informed if quirkily organized history centred on the town, rather than the parish, with an adequate index and brief bibliography. Its chief interest for this biography arises from the numerous political and personal asides, and the rhetorical devices by which Frederick reinforced his growing reputation as a sage and a seer. Like local readers in 1928, we must read such passages not merely as history but as glosses on contemporary debates.

Frederick's account of plantation was measured but notably unenthusiastic, Chichester being depicted as no more callous than his contemporaries: 'It will never be possible to use war as an instrument and not have frightfulness as its concomitant. ... While the Cromwells, and the Chichesters should not be white-washed, yet it should not be suggested that they were entirely black.' He admitted that Antrim was 'by far the most successful of the plantations'. Chichester had 'helped to provide the Presbyterians of Scotland with an opportunity which they knew how to use. He, in some sense, was the architect, and they in great measure were the builders of the Ulster that we know to-day, the Ulster whose three hundred years have helped to enrich the life of the world.' Having not quite justified the means of confiscation by its outcome, he introduced the Covenant debate in the context of 1644, when General Monro was among those subscribing to the Solemn League and Covenant in St Nicholas's church: 'In our judgment the promoters of the League and Covenant failed to discern the signs and needs of the hour. How men, with any knowledge of the English people, could have hoped by such a covenant to compel their conformity to a Presbyterian polity, and to Presbyterian discipline, passes our comprehension.' Touché! In a tilt at obsolete

Orange heroes, he remarked that 'next to nothing had been accomplished since the capture of Carrickfergus' by Schomberg's army before the arrival of William of Orange.[94]

The most delicate issue was that of Home Rule. Until 1914, Frederick had opposed Home Rule on religious grounds and believed that it might still be averted. Once convinced that the demand from nationalists was irresistible, if backed by the British electorate, he had reluctantly accepted that all-Ireland Home Rule would be preferable to partition. Fourteen years later, presumably addressing readers outside Carrickfergus who were unfamiliar with his views at the time, he antedated the unavoidability of Home Rule by a further thirty years:

> The extension of the franchise in 1884 made inevitable some form of Home Rule for Ireland. ... Election after election gave similar results. That surely was a writing on the wall. It was thought, however, that such warnings and verdicts could be disregarded. Arguments were reiterated for more than a generation which were a denial of the assumed meaning of democratic government. The true entity, it was urged, is Great Britain and Ireland. It is the majority in that unit that should count. Why should Ireland be regarded as a separate entity? ... Ireland in so far as it was educated and rich was against Home Rule! Such arguments, and they had a very Prussian ring about them, did duty for a time.[95]

Though quite persuasive as historical analysis, this account disingenuously suggests that the writer had indeed seen 'a writing on the wall' in 1884 rather than 1914, and that those arguments with 'a very Prussian ring' were not his own. Using a device much favoured by his son, Frederick was conducting a debate with his *alter ego*, in which the active voice of John Frederick MacNeice, the hindsightful historian, prevails over the passive voice of Frederick John McNeice, the contemporary actor. For those who remembered the facts, such passages must have provided quiet amusement. For later students, and perhaps even for his son, they fostered a myth that remains prevalent to this day. Likewise, the seemingly fair-minded treatment of Carson and the Covenant is subtly misleading: 'For the policy then contemplated there could not have been found one more competent to act as commander-in-chief, than Sir Edward Carson. He had great qualities of head and heart; he had courage, enthusiasm, quickness, eloquence. ... He stressed the things which appealed inside and outside Ulster. He did not worry about the Pope.'[96] Only initiates would have understood that Frederick, still convinced that Home Rule would be Rome Rule, worried greatly about the Pope in 1912. As for the rector's address declining to sign the Covenant, only the conclusion was quoted in his book, while his eloquent defence of unionism was entirely omitted. Taking these passages together, any intelligent but uninformed reader would have concluded, as so many have, that Frederick was that rare being, a pre-war Protestant Home Ruler in darkest Ulster.

In other respects, the political analysis accurately reflected his views at the time. The book points out the seductive sense of solidarity aroused by the Covenant and the UVF; the baneful effects of partition, whether that defined by national borders or by the informal barriers between parallel communities; the unifying potentiality of Ireland's widespread support for Britain and her wartime allies; the polarizing consequences of the 1916 rebellion; and the failure of the Churches to work for peace:

> It was too late to work for peace when war had begun. On a smaller scale the same was true of Ireland. The lesson to all churches from the Great War is to use the years of peace for their war against war, and that is the lesson to the Churches in Ireland from the dreadful years in which Ireland was a veritable hell.[97]

Nothing in *Carrickfergus* is foolish, unrealistic, or downright untrue; yet, on key issues, the archdeacon let it be known that the rector had seen earlier and further into the political future than the contemporary record attests. His purpose was not vaingloriously to falsify the past, but to give added authority to his continuing campaign for peace and unity.

Though straying far beyond parish boundaries, *Carrickfergus* was above all an affectionate tribute to the town in which Frederick had spent his middle age. His attachment was reaffirmed in July 1930, when he joined 'other well-known residents of Carrickfergus' in expressing 'mingled feelings' in the *Carrickfergus Church Review* about the transfer of the Castle from the army to the government of Northern Ireland. The new owner had economized by ceasing to fly the union flag from the Castle keep:[98]

> Why should the ritualism of flying the flag of St. Patrick, St. Andrew, St. George be encouraged? There were slogans that were very popular a few years ago. One was 'For King and Country'; another, 'Keep the Old Flag Flying'. They served a purpose. Now the thing of immediate importance is to save a few pounds, and so the flag must not fly!

Equally obnoxious was the letting out of grounds in front of the castle in July, bringing 'dishonour' to historic buildings and making the citizens 'humiliated and ashamed – but what can they do?' He asked if readers could 'imagine circus shows, or Punch and Judy shows, or gipsy camps up against the walls of Edinburgh Castle, or Stirling Castle, or Dublin Castle?' The response by the ministry of Finance to publication of his protest was unsatisfactory: 'The matter has not been officially brought to the notice of the Ministry. We do not propose to take any official action or make any answer.'[99] This episode was recounted in a letter to Louis by Beatrice: 'The Circus & Merry go rounds are again outside the Castle – Daddie wrote a sort of protest in his local Magazine, Church Review, & sent it to the Papers too some time ago – there have been several letters fierce[?] about it.'[100] Frederick's protest exhibited both his civic pride and his undiminished loyalty to the monarch and the union.

Frederick's second historical study, *The Church of Ireland in Belfast*, was a disjointed but illuminating account of the development of parishes in Belfast, with obvious lessons concerning the need for further church extension and rationalization. Though based largely on documentary sources and synod reports, it was also a personal record of 'high hopes and great sacrifices' on the part the part of Belfast's clergy and laity, by an observer who since 1898 had been 'watching at close range the fight that goes on for the Church year in, year out, in great city parishes'.[101] It offered a spirited vindication of Frederick's so far unsuccessful campaign for division of the diocese, and a persuasive defence of the sometimes unpopular assessment of individual parishes offered by the Belfast Church Commission. Though not free from the unctuous phraseology commonly used by clergymen when discussing their colleagues in public, its carefully graduated references to the attainments of clergymen of diverse political and doctrinal views illustrate Frederick's skill as a diplomat and as a judge of shades of character. The few autobiographical passages depict the younger Frederick as a hard-working clergyman experiencing the consequences of poor diocesan organization, forming firm friendships and alliances throughout the Church, yet without personal ambition. This work was at once a history, a blueprint for further reform, and potentially an electoral manifesto.

II. *Anointed*

WATERFORD, 1931–1934

I

On 29 April 1931, Frederick and Beatrice had a celebratory tea at Thompson's of Donegall Place. At the diocesan office, he had just heard of his election as bishop of Cashel, with responsibility for no less than three other dioceses (Emly, Waterford and Lismore).[1] Under the democratic but haphazard system whereby diocesan synods then elected bishops, any clergyman could be put forward on the day without prior notice, formal nomination or even the candidate's acquiescence. In practice, synods were presumably preceded by informal consultations between voters and with potential candidates. Frederick was avowedly reluctant to enter the contest in Clonmel, telling Elizabeth that 'I did my best to stop it'.[2] Though the front runner, he faced stiff opposition from the dean (later bishop) of Ossory before securing the requisite two-thirds majority of each order at the third attempt. Initially more popular among the clergy, he eventually won even stronger support from the laity. Though three decades had elapsed since his brief curacy in Cappoquin, virtually all of the Waterford and Lismore clergy backed him from the start.[3] Archbishop Gregg of Dublin, sometimes at odds with the new bishop on issues such as reunion, reassured the joint synod that 'he had known the Archdeacon for many years, and he knew the united diocese had made a wise choice'.[4]

Frederick's elevation aroused little surprise and widespread acclamation in the press. The *Belfast News-Letter* and *Church of Ireland Gazette* both observed that he was 'well-known throughout the [whole] Church', and 'Roamer' of the *News-Letter* devoted three articles to his achievements as 'a practical idealist', local historian, peace campaigner and 'friend of youth'.[5] The Carrickfergus select vestry, 'while deploring the severance occasioned by his removal from our parish', wished him 'long life and happiness in the new sphere of church service to which he has been called'.[6] The *Irish Churchman*, edited by his Belfast ally Richard Breene,[7] was particularly appreciative. While the honour was 'richly deserved', his loss would be 'severely felt' in the diocese 'which he has served so long and faithfully': 'The Archdeacon's interest in the work of the Church has not confined itself to one field only. He has thrown his weight into Church Extension in Belfast, into the World Call movement, and into the Movement for Re-Union. He has also found time for literary work.' The same issue contained many other references to Frederick, including his conjuring of 'order out of chaos' in St Clement's and his success in 'overcoming the initial difficulties' in Carrickfergus, under circumstances 'known to most Churchmen in the diocese'.[8]

Eight days before the parochial presentation on 19 June, he received 'a beautiful episcopal ring from the clergy of the diocese' at a ceremony in Belfast. An amethyst engraved with the diocesan arms was held by 'broad shoulders ... engraved with Celtic interlaced pattern, enclosing in each centre a cross of Celtic design'. Bishop Grierson praised 'his sincerity, his sympathy', his self-effacement, and the 'very real leadership' he had displayed in the campaign for church extension. Several colleagues transcended platitude when recalling his turbulent entry to Carrickfergus. Dean Dowse of Connor declared that he had 'turned hatred into love and bitter opposition into cordial affection', prevailing 'by force of character, Christian life, and the influence he exerted on those who were hostile to him'. Dean Brett of Belfast, himself a candidate for Cashel, revealed that he had acted as intermediary between Frederick and the diocesan authorities 'during those anxious discussions' in 1908. His 'singular gifts' included 'independence of judgment ... in that he did not follow the crowd', along with 'great powers of leadership, and courage'. Canon Clarke observed that 'he was never afraid to stand alone', while other speakers noted his 'interest in the junior clergy' and contribution in keeping the clergy 'abreast of the times in modern thought'. In response, Frederick referred to the 'mis-interpretations' and 'misunderstandings' that he had faced at St Clement's and Carrickfergus, his success in enlightening deluded parishioners, and his determination to avoid needless confrontation: 'I made up my mind that I was not going to fight or resist anything that should be conceded to them.' Likewise, the church as a whole should avoid 'extremes in one direction or another' and follow Bishop Creighton by standing simultaneously 'for truth, liberty and order'.[9]

When the archdeacon of Connor became bishop of Cashel, he exchanged a modest living for opulence, a missionary church for one in terminal decline, and high hopes for placid resignation. Like all bishops, he acquired an honorary Doctorate in Divinity from Trinity College. His annual stipend trebled from £460 to £1479, reflecting the stark class division between priest and prelate. Some forty-four clergymen in four dioceses were in his charge, but the combined church population only just exceeded 3000, compared with 2000 in Carrickfergus alone. Indeed, only one see in Ireland was significantly smaller. The Episcopalian population of Counties Waterford and Tipperary had fallen from 18,000 in 1861 (and 11,000 in 1911) to 6000 in 1926, when it comprised only 2.7 per cent of the census population. Admittedly, 'average' attendance at Sunday services was not far short of 2000 in 1934, suggesting a much higher rate of observance (about three-fifths of the diocesan population) than that in the Belfast region. But returns for 1934 indicate that the Church population had virtually ceased to reproduce itself, pointing to the prospect of imminent extinction. Only four marriages and twelve baptisms were celebrated during that year in Waterford and Lismore, along with nine baptisms in Cashel and Emly. By contrast, 316 baptisms had been performed at Holy Trinity during Frederick's first year as incumbent. Average attendance at the fifteen schools under Church management had fallen well below 200.[10] The new bishop had entered a mausoleum.

Yet there were compensations for a hitherto overworked and underpaid 65-year-old: money, leisure, tranquillity and a pleasant country house. On Ascension Day, 14 May 1931, the MacNeices took the train to Dublin (second-class) and then to Waterford, where they stayed with Dean Mayers. Next day, they were shown the old episcopal palace in Cathedral Square, Waterford, by Archdeacon Burkitt, Frederick's superior at Cappoquin, and then taken to Bishopsgrove, the slightly more modest home with its portico and colonial-style verandah where they were to spend the next three and a half years. Bishopsgrove was pleasantly situated on the north side of the Suir, convenient to the railway station and looking across the river to the city and the cathedral.[11] After lunch with two titled ladies, they retreated to Dublin in 'a comfortable 3rd-class carriage which had once been a 1st-class', as Beatrice recorded with satisfaction at the saving. Following a month devoted to packing the household and engaging servants, they farewelled Carrickfergus on 22 June.[12]

Two days later, the new bishop of Cashel was consecrated in Christ Church Cathedral by Archbishop Gregg, in the presence of six bishops, seven northern clergymen and about fifty parishioners from Carrickfergus. The preacher was Canon Clarke, who celebrated his protégé's unifying influence in the Church:

Never was there a more loyal and zealous colleague, never was there a more trusty, kinder, more tender friend, especially in every hour of need and sore distress. That one so universally esteemed and loved should be called to the See of Cashel they took as a sign from Heaven, as something tending to bind together the whole Church of Ireland.[13]

Luncheon, for sixty 'Carrickfergus people & Clergy of New Diocese', followed at the Royal Hibernian Hotel in Dawson Street.[14] Celebrations continued until the end of July, with separate enthronements in the cathedrals at Waterford, Lismore and finally Cashel (Emly's cathedral having been demolished in 1877). 'Cordial' and 'hearty' welcomes, along with promises of loyalty and co-operation, were also offered by the two diocesan synods meeting in Waterford and Clonmel.[15] The Church in the south-east might be doomed, but its flair for ceremony was undimmed.

II

Frederick did his best to animate his lethargic clergy and ageing laity. In September 1931, he was welcomed by the Waterford and Lismore clerical society with a paper on 'Some Church of Ireland Difficulties in the South'. In addition to 'Secularism', 'modern Criticism', 'Decline of church population', and 'Frequency of mixed marriages', the speaker was alarmed (perhaps unduly) by 'the menace of Dissenting Churches'. In June 1933, the bishop called a joint meeting of the two diocesan clerical societies to hear Chatterton Hammond discuss 'The Present Outlook in Ireland' in more positive vein. Hammond, 'so well known for his work with the I.C.M. Society', offered a 'keen insight into the current events of Ireland, both religious and political', finding 'the outlook hopeful, and the future of the Church of Ireland assured'. The bishop presided over papers ranging from 'The Limitation of Sacrifice in the Old Testament' to 'The Use of Oil in the Church in Connexion with Spiritual Healing', himself introducing discussions on the celebration of St Patrick's landing in Ireland and 'The Authorship of the Gospel of St. John' (his exposition being deemed 'clear and forceful').[16] He also appealed to the Mothers' Union, a shrinking sorority, to activate themselves:

The Bishop's address was listened to with rapt attention, and his appeal to mothers to stand fast by their Christian principles in these days of trials and temptations of youth found an echo in every heart. He dealt specially with the questions of mixed marriages and gambling, and exhorted all mothers present to a frequent attendance at Holy Communion, the unfailing source of inestimable blessings.[17]

Optimist though he was, Frederick must have been dispirited by the futility of preaching at his cathedral in Waterford, with only ten worshippers at morning service on 9 August 1931. That evening, as was his wont, he 'asked people to sit nearer together'.[18] The annual reports of his diocesan councils were invariably depressing, in keeping with the economy throughout the period of his episcopate. The mood was further darkened by the electoral triumphs of de Valera's Fianna Fáil in February 1932 and January 1933, leading to 'economic war' with the United Kingdom and the progressive dismantling of the Free State's connection with the British Commonwealth. As the Waterford and Lismore synod was informed by the diocesan council in June 1932: 'The general depression through which the world is passing has left its mark both directly and indirectly upon the finances of our Diocese. ... The future of our Church is, in many ways, disconcerting as to its outcome.' The prospect failed to brighten over the following year: 'What the days to come have in store for our Church in this land none can foresee – Our numbers have decreased, and at times the outlook is not encouraging.' As for Cashel and Emly: 'Economic depression and political uncertainty have borne heavily on our country and our Church, and yet, with some exceptions, our people and clergy have shown great self-sacrifice in supporting the funds and assessments of their parishes and have deepened their devotion in the service of the Church.'[19]

In his Waterford address in June 1932, Frederick declared that the numerical decline had far-reaching implications, since the Church was intrinsically capable of making 'a contribution of a distinctive kind not only to the spiritual life of Ireland, but also to the spiritual life of the world'. Its influence might help counteract the 'mental states, hatreds, distrusts, prejudices, plottings for revenge which are keeping people apart'. These divisive forces were exacerbated by de Valera's economic doctrine: 'If economic nationalism has broken down everywhere – in countries large and small – it is not likely to succeed here. Rigid economic nationalism to-day, with all its necessary protective devices, could not but result in lowering the standard of life for the masses of the people.' Still more insidious was Ireland's lingering attachment to violence:

> In the not too distant past, too, one of the tragedies in Irish life was that so many in every camp and every party, no matter how they differed on everything else, were in agreement as to the presumed necesssity and wisdom of putting their trust in force. This not only kept men apart, but helped to perpetuate suspicion and mistrust. ... If the world is to be saved, if Ireland is to be saved the way of the Cross must be taken.[20]

In his novel rôle as spiritual leader of a vulnerable minority, Frederick took care to establish cordial relations with his Catholic counterpart as bishop of Waterford and Lismore, Bernard Hackett. Having abandoned academic life in his forties to become a Redemptorist, Hackett presumably shared elements of Frederick's missionary and evangelical outlook, despite ugly past confrontations between Redemptorists and Soupers in the West of Ireland.[21] In September 1931, the two bishops converged at the funeral of a Protestant solicitor, a gesture almost inconceivable in Belfast if not in Carrickfergus.[22] A few weeks later, as Beatrice drily recorded: 'Derrick drove to call on R.C. Bishop – He was out.'[23] After Hackett's death in June 1932, 'a stream of sympathisers' visited the Palace, St John's Hill, to pay homage to his remains. The *Irish Independent* deemed it noteworthy that Frederick was 'amongst the early callers', though he was not listed among the clerical multitude attending the funeral.[24] Tentative as they were, Frederick's ecumenical overtures were never to be replicated after his return to Ulster.

III

Though his flock was minuscule, Frederick's influence in the Church of Ireland was vastly extended by his elevation. As a member of the House of Bishops, he belonged ex-officio to the Representative Church Body, which governed the church's finances, as well as the standing committee of the general synod. Like every Irish bishop, he also became a vice-president of the Society for Irish Church Missions to the Roman Catholics. Equally automatic was his election to the Dublin University Club, which served as a second home for the elders of the church: 'Regularly during synod week and RCB week almost all the episcopal bench would spend a few nights in the Club and when after dinner, the bishops, gartered and aproned, could be seen confabulating with the other dignities or joining with mellowed common sense in genial conversation, a whiff of pre-disestablishment days lingered in the air.'[25] At the time of Frederick's enrolment in 1931, every serving prelate belonged to the club, only four having joined before their ascension. Those living more than twenty-five miles outside Dublin paid only six rather than ten guineas per annum, and for four shillings could enjoy an ample dinner of soup, fish, joint, sweet, and savoury courses. The fine port would not have interested Frederick, and he was doubtless too venerable to play squash racquets on the court erected in 1930. But he presumably welcomed the company of the innumerable Trinity men who drifted in and out of the handsome house on St Stephen's Green, most of the lay members being lawyers or medical practitioners (women were not yet admitted even as visitors). By the 1930s, the club was no longer useful in cultivating judges, politicians, or senior civil servants, but it did include four peers and even one Roman Catholic priest.[26]

As bishop of Cashel he remained active in the general synod, but had little new to contribute in a period of falling revenues and institutional stagnation. In May 1932, he introduced yet another anodyne report from the Home Re-Union committee with some weariness: 'It had been accepted that if there was essential agreement between two churches – if each side believed that the other held the principles of the Christian faith – there might be considerable divergence on other points.' He left it to his old friend Canon Newport White, Regius Professor of Divinity at Trinity, to point out the boundaries of reunion in Ireland: 'One of the tragedies of Ireland to-day was that men of goodwill in the Roman Catholic Church were unable, owing to the domination of their clergy, to co-operate as they would wish with Protestants in trying to stem the tide of Communistic and revolutionary principles into this country.'[27] Two years later, Frederick addressed the annual service at St Patrick's Cathedral that preceded the synod, closely paraphrasing his celebrated words of July 1920:

> We are here, in the providence of God, in a small country, side by side, some in one communion, some in another. There must be a purpose in it, and an opportunity. It must be that we are here, not to destroy or hurt one another, but to help one another, and in the spirit of Christ, as His disciples, to bear a distinctive kind of witness. Ireland means much to us who are gathered together in this old church. Consistently with loyalty to Christ there is nothing we would not do for her honour and her peace. But He must be first, He must be Lord. Without reserve our first loyalty must be given to Him.[28]

A few days later, he reaffirmed the link between social reform and ecumenicism when seeking adoption of a report, resulting from prolonged consultations with like-minded Presbyterians, which advocated 'a common expression of the mind of Christ towards war' and deplored the depth of poverty revealed by a Dublin social worker. These views proved too radical for the synod, which eventually declined to endorse such sentiments.[29] Despite this minor setback, Frederick was appointed as one of the synod's five representatives to the Second World Conference on Faith and Order, to be held in 1937.[30] This resulted in an invitation to Hertenstein, on Lake Lucerne, where a preparatory meeting of the 'continuation committee' was held in September 1934. Frederick spent almost a fortnight discussing 'The Church and the Word' and 'The Church and the World' with representatives of Russian, German, French, Scandinavian and various British denominations under the adroit direction of William Temple, archbishop of York.[31] In his lakeside hotel, surrounded by kindred spirits, the prospect of bringing man to God must have seemed brighter than in lonely Bishopsgrove.

Untroubled by the incessant demands upon a northern clergyman, Frederick had ample leisure for reading, writing, and conferring on topics of global significance. Even in Carrickfergus, he had laced his sermons with references to world affairs: just before his elevation to Cashel, he had attributed the 'upheavals in Russia and Spain' to the fact that 'in both countries the masses of the people had been kept in ignorance for generations'.[32] In February 1932, he completed a collection of essays and addresses entitled *Spiritual Rebirth or World Revolution*, devoted to the evil of war and the duty of Christians 'to repent of our corporate love of militarism', to acknowledge the interdependence of all nations, and to follow Christ in the struggle against injustice and dangerous state experiments, especially in Russia.[33] He continued to publish individual sermons through the Church of Ireland Printing and Publishing Company in Dublin, one of which was advertised along with *Spiritual Rebirth* in the same issue of the *Church of Ireland Gazette*.[34]

In October 1932, he contributed a paper on 'War and Peace' to a conference in the Mansion House, Dublin, celebrating 1500 years of the Church of Ireland since the landing of St Patrick. Having pointed out that both Protestant and Catholic churches had adhered unquestioningly to St Augustine's doctrine of the 'just war' until 1914, he detected 'a profound change in Christian thinking' evident in the resolutions of the Lambeth conference in 1930. The development of air power meant that 'the war of the future would be against whole populations. The business of the attacking force would be to exterminate, quickly and mercilessly, whole and sick, old and young, men and women and children.' It would be possible 'to destroy enemy cities, but not possible to defend your own'. As the League of Nations developed, 'absolute national sovereignty must be somewhat abated'. It was surely time 'for a movement towards a true internationalism, a world community', which would transcend national antagonisms: 'In so far as the world is a world covenanted for peace, then within that world war would be a crime against God and man.'

As for Frederick's homeland:

Within Ireland to-day there is no problem, political or economic, which necessitates the use of physical force for its solution. ... An apostle would say, I think: 'Forget that past, the story of old feuds, old antipathies, old triumphs, old humiliations. They belong to a stage of human development that was immature. Many of the worst things were done in ignorance, or in violent passion, and few of the things, good or bad, have any relevance to the world in which we live.'

Like de Valera, Frederick believed that Ireland could contribute decisively to the new order: 'Her influence for the spiritual, and in the advocacy of peace, might be felt throughout the world.'[35] From the vantage-point of sleepy Waterford, the archaic passions of Ireland, so insistent in the fractious north, seemed mere ripples across the inexorable tidal wave of internationalism.

In June 1934, Frederick reminded the Waterford synod that 'no European nation was now an independent, economic unit. Conditions in the Far East and the Far West determined the standard of life in Cork or Waterford.' Any future war would entail 'ruin' for all those involved, whether combatants or non-combatants, since all countries were vulnerable to air attacks and chemical warfare:

> The world was largely without the right kind of leadership to-day, because the men who had the gifts for leadership died in the war. The unemployed still numbered millions, while there existed a great multitude, never yet accurately numbered, of broken men, blinded, maimed, paralysed, and those once the pride and glory of their families were now worse than dead. The Church should take the lead, for Christians must condemn war not merely because it was wasteful and a ruinous cause of untold misery, but because it was contrary to the will of God.[36]

IV

Agreeable though it was, Frederick was utterly unfulfilled by his life as bishop of Cashel. His missionary instinct, 'solitary and wild', propelled him towards more challenging and dangerous terrain. Throughout his tenure, he retained a close connection with northern affairs and kept his options open. The *News-Letter's* review of *The Church of Ireland in Belfast*, published just after his election as bishop, declared that it should be in the hands of all those at the forthcoming general synod, where 'the Belfast Church problem will again come up for discussion'. Frederick was 'a man of vision, who has frequently shown that he is also well able to appreciate practical difficulties and considerations'.[37] When successfully urging the synod to increase the allocation for Belfast church extension from £50,000 to £75,000, Frederick declared that the proposal involved 'the North and South working together, so that adequate witness might be borne by the Church as a whole'. He had already received a warm welcome as bishop-elect from Primate D'Arcy: 'His utterances have always commanded our deep attention.'[38]

Frederick repeatedly returned to his old diocese to preach in churches and cathedrals, reinforcing his reputation as a statesman of the church. At Knockbreda, in October 1931, he declared that the Church of Ireland 'is in Ireland, she is of Ireland, she is for Ireland. Free from all State and political entanglements she can to-day give her best to Ireland, and help to bring near the Kingdom of God.'[39] Six months later, at the dedication of St Polycarp's, Finaghy, he proclaimed that the Church of Ireland (as of England) was 'the true Catholic church of the country', embodying 'the historical succession, and, better still, she has preserved all the essentials of the faith which is Catholic'.[40] At the special commemoration service in Downpatrick for the landing of St Patrick in 432 AD, Frederick read the prayers; and at the general synod in May 1934, he supported Dean Kerr of Belfast in his spirited rejection of a 'revisionist' account casting doubt on Patrick's reputed landing at Saul.[41]

At St Anne's Cathedral, on 3 May 1933, he launched a ferocious attack on the contemporary 'ideals' of 'Communism, Fascism, and Americanism', each of which was a 'denial of Christ' demanding resistance from Christian youth world-wide. Speaking three months after Hitler's electoral triumph and one month after the inception of a national boycott of Jewish businesses and professions in Germany, he declared that 'Fascism, such as is dominant in Germany, means the revival of Paganism. ... By its brutal treatment of the Jews the Fascist Government has made sure of an inglorious immortality for itself.'[42] As Fauske suggests, Frederick may have been the first Irish bishop to denounce the persecution of German Jews; though in England condemnations had already been voiced by the Anglican bishops of Manchester and Fulham, the Catholic bishops of Salford and Nottingham, and the British organization of the World Evangelical Alliance.[43] Frederick's outlook had surely broadened since his crass response to Louis's engagement to a 'Jewess' in 1929.

Two months later, he resumed his assault on pew-rents with particular reference to St George's, stating that 'pew rents and appropriated sittings do not harmonize with the missionary idea, and when the Church loses the missionary spirit in her work she tends to become a sort of social club'.[44] These addresses were published in spring 1934 in Frederick's second book on the church in Belfast, which reminded the northern clergy that he was still deeply engaged with their local problems and opportunities. Far more than a local study, as one reviewer pointed out when praising the book for its broad scope and 'very wide reading', *Some Northern Churchmen* was indeed 'a splendid shilling's worth'.[45] Frederick's interest in his old diocese was reaffirmed in October 1934, when he gave a paper to the diocesan clerical society in Belfast on the recent conference at Lucerne on Faith and Order. Frederick averred that 'the outlook was very hopeful'. His paper drew a bumper attendance of sixty-three, with responses from many old associates including Canon Clarke, Dean Kerr, Richard Breene and John Bristow. Bristow, another delegate at Lucerne, may have unsettled the audience by observing 'that the Anglo-Catholic representatives at the Conference were the most charitably disposed of all'. Kerr, ever hopeful, 'spoke chiefly of the possibility of Re-union in Ireland'. The timeliness of Frederick's visit was underlined by a resolution regretting 'the approaching resignation of the Bishop of Down'.[46]

If the challenge of Belfast had not lost its rugged allure, the MacNeices (especially Beatrice) undoubtedly enjoyed the rustic surroundings and relative comfort of Bishopsgrove. Frederick's siblings and their families, who with the exception of Herbert had scarcely visited the rectory in Carrickfergus, now came to stay 'quite a lot'. According to Elizabeth, he had always 'kept in touch with all his brothers & sisters & their children', providing an indirect link between relatives long separated from each other 'because of their touchiness & quarrelling'.[47] In August 1931, 'Madre' wrote to Elizabeth about her visit to Italy and Corsica with John Nicholson, recalling her own past holidays and extolling the 'wonderful Summer weather' in Waterford, the succession of house guests, and the diverting sight of a small rat passing the drawing-room window in search of crumbs sprinkled by a servant. Frederick wrote to his daughter on the same day:

> 'I think we must get a small boat for the river. We have been over much of Tipperary. It is beautiful. … Let us know something of Corsica: I suppose you will see Napoleon's birth place. Send us even post cards so that we may know where you are & follow you on the map. I should like to pay for part of your holiday. Why should Sir Charles [Nicholson] have all the pleasure?'[48]

In the following month, 'men came to wire 3 lamps for Electric lights in afternoon. … Used Electric Standard for 1st time in Drawing room.'[49] Gone and unregretted were the flickering candles and gas lamps of Carrickfergus.

A few days later, Louis and Mary arrived for three weeks' holiday, amply recorded in a family photograph album. On Louis's twenty-fourth birthday, Beatrice reasserted her superior wealth despite her husband's inflated salary: 'I gave him cheque £10 & Derrick cheque for £6.' These gifts were perhaps more needful than Frederick's earnest offering a month earlier, on his wife's forty-ninth birthday: 'Derrick gave me a Prayer Book – & New Testament – a Gospel & Acts Oxford Student's Edition.'[50] As usual, there were occasional signs of family friction, exhibited in diary entries recording tours and lunches that Louis and Mary managed to avoid. Yet the frisky young couple 'made place in pig sty' for a new puppy named Dominic, played croquet with Frederick and Beatrice, dutifully attended the cathedral, visited the Rock of Cashel by car, and accepted gifts (Beatrice spent 16s. 6d. on a black shawl for her black-haired stepdaughter-in-law).

Shortly before retreating to Dublin and Liverpool, Louis 'looked up his old school photos etc.', a sure sign of amity as the holiday neared its end.[51] Free from the troubling associations of Carrickfergus and Belfast, Bishopsgrove supplied an agreeably neutral site for family reunions and reappraisals. Birmingham remained problematic, as Louis indicated to Anthony Blunt three weeks after the arrival of Daniel: 'My family are coming over tomorrow for a weekend in B'ham. I told you they have been much humanised by living in the South? But they will, I fear, want the creature to be christened; not that they will get it, & the nurse won't even let them see it having its bath.'[52] A less driven 68-year-old might have played out the mellow rôles of bishop, paterfamilias and grandfather by succumbing to dotage in drowsy Waterford.

Yet Frederick remained unsettled. In October 1933, he received considerable initial backing in the episcopal election for Cork, Cloyne, and Ross, a far more populous and important diocese than Cashel. Though rapidly losing support over the four rounds of voting, he scored almost as many lay votes in the preliminary contest for the 'select list' as the eventual winner, Archdeacon Flewett of Cork.[53] This well-publicized contest made it clear that the bishop of Cashel was not content to linger in his backwater by the Suir. Scarcely a year later, the retirement of old Bishop Grierson created the vacancy which Frederick had surely been anticipating for almost a decade. The prize was the still undivided diocese of Down and Connor and Dromore.

12. Saviour

BELFAST, 1934–1936

I

A fortnight before Christmas 1934, Frederick MacNeice was elected bishop of Down in a protracted contest. As usual, synodsmen had been subjected to extensive canvassing over the previous fortnight, leading to a warning through the press by eleven leading Churchmen that votes should not be pledged 'rashly or prematurely'. The signatories called for the appointment of 'a man of affairs' with 'deep spiritual power', 'proved learning', and 'broad outlook'.[1] They themselves were accused of indirect canvassing, since 'broad outlook' signified 'toleration and support for everything that is popular at the moment', while 'man of affairs' suggested 'clever manipulation, astute arrangement, and compromise'.[2] For some conservative synodsmen, Frederick would have seemed the very embodiment of these dubious qualities. Though the front runner, he required three ballots to achieve the required two-thirds majority in both orders, as a result of pronounced lay support for Dean Kerr of Belfast and James Quinn, the rector of St Jude's in Ballynafeigh. Kerr, a leading Orangeman who shared many of Frederick's evangelical and social views, scored almost as strongly in the preliminary vote for a select list, but lost most of his support to Frederick in subsequent ballots when synodsmen could support only one candidate.[3]

After the inconclusive second ballot, it seemed likely that the appointment would have to be referred to the Bench of Bishops with unpredictable consequences.

Canon Clarke of Carnmoney, Frederick's predecessor at Holy Trinity, reminded the synod that 'for 64 years, that great diocese had always elected its own bishop. Northern Irish people liked to do their own work, and every bishop had come to them assured beforehand of the hearty sympathy, support, and welcome of the whole diocese.' Though Clarke's motion for an hour's adjournment was rejected in favour of an immediate additional ballot, this left Frederick with 429 supporters among the 537 voters, including 88 per cent of the clergy and 74 per cent of lay synodsmen. William Dowse, the former dean of Connor, admitted that 'they had had their difficulties that day, but they were unanimous in expressing their delight in having with them the Lord Primate'. D'Arcy himself was more forthright in congratulating his old ally, assuring the synod that they had 'elected a true man to be their bishop'.[4]

Frederick was not caught off-guard by the synod's decision, dictating a well-rehearsed manifesto by telephone to the *Northern Whig* on the night of his election:

> I am returning to the scenes of over thirty years' labour with the desire, God helping me, to maintain and set forward quietness, love, and peace among all men. When I was consecrated Bishop I was charged to show myself gentle and to be merciful for Christ's sake to poor and needy people, to be to the flock a shepherd, holding up the weak, bringing again the outcast, seeking the lost. This I shall endeavour to do. I shall, I know, have many opportunities of encouraging the members of our Church to join with those of other Churches in bearing a common witness where there is a common conviction. ... In the distant past Ireland was a missionary nation to other nations. In another sense she could be so again.[5]

He seemed ready and eager to resume the campaigns and projects that he had pursued so boldly as a reformist archdeacon, thus renewing the missionary zeal of his own 'distant past'.

Frederick's translation from sleepy Waterford to stormy Belfast, at the age of sixty-eight, did not startle seasoned observers any more than himself. The *Church of Ireland Gazette* remarked that 'it would be a very difficult task for a stranger to take up the reins with rapidity, so that it was no surprise to see that all the votes were cast for well-known clergymen whose lives have been spent chiefly in Ulster. The many friends whom the Bishop of Cashel made in his brief stay in the South will pray that he may long have health and strength for the more exacting work to which he is now called.' He had already exhibited noteworthy 'powers of comprehension and concentration' while at Carrickfergus. These sentiments were echoed by the Cashel clerical union, which surprisingly farewelled him in Hayes's Commercial and Family Hotel, Thurles, in whose billiard-room the Gaelic Athletic Association had been conceived in 1884: 'During his short tenure of the See the Bishop proved himself a very practical man, well able to deal with the various problems that arose. And he was always sympathetic, kindly and helpful to his clergy in the Diocese of Cashel and Emly, who will miss him very much.'[6]

Various articles in the always sympathetic *Belfast News-Letter* remembered him as 'a cultured preacher and an indefatigable worker' when still a curate, whose appointment would 'be approved generally in the united diocese and throughout the Church of Ireland'. He had not only won 'the affections of his people' as 'a preacher and a pastor', but 'revealed administrative qualities of a high order' while officiating in Connor.[7] The *Northern Whig* likewise praised his 'pastoral work', 'administrative and organising qualities', and 'gifts of leadership': 'In the highest councils of the Church Dr. MacNeice will be a stimulating and progressive influence. To him the words of the Lord Primate may be applied without reservation: he is a man of learning, of wide outlook, of broad sympathies.'[8] The *Belfast Telegraph*, while noting his 'great energy and devotion', 'eloquence', 'high literary attainments', and involvement with 'progressive movements', was less fulsome:

> If the new Bishop has not been equally happy in dealing with the Irish political situation, he has been in good company, for here all those who venture tread on slippery ground. The events of the past few years have greatly widened the cleavage between North and South, and the aspirations of those who were reluctant to acknowledge the permanence of division have become less and less likely of fulfilment as time passed.[9]

Despite such warnings and his own repugnance for politics, Frederick would soon be drawn once more on to that 'slippery ground'.

He started work on New Year's Day by administering Holy Communion to one hundred worshippers at Downpatrick and burying one of his clergy. Next day, when welcomed by the diocesan council, he declared 'that the biggest task in the Church of Ireland was before him', but that 'the people of the diocese had never failed when called upon. They were good material.'[10] In February, he endured no less than four ceremonies of enthronement, notably in St Anne's Cathedral where the lesson was read by Canon Clarke and the induction performed by his friendly rival, Dean Kerr. More than one hundred 'surpliced clergy and lay readers' greeted the new bishop, resplendent in red, white and black vestments, by singing 'Hail to the Lord's Anointed'. He used this occasion to extol his predecessors, wittily beginning with Aengus Mac Nissi (who died in 514), but concentrating on Crozier (memorable for 'his energy, his enthusiasm, his eloquence, his joyousness') and D'Arcy ('our foremost man, trusted, honoured, loved by the whole Church').[11] For the time being, Frederick's manner had lost its sharper edge, as he mellowed into the persona of an eminent divine, at ease with prelates and primates, adept at selecting the appropriate cliché for every clerical occasion. Yet a touch of black humour enlivened his eulogy for Bishop Grierson, whose memorial service at St Anne's was performed on the eve of the Twelfth in 1935. He informed the congregation that the widowed bishop's 'last words were: "Oh, Christ," and then after a brief interval, "Here is my beloved wife." Beautiful this reunion in the heavenly places.'[12] Perhaps Frederick looked forward with equally mixed feelings to his own impending reunion with Lily.

His duties as bishop of three dioceses with about 230 clergymen and nearly a quarter of a million nominal Episcopalians were formidable, but punctiliously performed until recurrent illness intervened in the last 3 years of his life. The Church population of the Belfast region had continued to expand between the census-takings of 1926 and 1937, though remaining proportionately stable at 28 per cent.[13] Boundless energy and especially patience were required to maintain the relentless round of committee meetings, ceremonial services and addresses, ordinations, appointments, parochial visitations and confirmations. Bishops were also expected to preside at a host of meetings organized by church societies. As in Waterford, Frederick was particularly intent on broadening the minds of his clergy through the diocesan clerical society. Having graciously accepted his second episcopal ring at the first gathering after his enthronement, he attended all of its quarterly meetings up to the end of 1936. In October he responded to 'a graphic description of the Missionary conditions of the Church in China' by his old friend from Carrickfergus, Bishop John Hind of Fukien. Over the following year, he commented on topics as diverse as 'Social and Religious Conditions in Russia', 'The Present Position in Germany: Political, Ecclesiastical, and Religious', a controversial appendix to the Church Hymnal, and 'Bible References in English Literature'.[14]

He remained a vice-president and staunch supporter of the Society for Irish Church Missions, which organized sermons in thirty-one Belfast churches on the Sunday following his enthronement at St Anne's. Though unable to attend Monday's annual meeting of its Belfast Auxiliary, he 'wrote that the work of the Missions was primarily a work of witness for the faith in its primative [*sic*], uncorrupted form. That witness should be borne by everyone of them in a spirit of love. Nothing was accomplished by bitterness.' Dean Kerr was left to amplify Frederick's message of love by offering a stout defence of 'proselytism' while dismissing charges of 'souperism' as 'a ludicrous slander'. Chatterton Hammond, widely reviled as 'the prince of soul snatchers' in his capacity as superintendent of the Dublin Missions, rather testily concurred 'that religious controversy should be conducted without temper, bitterness, or unhappy reflections upon the method and motives of those from whom they differed. That, however, was exceedingly hard to maintain when there was a constant campaign of slander in the Roman Catholic Press.'[15] The rancour exhibited in the Omey conflict, more than half a century earlier, had not yet fully dissipated.

No bishop of such a diverse and volatile diocese could hope to avoid criticism and controversy arising from his actions and also inactions. His decision to send a deputy to the Armistice Day ceremony outside City Hall, involving representatives of all major denominations except the Roman Catholic Church, aroused public murmurs and several defensive statements in November 1935. As he explained in a rather convoluted explanatory letter to the press:

> I preached to two Armistice services on Sunday to large congregations. From the inception of the Poppy Day movement I have done everything in my power to encourage the public to give it whole-hearted support. But when circumstances permit, I prefer to be in one of our Cathedrals on Armistice Day itself, rather than elsewhere, for the observance of the Two Minutes' Silence.

Though Frederick 'volunteered to sell poppies if necessary' and constantly invoked the memory of fallen servicemen, his repeated avoidance of the main civic commemoration was understandably interpreted as an attempt to prevent political contamination of the spiritual sphere.[16]

As an indefatigable proponent of redirecting scarce resources from depopulated parishes to expanding suburbs with inadequate clerical provision, he was bound to arouse apprehension and sometimes hostility in embattled congregations. After Beatrice had opened a sale of work in support of his depopulated former parish, Holy Trinity, Frederick initially lulled his listeners with memories of 'the green fields stretching from its doors to the Antrim Road', as recounted by parishioners in 1899, and of his 'extraordinarily happy' seven and a half years in the parish. Yet there was latent menace in his subsequent observation that the vicar 'had a most difficult charge, for the character of the parish had changed in recent years'.[17] The bishop sometimes found it difficult to induce young clergymen to enter fractious parishes of the kind he had himself tackled so effectively. Particular problems arose when attempts were made to amalgamate shrinking parishes under a single incumbent. In March 1936, Dean Kerr informed him that two candidates for such a post had resisted appointment, one feeling that it 'would not suit him' and the other recoiling from the 'atmosphere of hostility'. As Kerr expostulated: 'The young clergy of today have "no guts". ... You were not afraid of atmosphere and hostility in St Clements or Carrickfergus! D— is keen to get back to Clogher and I fancy may have heard that Bishop of Clogher is retiring.'[18] The challenge was eventually accepted by the elderly rector of Billy, formerly a chaplain for the Irish Church Missions and also for the wartime forces.[19] He at least had spirit enough to outface the restive parishioners, after a surly initiation that Beatrice reported in her diary: 'D[errick] had early <u>dinner</u> & left at 6.55 for Institution of Canon Morrow in Ballyscullion at 8 p.m. People dis[s]atisfied with choice of Re[a]ding & resigned from Vestry & choir after D. left.'[20] Every attempt at rationalization and reform tended to expose fault-lines within the Episcopalian community, where issues of faith, doctrine, ritual and ecclesiastical authority were still passionately contested by laymen as well as ministers.

The persistence of economic depression throughout the 1930s, despite fluctuations in unemployment and production, restricted the opportunities for church extension and radical reorganization, these being dependent on the munificence of laymen. Collections and subscriptions in the united diocese fell short of £130,000 in the year of Frederick's election (about 10s. per capita), only once exceeding this modest tally in the remaining years of his episcopate.[21] Declining interest rates had drastically reduced the income from capital funds, both local and central, and the diocese could no longer provide emergency help to poor parishes without falling into debt. At his first diocesan synod as bishop, Frederick therefore advocated a Diocesan Endowment Fund to enable the Church to pursue its struggle against secularism and indifference. This inspired a rather sceptical leading article in the *News-Letter*, hoping 'that the response will be equal to those needs and worthy of the Bishop's leadership'. The initial aim of this appeal, launched in February 1936, was to induce the laity to raise £10,000 for parochial equipment, in addition to their normal contributions. Despite 'generous contributions' from the minister of commerce, John Milne Barbour, this target had barely been met by November 1937.[22] More ambitious financial remedies were clearly demanded.

As bishop of Ireland's most populous diocese, Frederick played a major part in the central government of the Church of Ireland. All bishops belonged *ex officio* to the Representative Church Body and the standing committee of the general synod, as well as several of its subsidiary committees. When bishop of Cashel, he had been a faithful participant in the RCB, the administrative and financial hub of the Church, but less zealous in attending bodies associated with the general synod, such as the standing committee and the board of education. After elevation to Belfast, he was even more assiduous in attending RCB meetings, despite being drafted on to two additional committees. Between 1935 and 1938 he attended over four-fifths of these meetings, though often neglecting his synod committees.[23] These commitments entailed frequent travel to Dublin, where all such meetings were held, always requiring an overnight or longer stay, presumably in the Dublin University Club. He spent thirty-nine days in the Free State in the financial year 1935/6, thirty in 1936/7, and twenty-eight in 1937/8.[24] In practical as well as ideological terms, Frederick remained an all-Ireland minister.

As a church politician, his initial preoccupation after returning to Belfast was to promote co-operation between the Church of Ireland and its major Presbyterian rival. Within a fortnight of taking up duty in Belfast, he joined the moderator and the Methodist president in supporting the League of Nations' Union in its demand that international disputes be referred to arbitration. If only the League could be empowered 'to guarantee peace to the world', then 'the sacrifices made by brave men in the Great War' would not have been in vain.[25] Joint advocacy of good causes did not, however, entail organizational unity. In May 1935, an 'animated debate' was initiated at the general synod by Dean Kerr of Belfast, who proposed that 'the Church of Ireland fully and freely recognises, as a basis for future progress towards union, the validity, efficacy and spiritual reality of both ordination and sacraments as administered in the Presbyterian Church'. This resolution embodied the recommendations of a synod committee, including Kerr and the bishop, which had for several years been trying to resolve or bypass the remaining points of contention between the churches. Archbishop Gregg of Dublin, once an eloquent advocate of collaboration, proposed an amendment stating that reunion along the lines proposed at the last two Lambeth conferences offered 'no present prospect of success', and deferring the issue 'until more promising methods of approach present themselves'. After an ugly procedural struggle between Gregg and the Primate's 'assessor', Lord Justice Best from Belfast, Kerr responded that Gregg's amendment 'would definitely mean the end of all efforts at reunion', an assertion that provoked further bickering.

Frederick, despite his long-standing alliance with Kerr, sensed that further pursuit of inter-church reunion would dangerously disunite their own church:

> It was quite obvious that the passing of this resolution would not further the cause of reunion, because the Synod itself was divided on the resolution. If they passed it, the division would be more pronounced. At this stage there were continuous calls from a part of the Synod for 'Vote, vote.' The Primate had to ring the bell for order.

Primate D'Arcy, who had hitherto appeared to favour Kerr's resolution, wobbled towards the same opinion, stating cagily that 'he was in favour of the original motion, but he would much rather that the Archbishop's amendment were passed (Laughter).' He wished at all costs to avoid the overt rejection of Kerr's resolution or its approval by a bare majority. Gregg's amendment was then passed by 'a considerable majority' of hands, and (despite D'Arcy's plea) the substantive motion was put and thrown out with only a few supporters.[26] The controversy simmered on for a week or so in the press, but the defeat of reunion became undeniable in early June when the Presbyterian General Assembly discharged its committee on Church Union (not 'Reunion') as 'further negotiations seem out of the question at present'.[27] In casting his weight behind Gregg rather than Kerr, Frederick exposed the degree to which he had become an episcopal insider.

Frederick never allowed his preoccupation with financial, managerial and tactical problems to deflect him from the broader battle against unbelief. He had long believed that the major threat to Christianity, in Belfast and the world at large, was no longer Roman Catholicism but secularism. In mid June 1935, he brushed off threats from an influential Low-Church layman obsessed by the influence in the Church of former Romanists:

> The issues which divide mankind to-day are far removed from those which seem to have most interest to you. There is increasing secularism. I have reason to believe that there is 'Red' propaganda in Belfast and that it is becoming more and more menacing. I am considering at present how this menace may be met, and the Community safeguarded against the assaults of Paganism. This is the enemy at our doors and the immediate need, I believe, is the deepening of the religious life of the whole community.[28]

He expanded this theme when addressing the diocesan synod in November:

> Unless there is increased activity on our part the drift to secularism will, I believe, be rapid and pronounced. ... Our country has to a far greater extent than is commonly realised come under the influence of Continental movements of a reactionary and anti-social character. The real issue to-day is, I believe, between two interpretations of the meaning of human life, one secular and materialistic, the other spiritual.

Whereas the old 'secular humanism' had merely 'ignored religion', contemporary movements aggressively rejected it: 'But the rejection of God results in the rejection of man also. His personality loses its sacredness. He becomes a thing which may be scrapped in the interests of some theory of class or state, or race.'[29] The vocation of the bishop of Down was not merely to build church halls, pay long-service annuituies, and tinker with prayer books, but to bring the soul of man to God.

II

Even as he cemented his episcopal alliances, Frederick was preparing for a notably unconventional attempt to apply his prestige in defence of the spiritual well-being of Belfast. The need for a moral crusade was heightened by worsening violence on the city's streets and further sectarian polarization, prompted by celebrations of the Silver Jubilee of King George V in early May. Political animosity was excerbated by heavy unemployment, widespread poverty and chronic shortage of working-class housing, which conspired to set Protestant and Catholic workers at each others' throats. The northern government's ban on demonstrations, imposed on 18 May but rescinded on 27 June (in time for the Twelfth), had further shaken stability by provoking many Belfast Orangemen and chaplains into open denunciations of Craigavon's government.

Frederick's first priority in this crisis was to discourage his clergy from becoming engulfed in sectarian conflict or illegalities. When dedicating a window in memory of Dean Brett of Belfast on 29 June, he observed that 'aloofness from party politics was another characteristic of his long ministry. I do not suppose he ever delivered a political speech. No pronouncement of his can be recalled in which there was even a trace of bitterness.' He further pronounced that 'the influence that is gained by a clergyman in the political sphere lessens his influence in the spiritual sphere'.[30] Eight days later, as rioting intensified and the resumption of sectarian civil war seemed imminent, he returned to the themes he had so eloquently and effectively pursued while rector of Carrickfergus. In a sermon at St Thomas's, Belfast, he expounded the text that 'Ye have heard that it was said, An eye for an eye and a tooth for a tooth; but I say unto you, resist not him that is evil' (Matt. 5: 38). He reasserted the precept that the state's function was 'to subordinate force to law, but it is the function of the Church to subordinate force to love'. Almost word for word, this address repeated his earlier warnings against dwelling 'on the wrongs, real or imaginary, of bygone days', likewise reminding listeners that they were 'here, in the providence of God, Protestants and Roman Catholics, side by side in a small country', and enjoining them that they 'must work and witness for peace, and thus become peacemakers'.[31]

His call for peaceful coexistence in the troubled Belfast of 1935 differed radically in its impact and implications from the same phrases when delivered to a sympathetic audience in St Patrick's Cathedral before the general synod of 1934. Living 'side by side' with one's Catholic neighbours had become simple enough in Dublin or Cork, but was not so easily achieved in the contested territories of Ulster, each a 'small country' in itself. Appealing 'to all ministers of religion to give a lead in this direction', he affirmed optimistically that their 'combined influence' would prove 'irrresistible'.[32] Though not explicitly advising cancellation of the forthcoming Twelfth demonstrations, his coded message was inescapable.

Though irenic in tone, his admonitions incensed many Churchmen, for whom politics and religion remained inseparable. Their position was most trenchantly expressed by Herbert Lindsay, rector of St Bartholomew's in Stranmillis,[33] when unfurling a banner for Queen Victoria's Temperance LOL 1541 on 1 July. Lindsay had abandoned a clerical career in Canada to settle in Belfast at the height of the 'Ulster Crisis' in 1913:

> There are dissenting people to-day ... who would find fault with ministers for having anything to do with such a ceremony as this. ... They think that ministers must sit dumb where politics are concerned, and that it is not for the Ambassador of Christ to redress political wrongs. ... As long as the Anglician [*sic.*] Communion is pledged to support its Prayer-Book with its state prayers, its Litany, and the last three of its 39 articles, it can never divorce itself fom the duty of condemning and righting political wrongs, and therefore of taking a part in politics. ... As far as the position of Ulster is concerned we were more secure under the Union Jack when we had men like Dr. Hanna, Dr. Cooke, and Dr. Kane to defend our cause than we are with the weaklings of to-day, who, while eating the bread and butter of Ulster, would condemn the Ulster Covenanters, and hand over the whole Six Counties to the Irish Free State.[34]

Other clergymen took more explicit issue with the bishop when addressing Orange anniversary services on 7 July. Canon Percy Marks, rector of Ballymore and District Master of Tandragee,[35] interpreted Frederick's reference to 'party politics' as meaning 'that no clergyman should be an Orangeman'. He could not see 'why a minister of religion should lose his spiritual influence because he belongs to the Orange Order, which was founded on the Bible. Religion and politics were never separated, nor would they ever be separated.' A yet more direct challenge to episcopal authority was mounted in Dromore Cathedral by Henry O'Connor, incumbent of Kilmegan (Dundrum) and a senior Orange chaplain. Also assuming that Orange clergymen had been impugned, O'Connor declared that the bishop's 'statement had wounded the feelings of many godly men in the ministry who were endeavouring to lead the Orangemen of Ulster in the paths of righteousness. The insinuation was not correct either in fact or experience. It was all the more painful when it came from one whom for many reasons they held in high respect and esteem.'[36]

The veiled reference to Frederick's past prominence as an Orangeman carried an equally veiled threat that the bishop was at risk of being denounced as a 'Lundy' who had betrayed his brethren. This may have provoked his rather unconvincing disavowal of any implied antagonism to Orangeism:

> I was not thinking of the Orange Order, and I was not insinuating anything whatsoever. ... The Orange society is not a political society. (See the Dean of Belfast's fine address reported in to-day's 'News-Letter'.)[37] I know well that many most excellent men have used the opportunity, which membership of the society has given them, in advocating the basic principles of Christian revelation.[38]

As always, Frederick's objection was not to Orangeism as a 'religious institution' but to the exploitation of the Order by politicians (not always adherents of the government). In a personal letter, O'Connor apologized for any 'pain' that his sermon had inflicted and declared himself 'quite satisfied' with Frederick's explication, even though 'clergymen of the Reformed Churches in this country do not as a rule identify themselves with politics' in any other guise.[39] Yet the sardonic tone of O'Connor's subsequent public letter suggested lingering scepticism:

> That the misinterpretation was widespread there is no doubt. ... The fact that the statement was made on the eve of the commemoration of the battle of the Boyne may have helped to the misinterpretation. We now know from his Lordship's letter that he does not consider the Orange Order a political organisation, and that his statement had no reference to the Order. We are relieved and thankful.[40]

Orange suspicion of the bishop's intentions may have been allayed by his explanatory letter, but not eliminated. When opening the Lisburn Orange arch on 9 July, the prominent barrister and unionist politician Edward Murphy claimed to be 'delighted' by Frederick's vindication of Orange chaplains, yet disturbed by the tenor of his recent appeals for peace:

> What did the Bishop mean by his sermon on Sunday last? It seemed that he really wanted Orangemen to give up their services and processions at this time of year, because, according to him, they would in that way promote peace. Every true Orangeman was devoted to peace at home and abroad, but they would not secure peace at home by abandoning their principles. (Applause)[41]

The assault was renewed from several Orange platforms on the Twelfth. The Grand Master of Belfast, Sir Joseph Davison,[42] failed to see how membership could 'in any way impair the spiritual influence of any minister of the Gospel. ... While their Order was essentially religious, they could not separate religion and politics in Ireland owing to the insidious Romanising propaganda.' As for the bishop's appeal to forget past wrongs, it 'had the special blessing' of the nationalist *Irish News* in its campaign against Davison and the Order. While expressing respect for his 'high ideals', Davison and his sighing, groaning audience could not forget the statements of 'Republicans, and even Nationalists that they will never be satisfied until they rule this land from sea to sea', the 'murderous campaign' of 1921–3, or, 'above all, … the heroic achievements of our forefathers'.[43] In Enniskillen, the aged Imperial Grand Master and former minister of Agriculture, Sir Edward Archdale,[44] had 'been astonished to read an appeal by Bishop of Down for the cessation of Orange anniversary demonstrations. A similar appeal had been made by a Southern bishop. He asked those gentlemen how the Protestant faith was progressing in the South of Ireland.'[45]

For nationalists, the bishop's apparent alienation from Orangeism was a welcome sign of unionist fragmentation. In Dublin, the *Irish Independent* praised his 'sound and impressive words', anticipated 'a sobering effect on the citizens of Belfast and the Six Counties', and detected an implied 'rebuke' against Craigavon's recent reference to 'a Protestant parliament for a Protestant state'.[46] In Belfast, as Davison noted, the *Irish News* was delighted, mischievously suggesting that the published resolutions to be affirmed on the Twelfth should be replaced by embodiments of 'the Bishop's message of peace and friendship'.[47] When its editor visited the Hebridean island of Barra in summer 1936, he told Compton Mackenzie 'about the great courage the Bishop of Down had shown in criticizing the behaviour of the Orangemen'. Mackenzie was taken aback by Louis's response to such compliments when he too visited the island in April 1937: 'Oh, I'm not interested in what my father is doing.'[48]

Frederick's stance also reassured liberal Churchmen that he had not abandoned the quest for spiritual regeneration and eradication of obsolete sectarian divisions. This view was lucidly expressed by Captain Terence Verschoyle from Fermanagh, a Clogher synodsman who as a youth had commanded the local UVF and served as a unionist on the county council.[49] Verschoyle had become a strong opponent of sectarianism, describing his neighbour Sir Basil Brooke as 'the Colebrooke Hitler' after Brooke's notorious appeal 'wherever possible, to employ Protestant lads and lassies'.[50] On 8 July, he addressed the bishop as a brother who had momentarily strayed when abandoning the ecumenical cause at the general synod:

A feeling of disappointment at a recent (to me) very apparent change in your attitude towards Reunion shall not deter me from expressing my thankfulness for the truly admirable and courageous sermon preached by you yesterday. I have long thought that a complete loss of memory is one of the chief needs of this country. … But I am also thankful to you for another reason, & that is – quite bluntly – that a bishop other than Dr. Gregg is now discovered to have a mind of his own, & to be not afraid to speak it.[51]

Despite earlier signs to the contrary, the Lord Bishop of Down had not yet been fully tamed by his own eminence.

His initial campaign failed to deter either side from sectarian riots, assaults, arson, intimidation and expulsions. The immediate cause of the renewed conflagration was a series of attacks, involving gunfire and causing two fatalities (one Catholic, one Protestant), on Orangemen returning from the field at Belmont on the evening of the Twelfth. As the *Irish News* observed on 13 July: 'Had the appeals for peace in our midst been listened to with respect, Belfast might have been spared the bloodshed and the turmoil of the past twenty-four hours.'[52] This savage outburst of violence in the names of both communities, leading to a fortnight of outrages, reprisals and feverish disputes about ultimate reponsibility, was an alarming aberration in the largely peaceable condition of Belfast during holiday seasons between 1923 and the 1960s.[53] Police returns showed that two-thirds of those injured were Catholics, though seven of the nine fatalities were Protestants. Catholics had also occupied five-sixths of the 421 houses evacuated because of arson, violence or intimidation.[54] The great majority of those arrested and convicted were Protestants, leading to furious but unjustified allegations that the Royal Ulster Constabulary had fallen into the clutches of disloyal papists.[55]

On Thursday, 18 July, the bishop broadened his peace campaign by using the press to convene a meeting of 'the clergy of Belfast' for the following evening, as well as calling for intercessory services on the Sunday: 'Without discriminating between Protestants and Roman Catholics there should be special prayer for all who have been bereaved through the recent mad outbursts of passion, and for those who are still suffering from wounds.' The 'immediate question' was not 'Who fired the first shot or struck the first blow?', but who was ready to 'bring about the relationship which should exist between neighbours who profess and call themselves Christians'. His aim in mobilizing the clergy was 'to help in creating an atmosphere without which we cannot hope for peace', something sought by 'the overwhelming majority of the people of Belfast'. The same issue of the *News-Letter* published an equally eloquent letter by Dean Kerr, Grand Chaplain of Belfast. Expressing equal indignation at the killing of a 'hard working boy ... by shots fired at the Orange procession', and 'the wrecked and burnt out homes of quiet inoffensive Roman Catholic families who lived under the shadow of the Cathedral', Kerr called for a joint appeal by 'representative citizens of any or no political affinities' for peace and an end to 'the devilry of revolver firing'.[56] The crusade for peace had reconciled bishop and dean after the collapse of their joint campaign for church reunion.

By Friday morning, Frederick had enlisted the current Presbyterian moderator and a former Methodist president in a joint appeal for 'ministers of all Churches' to attend that evening's peace conference.[57] Moderator Moody's separate statement to his clergy and flock was closely attuned to the bishop's, avoiding ascription of culpability to either side.[58] Some unconventional practical proposals were simultaneously put forward by James Haddick, a curate currently unattached to any parish who would soon become one of the bishop's private chaplains.[59] Deploring a 'lack of leadership', which had been 'somewhat removed through the efforts of our Bishop and the Dean of Belfast', he advocated a public meeting to hear the proposals of the clerical conference. He urged church leaders and clergy to 'hold frequent open-air meetings in the disturbed areas, and then back up these appeals by personal visiting … in the cause of peace. I have seen much good result from courageous action by the clergy during the worst of the rioting in 1920–22.' He also suggested preparation of 'a manifesto … signed by the heads of the Roman and Protestant Churches, placarded in the disturbed areas and distributed in the homes'.[60]

The clerical conference, chaired by the bishop, adopted Dean Kerr's resolution expressing 'distress and abhorrence at the bloodshed and disorder that have recently brought disgrace on our city. … We should suppress every symptom of animosity, and withstand every beginning of unruliness. … We advise strict obedience to, and co-operation with, the orders of those in authority.' A deputation was appointed to put 'several practical suggestions' before Sir Richard Dawson Bates, the minister of Home Affairs, and Craigavon himself was 'very pleased to see that representatives of the Churches and of trade and industry in Belfast were trying to create a better feeling amongst all sections of the population'.[61] Immediately after the conference, Frederick issued a 'personal appeal' to all those 'who in any capacity represent and serve the people', including both Orange and nationalist leaders: 'I appeal to the young men and young women to join in a great peace crusade. No question of loyalty to Church or political party arises. … From reprisals by one side or the other, no good has ever come, or ever could come.' Calling for an end to threats and taunts, he urged Belfast's Christians 'in their several spheres of influence [to] make known their desire and resolution to work with others, no matter who or what they are, for the restoration and preservation of order in Belfast'.[62]

That Sunday, Frederick reiterated his message in St Anne's Cathedral. Once again urging 'a common movement' of Christians rejecting 'anti-social activities' and the secularism that engendered them, he set out his familiar formulation of human rights as a basis for the movement (the rights to life, opinions and neighbourly relations, to be secured by the disarming of all citizens, stoppage of reprisals and protection of minorities). In a bold attempt to undo the damage caused by his supposed attack on the Orange Institution, he depicted it as a potential defender of law and order:

> To the Orange Society I make a very special appeal. I witnessed the great procession on the twelfth of July. It was magnificent. I was deeply impressed by the orderliness, one might say, the solemnity of it. . . . I believe that those men, worthily led, could, more than any other men, now find a way, an honourable way, out of a vicious circle. I implore the leaders of the Orange Society not to let such an opportunity go by.[63]

As in Carrickfergus, he lost no time in arranging publication of his address in leaflets available 'on easy terms' from James Haddick, for distribution in church porches and otherwise, before the end of the month.[64] The printed version was pointedly dedicated to 'the Men of the Queen's Island', loftily praising their 'craftsmanship' but warning them that 'we cannot live on hatred, and we could not live on a "boycott".'[65]

On the Sunday evening, Haddick drafted 'a message of peace' calling on citizens to refrain 'from saying or doing anything to injure in any way those who differ from you, whether in politics or religion'. Signatures were secured from leading figures in six denominations and the Salvation Army, though not from the Reformed Presbyterian or Roman Catholic churches. Dean Kerr and fourteen other Episcopalian, Presbyterian and Methodist ministers gathered at the gate of Queen's Island at 7.30 on Monday morning to distribute 8000 leaflets printed overnight. The recipients were presumably Protestants, since 'Roman Catholic workmen, almost without exception, stayed away from the yard, which was opening after the July holidays'. Bates duly discussed the crisis with Moody and Frederick (as church delegates) and also with officers of the Belfast Grand Orange Lodge, which dissociated itself from 'the disgraceful outrages – no matter by whom perpetrated – in our city'.[66]

The impact of the clerical campaign was intensified by extensive coverage and editorial support in the Protestant press, though the *Northern Whig* regretted that 'the Protestant clergy and ministers have not the active collaboration of representatives of the Roman Catholic Church'.[67] While one cannot measure the impact of the ecumenical peace crusade in discouraging Protestant reprisals, it surely contributed to the sharp reduction in attacks leading to withdrawal of troops from the streets on Wednesday, 24 July.[68] The Commonwealth historian Nicholas Mansergh, writing in 1936, cited Frederick's 'admirable words' in St Anne's cathedral as evidence that the churches could apply their 'very real influence on political life' to 'instil a spirit of tolerance and co-operation in the North'.[69]

Daniel Mageean, the Catholic bishop of Down and Connor, had just promulgated his own call for peace in a pastoral letter, which also denounced reprisals from all quarters but emphasized the 'great provocation' facing his flock. In phrases closely resembling those of Frederick and his associates, he praised 'the courage and vision of many high-minded non-Catholics of this city, clerics and laity, men and women, who are endeavouring to assuage the angry passions of men that have been evoked within the last few weeks, to establish tolerance and fraternal charity in our midst, to wipe out the bitter memories of the past, and to rehabilitate Belfast in the eyes of the civilised world.'[70] Even in this crisis, such shared sentiments were not strong enough to overcome the apparent aversion of the Catholic hierarchy to overt co-operation with their Protestant adversaries.

Nevertheless, the pan-Protestant crusade gave great encouragement to bodies such as the United Council of Christian Churches and Religious Communions in Ireland, whose joint secretary thanked Frederick for his 'noble letter' and remarked that 'if the sentiments you so beautifully express were held by all the religious leaders the hateful doings of the past few weeks could never have taken place'.[71] Major-General Hugh Montgomery of Blessingbourne, instigator of the anti-sectarian Irish Association formed in 1938–9, offered vigorous support in public and private and circulated Frederick's recent sermons to his wide circle of influential, liberal-minded, unionist acquaintances.[72] His collaborator Viscount Charlemont, the minister of Education, regarded the bishop as a key ally and urged Montgomery a few weeks later to seek the bishop's advice before approaching Craigavon in pursuit of a more conciliatory policy towards nationalists.[73] Frederick's reputation as a liberal leader was secure.

Despite his attempt to placate Orange fears and enrol Orangemen in his crusade, it provoked some lurid hate mail. Incoherent with rage, 'A Staunch Protestant' excoriated him as an enemy of Protestant workers:

> Regarding your call to the clergy for conference, concerning recent events – You are too late. The evil is done by you and your kind who are able to employ servants & give the preference to R. Catholice [*sic.*] servants and gardeners & such like who are constantly in & about your homes prying into affairs and then settling down & marrying in our midst ousting our young men and women out of jobs they are badly in need of jeering at our open Bible, & too often marrying our sons & daughters. The poor working class have then to fight your battles whilst you get down on your knees in safety & comfort to pray for peace. ... A protestant league is now getting formed who will now shoot & leave a card on the man who employs a catholic.[74] Tell your clergy to preach this from the pulpit a lot of Good your litanies & prayers will do poor harassed Protestants.[75]

Another correspondent, whose signature and address have been snipped off, indicated that the bishop and his associates were traitors:

> The papists were the offenders and should be severely punished. Those who think otherwise are apostates and traitors. The only thing an Irish Papist understands is the mailed fist applied with arrogance. ... But woe betide the betrayers. This pandering to papists means no good. ... There are enough protestants 'with guts' in Belfast to rid it of all papist roudies [*sic*.] if given an opportunity. If things go on as they are then Orangemen must drill and arm at once to drive out papists and all their ilk out and restore <u>the other three counties</u>.[76]

Where anger and bitterness reigned, the message of the peacemakers acted as a provocation.

III

The long-awaited death of Edward Carson on 22 October 1935 provided a further test of Frederick's ability to negotiate the 'slippery ground' of Ulster politics. Making no allusion to his rejection of Carson's past brinkmanship and partitionism, he issued an admittedly brief tribute on the following day: 'I learn with deep regret of the death of Lord Carson, one of the outstanding figures of his day, and one whose great gifts of head and heart gave him a place of his own in the hearts of multitudes.'[77] Five months before Carson's death in England, preparations had been made by the Northern cabinet for a state funeral in St Anne's cathedral. Lady Carson having made known her husband's wish to be buried in Ulster, Craigavon had proposed interment within the cathedral (an unprecedented honour) and secured her approval. The prime minister reported that Dean Kerr had 'cordially concurred in the proposal' and referred it to the cathedral chapter. The chapter, though assenting in principle, had the temerity to suggest that the body be cremated before interment, 'in view of possible difficulties arising under the Public Health Acts, and to make the erection of a permanent tomb less difficult'. Craigavon told the cabinet 'that this was repugnant to him and Lady Carson had informed him that she could not agree to that suggestion'.[78] Regardless of the public health, dust rather than ashes would represent her husband in his Belfast resting place.

Presumably because of the urgency of Craigavon's approach, the dean had in fact referred his request neither to the chapter (a ceremonial body) nor to the cathedral board, whose titular chairman was the bishop. Instead, he had convened an 'emergency meeting of the select vestry', attended only by the churchwardens, seven laymen, and himself.[79] The meeting learned that Carson was averse to burial in a cemetery and that his wife had proposed a hill-top, Craigavon preferring the cathedral. The select vestry 'was decidedly of opinion that the body should be cremated', and laid down various 'conditions' for acceding to the request. All designs must be approved by the cathedral architect (Sir Charles Nicholson, Elizabeth's father-in-law), and all expenses met by the government. Perhaps in anticipation of the prime minister's own demise, 'it was further agreed that if the burial should be in the Cathedral a precedent should not thereby be established'. Arrangements, 'in case of immediate necessity', were left with a sub-committee of the dean, the churchwardens, and two vestrymen. The cathedral board was not convened until 21 October, on the very eve of Carson's death, when 'the Dean reported that Sir R. Dawson Bates & other members of the Government had met the sub-committee and had selected a site in the nave where interment should take place, and that when the occasion should arise it was intended to pass a special Act of Parliament which would overcome any legal difficulties'. Once again, the bishop was absent from the meeting (having never yet attended the cathedral board) and had no recorded part in the arrangements.[80]

Carson's remains reached Belfast on 26 October. After a ceremonial procession from Queen's Square, the coffin was delivered by gun-carriage to the west door of the cathedral. The funeral address and committal sentences were delivered by Primate D'Arcy, and a former president of the Methodist Church in Ireland was assigned the task of sprinkling soil from a silver bowl supplied by the cabinet. In the mawkish words of the *Belfast Telegraph*:

> As the coffin slowly disappeared from sight it was committed to the grave in sure and certain hope, Rev. Mr. [John A.] Duke dropping the mingled earth of the Six Counties on the lid, from which the Union Jack had automatically been withdrawn. It was a never-to-be-forgotten scene, and many were moved to tears as the sacred dust of the man they loved was lost to mortal sight for ever. The silence was broken by the prayers of the Lord Bishop, with the responses sweetly sung from the distant choir.[81]

When embroidering this event for the amusement of Anthony Blunt, Louis alleged that 'that great man', his father, 'had to sprinkle earth from the 6 Northern Counties on the coffin of Sir Ed. Carson his lifelong bête noire out of a large gold chalice'.[82] In fact, apart from intoning the final prayers, the bishop's only recorded contribution was to accompany the Primate, Moderator Moody, ex-President Duke, and a host of lesser clergy in procession through the cathedral before the arrival of the cortège.[83]

As chairman of the cathedral board, the bishop shared responsibility for granting the privilege of interment in the cathedral to a controversial politician whose Ulster credentials did not include birth, death, or residence. This issue provoked angry protests from several directions. A Catholic correspondent, while admitting 'the difficulty you would find yourself in had you refused permission', remarked that 'St. Annes has now become a fashionable graveyard for "Sham Statesmen".' He warned the bishop 'that in future you will have to be very careful in allowing burials in St. Annes. Craig cant have very long to live, and it would be making things more ridiculious [sic.] to have him embalmed and placed in a "niche" and people to admire him as one of the greatest statesmen that ever lived, showing the puppet he made of religion both in life and after death.'[84] For Marrable Williams, rector of St Luke's and precentor of Connor, this constituted 'a very dangerous precedent', which led him to contemplate resigning his canonry and therefore his membership of the cathedral's governing bodies. In a letter of protest to Dean Kerr, which he copied to the bishop, Williams enquired rhetorically whether the board or chapter had been consulted on the issue, and when the chapter had discussed 'sending out tickets for a service in the Cathedral stamped by the Northern Government'. He objected to the government's appropriation of the cathedral 'as a Mausoleum', and to the chapter's use 'as a puppet'. Stormont, he felt, 'would have been the proper place to Bury a Political Hero whom Ulster delighted to honour'.[85]

Instead of resigning his offices, Williams pursued his protest through the *Lower Falls Magazine*, remarking that the sprinkling of earth from six (rather than nine) counties meant that 'a broken covenant will inevitably be inseparable for Ulster pilgrims from Monaghan, Cavan and Donegal, when they visit Belfast Cathedral'. This evidence of a rift in the cathedral board was taken up by the *Irish News*, leading to searching enquiries by the unionist press about rumours that the board had ruled against the permanent display of the union flag above Carson's grave. This was to have adorned the permanent memorial as specified by the government, a granite slab inscribed 'Carson' and surrounded by brass railings. The dean and the bishop both refused to comment, but the Press Association stated that Craigavon's proposal for a flag had been rejected because of opposition from the bishop and other members of the board.[86] Such reports provoked 'an avalanche of letters' to the *Belfast Telegraph* expressing indignation at this insult to the great leader, an appeal for reconsideration of the decision from Sir Joseph Davison, and a report that Dean Kerr was 'wholeheartedly in favour of accepting the flag so that it can be placed over Lord Carson's grave'.[87]

On 13 December, the board disowned Williams's article,[88] stated that a flag flying over the temporary tomb had been put up and taken down by persons unknown, revealed that no proposal for a flag had been submitted by the government, and promised further consultation. When approving other elements of the permanent memorial on 8 November, the board had 'after a short discussion' rejected the offer of a union flag made by a 'personal friend' of the dean: 'Any suggestion that this result was due to any "veto" or "ban" of the Lord Bishop ... [was] without foundation.'[89] The *Irish News* denounced recent articles 'attacking the Lord Bishop in particular in the bitterest and most unjust way, though of all those who were engaged in the matter on the side of the Board he was probably the least consulted or responsible'.[90] It seems that Frederick was not the primary source of opposition to Carson's perpetual veneration as a defender of the union.

The minutes of the cathedral board demonstrate the inadequacy of contemporary and later accounts suggesting a sharp opposition between an anti-partisan bishop and a Carsonite dean parroting the government's views. Instead, they illuminate the mechanisms of negotiation and compromise that allowed Churchmen and politicians of all shades to co-exist, and often to collaborate, in the miniature world of élite Belfast. At its meeting on 8 November, the first to be chaired by the bishop, the board had referred the government's design for the tomb to Sir Charles Nicholson and agreed that Lord Carson should not be joined by any member of his family under the granite slab. At this point, Kerr announced a generous offer from the Minister of Commerce, a major benefactor of the cathedral who had recently endowed special seating for members of the government:

> The Dean informed the meeting that he had received from Mr. J. Milne Barbour the offer of a Union Jack to be placed on a pole and suspended from the wall over Lord Carson's grave. After some discussion, in the course of which it was evident that the suggestion did not commend itself, the offer was not accepted. A proposal that the Colours of the 5th. Batt. of the [R. I. Rifles: erased] U.V.F. South Belfast be received and placed in the Cathedral was also negatived on the ground that the Corps had been identified with a political organization.

The minutes do not record any amendments or expressions of dissent at a meeting attended by five clerical and eight lay members of the board.[91]

The next meeting on 13 December, chaired by the bishop and attended by no fewer than ten of his clergy and fourteen laymen, was summoned to refute 'certain misleading statements' about its earlier proceedings. The Recorder of Belfast, Frederick's close ally Judge Herbert Thompson, proposed the formation of a new sub-committee to confer 'with the Government at an early stage on the whole subject of Lord Carson's Memorial'. Only then was dissent expressed by two influential laymen absent from the previous meeting. An amendment to accept 'the offer of Mr. Milne Barbour to present a flag to float over Lord Carson's tomb' was proposed by the Lord Chief Justice of Northern Ireland, Sir William Moore, who as an Ulster Unionist MP had seconded the party's welcome to Carson as its new leader in September 1911.[92] It was seconded by Henry Kinahan, a wine and spirit merchant and Orangeman belonging (like Bates) to the influential Eldon lodge. The amendment was shelved after 'some discussion', and a sub-committee appointed to interview the government, which included the bishop and the Recorder, but neither Moore nor Kinahan. After a fierce condemnation by Dean Carmody of Down of those leaking board proceedings to the press, Frederick finally intervened:

> The Bishop spoke strongly in deprecation of controversies of the kind that we had had under consideration as being injurious to the Church and prejudicial to the great work of promoting the Kingdom of God on earth. Neither the Government nor any outside body or party has any right to interfere, and it must be clearly understood that the Church is mistress in her own house. The meeting was closed with Benediction.[93]

Within that 'house', the true mistress was the bishop, who had the power to with-hold the required 'faculty' even if the chapter had agreed to fly a flag permanently over Carson's tomb.[94]

In preparation for the proposed conference between representatives of the board and the government, Frederick (on behalf of the sub-committee) wrote to the deans of English cathedrals to enquire whether flags were displayed over their tombs. Fourteen replies were received, all denying the display of union flags except in the case of certain military, naval, and royal monuments and memorials. Somerset Herald did 'not think the Union Flag should be used over the grave permanently of any civilian subject'.[95] This investigation pointed towards an ingenious resolution of the dispute, which Judge Thompson outlined to another crowded meeting of the board on 5 February 1936. Fortified by the evidence of English practice, he had interviewed Bates and the minister of Agriculture, Sir Basil Brooke:

> In the course of a long discussion it transpired that the proposal to place the flag over Lord Carson's tomb had not in the first instance emanated from the Government, nor were they insistent upon it until, following the Press notices, pressure from outside sources had been brought to bear with them with which they found some difficulty in coping. He, the Recorder, suggested as a solution of the difficulty, and by way of compromise that the Union Jack might be placed over the War Memorial Lectern, which contains the list of the names of those

who had served in the Great War with the Ulster Division in whose formation the late Lord Carson had taken a leading part and also, if so wished, over the Western Memorial porches.[96] His suggestion had been sympathetically received, but the Government representatives preferred that if possible the suggestion of having it over the tomb be adopted by the Board.

Thompson, seconded by Dean Kerr, then proposed a delicately worded resolution 'gratefully' accepting any offer of a union flag, from the government or a private donor, along these lines. Sir William Moore again counter-proposed 'that a flag be accepted to be placed over the tomb', but only two of the twenty-one attenders supported his amendment. The hypothetical resolution was approved, and 'it was arranged that the Recorder should communicate the Board's decision unofficially to Sir Dawson Bates and that negotiations should be continued by the sub-committee who would prepare a statement – for submission to the Board before its issue to the Press'.[97]

Thompson broke the board's decision to Bates by letter, and received 'a reply stating that the Government will be happy to supply a Union Jack as suggested'. On 21 February 1936, the cathedral board confirmed the compromise and announced the final format of the permanent memorial:

> To commemorate the intimate connection that existed between Lord Carson and the Ulster Division the Government has offered and the Cathedral Board has accepted a Union Jack to be displayed over the memorial rolls of honour of the Division now placed at the west end of the building and to be flown on occasions of national joy and mourning over the western porches built as a memorial to the Division.

'A hearty vote of thanks to the Recorder' was passed by acclamation (having been seconded by one of Moore's allies), the Recorder responded, and the meeting closed in a glow of mutual admiration with Benediction.[98] In due course, the government was presented with a bill for £23 for a flag, pole and oak tablet over the lectern, while Milne Barbour donated a much larger union flag for the north side of the western gable as well as an ever expanding suite of 'seats of honour' for politicians and dignitaries.[99] Having settled the issue of the flag, Frederick never again attended a meeting of the board except in November 1936, when Viscountess Craigavon, on behalf of the Ulster Unionist Women's Council, returned to the offensive by offering to place a memorial tablet over the tomb. After further negotiation between the dean, Bates and the Craigavons, the Recorder's perhaps mischievous suggestion of a recumbent statue was discarded in favour of a bronze plaque in bas-relief by Rosamond Praeger.[100] The tomb, plaque and oak tablet remain in place, the lectern has been moved, but of that vexatious flag no trace remains except the bracket that once fastened its pole to the wall.

The compromise put an end to public debate and silenced the insinuation that the bishop had desecrated Carson's memory. It left the Church's autonomy intact, the government relieved, and (crucially) Milne Barbour's goodwill undiminished. It was achieved by discreet discussions within a small group of men already closely connected. The dean, the Recorder, Bates and Barbour were all Prince Masons and members of the Ulster Club, Kerr and Barbour having penetrated still more exalted Masonic circles. Gerald Ewart, who was prevented by illness from accompanying the Recorder on his mission to Bates and Barbour, was also a Prince Mason.[101] Sir William Moore's eventual acquiescence in the decision may have been eased by the fact that he, too, belonged to the Ulster Club. Beatrice, presumably relieved, took note of the final flurry of press reports in her diary.[102] Frederick remained apprehensive in a letter sent to his son a few days later, referring to a report of the board's decision and implying that the flag controversy was symptomatic of a wider assault on his campaign for peace and tolerance: 'However there is much to rejoice over: the Clergy, in the main, and the respectable people, including the working men, are with us. But in every large city there are "lewd fellows of the baser sort" and the professional politicians, now & again, use them as tools for the doing of a very poor kind of work.'[103]

To the extent that Frederick resisted government pressure in this instance, he was probably inspired less by aversion to Carson than by determination to assert the Church's independence of the state. In mid March, Dean Kerr sent him a memorandum from Craigavon proposing a series of ecumenical services to be attended by government ministers, judges and other 'prominent citizens' in St Anne's Cathedral and, alternately, in the Assembly Buildings of the Presbyterian Church. The prime minister, doubtless encouraged by his spectacular deployment of the three major Protestant churches in a political funeral, had proposed an elaborate protocol for such services whenever necessitated by 'an occasion of National importance'. Though not dismissing the possibility of allowing such events for 'a particular occasion', Frederick refused any general dispensation for allowing his clergy to attend services in other churches, or allowing ministers of other churches to participate in services within his domain. He informed Craigavon that the reponsibility was his alone, and 'that responsibility I could not delegate to any man or men on earth'. Though members of the government and judiciary would always be welcomed in the cathedral, and given 'special accommodation', with respect to the conduct of services and selection of officiating clergy 'the control and authority must always be our own'.[104]

As usual, Kerr acted as intermediary between bishop and prime minister, ensuring that episcopal authority would be respected:

> I am sure the P.M. will understand that you cannot pledge the church in any indefinite way. I have suggested to him (1) to leave altogether to each church the conduct of its services. This frees the Government, I said, of any further responsibility. (2) to express a wish that representatives of other churches may be invited to take part in the Service. The Government seems to long for united Services.[105]

Frederick later told Primate D'Arcy that Craigavon had assured him by letter that he was 'quite satisfied' with the assertion of Church autonomy, subsequently repeating this in conversation 'when he, the Archdeacon of Connor [Shirley] and I met at a city function'. Frederick had heard 'on excellent authority' that Craigavon's proposal had been prompted by 'pressure from the Presbyterian side'.[106] The bishop still favoured co-operation with other Protestant churches, but only on terms agreeable to himself and his own church, that *ecclesia dei* whose authority he had so skilfully defended against the rebels of Carrickfergus in 1908. Caesar, whether or not an Ulster unionist, must be kept within his own province.

IV

During the sectarian off-season following the riots of July 1935, Frederick had continued to marshal the forces of Christianity against the godless pursuit of violence. On 16 September, after thanking Louis for his 'wonderful' second volume of poems,[107] he referred to some of the obstacles facing peacemakers in Belfast:

> Yes, I fear the R.C. bishop [Mageean] & I were a bit mixed up in the English papers. He was given credit for some of my appeals for fairmindedness &c, & I suffered occasionally because of some of his criticisms & attacks! I see in today's paper a speech by Craigavon. In it he said one thing that I think was inspired by a letter I wrote, & which was signed by me & 3 others – a letter to his Chief Lieutenant.[108]

This referred to a notable utterance at the opening of an Orange hall near Bessbrook, County Armagh, when the prime minister had stated that there was 'no room' for 'defence organisations, as they are called', and that he would 'be no party to any terrorism against a minority in our midst … [or] to victimisation or to a pogrom in Ulster'.[109] Moderator Moody commended Craigavon for his 'timely, statesmanlike, and courageous speech', which might discourage 'misguided people' such as those calling for the release of 'certain convicted prisoners, not on the ground that they were innocent, but on the ground that they were Protestants'.

Craigavon forwarded Moody's letter to Bates, noting that this passage would 'afford you great encouragement'.[110]

Further outrages and murders occurred a few days after Craigavon's pronouncement, leading Dean Kerr, when addressing a Masonic service on 22 September, to renew his repudiation of 'criminal retaliation' leading to 'a vendetta of blood'.[111] Two days later, the police rounded up ten suspected gunmen and sectarian ringleaders, eight of whom were Protestants, for temporary detention under the Civil Authorities (Special Powers) Act. Their detention, more decisively than the earlier arrest of scores of petty criminals and perennial troublemakers, manifested the government's determination to suppress disorder in its own constituency. Equally, their release on 7 October, following demonstrations and deputations organized by the Protestant Defence Associations, exhibited the government's weakness in the face of concerted unionist opposition.[112]

Louis had been offered a further hint of the extent of his father's immersion in local politics: 'I am to speak tonight – in a private way – to a group of people interested in the condition of Belfast. Now I must be off.'[113] This group may have been the Belfast Peace League, a pacifist body whose organizers included the Quaker historian T. W. Moody and the poet John Hewitt.[114] A few days later, when addressing the Church Missionary Society, Frederick renewed previous appeals for the formation of 'peace committees' in troubled districts:

> The ministers of all churches and Salvation Army officers have done nobly, but something more remains to be attempted. Lay people of every rank who acknowledge the leadership of Jesus Christ should now come forward and offer their services for the creation of a better atmosphere in the promotion of peace and goodwill. Let those who are willing to work and witness in this way, visiting every street in the danger zone and every house – ... give their names to the ministers of their congregations or Salvation Army officers.[115]

As usual, he left it up to others to give practical effect to his missionary ideals.

One outcome of his campaign was a meeting in the Assembly Buildings on 8 October, convened by Moderator Moody and chaired by Frederick, which resolved to establish a council of 'representatives of the Christian communities in Belfast willing to join in united efforts to promote goodwill in the community, to seek to ensure that the fundamental rights of civil and religious liberty and personal safety shall be assured to all citizens, and to deal with matters of public interest from the religious point of view'.[116] Once again, only Protestants joined this ecumenical body. According to Moody, 'the Roman Catholic bishop refused to join the Council or to co-operate officially with it', while 'some Roman Catholic priests, though holding aloof from the Council, nevertheless played a very worthy and efficient part among their own people'.[117] In early November, the Belfast Council of Christian Churches issued 'An Appeal for Tolerance and Goodwill', declaring that 'all those who refuse to leave room for opinions differing from their own in the religious and political worlds – so long as these are not subversive of public order or public morality – are branding themselves, however great the provocation, as enemies of Christ and His Church'. The new body promised 'to assist in seeing wrongs righted, and in drawing the attention of the Government and other authorities to any abuse that may exist or arise in the community'.[118]

The appeal was signed by three honorary secretaries, representing the major Protestant churches and a notably broad range of viewpoints and affiliations. Reginald McDonald, the rector of St Matthew's, served on the Grand Orange Lodge of Ireland for half a century.[119] John Spence, who became secretary of the Methodist Church in Ireland in 1937, spent most of his career in the Dublin and Belfast central missions.[120] Of the three signatories, the closest in spirit to Frederick was John Waddell, the controversial minister of Fisherwick Presbyterian church, who had offended orthodox unionist opinion on many occasions yet secured election as moderator in 1937.[121] Waddell, like Frederick, had expressed radical views in a sermon on 'Christianity and Socialism' in 1912, refused to sign the Ulster Covenant or join the UVF, and warned the unionist clubs against 'any resort to armed force'. He too had been involved in struggles for church reform and church extension, which closely paralleled those engrossing the Church of Ireland in the aftermath of the Great War. Unlike Frederick, he had 'never joined any political party', and seems never to have pursued his crusade for temperance and moral reform through Orange lodges.[122] For informed readers, the choice of secretaries clearly indicated that the council hoped to influence Orangemen as well as liberals, workers as well as people of property and education.

Among the first laymen to endorse the council's appeal was Hugh Montgomery, who promised a 'small cheque' and then a 'larger one', if the campaign were extended to the countryside.[123] After some days of silence in the correspondence column of the *News-Letter*, whose relations with the impetuous Montgomery were increasingly strained, one of his closest allies expressed the discouragement felt by those who had 'long cherished dreams of a community animated by such qualities', upon observing 'so little public support' for the appeal.[124] Montgomery's cronies thereupon bombarded the press with messages of support, provoking protests against the suggestion that Protestants were solely to blame 'for any trouble in our city' and warning that the campaign was 'liable to offend Protestant sentiment'.[125] Before long, the initial appeal had been submerged by the frothy exchange of insults between exponents of various strains of Christianity. Undaunted, the council (like the bishop) renewed the campaign for peace and tolerance in summer 1936.

Having delegated the ecumenical peace crusade to other organizers, Frederick concentrated on appeals to his own people. On 1 November, he attempted to harness the forthcoming Armistice commemorations to the cause of international peace. When issuing guidelines for lessons and prayers to be delivered on Armistice Day and the preceding Sunday, he added instructions for his ministers which, if implemented, would have required radical departure from the customary format: 'Armistice memories and Armistice hopes will determine the character of the sermon. From every pulpit there should be appeals for peace at home and abroad, and peace not simply as the absence of conflict. For peace there must be a mind, a temper, a goodwill. In this sense Europe does not now know peace.'[126]

A few days later, when addressing the diocesan synod, he renewed his condemnation of the summer riots but pointedly dissociated himself from nationalist accounts of their origin and scale:

> It is true that the reports that went abroad were much exaggerated, that the exaggerations seriously misled many at a distance, and that their one-sidedness provoked criticisms which were grossly unfair to the law-abiding people of this great city. The fomenters of strife and the actual perpetrators of outrage were few in number, and yet for some weeks and in some areas they were a terror to their neighbours and a menace to the peace of the whole community. It is, I think, a gross misuse of language to describe anti-social, lawless individuals, some of whom have had at one time a nominal connection with one side and some with another, by the names of any religious communion. They should rather be regarded as anarchists.

He called for all present to support the use of force by the state in suppressing 'mob violence', for in so doing 'its ministers may be God's ministers'.[127]

As the prospect loomed of a second bloody summer, the bishop issued a 'pastoral letter' for delivery at all services on 28 June 1936. After some introductory *plámás*, he called for the building of a bridge between 'communities' defined not by religion but by wealth:

> From a long and intimate knowledge of Belfast I am convinced that its people are tolerant, fair-minded, chivalrous, kindly. But something is wanting. There are two communities, the community of the well-to-do, and the community of the poor. They live apart, far too much so, and know hardly anything of one another. The clergy know both, and they, perhaps, more than others, could be influential in bringing about the relationships which ought to exist. I plead for real neighbourliness.

This attitude would render 'lawless activities much more difficult'. Having reiterated his analysis of the riots already delivered to the synod, he called on each man or woman of social, political and religious influence 'to make sure that his loyalty to his party does not conflict with his loyalty to his Lord'. On the same day, the bishop delivered a sermon on international peace in St Anne's cathedral, in which he repeated his appeal for the mobilization of laymen of all Protestant denominations in peace committees. Clearly, so far, his advice had carried less weight with the laity than with the clergy.[128]

The force of these appeals was enhanced by the simultaneous delivery and then publication of Bishop Mageean's pastoral letter, which likewise urged co-operation with 'those who have the maintenance of law and order in our midst' and called for the promotion of 'peace and goodwill among all sections of the community'. Mageean, unlike Frederick, explicitly referred to the 'present state of tension', which many feared would soon explode into further riots, burnings and expulsions. The *News-Letter* offered qualified editorial support for both pastoral letters. Mageean's 'wise advice' was 'wise enough, perhaps, to compensate for the somewhat doubtful note which is struck in some of his exhortations'. Though Frederick's letter contained 'passages which some members of his flock will find a little obscure', there would be 'common agreement' as to the 'general trend' of his remarks. The origin of the editor's perplexity was exposed by a corrective letter from 'John F. Down', who rather testily explained that his advice had been to 'avow' rather than 'avoid' liberal sentiments expressed by Presbyterians and Methodists.[129]

Better prepared than in 1935, Frederick was ready well before the Twelfth to broadcast his views through his ecumenical auxiliary, the Belfast Council of Christian Churches. Its appeal for 'The Peace of the City', though signed by the same secretaries as in November 1935, was surely the bishop's work:

> We beg that those who live [?near] to people of a different religious or political persuasion will refrain from every provocative word or action, and seek to promote true neighbourliness and the Christian spirit of brotherhood and goodwill. We appeal for vigilance in restraining any foolish and unruly members so that the just rights of all citizens, and civil and religious liberty be preserved inviolate.[130]

While the clerical campaign for a peaceful holiday season contributed to the absence of renewed sectarian conflict, other forces such as the Orange Institution and indeed the government had a strong interest and influence in preventing its recurrence. Rain, and the revival of employment in the shipyards, also helped.[131] Beatrice noted the 'bad weather' that afflicted the 'Orange procession' on Bank Holiday Monday, 13 July, when 'we all went to Lisburn Rd. to see it' from the sanctuary of two motor cars.[132] For the time being, the dark passions of 1935 had subsided. If he was not quite the saviour of Belfast, Frederick MacNeice was now widely recognized as the chief prophet of a more harmonious way of life.

V

The duties of an episcopal prophet, though onerous, were well rewarded. His annual stipend of £1750 was among the highest in the Church of Ireland, exceeding that of the bishop of Cashel by about £200. Admittedly, there was no regular palace or episcopal residence, D'Arcy having been the last bishop to reign in the splendour of Culloden at Cultra (now an hotel). Grierson had lived successively in two houses on opposite sides of the Antrim Road, the second being eventually reoccupied by Frederick's successor in 1943.[133] The MacNeices lived temporarily in Green Road, next to the Knock Lawn Tennis Ground, in 'a very unromantic & unglamorous villa' formerly occupied by the MacGregor Greers.[134] At the end of June, they moved into 'Dunarnon', a somewhat Italianate building on the Malone Road, close to the Queen's University, whose purchase by the diocese had been 'met entirely from episcopal income funds'.[135] Frederick was the only bishop to occupy this almost garish mansion, with its then unattractive stucco redeemed by fine bay-windows, elegant mouldings, and hexagonal piers at the gateway. It had been built in 1889 for James Johnston, a Presbyterian tea merchant and builder whose grandson was the playwright and broadcaster, Denis Johnston.[136] Contrary to popular belief, the 'great bay-window' of 'Snow' cannot have been located in Dunarnon, since Louis's celebrated lyric poem was composed five months before the MacNeices moved in.[137] Louis, writing to Anthony Blunt from his rented cottage in Birmingham, detected alarming signs of suburbanism in the bishop's household:

> Talking of life, my family came to see us the other day. Being all these bishops has made them more material; they could do nothing but tell us how many garages & lavatories they would have in their new house. And every post brings us press-photographs from the step aunt who lives with the Folk Poetess, of them shaking hands with the Duke of Gloucester or presenting prizes at the Home for Lost Seamen.[138]

Though Louis playfully treated Beatrice and the bishop as indivisible, he surely had in mind his house-proud stepmother.

The shift from Waterford to Belfast allowed Beatrice to entertain and visit her innumerable Ulster relations and friends as she had once done at Sea Park. Her diary for 1936 suggests that she relished her new demesne, with its substantial garden and large retinue of servants, despite the surprisingly small number of guest bedrooms. Beatrice remained in constant contact with her unmarried sister Eva and Gertrude Hind, often visiting their celebrated garden at Glasdrumman on the coast between Newcastle and Annalong in south Down.[139] On one night in February, Bishop's House was crammed with seven visiting Greers and spouses, though Beatrice's brother Mac skipped the teetotal family meal to attend a Masonic dinner. The MacNeices enjoyed the novel luxury of central heating, which in a rare spasm of extravagance was even 'relighted' on one 'very cold and wet day' in April.[140] By comparison with Waterford, their social round was quite varied: not merely frequent meetings with clerical friends such as Canon Clarke, but also grand events such as a levée put on by that inveterate Carsonite, Lord Chief Justice Moore. There was even a day tour skirting the Mournes with lunch at the rectory in Castlewellan, tea with the Rodens at Bryansford, and supper at Montalto with the Clanwilliams. Frederick's engagement with the liberal intel-ligentsia probably livened up dinner parties at Dunarnon, as on 16 May when the guests included the egregious Hugh Montgomery as well as the ever loyal Recorder of Belfast and his wife.[141]

Having left Munster and displacement behind, Beatrice was all the better able to enjoy their brief return visit in March. Three hundred people were assem-bled on 25 March to hear Frederick preach in Cashel cathedral, with tea and a sale afterwards in the deanery: 'Saw lots of our own friends – Have a lovely bed-room overlooking the Rock.' Less satisfactory was an overnight stay in Waterford, in a house not yet enlightened by rural electrification: 'They have only lamps.' On the following Sunday, Frederick preached twice in his old parish of Cappoquin, and they motored on through Queenstown and Fermoy before returning to Dublin. The climax of this tour awaited their return to Belfast: 'Got framed photograph & names of presentation to Derrick from Cashel & Waterford.'[142] Despite the brevity of his term in Cashel, he had as before managed to avoid the resentment that might have been aroused by a more openly ambitious high-flyer.

Meanwhile, the collapse of Louis's marriage to Mary Ezra had helped to bring the MacNeice family closer together after five rather difficult years. Her elopement with the American Charles Katzman, in November 1935, left Louis singularly ill equipped to cope with their infant son Daniel, born in May 1934. Elizabeth Nicholson, who was childless, came to his aid in Birmingham, while Mary's mother schemed and raged against Katzman and Mary as she had once done against Louis.[143] On 1 February 1936, Frederick and Beatrice began a three-day visit to Birmingham, treating Louis to numerous meals in the Queen's Hotel, taking tea and playing with Daniel at his home (Highfield Cottage), risking their lives as passengers in Louis's car, and buying 'a divan for his sitting-room'.[144] This visit persuaded Frederick that his son needed practical help. Three weeks later, he sent Louis a cheque for £50 with the possibility of more, once he had escaped the stranglehold of double taxation caused by relocation from the Free State to Northern Ireland. He also suggested an extraordinarily generous remedy for Louis's household problems: 'It might be wiser – for a time – to let us have Daniel. I know it would be a great wrench, & am not pushing it at all. I am awfully busy at present.'[145] Even with a plethora of servants, it was a formidable challenge for two sexagenarians to undertake responsibility for a motherless toddler in addition to a dependent 30-year-old. Six months later, their offer was accepted.

After an exhilarating visit with Blunt to Spain, at the brink of civil war, Louis summoned up courage enough to inform 'Daddie & Madre' that he was seeking a divorce. In a skilfully composed letter that his biographer deems 'considerate', Louis explained that 'I had meant to tell you that I was taking divorce proceedings against Mary but had postponed doing so in case an opportunity should arise for me to drop the whole business. ... I naturally get the custody of Daniel.'[146] Even more considerate was the absence of any sanctimonious response from two pious Christians, for whom presumably the dissolution of marriage was anathema. Instead, they offered a warm welcome to one of Louis's most decadent associates in early July, when Blunt came to lunch at Dunarnon with his Cambridge boyfriend Peter Montgomery, son of the Major-General. Frederick rather grandly assured Montgomery that 'all the maids will be out on Monday, but we shall be able to manage quite well'. Blunt, who had been invited to stay in Carrickfergus eight years earlier, also accompanied the MacNeices to an afternoon reception for the Londonderrys at Queen's University.[147] Louis himself seems only to have made a single lightning visit to Belfast during 1936, being preoccupied by his divorce, exploring Iceland with Wystan Auden, and moving from Birmingham to London. But on Sunday, 12 July, his sister Elizabeth arrived in Belfast with a psychiatrist colleague from the Tavistock Clinic: 'Derrick to Abbey Ch. Bangor, & outdoor service in Millisle – Elizabeth & Dr. Hermia Mills arrived with car from England – Took me to Millisle.' Three decades earlier, a holiday near that seaside village had ended abruptly with the death of Lily's father and his burial in Carrowdore. This time, the climax of the visit was tea with the Pack-Beresfords at Woburn.[148] Despite background murmurs, all seemed harmonious within the family circle. Beyond the bay-windows, astonishingly, Belfast remained at peace.

13. *Sage*

BELFAST, 1936–1939

I

At seventy, Frederick MacNeice's achievement seemed impregnable. Having given new urgency to the Church's spiritual mission and fought so successfully to fend off the forces of darkness and violence in Belfast, he was widely admired as one of Ulster's foremost men. No door was closed to him, as Beatrice's diary made clear. During the holiday season following the uneventful Twelfth in 1936, she reported lunch with the Londonderrys at Mount Stewart and the Dunleaths at Ballywalter, and more tea with the Pack-Beresfords at Millisle followed by an evening service at Carrowdore. In early August, the MacNeices motored to Donegal for a week's holiday, staying initially in the Fort Hotel in Greencastle, at the mouth of the Foyle. Beatrice discussed the servant problem with the proprietress, noting her faintly ecumenical employment policy and success in retaining staff: 'Had chat with Miss Little proprietress – Her Housekeeper has been with her 15 years – Miss Forbes – a Housemaid & cook about 9 years – all protestants. Parlourmaid some years too, R. C. Man (Protestant) with her since a boy.' In nearby New Park, they had tea with Mrs Montgomery, widow of a bishop of Tasmania and mother of the future field-marshal, and were shown over the 'garden & her husband's grave with Irish Cross on it'.[1]

On 17 September, Frederick's widowed sister Charlotte Kavanagh died from a stroke in Marlborough Road, Dublin. Of the ten children of William and Alice

McNeice, only four were now living. Frederick attended the funeral at Mount Jerome Cemetery in Harold's Cross, where the family headstone had recently been blown down and broken. Though he had requested and received drawings for a new memorial costing £23, Frederick let the matter lapse and no identifiable fragments of the grave can now be traced.[2] A few days after the funeral, the family circle in Belfast was rejuvenated through a fleeting visit from Louis, just back from Iceland and about to move to his new post at Bedford College, London. He had belatedly accepted 'Daddie's' proposal to take over temporary responsibility for the toddler that Mary had abandoned: 'Louis & Daniel & Nurse Mairs arrived via Heysham – Daniel's 1st. visit – aged 2 years 4 months. Derrick met boat – Daniel, Eva [Greer], Louis & I to Maralin Church at 11.30 – back for lunch – Louis & I took Daniel for a walk at 3 p.m. – & sat in summer house.' Next day, the forty-first anniversary of Frederick's ordination, they introduced Daniel to the delights of Millisle:

> Louis & Derrick & Daniel Nurse & I in our car & Gertrude [Hind] & Eva in theirs to Mill Isle to see Baby on the sand for 1st time – Bought him a spade & bucket. ... Louis & I went to see about pram for Baby – at shop for blind – D & I saw Louis off on Heysham boat.[3]

Though evidently less active as a grandparent than Beatrice, Frederick was quite capable of rolling up his trousers to take Daniel for a paddle, as several touching snapshots record.

Beatrice clearly relished her renewed rôle as substitute mother, and gave no hint of irritation when recording the precipitate departure of Daniel's nurse for a fortnight's holiday in Glasgow, after less than a fortnight in Belfast. Though the nurse returned to duty, 'Madre' did much of the child-minding herself. On 7 November, for example, she 'took Baby out in pram 10.30 to 11 oc then in car to town – & found way back by tram.'[4] On the previous day, Louis had moved into a chic garden flat in Keats Grove, Hampstead, where Daniel and Nurse Mairs soon joined him.[5] Louis assured his former wife that 'the old chaps in Ireland have been treating him very nicely & sensibly, doing exactly what the Nurse (& I) tell them'. Indeed, 'he has had the time of his life there, & there was nowhere else to send him at the moment'.[6]

After Daniel's departure, Beatrice reverted to the more sedate life of wife and household manager to an elderly bishop – attendance at the opening of the parliamentary session at Stormont; visits to Carrickfergus, where electric light had at last been installed in the church; allocation of Christmas tips to a host of tradesmen and menials. But Beatrice's maternal longings still had an alternative outlet in her elder stepson William, now in his thirties. Boxing Day was a 'beautiful day – sunshine – Willie & I walked to City Hall visited Garden of Remembrance & saw Christmas Tree – came home in tram.'[7] And Daniel was not forgotten, receiving a xylophone for Christmas along with 'a large hamper of foods' for Louis from 'the old stepdame'.[8]

Throughout the last three years of phoney peace, father and son edged closer together, encouraged by the removal of Mary and the advent of Daniel. Even after Louis had secured his decree of divorce 'absolute', the shared nuisance of Marie Beazley lingered on. When Frederick visited University College, Oxford for an ecumenical conference in July 1937, he sent some disagreeable news to Louis:

> I have just had a most painful experience. Mrs B called round: how she found my rooms I do not know. … She wished to unburden her mind, but I refused. It was, possibly, unkind on my part, but I felt I could not go through it. I'm sure she will be furious. … I suffered too much, years ago, at her hands. She wounded me in the most tender parts & seemingly exulted in it. I could not go over the things that have happened.

The meeting had reawakened memories not merely of an unsatisfactory and collapsed marriage, but of her insinuation that Louis's pedigree was sullied by hereditary physical and mental failings. Another painful recollection perhaps lay behind a reference to his son's forthcoming visit to Scotland, scene of one of their least harmonious family holidays in 1925: 'I hope you will not find things very monotonous in the Hebrides.' Frederick also offered a gentle reminder that Louis, in full pursuit of Nancy Coldstream, had fallen out of touch with his son: 'Madre has been with Dan, & has written interesting accounts of him.'[9] But Frederick's letter also established an unexpected positive link between father and son: T. S. Eliot, that quintessentially 'modern' poet, was about to address the Oxford conference.[10] Through Faber and Faber, Eliot had published Louis's second book of poems in 1935 and remained a critical but appreciative reader and publisher throughout his life.

In February 1938, Louis visited Dublin for a rugby international at Lansdowne Road, which he watched with his father. After the match, presumably as Frederick's guest, he had 'tea and toast with Fellows and Bishops' at the Dublin University Club.[11] Two months later, Louis once again deposited Daniel at Bishop's House for a few weeks while searching for 'a new flat and nurse or nanny'.[12] His published account of revisiting Belfast after a year's self-conscious exile was relatively benign: 'Breakfast in my family's home was as ample as always. The same porridge on the side table – each one helping himself – the same breakfast service, the same triangular loaves of shaggy bread. But the house was not the same.'

Mimicking the condescending tone of mentors like Anthony Blunt, he described it as a 'large, ugly but comfortable mansion', indeed 'a hideous house, but very comfortable – run by five maids who slept in a wing over the garage'. He could not resist sneering at the wallpaper and the absence of wooden panelling in the upper stairwell. When accompanying his stepmother to the cathedral, he mocked 'the strictly vertical worshippers in front of me'. Despite such jibes, the publication of *Zoo* marked a public reconciliation with Ulster, Belfast and his family, which must have gratified the long-suffering MacNeices.[13]

By May 1939, Louis was clearly worried by reports of his father's failing health, telling his American beloved Eleanor Clark that 'he has been ill – heart I think', and later that he had 'very high blood pressure & has been ordered a rest for six weeks'. After hearing that Frederick was 'feeling a lot better', he wrote to 'Daddie' to correct various misconceptions about Americans and to propose, rather unenthusiastically, a brief trip to Belfast: 'Well, I might come over for a weekend before the end of June'.[14] This was followed by an extended visit in August and September, when Louis, his friend Ernst Stahl, Daniel, Sophie Popper (the new Hungarian nanny), her father Wilmos and the Nicholsons joined the bishop and his retinue in 'a beautiful house at the end of Cushendun bay', below the Glens of Antrim.[15] As Louis exclaimed in 'Cushendun', 'What a place to talk of War.'[16]

II

Meanwhile, Frederick had been working tirelessly to maintain and develop his vast diocese. His attendance at major meetings associated with the Representative Church Body was even more punctilious in 1937–8 than before, though he remained an irregular participant in committees of the general synod.[17] When unable to attend key meetings, he took care to ensure that Belfast's claim to a greater share of church income would not be shelved or mishandled. Just before leaving for the Oxford conference in July 1937, he reminded an unidentified synodsman of his earlier proposal to plead Belfast's case before a private session of the next general synod. Now that Primate D'Arcy was pressing for a speedier decision, Frederick wished to reassure synodsmen that no attempt was being made to penalize small southern dioceses: 'No man in the Church of Ireland is less inclined than I am to take a penny from the South which could be used there.' Instead, the RCB should be urged to provide expanding northern parishes with funds 'not tied up to any particular place'. Cannily appealing to the competitive instincts of his colleagues, he declared: 'I have the most difficult job in the Church of Ireland. I did not seek it. But here I am. I know that Methodists and Presbyterians are giving large sums of money for the strengthening of their positions in Belfast and N. E. Ireland.' Having outlined his case, he requested that the matter should not be referred to the RCB or the synod's standing committee until his return from Oxford.[18] Experience had shown that few voices except his own were capable of defusing the distrust and rivalry between north and south, which had so often fractured an ostensibly national church.

When addressing the diocesan synod in November 1936, he urged practical measures to counteract the drift away from religion, such as church extension, missionary activity, 'systematic religious instruction' in state schools, the encouragement of youth fellowships, and renewed struggle against gambling and intemperance.[19] A year later, he expressed 'shock' that thirty-nine parishes had disregarded an appeal for funds issued by the Religious Education Board, but satisfaction that the modest target of £10,000 to sustain struggling parishes had at last been reached.[20] By now, however, he was on the point of securing a much larger sum for church extension, his forte as an archdeacon. In an interview shortly after the synod, Dean Kerr and he revealed that the RCB had recommended an allocation of up to £40,000 for the building of churches and halls in the Belfast district, subject to proportionate amounts being raised locally. Kerr congratulated the bishop on his astute handling of Provost Thrift of Trinity College and the secretary of the RCB, who had visited Belfast to assess its needs. 'He took them on a tour round the city, showing them the new districts where the churches were urgently needed.' Simultaneously, in association with the dean, he was vigorously raising funds for the never-to-be-achieved completion of St Anne's Cathedral, holding an 'at home' (away from home) for clerical and lay 'Cathedral Builders', at which he outlined an elaborate scheme involving at least 200 'Parish Patrons' and 1000 collectors. The dean's 'Quarter of a Million Shilling Fund' directed at working-class members had yet to take off, having raised only 17,000 shillings (£850) so far.[21]

The climax of Frederick's struggle for money came at the general synod in May 1938, which appropriated much of the Central Church Fund for church extension in Belfast. Provost Thrift strongly supported Frederick's proposals, confirming from his own observation the 'amazing … redistribution of population' and the unavailability of funding from local sources. Despite some residual opposition, the synod offered almost unanimous approval. When reporting this triumph to the dicoesan synod in November, Frederick emphasized that at least £20,000 must be raised locally to avoid forfeiting part of the central allocation, £15,000 having been squandered for this reason under the previous church extension scheme.[22] By the end of 1939, four-fifths of the promised £40,000 had been advanced to fourteen parishes, supplemented by diocesan and parochial contributions amounting to almost £20,000.[23] Frederick had not lost his golden touch.

The public duties of a bishop ranged from personally confirming every new member to hobnobbing with royalty. As a senior prelate, he was expected to represent the Church on great state occasions, such as the coronation of King George VI on 12 May 1937. As Louis wrote to Annie Dodds in Oxford: 'I hear Westminster Abbey is going to fall down on the Coronation. My father is going to be there complete with crozier.'[24] In July, six days after attending a garden party at Buckingham Palace, Beatrice and the bishop visited City Hall for the presentation of Loyal Addresses to George VI and Queen Elizabeth. These included a combined address from leaders of the major Protestant churches and Rabbi Shachter, whose inclusion underlined the continued abstention of the Roman Catholic hierarchy in Northern Ireland from all expressions of loyalty to the Crown. The MacNeices had to be content with seats in Block C in the crowded banqueting hall, albeit in the front row.[25] The bishop's dissociation from party politics did not prevent him from attending a garden party for 750 unionists, a few weeks before the royal visit, to meet the prime minister and Lady Craigavon. Like his fellow guest John Waddell of the Belfast Council of Christian Churches, now the Presbyterian moderator, Frederick doubtless relished the opportunity to engage in 'happy social intercourse' with leading unionist politicians of all factions, including the short-lived 'Progressive Unionists' with their New-Deal programme for state intervention and economic regeneration. As usual in Ulster, the occasion was spoiled by 'incessant rain'.[26]

His routine episcopal duties were more onerous: in a single quarter of 1937, he performed 2626 confirmations.[27] Though demonstrating that the Church was still in working order, mass ceremonies of initiation were probably less gratifying to a son of the missions than the occasional reception of an adult convert. In December 1938, Frederick confirmed three men in the Chapel of the Resurrection below Belfast Castle and 'enjoyed Service very much'.[28] The converts included 'a Hungarian Jew, Mr Popper', perhaps the father of Daniel's nanny. Wilmos Popper was to spend several months living with the MacNeices before moving to the refugee settlement at Millisle.[29] The bishop remained a regular attender at meetings of the diocesan clerical society, invariably offering 'a masterly and comprehensive summing up' of the preceding discussion, whether this concerned the 'Faith and Order' movement, 'Parochial Discipline', the Quatercentenary of 'The English Bible', or the 'New Constitution of India'.[30]

He relished having the last word, as in a warm obituary tribute to Primate D'Arcy, 'our foremost man', whose reputation as a scholar and theologian 'extended far beyond the shores of Ireland'. D'Arcy had displayed 'a wide and accurate knowledge of literature', 'a poet's appreciation of style', and a 'power of compression' comparable to Bacon's. He was also a connoisseur of Ireland and the Irish: 'He knew Ireland as a mountain climber and walker, knew its flowers, shrubs, trees. He knew its people, too, and had very definite opinions as to their racial origins and characteristics.'[31] D'Arcy had believed that 'the very same racial elements which went to the making of the English people are blended in the Irish', the Anglo-Irish antagonism being not 'mainly racial' but 'the outcome of historical causes'. It followed that 'that the people of Ireland' could not be defined as 'a nation apart, having no racial affinity with the people of England'.[32] D'Arcy's analysis resembled Frederick's view that 'the term "Irish" is not now a race term', and that 'in Wales, in the Highlands of Scotland, and in parts of England, there are populations more pronouncedly Celtic than are to be found in Ireland, except perhaps along her western coast'.[33]

The primacy was offered to Archbishop Gregg, who after much dithering decided that he was too old and politically ill-attuned to Ulster to accept the honour.[34] Frederick was reportedly one of the three candidates subsequently under consideration as D'Arcy's successor, but his election by the House of Bishops would have had disastrous repercussions for the diocese of Down. Under the arcane laws then governing the Church, his place in Belfast would automatically have been filled by the 76-year-old dean of Armagh, who could scarcely be expected to cope with the demands of so tumultuous a diocese.[35] Instead, Bishop Godfrey Day of Ossory was elected primate, being welcomed in Belfast by Frederick as one possessing 'the goodwill and approval of the People of the Church, North and South'. Only five months after exclaiming 'Long may he live', Frederick found himself officiating at Day's own memorial service at St Anne's cathedral. Day's virtues, as he depicted them, were those to which he himself aspired:

> He had a man's interests to the full – cricket, rowing and football being among them. ... He was at his best when stressing that the world was the church's parish. ... He did not seek or desire the Primacy, because he was a humble-minded man and singularly unselfish. ... He was nothing of a partisan. He put his strength into the things that made for peace, and his ministry was indeed a ministry of reconciliation.[36]

Once again, Frederick was named as a serious contender for the primacy, and on this occasion his successor in Belfast would have been a younger man, admittedly with no pastoral experience outside Dublin.[37] This time, however, Archbishop Gregg overcame the scruples arising from his southern background and advanced age, only to preside over the Church in Armagh for two decades.[38] Gregg's elevation gave Frederick his final opportunity for promotion, and his name appeared in the select list of four bishops contesting the united diocese of Dublin, Glendalough and Kildare. At the electoral synod in February 1939, he received surprisingly little clerical or lay support and came in last.[39] There was to be no escape from Belfast.

III

For Frederick MacNeice, the manoeuvrings associated with synods and elections were always secondary to his deeper mission. Yet, even in his passionate pursuit of peace and reconciliation through ecumenicism, he was undeniably constrained by his office. A tireless advocate of the movement towards Protestant reunion, he resisted practical co-operation whenever this compromised his own church's discipline and authority. His stern rejection in March 1936 of Craigavon's proposal for ecumenical services on state occasions, though apparently accepted by the prime minister, only briefly alleviated the pressure. In April 1937, when urged to participate in a Presbyterian service to be held two months later, he informed D'Arcy that he would be absent in Oxford and saw 'no reason at all why I should be represented'. Though happy for the Primate or his representative to attend, and himself 'on the friendliest terms with the Moderator', he resisted any encroachment on his independent authority as bishop. He continued to 'feel very strongly that our own Control of services at the Cathedral or in any of our Churches should not be shared with others'.[40] He must have been relieved in November 1940 by the government's decision to bury Craigavon beside the parliament building at Stormont and to hold the public ecumenical service at Belmont Presbyterian church. Frederick, like the Presbyterian moderator and the president of the Methodist Conference, offered up a prayer.[41]

Frederick's distrust of pan-Protestant movements outside his own control re-emerged in January 1938, when he made his first appearance as bishop at a meeting of the Diocesan Temperance and Social Service Committee. As usual, the committee was attempting to counteract the menace of 'Red Biddy' (a toxic but widely sold blend of wine and methylated spirits), and associated 'evils' such as 'Toney Wine' (a potent effusion of British and colonial vineyards). A lay speaker urged a joint campaign by all Protestant denominations in Belfast, with their armoury of 188 places of worship; and Dean Kerr reported on investigations by the Presbyterian city missionaries. In response, 'the Bishop expressed the view that it was primarily a matter for our own parishes to take up the Temperance

Question more seriously' and proposed a meeting of his entire Belfast clergy on 25 February. Meanwhile, Craigavon offered a vague assurance that the government was considering how best to counteract Red Biddy. The outcome of the monster meeting was an anodyne resolution calling for heavier taxation on Toney Wine.[42] As in 1926, Frederick had sensed the danger that a pan-Protestant moral crusade would lead to confrontation with the government and espousal of a political party on the lines of the failed Local Option movement. The Church of Christ should not bind itself to any political faction, moralistic or otherwise.

Though often distrustful of the implications of ecumenical enterprises at home, Frederick had become involved in two worldwide movements that would eventually spawn the World Council of Churches in 1948. In July and August 1937, he attended two international conferences aiming to extend and refine the ecumenical aspirations advanced at Edinburgh in 1910, Stockholm in 1925 and Lausanne in 1927. The agenda for both meetings had been carefully prepared by a 'Committee of Thirty-Five' representing the two movements. It included one Irish representative, Frederick's old ally Canon Drury. First, he spent a fortnight in Oxford contemplating 'Church, Community, and State' in the company of 300 official delegates and 125 others, from about 45 countries. Despite the vast catalogue of Christian denominations represented in Oxford, there were no official delegates of either the Roman Catholic or the German Evangelical churches. No Irish delegate presented a paper, but Frederick was a keen participant in the section considering 'Church and State', which concentrated on the contemporary 'wave of secularism', the 'exaltation of the state', and the menace of 'totalitarianism' (embracing Fascism, Nazism and communism). As usual with such festivals, the conference created a renewed sense of goodwill, optimism and shared purpose without agreeing on any specific programme or future ecumenical organization.[43]

After a week's respite in London, Frederick proceeded to Edinburgh for the second World Conference on Faith and Order, which (but for the gloomy international outlook) would have again met in Lausanne. The president and architect of the conference was Archbishop William Temple of York. Enrolment slightly exceeded that in Oxford, with 504 attenders including delegates from 122 'Christian Communions' in 43 countries. Frederick was one of a dozen Irish delegates from the Church of Ireland, the Presbyterian and Methodist churches, and the Society of Friends. His companions included Drury, Archbishop Gregg, Principal Davey of the Assembly's College and the prominent Presbyterian unifier, James Spence Rutherford. Gregg was the only prominent Irish participant in conference debates, though Drury and Rutherford served on a key committee. Frederick's one recorded contribution to the fortnight's proceedings was to move unsuccessfully for adjournment of an interminable debate on granting a 'sympathetic welcome' to a proposal by the Committee of Thirty-Five to prepare plans for a future 'World Council'.[44] But a well-informed obituarist described him as 'one of the outstanding representatives of the Anglican Communion' in Edinburgh, where 'his addresses and advice in committee attracted much attention'.[45] He was one of 6 Irish delegates elected to the 'Continuation Committee' of 120 members, whose task was to meet regularly in attractive European locations to prepare for further conferences.[46] The bishop of Down had joined the motley team of cosmopolitan seers and dreamers who believed that, if only Christians of the world would unite, the forces of materialism might yet be vanquished.

Though without immediate practical consequences, these gatherings created a sense of brotherhood among unifiers worldwide, which deeply touched Frederick's fraternal instincts. In May 1938, when proposing further co-operation with the Presbyterian Church to an 'attentive House' at the general synod, 'he referred to the Oxford Conference and said that questions of race colour and class never were absent from their thoughts. – What he had thought specially significant was the actual unity realised in worship, and he had thought that in that unity was promise that ultimately would be fulfilled.'[47] Six months later, he gave a striking account of the two conferences to the diocesan synod:

> At each there were delegates from almost every professedly Christian Communion, and from almost every race. What I thought amazing and encouraging was the unity achieved in worship. At the daily services in the University Church, Oxford, and in St Giles' Cathedral, Edinburgh, black and white, brown and yellow, knelt side by side. An actual Christian fellowship was realised.[48]

These colourful images lingered in his memory, re-emerging three years later in the wake of the Blitz:

> The Conferences themselves, in their very composition, held out a real hope of the things that could be – if Society were but based on the right foundation. … Brown and black, yellow and white had meals together, studied together, prayed together. All were one in Jesus Christ. Some of the most hopeful members were negro gentlemen and negro ladies.[49]

Through these personal experiences of international fraternity, he sensed how it might feel to inhabit an ecumenical world.

IV

More than ever, Frederick was preoccupied with the duty of Christians to pursue both domestic and international peace. He continued to ruminate about reconciliation in Ireland with Major-General Montgomery, his ardent supporter in the aftermath of the 1935 riots. Throughout his protracted attempt to prepare the public mind for organized pursuit of reconciliation, Montgomery regarded Frederick as a soulmate and natural ally. When Molly McNeill, 'northern' secretary of the Irish Christian Fellowship, suggested that he circulate a school syllabus entitled *Good Neighbours*, he decided to 'get a few wise & moderate men like the Bishop of Down … to look through it carefully & see if there are any other points worth considering'. After minute revision of the pamphlet, he proposed giving Frederick and half a dozen others 'a bundle of "Good Neighbours" to distribute among their friends', as well as planting 150 copies at the general synod in May 1938. Though Frederick's comments are untraced, he was again asked to copy-edit a leaflet drafted by Montgomery in the following month.[50] In a non-partisan crusade for peace and reconciliation, the bishop's sharp eye for hidden snares was indispensable.

In November 1937, Montgomery sought his opinion on proposals submitted by the Australian-born historian Keith Hancock, who had recently completed the first volume of his monumental *Survey of British Commonwealth Affairs*. For Hancock, de Valera's recent introduction of a proto-republican constitution offered Britain and the Commonwealth a stimulating challenge rather than a terminal rebuff. He remained guardedly optimistic that Britain and Ireland would eventually discover 'the secret of friendship', given the strength of 'objective factors' favouring interdependence, co-operation and reconciliation. The main obstacle, apart from lingering revolutionary romanticism, was 'The hard cold fire of the northerner | Frozen into his blood from the fire in his basalt'. This metaphor, minted by Louis, encouraged Hancock to speculate that 'the fighting creed' of 'the Orange rulers in Ulster' could only be shaken by an equally fanatical creed such as communism.[51]

Despite admitting that he 'did not know the North well', Hancock bombarded Montgomery with suggestions for his campaign. British, Irish and Ulster economists should jointly advocate an Irish Customs Union based on selective protection, and persuade northern businessmen of the material benefits of 'Irish Economic Unity'. To achieve Anglo-Irish reconciliation, it was essential to persuade British Conservatives that some Ulstermen were prepared to do their 'best to build a bridge between Belfast and Dublin', acting 'both as Irishmen and as believers in the British Commonwealth'. While 'particular schemes' might be premature, the issue of partition should not be ruled out of discussion.[52] Hancock's approach clearly appealed to Frederick's long-standing aversion to the division of

Ireland: 'I am returning Prof. Hancock's letter which I think extremely valuable. He indicates the lines – & I believe the only lines at present – on which advance might be possible. It ought to be possible for the two Governments, without any surrender on the part of either, to confer as to the boundary & other problems.'[53]

Yet there were signs that Frederick was growing weary of Montgomery's missionary idealism, relentless exuberance, and almost ludicrous political innocence. In January 1938, Montgomery told Molly McNeill of a dispiriting visit to Bishop's House:

> After seeing you on Thursday I had a talk with Bishop McNeice, but found him very 'tired', and lacking in his ordinary enthusiasm. He is evidently suffering from overwork, and ought to go on a holiday; that diocese is ridiculously top-heavy, & much more than one man can cope with, if he is conscientious. However, he promised to go & see Profr Henry and arrange for us to meet and discuss Profr Hancock's proposal.[54]

The test of Frederick's commitment to Montgomery's cause came a year later, when the long-heralded Irish Association was finally launched.[55] In its first year, 248 liberal-minded well-wishers, from both Irish states and beyond, showed their rejection of sectarianism and espousal of tolerance by paying at least half a crown for an annual subscription, or occasionally two guineas for life. The great majority were well-heeled and highly educated Protestants, with a scattering of gentry and clergy. Several were old associates of Frederick, such as Alexander Moody (the former Presbyterian moderator), John Heron Lepper from Carrickfergus (now in London), and R. J. Pack-Beresford of Woburn, Millisle and the general synod. The bishop's name appeared in the address book kept by Molly McNeill, now northern secretary of the Irish Association as well as the Irish Christian Fellowship, but he did not join or pay any subscription.[56] Like his son, Frederick remained a fellow traveller rather than a party member.

The bishop's reluctance to join political organizations, however laudable, was grounded in theology as well as prudence and parsimony. He called on his own clergy to renounce the part of 'a politician' in favour of 'an apostle of peace' in the 'great tug-of-war', occurring in every country, 'between Christ and anti-Christ'. When introducing a new rector to a north Antrim parish in May 1937, he remarked that clergymen participating in political meetings should be reminded by 'someone' of their vocation: 'What doest thou here, Elijah? Is this the thing for which you were ordained or set apart?' His advice was unheeded, in that the rector promptly became a stalwart of the County Grand Orange Lodge of Antrim.[57] The bishop's private impatience with conventional Orange unionism, still implacably opposed to any compromise with Éire, was evident in his diary entry for 12 July 1938: 'About 11 went down to the Lisburn Rd: Watched Orange procession, in a Car [?], from front of St Thomas's Rectory: then went to junction of Lisburn & Malone Roads & watched from there. A very large procession. But what does it all mean, & why are Clergymen in it?'[58] If anyone knew the answers to those questions, it was Frederick MacNeice.

As the crisis in Belfast subsided, his focus had shifted to international problems. On Armistice Day in 1936, he declared that 'war solved no problems; it never did. ... If Germany, France, or Great Britain had been Christian in 1914 there would have been no war, and if Germany, France, and Great Britain were Christian to-day the war that is now dreaded would be averted.' The responsibility of the churches, unlike the state, was 'not to determine when and in what circumstances war might be justified', but 'to convert, to change, and to prepare the way of the Lord'.[59] On the following St Patrick's Day, he prefaced another volume of letters and addresses, often 'written very hurriedly', with the hope that his thoughts on peace and reconciliation might 'have some guidance for those who are responsible for leadership'.[60] *Our First Loyalty* certainly impressed ecumenical reformers, if not political leaders, being cited approvingly in a volume of essays on religion in Ireland published a few months later for the Irish Christian Fellowship.[61] At the diocesan synod, he again left it to the state 'to decide when and in what circumstances war might be permissible', whereas the Church's responsibility was 'to plead for the better way of conference and arbitration'.[62]

This distinction between the provinces of God and Caesar masked his deep disenchantment with all states and politicians in the post-war world, expressed on Armistice Day in 1937: 'The war was won by the men who suffered and died, but peace was lost by the politicians; and it was lost because the politicians carried the war spirit into the peace negotiations.' Speaking in St George's church at a 'service of intercession for peace', he outlined an unusually elaborate 'peace programme for peace workers'. They should support the government's declarations of support for the League of Nations; 'strengthen the forces making for peace' by funding them; 'recommend justice' for aggrieved nations as a basis for peace; consider national demands 'for access to raw materials'; advocate that all colonies 'should be collectively administered' by an 'international civil service', especially 'where peoples were undeveloped'; and ask if trade tariffs and treaties were not 'war in the economic sphere'.[63]

As Germany and therefore the world lurched towards war, Frederick began to inscribe ominous observations in his diary for 1938. On 26 September: 'International situation very serious. Appeal from Roosevelt not to break off negotiations.

Bellicose speech by Hitler.' Two days later, he cautiously welcomed the meeting at Munich: 'Anniversary of Ulster Day – 1912!! … Development in the International Situation. Hitler, at request of Chamberlain, consented to meet Mussolini, Daladier, and Chamberlain, and to postpone mobilisation. This was welcome news. I wish, however, America could be brought into the Conference, and that some one such as Churchill should accompany Chamberlain.'[64] On 30 September, he opened the memorial service for Primate Day, in St Anne's Cathedral, with a strikingly warm endorsement of the Munich agreement:

> Today's great news fills us with thankfulness. We may, I think, believe that God has intervened. … We have had a signal illustration of the power of a great appeal. We hope it is but the beginning and that the problems which divide the nations will be approached in the spirit that puts its trust in conference and conciliation rather than in violence and force. There are questions still unsettled. There may be a case – most reasonable people think there is – for revision of some treaties and re-adjustment of some boundaries; for the removal, too, of economic barriers, so as to improve the standard of life for the poor and under-privileged in all countries. … For what has been done we give thanks to God.[65]

His euphoria soon dissipated. On 11 November, he spoke of '20 years of disillusionment' since the Armistice and lamented 'a tremendous lack of real statesmanship', especially in the failure to regard economic issues 'as moral questions'.[66] By 20 December, it was apparent that the Munich agreement was a mere cover for continued German aggression: 'Chamberlain is leading the country to disaster.' On New Year's Eve, he composed a sombre reflection adorned by his favourite Greek exclamation in times of crisis, 'God help me': 'Another year comes to an end. κγριε βονθει μοι. It has been an eventful year: witnessed more than one international Crime. British prestige has been lowered, & for the time Hitler & Mussolini have scored. But surely their day will pass, as did that of Sennacherib, Nebuchadnezzar, & in modern times that of Napoleon.'[67] Like Nebuchadnezzar, today's dictators would be humiliated and reminded 'that the Most High God ruleth in the kingdom of men, and that he setteth up over it whomsoever he will' (Dan. 5: 21).

14. *Apostle*

BELFAST, 1939–1942

I

When Germany's invasion of Poland finally induced Britain to declare war on 3 September 1939, Frederick's 'peace programme' became irrelevant. A quarter of a century earlier, he had greeted the outbreak of war with pained silence while searching for a moral formulation that would satisfy his duties to both God and Carrickfergus. This time, he instantly supplied unqualified moral support in a letter to the press on behalf of his people:

> I feel certain they will, at this critical time, render all assistance in their power to the British Government in the heroic stand which it is making for the liberties of Europe and mankind. The issue is perfectly clear. Never was there a war more unnecessary than that forced by Herr Hitler, and never did more powerful and representative individuals and governments offer their services as mediators. I am confident that our people, whatever their spheres, will play their part with unflinching determination to defend the right of plain people, no matter what their politics or religion, in any country, weak or strong, to live their lives and think their thoughts.[1]

Yet his analysis of the roots of war, and the conditions for its eradication, remained unaltered. On 7 November, when addressing the diocesan synod, he declared that 'there are not a few living devils challenging, at the present time, all that is Christian', implying that these devils were not confined to Britain's enemies. He rejected the fallacy that there were any 'Christian nations', declared that 'war as it is to-day must be outlawed, and outlawed speedily if civilization is to survive', and urged that 'we should think not only of the military aim of winning the war, but of the distinctively spiritual aim of winning the peace'. His reversion in wartime to a familiar peacetime theme raised delicate issues, which led him to publish the full text of his address as a pamphlet.[2] He also upheld an objection to the report of the diocesan council, which had exonerated Britain from blame: 'The whole Church is aghast that such a catastrophe, outraging the teaching of Christ, could happen in our era. Whilst we feel that our country is free from the guilt of causing it, we are horror-stricken at the sufferings involved.'[3] When a young Clareman ministering in Dunmurry protested that 'they all shared in the guilt and to him the statement savoured of the Scribe and the Pharisee', Frederick advised modification of the offending phrase. Despite the 'Loud Applause' greeting Dean Kerr's retort that 'he distinctly felt that Germany was responsible for the war', the bishop reiterated that 'they all shared the guilt to some extent'.[4] Patriotic senti-ment had not overwhelmed his deeper beliefs. *The Irish Times* cited the address as proof that there was 'life left in the Church of Ireland', inferring that 'his rebuke to the democractic nations is not less severe than his rebuke to their adversaries', and concluding that he had brought Britain's war aims under much-needed critical scrutiny.[5] The issue was not, on reflection, 'perfectly clear'.

During the first two months of phoney war Frederick seems to have suffered a breakdown, as he had done on several previous occasions when his severe daily regimen suddenly succumbed to overwork compounded by anxiety. The diocesan council hinted, in its report of 31 October, that the problem was not primarily physiological:

> The illness of our beloved Bishop has aroused the keenest sympathy with him. We realise how unsparing and self-sacrificing he has been since he returned here to be Bishop of this great Diocese. The enthusiastic way in which he threw all his intense energies into meeting the special needs of the Church here, the wholehearted devotion which has already accomplished so much, has won our abundant admiration and gratitude.

Frederick resumed his 'inspiring leadership' sooner than expected.[6] In a hall 'packed to capacity', he was welcomed by 'a rousing and prolonged reception on rising to deliver his address', by which he was 'visibly touched'. As the *Church of Ireland Gazette* observed, he was 'evidently restored to much of his former strength and health'.[7] Perhaps, in recovering the moral independence that he had momentarily surrendered at the outbreak of war, he had released untapped reserves of energy.

Over the next two years, his analysis of the war remained ambivalent to a degree unusual among church leaders. When opening a naval canteen on New Year's Day, he dismissed the vulgar misconception 'that, if it had not for the war, there would have been a dying out of all the heroic virtues': 'That was not their conviction; they believed that war was a brutal thing, a cruel thing, a horrible thing; but yet in some circumstances it was a regrettable necessity. Britain at the present time was engaged in war, not for the acquisition of territory or power, but in defence of small and weak nations.'[8] On 10 May 1940, Germany's invasion of France and the Low Countries precipitated the crisis that led to evacuation of the British Expeditionary Force from Dunkirk a few weeks later. Frederick's tone was uncharacteristically pessimistic when addressing the Church Missionary Society in Belfast on 20 May: 'He supposed that, even during the last war few of them had contemplated the possibility of defeat, not in battle but in war. Yet to-day there were some who contemplated that possibility. … [B]elieving that it was a worthy cause, they must put their whole strength into it so that the right side might win – as he believed it would.'[9] Two days later, when endorsing the King's appeal for a 'national day of prayer', he interpreted this as 'a call to repentance, for victory, if we remained impenitent, would not be a blessing at all'. He did not reportedly participate in the main service in St Anne's cathedral, conducted by Dean Kerr in the presence of the Craigavons, the Abercorns and 1400 others.[10]

At the diocesan synod of November 1940, there was again a striking contrast between the assessments of the war offered by the bishop and the diocesan council, dominated by rich unionist laymen. For the council, it was 'an awe-inspiring thought that on our race is laid the tremendous but glorious mission to save the world from spiritual enslavement. The struggle and its issue depend vitally on the religious convictions of our people.'[11] Frederick's address concurred that 'there are forces now dominant in Europe which would rule out the decencies of human life. So to-day, while we are fighting against a soulless despotism which, if it were permitted to succeed, would make the world a hell, and human life intolerable, we have also to make clear to ourselves and others why we fight at all.' In a rather scholastic rejection of the pacifist axiom that the use of force was against Christian principles, he stated that 'Great Britain was morally bound to enter the war' and that the civil magistrate was entitled to take 'coercive action': 'He has authority from God, and if he exercises his authority rightfully he is God's minister.' Yet neither the Church nor the individual Christian was 'the minister of God's retributive justice', being answerable to higher moral responsibilities. He hoped that the chastening experience of wartime deprivation would encourage those at home to cast aside their 'ostentatious expenditure' and vulgar 'extravagance in pre-war days': 'Necessity may compel us, I hope it will, to re-think the whole question of the getting and spending of money. ... But more than military victory would be needed if they were to be in any degree worthy of the heroic men who, in their tens of thousands, had offered themselves in service.'[12] Many lay synodsmen should have stirred uneasily as their bishop pilloried the relentless materialism that had once made Belfast the envy of Europe.

The war had a crushing impact on the institutional church, stalling or negating most of Frederick's strategies for church extension and missionary activity. At each diocesan synod, he lamented the impracticality of pursuing his attempt to replenish its material strength and moral power. In November 1939, he 'had intended to speak of the special needs of the Church in Belfast and of the efforts that should be made if those needs were to be so met as to become opportunities for a real advance. He was working on a plan, but he felt it must be held over for the present.'[13] His earlier success in securing central funds for church extension ensured that several halls were opened during the war, leading Dean Kerr to observe that 'our present Bishop, from his appointment, faced the problem with courageous initiative and untiring advocacy'. In response to Kerr's 'excellent sermon', Frederick stated that wartime demands had caused him to defer an appeal for further subscriptions from the laity.[14] In its report to the synod of November 1940, the diocesan council admitted that Church work had been somewhat 'circumscribed by the war conditions', leading to postponement of church building and the long-awaited extension of the cathedral. Yet it could still 'rejoice in the restored health of our Bishop and gratefully record our appreciation of his tireless labours'.[15]

II

In April and May 1941, the work of decades was undone in four fearful nights of aerial attacks lasting for ten hours. As Frederick had long predicted, no country was capable of repelling air attacks on its cities and their inhabitants. Outside London, only Glasgow and Liverpool suffered comparable fatalities, though eleven British cities were subjected to even heavier bombardment than Belfast. About 1100 civilians were killed, mostly on the night of 15 April, when the deficiency of provision for air-raid shelters, evacuation, and anti-aircraft defence was cruelly exposed. The raid on the night of 5 May, though involving more aircraft, more bombs, and more incendiaries, resulted in far fewer deaths as a result of mass evacuation from the city and improved precautions. More than half of the city's housing stock suffered, 3200 houses being demolished, 4000 acutely damaged, and almost 50,000 others hit or blasted. Organized temporary evacuation from the city affected 50,000 people, while tens of thousands of others fled independently: according to one official estimate, 220,000 had left the city by the end of May.[16]

The impact on all denominations in Belfast was devastating, as buildings were razed or rendered unusable, congregations scattered across Ulster, and urban employment severely curtailed. No less than seventy churches and gospel halls (over one-third of all places of worship in the city) were reportedly destroyed or damaged.[17] The fabric of the Church of Ireland was laid waste. Three churches were demolished, fourteen others were damaged, and serious injury was inflicted on six church halls, nine parochial halls, four schoolhouses and five rectories.[18] Holy Trinity church was so badly damaged that the spire had to be demolished (with some difficulty) by the army, while the congregation met in Clifton Street Orange hall. Two years later the parish was transferred to Joanmount, an expanding northern suburb, and the old site was cleared and sold.[19] After the first waves of attacks, the *News-Letter* published a grim account of the resultant disruption of church business:

> Owing to damage to church property in the city, and the consequent distur-
> bance of the normal financing of parochial life in some areas, there will have
> to be a measure of re-arrangement of services and meetings on Sundays and
> week-days for the time being. We can be assured that clergy and people will pull
> together in the untouched parishes to give every aid and convenience to their
> brethren who have felt the weight of the enemy's malice.[20]

Frederick, who had again fallen ill, 'resumed active work' about a week after the first attack: 'He has already inspected some of the damage done to church property in Belfast, and has made a handsome contribution to the Lord Mayor's Air Raid Distress Fund.'[21] Following further attacks in early May, Frederick appealed through the press for 'emergency help' from outside Belfast, while not 'mentioning special cases of distress' since these might be 'too harrowing' (not a scruple that would inhibit today's fundraisers).[22] On 22 June, an appeal from the bishop for a new Diocesan Church Maintenance fund, arising from the air raids, was read in every remaining church in the united diocese. As usual, Frederick offered inspiration rather than specific instructions, though he presided over a committee designed to 'act in an advisory and administrative capacity'. Collec-tions might be held on a designated Sunday, over several weeks, or through weekly penny offerings over an entire year.[23] Nearly £4000 was eventually raised by such means.[24] Despite the depletion and impoverishment of congregations caused by air raids, the sum raised in parochial subscriptions and collections during 1941 actually exceeded that in 1940, the recovery being sharpest in Connor.[25] State compensation covering temporary repairs and loss of contents (where insured) was available under the War Damages Act, 1941, and some modest supplementary grants and advances were also dispersed by a committee of the RCB with authority from the general synod.[26] Through state assistance and a combination of parochial, diocesan, and central funding, the Church in Belfast was saved from financial ruin.

In his address to the synod in December, which he could not deliver in person because of 'indisposition', Frederick 'wrote that the work on reconstruction must be the people's'. If £10,000 could be raised, then 'essential aid' could be given to 'several struggling parishes'. As he surveyed the wreckage of his Church, he was less concerned with the practical problem of reconstruction than with the dreadful intimation of divine displeasure that it embodied: 'The war,' declared the Bishop, 'had come not accidentally, but as a harvest of what the nations have sown. In that sense, it was a judgment on and a revelation of the aims and ambitions of sinful men.'[27] Yet his address detected moral compensations arising from the disaster, 'the most serious crisis that our Church in Belfast has ever been called upon to face': 'But there are, thank God, things which cannot be shaken. During a time of great strain our people in the city showed unshakable fortitude, while the clergy, young and old, were foremost in ministering to those who had suffered.'[28] The spirit of the Church of Christ lay not in its fabric, but in its people.

The human cost of the war was gruesomely exhibited on 18 April, when 255 unidentified bodies were assembled in St George's Market, encased in open coffins to ward off rats. After 3 days, relatives or friends had identified 151 corpses, of which 92 were removed for private burial. The remainder, with 'comparatively few' exceptions, were classified as either Catholics or Protestants, apparently according to the presence of religious emblems such as rosary beads and crucifixes.[29] Two services were held there, the first by Bishop Mageean and the Catholic clergy, the second by leading Protestant ministers (including Frederick) and Rabbi Shachter in the presence of John Andrews (Craigavon's successor) and many of his ministers. The coffins were then conveyed in covered military wagons to the Milltown and City cemeteries, catering respectively for Catholics and Protestants. Separate burial services were performed at each cemetery, with four coffins in each grave. The News-Letter reported that 'two wreaths were sent by the Ulster Government, one for the Protestants and one for the Roman Catholics'.[30] Despite subsequent official claims that 'religious differences were set aside' as 'Protestants and Roman Catholics joined in prayer', it is apparent that even the indiscriminate carnage of the Blitz had failed to unite the two communities in shared ceremonies of mourning.[31]

The bishop's address to Protestant mourners at the City cemetery expressed not recrimination but compassion, not despair but hope:

> We here to-day represent several Communions, but we are absolutely united by a common sorrow and sharers in a common suffering. Many of our people have been severely tested. Thank God they endured the test nobly. Not a few have, alas, lost homes – lost some of their nearest and dearest – but they have not lost heart. Their homes have been broken, but not their spirit. Our people cannot be overcome by bombs or mines. For their courage and fortitude we give thanks to God, the Author and Inspirer of every good thought and deed. The people we have the privilege of serving would not care to live at all unless as free men and free women. ... It would be an easy thing in a city like this to cry to Heaven for vengeance, but such prayer is not for us. It is not for us to sit as judges.[32]

Frederick did not witness the 'pathetic scenes' at the next such funeral on 7 May; but he could never 'forget the first of the mass funerals of our air-raid victims, when the bodies of men and women and children, some whose names were unknown, were committed to the dust'.[33]

III

Immediately after the outbreak of war, Louis had rejoined Daniel, the Poppers, and the family in Cushendun before they all returned to Bishop's House. There for the most part Louis remained, predictably restive, until his departure for New York in mid January 1940. He wrote to Eleanor Clark in America that staying with his family was 'a mistake – except financially', the atmosphere 'demoralising in the extreme, the life in Belfast 'piano & grey'. Likewise, he told E. R. Dodds defensively that 'it saves money staying with my family'; that '*it is vastly boring here*'; that 'the family tempo here is impossible' since 'no one can take in anything until one is round the corner'; and that 'it is lovely being quit of my family for a little'.[34]

As always, Frederick and Beatrice declined to be offended by his ungrateful, even graceless response to their hospitality. Once again, Frederick, Beatrice and the Poppers took responsibility for Daniel while his father pursued fame, fortune, adventure and women in the safe haven of America. In May 1940, Daniel contracted scarlet fever and Miss Popper got married, though she undertook to resume her duties in Belfast until late June. Despite a demand from Louis that his son be sent across the Atlantic, Daniel remained in Ireland. In August, Frederick advised Louis that 'the danger of travelling to America should be far greater than that of staying where one is', and assured him that Dungannon, where the boy was then staying, was a safe as well as 'a lovely spot'. Though dismissive of the opinion of 'my old man' when writing to his former wife ('Of course we know what <u>his</u> opinion is worth on such matters'), Louis eventually concurred.[35]

After nearly a year spent mainly with Frederick and Beatrice, Daniel was despatched to distant cousins of Beatrice near Cootehill, County Cavan. This decision was reportedly prompted by the discovery of a bomb in the bishop's garden, though the Blitz had yet to strike Belfast. He was briefly reunited with his father in March 1941, three months after Louis had returned from America with no immediate prospect of employment (having resigned his lectureship at Bedford College while at Cornell). Another fifteen months seem to have passed before their next meeting, again at Cootehill, shortly after Frederick's funeral.[36] Though Louis's visits to Ireland were infrequent, Daniel's presence in Belfast and then Cootehill sustained the sense of a functioning MacNeice family, organized by Beatrice, anchored by Frederick.

Yet the anchor was beginning to falter. His recurrent illnesses had become alarmingly frequent since 1939. Beatrice's diary for 1942 began ominously: '<u>Derrick in his room</u> since Nov 27.' By Monday, 5 January, he had recovered enough to venture out of the house: 'Derrick got up & dressed by 11.30. … D & I in car to office & I came back by tram & Archdeacon Manning with Derrick to lunch at 1 oc (cold mutton). The Primate called 3.30 to 4.30 – & had tea in Drawing R. D to bedroom about 6. p.m. dinner upstairs.'[37] On the previous day, 'Madre' had chirpily written to her 'dearest Louis' that 'Daddy is still upstairs – He is plotting to attend his Diocesan Council on Wednesday at 11.30 – I hope it will not be too much for him – after 5 or nearly 6 weeks in his room – Of course he has seen heaps of people – mostly clergy.' She thanked Louis, who had recently secured a decent salary from the BBC Drama department (temporarily based in Bedford College), for repaying a long-standing loan from his father: 'Wonderful how you remembered about it!'[38] Three weeks later, she reported that Frederick's illness had its compensations:

> All going as usual here. Daddy still living a quiet life – Mostly in his bed-room. He is warmer up here with a nice fire & he is away from the telephone & from too free access – He goes out each week to necessary Committees or Councils – & sees some of the Clergy here – Archdeacon (Manning) of Down – is acting as his Commissary at present – till we see how Daddy gets on – It will be nice to see you before the end of March.[39]

Louis eventually cancelled the visit, and never again saw his father alive.[40]

Beatrice's diary recorded the fluctuations in Frederick's condition, more mundane problems such as the advent of tea coupons, and moments of delight as she put on her red felt hat and red dress for '1st. time this winter'.[41] Frederick paid his last visit to Carrickfergus on 11 March, and next day they both 'listened in to Louis' "Vienna" 8 to 9 p.m. – very good'. Conscious that she had been neglecting mundane duties during the prolonged crisis, she took both William and Frederick to have their hair cut and teeth inspected, as a result of which the dentist 'took wax impression of mouth to fix new front teeth' for the bishop on 8 April.[42] Despite these tokens of confidence in his recovery, Frederick telephoned the press on the following day to announce his impending resignation as bishop of Down at the age of seventy-one. This was to take effect in May. On 12 April, he performed his last public duty, a confirmation service in which he remained seated. Afterwards, he and Beatrice went 'round garden about 6 p.m. – windy & dull – He had no coat on.'[43]

On Tuesday, 14 April, a multitude of visitors and relatives descended on Bishop's House, and late in the afternoon his old mentor, Richard Clarke, 'called & chatted to D'. The end came quickly: 'Derrick passed peacefully away about 8 p.m. tonight. Was taken ill when in the Drawing room Sofa about 6.30. Dr. Colquhoun came in 15 minutes after being called – & later Dr. Smith – Derrick did not respond to blood Extraction – & became unconscious.'[44] The certified cause of death was hyperpiesis, signifying high blood pressure of uncertain origin.

IV

Beatrice gave no hint of weakness or disorganization as she dealt with the aftermath of her husband's death, even though he had expired without bothering to make a will or to secure a burial plot. Next morning: 'We all had breakfast in bed – a lot of callers – notice had got into papers – Canon Crooks, Dean of Belfast, Mr. Deane, Arch [Manning] of Down, Dr. Breene, came. Went 1st. to Drumbo grave-yard & found no place … Cloudless & beautiful day – We chose the burial place in Drumbeg New Cemetery.' This charmless expanse of ugly new gravestones, consecrated by Frederick in December 1935, belonged to a parish with which he had no personal association. On Thursday, the house filled up with family, with Louis occupying the dressing-room and Uncle John MacNeice a servant's room. Beatrice was gratified by the flood of telegrams – seventeen arrived in two days.[45] All was set for the 'strictly private' funeral on Friday.

The ceremonies began at Bishop's House, where Archdeacon Clarke and Dean Kerr participated in a service performed by Richard Deane, the rector of St Thomas's in the Lisburn Road.[46] At 11.30, on another 'Cloudless, Beautiful day', the family left the house in two cars for Drumbeg, where all of the clergy who had visited on Wednesday (with the exception of Dean Kerr) took part in services in the church or at the graveside. Archdeacon Clarke delivered the 'short address', of which the only record appears to be Louis's haunting but puzzling account in 'The Kingdom': 'All is well, said the voice from the tiny pulpit, | All is well with the child.'[47] After lunch for eleven, the family drove to St Anne's cathedral for the memorial service. Press coverage of the service was truncated by shortage of news-print and competition from war news. There were no reports of tearful crowds inside or outside the cathedral, and only brief accounts of the Primate's address and the names of attendant dignitaries. Even so, space was found to list a few mourners, including the prime minister (John Andrews), the minister of Finance (James Milne Barbour), the minister of Education (John Robb), the secretary of the Church Missionary Society (Bishop John Hind) and other clergy, leading ministers of the Presbyterian, Unitarian ('Non-Subscribing'), and Methodist Churches, and grandees such as Sir Thomas Dixon and Judge Herbert Thompson, ex-Recorder of Belfast. The nationalist *Irish News* carried only a brief and neutral report, which made no reference to the alleged presence of Bishop Mageean praying for his old rival in the cathedral porch.[48]

John Nicholson and Uncle John MacNeice left Belfast that evening, and Louis left for Monaghan next morning on his way to Cootehill and his seldom-seen son, now almost eight years old. Daniel, who had a close bond with his grandfather, had missed the funeral. After driving Louis to the station, Elizabeth sat with Beatrice 'in the summer house after tea & opened & read letters – I sorted some of Derrick's letters – We sat in study by fire after dinner & talked – listened in, in dining room.' The obsequies resumed on Sunday, with memorial services in most Belfast churches including St Thomas's, the MacNeices' parish church, where 'Mr. Deane spoke about Derrick fm Reading desks'. Next day, 'Louis came back for lunch & staying tonight – He & Eliz worked all Evening at Derrick's desk … I sorted out Income papers.' The extended family briefly regrouped, Eliza-beth being despatched to Monaghan to meet Daniel and bring him to Bishop's House: 'Darling Dan looking well – 2 front top teeth out & others coming on.' Elizabeth returned Daniel to Cootehill on 24 April, but stayed on with Beatrice for some time to prepare for her evacuation.[49] Louis seems to have accepted his father's death with equanimity, at least when writing to E. R. Dodds shortly after his return to London:

> I don't know if you heard that my father had died – suddenly – on April 14th. I went over there immediately & stayed a few days. He had been in very good form all that day & died quickly in the evening; it seemed a good way. He had just announced that he was going to retire this year & he wouldn't have liked being retired at all.[50]

Within a month, Bishop's House had been emptied. Beatrice went to stay with Eva and Gertrude at Glasdrumman: 'Very tired – glad to be well. Evening – new life begun – Emmanuel – <u>Last chapter</u>.' Clearly, Beatrice was not ready to succumb to supine widowhood. After three months at Glasdrumman and a few weeks at Tullylagan with her late brother's family, she moved to Oakfield, Carrick-fergus, on 1 October 1942.[51] Oakfield was a large house in a substantial demesne, about a mile up the North Road from the rectory. Like the reluctant Louis on his daily trudge as a boy, Frederick had often walked past its gate lodge on his way to and from Mile Bush with its panoramic view of Belfast Lough and the north Down coast. The house had previously belonged to James Love McFerran of the Barn Mills, the Orange Freemason who had initially resisted Frederick's appointment as rector, only to become one of his closest allies on the vestry. Oakfield was Beatrice's home for the remaining fourteen years of her life.

In the absence of a will, Beatrice was left to administer a personal estate amounting to almost £4800. Clearly, his simple way of life had made it possible to save a large part of the annual episcopal stipend of £1750. Frederick had made some provision for William through shares in the Church of England Building Society, and William evidently lived with Beatrice and then with the Nicholsons until his death in 1968.[52] He outlived Louis, who had died five years earlier, just before his fifty-sixth birthday, leaving a slightly smaller personal estate than his father's after the deduction of substantial debts.[53] Elizabeth Nicholson, custodian of the family papers and tradition, died in Herefordshire in 1981. Frederick was survived by three of his siblings: (Ferguson) John, Margery Scott and Herbert, who died at advanced ages in 1948, 1958 and 1969 respectively. Of these, only 'Uncle John' was interred with his parents in Mount Jerome Cemetery.

Throughout her widowhood, Beatrice remained a MacNeice in practice as well as in name. Louis did not hesitate to take advantage of her generosity, as when his second wife developed a 'very tired heart' in April 1945: 'We both think it best that Hedli should stay on a bit in my stepmother's house over here where they really do have facilities.'[54] In 1949, Beatrice willed her residual estate in equal portions to her nephew, her two married nieces and Elizabeth Nicholson, each of whom eventually received over £7000. She also set aside £3000 in a lifetime trust for William and £2000 for Louis, to provide William with 'support and mainte-nance' and Louis with an annual income of about £100.[55]

She died at Oakfield on Saturday, 7 April 1956, aged eighty-four, and was buried with the bishop in Drumbeg. The certified cause of death was 'Chronic Myocarditis' (disease of the heart muscles) recently compounded by broncho-pneu-monia.[56] St Nicholas's church was 'well filled' for the funeral service on Wednesday afternoon, in the presence of Louis and Elizabeth but not, reportedly, William. Bishop Mitchell of Down and Dromore delivered a standard panegyric to the 'bright spirit' of one whose 'constant companionship' had helped 'to lighten the large burden he had to bear in that then very large diocese'.[57] Beatrice would surely have winced at the 'fashion show' in aid of Church funds on the evening of her funeral, featuring 'cocktail and party dresses, sun frocks, model coats and suits, and evening dresses'. The outstanding garment was a coat of 'sapphire tweed, lavishly lined with white nylon fur', so much more showy than the red dress and red hat that she used to lovingly take out of mothballs each year as spring approached.[58]

As for the diocese of Down and Connor and Dromore, it remained united until 1945, when Charles King Irwin relinquished Down and Dromore while retaining Connor. Irwin, formerly bishop of Limerick, had been imposed by the House of Bishops after failing dismally in the diocesan election for a new bishop in June 1942. Dean Kerr had been narrowly out-voted by Dean Elliott of Down, but neither could secure two-thirds of either the clerical or lay electorates.[59] Justice was eventually done to the local favourites, both stalwarts of the Orange Order, when Kerr became bishop of Down and Dromore in 1945, and Elliott bishop of Connor in 1956. Division made the diocese administratively viable, but came too late to unleash the massive missionary crusade by which Frederick MacNeice had hoped to rescue his people from the Devil.

V

The public tributes that followed Frederick's death offered only an oblique impression of his character and achievement. Press obituaries, though largely bland and respectful as befitted the memory of a bishop, gave hints of his extraordinary spirit and independence of mind. An anonymous 'friend', writing in *The Irish Times*, remembered him as 'one of the most forceful preachers of the Church of Ireland', notable for his 'courage' in taking 'a somewhat unpopular line – at least in the eyes of many of Northern brethren – on more than one occasion'. Yet he had retained their 'respect' and 'admiration', and had displayed 'something like a crusading spirit' in his work for church extension in Belfast.[60] The *Northern Whig* recalled his triumph over local opposition to his appointment in Carrickfergus, where he eventually became 'the most widely and best beloved person of the parish'. He had 'worked for the brotherhood of the peoples of Ireland' and rejected politics in the pulpit. The *Whig* also gave his place of origin as Ballysadare, claimed that he had refused the use of St Nicholas's for a service on Covenant Day in 1912, alleged that his objection had prevented the flying of the union flag over Carson's grave, and misidentified Beatrice as a sister-in-law to the unfortunate Arthur Percival.[61] Two of these errors were reiterated in the *Belfast Telegraph*.[62] Already, the facts of his career were fading from the public mind.

Little attention was paid to his passing in the Catholic press, with the exception of the *Irish Independent*. In an obituary starkly headed 'Protestant Prelate Dead', it recalled his appeals 'for a non-party settlement to the Irish problem' and his condemnation of 'all methods that could not be reconciled with their Christian profession'.[63] The most misleading encomium came from its social columnist, who depicted him as a naively heroic outsider in the Black North:

> I came in contact with his efforts to fight the bigotry of the North during the Belfast anti-Catholic pogrom in 1935. Only a year before arrived from the easy, tolerant atmosphere of the South, the intolerance of Orange Belfast deeply distressed him; he could not understand it, and courageously he set out to try to subdue it; and though he fought a losing battle the Belfast Catholics appreciated his efforts.[64]

Posthumous elaboration of the myth of Frederick MacNeice, which he himself had fabricated, was underway.

The assessments offered by senior colleagues were more apposite but scarcely more revealing. The rather dry memorial address at St Anne's had been delivered by Primate Gregg, who declared that 'he was a man who had no ambition for high office' and that, when elected bishop of Cashel, 'he wrote that he had been selected against his wishes'. Gregg spoke candidly about the personal impact of the air raids: 'The last year of Dr. MacNeice's life as Bishop was marred by the calamity which befel this city last spring. Damage to church property as a result of enemy action had dealt him a blow which he found it hard to bear, and the strain began to tell seriously on a man of his years.'[65] When addressing the general synod in the following month, Gregg paid tribute to his widely recognized 'courage, his independence of judgment, and the practicalness of his religion', an odd phrase whose very awkwardness suggests authenticity.[66] His 'deep interest' in ecumenicism, and the United Council of Christian Churches in Ireland, was noted by the general synod's committee that for decades had been fruitlessly seeking closer relations with the Presbyterian church.[67] The *Church of Ireland Gazette* recalled the 'sympathetic nature' of one who was 'always a peacemaker'. Its diocesan correspondent lauded the 'keen intellect, penetrating insight, charitable disposition, [and] tireless energy' of 'a man of vision, a man of God', who was 'fearless in his support of what he believed to be right'. Perhaps for the first time, lines by Louis were cited to illuminate his father's character:

I leave my father half my pride of blood
And also my admiration who has fixed
His pulpit out of the reach of party slogans.[68]

One of the least formulaic tributes was offered by Judge Thompson on behalf of the diocesan council. As archdeacon, he had 'displayed qualities of vision and courage and developed gifts of planning and organization which ranked him as a leader in the Church'. Having left for Cashel 'with reluctance, and having had a happy and fruitful Episcopate in the South', he had returned 'well knowing the almost insupportable burden of work he was undertaking but never shrinking from the task':

> As a Bishop he was wise, firm, far-seeing, tolerant and courageous. As a Pastor he gained everywhere the respect, the confidence and the affection of his parishioners. As a friend he was beloved because he was kindly and warm-hearted and true. An earnest student, a deep thinker, an eloquent and impressive preacher he did not fear to face the manifold problems of present day life never doubting that right would triumph: God was in His Heaven.

Many present had reason to agree that 'in him is lost a leader and a friend'.[69]

Obituaries of public men, particularly clergymen, are heavily coded and censored documents designed to be read, if at all, between the lines. References to 'courage' and 'fearlessness' reminded readers of Frederick's many confrontations with locally dominant groups whose behaviour offended his moral principles. 'Independence of judgment' carried overtones of prickliness, lack of deference, and contempt for consensus. As a 'leader', he had not hesitated to exercise the full authority of his office, and to outmanoeuvre or subdue those who questioned his strategy. If he was 'tireless' in undertaking ridiculously heavy burdens, this reflected a reluctance to delegate vital tasks unless he could maintain close personal supervision. If his task was 'almost impossible', this was borne out by his ultimate inability to achieve church reunion and revitalization of the Church's urban mission, through which he had dreamt of winning the 'tug-of-war' against secularism. To be 'forceful' as a preacher was also, in the eyes of many Churchmen, to breach decorum by seeking to influence people rather than merely to reassure them.

His reputation for breaking down 'religious prejudice' and denominational barriers had different meanings for different denominations. His colleagues knew that he had developed close personal associations with Jews as well as Presbyterians and Non-Conformists, whereas he seems to have had little personal contact with Catholics apart from servants such as jolly Annie Bogue from Tyrone.[70] He imagined Protestants and Catholics co-existing 'side by side' as good neighbours in parallel communities, rather than as brethren in an integrated community. More surprising is the sympathetic concern for the plight of Jews that he had developed in later life, despite his horrified reaction to Louis's engagement to Mary Ezra in 1929. Frederick was among the first Irish church leaders to abhor the 'brutal treatment of the Jews' in Hitler's Germany, in St Anne's Cathedral on 3 May 1933.[71] Five years later he was thanked by Rabbi Shachter for his denunciation of German despotism at a school prize-giving.[72] Several factors had transformed his attitude from abstract distaste to active interest: personal acquaintance with Jews that he met through Louis, involvement in the ecumenical movement for which German persecution of the Jews was a major issue from 1933, and admiration for the civic virtues and imperial loyalty so conspicuously displayed by Belfast's Jewish community. He had observed Mary's exotic tastes and habits in Achill and Waterford, doted on Mary's son with his Jewish nurse, Sophie Popper, and put his principles into practice by offering her father refuge in Bishop's House. Wilmos Popper tested Frederick's tolerance by eccentric habits such as joking and punning in broken English, acting out the crudely onomatopoeic origins of language, swimming and running naked at Millisle, and even borrowing the bishop's hat when instructed by Shachter to cover his head on the *Shabbat*.[73] Unshaken by the apparent defection of his former adherent to the Church of Ireland, Shachter remembered Frederick as 'a great Churchman who has helped to break down barriers of racial and religious prejudice' and as 'a mighty agency for good'.[74]

As for the bishop's disparagement of clergymen who engaged in 'politics', another theme of his obituarists, this would itself have been interpreted by contemporary readers as a political declaration. Yet few informed contemporaries would have inferred a rejection of the traditional precepts of unionism or loyalty to the Crown. Those familiar with Frederick's view of the Ulster Covenant knew that his objection was to clerical participation in a party condoning violence, the partition of Ireland, and (in due course) Home Rule for Ulster. Even the *Irish Independent* did not imply that he was, or had been, a Home Rule nationalist. Those who knew something of his early ministry in Belfast and Carrickfergus would also have realized what lay behind the observation that those initially in conflict with him eventually regarded their minister with 'respect', 'admiration', 'confidence' and even love. In the tightly organized fraternal world of Protestant Ulster, it was not argument or charm that won over doubters, but initiation in the brotherhoods within which mutual trust was nurtured and tested. The sign in which he conquered was not that of the Cross alone, but also of the Orange and Masonic orders that had given him paths of access to the hearts of the brethren.

Yet, as Frederick would say when shifting gear in a sermon, there is still something more to be said. No published obituary or tribute probed, even indirectly, the deeper springs of Frederick MacNeice's personality. None alluded to his upbringing with the Irish Church Missions in Connemara, or to the missionary fervour with which he corrected the errors of the Church of Rome before the Great War. Since his writings and reported addresses contain no known reference to his ordeal on Omey Island or his employment as a missionary teacher, it is conceivable that this seminal episode in his life was actually unknown to obituarists. Neither was any hint given of his humble origins, his first marriage to a small farmer's daughter, or the social gulf between himself and most of his peers in the Church of Ireland. Instead, frequent references were made to the grand family connections he had acquired through marriage to Beatrice Greer, without which he might never have been considered as a potential bishop. Nor did any memorialist speak of the fearful suffering he had endured as a child under siege, as the husband and then widower of a deeply depressed and suicidal woman, or as the father of a boy and man afflicted with Down's Syndrome. Perhaps there was a faint echo of these ordeals in the diocesan synod's recollection of one who was 'kindly and warm-hearted and true'. None detected those elements in his personality which his son so strangely, so truly described as 'something in him | solitary and wild'.[75] In death as in life, his secrets and therefore the sources of his extraordinary spiritual power remained shielded from the world.

Nor have all his secrets succumbed to biographical scrutiny. The books, sermons and addresses only occasionally illuminate his personal experiences and relationships. The few available diaries and letters reveal tantalizingly little about his emotions and sexuality, which, when expressed at all, are invariably filtered through the language and precepts of Christian virtue. His sorrow and alarm at Lily's decline becomes an appeal for divine assistance, couched in the imperative ('God help me') rather than the resigned subjunctive ('Thy will be done'). The attraction that he feels towards Miss Hunt on the boat to Portugal is justified by admiration for her moral strength in avoiding the card table, coupled with almost exultant dismissal of her physical attributes. His Christmas soliloquy about the handsome nephew from Canada is, for the most part, a cerebral celebration of Christian manliness with the underlying attraction kept strictly under control. We sense the wildness, but cannot cage it.

Visitors and acquaintances found his personality elusive, by contrast with the playful extroversion of Beatrice, and even John Hilton was reduced to paradoxical abstractions in 1928 (impressive and awe-inspiring, warm and humane).[76] Margaret Gardiner, who accompanied Louis to Bishop's House in October 1939, found him 'a magnificent looking man' who took almost mischievous pleasure in his privileged position. When needled by Louis about his disregard of the black-out, as 'the hall lights blared out into the night', he replied: 'That's the best of being a bishop. People won't be pestering you about such matters.'[77] His air of self-sufficiency sometimes suggested haughtiness. A young Presbyterian woman in Carrickfergus, who used to pass the rectory on her way to and from piano lessons, recalled that most clergymen and gentlemen 'would have raised their hat to her as they passed, but Canon MacNeice would just lower his head, pull his hat over his brow, and keep looking at the ground as he passed as if he had not noticed her'. Whereas the priest and other ministers in the town would stand 'in a huddle on the pavement chatting with each other', Frederick would merely acknowledge them and walk on: 'She believed he was rather grand and kept himself aloof from them.'[78]

Though many of his clerical contemporaries wrote reminiscences, his rather taciturn and remote manner seldom inspired amusing or even dull anecdotes. When Canon John Barry rose to the challenge in 1993, describing two meetings when a young curate, he recalled only abruptness, embarrassment and a touch of authoritarianism on the part of the bishop. He and his fellow curate at St Matthew's, Shankill (Arthur Campbell), were not pleased by the unheralded visit of their ill-groomed chief: 'Stocky figure, long face, mouse-coloured hair straight across the top of his head and falling down over the right eye in a dank sort of cow's lick, low voice, deep brogue.' After ordering Campbell to give an impromptu sermon should the rector fail to show up (he eventually did), and sitting silent and morose in the sanctuary throughout the service, Frederick complained to poor Campbell about the omission of one of the listed psalms before apologizing for his unfairness. Their second meeting resulted from a telephoned summons to Bishop's House, where Barry found him 'sitting humped up in a big chair at the fireside with a shawl around his shoulders, asleep'. In between dozes, the bishop tersely instructed him to move to another parish and to tell his rector 'you're to be there by the end of next week'.[79] In old age, though Frederick had lost some of his considerate manner, he remained a formidable and disturbing presence.

Many of the inner forces driving Frederick through life thus remain obscure. Yet the ample public and institutional record of his later career has enabled us to recover one vital but submerged characteristic: his keen strategic sense of how to win the trust of those whose help he needed in battling the Devil. With tact and patience, he formed and sustained fraternal alliances with bishops, deans, missionaries, Orangemen and Freemasons, whose friendship and influence protected him from vilification whenever he adopted a controversial stance. His marriage to Beatrice gave him entry to the most exalted circles in 'the Province', providing further shelter when he took on the governing party or the prime minister. The very antithesis of the guileless idealist so beloved of MacNeicians, he was closer in spirit to Alexander Dallas, who deployed the skills and savvy of a general in a campaign that was ultimately doomed. If one word could encapsulate him, it was not 'Bishop', that terse designation on his headstone at Drumbeg, but 'Apostle'. If any man could have brought salvation to Ulster, if not Ireland, it was surely Frederick John MacNeice.

15. His Father's Son

I

As a person and a writer, Louis MacNeice never could escape the formative influence of his family, and his father in particular. True, few of us do. What marks out MacNeice is his lifelong and obsessional interest in his childhood, and the extent to which childhood dramas were re-enacted and embellished in his later life and work. The bequest of childhood and upbringing is equally obvious in the pious little boy; the rebellious adolescent (a protracted phase) rejecting his father's temperance, prudishness and Christian morality; and the troubled adult embarking on the 'Quest' for certainty, virtue and redemption. The psychological consequences of losing his mother and blaming his father were not only far-reaching but the subject of relentless introspection and Freudian self-analysis, as one would expect of a 'Thirties' poet. Yet, even as a rebel, Louis maintained close contact with his family, writing affectionate letters to 'Daddie' and 'Madre', staying with them at home or on holiday, entertaining them in England, borrowing their money, and accompanying his father to rugby matches and the Dublin University Club as well as church. Frederick left a strong imprint on Louis's likes as well as dislikes: his intellectual curiosity, fondness for manly games, social radicalism, love of Ireland, distaste for Roman Catholicism, unwillingness to surrender his political independence to the Communist Party or any other, and (sometimes appalled) fascination with exotic races and cultures. Frederick's influence was also evident in Louis's long head and wide mouth, his lack of an Ulster accent, his gruffness with strangers and his warmth with trusted friends.

These likenesses do not imply that Louis was his father reincarnate: Frederick was too grave, Louis too playful to swap personalities at will. Nor were they easy companions: as Louis reportedly told his acolyte Margaret Gardiner in about 1954, 'I somehow couldn't break through to him just as he couldn't break through to me, though we both wanted it so much.'[1] His letters are littered with disparaging references to his father and family, evoking the irritation and ennui associated with visits home. Writing from London in 1927, he told Beatrice that 'I don't think I shall come home yet – especially as you are coming over soon, and I do not want the North Ireland melancholy to get its teeth into me.' In a mawkish self-justification addressed to Eleanor Clark in 1940, he claimed to have developed such keen insight into other minds that he would wince 'in advance on behalf of one's family's reactions in any possible situation'. As for the apparently warm and respectful tone of many of his letters home, he instructed his literary executor to ignore all such utterances: 'I do not want any letters to my father or stepmother to be published as they nearly always contain some falsity.'[2]

The ambivalence of Louis's relationship with his father continued to preoccupy him long after Frederick's death, as his son Daniel developed similar feelings of rejection and alienation:

> I think you had a rough deal for a number of years, yet I'm not sure I wouldn't prefer it to my own upbringing. Talk about not knowing one's parents! ... I never can remember being at ease with my father (not but what I have things in common with him, including some of the things which put me off in *him*!) until perhaps the last few years of his life. On the other hand I remember my step-mother bursting into tears at breakfast because she thought Elizabeth & I only owed allegiance to my father & were excluding her from 'the family'. Whereas some years later she was reproving us both bitterly because, she said, we always left the room whenever my father entered it. Which, I think, was true! It gave us both guilt feelings of course & I think we'd have tried to meet him half-way if he on his side had been more elastic.[3]

Though obviously designed to win over his own son, this analysis illuminates the deep affinity between Louis and his father that outlasted their spectacular differences in morality, manner and opinion. As Louis observed in 'The Strand', there was something in his father (as more obviously in himself) that was 'solitary and wild'.

As a writer and master of language, he was also strikingly indebted to his father. Both were precise and logical, avoiding flashy phrases and epigrammatic swagger. Though self-consciously dismissive of his own facility in Greek, Louis too relished command of an esoteric medium giving access to a secret world. Like

Frederick, he resisted flaunting his classical education through arcane allusions, preferring to utter complex thoughts in everyday phrases. For initiates, layers of less accessible resonances and references cushioned the surface banality of so much of his poetry and prose. Louis was conscious of the likeness between poems and sermons, properly conceived, with their expository and didactic functions and their amalgam of intellectual, emotional and moral elements. In 1937, he remarked in an open letter to Auden that 'poetry is related to the sermon and you have your penchant for preaching, but it is more closely related to conversation'.[4] As he proclaimed in the following year: 'The poet is primarily a spokesman, making statements or incantations on behalf of himself or others. ... Good poets have written in order to describe something or to preach something.'[5] The didactic strand is dominant in discursive works such as *Autumn Journal* and *Autumn Sequel*, whereas the lyric poems, with their flashes of revelation and subterranean tremors, share the clergyman's mission to jolt the congregation into some sense of mystery and transcendence.

The alternation between common sense and inspiration, so characteristic of Louis's poetry, has much in common with the structure of Frederick's finest sermons. Though not a linguistic magician like his son, he was capable of dramatic changes of register when pointing out the alarming implications of actually loving one's neighbour or turning the other cheek. The unsuspecting listener or reader is first lulled by familiar truisms, then guided towards something novel or disconcerting, finally calmed by a second flurry of truisms. Both, in short, were expert practitioners of Ciceronian rhetoric, in which the audience of a speech or letter is won over by an informal, conversational style. The impact of the 'petition' is enhanced by a preliminary 'exordium' (such as a proverb or passage from scripture), and a 'narration' providing context for the crucial appeal that follows. Frederick, like his son, was a truth-teller who had no compunction in guiding his readers or listeners towards false but beneficial inferences from his carefully chosen words. For father and son alike, words were tools serving a higher purpose, though only Frederick had a clear and consistent sense of what that purpose was.

The language of the Bible intoxicated Louis from childhood, leaving an indelible impression. As he wrote in *Modern Poetry*: 'My father was a clergyman, and from a very early age I was fascinated by the cadences and imagery of the Bible.'[6] It is worth noting that Frederick, being a fairly Low-Church evangelical, preferred the flattened cadences and less colourful imagery of the 'revised version' of 1885, rather than the more opulent translation authorized by King James I in 1611 and last modified in 1769.[7] For the liturgy, however, he was required to follow the relatively archaic version of *The Book of Common Prayer* adopted by the Church of Ireland in 1878, which remained in use until timidly vulgarized in 1926. Other religious texts in plainer language also left their mark on Louis's imagination and in due course on his prose. The little boy's 'most melancholy hymn' was his mother's favourite, 'There is a Green Hill Far Away', though by the 1920s none of the family in Carrickfergus listed it among their ten preferences for Sunday services.[8] Louis never lost his affection for plain-spoken evangelical writers such as Bunyan, whose 'very naturalistic dialogue' he praised when lecturing at Cambridge in 1963. Though *The Pilgrim's Progress* 'ran the risk of being a dull dressed-up sermon' and had no literary influences except the Bible, it had 'the virtues of good conversation' as well as a deceptive, even haunting subtety of construction: 'the pulpit abstractions become concrete and speak with the voice of human beings'.[9] The same might be said of Frederick MacNeice's preaching.

At St Nicholas's, Louis had soon progressed from enjoying the spectacle, notably that of his father in a surplice, to listening to what was said and allowing it 'to seep in on me'. At first, Louis was encouraged to read the Book of Revelation while his father preached:

> But now I was old enough for the sermon and I attended to the rest of the service and the hymns made me feel like crying, in a rather pleasant sugary way, but the parts about sin made me terrified. Religion never left us alone, it was at home as much as in church, it fluttered in the pages of a tear-off calendar in the bathroom.[10]

Since Frederick, like his son, was alert to the musical power of the spoken word, Church was a pleasure rather than an ordeal: 'I very much enjoyed my father reading the lesson because, unlike many Anglican clergymen I came across since, he could deliver the English language with rhthym and dignity.'[11] His father's voice was 'soft and rich', blending words like 'heron' and 'orange' into a single syllable.[12] Yet enjoyment was tinged with fear, aroused by 'the frightening intonations about *sin, hell, death*' evoked in Louis's early novel *Roundabout Way*. 'The monosyllables hung in the air, seemed plucked out on wires.'[13]

II

Frederick MacNeice's influence on his son's outlook and writing was anything but static, reflecting profound changes in his own situation. His puritanism and missionary zeal were constants, but his place in Ulster society was transformed during Louis's childhood and youth. At the time of Louis's birth in 1907, Frederick was an impoverished minister in an inner Belfast parish, without any of the benefits of inherited wealth or status enjoyed by most clergymen of the 'anglican order'.

Remarriage to a rich spinster gave access to an ever-widening circle of influential relatives and friends, without whose support he could scarcely have contemplated becoming a bishop and a formidable figure in the Church of Ireland. Louis was understandably disorientated by his father's sudden social elevation, not knowing from what pedestal to bestow his disdain on all and sundry. According to his autobiography drafted in 1940: 'The Lower Classes were dour and hostile, they would never believe what you said. Not that the Gentry were much better; even then I was conscious that to be the son of a clergyman was to be something the Gentry only half accepted and that in a patronising way.'[14] Perhaps out of filial loyalty, Louis ascribed their condescending attitude to his father's profession rather than his humble origins.

Three years earlier, he had recalled a 'great gulf between myself and the bare-foot boys in the streets', leading to 'perpetual embarrassment' at being 'the rector's son'. Reporting the hostility of the 'gentry' to his father's radical views, he pronounced that 'the Ulster gentry are an inferior species', being 'comparatively new to their class' and therefore lacking 'the traditions and easy individuality of the southern Anglo-Irish landowners'.[15] In lampooning Ulster's *arrivistes*, he must have been aware of his family's tenuous claim to social superiority, epitomized in his own status as a scholarship boy at Marlborough College. He may also have been venting resentment against the Greers, whose wealth derived from linen. They could not, however, be accused of being too 'fast', another alleged reason for his family's avoidance of the gentry of Carrickfergus. Already 'very snobbish about accents' as a child, Louis continued for much of his life to patronize all classes, especially his own 'middle class'. When visited in Merton College by 'some Poor Relations', he cravenly 'sported the oak' (closed his outer door) in order to 'protect my snobbery from callers' and their expected sneers.[16] Whereas many of his grander friends, confidently dismissive of their own kind, amused themselves by cultivating the common man, Louis was an alien in every social class. His indiscriminate snobberies were surely the outcome of social insecurity, compounded by his father's unexpected elevation. Frederick himself was subtler and more discreet in coping with his changing status in Carrickfergus and the world. Never contemptuous, never ingratiating, somewhat aloof, he treated all classes with respect and was trusted in return.

Frederick's social advance was accompanied by gradual retreat from active involvement in unionism and Orangeism, though he never truly became a political nationalist. His struggle against the Anti-Christ was redirected from popery to secularism, in keeping with his conviction that the alliances and antagonisms driving humanity had been transformed by the disaster of the Great War. The security conferred by wealth and influence made him in some respects a rebel rather than a conformist, enabling him to become a fearless opponent of sectarianism, a passionate internationalist and a dogged advocate of the autonomy of the Church of Christ when imperilled by political interference. These changes in public persona entailed disregard of certain facets of his earlier career, a process in which Louis willingly colluded. This is evident in Louis's strange and contradictory utterances about nationalism and Orangeism, and the loyal manner in which he asserted and antedated his father's liberal credentials. As he came closer to Frederick in later life, Louis took an active and imaginative part in recasting the family narrative into the plausible and attractive form now generally accepted by MacNeicians. He became his father's protector.

Louis's lifelong preoccupation with Irishness was shaped not merely by his actual family background, in which so many incongruous strands were tangled, but also by the need to portray his father as a southern Home Ruler who was never at home in unionist Ulster. Though Frederick was not in reality an outsider in Ulster, his evolving reputation as a fearless critic of Ulster shibboleths supplied Louis with a convenient cover. Instead of appearing before the world of schoolboys or intellectuals as a typical product of the Black North, born and raised among Orangemen and unionists, Louis could assume the more interesting rôle of a son rebelling against his rebel father, doubly separated from the widely despised stereotype of a narrow-minded Protestant Ulsterman. This posture entailed an awkward dissonance between the rebel rejecting his father's puritanical faith, and the dutiful son emulating his father's attachment to Dublin, Connemara and the Irish nation. As a child, he put on 'the Wild Irish act' to impress an English housekeeper, and resolved to 'exploit the fact that I was Irish' when despatched to Sherborne.[17] Dublin, which he first visited on the way home from Sherborne, was 'a glorious name in our family and had pleasurable associations of violence'. But his primary imagined home was 'The West of Ireland', a phrase that in 1957 still stirred him 'like a fiddle half heard through a cattle fair'. Having never visited Achill or Connemara until 1927, 'for many years I lived on a nostalgia for somewhere I had never been'.[18] On that first encounter with Connemara, he imagined himself as his father on his 'home-coming', and sensed that they were both agitated by the same nostalgia: 'It was a country I had always known, mournful and gay with mournful and gay inhabitants.'[19] Divided in matters of faith and morality, father and son were united in their Irishness. Or so Louis, writing just before his father's death, wished the world to believe.

On close inspection, this comforting narrative unravels. Though indeed fond of Dublin and Connemara, Frederick was thoroughly at home in Carrickfergus and dismissive of many aspects of southern life. Even by Louis's account, he found the people of Connemara 'terribly backward' in 1927, having refused to take southern holidays during 'the Troubles' because of his aversion to violence. Frederick, 'in spite of his nationalism', had exclaimed: 'How can you mix with people who might be murderers without you knowing it?'[20] Nor is it likely that young Freddie's initial impersonation of a 'rebel against England' had nationalist overtones. The only potential rebels on view in pre-war Carrickfergus were loyalists and Ulster Volunteers, on parade or at drill, preparing for possible confrontation with the forces of the Crown. This helps us to decode the 'odd paradox' that Louis noticed when reading Yeats's *Autobiographies*: 'Yeats, as a little boy in the west, read Orange songs and fancied himself dying facing the Fenians; I, as a little boy among Orangemen, imagined myself a rebel against England.'[21] In each case, the child's chosen rôle was that of a militant loyalist, reflecting strong unionist and Orange influences within his family circle. Freddie's game was surely a melodramatic expression of his father's unionism, not of nationalism.

Even at the height of his rebellion against paternal authority, Louis never adopted a view of Ireland sharply at odds with that of his father. Given Frederick's distinctive combination of devotion to the monarchy and the British constitution, rejection of partitionism, love of Ulster and strong sense of Irish nationality, finding a diametrically opposite stance would have been a daunting task. Instead, Louis pronounced maledictions against southern and northern cultures alike, while admitting his inherent susceptibility to both ways of life. In 'Valediction', though intoning 'Farewell, my country, and in perpetuum' in order to 'exorcise my blood', he proclaimed that 'the woven figure cannot undo its thread'. This applied as much to the bequest of his 'mother-city', 'a heart that leaps to a fife band', as to that of his father's West, with its 'dolled-up Virgins' and 'ignorant dead'.[22] These farewells pronounced in January 1934 were purely rhetorical, as implied by the antiphonic design of the poem (alternating between affirmation of indissoluble bonds and ineffectual yelps of disgust). Dublin 'always' seemed 'a home from home',[23] the West of Ireland a romantic holiday resort.

While his Ulster allegiance remained problematic, Louis was parading his Irishness by the time of Frederick's death. This may have been in part a consequence of Éire's neutrality in the Second World War, which made Louis's Irish nativity a valuable asset. As he told T. S. Eliot in connection with his planned autobiography just after the declaration of war: 'Being an Irish citizen I am exempt from conscription, so shall no doubt have time to write it long before a year's time.'[24] In a biographical notice published in 1942, he wrote 'both parents Irish, from Connemara', adding that in politics he was 'opposed to Partition in Ireland'.[25]

A decade later, he reaffirmed his national credentials for the benefit of an agent in Chicago: 'Self. Irish parentage (Gaelic family). Father a Protestant bishop, but a nationalist.'[26]

His attitude towards Ulster, though always guarded, mellowed upon rein-spection in summer 1938. In *Zoo*, he apologized to Belfast for his long-standing assumption 'that it should always be grey, wet, repellent and its inhabitants dour, rude and callous'. The sun shone, and the denizens 'were not really grandiose monsters' as he had imagined them from the sanctuary of Carrickfergus (itself, of course, not without menace).[27] Like his father, Louis had finally come to terms with the vying loyalties and prejudices of an Irishman who was also an Ulsterman. In 1944, he drafted a relatively mild and balanced booklet on 'Northern Ireland and Her People' for the British Council's series, *Peoples of the United Kingdom*. MacNeice (along with R. V. Williams, the poet and playwright 'Richard Rowley') was deemed suitable by the Council, which had rejected the Ulster Office's sugges-tion of Craigavon's future biographer, St John Ervine.[28] Ervine had recommended Robert Lynd and Stephen Gwynn as possible authors if he himself were not appointed, but government officials were unhappy with entrusting the province's reputation to any nationalist intellectual, however able.[29] Louis's political stance was sufficiently convoluted to pass the test, and he was engaged.

The Ulster Office regarded Louis's first draft, which has not been located, as 'largely a travesty': 'It deals prominently with religious and political differ-ences in Ulster and throws into bold and altogether disproportionate light various matters which are best omitted. … It is full of comparisons with Eire, it mentions 'partition' and talks about the "Six Counties", and is in many respects somewhat insulting to Ulster.' The British Council had agreed that 'Macneice [*sic.*] must re-cast it completely'. Even though it was indeed 'revised on the lines which we had suggested', the Ulster Office found even the revised version 'quite unsuit-able': 'It is clear that Macneice writes with a peculiar complex about Ulster. His script emphasizes that Northern Ireland is very rainy, has mud floor cottages, and is a land of strife!' While admitting that 'Macneice's stuff was, in fact, quite well written – bright, reasonable and in a style suited to the Council', the Ulster Office persuaded the British Council to 'pay off' the author, who 'took the decision in the most friendly spirit'.[30]

Though removing tendentious phrases and adopting a relatively benign tone in the revised version, Louis had been unable to resist jibes about his native prov-ince. Belfast was 'an ugly city in a very beautiful setting'; the Ulsterman's character was hospitable but 'dour'; and partition, 'from a purely geographical point of view', looked 'odd'. Nor did he spare the English as viewed by the Irish, whether northern or southern: 'However much they both differ from each other they both think of the Englishman as a foreigner.' Louis's warmest words and hopes were reserved for the 'Decent Wee Men' who might soon be 'ready at last to sink their differences' as the 'Good Haters' passed away.[31] With Ervine, Lynd, Gwynn, Williams and Louis eliminated, it proved difficult to find a politically acceptable writer with sufficient knowledge and panache for the tricky task of restoring the province's rather tarnished international image. Captain Cyril Falls submitted another 'unacceptable' draft, Dame Helen Waddell withdrew after her 'political convictions' had been brought into question, but eventually the task was satisfactorily performed by W. R. (Bertie) Rodgers, soon to desert the Presbyterian ministry for the BBC.[32]

Despite lingering distaste for many aspects of Ulster, Louis became ever more mellow in depicting his native place. In 'Carrickfergus Revisited' (1945), he wrote, as if from an immense distance, of the childhood 'interlude' between the 'pre-natal mountain' in the West of Ireland and an English schooling:

> Whatever then my inherited or acquired
> Affinities, such remains my childhood's frame
> Like a belated rock in the red Antrim clay
> That cannot at this era change its pitch or name.

The sombre simile of pitchstone, that blackened residue of extinct volcanoes, embodies the ominous shadow still cast by his Carrickfergus childhood, troubled by 'Fog-horn, mill-horn, corncrake and church bell'; yet, by comparison with 'Carrickfergus' (1937), the tone is mild, even sentimental: 'Our past we know | But not its meaning – whether it meant well.'[33]

Louis shared his father's view that Ulster and Ireland were inseparable, the Irish nation being defined not by race but by the historical conflict and convergence of many different races. Equally disparaging about north and south in early poems such as 'Valediction', he came to regard both elements of Ireland with indulgent familiarity instead of bitter contempt. The 'meaning' of Irishness remained elusive, as shown by his inability to complete *The Character of Ireland*, the volume of essays that Bertie Rodgers and he had undertaken to edit for the Oxford University Press in 1951. In a rambling poetic 'Prologue' (1959), he pronounced: 'Let us dump the rubbish | Of race and talk to the point: what is a nation?'[34] An article published in the same year reiterated his belief that the Ulsterman and the southerner had 'much more in common with each other, I realize now, than either has with the Englishman'. Reworking his rejected script for the British Council, he remarked of the border that 'the ordinary Irishman on both sides, being a magnificent hypocrite and also basically practical, manages largely to ignore it'. He drew hope from a rather hackneyed vision of the miniature united Ireland of rugby football: 'A "good hater" of an Orangeman will serve most devotedly in an Irish XV under a "papish" captain. And vice versa.'[35]

III

Louis, like his father, never lost his aversion for what he deemed the vulgarity and tawdriness of Irish Catholicism, despite his adoration for Annie Bogue, the bonny cook from Tyrone who was his only Catholic acquaintance when a child. In 'Belfast' (1931), written three years before 'Valediction', he had already coupled the 'garish Virgin' in the chapel porch with the 'banging of Orange drums' as twin tokens of sectarianism.[36] When 'running away from the war' in Dublin in late 1939, so he recalled eighteen years later, he found Catholic supremacy unshaken by the world's crisis: 'There was still a pot of flowers in front of Matt Talbot's shrine. The potboy priests and the birds of prey were still the dominant caste.'[37] In 1941, he observed that Yeats, with whom he claimed a strong background affinity, was too sceptical to have 'turned Roman Catholic' (despite his envy of true believers), and that he 'had come to realize more vividly the drawbacks of Catholic Ireland' as a result of settling there after the Great War.[38] Twelve years later, he quoted Honor Tracy's unflattering reference to the arrogance of the Catholic clergy, 'their pride, their vindictiveness, their greed', only regretting 'that Miss Tracy has not attended in equal detail to the Orangemen'. He did not contest her diagnosis of the 'error' afflicting the Irish clergy, that 'they were running a country' instead of pursuing 'the Way and the Truth'.[39] Louis is alleged to have contemplated 'turning back' to the baptismal faith of his grandfather, Martin Clesham, in conversation with a devout Catholic lodger in 1957.[40] Yet his distaste for the outward and visible signs of Catholicism endured, a lingering bequest of the sentiments of his father and the Irish Church Missions. In 1959, he still shuddered at the image of 'cormorants | Waiting to pounce like priests'.[41] Three years later, he called upon 'Master Blackthorn' to 'Provide the black priest with a big black stick | That his ignorant flock may go straight for the fear of you'.[42] He died as he had lived, a Protestant unbeliever.

Louis MacNeice's animosity to Orangeism, as to Catholicism, was rooted not in issues of doctrine or morality but of politics and public display. When drunkenly accused by his publisher Dan Davin of being 'a black Ulster Protestant' and therefore essentially 'orange', he 'only gave his lopsided smile. I could not get behind the guard of his good humour.'[43] As a child, he had three sources of insight into Orangeism: his father's involvement as a chaplain, to which he never referred; his friendship with the gardener Archie White; and the ominous beat of the Lambeg drum, which became a lifelong emblem of violence in his poetry and prose. The sound of the Lambeg is more mellow and muffled than outsiders imagine, its beat is slow and deliberate, but none the less disturbing for that. When a new mother's help arrived from England early in the Great War, Elizabeth and Louis delighted in unveiling the awful secret of 'blood on the drums':

> We often heard those drums as we were walking through the country; a couple of men might spend a whole day practising. One would walk in front with a great drum the size of a cartwheel strapped on his back and the sweat running down his face and the other would walk behind with the sweat running down his face and flail the drum on each side with a couple of canes. ... And sometimes, we explained to Miss Hewitt, if you did the job properly you cut your wrists on the rim of the drum and the drum got bloody and proved you were a good Orange Protestant.[44]

This was no childish fantasy, as shown by a critical comment in the *Carrickfergus Advertiser* just before the Twelfth in 1925:

> Before the day mentioned arrives there appears in our narrow and confined streets a man and fife, two men and two drums; the former blows on his fife till the veins stand out on his temples and his face grows scarlet; the men with the drums slash thereat with canes until their knuckles are skinned and the blood flows therefrom.[45]

The dreaded drumbeat first heard in Carrickfergus resonates in *Letters from Iceland* (1936), where his father rejects 'the sordid challenges and the mixed | Motives of those who bring their drums and dragons | To silence moderation and free speech'. In *Autumn Journal* (1938), he abhors 'the voodoo of the Orange bands | Drawing an iron net through darkest Ulster', and derides 'The grocer drunk with the drum'. As in 'Valediction', these nightmarish images of Orangeism are balanced by the equally unsettling 'shawled woman weeping at the garish altar'.[46] The Orange cult of the Lambeg, like the Catholic cult of saints and martyrs, carried sinister yet thrilling overtones of masochism and primitive sorcery.

Though Frederick MacNeice played no recorded part in Twelfth demonstrations after 1902 (except as a spectator), he remained an intermittently active Orangeman until about 1915 and a lifelong believer in the potential moral and civic benefits of lodge membership. In denouncing Orangeism, therefore, Louis was to some degree repudiating the father he had known when a child. This engendered feelings of guilt and betrayal, which underlie a perplexing autobiographical cameo from his last term at Sherborne. On 12 July 1921, the headmaster (Littleton Powys) visits his dormitory, asking: 'What is all this they do in your country today? Isn't it all mumbo jumbo?' Louis offers an elaborate explanation for his response:

> Remembering my father and Home Rule and the bony elbows of Miss Craig [Margaret McCready] and the black file of mill-girls and the wickedness of Carson and the dull dank days between sodden haystacks and foghorns, I said Yes it was. And I felt uplifted. To be speaking man to man with Powys and giving the lie to the Red Hand of Ulster was power, was freedom, meant I was nearly grown up. King William is dead and his white horse with him, and Miss Craig will never put her knuckles in my ears again.

Unable to admit in 1940 that his response was a betrayal of his father, the alleged Home Ruler, Louis displaces his guilt by introducing 'Mr Cameron' from Portadown, in fact Frederick Lindsay, Powys's deputy.[47] With his rough manner and harsh accent he reminds Louis of Miss McCready, though both had redeeming features. Having overheard Louis's remark, Lindsay, 'his underlip jutting and his eyes enraged', asks 'What were you saying to Mr. Powys?' This provokes another disingenuous commentary: 'Oh this division of allegiance! That the Twelfth of July was mumbo-jumbo was true, and my father thought so too, but the moment Mr. Cameron appeared I felt rather guilty and cheap. Because I had been showing off to Powys and because Mr. Cameron being after all Irish I felt I had betrayed him.'[48]

This evasion is matched by the story of the 'dear old gentleman' shepherding Louis from Belfast to Dublin just after the Armistice, 'who was pestered on the way by a drunken American soldier' full of loathing for Germans, including King George V. Louis's chaperon, 'being a loyal Orangeman, was outraged, so the American appealed to me and I, as an Irish nationalist, sided with him'. Subsequently, 'I felt guilty.'[49] In an earlier version, the source of guilt is made explicit: 'Feelingly shockingly disloyal to the dear old man but remembering my father and Home Rule, I said I thought Carson was a pity.'[50] As in the conversation with Powys two years later, the true betrayal was surely that of Frederick MacNeice, monarchist, unionist and former Orangeman.

By 1939, Louis had rediscovered curiosity about the Orange rituals of his youth in Carrickfergus. As he told Eleanor Clark in late June: 'In a few weeks, darling, I am going over to Belfast to broadcast & shall be there for the twelfth of July. Haven't seen the processions (one of the most extraordinary sights in the world) since I was a little boy; I expect they may have trouble this year.' If so, as he promised his Trotskyite muse a week later, 'I shall write an article anti-Orange.' The riots of 1935 did not in fact recur, and Louis left Belfast with a sense of exhilaration at the blaze of incongruous images invading the streets: 'The Orange procession was crazy – banners depicting Samson fighting with the Lion, Christ giving water to Total Abstainers, The Storming of Jhansi, William III of course ad nauseam, Queen Victoria pretty often, Lord Beaconsfield quite a bit, plenty of local worthies, a number of local churches & also some allegoricals like Justice & Truth.'[51]

Unlike many nationalist observers, he did not deny the force of those 'allegoricals' in the mental world of Ulster Protestants. In his script for the British Council in 1944, Louis paid a striking tribute to the essential decency of Orangeism, distancing himself from the harshly melodramatic portrayal in his own earlier work, when discussing 'The Glorious Twelfth':

> You will not normally find the Northern Irish practising in private life the more narrow tenets they may hold as party members. This is proved *a fortiori* by the case of the Orangemen. … To an English spectator these processions, and the speech-makings which follow them, appear not only primitive but sinister, smacking even of fascism. In fact, however, they probably serve for most Orangemen, who in private life are quiet and unemotional, as an emotional safety-valve – a case of what the Greeks called 'catharsis'. … For the great majority of Orangemen their idea of goodness is summed up in the common phrase: 'a decent wee man'. The Decent Wee Man is unostentatious, sober, industrious, scrupulously honest, and genuinely charitable.[52]

These Christian virtues, the 'Truisms' of the celebrated poem, were precisely what Frederick hoped to instil in the brethren when a chaplain. Through his sympathetic treatment of Orangeism as a moral institution, Louis belatedly expunged his guilt and placated his father's ghost.

IV

Such civic virtues and moral precepts were deeply embedded in the rituals of both Orangeism and Freemasonry, which may well have become familiar to Louis through his father's involvement. The rituals of Royal Arch Masonry in particular should have appealed strongly to an imagination fired by fantasy, allegory and nightmare. 'Flight of the Heart', written during his American convalescence in October 1940, is a moral fable occasioned by his impending return to England to share (in the comfortable rôle of occasional propagandist) the burdens of war – as well as childcare and petcare. As Edna Longley observes, it represents an internal dialogue between 'the would-be good citizen' and 'the defeatist'.[53] It may also be interpreted as a poetic variation of the 'exaltation' ceremony for the Royal Arch degree, which Frederick had undergone in October 1914. Despite extraneous elements, startling parallels are detectable between the poem and the ritual:

> Heart, my heart, what will you do?
> There are *five lame dogs* and one deaf-mute
> All of them with demands on you.

According to a well-informed Masonic exposure by John Fellows, 'the royal arch ... contains a scenical representation of a journey from this world to the next. In the way are four guarded passes, called *vails* ... allegorically denominated gates of heaven, through which lies the sun's course.'[54] In the first part of the initiation drama, the candidates are submitted to tests by five officers: the 'captains' protecting each of the four Veils and the 'Excellent King' (otherwise known as 'first principal'). Their journey corresponds to that of Moses through the desert in the Book of Exodus, as God reveals his might in miracles such as the Burning Bush.

> I will *build* myself a copper *tower*
> With *four ways out* and no way in
> But mine the glory, mine the power.

The second part re-enacts the rebuilding of Solomon's temple by Zerubbabel, seventy years after its destruction by Nebuchadnezzar leading to the Babylonian Captivity. According to a handwritten Irish ritual, the three candidate 'companions' are 'prepared as workmen shirt sleeves rolled up', carrying pick, shovel, and crow, their mission being to 'repair the temple'.[55] The second stanza may be read as an inversion of the candidate's progress towards enlightenment, the 'four ways out' of the tower corresponding to the four Veils leading towards the Masonic ruined temple.

> And what if the tower should shake and fall
> With *three sharp taps* and *one big bang*?
> What would you do with yourself at all?

Before allowing the party into the temple, the tyler gives three knocks. The workmen loosen the rubble and find 'a large cut stone with a ring set in it. Upon striking it a hollow sound is heard indicating a cavity below', which turns out to be 'a vaulted chamber'. This is sometimes termed 'the vault of the Nine Arches'. A shaft of sunlight discloses the depth but not the contents of the chamber.

> I would go in the *cellar* and drink the *dark*
> With two quick sips and *one long pull*,
> Drunk as a *lord* and gay as a lark.

In the chamber are various objects on a pedestal, including the Book of the Law and a plate engraved with the three Hebrew letters for 'Jehovah', the Lord. There is also a cubical stone incised with the initials JBO, signifying three more terms for God, 'Jao-Bul-On' or 'Jah-Bul-Lun'. The three syllables are 'divided' between the candidates, who utter them one at a time. The stressed final syllable may correspond to the 'one long pull', itself a mollossus reminiscent of the sacred words.

> But what when the cellar roof caves in
> With *one blue flash* and *nine old bones*?
> How, my heart, will you save your skin?

In the first part of the ceremony, according to Fellows, the candidates witness the destruction of the temple by Nebuchadnezzar (2 Chron. 36: 11–20). The words 'and brake down the wall of Jerusalem' are followed by 'a tremendous noise, by firing pistols, clashing swords, overturning chairs, rolling cannon balls across the floor, etc.' (the pistols doubtless emitting blue flashes).[56] Blue is also the colour of the degree, and of the banner held by the Captain of the First Veil. The 'nine old bones' correspond to the nine arches of the vault preserving the sacred objects after the temple's destruction.

> I will go back where I belong
> With *one foot first* and *both eyes blind,*
> I will go back where I belong
> In the fore-being of mankind.

The three candidates, 'hoodwinked' or blindfold and bound together by ropes according to Fellows, seek admission to each Veil on their hands and knees, beneath a human arch formed by the brethren. Having endured all these ordeals, they are ready to hear explanations of their spiritual meaning and to become members of the degree.

The Masonic resonances of this otherwise enigmatic poem seem too rich and intricate to be coincidental. There are no comparable echoes of Orange ritual, despite the existence of a 'Royal Arch Purple' degree into which many Orangemen of his father's generation would have been initiated.[57] 'Flight of the Heart' is not his only poem suggesting Masonic knowledge, though other examples are less esoteric in their allusions. In 'Autumn Journal', the motif of the 'falling castle' distinctly recalls the allegory of the temple: 'I must go out to-morrow as the others do | And build the falling castle; | Which has never fallen'.[58] In 'Débâcle', with its bleaker allegory of civilization crumbling away in the guise of a building, the work of the 'red-eyed pioneers' is conjured up by Masonic themes of honest labour and enlightenment: 'Vision and sinew made it of light and stone'.[59]

Admittedly, there is no reason to suppose that Louis was ever a Freemason.[60]

His writings on allegory and astrology make no reference to Masonic narratives and betray no interest (other than amused scepticism) in the occult or in arcane rites.[61] Though acknowledging the importance of mystical theories and magical conceits in feeding Yeats's poetic imagination, he showed no curiosity about the intricate astrological symbolism codified in *A Vision*, leaving 'the phases of the moon | To Mr. Yeats to rock his bardic sleep'.[62] Yet his own poetry draws heavily on dream sequences originating in fairy tales, biblical parables, and romances of chivalry, which are also the raw materials of Masonic ritual.

His apparent susceptibility to Masonic imagery was surely aroused by Frederick's immersion in its mysteries during and after Lily's final illness, and he may well have become familiar with its fabulous narratives through some volume in his father's library. At a deeper level, his poetic deployment of Masonic allegories (notably the attempt to rebuild the shattered temple) betokens a lifelong Quest for the place where his heart belonged. In some moods, that place was the moral sanctuary constructed by his parents, in which the child had been taught the simple virtues of honesty, decency, and restraint in preparation for salvation. Though Louis MacNeice never completed the return pilgrimage, his father's ghostly presence was always coming up behind him.

16. Eight Poems and Commentary

Louis MacNeice's family is a powerful, often disturbing, presence in his poetry. His treatment of family and childhood themes mellowed over time, evolving from angry rejection of his father's morality in 1930 towards acceptance of their essential affinity by the 1940s. MacNeice's exploration of family in verse and prose intensified after his father's death in 1942, contributing to a faltering and uncompleted return journey towards the faith and moral certainties of his 'oracular home'. My intention here is to apply the historian's eye to eight familiar poems, which together offer a kaleidoscopic view of his response to the lives and deaths of his three parents and to the 'values' that they embodied. In several cases, the obvious and accepted interpretation of key passages may be undermined by looking closely into the local and personal contexts of their creation.[1] These poems may therefore be read in two registers, either as straightforward and disarmingly candid declarations of feeling and fact, or as coded intimations of a reality largely hidden from the world beyond Protestant Ulster.

I

The Prodigal Son, or, The Dog Returns to his Vomit (1930)

Becoming at last bitter
After having been mild year in and year out

After having so let them bungle bungle me (with a small m
But capital T Them)
Subserving their ideals because of the something right
Which happened to be in them,
And all that much wronger efflorescence
Putting up with, pretending to enjoy.
As a little boy
Cowed into perseverance, too frightened
Ever to run from the vampire of imbecile kindness;
Alloying cowardice with filial sentiment.
And if I run now, called ungrateful
Corrupted by strange influences
Away from the dominance of an oracular home.

Vampires who take things for granted,
Who do everything for one and ask in return
Only the complete mortgage of one's soul.
There is no point anyhow in pouring
Venom. For that one keeps for the really bad,
Not for the really harmful.

Having been thus a scapegoat I have pretended
A filial martyrdom. Or have had recourse
To buffooneries drunk and sober,
With pretence of initiative
With claims to be original,
Sticking in flags on alien territories
The brighter the bunting the less its anyhow little

Almost negligible meaning.
One can never pay, they say, the debt to one's parents
However much one spends their money or forces
Them to assist one against their better judgements;
One never can cancel out their taking for granted
That everything is Theirs,
(Taking for granted is robbery of the worst
Order. Family kindness the worst coercion.)

But for all that I will give them one more chance,
Will try once more to see if they can see
Me for once instead of their blasted son;
Will go home after the pigs and whores
And see if they treat me reasonably, or if as always
… inevitable swamp.
Father I have sinned
In the sight of the morons and am no more worthy
(Thank God) to be called thy son.

The fatted calf smiled a superior bland
Smile of long calculated martyrdom,
The cricket bats chirruped on the family hearth,
The whole ghastly pack of comedy cards,
My father's words, fell
Like the droppings of a cow on my trampled mind.

My challenge had passed unnoticed;
In killing the fatted calf they had killed off also
My weakling hope pastured on foreign acorns –
Had damned me once for all
By taking my ultimate salvation for granted.

'The Prodigal Son, or, The Dog Returns to his Vomit', was published in an Oxford magazine in May 1930, a few weeks before Louis's marriage to Mary Ezra.[2] He had spent the previous Christmas at Carrickfergus 'under clouds of parental disapproval', partly stirred up by his fiancée's exotic, Jewish background. This 'shocker' of a poem, in McKinnon's view, is 'surely the high-water mark of his anti-father, anti-religion, anti-family attitude'.[3] The unrepentant Prodigal's target is not 'Him' but 'Them', so implicating his stepmother in 'the dominance of an oracular home' with its 'imbecile kindness'. But the most scathing jibes are reserved for the rector, who sits in judgment over the sinner, his moral code reinforced by 'the morons', his words a 'ghastly pack of comedy cards'. Though there was admittedly 'something right' in his 'ideals', this was outweighed by 'all that much wronger efflorescence'. This poetic rant is deliberately subverted by its manifest unfairness, culminating in the impotent protest that, as a believer in the forgiveness of sins, his father had taken 'my ultimate salvation for granted'.

Ostensibly an appeal for the respect due to an errant adult, it is essentially a howl for attention from an anarchic adolescent. Louis wisely omitted this revealing but truly nauseating diatribe from all collections of his work.

II

Auden and MacNeice: Their Last Will and Testament (1936)
Extract

And to my own in particular whose rooms
Were whitewashed, small, soothed with the smoke of peat,
Looking out on the Atlantic's gleams and glooms,

Of whom some lie among brambles high remote
Above the yellow falls of Ballysodare
Whose hands were hard with handling cart and boat

I leave the credit for that which may endure
Within myself of peasant vitality and
Of the peasant's sense of humour and I am sure

That those forefathers clamped in the boggy ground
Should have my thanks for any Ariadne's thread
Of instinct following which I too have found

My way through the forking paths of briars and mud,
My thanks I leave them therefore double and next
I leave my father half my pride of blood

And also my admiration who has fixed
His pulpit out of the reach of party slogans
And all the sordid challenges and the mixed

Motives of those who bring their drums and dragons
To silence moderation and free speech
Bawling from armoured cars and carnival wagons;

And to my stepmother I leave her rich
Placid delight in detailed living who adds
Hour to hour as if it were stitch to stitch

Calm in the circle of her household gods;
Item, to my sister Elizabeth what she lacks –
The courage to gamble on the doubtful odds

And in the end a retreat among Irish lakes
And farmyard smells and the prism of the Irish air;
Item, to Dan my son whenever he wakes

To the consciousness of what his limits are
I leave the ingenuity to transmute
His limits into roads and travel far;

Lastly to Mary living in a remote
Country I leave whatever she would remember
Of hers and mine before she took that boat,

Such memories not being necessary lumber
And may no chance, unless she wills, delete them
And may her hours be gold and without number.

More than six years elapsed before Louis's next depiction of his family in verse, in 'Auden and MacNeice: Their Last Will and Testament'.[4] This jocular by-product of a memorable visit to Iceland coincided with Mary's remarriage to Charles Katzman, a year after her abrupt desertion of Louis and their infant son Daniel.[5] Dissolution of the unwelcome marriage was rapidly followed by reconciliation with his father, who had become bishop of Down and Connor and Dromore in 1934. Louis's new-found 'admiration' for a father who had 'fixed | His pulpit out of the reach of party slogans' was doubtless prompted by news of Frederick's attempt in summer 1935 to counteract sectarian conflict by an ecumenical crusade for peace. The 'armoured cars' were possibly the Lancia 'Cage cars' used by the Royal Ulster Constabulary (eventually aided by the army and part-time 'B' Special Constabulary), when endeavouring to suppress the spiral of reprisals and counter-reprisals occasioned by attacks on Orangemen and loyalists celebrating the Jubilee and the Twelfth.[6]

His stepmother no longer appears as an accessory in moral repression, but as an efficient if 'placid' household manager who is 'rich' in delight as well as wealth. Ever generous, she bought a fine car for Louis and Mary in 1931, later willing her profligate stepson the income from a bequest of £2000, to be set aside in trust for his lifetime.[7] Louis expressed his gratitude in 'Death of an Old Lady', written soon after her funeral service in Carrickfergus on 11 April 1956, which Louis attended. Though old and tired (in her eighty-fourth year), her approach to death was 'calm and slow', just as, two decades earlier, she had reigned 'calm in the circle of her household gods'. In his obituary poem, Louis likened Beatrice's dying to the destruction of the *Titanic* in 1912, an unexpected comparison that Stallworthy attributes to a 'subconscious association' with 'the loss of his mother (to a psychiatric institution) in the same year, 1912'.[8] Since Lily was not admitted to her first hospital until March 1913, it seems more likely that the metaphor was inspired by the well-publicized anniversary of the fatal collision on 14 April.[9] It is worth noting that publication of Beatrice's death notice coincided precisely with a broadcast on 'The Sinking of the Titanic' over the BBC's Home Service.[10]

In 'Their Last Will and Testament', 'L.' not only left his father 'half my pride of blood', but specified his Sligo rather than his Connemara ancestors when declaring the origins of his own 'peasant vitality' and 'peasant's sense of humour'. His sister, when discussing a draft of McKinnon's study of MacNeice published in 1971, recalled that 'when my father first read Louis' tribute to himself (which he liked) in *Letters from Iceland* he said to me "There is just one mistake in it". When I said "What is that?" he said to me "The MacNeices were never peasants" and said "Oh well you know, I expect Louis would rather think that they were".' Having investigated their Sligo origins, Elizabeth concluded that Louis had been deceived by the apparent poverty of some descendants whom they had visited in 1927. They were in fact 'small farmers, and for that matter, a great deal more prosperous even than Louis thought'. She surmised that any 'peasant characteristics' were 'probably from our mother's side of the family', which provided 'some real Connemara peasant ancestry' with earthy values helping to counteract the 'fecklessness' of some of the MacNeices.[11] Though Louis toured Connemara as well as Sligo with his family in September 1927, the climax of this atavistic visit was his father's birthplace, Omey Island, not his mother's native Killymongaun. This was the townland slightly eastwards of Clifden where his maternal grandfather, the convert Martin Clesham, had farmed some thirty acres of extremely arid land. The holding of Frederick MacNeice's grandfather in Ballysadare, though only half as large, consisted of relatively fertile land twice as valuable as the Cleshams' farm in Connemara.[12] Louis's misleading account of his Connaught origins reflects the dominance of 'forefathers' rather than foremothers in his personal myth of origin. Despite Louis's lifelong grief at the loss of his mother when he was barely seven years old, he remained profoundly ignorant of her background in what he romantically termed 'the West of Ireland'.

III

Carrickfergus (1937)

I was born in Belfast between the mountain and the gantries
    To the hooting of lost sirens and the clang of trams:
Thence to Smoky Carrick in County Antrim
    Where the bottle-neck harbour collects the mud which jams

The little boats beneath the Norman castle,
    The pier shining with lumps of crystal salt;
The Scotch Quarter was a line of residential houses
    But the Irish Quarter was a slum for the blind and halt.

The brook ran yellow from the factory stinking of chlorine,
    The yarn-mill called its funeral cry at noon;
Our lights looked over the lough to the lights of Bangor
    Under the peacock aura of a drowning moon.

The Norman walled this town against the country
    To stop his ears against the yelping of the slave
And built a church in the form of a cross but denoting
    The list of Christ on the cross in the angle of the nave.

I was the rector's son, born to the anglican order,
    Banned for ever from the candles of the Irish poor;
The Chichesters knelt in marble at the end of a transept
    With ruffs about their necks, their portion sure.

The war came and a huge camp of soldiers
    Grew from the ground in sight of our house with long
Dummies hanging from gibbets for bayonet practice
    And the sentry's challenge echoing all day long;

A Yorkshire terrier ran in and out of the gate-lodge
  Barred to civilians, yapping as if taking affront:
Marching at ease and singing 'Who Killed Cock Robin?'
  The troops went out by the lodge and off to the Front.

The steamer was camouflaged that took me to England –
  Sweat and khaki in the Carlisle train;
I thought that the war would last for ever and ever and sugar
  Be always rationed and that never again

Would the weekly papers not have photos of sandbags
  And my governess not make bandages from moss
And people not have maps above the fireplace
  With flags on pins moving across and across –

Across the hawthorn hedge the noise of bugles,
  Flares across the night,
Somewhere on the lough was a prison ship for Germans,
  A cage across their sight.

I went to school in Dorset, the world of parents
  Contracted into a puppet world of sons
Far from the mill girls, the smell of porter, the salt-mines
  And the soldiers with their guns.

'Carrickfergus', perhaps MacNeice's most widely quoted work, was the declamatory opening salvo in *The Earth Compels*, published in 1938.[13] Here, his father is treated not as a living being but as a factor in the poet's social conditioning: 'I was the rector's son, born to the anglican order, | Banned for ever from the candles of the Irish poor'. It would be easy to assume, given Louis's frequent and disparaging references to impoverished devotees of the Blessed Virgin, that the 'Irish poor' signified candle-venerating Roman Catholics, segregated in a ghetto from which the Protestant majority was excluded: 'The Scotch Quarter was a line of residential houses | But the Irish Quarter was a slum for the blind and halt.' For Brearton, for example, this passage indicates that 'past invasions are responsible for the divisions and inequalities of the present', still redolent of the conflict between the 'invader' (epitomized in 'the anglican order') and 'his slave' (the 'Irish poor').[14]

This inference is more blatant in Banville's *The Untouchable*, where 'Victor Maskell' defies his upbringing by undertaking nocturnal rambles in forbidden territory:

> When I was a boy in Carrickdrum I often ventured at night into Irishtown, a half acre of higgledy-piggledy shacks behind the seafront where the Catholic poor lived in what seemed to me euphoric squalor. … I would creep up to Murphy's Lounge or Maloney's Select Bar and stand outside the shut door, my heart beating in my throat – it was known for a fact that if the Catholics caught a Protestant child he would be spirited away and buried alive in a shallow grave in the hills above the town.[15]

Banville's rigmarole is paraphrased from a graphic passage in *The Strings are False*, in which no reference whatever is made to religious distinctions:

> We rarely went into the Irish Quarter and I used to hold my breath till I got through it. There was a dense smell of poverty as of soot mixed with porter mixed with cheap frying fat mixed with festering scabs and rags that had never been washed. … And in Irish Quarter West there was a place which I knew was bad – a public house with great wide windows of opaque decorated glass.[16]

MacNeice's autobiographical account refers exclusively to divisions of class rather than religion, and would have been so interpreted by anyone familiar with the social geography of Carrickfergus. By the early twentieth century, all trace of the ethnic origins of the seventeenth-century 'Irish' and 'Scotch' Quarters, apart from their names, had been eradicated. Examination of the unpublished enumerators' abstracts of the 1901 census reveals that less than one-fifth of the 800-odd residents of the two Irish Quarters (South and West) were Catholics, only slightly above the proportion for the entire town, whereas two-fifths adhered to the Church of Ireland, easily the highest proportion for any sector of Carrickfergus. Though undoubtedly poor, most of the cripples, shopkeepers and drinkers of the Irish Quarters were Protestants, half of them Frederick MacNeice's parishioners. Presbyterians accounted for only two-fifths of the 300 inhabitants of 'residential houses' in Scotch Quarter, being greatly outnumbered by Protestants of other denominations.[17]

By no means a preserve of the rich and powerful, as superficially suggested by the image of the Chichesters kneeling in marble in the north transept of St Nicholas's parish church, 'anglicanism' in Antrim embraced all classes, the mercantile and professional élite being disproportionately Presbyterian and Methodist as in most of Ulster.[18] The Church of Ireland laity in urban Ulster was far humbler than its southern counterpart, whose ever tinier congregations were indeed dominated by the residue of the fallen 'Ascendancy'. In Carrickfergus, as in 'Carrickfergus', most of the 'candles of the Irish poor' illuminated Protestant hovels rather than the 'garish altars' or 'garish Virgin' ridiculed in 'Autumn Journal' and 'Belfast'.[19] The contrast between the candles of the poor and the rectory's oil lamps is explicit in 'Country Week-End', which evokes the comforting association between the dim, steady light of oil lamps and 'Bustling dead women with steady hands, | One from Tyrone and one from Cavan | And one my mother'. The lamps offered:

> Assurance, not like the fickle candles
> Which gave the dark a jagged edge
> And made it darker yet, more evil,
> Whereas these lamps, we knew, were kind.[20]

Far from symbolizing an idealized Catholic Ireland from which MacNeice was unfairly excluded by his upbringing, the candles of the poor betokened the menace of an underclass latent within his father's own flock. Since Louis MacNeice was a stickler for the literal truth, adept though he was in deluding the uninitiated through studied ambiguities, the term 'anglican order' must refer not to the laity, but to the clerical order that his father had entered in 1895. For the historically alert reader, 'Carrickfergus' encapsulates the profound class divisions within twentieth-century Ulster Protestantism rather than some eternal contest between Protestant invader and Catholic slave.

IV

Autobiography (1940)

In my childhood trees were green
And there was plenty to be seen.

Come back early or never come.

My father made the walls resound,
He wore his collar the wrong way round.

Come back early or never come.

My mother wore a yellow dress;
Gently, gently, gentleness.

Come back early or never come.

When I was five the black dreams came;
Nothing after was quite the same.

Come back early or never come.

The dark was talking to the dead;
The lamp was dark beside my bed.

Come back early or never come.

When I woke they did not care;
Nobody, nobody was there.

Come back early or never come.

When my silent terror cried,
Nobody, nobody replied.

Come back early or never come.

I got up; the chilly sun
Saw me walk away alone.

Come back early or never come.

'Autobiography' is one of eleven poems that MacNeice composed during a week's convalescence, from peritonitis, on a Connecticut island in August and September 1940.[21] As he self-deprecatingly informed his recalcitrant American muse, Eleanor Clark, it is 'a naive-seeming kind of little ballad with refrain'.[22] The poem crystallized the painful memory of his mother's illness and death that he explored so powerfully at the same period in *The Strings are False*, and to which he would return in his final (posthumous) broadcast, 'Childhood Memories'.[23] The rector appears as a forceful, almost frightening figure, who 'made the walls resound, | He wore his collar the wrong way round'. By contrast, his mother eludes specific recollection, leaving the the bereft seven-year-old of the poem to clutch at straws: the colour of a dress, a vague aura of 'gentleness'. His sister Elizabeth, more than four years older, cast some doubt on this 'naive-seeming' failure of precise recollection when she remarked that 'his memories of her before that time [1913] were fragmentary and shadowy, at least so he said'.[24] Her own memories were of 'warmth and love and vitality', expressed through Lily's creation of 'a placid, orderly kind of household' abounding with pets, rituals and games, and also through her gaity, love of dancing, and emotional responsiveness. But Elizabeth also recalled elements of 'tension' arising from Lily's dislike of 'the Ulster atmosphere' and the first signs of physical breakdown and 'mental disturbance' that culminated in a successful hysterectomy, followed by unsuccessful treatment for depression.

Louis, like Elizabeth, must have been aware that Lily 'developed ideas of having committed unforgivable sins and was inclined to talk even to the children about Death and Judgement, Hell and Heaven and kindred subjects'.[25] As Elizabeth makes clear, the images of Hellfire that may have intensified Louis's 'black dreams' are more likely to have emanated from Lily MacNeice than either her husband or poor 'Miss Craig' (Margaret McCready) from County Armagh, the reputedly Calvinist (in fact Episcopalian) 'mother's help' on whom Louis heaped so much probably undeserved odium.[26] By vilifying his substitute mother in prose, and poetically contrasting his father's forcefulness with Lily's 'gentleness', Louis did his best to cleanse his memory of the more alarming maternal images recorded by Elizabeth. Yet, even in 'Autobiography', there is an undertone of anger in the refrain, *'Come back early or never come'*. It was not his mother's help or father that failed Freddie as he shivered in the dark, but his mother. It was 'the dead' that 'did not care', that were not there, that did not reply, that left the child to 'walk away alone'. While the music of the poem wraps his mother in a protective layer of sentimentality that reproaches those that survived her, the syntax conveys unrequited anger against the mother who had betrayed her child by dying too early.

V

The Kingdom, VII (1943)

All is well, said the voice from the tiny pulpit,
All is well with the child. And the voice cracked
For the preacher was very old and the coffin down in the aisle

Held the body of one who had been his friend and colleague
For forty years and was dead in daffodil time
Before it had come to Easter. All is well with
One who believed and practised and whose life
Presumed the Resurrection. What that means
He may have felt he knew; this much is certain –
The meaning filled his actions, made him courteous
And lyrical and strong and kind and truthful,
A generous puritan. Above whose dust
About this time of year the spendthrift plants
Will toss their trumpets heralding a life
That shows itself in time but remains timeless
As is the heart of music. So today
These yellow fanfares in the trench re-echo,
Before the spades get busy, the same phrase
The preacher lost his voice on. All is well,
The flowers say, with the child; and so it must be
For, it is said, the children are of the Kingdom.

Frederick MacNeice's death on 14 April 1942 unleashed a rich sequence of positive filial memories, beginning with an affectionate post-funeral tribute incorporated in 'The Kingdom'.[27] As in 1930 and 1936, the years of his first marriage and divorce, Louis's poetic treatment of his father was clearly influenced by major changes in his personal life (as an astrologer might put it). If Frederick's opposition to his marriage to a Jewess added rancour to 'The Prodigal Son', while divorce facilitated the renewed goodwill expressed in 'Their Last Will and Testament', the bishop's death released Louis from the risk of an equally negative paternal response to his second marriage (to Hedli Anderson), which occurred on 2 July.[28] No longer a threatening or awesome figure, his father in death had become as gentle as a mother and as vulnerable as a child: 'All is well, said the voice from the tiny pulpit, | All is well with the child.' The 'child' of the biblical text appears to be dead, but subsequently returns to life in an emblem of resurrection.[29]

The voice from the pulpit was that of Richard Clarke, archdeacon of Connor, who delivered 'a short address' to mourners at St Patrick's church, Drumbeg.[30] The preacher was indeed 'very old' (in his eighty-sixth year, with a decade yet to come), and had played a crucial part in Frederick's advancement in the Church. As rector of Holy Trinity (1894–1903), Clarke had first engaged him as his curate and later welcomed him back to the parish as his successor, deeming him a man of 'ability, energy, and a sympathetic mind'.[31] Preaching at his consecration as bishop of Cashel at Christ Church Cathedral in 1931, he had depicted MacNeice's election 'as a sign from Heaven, as something tending to bind together the whole Church of Ireland'.[32] At the election for the new bishop of Down in December 1934, Clarke's intervention had helped to persuade the synod to hold an additional ballot after the inconclusive outcome of earlier rounds, so ensuring that the synod rather than the Bench of Bishops would determine the result and enabling MacNeice to secure the required majorities.[33] Like his protégé, Clarke was a Trinity man with an unremarkable academic record, from a 'Southern' background (Virginia, County Cavan), who adjusted to Belfast conditions by becoming an active Orangeman. Like Frederick, he has been misleadingly portrayed as a 'Protestant Home Ruler' despite his support for the Orange Order, the Union, and also (unlike Frederick) the Ulster Covenant.[34] He was not merely his 'friend and colleague' but, in several senses, his brother in spirit.

The 'generous puritan' of this poem gained his serenity from authentic faith, as 'One who believed and practised and whose life | Presumed the Resurrection. What that means | He may have felt he knew'. According to a sermon delivered in Carrickfergus in 1925, MacNeice adhered to St Paul's teaching 'that there will be a resurrection of the body, but that there will not be a resurrection of flesh and blood'. The 'raising' of the 'Spiritual' body referred 'to the whole career of the same personality, beginning with the birth, through death into that spiritual order in which each, according to his capacity, will be able to share in the unexplored and inexhaustible wealth of the world to come'.[35] This doctrine, literally interpreted, allowed Frederick to pay so little attention to the fate of the physical body that he neglected to reserve any plot for his own burial, bishop though he was. The survival and rebirth of his 'personality' was achieved, irrevocably, in the poetry of his agnostic son.

VI

The Strand (1945)

White Tintoretto clouds beneath my naked feet,
This mirror of wet sand imputes a lasting mood
To island truancies; my steps repeat

Someone's who now has left such strands for good
Carrying his boots and paddling like a child,
A square black figure whom the horizon understood –

My father. Who for all his responsibly compiled
Account books of a devout, precise routine
Kept something in him solitary and wild,

So loved the western sea and no tree's green
Fulfilled him like these contours of Slievemore
Menaun and Croaghaun and the bogs between.

Sixty-odd years behind him and twelve before,
Eyeing the flange of steel in the turning belt of brine
It was sixteen years ago he walked this shore

And the mirror caught his shape which catches mine
But then as now the floor-mop of the foam
Blotted the bright reflections – and no sign

Remains of face or feet when visitors have gone home.

In 'The Strand',[36] Louis evoked his father not as a disembodied 'personality' but as a fully visualized physical being, though the force of his faith is obliquely fixed in the image of 'a square black figure whom the horizon understood' (the horizon being itself understood as 'the line at which earth and sky appear to meet'). The memory of his father 'Carrying his boots and paddling like a child' echoes Frederick's own account of a visit to Omey in 1930: 'Bea and I crossed Omey strand, carrying our footwear'.[37] The poem, however, emerged from a visit with Hedli to Achill Island in 1945, which re-enacted the presumably fraught family holiday, sixteen years earlier, in which Louis's unsuitable fiancée Mary Ezra had spent nearly a month getting to be known by his father, stepmother and brother William. They had rented the Old Rectory at Dugort, once the headquarters of Edward Nangle's celebrated Protestant 'colony', which the Irish Church Missions had attempted to revive in the 1850s. Though none of his 'fathers' had dwelt in Mayo, its mountainous terrain and Atlantic seaboard gave it enough in common with Ballysadare, Omey and Killymongaun to serve as an outpost of the generalized, faraway 'pre-natal mountain' of

'Carrick Revisited' (another product of the summer holiday in 1945).[38] 'Slievemore | Menaun and Croaghaun' were rugged Achill surrogates for the Twelve Pins outside Clifden, or Knockalongy a few miles to the west of Ballysadare.

Beatrice's diary of the holiday in 1929 suggests that the rector was indeed intoxicated, if not 'fulfilled', by the island's mountainous challenge.[39] Their third Sunday in Achill was a *'Lovely day*. Service 11.30, Dugort. Derrick & I had walk after tea towards Keel – I came Home alone & he went up Slievemore – not Home till 11.15 p.m. – I was anxiously looking out for him.' Next Sunday, he kept the family waiting for an hour at the Bull's Mouth before returning from 'the Island service' on Inishbiggle, while they watched a 'beautiful sunset behind Slievemore'.[40] These rambles allowed possibly welcome escape from domestic tension at the Old Rectory, where Mary plied them with lobsters spirited out of Keel while Beatrice countered this display of Oxford hedonism with a homely macaroni cheese. Consumption of the lobsters was postponed, perhaps unfortunately, till the following lunchtime.[41] Frederick, Beatrice and William returned briefly to Achill in the following summer, without the company of Louis and his new wife, and once again the rector made for the mountains. As he noted in his holiday diary (one of those 'account books of a devout, precise routine' which failed to conceal 'something in him solitary and wild'): 'We attended service in Dugort Church. – There were about 50 persons present. It was about 1.45 before we had lunch. After lunch we drove to the entrance of what is known as "Captain Boycott's place".[42] Bea remained there and William and I essayed to climb Croaghaun. It was a perfect day with a cloudless sky.' After some faltering, they reached the summit (2192 feet) before collecting the patient Beatrice on their way to supper at the Slievemore Hotel.[43]

VII

Autumn Sequel, Canto XXII (1953)
Extract

One stockstill man on the road comes westward like a sprinter
And soon we are back in Wilts; and the downs climb
Where early man spent hours, spent weeks, upon a splinter

Of flint; and now I am back in my own early time
Where I spent days, spent years, learning to doubt
Whether I had not already passed my prime

Before I was even of age. Loping about
On these bare downs, the haunt of ancient man,
With the turf skin-deep and the chalk showing through and the knout

Of the hail-studded wind on each stud in my spine, I began
To feel I had never been young. It was here that asleep
In a high long panelled room from the time of Queen Anne

I once had the worst of my dreams, when climbing a steep
Dune with my father, one clear and silent day, I went
Ahead of him towards the skyline, he could not keep

Up with me, being heavy; I climbed with my head bent
When suddenly on the skyline there stood a tall
Redcoat rigid as lead and the sky was rent

With the motley noise of a funfair, the brangle and brawl
Of hooters and concertinas and snatches of cockney song,
And I passed that towering sentry and crossed the rim with all

My premonitions on edge, and I looked down and a gong
Rang in my guts for time. Below me, cut in the dead
White chalk lay an amphitheatre packed with a holiday throng,

Tom, Dick, and Harry, peeping, dirty, red
In the face with shouting, bunting and paper caps,
While tiers and tiers below, where all the gangways led,

Down to the round arena, newspaper scraps
Capered around the foot of three tall black
Crosses and through the noise I foresaw the world collapse

In my father's mind in a moment, who at my back
Was still coming up, coming up. This was the worst
Of my dreams and I had the worst of it, in the lack

Of my own faith and the knowledge of his, the accursed
Two ways vision of youth. Childhood was left behind
In the limestone belt with Owen, and here in the first

Inhabited heights of chalk I could feel my mind
Crumble and dry like a fossil sponge, I could feel
My body curl like a foetus and the rind

Of a barrel harden round me, to reveal
Millennia hence some inkling of the ways
Of man before he invented plough or wheel

Or before England, still in her foetal daze
Of forest and fen, had cut the unbilical cord
That bound her to the Continent.

The association between his father and ascent reappears in *Autumn Sequel*, no longer as a symbol of fulfilment but as a premonition of death in 'the worst of my dreams'.[44] In 'The Strand', the poet traces his father's sturdy steps along the seashore; in *Autumn Sequel*, written eight years later in 1953, both father and son seem older: 'he could not keep | Up with me, being heavy', while 'I began | To feel I had never been young'. Yet the dream originated in his time as a pupil at Marlborough College, six or seven years before that first holiday in Achill. For two years after his promotion as a fifteen-year-old to Upper School and 'C. House', he had slept in a dormitory of the former Seymour mansion clearly identifiable as that 'high long panelled room from the time of Queen Anne'.[45] Though the poem's setting is in Wiltshire, the 'steep dune' with its sinister hidden amphitheatre does not belong to the English landscape of 'Woods' – each 'moored | To a village somewhere near' – which his father had found so 'tame' by comparison with the West of Ireland.[46] In the dream, there is no reprieve (as in 'Woods') from 'the neolithic night', as the poet feels his 'mind | Crumble and dry like a fossil sponge' and his body 'curl like a foetus'. The poem draws a theological fable out of the grotesque vision of funfair, 'holiday throng', and 'newspaper scraps' that 'capered around the foot of three tall black crosses'. For the boy who has lost his faith, these images of Armageddon inspire sheer fear of death; for his father, faith in salvation makes the imminent collapse of the world a triumph rather than a catastrophe. As so often, the poet's imposed interpretation fails to conceal a still more alarming undercurrent: the possibility that Louis's scepticism, the very spark of his creativity, might eventually succumb to the certainties of his father, 'still coming up, coming up' behind him.

VIII

The Truisms (*c.*1960)

His father gave him a box of truisms
Shaped like a coffin, then his father died;
The truisms remained on the mantelpiece
As wooden as the playbox they had been packed in
Or that other his father skulked inside.

Then he left home, left the truisms behind him
Still on the mantelpiece, met love, met war,
Sordor, disappointment, defeat, betrayal,
Till through disbeliefs he arrived at a house
He could not remember seeing before,

And he walked straight in; it was where he had come from
And something told him the way to behave.
He raised his hand and blessed his home;
The truisms flew and perched on his shoulders
And a tall tree sprouted from his father's grave.

Eight years later, this possibility was made manifest in 'The Truisms', which portrays a world-weary son welcomed by tokens of his dead father's approval.[47] Unlike 'The Prodigal Son' of 1930, whose challenge to 'the dominance of an oracular home' had 'passed unnoticed', he remembers how to bless his father's home. In response, he too is blessed: 'The truisms flew and perched on his shoulders | And a tall tree sprouted from his father's grave.' Through some enchantment, the son seems ready at last to embrace his father's long-discarded moral precepts and so reclaim the lost 'home'. The very term 'truisms' suggests, deceptively, that the character of these precepts is self-evident: presumably the plain Christian virtues which, according to 'The Kingdom', 'made him courteous | And lyrical and strong and kind and truthful'. Conspicuous among those virtues, according to the prevalent view, were courage, tolerance, hatred of violence and rejection of sectarianism. Closer inspection of his career has indicated that Frederick MacNeice's world view was less conventionally liberal, more complex, and altogether more interesting. The truisms that 'perched on his shoulders' were, in my view, decidedly unsettling. The apparent theme of the poem – redemption – is further subverted (for literal-minded historians) by the fact that no tree shelters the grassy plot at Drumbeg where Frederick MacNeice, 'Bishop', lies buried.

Statistical Appendix

Table 1. Protestant Episcopalian Population of West Connemara, 1834–1901

Census	1834	1861	1871	1881	1891	1901
Parish of Omey						
Episcopalians	191	827	772	597	319	238
Total Population	7200	6357	6418	5886	4584	3991
% Episcopalians	2.7	13.0	12.0	10.1	7.0	6.0
Barony of Ballynahinch						
Episcopalians	454	1668	1653	1223	832	689
Total Population	31,067	23,764	23,969	23,094	19,572	17,877
% Episcopalians	1.5	7.0	6.9	5.7	4.3	3.9

Note: The barony of Ballynahinch, Co. Galway, comprised the civil parishes of Ballindoon, Ballynakill, Moyrus and Omey (Inishboffin, transferred from Co. Mayo in 1873, is excluded from these calculations). Its boundaries coincided with those of the poor law union of Clifden and the pre-Famine benefice of Ballynakill, encompassing Connemara westwards of Kilkieran Bay and Leenane.

Sources: Commissioners of Public Instruction, Ireland, *First Report*, HCP 1835 (45), xxxiii; Census of Ireland, County Reports for Galway (1861–1901).

Table 2. Religion and Illiteracy in West Connemara, 1861–1891

Census		1861	1871	1881	1891
	Parish of Omey				
Episcopalians	No. illiterate	209	131	64	19
Episcopalians	% illiterate	28.8	19.2	11.9	6.5
Roman Catholics	% illiterate	64.1	59.8	56.1	37.7
Total population	% illiterate	59.1	54.6	51.0	35.3
	Barony of Ballynahinch				
Episcopalians	No. illiterate	363	252	132	78
Episcopalians	% illiterate	25.5	17.8	11.1	10.4
Roman Catholics	% illiterate	75.1	71.8	64.0	49.5
Total population	% illiterate	71.4	67.9	60.6	47.6

Note: All figures refer to the population aged 5 years or more who could neither read nor write.

Sources: Census of Ireland, County Reports for Galway (1861–1891).

Table 3. Occupations of Episcopalian Males in Three Counties

Nos.	Order	% of Episcopalians			Episc. % of Order			IOR		
		Gal	Wat	Ant	Gal	Wat	Ant	Gal	Wat	Ant
1	Government	12.8	9.8	1.9	19.9	14.3	29.5	601	516	141
2	Defence	35.5	11.1	1.4	53.0	42.2	54.5	1600	1520	260
3	Professions	9.1	12.3	2.7	19.3	16.9	24.1	581	608	115
4	Service	4.8	10.7	2.6	8.7	13.2	36.8	262	476	176
5	Commerce	2.2	9.3	2.8	16.8	24.3	25.8	506	876	123
6	Conveyance	1.3	7.5	5.3	3.7	9.6	27.9	111	346	133
7–8	Agriculture	25.6	25.7	33.1	1.1	1.0	14.5	34	36	69
9–23	Other	8.6	13.7	50.2	1.9	2.0	27.2	56	73	130
Total	*Specified Occ.*	*100*	*100*	*100*	*3.3*	*2.8*	*21.0*	*100*	*100*	*100*

Note: Figures refer to Co. Galway (including the town), 1881, Co. Waterford (excluding the city), 1901, and Co. Antrim (excluding Belfast), 1911. Orders refer to the occupational classification in the published census. The Index of Over-Representation (IOR) gives the percentage ratio of the Episcopalian proportion in each order to that in the total male population with specified occupations. When IOR exceeds 100, the order is over-represented.

Sources: Census of Ireland, County Reports (1881–1911).

Table 4. Occupations of Vestrymen in Holy Trinity Parish, 1902

Occupational Group	Fathers of Baptised	Vestrymen	Officers	Others
	1903–4	1902	1902	1902
Professional	3	3	3	0
Government, Defence	12	21	7	14
Managers	0	4	2	2
Other White-Collar	6	13	7	6
Merchants	0	2	1	1
Shopkeeping	10	8	2	6
Sub-Total	*31*	*51*	*22*	*29*
As % of Sample	9.9	66.2	64.7	67.4
Conveyance	15	1	1	0
Workers in Building, Furniture, Wood	26	9	7	2
Other Skilled Workers	82	12	2	10
Labourers, Servants	158	3	1	2
Agriculture	1	1	1	0
Sub-Total	*282*	*26*	*12*	*14*
As % of Sample	90.1	33.8	35.3	32.6
Sample	*313*	*77*	*34*	*43*

Notes: Occupations of vestrymen are derived from family census schedules (1901), supplemented where untraced by information from directories; occupations of fathers are those given in the Register of Baptisms. The occupational classification differs slightly from that in the published census, being organized by status rather than industrial sector. Columns refer to fathers of children baptized (25 Mar. 1903–23 Mar. 1904); registered vestrymen (Apr. 1902); those elected to parish offices or the select vestry (1902–4); and those not elected to such offices. A few names of vestrymen could not be confidently matched with census returns.

Sources: Registers of Baptisms, giving father's occupation and address (1893–1919), CR/1/3/1/4–5, PRONI; Register of Vestrymen, giving precise address and subsequent changes (1870–1935), CR/1/3/8/1; Trinity Church Vestry Book (1892–1942), CR/1/3/5/2, PRONI; family schedules, Census of Ireland (1901), NAD.

Table 5. Characteristics of Vestrymen in Holy Trinity Parish, 1902

Characteristic		Vestrymen	Officers	Others
Age	Median (years)	47	47.5	46.5
H'hold Size	Median (no.)	5	5	5
Rooms	Median (no.)	6	8	6
House	% First-Class	17	23	12
Marital Status	% Single	18	19	17
H'hold Status	% Heads	82	84	83
Birthplace	% Belfast Region	68	69	67
Sample		*74*	*32*	*42*
Residence	% > 1 Kilometre from Church	42	50	33
Sample		*79*	*34*	*43*

Notes: For specification of columns, see Table 4. A few names could not be confidently matched with census returns. In other cases, the enumerator's abstract giving information on housing was unavailable. Information on residence was available in all cases. The Belfast Region incorporates Antrim and Down.

Sources: See Table 4.

Table 6. Religious Affiliation by Sector, Parish of Carrickfergus, 1901

Sector	% by denomination	Episc.	Pres.	R. Cath.	Other
	Urban District				
North-Central		33.2	33.7	21.1	12.0
South-Central		23.4	48.6	12.5	15.5
Irish Quarters		40.1	26.7	18.2	15.0
Other Western		21.7	35.0	22.6	20.7
Northern		20.6	45.5	10.6	23.4
Eastern		25.2	45.5	8.3	21.0
Urban District Total		*27.9*	*38.7*	*15.2*	*18.2*
	Rural District				
West Division		16.2	61.8	8.0	13.9
Commons & Middle Division		10.9	69.3	2.6	17.2
North-East Division		15.9	62.4	2.3	19.4
Rural District Total		*14.3*	*64.5*	*4.7*	*16.5*
Parish Total		*21.0*	*51.8*	*9.9*	*17.3*

Note: The rural divisions are townlands; the urban sectors are streets grouped by the author according to location. The parish of Carrickfergus coincides precisely with the District Electoral Division used in census tabulations. The aggregate populations for each religion derived from manuscript sources vary only slightly from those in the printed County Report.

Sources: Census of Ireland, enumerators' abstracts for each townland and street, supplemented where necessary by family schedules, Census of Ireland (1901), NAD.

Table 7. Occupations of Selected Groups in Carrickfergus, 1911

Occupational Group	Unionist Club	Parish Off.	Protestors	ML 346	LOL 1537
	1914	1908–12	1908	1913–16	1909–12
Professional	15	8	8	8	1
Government, Defence	9	8	5	5	2
Managers	5	4	6	4	2
Other White-Collar	3	9	7	6	2
Merchants	3	0	1	4	1
Shopkeeping	0	2	2	6	5
Sub-Total	*35*	*31*	*29*	*33*	*13*
As % of Sample	70.0	81.6	82.9	58.9	17.8
Conveyance	3	3	0	1	13
Salt-mining	0	0	0	0	6
Workers in Building, Furniture, Wood	4	1	2	7	9
Other Skilled Workers	4	3	3	13	18
Labourers, Servants	1	0	1	1	6
Agriculture	3	0	0	0	8
Sub-Total	*15*	*7*	*6*	*23*	*60*
As % of Sample	30.0	18.4	17.1	41.1	82.2
Sample	*50*	*38*	*35*	*56*	*73*

Notes: Occupations are derived from family census schedules (1911), supplemented where untraced by information from directories, registers, etc. The occupational classification differs slightly from that in the published census, being organized by status rather than industrial sector. Columns refer to officers of the Carrickfergus unionist club (13 Feb. 1914); parish officers and select vestrymen elected at the Easter vestry (1908–12); parishioners attending the first protest meeting (10 Nov. 1908) or contributing to the petition drawn up after that meeting; enrolled members of Masonic Lodge 346 (1913–16); and enrolled members of LOL 1537 (1909–12). A few names could not be confidently matched with census returns.

Sources: Reports of meetings of unionist club, Easter vestries, and protest meetings, *CA*; Grand Lodge Register (1900–22), Freemasons' Hall, Dublin; LOL 1537, Minutes Books and Registers (in private hands).

Table 8. Characteristics of Selected Groups in Carrickfergus, 1911

Characteristic		Unionist Club	Parish Off.	Protestors	ML 346	LOL 1537
		1913	1908–12	1908	1913–16	1909–12
Age	Median (years)	45	44	43	30.5	28
H'hold Size	Median (no.)	6	6	5.5	5.5	6
Rooms	Median (no.)	10	11	9.5	8	4.5
Front Windows	Median (no.)	6	6	6	4	3
House	% First-Class	64	74	64	38	7
Denomination	% Episcopalian	49	100	100	33	26
Marital Status	% Single	23	26	33	50	52
H'hold Status	% Heads	82	75	67	48	47
Birthplace	% Antrim	63	58	67	81	92
Sample	*Number*	*44*	*31*	*28*	*42*	*73*
Covenant	% Signatories	84	68	85	59	77
Sample	*Number*	*51*	*40*	*40*	*56*	*83*

Notes: For specification of columns, see Table 7. All names in each group have been checked against the lists of Covenant signatories, but some could not be confidently matched with census returns. In a few other cases, the enumerator's abstract giving information on housing was unavailable.

Sources: See Table 7.

Table 9. Religious Affiliations in the Belfast Region, 1861–1937

Denomination	Down & Connor & Dromore						Belfast, Antrim, & Down		
	1861	1871	1881	1891	1901	1911	1911	1926	1937
% of Population									
Episcopalians	21.3	23.2	24.2	25.4	26.1	27.0	26.4	27.8	27.8
Other Protestants	48.9	47.9	48.3	48.4	48.5	47.7	48.4	48.0	47.5
Roman Catholics	29.9	28.9	27.5	26.3	25.4	25.3	25.2	24.3	24.7
% of Denomination throughout Ireland									
Episcopalians	22.1	25.7	27.9	31.2	35.2	38.5	36.0	45.0	48.0
Other Protestants	58.8	59.9	61.9	63.9	67.0	68.8	66.6	70.7	72.4
Roman Catholics	4.8	5.2	5.1	5.5	6.0	6.4	6.1	6.2	6.5

Notes: The united diocese of Down and Connor and Dromore incorporated Belfast, Down, and almost all of Antrim, with small sections of Londonderry and Armagh. Returns by Church of Ireland dioceses were not published after 1911. Figures in the last column are derived from the Census of 1937 for Northern Ireland but 1936 for the Irish Free State.

Sources: Census of Ireland, General Reports (1901, 1911); W.E. Vaughan and A.J. Fitzpatrick, *Irish Population Statistics* (Dublin, Royal Irish Academy, 1978).

Table 10. Attendance (%) of Bishop MacNeice at Church Committees, 1932–1941

Period	RCB	RCB Committees	General Synod Committees
1932–4	87	68	49
1935–6	85	83	33
1937–8	89	84	39
1939–41	59	52	8

Notes: Percentage of meetings of the RCB and its committees attended by FM in each calendar year, and of the general synod's standing committee and board of education during the year to the following 31 March. The figure for general synod committees, '1932–4', incorporates the period from 1 Apr. 1931.

Sources: General Synod of the Church of Ireland, *Journal* (1933–42).

Abbreviations

Banner	*The Banner of the Truth in Ireland* (London, Dublin and Wonston, monthly, later quarterly)
Belfast Directory	*Belfast and Province of Ulster Directory* (Belfast, *BNL*, annual): variant titles
BLL	British Library, London
BLO	Bodleian Library, Oxford
BM	Georgina Beatrice MacNeice (née Greer)
BNL	*Belfast News-Letter*
CA	*Carrickfergus Advertiser*
CIG	*Church of Ireland Gazette* (Dublin)
CMMC	Carrickfergus Museum, MacNeice Collection
CMS	Church Missionary Society
CRL	Church Reform League
DED	District Electoral Division
(D)GC	(Deputy) Grand Chaplain, LOII
(D)GM	(Deputy) Grand Master, LOII
DL	Deputy Lieutenant (of County)
DU Calendar	*The Dublin University Calendar for the Year—* (Dublin, Hodges, Figgis, annual)
EN	(Caroline) Elizabeth Nicholson (née McNeice)
Fauske, *'Side by Side'*	Christopher Fauske, *'Side by Side in a Small Country' Bishop John Frederick MacNeice and Ireland* (Newtownabbey, Church of Ireland Historical Society, 2004)
FM	Frederick John (John Frederick) McNeice (MacNeice)
FM, *Carrickfergus*	John Frederick MacNeice, B.D., *Carrickfergus and Its Contacts: Some Chapters in the History of Ulster* (London, Simpkin, Marshall and Belfast, W. Erskine Mayne, 1928)
FM, *Church of Ireland*	John Frederick MacNeice, B.D., *The Church of Ireland in Belfast: Its Growth, Condition, Needs* (Belfast, *Belfast News-Letter*, 1931)

FM, *Our First Loyalty*	John Frederick MacNeice, D.D., Bishop of Down, *Our First Loyalty* (Belfast, W. Erskine Mayne, 1937)
FM, *Northern Churchmen*	John Frederick MacNeice, D.D., Bishop of Cashel, *Some Northern Churchmen and Some Notes on the Church in Belfast* (Belfast, W. Erskine Mayne and Dublin, Church of Ireland Printing and Publishing Co., 1934)
GE	*Galway Express*
GOL(I)	Grand Orange Lodge (of Ireland)
GRO	General Register Office, Dublin
GS, *Journal*	General Synod of the Church of Ireland, *Journal of Proceedings* (Dublin, Association for Promoting Christian Knowledge, annual)
GV	*Galway Vindicator*
HCP	House of Commons Papers
HS	High Sheriff (of County)
ICD	*Irish Church Directory and Year-Book* (Dublin, Church of Ireland, annual)
ICF	Irish Christian Fellowship
ICM	Society for Irish Church Missions to the Roman Catholics
ICM, *Report*	*Report of the Committee of the Society for Irish Church Missions to the Roman Catholics, Read at the Annual Meeting; Report for [preceding year]* (London, ICM, annual)
ICM (IB), *Report*	*Report of the Irish Branch of the Society for Irish Church Missions for [previous year]* (Dublin, ICM, annual): variant titles
IRA	Irish Republican Army
IT	*Irish Times* (Dublin)
JL	Jane Leonard
JP	Justice of the Peace
LHL	Linen Hall Library, Belfast
LM	Frederick Louis MacNeice
LM, *CP*	Louis MacNeice, *Collected Poems*, ed. Peter McDonald (London, Faber, 2007)
LM, *SL*	*Selected Letters of Louis MacNeice*, ed. Jonathan Allison (London, Faber, 2010)
LM, *Selected Prose*	*Selected Prose of Louis MacNeice*, ed. Alan Heuser (Oxford, Clarendon Press, 1990)
LM, *Strings*	Louis MacNeice, *The Strings are False: An Unfinished*

	Autobiography, ed. E. R. Dodds (London, Faber, 1982; 1st edn. 1965)
LOII	Loyal Orange Institution of Ireland
LOL	Loyal Orange Lodge
MP	Member of Parliament
NAD	National Archives, Dublin
NAL	National Archives, London (Public Record Office)
NI	Northern Ireland
NLI	National Library of Ireland, Dublin
NW	*Northern Whig* (Belfast)
PD	The Parliamentary Debates: variant titles
PRONI	Public Record Office of Northern Ireland, Belfast
RCB(L)	Representative Church Body (Library), Dublin
RCB, *Report*	*Report of Proceedings of the Representative Body Laid before the General Synod* (Dublin, Hodges Figgis, annual), with GS, *Journal*
RIC	Royal Irish Constabulary
Rutherford, 'FM'	George Rutherford, 'John Frederick MacNeice', in *Carrickfergus and District Historical Journal*, vii (1993), 38–46
Rutherford, *Old Families*	George Rutherford (comp.), *Old Families of Carrickfergus and Ballynure*, ed. Richard Clarke (Belfast, Ulster Historical Foundation, 1995)
SCM	Student Christian Movement
Stallworthy, *LM*	Jon Stallworthy, *Louis MacNeice* (London, Faber, 1995)
TCD(L)	Trinity College, Dublin (Library)
Thom's Directory	*Thom's Official Directory of the United Kingdom of Great Britain and Ireland* (Dublin, Alex Thom, annual): variant titles
Time was Away	*Time was Away: The World of Louis MacNeice*, ed. Terence Brown and Alec Reid (Dublin, Dolmen Press, 1974)
United Diocese, *Proceedings*	United Diocese of Down and Connor and Dromore, *Report of the Diocesan Council for [preceding year] and also the Proceedings of the Diocesan Synod* (Belfast, Synod, annual)
UP	University Press
UVF	Ulster Volunteer Force
VOD	Valuation Office, Dublin
WM	Worshipful Master (LOL)
YMCA	Young Men's Christian Association

$\mathcal{N}otes$

I. HIS SON'S FATHER

1. John Banville, *The Untouchable* (London, Picador, rev. ed. 1998), p. 72. Stallworthy, *LM* is among the eight authorities acknowledged by Banville (p. 406).

2. See, for example, Terence Brown, 'MacNeice: Father and Son', p. 23, in *Time was Away*, pp. 21–34; Brown, *Louis MacNeice: Sceptical Vision* (Dublin, Gill and Macmillan, 1975), pp. 8–10; Albert Haberer, *Louis MacNeice, 1907–1963: L'homme et la poésie* (Talence, Presses Universitaires de Bordeaux, 1986), p. 15; Declan Kiberd, *Irish Classics* (London, Granta, 2000), pp. 550, 554; Edna Longley, *Louis MacNeice: A Study* (London, Faber, 1988), pp. 19, 22; Longley, ' "Defending Ireland's Soul": Protestant Writers and Irish Nationalism after Independence', p. 199, in *Literature and Nationalism*, eds Vincent Newey and Ann Thompson (Liverpool, UP, 1991), pp. 198–214; William T. McKinnon, *Apollo's Blended Dream: A Study of the Poetry of Louis MacNeice* (London, Oxford UP, 1971), pp. 9–10; Seán McMahon, 'A Heart that Leaps to a Fife Band: The Irish Poems of Louis MacNeice', pp. 129–31, in *Éire–Ireland*, xi, 4 (1967), 126–39; Robin Marsack, *The Cave of Making: The Poetry of Louis MacNeice* (Oxford, Clarendon Press, 1982), p. 1; Stallworthy, *LM*, p. 34. Among the few critics who have examined Frederick MacNeice's influence on Louis *without* the explicit attribution of nationalist sentiments are Peter McDonald, *Louis MacNeice: The Poet in His Contexts* (Oxford, Clarendon Press, 1991) and also McKinnon, in his enigmatic but suggestive reappraisal of 'The Rector's Son', in *The Honest Ulsterman*, 73 (1983), 34–54.

3. This interpretation is implicit in Stallworthy's superbly crafted biography, and explicit in Fauske's statement that 'his experience of the flight from Omey led the man later to understand the dangers of division': Fauske, *'Side by Side'*, p. 4.

4. 'Landscapes of Childhood and Youth' (*c.*1957), p. 223, in LM, *Strings*, pp. 216–38.

5. LM, *Strings*, p. 62.

6. Stallworthy, *LM*, p. 65.

7. Elizabeth Nicholson, 'Trees were Green', pp. 14–15, in *Time was Away*, pp. 11–20; LM, *Strings*, p. 53.

8. LM to BM, 30 June [1927]: LM, *SL*, p. 171.

9. Fauske, *'Side by Side'*, p. 15.

10. FM, *Carrickfergus*, pp. 70, 75.

11. See, for example, Stallworthy, *LM*, esp. pp. 34–7, 172–4; Fauske, *'Side by Side'*; Rutherford, 'FM'.

12. John Hilton, 'Louis MacNeice at Marlborough and Oxford', p. 255, in LM, *Strings*, pp. 239–84 (referring to his visit to Carrickfergus in 1928).

13. LM, *CP*, p. 263.

2. CHILD OF THE MISSIONS: OMEY, 1866–1879

1. FM, 'Diary of Holiday in West of Ireland in 1930', transcribed by EN, CMMC.

2. 'After twelve hours' fasting and an hour's bell-ringing and scolding', Thackeray was served 'one very lean mutton-chop and one very small damp kidney, brought in by an old tottering waiter to a table spread in a huge black coffee-room': W. M. Thackeray, *The Irish Sketch Book of 1842* (London, Smith Elder, 1869; 1st edn 1843, pseud. M. A. Titmarsh), pp. 231–2.

3. 'The Strand' (1945): LM, *CP*, p. 263.

4. LM, *Strings*, pp. 111–12. Frederick's age was 13, not 9, when he left the island in 1879.

5. Parish of Omey, Valuation Field Book (29 Mar. 1842), 4.0539, NAD.

6. 'A. Nicholson, of New York', *Ireland's Welcome to the Stranger: Or, Excursions through Ireland, in 1844 and 1845, for the Purpose of Personally Investigating the Condition of the Poor* (London, Charles Gilpin, 1847), pp. 395–6; also quoted in Stallworthy, *LM*, p. 3.

7. Joseph Denham Smith (Congregational minister, Kingstown), *Connemara: Past and Present* (Dublin, J. Robertson, 2nd edn 1853), p. 72: copy in BLL.

8. Parish of Omey, Valuation House Book (Nov. 1853), 5.0963, NAD.

9. Nicholson, *Ireland's Welcome*, pp. 396–8.

10. Primary Valuation (31 Mar. 1855) and Revision Books, Sellerna DED, VOD; Landed Estates Court Rentals, vol. 1, no. 16 and vol. 2, no. 52 (D'Arcy estate, early 1850 and 2 Aug. 1850); vol. 17, no. 35 (Martin estate, 14 July 1852), NAD. Law Life, having previously gained possession of the Martin estate and put it up for auction in August 1849, finally disposed of the estate in 1872 to Richard Berridge, a London brewer, for £230,000. The much smaller D'Arcy estates were again offered for sale on 18 Nov. 1850, being bought for £21,245 by Thomas and Charles Eyre: *Connemara after the Famine: Journal of a Survey of the Martin Estate by Thomas Colville Scott, 1853*, ed. Tim Robinson (Dublin, The Lilliput Press, 1995), pp. ix–xi; Kathleen Villiers-Tuthill, *Beyond the Twelve Bens: A History of Clifden and District, 1860–1923* (no provenance, 1986), p. 15.

11. Report to Congested Districts Board by Major Robert Ruttledge-Fair (Inspector, Clifden district, 26 Aug. 1892): 'Baseline Reports', no. 49 (confidential print, Dublin, HMSO, 1898), pp. 453–9: copy (and microform) in TCDL (OLS X.1.324).

12. Bernard H. Becker, *Disturbed Ireland: Being the Letters Written during the Winter of 1880–81* (London, Macmillan, 1881), pp. 146–9.

13. Census of Ireland, County Reports for Galway (1841–1901).

14. 6-inch Ordnance Survey map (Galway, sheet 21, 1841: surveyed 1839; 1st rev. edn 1900: surveyed 1898).

15. Census of Ireland (1901), family schedules and enumerator's abstracts for townlands of Omey Island, DED Sellerna, NAD.

16. The percentage of females speaking Irish only was 36.6 in 1851 and 17.1 in 1881, corresponding percentages for males being 31.1 and 13.1. The percentage of persons under 20 who spoke no Irish was 22.1 in 1851 and 37.0 in 1881, corresponding percentages for adults being only 6.4 in 1851 and 7.4 in 1881. Figures are derived from tables of Irish-speaking by barony and of age-groups for each of the civil parishes in the barony of Ballynahinch (including Inishbofin, 1881).

17. See appendix, Table 2. The proportion illiterate among females aged 5 or more declined from 77.9% (1861) to 52.2% (1891), while that for males declined from 64.5% (1861) to 43.1% (1891).

18. Desmond Bowen, *The Protestant Crusade in Ireland, 1800–70: A Study of Protestant–Catholic Relations between the Act of Union and Disestablishment* (Dublin, Gill and Macmillan, 1978), pp. 203–4; Revd Henry McManus, *Sketches of the Irish Highlands: Description, Social, and Religious. With Special Reference to Irish Missions in West Connaught since 1840* (London, Hamilton, Adams, 1863), p. 208.

19. Revd Alex Dallas, *The Story of the Irish Church Missions, part I: An Account of the Providential Preparation which Led to the Establishment of the Society for Irish Church Missions to the Roman Catholics in 1849* (London, ICM, 1867), pp. 125–6.

20. For the career of Dallas (*1791–1869*), Rector of Wonston from 1829, see [Mrs Alexander Dallas], *Incidents in the Life and Ministry of the Rev. Alex. R. C. Dallas, ... by His Widow* (London, James Nisbet, 1871); Bowen, *Protestant Crusade*, esp. ch. 5; Miriam Moffitt, *Soupers and Jumpers: The Protestant Missions in Connemara, 1848–1937* (Dublin, Nonesuch, 2008). I am grateful to Dr Moffitt for allowing me to consult sections of her thoroughly documented and well-balanced study in advance of publication.

21. *Banner*, iv (1 July 1854), 87–8.

22. *Banner*, i (1 Feb. 1851), 74.

23. On 16 Jan. 1846, 20,000 packets containing texts, some in Irish translation, were anonymously despatched to 'Romanists of the respectable and middle class' who had been identified by Dallas's agents, doubling as distributors of an official form enquiring into the state of the crops. Six months later, a second postal campaign was directed towards the priesthood: Dallas, *Story of the ICM*, pt. I, pp. 52–7.

24. About a thousand handbills advertising ICM sermons in Dublin (1852–7), tightly bound in two volumes, survive in TCDL (Gall.6.m.71–2).

25. Bowen, *Protestant Crusade*, p. 228.

26. *Mission Tour-Book in Ireland; Showing how to Visit the Missions in Dublin, Connemara, etc., together with an Explanation of a Set of Six Diagrams, Exhibiting the Work of the Irish Church Missions to the Roman Catholics* (London, ICM, *1860*): copy in NLI.

27. The ICM's library in Dublin holds extensive but incomplete sets of the *Banner* for 1850–99 (monthly, then quarterly issues from 1864); ICM, *Reports* presented to the annual spring meetings in London (1850–1939); and the series of corresponding reports presented to the annual meetings of the Irish Branch in Dublin (1868–1939), which often included additional lists of Irish subscribers. Most missing issues of the first two series, apart from

the first and second *Reports* (1850–1), may be found in BLL.

28. [3rd] Earl of Roden, *Progress of the Reformation in Ireland: Extracts from a Series of Letters Written from the West of Ireland to a Friend in England in September, 1851* (Stoke-on-Trent, Tentmaker Publications, 2003; 1st edn 1851), pp. 34–6. [JL]

29. *Banner*, i (1 Mar. 1851), 82–5.

30. Just over half of the ICM's agents throughout Ireland at the end of 1856 (apart from the 274 Irish teachers) spoke Irish, including 32 of the 68 masters but only 9 of the 73 mistresses. 149 of the 215 lay agents and scripture readers spoke Irish, as well as 14 of the 45 ordained missionaries: ICM, *Report* (1857), p. 16.

31. *Banner*, v (1 Mar. 1855), 37–40. The Society's original 'Principles and Arrangements ... Adopted by the Committee, for the Guidance of the Agents, January, 1851' had emphatically discountenanced 'political advocacy or party distinctions', and pledged that the Committee's funds would never 'be employed for temporal relief' (though missionaries might use 'private funds' for that purpose while showing 'the greatest caution'): *Banner*, i (1 Feb. 1851), 75–6.

32. Dallas, *Story of the ICM*, pt. I, pp. 137–9; Mrs Alexander Dallas, *Incidents*, p. 367; *The Story of the Irish Church Missions: Continued to the Year 1869* (London, James Nisbet, 1875), p. 82 [hereafter, *Story of the ICM*, pt. II].

33. Thomas Span Plunket (1792–1866), 2nd Baron Plunket (succ. 1854), consecrated as bishop of Tuam, Killala, and Achonry in 1839, was initially a neglectful absentee before unexpectedly succumbing to evangelical fervour.

34. William Conyngham Plunket (1828–97), 4th Baron Plunket (succ. 1871), archbishop of Dublin from 1884. By 1875, the area covered before 1851 by the rector and curates of Ballynakill was served by 16 clergy, of whom 13 were maintained by the ICM backed by the West Connaught Church Endowment Society (as it became known): *Story of the ICM*, pt. II, pp. 95–6; *Banner*, viii (1 June 1858), 89; x (1 Apr. 1860), insert.

35. Roden, *Progress*, p. 31. Hyacinth D'Arcy (1801–74), rector, Omey (1851–74) and Arran (1852–5).

36. *Banner*, i (1 Oct. 1850), 10–11.

37. *The Story of the Connemara Orphans' Nursery from its Commencement to the Year 1876* (Glasgow, Campbell and Tudhope, 1877), pp. 75–7: copy in BLL.

38. Report by missionary, Sellerna, 1 Aug. 1850: *Banner*, i (1 Oct. 1850), 13.

39. Letters from missionary's wife, Sellerna: *Banner*, i (1850–1), 19–20, 32–3, 51.

40. Parish of Omey, Register of Marriages (1845–57): P 491.3.1, RCBL.

41. EN's unpublished family memoir (as summarized by Stallworthy, *LM*, p. 3), incorrectly describes the College as serving the ICM, and states that McNeice was teaching at 'Aughrus' at the time of his marriage in '1855' before moving to Omey in the following year.

42. Thomas de Vere Coneys founded the College with the Revd James Lancaster, secretary to the Connaught Auxiliary of the Irish Society (whose Irish missionary operations remained distinct from those of the ICM). By 1854, the Irish Society's superintendent and missionary at Ballinasloe had become, respectively, the College's honorary treasurer

and joint secretary. See *The Seventh Annual Report of the Irish Missionary School, Ballinasloe* (Dublin, pr. James Charles, 1854) and *The Irish Society Record*, 15 (Mar. 1854), 146: copies in NLI; Revd Patrick K. Egan, *The Parish of Ballinasloe: Its History from the Earliest Times to the Present Day* (Dublin, Clonmore and Reynolds, 1960), pp. 252–4.

43. Scottish Association for the Relief of Irish Children Attending Scriptural Schools, *Report for 1851, with Notes of a Two-Months' Residence among the Irish Church Missions in West Galway and Mayo* (Edinburgh, Paton and Ritchie, 1851), p. 3: copy in BLL. Average attendance at Moyrus between 27 July and 3 Aug. 1851 was 70 pupils out of 102 on the roll. The school was not listed among ICM schools operating on 1 Aug. 1850: *Banner*, i (1 Oct. 1850), 10–11.

44. Tim Robinson, *Connemara: The Last Pool of Darkness* (Dublin, Penguin, 2008), p. 237 (no source given). This nickname may account for 'folklore' references to an otherwise unrecorded teacher on Omey Island called 'Crusheen': Moffitt, *Soupers*, p. 169.

45. William Lindsay McNeice (died 13 Dec. 1906, aged 77, according to Civil Register of Deaths, GRO; but 81, according to Registry of Grants, Mount Jerome Cemetery (7875/1889): microform copy in Gilbert Library, Dublin; aged 74 on 31 Mar. 1901, according to his own census schedule, NAD).

46. The published census returns show that the percentage of Protestant Episcopalians in the civil parish of Ballysadare was 20.2 in 1831 (religious affiliation retrospectively returned in 1834, with some adjustment for changes in population), 19.1 in 1861, 18.6 in 1871, 18.5 in 1881, 19.9 in 1891, and 18.9 in 1901. The percentage of Catholic males (and females) who could neither read nor write (excluding children under 5) fell from 48.4 (56.8) in 1861 to 22.3 (23.9) in 1891. The corresponding percentage for non-Catholics fell from 12.0 (14.5) in 1861 to 6.9 (3.0) in 1891. See Commissioners of Public Instruction, Ireland, *First Report*, HCP 1835 (45), xxxiii; Census of Ireland, County Reports for Sligo (1861–1901); see also Miriam Moffitt, *The Church of Ireland Community of Killala and Achonry, 1870–1940* (Dublin, Irish Academic Press, 1999).

47. Undated MSS notes in hand of EN, clearly referring to a draft of William T. McKinnon, *Apollo's Blended Dream: A Study of the Poetry of Louis MacNeice* (London, Oxford UP, 1971), in notebook entitled 'The World Call': FM Papers, Dep. c. 757, BLO. See also Stallworthy, *LM*, p. 2.

48. EN, notes on McKinnon.

49. Thomas Bartlett, 'The O'Haras of Annaghmore, *c.* 1600–*c.* 1800', p. 34, in *Irish Economic and Social History*, ix (1982), 34–52.

50. Andrew Shields and Victoria Perry, introduction to calendar of O'Hara Papers, Collection List 66, NLI.

51. The family name is variously rendered in the O'Hara Papers as McNees, McNeese, McNeess, McNeesse, McNess, McNiess and McNeiss, and in Valuation returns as Macnice, MacNice, MacNeece and McNiece. The forms McNeice and MacNeice, successively preferred by Frederick John (otherwise John Frederick), never appear.

52. O'Hara Papers, MS 36318/12, NLI. Rent figures exclude quit rent, taxes and fees.

53. Lease (15 June 1758), O'Hara Papers, MS 36305/14.

54. Rental (1785), O'Hara Papers, MS 36318/18.

55. In the townland of Carrownageeragh, where no tenants of the name are recorded.

56. Record of leases and rentals (1775–1811), O'Hara Papers, MS 16712.

57. Parish of Ballysadare, Tithe Applotment Book (1 May 1825), TAB 26/16, NAD; Rental (Nov. 1846), O'Hara Papers, MS 36319/9.

58. At its peak, Anthony's annual rent in Lugowarry exceeded £35, under 3 separate leases signed in 1775 and 1779. By 1785, his rent for 16 acres of arable and meadow, with a share of mountain, had fallen below £18: Record of leases and rentals (1775–1811) and Rental (1785), O'Hara Papers, MSS 16712, 36318/18.

59. [Revd J.] T. O'Rorke, *History, Antiquities, and Present State of the Parishes of Ballysadare and Kilvarnet, in the County of Sligo* (Dublin, James Duffy, *1878*), p. 403.

60. Rental (Nov. 1822), O'Hara Papers, MS 36319/5; Tithe Applotment Book.

61. Index of Marriage Licence Bonds, Diocese of Killala and Achonry (1787–1842), NAD. The ability to circumvent the banns by providing a bond for a marriage licence suggests that the couple was relatively well off. Margaret may have been related to John Lindsay, another Lisduff tenant (see Rental (Nov. 1814), O'Hara Papers, MS 36318/22). Ferguson, then Anthony's 'only son', was among the lives named in a lease dated May 1779: Record of leases and rentals (1775–1811).

62. Parish of Ballysadare, Valuation Field Book (19, 22 Sept. 1840), 4.1676, NAD. The Primary Valuation for Ballysadare DED (18 Jan. 1858) confirms that the McNeices' 51 acres in Lisduff, valued at £38 per annum, were more fertile holdings than their 30 acres in Lugawarry, valued at only £12.

63. Ballysadare West DED, Valuation Revision Books (1858–1928), VOD. The descendants returned in the 1901 Census still adhered to the Church of Ireland: family schedules for Ferguson McNeice (Lisduff) and Kate McNeice (Lugawarry), Ballysadare West DED, NAD.

64. Rental (Nov. 1846). O'Hara, as chairman of the Lower Leyny Relief Committee and the Sligo Board of Guardians, was active in soliciting emergency funds: see calendar to Relief Commission Papers, RLFC 3/1/5492, NAD (original document mislaid).

65. His annual rent exceeded £24 in Lisduff and £8. 18s. in Lugawarry, compared with Ferguson's 8 guineas: Rental (Nov. 1846).

66. Petitions addressed to Richard Beere, agent, Annaghmore (1847), O'Hara Papers, MS 20376.

67. Anthony occupied the land formerly held by Thomas and Ferguson in Lugawarry, while Anthony and John each held sections of the land formerly occupied by Thomas in Lisduff: Primary Valuation (1858); family tree by Dan MacNeice, CMMC. No estate rental is available for the period between 1846 and 1868; but Ferguson was listed as a 'farmer' when his son's marriage was registered in 1851.

68. Alice Jane McNeice, née Howell (married as a minor, 22 Mar. 1851; died 4 Mar. 1904, aged 70, according to both Civil and Burial Registers; aged 66 on 31 Mar. 1901, according to census schedule, NAD); John Howell (buried at Roundstone, 24 Dec. 1879, aged 74: Parish of Moyrus, Register of Burials (1849–2000), P 175.4.1, RCBL). Howell's second wife (Elizabeth

Trewhela) bore him at least two more children, in 1854 and 1864: Registers of Baptisms, Parishes of Moyrus (1841–1997) and Ballinakill (1851–2000), P 175.2.1 and P 742.2.1, RCBL; family tree. The reputed birthplaces of Alice Jane's parents appear in Stallworthy, *LM*, p. 3.

69. William Webb, *Coastguard: An Official History of HM Coastguard* (London, HMSO, 1976); James P. Murray, 'The Coastguard in Famine Relief on the West Coast', in *Journal of the Galway Family History Society* (posted on 'Coastguards of Yesteryear' website, 29 Oct. 2007).

70. The corrected returns for the civil parish of 'Umma' recorded 191 members of the Established Church (2.7% of the population), with 106 (1.0%) in Moyrus: Commissioners of Public Instruction, Ireland, *First Report*.

71. Both fathers-in-law were farmers: Parish of Omey, of Marriages (1857–91; 11 June 1861, 8 Sept. 1864), P 491.3.1, RCBL; ICM, Agency Books (1856–79), ICM Office, Dublin. McNamara retired in 1905 after more than half a century's service with the ICM, while his wife retired after more than 40 years' service in 1906; Michael Couhill had left the Connemara mission in 1872: Moffitt, *Soupers*, p. 67.

72. ICM, *Report* (1865), p. 59.

73. The available information from Civil Registers, supplemented where so stated by other sources, indicates a somewhat different sequence from that in Stallworthy, *LM*, p. 498: (1) Caroline Matilda (baptized 7 Nov. 1852: Parish of Omey (and Ballindoone), Register of Baptisms (1852–87), P 491.2.1, RCBL; died 8 Mar. 1895, reportedly aged 40); (2) Ferguson John (died 21 Apr. 1867, aged 12); (3) Charlotte Ann (died 17 Sept. 1936, aged 78); (4) William Lindsay (died 28 Aug. 1889, aged 29); (5) [Frederick] John (born 20 Mar. 1866, died 14 Apr. 1942); (6) Ferguson John (born 24 Sept. 1868, died 14 July 1948); (7) Alice Jane Eccles (died 5 Apr. 1917, aged 46; aged 30 on 31 Mar. 1901, according to census schedule, NAD); (8) Margery [Hannah] Elizabeth (born 23 Mar. 1871, died 1958 according to family tree); (9) Lindsay Edwin Shaw (born 19 July 1873, died 22 May 1878); (10) Herbert Henry Howell (born 18 Dec. 1876, died 1969 according to family tree).

74. ICM, Agency Books (1856–79). Alice Jane's salary was raised to £1 15s. (Oct. 1870) and finally £2 (Aug. 1871), with 2 gratuities of £2 (Nov. 1871, Mar. 1873).

75. ICM, Agency Book (1856). According to the Primary Valuation (31 Mar. 1855), the annual rent of the ICM schoolhouse was £4, equivalent to 6s. 8d. monthly.

76. *Mission Tour-Book*, p. 43.

77. Sellerna DED, Revision Books (1855–79), VOD. Schools were exempt from the rates normally levied on the net annual valuation of land and buildings. No school is marked on the earliest 6-inch Ordnance Survey map (Galway, sheet 21, 1841), while only the 'Omey [National] School' in Cartoorbeg appears in the first revised edition (1900). The former (third) schoolhouse in Sturrakeen is marked, however, as a 'Church (*Disused*)'.

78. Scottish Association, *Report for 1851*, p. 3; ICM, *Reports* (1867), p. 77, (1869), p. 70.

79. Royal Commission of Inquiry, Primary Education (Ireland) [hereafter, Powis Commission], vol. vi, *Educational Census: Returns Showing the Number of Children Actually Present in Each Primary School on 25th June, 1868*: HCP, 1870 [C.6–V], xxviii pt. V. The

census returned 723 pupils at 33 ICM schools in Co. Galway, 10 other schools being listed but closed (mainly because of fair-day at Clifden). By contrast, a return by Revd Henry Cory Cory (missionary secretary of the ICM) enumerated 1187 pupils attending 53 schools in the county on Tuesday, 12 May 1868: Powis Commission, vol. iii, *Minutes of Evidence*, p. 494: HCP, 1870 [C.6–II], xxviii pt. III.

80. Attendance at ICM schools (with the percentage of Episcopalians) in Galway was 1173 (76%) in the week ending 17 June 1871; 673 (94%): 14 May 1881; 400 (90%): 30 May 1891; and 231 (90%): 11 May 1901. See Census of Ireland, County Reports for Galway (1871–1901).

81. Evidence of Revd H. C. Cory, 10 July 1868: Powis Commission, *Minutes*, pp. 488–94.

82. William Jack, *Report upon the State of Primary Education in the West Connaught District*: Powis Commission, vol. ii, *Reports of Assistant Commissioners* (pt. L), pp. 352–4: HCP 1870 (C.6–I), xxviii pt. II.

83. Application for Aid and Register of National schools, District 34, Galway, Roll no. 8870, ED 1/35, no. 39 and ED 2/136, ff. 186–7, NAD; *Returns, by Counties and Parishes, of the Names of all Schools in Connection with the Board of National Education in Ireland ... in Operation on the 31st Day of December 1862*: HCP, 1864 (481), xlvii. In 1882, aid was provided for a new National school on Omey.

84. Annual *Reports of the Commissioners of National Education in Ireland* (for 1862–74), app. I: 'List of Schools in Operation': HCP.

85. Of 1219 pupils attending schools in the civil parish of Omey in the week ending 17 June 1871, 405 (33.2%) were at 13 ICM schools, 376 (30.8%) at 7 National schools, 158 (13.0%) at 3 non-convent orphanages, 243 (19.9%) at 3 schools conducted by Catholic religious orders, and 37 (3.0%) at 2 other institutions: Census of Ireland, County Report for Galway (1871).

86. *Mission Tour-Book*, p. 43.

87. ICM, *Reports* (1852–81); ICM, Agency Books (1856–79); Jack, *Report* for Powis Commission, p. 353.

88. Clergy lists for all denominations appeared annually in *Thom's Directory*.

89. ICM, *Report* (1875), pp. 78–9. George Shea, a merchant's son from Co. Cork, was not, however, returned as a Roman Catholic when he entered Trinity College in 1849.

90. The number of reported confirmations performed in Clifden, and other churches in the barony of Ballynahinch, was 548 in 1851, 163 in 1852, none in 1853, 193 in 1855, 201 in 1860, 190 in 1863, 189 in 1867, 157 in 1870, 191 in 1874, 255 in 1880, 139 in 1883 and 110 in 1890. In all ICM districts, 401 converts were confirmed in 1849, and it seems likely that further confirmations were bestowed between 1855 and 1860. On the conservative assumption that west Connemara accounted for 250 confirmations in 1849 and 200 in the later 1850s, the total for 1849–80 (including 2087 enumerated above) would exceed 2500. Of 1295 recorded confirmations in west Connemara between 1851 and 1863, 1196 (92.2%) were of converts. See Bishop of Tuam, *Convert Confirmations: A Discourse Delivered to the Converts from Romanism in West Galway, in September 1851; together with a Report of the Tour for Missionary Confirmations upon the Same Occasion* (London, James Nisbet, 1851), pp. 17–29. *Banner*, ii (1 Sept. 1852), 125–7; iii (1 Dec. 1853), 172; v (1 Sept. 1855), 151–2; x (1 Nov. 1860), 170–1; xl (1 Oct.

1890), 49. ICM, *Reports* (1864), p. 46, (1868), p. 65, (1881), pp. 32–3, (1884), p. 35.

91. Of 548 persons confirmed in 5 churches in west Connemara in Sept. 1851, the number in each age group was as follows: under 15 years, 209 (38.1%); 15–19, 209 (38.1%); 20–29, 55 (10.0%); 30–39, 47 (8.6%); 40 or more, 28 (5.1%). 272 (49.6%) were female: Bishop of Tuam, *Convert Confirmations*, pp. 17–29.

92. *Banner*, xi (1 June 1861), 81–4.

93. See appendix, Table 1.

94. *Banner*, xi (1 June 1861), 83.

95. Bowen, *Protestant Crusade*, p. 146.

96. In the civil parish of Omey, the proportion of Catholic illiterates was lower than that elsewhere in west Connemara, whereas the proportion of Episcopalian illiterates was higher: see appendix, Table 2.

97. See appendix, Table 3.

98. Parish of Omey, Registers of Marriages and Baptisms.

99. Parish of Sellerna, Register of Marriages (1857–1906), P 185.3.1, RCBL.

100. 25 of the 53 vestrymen could not be matched with occupational data, including 9 (probably coastguards or policemen) from Cleggan: Parish of Sellerna, Register of Vestrymen (1871–2, 1877), P 185.6.1; Parishes of Omey and Sellerna, Registers of Baptisms and Marriages; ICM, Agency Books (1871–7); testimony of ex-'Jumpers' circulated by Revd William Rhatigan, *Galway Vindicator*, 2 Aug. 1879 (I am grateful to Dr Miriam Moffitt for alerting me to this source).

101. *Banner*, i (1 Aug. 1851), 149; ii (1 July 1852), 109.

102. 'M—', *Misssionary Scenes, Second Series: A Letter from an Eye-Witness, after a Missionary Tour during the Summer and Autumn of 1853* (London, ICM, 1854), pp. 12–14: copy in NLI.

103. *Banner*, iii (1 Dec. 1853), 160–3 (reproduced in *Mission Tour-Book*, 'explanation' of diagram showing Omey Island, pp. 41–3).

104. ICM, *Report* (1854), p. 68. The new landlord was Thomas Eyre, whose nephew's will anticipated that he would 'die in the true faith of the Holy Roman Catholic Church' under the protection of 'the Blessed Virgin Mary, and all the saints of heaven': report of probate for John Joseph Eyre (Thomas's successor in Clifden Castle), *Irish Times*, 6 Aug. 1894.

105. *Erin's Hope: The Irish Church Missions' Juvenile Magazine* (Oct. 1854), pp. 158–9.

106. ICM, *Two Months in Clifden, Co. Galway, during the Summer of 1855* (Dublin, George Herbert, 1856), pp. 16–18: copy in BLL.

107. The basis of this derivation, also given by Smith, *Connemara*, p. 72, is unknown.

108. Robert Stephen Hawker's tribute to Sir Jonathan Trelawny, bishop of Bristol, when awaiting trial after his defiance of King James II in 1688, became an anthem for Protestants as well as Cornishmen after its publication in 1832. It was cherished most for its borrowed refrain, 'And shall Trelawny die? | Here's twenty thousand Cornish men | Will know the reason why!'

109. It was reproduced in William Conyngham Plunket, *Short Visit to the Connemara*

Missions: A Letter to the Rev. John Garrett (London, Hatchard, 1863), p. 54; and thence in John Garrett, *Good News from Ireland: An Address to the Archbishops and Bishops of the Church of England* (London, Hatchard, 1863), p. 138: copies in BLO.

110. ICM, *Reports* (1857), p. 69, (1858), p. 66.

111. *Banner*, vii (1 Apr. 1857), 49–51.

112. ICM, *Report* (1859), p. 60.

113. *Banner*, x (1 Sept. 1860), 138.

114. Having asked his congregation at Sellerna, 'Why persecutest thou me?' (Acts 9: 4, and elsewhere), Dallas pondered a gentler text in Omey: 'And this is life eternal, that they might know thee the only true God, and Jesus Christ, whom thou has sent.' (John 17: 3)

115. ICM, *Report* (1864), p. 49.

116. *Story of the ICM*, pt. II, p. 265.

117. *Banner*, xvi (Apr. 1866), 31–2; ICM, *Reports* (1866), p. 60, (1867), p. 78. The landlord was presumably John Joseph Eyre, whose uncle Thomas Eyre had expressed such hostility in 1854.

118. ICM, *Reports* (1869), pp. 71, 75, (1871), p. 60, (1876), p. 68, (1878), pp. 69–70.

3. OUTCAST: OMEY, 1879

1. Register of Marriages, GRO; ICM, Agency Books (1869–78), ICM Office, Dublin; RIC General Registers, HO 184/19 (36702) and 184/3 (5427), NAL (microform copies, NAD). John Henry Frizelle, enrolled (1870), pensioned as sergeant (1900), 6′1″; William Frizell, enrolled (1843), pensioned as constable (1875), 5′9″.

2. ICM, Agency Books (1869–78).

3. In 'Valediction' (1934), Louis recalled his father talking 'about the West where years back | He played hurley on the sands with a stick of wrack' (dried seaweed): LM, *CP*, p. 9.

4. *Banner*, xxviii (1 Oct. 1878), 63–4. Since William McNeice was now officially a reader, the confrontation may have involved John King, schoolmaster on the island in Aug. and Sept. 1878.

5. *Daily Express* (Dublin), 13 Dec. 1878, quoted in *Banner*, xxix (1 Jan. 1879), 3. For a detailed study of the wider disturbances arising from the confrontation between McNeice and Rhatigan, see Miriam Moffitt, *Soupers and Jumpers: The Protestant Missions in Connemara, 1848–1937* (Dublin, Nonesuch, 2008), ch. 16, esp. pp. 138–44. I am grateful to the author for offering several leads and suggestions.

6. *Banner*, xxix (1 Apr. 1879), 19.

7. Bernard H. Becker, *Disturbed Ireland: Being the Letters Written during the Winter of 1880–81* (London, Macmillan, 1881), p. 146. For Rhatigan's clerical career, including his brief curacy in Clifden, see *Thom's Directory* (1875–90).

8. *Banner*, xxix (1 Apr. 1879), 20–1. Though the letter is attributed only to 'the daughter of the teacher of Omey', it is almost certainly the work of Charlotte rather than the newly wed Caroline or a daughter of the recently appointed schoolmaster (Michael Davies).

9. Copies of police statements sworn before the Galway Crown Solicitor, Thomas

O'Farrell, 26–8 Mar. 1879, are in Chief Secretary's Office, Registered Papers [hereafter, RP], 1879/5309, NAD. They were quoted at length in press reports of Clifden petty sessions, as in the unionist *Galway Express*, 19 Apr. 1879. Police accounts of the sermon differed on whether the reader, Stephen Coursey, had been accused of assaulting Rhatigan.

10. T. H. Burke (Under Secretary) to James Lowther (Chief Secretary), 19 Mar. 1879; O'Farrell to Burke, 31 Mar. 1879; Hugh Holmes (Solicitor General) to Burke, 2 Apr. 1879, RP 1879/5309 (inc. 4872); *GE*, 12 Apr., 3 May 1879.

11. Police statements, RP 1879/5309; *GE*, 19 Apr. 1879.

12. Statements of Sub-Constables Hanlon and Roarke, RP 1879/5309. Honor Gorham and Celia Gordon were misidentified by Hanlon as Honor Graham and Celia King.

13. *GE*, 8 Mar. 1879.

14. *Banner*, xxix (1 Apr. 1879), 23.

15. Original memorial, signed by John Conerney and nine others, RP 1879/4436 (in 5309); reproduced in many newspapers and in *Banner*, xxix (1 Apr. 1879), 18.

16. Burke to Lowther, 19 Mar. 1879, RP 1879/4872 (in 5309). The index to Registered Papers for 1879 lists several hundred files relating to the Connemara disturbances, of which only about one-tenth can now be located.

17. *GE*, 29 Mar. 1879.

18. RP 1879/5309.

19. Report by Constable Patrick Gorman (Cleggan), 26 Mar. 1879, RP 1879/5018.

20. O'Farrell to Burke, 31 Mar. 1879; Holmes to Burke, 2 Apr. 1879, RP 1879/5309.

21. *GE*, 5 Apr. 1879.

22. *PD*, 3rd series, vol. ccxlv (3, 7 Apr. 1879), cols 270, 438–9.

23. *GV*, 5 Apr. 1879.

24. Parish of Omey, Vestry Minute Book, P 491.5.1, RCBL.

25. *The Times*, 16 Apr. 1879.

26. *GE*, 19 Apr. 1879; ICM, Agency Books; Parish Registers for Omey and Sellerna, RCBL; lists of converts, orphans, marriages, and baptisms in Moffitt, *Soupers*.

27. *GE*, 19 Apr. 1879. Coursey's salary as reader is returned as £4 10s. in ICM, Agency Book (1879).

28. *GE*, 26 Apr. 1879; *GV*, 26 Apr. 1879.

29. *GE*, 3 May 1879.

30. *GE*, 3 May 1879.

31. *GV*, 17 May 1879.

32. ICM, Agency Book, 1879.

33. County Inspector F. N. Cullen to Inspector General, RIC, 24 Apr. 1879, RP 1879/8324.

34. Letter from Father McManus and four other signatories to *Freeman's Journal*, 6 May, in *GV*, 14 May 1879; letter from Cory, 9 May, in *GE*, 17 May 1879.

35. *IT*, 6, 7 May 1879; *GE*, 10 May 1879.

36. Cullen to Inspector General, 13 May 1879, RP 1879/8324.

37. *PD*, 3rd series, vol. ccxlvi (19 May 1879), cols 686–91.

38. ICM, *Report* (1879), pp. 24–5.

39. *Ibid.* p. 59.

40. *GE*, 7 June 1879. I am grateful to Miriam Moffitt for sending me a copy of this letter as published in the Dublin *Evening Mail*.

41. *GE*, 14 June 1879.

42. Report by Sub-Inspector W. J. Greene, 12 June 1879, RP 1879/9800 (in 9967).

43. *Banner*, xxix (1 Oct. 1879), 60–5.

44. *Ibid.* 65–6. This report was followed by an appeal for the Connemara Outrage Fund, citing further confrontations.

45. *GE*, 28 June 1879.

46. *GV*, 2 Aug. 1879. I am grateful to Miriam Moffitt for sending me transcripts of these statements, reproduced in Moffitt, *Soupers*, pp. 195–8.

47. Not Michael Davies, teacher at Omey from Oct. 1878 to May 1879, who was transferred to Portarlington: ICM, Agency Books, 1878–9.

48. Since there were two Stuffle households on the island according to the Primary Valuation, there may have been two Marys.

49. An orphanage associated with the ICM in York St, Kingstown (Dún Laoghaire).

50. *GE*, 2 Aug. 1879.

51. *Ibid.*; *GV*, 2 Aug. 1879; *IT*, 2 Aug. 1879.

52. No reference to the case appears in local press reports of the Connaught Winter Assizes or the Galway Spring and Summer Assizes.

53. Report of cases at petty sessions, 14 Aug.: *GE*, 16 Aug. 1879.

54. *GV*, 6 Aug. 1879. 'The witnesses on behalf of the prisoners met with a similar demonstration' on the previous evening.

55. *GV*, 9 Aug. 1879.

56. ICM, *Reports* (1881), p. 61, (1882), pp. 45–6, (1883), pp. 54–5, (1884), p. 49.

57. Moffitt, *Soupers*, p. 152; *Banner*, xxxv (1 Jan. 1885), 16.

58. Mission statistics in ICM, Agency Books (1878–90) and *Reports* (1879–92).

59. See appendix, Table 1.

60. Census of Ireland (1901), family schedules, NAD; Parish Registers for Omey and Sellerna.

61. Moffitt, *Soupers*, p. 258 (note 622).

4. APPRENTICE: DUBLIN AND BEYOND, 1879–1898

1. Nothing in Frederick's writings, however, indicates knowledge of Irish; and neither Frederick nor his father declared himself able to speak the language in their family Census schedules for 1911 and 1901 respectively.

2. Stallworthy, *LM*, pp. 5–6.

3. *Ibid.* p. 5.

4. RIC, General Register, HO 184/19 (36702), NAL (microform copy, NAD).

5. He was briefly listed as a probationer, with a monthly salary of £2 5s., from Aug. 1879 to Jan. 1880: ICM, Agency Books (1879–80), ICM Office, Dublin.

6. ICM, Agency Books (1879–1905); Stallworthy, *LM*, p. 6.

7. McNeice was returned for this address in the issues for 1882 and 1883 only, the house being occupied thereafter by a bootmaker: *Thom's Directory* (1881–4).

8. This was the registered place of death of William the younger, no longer employed by the ICM, in 1889.

9. ICM, *Report* (1883), pp. 11–12.

10. *Ibid.* (1884), pp. 11–14; *Thom's Directory* (1883, 1891). The Society's office was in nearby D'Olier Street, next door to those of a cluster of kindred bodies such as the Priests' Protection Society, the Italian Mission, and the Home Mission to All the Churches.

11. ICM, *Report* (1882), pp. 19–20.

12. Register of Marriages, GRO.

13. RIC, General Register, HO 184/22 (41,873). James Livingstone Kavanagh, enrolled (1876), pensioned as sergeant (1905), 5′10″.

14. Register of Deaths, GRO; Registry of Grants, Mount Jerome Cemetery (7875/1889): microform copy, Gilbert Library, Dublin. William, returned as a stationer, died in Townsend St.

15. ICM, *Report* (1889), pp. 16–19.

16. Intermediate Education Board for Ireland, *Results of the Examinations* (Dublin, 1881–7): copies in NLI (Attic).

17. Stallworthy, *LM*, p. 6.

18. On display in Carrickfergus Museum (CMMC).

19. *Daily Express* (Dublin), 15 Oct. 1887.

20. The Dublin YMCA, founded in 1849 and located in Sackville Street and later Abbey Street, was a more plebeian organization not associated with the Church of Ireland. Its general secretary was the leading Orangeman John R. Fowler, eponym of Fowler Hall in Rutland Square: *Thom's Directory* (1883), p. 845.

21. *Thom's Directory* (1883), p. 845; *IT*, 12 Sept. 1884 (obituary of Harden), 15 Oct. 1887 (prize-giving); *Daily Express*, 15 Oct. 1887 (names of prize-winners).

22. *Fourteenth Annual Report of the Church of Ireland Young Men's Christian Association* (Dublin, pr. Porteous and Gibbs, 1875): copy in NLI. In 1874, the Association had 413 full members and 160 'subscribers' (paying £1 for the same privileges).

23. FM, *Church of Ireland*, p. 17. The references to Gibson suggests that Frederick heard him speak before his elevation to the peerage in July 1885.

24. Edward Gibson (1837–1913), cr. Baron Ashbourne (1885), QC (1872), MP, Dublin University (1875–85), Lord Chancellor of Ireland (1885–6, 1886–92, 1895–1905); Thomas Sexton (1848–1932), Chairman, *Freeman's Journal* (1892–1912), MP (1880–96), Lord Mayor of Dublin (1888–9); Timothy Michael Healy (1855–1931), MP (1880–1910), imprisoned (1883), QC (1899), Governor-General, Irish Free State (1922–8); Gerald Fitzgibbon (1837–1909), QC (1872), Solicitor-General for Ireland (1877–8), Lord Justice of Appeal (1878–1909); David Robert

Plunket (1838–1919), cr. Baron Rathmore (1895), QC (1868), MP, Dublin University (1870–95), Solicitor-General for Ireland (1875–7), 1st Commissioner of Works (1885–6, 1886–92).

25. ICM, Agency Books (1887–9). His initial salary as a student was £2 5s., rising as a probationer to £3 5s. and then £4 in July 1888. Since the orphanage was not funded directly by the ICM, its records provide no information on his appointment beyond noting his departure from Dublin to 'Ballyconree O.H.'

26. Scottish Association for the Relief of Irish Children Attending Scriptural Schools, *Report for 1851, with Notes of a Two Months' Residence among the Irish Church Missions in West Galway and Mayo* (Edinburgh, Paton and Ritchie, 1851), p. 12. The house was extended and out-offices added in 1861, whereupon the annual valuation was trebled to £30. See Clifden DED (townland of Ballmaconry), Valuation Revision Books (1858–64), VOD.

27. *Banner*, xxv (1 Jan. 1875), 14; ICM, *Report* (1879), p. 24.

28. *Banner*, xxxvi (1 Jan. 1886), 11.

29. The number of boys attending orphanages in the civil parish of Omey (including one male orphanage, and one or two 'mixed' institutions not associated with the ICM), was 76 in 1871, 40 in 1881, 33 in 1891, and 27 in 1901: Census of Ireland, County Reports for Galway (1871–1901).

30. *IT*, 5,14 July 1922, 1, 4 Jan. 1923. [JL] See also Miriam Moffitt, *Soupers and Jumpers: The Protestant Missions in Connemara, 1848–1937* (Dublin, Nonesuch, 2008), pp. 166–7.

31. Like her husband and son, she was ill at ease with her names. Born, baptized, and married as Eliza, she died as Elizabeth, but was known to her husband as Lily. In the ICM's Agency Books, she was listed initially as Miss M. C. Clisham, later as Miss E. C. Clesham (the spelling on her marriage certificate).

32. ICM, Agency Books (1883–1902); ICM (IB), *Reports* (1899), p. 81, (1902), p. 70; Census of Ireland (1901), DED Clifden (townland of Kingstown), family schedule.

33. Stallworthy, *LM*, pp. 7–8.

34. Parish of Omey, Register of Baptisms (1852–87), P 491.2.1, RCBL.

35. Stallworthy, *LM*, pp. 6–7.

36. When the change of occupancy from William 'Cleshan' to Martin 'Clishan' ('Clesham' from 1867) was recorded in 1866, the land was valued at £2 15s. and the buildings at 15s.: DED Derrylea, Valuation Revision Books (1857–98). His landlord from 1873 was Moreton Frewen, a prominent Home Ruler whose sister Ruby married Edward Carson and became a senior Orangewoman.

37. William Clisham's annual rent was £3 1s. 2d.: Auction Notice, D'Arcy Estate (early 1850), Townland of 'Killewungane', Landed Estates Court Rentals, vol. 1, no. 16, NAD.

38. Parish of Omey, Registers of Marriages (1857–91) and Burials (1832–1900, with Ballinakill entries), P 491.3.2 and P 742.1.2.

39. In the Census of 1901, Martin Clesham returned himself in the family schedule as a widowed and retired farmer, aged 67, able to read and write and (unlike his daughter) to speak Irish as well as English. He ceased to be returned as occupier of the farm at Killymongaun in 1898: Valuation Revision Books.

40. *GE*, 19, 26 Dec. 1863.

41. Parish of Omey, Register of Burials. A Michael Clisham sponsored a Catholic baptism in Omey Parish on 13 Mar. 1838: (Catholic) Parish of Omey and Ballindoon, Register of Baptisms (microform copy, NLI).

42. *Banner*, xxv (1 Oct. 1875), 57–8; see also Moffitt, *Soupers*, p. 122. I am grateful to Miriam Moffitt for alerting me to the existence of this report.

43. Timothy Clesham (*1839*–94), son of John, farmer near Clifden (perhaps Lily's great-uncle); ICM student and agent (1856–72); Bedell (extra) prizeman in Irish, Trinity College (1873), BA (1874); incumbent (ICM missionary), Aasleagh, Tuam diocese (1875–94): ICM, Agency Books (1856–89). His widow Isabella (d. 1937) and daughter Mary were still living in Mayo (at Caherduff, Cong) when the MacNeices visited their home on 29 Aug. 1930. See FM, 'Diary of Holiday in the West of Ireland in 1930', transcribed by EN, CMMC.

44. According to the ICM's juvenile magazine, *Erin's Hope*, his mother and uncle had succumbed to the pressure of being ostracized and excommunicated by bowing to priestly authority and expelling 'Tim Cl.' from the household: Moffitt, *Soupers*, pp. 41, 87.

45. Entrance Book (1896–1915), MUN/V/23/7, TCDL (Manuscripts Department). Of 262 candidates for entrance in 1892 who stated their schooling, only 30 had been educated privately or at home: Entrance Examination Book (1886–97), MUN/V/26/6.

46. *DU Calendar* (1892). An entrance fee of £15 was added to the half-yearly fee of 8 guineas.

47. Entrance Examination Book (1886–97); *DU Calendar* (1901–2), pp. 241–3 (Entrance Papers for Oct. 1900, the first to be published in the *Calendar*). His aggregate mark was 69%.

48. In 1892, the annual rent per Pensioner for a shared room varied between £2 and £9, with a deposit of up to two years' rent; while the cost of compulsory Commons was about 10s. weekly: *DU Calendar* (1892), pp. 20–2. For a student in residence for 30 weeks in a typical room, the annual cost was therefore about £20 (excluding various additional charges and tips for Scouts). Only Scholars (and Sizars, in the case of Commons) were exempt from these charges.

49. Buttery Books (1892–3, 1894–5), MUN/V/94/4–5; Commons Day Books (checked for 1892–5), MUN/V/92/10–11.

50. *TCD: A College Miscellany*, i, ii (1895–6) carried regular and detailed reports of the proceedings of the major College debating bodies, including the 'Hist.' (Historical), 'Phil.' (Philosophical), and Theological Societies: copies in NLI, TCDL.

51. [Rathmines School], *Blue, White and Blue*, x (n. s.), 1 & 2 (April 1894), 1, 20: copy in NLI.

52. *Ibid.*, vii, no. 2 (June 1891), 39 (occupations of fathers of 190 pupils currently on the school roll, as reported by Benson to the annual Old Boys' Dinner, 9 Feb. 1891); see also *Rathmines School, Ora et Labora: The School Roll from the Beginning of the School in 1858 till its Close in 1898*, ed. T. F. Figgis and T. W. E. Drury (Dublin, University Press, 1932): copy in NLI.

53. T. W. E. Drury, *Unforgotten* (Dublin, APCK, 1951), pp. 64–5.

54. *Blue, White and Blue*, x, no. 3 (Sept. 1894), 75; xi, no. 1 (Dec. 1895), 15.

55. Frederick averaged only 48.6% in Science examinations, with mediocre results except in Euclid. His average score in Classics was 66.7%, with relatively high marks in Logic and Ethics and a sounder record in Greek and Latin *viva voce* examinations than in Composition. His aggregate scores in Little-Go and the Degree examination were 64.2% and 65.0%, the threshold for Firsts being 60% and 65% respectively: *DU Calendar* (1892–6); Term and Examination Returns (1892–5), MUN/V/30/51–54; Trinity College, Classes of 1889/90–93/4 (summaries of each entrant's College career), MUN /V/29/8.

56. Papers for Degree examination, Michaelmas Term, 1900: *DU Calendar* (1901–2), pp. 247–50.

57. Frederick was stronger on Locke (5 out of 10) than Stewart (4): Divinity School Entrance Examination Book (1888–1915), MUN/V/85/7.

58. In the separate Divinity examinations he received 42% for his work as a Junior Sophister and 57% in his Finals: Divinity Examination, Junior Class (1863–1911) and Senior Class (1864–1924), MUN/V/85/4–5; *DU Calendar* (1895–7).

59. Drury, *Unforgotten*, pp. 92–3. Thomas William Ernest Drury (1872–1960), BA and deacon (1896), curate, St Anne's, Belfast (1896–1901) and Kilbroney, Dromore (1901–4), incumbent, Kilbroney (1904–18) and Raheny, Dublin (1918–49).

60. *The Parallel New Testament Greek and English* (London, Oxford UP, 1887): CMMC.

61. Heb. 8: 6–13, in *Parallel New Testament*, pp. 930–1.

62. See FM, Diaries (1913, 1938), 27 July, 11 Sept. 1913, 31 Dec. 1938, FM Papers, Dep. c. 758, BLO. According to Robin Bryans, the Greek words for 'God Help Me' appeared in the notes for 'every sermon he preached': Robert Harbinson (pseud.), *Ulster: A Journey through the Six Counties* (London, Faber, 1964), p. 42.

63. LM, *Strings*, p. 59.

64. William McNeice was first listed as occupier of this tenement (valued at £1 per annum) in Feb. 1893, being succeeded by William Jackson in 1908: Valuation Revision Books, DED, Parish, and Townland of Clonsilla.

65. Census of Ireland (1901), family schedule.

66. Herbert McNeice received 14% for the Sizarship examination in 1894 and 47% in 1895, along with 7% in the general Entrance examination in 1894 and 27% in 1895: Term and Examination Returns (1894–5), MUN/V/30/53–54; Index to Entrance Books (1880–96), MUN/V/24/6; *DU Calendar* (1896), pp. 29–31.

67. He took two of the six papers required for the degree of Bachelor in Divinity in Trinity Term 1904, scoring 20% in Hebrew and 49% in Ecclesiastical History: BD Examination Book (1890–1937), MUN/V/85/6. Ordained for Durham (1904–5), he held three curacies in England before serving as vicar of Melbourn, Ely (1922–51). His name last appeared in *Crockford's Clerical Directory* in the edition for 1971–2.

68. The *Parallel New Testament* is doubly inscribed 'Frederick J. McNeice 1894' and 'John Fredk. McNeice, Cappoquin, 1896'.

69. So far as can be guessed from other photographs, Alice Jane is seated on Margery's right, while Herbert (with beard) is standing on Frederick's left.

70. Sealed parchment licence, 21 Sept. 1895, FM Papers, Dep. c. 759, BLO.

71. G. B. MacNeice, Diary (1929), CMMC. On 29 Sept. 1929, she noted 'Anniversary of Derrick's 1st. Sermon preached in Cappoquin, 34 years ago.'

72. Robert Scott Bradshaw Burkitt (1857–1940), curate, Cappoquin (1881), then curate-in-charge (1894), and perpetual curate (*1896*–1940), archdeacon of Lismore (1912–40).

73. The Episcopalian percentage for Cappoquin DED was 4.5%; for the encompassing Rural District of Lismore, it was 4.0%: Census of Ireland, County Report for Waterford (1901).

74. See appendix, Table 3.

75. *Waterford Standard*, 28 Apr. 1897 (report of Easter vestry, union of Cappoquin and Whitechurch). Names have been matched principally with U. H. Hussey de Burgh, *The Landowners of Ireland: An Alphabetical List of the Owners of Estates* (Dublin, Hodges, Foster and Figgis, 1878), and various editions of *Burke's Landed Gentry* and *Peerage*, *Walford's County Families*, and *Thom's Directory*.

76. Average attendance at Sunday services was 175 (1891) and 158 (1909); at Sunday school, 26 (1899) and 28 (1909); at day school, 18 (1909). See Parish Returns, Cappoquin (including Whitechurch), for 1891 and 1909 (with figures for 1899); Rural Dean's Visitation Returns, Dioceses of Waterford and Lismore (with Cashel and Emly, 1909), D 9.2.3.2–3, RCBL.

77. Sealed parchment licence, 13 July 1896, FM Papers, Dep. c. 759.

78. Frederick gained unimpressive results in Old Testament (41.5%), Ecclesiastical History (49%) and Hebrew (50%), but stronger marks in New Testament (61%), Patristic Theology (65%) and Articles and Liturgy (68%): B.D. Examination Book (1890–1937), MUN/V/85/6. There is no record of his submission of the compulsory thesis.

79. FM, Diary, 30 Dec. 1938.

80. John McKee, millwright, and subsequently his widow, kept a boarding house at 19 Brookhill Ave., a first-class house with 5 front windows and 12 rooms according to the family schedule, Census of Ireland (1901).

5. ORANGEMAN: BELFAST, 1898–1908

1. Stallworthy, *LM*, p. 8.

2. After Frederick returned to the parish as incumbent, his curate was paid £110, £10 less than Frederick's annual stipend in Cappoquin: *ICD* (1906).

3. FM, speech at opening of sale of work, Trinity church, recalling the stories of parishioners when he first arrived as a curate: *CIG*, lxxx (6 Dec. 1935), 780.

4. The number of communicants on ordinary Sundays in 1905 varied between 2 and 37, the median being 22: Holy Trinity Parish, Preachers' Book (1905–20), CR/1/3/6/2, PRONI. The number receiving Communion throughout the year was 805, compared with 626 in Cappoquin in 1899 and 587 in 1909: sources cited in ch. 4, note 76.

5. Charles Frederick D'Arcy, *The Adventures of a Bishop: A Phase of Irish Life, a Personal and Historical Narrative* (London, Hodder and Stoughton, 1934), pp. 99, 178.

6. Thomas James Welland (1830–1907), Dubliner; deacon (1854), rector, St Thomas's, Belfast (1870–92), bishop of Down and Connor and Dromore (1892–1907).

7. FM, *Some Northern Churchmen*, pp. 77–8. FM's list of new churches excludes St Matthias, Glen Road (1892) and All Saints (1895). Several of the new livings were initially districts administered by 'perpetual curates' or 'curates-in-charge', only later being accorded the formal status of parishes with incumbents.

8. *TCD: A College Miscellany*, ii, 32 (14 Nov. 1896), 135.

9. Richard Rutledge Kane (*1841*–98), Primitive Wesleyan Methodist minister (1859–68), curate in Down and Salisbury (1868–71), curate, Tullylish, Co. Down (1871–2) and rector (1872–82), incumbent, Christ Church, Belfast (1882–98); Grand Master, Belfast GOL (1885–98).

10. FM, *Some Northern Churchmen*, pp. 39–40 (sermon at Christ Church, Belfast, 2 July 1933); FM, *Church of Ireland*, p. 17.

11. Frederick was elected annually as chaplain of LOL 440 (1898–1901) and as a District chaplain (1899–1902), with addresses in Cappoquin (1898), Clonsilla (1899), and Belfast (1900): City of Dublin District no. 3, Minute Book (1898–1917), D/2947/5/1, PRONI.

12. Idem; Minute Books for City of Dublin GOL (1901–17), District no. 2 (1889–1907), and Cumberland LOL 440 (1870–8): D/2947/2A/1, 4/1, and 6/3. The 7 lodges in District no. 2 had 272 members in 1897; membership returns are not preserved for the 8 lodges in District no. 1.

13. Sean O'Casey, *Pictures in the Hallway* (1942) in *Autobiographies*, vol. i (London, Macmillan, 1963), pp. 389–90; Christopher Murray, *Sean O'Casey, Writer at Work: A Biography* (Dublin, Gill and Macmillan, 2006; 1st edn. 2004), pp. 50–60.

14. For Crawford's remarkable trajectory, see J. W. Boyle, 'A Fenian Protestant in Canada: Robert Lindsay Crawford, 1910–22', in *Canadian Historical Studies*, lii, 2 (1971), 165–76.

15. District no. 3, Minute Book, 5 Jan., 4 May, 3 Aug. 1900; 2 Sept. 1898.

16. Philip Bernard Johnson (1847–1926), curate, Townsend St Mission Church (1892–4) and superintendent, Dublin mission (1894–1903); organising superintendent, ICM (1903–6); incumbent, Wicklow (1906–25). Johnson was admitted to LOL 440 as an 'Old Member rejoining' (10 May 1904), returned as lodge chaplain (3 Nov. 1904) and elected chaplain, District no. 3 (5 Oct. 1905): District no. 3, Minute Book. The three ICM candidates joined Cumberland True Blues LOL 1738: District no. 2, Minute Book, 7 Jan. 1902.

17. *Report[s] of the County Grand Lodge of Belfast* (Belfast, LOII, 1891–1921): copies in LHL and Schomberg House, Belfast.

18. Belfast GOL, *Report* (1908). Of the 21 Episcopalian DGCs elected for that year, 5 were rejected by GOLI, as were 3 of the 6 Presbyterians.

19. Belfast GOL, *Report* (1911).

20. Richard James Clarke (1856–1953), curate, Holy Trinity, Belfast (1882–4) and incumbent (1894–1903); rector, Carnmoney, Co. Antrim (1903–45); appointed prebendary, chancellor and archdeacon of Connor (1922, 1933, 1941).

21. *BNL*, 10 July 1899, 2 July 1900.

22. He was elected as DGC, Belfast (1903–5, 1907–8), and chaplain, District no. 1 (meeting in Clifton Street Orange Hall), but never held office in GOLI or in the Antrim GOL.

23. E. R. Dodds, *Missing Persons: An Autobiography* (Oxford, Clarendon Press, 1977), pp. 23–4, 34. Dodds, LM's close friend and professor at Birmingham, befriended Clarke's sons (Brice and Stewart) at Campbell College between 1908 and 1912, and stayed with the family at Carnmoney rectory. Dodds's perplexing account of the family's politics bears a striking resemblance to LM's repeated assertion that his own father was a Home Ruler.

24. Both Richard and his son Brice (described by Dodds as 'an idle and rebellious member of a talented family') signed the Covenant in Carnmoney, heading two separate sheets: PRONI (online); Dodds, *Missing Persons*, p. 23. For Clarke's election as a vice-president of the Unionist Association, see *CA*, 14 June 1912, 28 June 1918.

25. As with all of Frederick's Belfast lodges, LOL 410 no longer exists and its records have not been traced. He was probably admitted two or three years before his first election as DGC, Belfast, in Nov. 1902: Belfast GOL, *Report* (1903).

26. William Dowse (1856–1939), incumbent, St Thomas's (1892–1931), dean of Connor (1910–31); Samuel Patton Mitchell (d. 1943), curate-in-charge, St Nicholas's (1900–1), then rector (1901–43).

27. FM, *Church of Ireland*, p. 50.

28. William Harloe Dundas (d. 1941), curate, St Thomas's (1898–1907), vicar, Magheragall (1907–40), treasurer of Connor (1932–40); DGC, Belfast (1901–5, 1907); Francis Matchett (*1870*–1949), rector, Annahilt (1899–1913) and Hillsborough (1913–49), precentor of Down (1945–9); DGC, Belfast (<1900–2); Mervyn Archdall (1868–1939), curate, St Thomas's (1894–7); chaplain to the Forces (1897–1924), incumbent, Ballywalter (1925–37); DGC, Belfast (from 1906); James Craig, Congregational Church, Windsor; DGC, Belfast (1902). Matchett delivered the opening prayers at Orangefield on 12 July 1899: *BNL*, 13 July 1899.

29. Preachers' Book (1885–1904), CR/1/3/6/1; Diocese of Down and Connor and Dromore, Roll Book (1886–1924), DIO/1/20/1, PRONI. Visiting clergymen also took a few of the 110 services performed during 1899.

30. *BNL*, 27 Jan. 1899, 22 Oct. 1900.

31. *BNL*, 10 Apr. 1899.

32. 'A real help to him in his work and a power for good in the parish': Vestry Minute Book (1892–1942), 19 Apr. 1900, CR/1/3/5/2.

33. Preachers' Book.

34. Diocesan Roll Book, 6 Mar. 1901; watch on display in Carrickfergus Museum (CMMC); Vestry Minute Book, 11 Apr. 1901.

35. William Peoples (b. *1869*), deacon (1891), curate, Ballymacarrett (1894–7), incumbent, St Clement's (1897–1900), curate in English parishes (1903–20).

36. William Peoples, *Roman Claims in the Light of History* (London, W. Walker, 1904), p. iii.

37. FM, *Church of Ireland*, p. 52.

38. *BNL*, 23, 24 Mar. 1899.

39. *BNL*, 25 Mar. 1899.

40. *BNL*, 3 Apr. 1899.

41. FM, *Church of Ireland*, pp. 52–5.

42. William Henry Askins Lee (*1866*–1954), deacon (1893), curate, Carrickfergus (1893–6), vicar, Magheradroll (1896–1900), rector, St Aidan's, Belfast (1905–11) and Ahoghill (1911–45), treasurer of Connor (1940–5); DGC, Ireland (1901–54), at various times DGC, Down, Belfast, and Antrim; Heredom Chapter no. 15 of Prince Masons, Belfast (formed 1921). He was licensed as curate-in-charge, St Donard's, on 27 Sept. 1900, as incumbent, St Clement's, on 28 Nov. 1900, and as incumbent, St Donard's (having resigned St Clement's) on 10 July 1902, remaining there until 1905.

43. Minute Book, LOL 1537 (26 Sept. 1895), in private hands.

44. FM, *Church of Ireland*, pp. 54–5. Edward Bouverie Pusey (1800–82), Regius Professor of Hebrew and Canon of Christ Church, Oxford (1829–82), one of the few luminaries of the Oxford Movement who did not convert to Rome, framed his otherwise effeminate features with attenuated side-whiskers (as did Kane).

45. FM, *Church of Ireland*, pp. 52–4.

46. *BNL*, 8 July 1901.

47. *BNL*, 1 Apr. 1902.

48. FM, *Church of Ireland*, pp. 52–4.

49. The marriage was performed in Clonsilla Parish Church on 29 Jan. 1902, after banns: Register of Marriages, GRO. Thomas Cecil Magee (*1878*–1935), son of James Magee of Kinconla, Tuam; deacon (1901), curate in Scotland and Clogher (1901–6), rector, Drumsnatt (1906–8), Templecarne (1908–17), and Tydavnet (1917–28), curate-in-charge, Kilskeery (1928–35). After Alice's death in 1917, he married Marjorie Kane, a doctor's daughter, in 1919.

50. *BNL*, 4 Apr. 1902.

51. FM, *Church of Ireland*, p. 54.

52. His marriage certificate (25 June 1902) was signed John Frederick, but Frederick John appears on his certificate of institution and in a letter also written on 25 July: Register of Marriages, GRO; certificate with seal in FM Papers, Dep. c. 759, BLO; *BNL*, 26 July 1902.

53. The family census return for 31 Mar. 1901 omits John Sweet, who was staying near Kilkeel with the Presbyterian family of his daughter Mary: NAD [JL]. A decade later, the unity of the 'Sweet Home' had been restored. The Sweets' census address in 1901 is oddly given as 6 Martinez Ave. (a new development on the opposite side of Beersbridge Rd. and of the railway line); but valuation and directory records confirm that throughout the decade the Sweets resided at the house eventually listed as no. 410, a few doors from the Upper Newtownards Rd.

54. Elizabeth Nicholson, 'Trees Were Green', p. 14, in *Time was Away*, pp. 11–20.

55. *BNL*, 14 July 1902.

56. *BNL*, 26 July 1902.

57. *BNL*, 18 Apr. 1903.

58. *BNL*, 4 Apr. 1899, 4 Apr. 1902.

59. His congregations at St Clement's and Holy Trinity contributed £1 in 1903/4 and 1905/6 respectively, following sermons by Frederick. FM was elected to the executive committee for each of the six years 1907/8–1912/13, the last year for which this information is available: ICM (IB), *Reports* (1904–13).

60. The meeting of 21 December 1902 was attended by 10 of the 12 select vestrymen and the people's churchwarden, Job Cherry: Cherry to FM, 22–3 Dec. 1902, FM Papers, CMMC.

61. In his family census schedule for 1901 (DED Breda, village of Newtownbreda, Co. Down), Cherry returned himself as a Master Plumber aged 42, with an older wife and 3 children, 2 of whom were born in England: NAD.

62. Preachers' Book, 14 Apr. 1901, 15 June 1902.

63. FM, *Church of Ireland*, p. 54.

64. *BNL*, 18 Apr. 1903.

65. William Ralph (*1862*–1914), merchant's son from Gorey, Co. Wexford; deacon (1877), curate in Derry (1888–90) and England (1890–9), rector, Cloncha, Derry (1899–1903), incumbent, St Clement's (1903–5), curate-in-charge in Lancashire (1906–14); Francis Doherty (*1863*–1930), from Lurgan, Co. Armagh; deacon (1888), curate in England (1888–91) and Clones (1892–5), incumbent, Augher (1895–1900), Trillick (1900–6), and St Clement's (1906–13), vicar in England (1915–30).

66. *BNL*, 9 Apr. 1906.

67. *BNL*, 20 Apr. 1903. In 'proprietary churches', the right of patronage in appointing an incumbent was preserved after Disestablishment, though in Holy Trinity the parish was represented on the board of trustees: Trinity Church Vestry Book (1892–1942), 4 Jan. 1909, CR/1/3/5/2, PRONI.

68. In the year of his appointment, the 'annual income' of Holy Trinity parish was £430 compared with £200 for St Clement's. Within two years, Holy Trinity's income had been reduced to £302, reflecting a separate allocation of £110 for a curate who would hitherto have been paid out of the incumbent's stipend: *ICD* (1904–9).

69. Preachers' Book, 3 May, 31 May 1903; *Irish Church Directory* (1906); Register of Baptisms (1893–1919), CR/1/3/1/4–5, PRONI. The baptismal entry (31 May 1903) was subsequently altered from Frederick John McNeice to John Frederick MacNeice, while John Frederick McNeice appears on Elizabeth's birth certificate!

70. Lily McNeice to unnamed sister-in-law, Sept. 1906: extract in Stallworthy, *LM*, p. 12.

71. See appendix, Table 4.

72. See appendix, Table 5. The collective profile of those elected to parish offices differed only slightly from that of vestrymen.

73. The counties of birth of 74 vestrymen were as follows: Belfast 19, Antrim 18, Down 13, Armagh and Tyrone 4, Cavan and Fermanagh 3, other Ulster 2, other Ireland 8.

74. Comparison of the 79 street addresses in the Register with a street plan for 1901–2, based on the Ordnance Survey sheets (1: 2,500) for Antrim and Down, indicates the

following distribution according to distance in kilometres from Trinity church: 8 (< 0.25), 23 (0.25<0.5), 7 (0.5<0.75), 8 (0.75<1), and 33 (1 or more): Stephen A. Royle, *Irish Historic Towns Atlas No. 17: Belfast, Part II, 1840 to 1900* (Dublin, Royal Irish Academy, 2007), map 4.

75. FM was listed as occupier of 38 Cliftonville Avenue (1904–6), 25 Cliftonville Avenue (1907), and 1 Brookhill Avenue (1908–9): *Belfast Directory* (1904–9), corrected to Nov. or Dec. of year preceding each issue.

76. Louis Augustus Plunkett (*1853–1918*), Belfast manager, Royal Exchange Assurance Corporation, marine insurance broker, company director; died at his jokily named residence 'Canmore' in Windsor Park, Belfast.

77. *BNL*, 9 Apr. 1904, 2 May 1905, 23 Apr. 1906, 8 Apr. 1907, 27 Apr. 1908.

78. [S. H. Reid], *The Story of Holy Trinity Church Belfast, 1843–1941–1956* (Belfast, Howard Publications, 1956), p. 15; *BNL*, 10 June 1918. Plunkett left a substantial personal estate of £17,920, following earlier settlements in favour of his wife and children: Will and Probate Papers (4 Nov. 1918), PRONI.

79. Holy Trinity Parish, Pew Register (1883–1901), CR/1/3/7/1; *Irish Church Directory* (1913), p. 181. In later years, he transferred his parochial energies to St Thomas's: *BNL*, 10 June 1918.

80. Plunkett belonged to the élite Acacia Lodge 7, Belfast (initiated, 1877) and Chapter 8, Belfast (Prince Masons).

81. McNeice (variously identified as F., J. F., F. J. and T. J.) was elected annually from Nov. 1902 to Nov. 1908, with the exception of 1904. His only attendance was in 1908, and he was last recorded as a non-attender in 1910: Belfast GOL, *Reports* (1902/3–1910/11).

82. John Baptist Crozier (1853–1920), bishop of Ossory, Ferns, and Leighlin (1897–1907) and Down and Connor and Dromore (1907–11), archbishop of Armagh (1911–20); DGC, Ireland (1877–92) and GC (1893–1920), GC, Down (1896–8), GC, Belfast (1908–12); Senior GC, GL of Freemasons and of Prince Masons, member of Supreme Council of 33°.

83. McNeice (variously identified as F., J. F., F. J., J. C. and W. F.) was returned as chaplain, District no. 6 (meeting in Ballymacarrett Orange Hall), for the years 1903–4 and 1907–9; no. 10 (Ballynafeigh), 1903–5; no. 3 (Clifton St), 1904, 1906; and no. 1 (Clifton St), 1908–9: Belfast GOL, *Reports*. Despite the inconsistent ascription of initials, collation of addresses and lodge numbers in these returns indicates that all refer to the same person.

84. Holy Trinity, Register of Baptisms, 26 Apr. 1905. Edward Moore (*1871–1951*), from Co. Cork; deacon (1900), curate, Ballynafeigh (1900–5), incumbent, Glencraig (1905–15), vicar in Somerset (1915–18) and then Croydon.

85. George W. L. Hill, Alwyn Maconachie, and William Mercer, *Still Other Seed: A History of the Parish of Glencraig in the Diocese of Down and Dromore* (no provenance, 1996), pp. 19–21.

86. Moore deplored the diocesan synod's decision to endorse the Covenant, while 'not opposed to the general resolution ... against the Home Rule Bill': *BNL*, 7 Nov. 1912.

87. Holy Trinity, Register of Baptisms, 14 Oct. 1907.

88. Louis Augustus Le Pan (1808–83), chaplain, King's Hospital (1849–77) and

reportedly headmaster (1839–77); son of 'Monsieur' Louis N. Le Pan, French master at the Armagh Royal School and Belfast Royal Academy, first WM, Masonic Lodge 199, Armagh (1812): marriage notice of Juliana Louise Le Pan in *BNL*, 24 June 1831 (card index, LHL); William Jenkinson, 'Two Hundred Years of Masonry in the City of Armagh', p. 89, in Lodge of Research, no. CC., Ireland, *Transactions for the Year 1925* (Dublin, G. F. Healy, 1933), pp. 72–133. King's Hospital, a boarding school still in existence in Palmerstown, Co. Dublin, was formerly known as the 'Blue Coat Hospital, or Free School of Charles II' and located in Blackhall Place, Oxmantown. Its original function was 'maintaining, clothing, educating, and apprenticing the sons of reduced citizens of Dublin': *Thom's Directory* (1852), pp. 723, 751.

89. The mug, made by Gibson & Co., Donegall Place, and engraved 'FLMcN', with a card inscribed 'Louis A. Plunkett. With his Godfather's best wishes', is on display in the Carrickfergus Museum (CMMC).

90. 'Godfather', published in *Holes in the Sky: Poems 1944–1947* (London, Faber, May 1948): LM, *CP*, pp. 269–70.

91. Register of Deaths, GRO. On the basis of his own census return for 1901 (NAD), William's true age at death was at least 79.

92. ICM, *Report* (1907); ICM, Agency Book (1905), ICM office, Dublin.

93. Register of Deaths, GRO; Registry of Grants, Mount Jerome Cemetery (7875/1889): microform copy in Gilbert Library, Dublin.

94. Lily McNeice to sister-in-law, 27 Sept. 1906: extract in Stallworthy, *LM*, p. 12.

6. DIPLOMAT: CARRICKFERGUS, 1908–1912

1. George Chamberlain (1852–1910), deacon (1875), rector, Drumbo (1881–4), Christ Church, Lisburn (1884–6) and Carrickfergus (1886–1908).

2. James L. McFerran to protest meeting, 10 Nov. 1908: *CA*, 13 Nov. 1908.

3. See above, ch. 5, note 41.

4. Sermon in St Nicholas's, 19 Feb. 1933: FM, *Northern Churchmen*, p. 23.

5. William Herbert Bradley (1878–1939), deacon (1902), curate, Bangor (1902–7) and Carrickfergus (1907–9), rector, Jordanstown (1909–18) and ultimately Bangor (1930–9).

6. Of 10 curates appointed by Chamberlain, 2 were Ulstermen, 5 'southerners' and 3 of unknown birthplace.

7. After moving to Jordanstown, Bradley became DGC, Antrim, and subsequently for Down and then Ireland.

8. The candidates and their nominators were publicly named by Henry Blackburne, a prominent Carrickfergus and select vestryman: *CA*, 27 Nov. 1908. The diocesan nominators were Canon Charles Scott (d. 1910), deacon (1870), curate (1870–9) and incumbent, St Paul's, Belfast (1879–1910); Canon William Dawson Pounden (1830–1917), deacon (1855), rector, Lisburn (1884–1917), treasurer of Connor (1893–1917); GC, Ireland (1887–1917); and George Herbert Ewart, JP (1857–1924), of William Ewart and Son, Ltd, flax spinners, linen manufacturers, merchants, and bleachers; son of William Ewart (1817–89), cr. Bt (1887),

MP, Belfast and North Belfast (1878–89). The bishop exercised both an independent and a casting vote in the board of nominators.

9. Samuel Patrick Close (1843–1925), rector's son from Mayo, architect initially in Lanyon's firm: Rutherford, *OFC*, p. 66 (citing F. J. Bigger's description).

10. Oswald William Scott (d. 1936), deacon (1885), incumbent, All Saints, Belfast (1890–9), rector, Inver, Larne (1899–1904), vicar, Gilford (1904–15) and St Paul's, Belfast (1915–32); DGC, Belfast (1907).

11. Lawrence Parsons Story (*1861*–1956), land agent's son from Galway; deacon (1888), rector, Ardclinis (1892–1901), incumbent, Christ Church, Belfast (1901–26).

12. Blackburne's identification of 'Storey' as Greer's 'relative' has not been confirmed.

13. Extracts from FM, Diary (lost), via EN's unpublished memoir (unavailable): Stallworthy, *LM*, pp. 12–13.

14. *CA*, 13 Nov. 1908.

15. *Ibid.*

16. As Junior Sophisters in 1899, both men received First-Class Honors in all three term examinations, Lepper in Modern Literature and McNeice in Modern History. Lepper was the only 'Fellow Commoner' of his year (entitled to the honorific 'Mr' at the cost of double fees): *DU Calendar* (1900).

17. Condolence for Alfred John Adolphus Lepper, JP: *CA*, 24 Apr. 1908. Alfred John Adolphus Lepper (d. 1908), formerly of the Barn, Carrickfergus, director, Smithfield Flax Spinning and Weaving Co. Ltd, Belfast; member (like his son) of Acacia Lodge 7, Belfast and Harmonie Lodge 282, Carrickfergus; commissioned the celebrated 36-foot cutter, the *Peggy Bawn*.

18. John Heron Lepper (1878–1952), in Ministry of Information and Admiralty, Great War; editor and lexicographer, Cassell and Co.; author of several historical novels, *Famous Secret Societies* (London, Samson Low, Marston, 1932), and (with Philip Crosslé) *History of the Grand Lodge of Free and Accepted Masons of Ireland*, vol. i (Dublin, Lodge of Research, 1925); curator, Library and Museum, Freemasons' Hall, London (1943); Master, Quatuor Coronati Lodge (reponsible for Masonic history), in 1925: *The Times*, 22 Apr. 1925, 9 Jan. 1953.

19. Lepper was admitted to the Eldon lodge in Dec. 1904 and resigned in Oct. 1907: Minute Books, Eldon LOL 7, GOLI Archives.

20. George Edmonstone Kirk (1858–1909), DL, JP, HS; son of George Bull (1812–86), rector, Carrickfergus (1870–86), dean of Connor (1855–86); inherited his aunts' estates on condition that he assume the surname Kirk; buried at sea on voyage home from China. Agnes Beatrice, his second wife, was the daughter of Sir George Armstrong, proprietor of the London *Globe*: *CA*, 26 Mar. 1909. Kirk was admitted to Eldon LOL 7 on the same day as Heron Lepper.

21. *CA*, 20 Nov. 1908.

22. *CIG*, l (20, 27 Nov. 1908), 1006, 1031.

23. *CA*, 27 Nov. 1908.

24. *CA*, 4 Dec. 1908.

25. Stallworthy, *LM*, p. 17.

26. On 7 Nov. 1939, he told the annual diocesan synod that 'it is far too generally assumed that Parochial Nominators, if only they agree, have the sole right to choose Incumbents', adding that they should never come 'pledged to any particular man' in advance: FM, *On Matters relating to Church and State* (Belfast, Diocese of Down and Connor and Dromore, 1939), p. 3.

27. *CA*, 27 Nov. 1908.

28. Elizabeth's account was presumably based on later discussions with her parents or other eye-witnesses: Stallworthy, *LM*, pp. 18–19.

29. *CA*, 27 Nov. 1908; certificate of institution, 25 Nov. 1908, FM Papers, Dep. c. 759, BLO.

30. *CIG*, 1 (4 Dec. 1908), 1045.

31. Parish of Holy Trinity, Preachers' Book (1905–20), 29 Nov. 1908: CR/1/3/6/2, PRONI; *CIG*, 1 (4 Dec. 1908), 1051.

32. Bradley also sent an appeal for harmony to the editor: *CA*, 4 Dec. 1908; *CIG*, 1 (11 Dec. 1908), 1066.

33. *CA*, 4, 11 Dec. 1908.

34. *CA*, 25 Dec. 1908; *CIG*, 1 (24 Dec. 1908), 1110–11.

35. *CIG*, 1 (24 Dec. 1908), 1111; li (29 Jan. 1909), 103.

36. *CA*, 29 Jan. 1909. The term 'Independent' was commonly used to signify members of the Congregational Churches in Ireland.

37. John Barbour Pirrie (1863–1910), son of William Pirrie (shipowner); manager (1893–1904), then managing director (1904–10) of James Taylor and Sons Ltd, Barn Mills.

38. *CA*, 1 Apr. 1910.

39. Stallworthy, *LM*, p. 21.

40. Rutherford, 'FM', p. 39.

41. George Henry Bassett, *The Book of Antrim* (Dublin, Sealy, Bryers & Walker, 1888), p. 343. Twenty years later, the decline of the port and shipbuilding had been somewhat alleviated by harbour improvements and the introduction of a yacht-yard, and there were four salt works in operation: *Belfast Directory* (1909), pp. 1548–9.

42. Census of Ireland, County Report for Antrim (1911), tabulating occupations by rural and urban districts, including Carrickfergus.

43. William Hamilton Davey (*1880*–1920), OBE, barrister and editor, *Ulster Guardian*, 'Organ of the Liberal Party in Ireland' (weekly, Belfast); joined Tyneside Irish, Great War, rising to Major; contested Duncairn against Carson as a nationalist (gaining 17% of votes), Dec. 1918. [JL]

44. James Bell (*1844*–1920), printer and stationer in High St; native of Kilmarnock, Ayrshire. The paper was evidently edited by his son David Samuel Milliken Bell (*1879*–1952), a qualified journalist: *CA*, 3 Sept. 1920. A newspaper under the same name is still published.

45. 'Carrickfergus' (1937): LM, *CP*, p. 55; discussed in ch. 16, below.

46. For details by sector, see appendix, Table 6. This analysis is based on returns of

religious denomination for every street in Carrickfergus, derived from the enumerators' abstracts (imperfect) and family schedules of the Census (1901): NAD.

47. See appendix, Table 3, for summary of male occupational statistics (excluding Belfast) derived from the Census of Ireland, County Report for Antrim (1911).

48. For sources, see note to appendix, Table 7. Lists of parish officers elected at the Easter vestries (1908–12) were abstracted from the *CA*.

49. See appendix, Table 8.

50. The total number of persons elected to parish office (1908–12) was 36, of whom 23 were among the 37 protesters reportedly attending the first meeting or contributing to the petition. 10 of those elected in Apr. 1908 were involved in the protest.

51. The renovations, whose cost greatly exceeded the original estimate, were directed by the architect Samuel Close: *CA*, 24 Apr. 1908.

52. In the year to Easter 1908, the 11 largest contributors to pew rent and the sustentation fund included the protestors George Kirk, John Pirrie, Heron Lepper, William Coates and Tyndall Johns, but only Mrs Greer and John Hind among those favourable to Frederick. See *St. Nicholas Church, Carrickfergus. Statement of Accounts for the Year, from Easter, 1907, to Easter, 1908* (Carrickfergus, pr. James Bell, Sept. 1908): annotated copy in CMMC.

53. This analysis is based on minute books of LOL 1537 and lists of masters and secretaries of other Carrickfergus Lodges; Grand Lodge Registers for Carrickfergus's 3 Masonic lodges, and returns of their officers; and lists of rugby club officers elected in Sept. 1909 along with members of the club between 1932/3 and 1934/5. I am grateful to Jane Leonard for alerting me to Frederick's association with this club and arranging access to its records (in private hands). For details of Orange and Masonic sources, see note to appendix, Table 7.

54. James Love McFerran was admitted on transfer in Mar. 1893, George Kirk joined with Heron Lepper in Dec. 1904, and William Coates followed suit in Nov. 1919: Minute Books, Eldon LOL 7, GOLI Archives.

55. Stallworthy, *LM*, pp. 20–1.

56. The incumbent's annual stipend in Holy Trinity was £302 compared with £307 in Carrickfergus (raised to £347 in 1912 and £440 in 1922). In 1913, only 7 of Connor's 62 incumbents outside Belfast received a higher stipend: *ICD* (1908–31).

57. Stallworthy, *LM*, p. 21; LM, *Strings*, p. 37.

58. *My Mother Wore a Yellow Dress*, ed. Kate Newman (Carrickfergus, Borough Council, 2008), pp. 97–8 (recollections of June Thunder's grandfather). [JL]

59. On the same occasion, a presentation was made to Frederick's former curate (1905–9), John Donnelly (*1880*–1922), and welcome was offered to his successor as incumbent (1909–15), Bedell Stanford (1873–1945): *CA*, 12 Mar. 1909.

60. St Nicholas's Church, *Accounts*. Kirk soon ceased to be a threat, as Frederick drily noted: 'died, March 1909'.

61. Of the six former officers, one had shown 'moderate change', one was 'B unrepentant', one escaped censure, and three were not classified by FM.

62. *CA*, 16 Apr. 1909.

63. Stallworthy, *LM*, p. 20. Maria Noy Johns (1828–1916) was an aunt of the solicitor Tyndall Stuart Johns (1868–1947), a protestor displaying 'moderate change' who became a parochial nominator in 1909: Rutherford, *Old Families*, pp. 88, 90.

64. Co. Antrim GOL, *Annual Reports* (1907–16). No District membership returns were published until 1923, when 443 brethren belonged to six lodges.

65. Joseph John Hamilton Bennett (1844–1915), curate's son, born Monkstown, Co. Cork; deacon (1870), curate, Glenavy (1870–6), vicar, Kilroot and Templecorran (1876–1915); WM, Harmonie (Masonic) Lodge 282; District Master, Carrickfergus LOL 19 (1883–1915).

66. *CA*, 14 July 1911.

67. Preachers' Book, 16 June 1907.

68. *CA*, 16 July 1909. LOL 1537 was notified in early June of Frederick's sermon: LOL 1537, Minutes, 4 June 1909.

69. Sir Horace Plunkett, *Ireland in the New Century* (London, John Murray, 1905; 1st edn 1903), p. 26.

70. *CA*, 16 July 1909.

71. *Ibid.*

72. *CA*, 6 Aug. 1909; LOL 1537, Minutes, 2 Aug. 1909.

73. LOL 1537, Minutes, 26 Sept. 1896. Unfounded accusations were also to be punished by a fine.

74. Between 1909 and 1918, 24 brethren were punished for 39 violations, no fewer than 10 of which occurred in 1912. 19 offenders (23%) were among the 83 brethren returned on the rolls between 1911 and 1914: LOL 1537, Minutes, 1909–18.

75. LOL 1537, Minute Books and Roll Books.

76. Lee and his 3 immediate successors in the curacy were all admitted to 1537 between 1898 and 1903, but Chamberlain's last three curates played no part. Since none of Frederick's 4 curates joined, the lodge again lacked a chaplain until the arrival of his successor James Cooper Rutherford (d. 1971), deacon (1915), rector, Carrickfergus (1931–58), treasurer of Connor (1950–8); chaplain, LOL 1537 (1932–71).

77. See appendix, Tables 7, 8.

78. The July service rotated between four or five churches in the town. Frederick is known to have preached at anniversary services in July 1909, Nov. 1911, July 1917 and July 1922.

79. He was elected chaplain in Nov. 1911 and Nov. 1912, and listed as a member in 1915: LOL 1537, Minute Books and Roll Books.

80. The banner, made by William Bridgett, Belfast, cost 18 guineas: *CA*, 21 Apr. 1911; LOL 1537, Minutes, 7 Nov. 1910, 3 Apr. 1911.

81. Sir Antony Patrick MacDonnell (1844–1925), cr. Baron MacDonnell of Swinford (1908), Lieut.-Gov., North-Western Provinces and Oudh (1895–1901), Under Secretary, Ireland (1902–8), architect of 'devolution' scheme (1907).

82. For the McCann case (Nov. 1910), see Raymond J. Lee, 'Intermarriage, Conflict and Social Control in Ireland: The Decree "Ne Temere"', pp. 13–17, in *Economic and Social Review*, xvii, 1 (1985), 11–28.

83. James Martin McCalmont (1847–1913), Conservative MP, East Antrim (1885–1913); brother of Major-General Sir Hugh McCalmont, MP, North Antrim (1895–9); DGM, Co. Antrim GOL; Prince Mason, Chapter no. 6, Belfast: obituary in *CA*, 7 Feb. 1913.

84. *CA*, 21 Apr. 1911.

85. LOL 1537, Minutes, 1 May, 4 Sept. 1911.

86. *CA*, 17 Nov. 1911.

87. LOL 1537, Minutes, 4 Dec. 1911.

88. *CA*, 2 Feb. 1912.

89. John Young Minford (*1872*–1936), Antrim farmer's son; licensed (1897), minister, Carrowdore (1899–1908), Joymount (1908–36).

90. *CA*, 1 Mar. 1912.

91. *CA*, 12 July, 27 Dec. 1912.

92. Carrickfergus Rugby Football Club, Minute Book (1908–19), 13 Sept. 1909 (in private hands). I am grateful to Jane Leonard for alerting me to this fact.

93. Minute Book, 23 Nov., 14 Dec. 1908.

94. According to Louis, his father showed that he 'did not really understand the code' when they watched their only match together at Lansdowne Road, Dublin. As they witnessed Ireland's defeat by England by 36 points to 14, Frederick ingenuously remarked: 'Sure, they're much bigger than our men and anyway haven't they far more to pick from!': LM, 'Nine New Caps', in *New Statesman*, 63, 1614 (16 Feb. 1962), in LM, *Selected Prose*, p. 242. [JL] For photographs from the match, see *Irish Independent*, 14 Feb. 1938.

95. *CA*, 26 Nov. 1909, 25 Mar. 1910.

96. *CA*, 19 Jan. 1912.

97. *CA*, 11 Mar. 1910. Both visiting clergymen had been Bedell scholars in Irish at Trinity College: Patrick Percival O'Sullivan (d. 1919), deacon (1902), curate in southern parishes (1902–9), general licence, Down (1909), curate-in-charge, Loughguile, Connor (1916–18); Frederick William O'Connell (d. 1929), deacon (1902), curate in southern parishes (1902–9), lecturer in Gaelic Language and Literature, Queen's University, Belfast (1909), curate, St George's, Belfast (1911), assistant director, Dublin broadcasting station (1927–9, following conversion to Roman Catholicism), author of several works on the Irish language and translations.

98. Robert Newett Morrison (d. 1949), deacon (1907), curate, St Luke's, Belfast (1907–10), Carrickfergus (1910–14), and Hillsborough (1914–21), curate-in-charge, Magherahamlet (1921–48).

99. *CA*, 1 Apr. 1910.

100. *CA*, 21 Apr. 1911.

101. *CA*, 30 June 1911.

102. *CA*, 19 Apr. 1912.

103. *CA*, 14 June 1912.

104. *BNL*, 1 Nov. 1907.

105. In the following year, Frederick topped the list of four clerical supplementals

from Connor elected to the diocesan council, an achievement not replicated until 1913: *BNL*, 30 Oct. 1909, 5 Nov. 1910, 1 Nov. 1913.

106. *CIG*, liv (22 Mar. 1912), 235–6.

107. *Ibid.* 192; A. E. Hughes, *Lift up a Standard: The Centenary Story of the Society for Irish Church Missions* (London, ICM, 1948), p. 38. Thomas Chatterton Hammond (1877–1961), deacon (1903), curate (1903–10) and incumbent, St Kevin's (1910–19), Dublin superintendent, ICM (1919–36), principal, Moore Theological College, Sydney (1936–53), archdeacon of Sydney (1949–61); biography by Warren Wilson, *T. C. Hammond: His Life and Legacy in Ireland and Australia* (Edinburgh, Banner of Truth Trust, 1994).

108. The house in Governor's Place had 14 rooms but only 8 front windows and no out-offices: family schedules and enumerators' abstracts, Census of Ireland (1911), NAD.

109. Robert and Edna Wright, 'Carrickfergus Rectory and Louis MacNeice', in *Carrickfergus and District Historical Journal*, vii (1993), 21–31.

110. EN, 'Trees Were Green', pp. 11–12, in *Time Was Away*, pp. 11–20.

111. Family schedules, Census of Ireland (1911).

112. LM, *Strings*, pp. 41–2; Stallworthy, *LM*, p. 26; EN, MSS notes on draft of LM, *Strings*, presumably for E. R. Dodds, CMMC.

7. DISSIDENT: CARRICKFERGUS, 1912–1914

1. The declared number of signatories in Ulster (218,206) amounts to 76.7% of the male non-Catholic population aged 16 years or more in 1911. A 'Women's Declaration', dutifully pledging support for the men in their struggle, was signed by 72.2% of non-Catholic women over 16 (228,999). These numbers were swollen by allowing persons absent on 28 September to sign up to 14 October: *BNL*, 1, 2 Oct., 23 Nov. 1912. The number of signatories in Ulster accessible digitally on surviving sheets is 215,960 men (99.0% of those officially returned) and 215,594 women (94.1%): PRONI, online.

2. Charles Frederick D'Arcy (1859–1938), Dubliner; deacon (1884), dean of Belfast (1900–3), bishop of Clogher (1903–7), Ossory (1907–11), and Down and Connor and Dromore (1911–19), archbishop of Dublin (1919–20) and Armagh (1920–38).

3. Charles Frederick D'Arcy, *The Adventures of a Bishop, a Phase of Irish Life: A Personal and Historical Narrative* (London, Hodder and Stoughton, 1934), pp. 188–91.

4. *CIG*, liv (13 Sept. 1912), 760.

5. Ven. E. D. Atkinson, *Recollections of an Ulster Archdeacon* (Belfast, Carswell, 1934), p. 52. Edward Dupré Atkinson (1855–1937), Dubliner educated at Rugby and Cambridge; deacon (1880), curate, Seapatrick (1880–4), incumbent, Donaghcloney or Waringstown (1884–1919) and Kilbroney (1919–30), archdeacon of Dromore (1905–30); church historian.

6. *CIG*, liv (30 Aug. 1912), 733.

7. John Presbyter's letter elicited a variety of anonymous responses, including supportive letters from 'A "True Blue" Churchman' and 'E'; Berry's sermon was praised by B. R. (Blayney) Balfour of Townley Hall, Drogheda: *CIG*, liv (6, 13, 20, 27 Sept. 1912), 754,

772, 779, 818. Thomas Sterling Berry (1854–1931), clergyman's son from Ballysadare, Sligo; deacon (1877), incumbent, Booterstown, Dublin (1892–1913), bishop of Killaloe (1913–24).

8. LOL 1537, Minutes (1910–14), 2 Sept. 1912 (in private hands).

9. *CA*, 6 Sept. 1912.

10. *CA*, 20 Sept. 1912.

11. *CA*, 4 Oct. 1912.

12. Archibald Edward Dobbs (1838–1916), JP, HS (1909), barrister-at-law, succ. cousin at Castle Dobbs (1906).

13. Excerpt from *CA*, 4 Oct. 1912, in FM, *Carrickfergus*, pp. 72–3.

14. Covenant, signature sheet 575/8, PRONI (online).

15. EN, 'Trees were Green', p. 15, in *Time was Away*, pp. 11–20. Thomas Gray Robinson, flesher of Market Place, was a select vestryman, protestor, and future Freemason.

16. *CA*, 4 Oct. 1912.

17. 'A Brave Act' (second leader), *Ulster Guardian*, 5 Oct. 1912, taking up report in *CA*.

18. The number of signatories recorded at places within the parish was 1687 men and 1866 women, equivalent respectively to 64.0% and 59.3% of the estimated non-Catholic populations over 16 in 1911. The corresponding proportions for the remainder of the East Antrim constituency were 80.2% and 75.8%; those for Co. Antrim (excluding Belfast) were 67.4% and 69.8%. These figures, derived from a problematic digital search of the slightly incomplete surviving returns, may understate the true proportions.

19. See appendix, Table 8. These proportions represent those who could not confidently be matched with names on the signature lists, possibly because of deficiencies of data, faulty transcription of signatures, or migration between the census (2 April 1911) and Ulster Day. Where the available details are consistent with more than one local signatory, a match has been recorded.

20. 'Novelettes, IV. The Gardener' (summer 1939), published in *The Last Ditch* (London, Faber, 1940): LM, *CP*, pp. 694–6; cf. LM, *Strings*, pp. 47–8. Louis confirms White's illiteracy, though the census schedule for 1911 indicates that Archibald White, an Episcopalian labourer aged 57, born in Co. 'Derry', could 'read and rite' (in 1901, the assertion that he could 'read and write' was added by the enumerator): family census schedules for Scotch Quarter, Carrickfergus (1901, 1911).

21. FM, *Carrickfergus*, p. 72.

22. Hans McCoubrey Douglas (1821–1915), licensed Athlone (1861), agent, Belfast Town Mission, Presbyterian minister, Woodburn (1866–*1914*); Henry James Eakin (1879–1949), licensed Glendermott (1908), Presbyterian minister (initially Douglas's assistant), Woodburn (1908–27), Newmills (1927–31) and Carryduff (1931–49); Hugh M. Watson, ordained Belfast (1902), Methodist minister, West St (1912–15). Eakin was also an agent on Ulster Day.

23. Alexander Cuthbert (1882–1948), licensed Coleraine (1884), Presbyterian minister, 1st Carrickfergus, North St (1898–1920); John Young Minford (*1872*–1936), Antrim farmer's son, licensed Templepatrick (1897), Presbyterian minister, Carrowdore (1899–1908)

and Joymount (1908–36); father of Hugh Minford (d. 1950), unionist MP (NI, Antrim town) and Orangeman; James Lyon (*1865–1925*), native of Cambridgeshire, Congregational minister, Albert Rd (1888–1921) and then Zion church, Bristol: obituary in *CA*, 20 Feb. 1925; John McCleery (*1862–1950*), Unitarian minister, Joymount Bank and later Raloo (1903–42).

24. *Ulster Guardian*, 5 Oct. 1912. The only Episcopalian dissentient identifiable from these reports is Edward Albert Myles (1865–1951), from Limerick, deacon (1889), incumbent, Tullylish (1896–1951), dean of Dromore (1933–51).

25. Fauske, *'Side by Side'*, p. 6. Thomas Arnold Harvey (1878–1966), clergyman's son from Meath, deacon (1903), curate, St Stephen's, Dublin (1903–7), rector, Lissadell, Elphin (1907–12), Ballywillan, Connor (1912–16), and Booterstown, Dublin (1916–33), dean of St Patrick's, Dublin (1933–5), bishop of Cashel and Emly and Waterford and Lismore (1935–58); name not digitally traced as a Covenanter. No report of such an address has been traced in reports of Ulster Day in Portrush in Belfast or Antrim newspapers or in the *CIG*.

26. Henry Lyle Mulholland (1854–1931), 2nd Baron Dunleath (succ. father 1895), of Ballywalter Park, Co. Down, DL, JP, HS (1884); fortune derived from family firm, York Street Flax Spinning Co. Ltd.

27. *CIG*, liv (8 Nov. 1912), 963; *BNL*, 6 Nov. 1912; *NW*, 6 Nov. 1912.

28. *BNL*, 7 Nov. 1912.

29. *BNL*, 7, 9 Nov. 1912; *CIG*, liv (22 Nov. 1912), 1003.

30. *BNL*, 4 Oct. 1912.

31. *BNL*, 7 Nov. 1912. He came third among the Connor clergy elected as supplementals for the general synod, as in the previous triennial election, and second (as in 1911) for the diocesan council.

32. *CA*, 25 Oct. 1912.

33. Arthur Frederick Dobbs (1876–1955), DL, JP, HS (1921), Capt., Antrim RGA, ed. Wellington College and King's College, Cambridge, senator, Northern Ireland (1921–33).

34. *CA*, 18 Oct., 22 Nov. 1912. The family business was headed by Robert Cambridge ('timber merchant', aged 52), who lived with his son Thomas Reid Cambridge ('explosives merchant', aged 24): census of 1911, family census schedule, High St (1911).

35. *CA*, 21 Mar. 1913. Samuel Mains Shaw (1870–1932), licensed Belfast (1898), Presbyterian minister, Loughmorne (1903–32).

36. *CA*, 18 July 1913. The speakers were Canon John Clarke (*1845–1922*), graduate of Queen's College, Belfast, deacon (1872), vicar, Killead (1882–1922), prebendary of Connor (1907–22); and Samuel Thomas Nesbitt (1863–1931), deacon (1892), curate (1892–6) and rector, Ballynure and Ballyeaston (1896–1926).

37. FM, Diary (1913), 2, 3, 12, 13 Jan. 1913, Dep. c. 758, BLO.

38. In a by-election to succeed the new Duke of Abercorn as MP for Londonderry City, David Clegthorne Hogg (liberal) defeated Col. Hercules Arthur Pakenham (unionist) by 57 votes in a poll of 5341.

39. McCalmont was elected unopposed on nomination day (19 Feb. 1913) in the presence of several ministers but not Frederick: *CA*, 14, 21 Feb. 1913. Sir Robert Chaine

Alexander McCalmont (1881–1953), KCVO (1952), CBE (1946), DSO (1917); MP, East Antrim (1913–19); 2nd Lt., Irish Guards (1900); raised and commanded 12th (Service) Battalion, Royal Irish Rifles (1914–15), commanded 1st Battalion, Irish Guards (1915–17), 3rd Infantry Brigade (1917), Irish Guards Regiment (1919–24), 144th Infantry Brigade (1924–5); retired as Brigadier-General; various home service posts (1939–51).

40. LOL 1537, Minutes, 13 Mar. 1913.

41. *CA*, 26 Sept. 1913.

42. *CA*, 3 Oct. 1913; FM, Diary, 9 Sept. 1913.

43. FM, Diary, 1 Oct. 1913.

44. Dorinda MacGregor Greer, Diary (1913), 1 Oct. 1913, D/2339/4/8/22, PRONI.

45. EN, 'Trees were Green', pp. 15–16.

46. Sir John Campbell (1862–1929), Kt (1925), FRCS (Eng.), MP, Queen's University, Belfast (1921–9).

47. FM, Diary, 13, 14 Jan. 1913.

48. Sir William Josiah Smyly (1850–1941), Kt (1905), master of Rotunda hospital, Dublin (1888–96), president, Royal College of Physicians in Ireland and British Gynaecological Society.

49. FM, Diary, 21–5, 29 Jan. 1913.

50. 'Organised Religion and the Medical Profession' (St Anne's Cathedral, 24 Jan. 1924), p. 66, in FM, *Some Northern Churchmen*, pp. 61–8.

51. FM, Diary, 11 Feb., 18 Mar. 1913.

52. *Belfast Directory* (1923), p. 63. In 1911, the 15 patients included 6 Presbyterians, 3 Episcopalians, 3 Catholics, 2 Brethren and 1 Methodist; 6 patients had been suffering for over a year: hospital census return, Lisburn Rd, Belfast (1911), NAD.

53. 'Thou shalt not be afraid for the terror by night: … nor for the destruction that wasteth at noonday' (Ps. 91: 5–6); 'Preserve me, O God: for in thee do I put my trust. … I will bless the Lord, who hath given me counsel: yea, my reins instruct me in the night seasons' (Ps. 16: 1, 8).

54. FM, Diary, 18, 19, 21, 24, 25 Mar., 18 Apr. 1913.

55. EN, 'Trees were Green', pp. 16–17.

56. *CA*, 6 June 1913.

57. The only earlier known use of 'MacNeice' occurs in William's baptismal entry (26 April 1905); but this may be a later interpolation as the spelling was visibly altered from 'Mc' to 'Mac', in different ink, in the entries for both Elizabeth and Louis: Parish of Holy Trinity, Registers of Baptisms, CR/1/3/1/4–5, PRONI. No reliance should be placed on the form 'J. F. MacNiece' in *BNL*, 22 Oct. 1900.

58. These events occurred on 16 July, 13 Aug. and 20 Sept. 1913: Grand Lodge Register (1900–22), Freemason's Hall, Dublin. 346 is identified as a Temperance lodge in *CA*, 4 July 1930.

59. Initiated 13 Oct., certificate issued 19 Oct. 1914: Register of Royal Arch Chapters (1904–22), Freemason's Hall, Dublin.

60. See appendix, Tables 7, 8.

61. Thomas MacGregor Greer (1869–1941), JP, DL, OC, 5th Battalion, Tyrone UVF, treasurer, East Antrim Unionist Association, member of Vernon Masonic Lodge 127, Coleraine, agent for Ulster Covenant (1912), chairman, Harry Ferguson Motors, Belfast; married Dorinda Florence Lowry (1892, d. 1930) and Leone Caroline Esther Handcock (1931, d. 1941).

62. Dorinda Greer, executive committee, Ulster Women's Unionist Association, president, East Antrim Women's Unionist Association, worshipful mistress, Women's LOL 7 Carrickfergus (1927). For graphic accounts of their involvement in the Ulster campaign, see Dorinda's Diary, 28 Sept. 1912, 24–5 Apr. 1914, D/2389/4/8/21 and 23, PRONI.

63. 'Soap Suds' (1961), in LM, *CP*, p. 577. The enumerator's census abstract for Carrickfergus, West Division (1911), records a house of 30 front windows and 25 rooms with 11 out-offices: NAD.

64. Thomas Greer (1837–1905), of Tullylagan, Grove House, Regent's Park, and formerly Bushy Park, Co. Dublin; MRIA, JP, DL, HS (1876), MP, Carrickfergus (1880–5); married Margaret Owden, heiress of Sea Park (d. 1917); daughters Helena MacGregor (1865–1948), who married Capt. Robert Swinburne Lowry, RN, in 1893, Georgina Beatrice (1872–1956) and Eva Mildred (1874–1951).

65. *CA*, 11 May 1917.

66. Mac's daughter Margaret Elizabeth MacGregor Greer (1897–1953) married Lt-Col. Arthur Ernest Percival, DSO, MC, in 1927; the step-mother of Thomas Greer, MP, was a Bowen-Colthurst, whose daughter married a Bowen-Colthurst and bore the notorious John Colthurst Bowen-Colthurst (b. 1880).

67. Gertrude Elizabeth Heron Hind (1877–1951), orchestral violinist and teacher, playwright, poetess: Tomás Ó Cuireáin, 'Elizabeth Shane, the Forgotten Poetess', in *Donegal Annual*, 42 (1990), 33–7.

68. Until 1886, the dean of Connor was also rector of Carrickfergus, the last such dean being George Edmonstone Kirk's father (George Bull).

69. John Hind (*1847–1932*), revived firm as John Hind and Sons, engineers and machine makers: Ó Cuireáin, 'Elizabeth Shane', p. 33; occupant of first-class house with 14 rooms and 12 front windows, Scotch Quarter, with 3 servants (2 Episcopalian, 1 Presbyterian): family Census schedule (1911).

70. John Hind (1878–1958), deacon (1902), missionary, China (1902–18), bishop of Fukien (1918–40), Northern secretary, Hibernian CMS (from 1940): John Hind, *Fukien Memories* (Belfast, pr. James A. Nelson, 1951).

71. Six of the 7 children of John Hind and Margaret Grey McVicker were buried in the New Graveyard, Drumbeg: Agnes (1875–1943), Gertrude (1877–1951), John (1878–1958), Adelaide Margaret (1882–1976), James Alexander (1886–1976) and Norah (1888–1972).

72. Agnes Hind was listed in *Thom's Directory* as Matron or Lady Superintendent of two hospitals, at 21–2, Belgrave Rd, Rathmines (1912–18) and 7–8, Charlemont St (1910–*19*).

73. FM, Diary, 25–28 Aug. 1913.

74. *Ibid.*, 1, 3–6, 16, 7, 11, 12 Sept. 1912.

75. 'The weary find eternal rest | And all the sons of want are blest' (Isaac Watts).

76. Richard Robert Leeper, FRCSI (1890), LRCPI (1886); medical superintendent, St Patrick's hospital (1899–1941); president, Royal Medico-Psychological Association (1931/2).

77. Elizabeth Malcolm, *Swift's Hospital: A History of St Patrick's Hospital, Dublin, 1746–1989* (Dublin, Gill and Macmillan, 1989), pp. 216–57, 317–18 (analysis of 154 admission forms, 1874–83).

78. Brochure for *St Patrick's Hospital, Dublin, established by Royal Charter* (Dublin, Ormond Pr. Co., 1909 edn), pp. 17, 19: copy in NLI.

79. George Patrick Cope, LRCPI (1884), LRCSI (1883), Certificate in Psychological Medicine (1888), assistant resident medical superintendent, Richmond District Asylum, Dublin.

80. Admission form 1874 (13 Oct. 1913) with associated documents; Registry of St Patrick's Hospital (1795–1925), E/33, E/106, St Patrick's Hospital Archive: kindly made available by Andrew Whiteside, consultant archivist.

81. Case-Notes (kindly transcribed by Andrew Whiteside).

82. Admission form (13 Oct. 1913).

83. FM to Leeper, 22 Oct. 1913 (with admission form).

84. FM to Leeper and application form, 7 Feb. 1914; A. E. Coe (registrar) to FM, 2, 11 Mar. 1914 and FM to Coe, 14 Mar. 1914 (with admission form). The remission was continued to the end of Lily's life.

85. FM, Diary, 18 Oct., 17, 22 Nov. 1913.

86. In 'Off the Peg' (1962), Louis likewise wrote of 'occasions of love or grief', when 'the weather broke | In our veins or the golden bowl in our hands': LM, *CP*, p. 609.

87. Henry Richard Charles Rutherford, FRCSI (1909), DPH, RCPSI (1907), LRCPI (1904); assistant medical superintendent, St Patrick's Hospital; later medical superintendent, Farnham House, Finglas.

88. FM, Diary, 25 Nov., 25 Dec. 1913.

89. LM, *Strings*, p. 45.

90. Interval address at concert in support of the Ungava mission, 13 Mar. 1914: *CA*, 20 Mar. 1914.

91. This patient spent 490 hours in the jacket, dying in Sept. 1914 after nearly 2 years in the hospital: Registry; Medical Journal (1911–21), E/150, St Patrick's Hospital Archive.

92. Case-Notes, 19, 27 Oct., 5, 13 Nov., 8 Dec. 1913, 9 Jan., 11 Feb., 12 June 1914 (last report before Sept. 1914).

93. See appendix, Tables 7, 8; *CA*, 20 Feb. 1914.

94. *CA*, 13 Mar. 1914.

95. *CA*, 27 Mar. 1914.

96. Letters from Charles T. P. Grierson and 'Pro Pace', *Guardian*, 27 Feb., 6 Mar. 1914: cuttings in CMMC. The *Guardian*, incorporating the *Churchwoman*, was a London weekly (1846–1951) catering primarily to 'the High Church party' in the Church of England.

97. *CA*, 13 Mar. 1914.

98. *CA*, 27 Mar. 1914.

99. FM, *Carrickfergus*, p. 77.

100. The address was circulated by James Bell as a penny pamphlet: *CA*, 27 Mar. 1914; and summarized in FM, *Carrickfergus*, pp. 77–8.

101. Also sold as a penny pamphlet: *CA*, 3 Apr. 1914.

102. *CA*, 17 Apr. 1914.

103. Dorinda MacGregor Greer, Diary, 24–5 Apr. 1914.

104. EN to John Hilton, 30 Aug. 1977: LM, *SL*, p. 716. Dorinda ('Dindie') is there identified as the 'Belfast aunt, lately engaged in gun-running', with whom Louis and his friend John Hilton dined in 1928: Hilton to his parents, 20 Sept. 1928, in LM, *Strings*, p. 269.

105. *CA*, 29 May 1914.

106. *CA*, 10 July 1914.

107. Loreburn to FM, 12 Apr. 1914, CMMC. Robert Threshie Reid (1846–1923), Baron (cr. 1905) and Earl Loreburn (cr. 1911) , supporter of Boer cause, Liberal MP (1880–1905), Lord Chancellor (1905–12).

108. Sanday to FM, 1 Apr. 1914, CMMC. William Sanday (1843–1920), Lady Margaret Professor of Divinity (1895–1919), author of *The Life of Christ in Recent Research* (1907).

109. Undated drafts (three fragments), *c.*July 1914, CMMC. Likely recipients include Sir Horace Plunkett and the Earl of Dunraven, another prominent ex-unionist reconciler.

110. Horace Curzon Plunkett (1854–1932), KCVO (1903), English-born son of Lord Dunsany, unionist MP, S. Dublin (1892–1900), 1st president, Irish Agricultural Organisation Society (1894), vice-president, Department of Agriculture and Technical Instruction for Ireland (1899–1907), chairman, Irish Convention (1917–18), member, Seanad Éireann (1922–3); author of *Noblesse Oblige: An Irish Rendering* (Dublin, Maunsel, 1908).

111. Sir Horace Plunkett, *A Better Way: An Appeal to Ulster not to Desert Ireland* (Dublin, Hodges, Figgis, 1914), pp. 2, 7, 22, 38.

112. FM to Plunkett (draft), 24 July 1914, CMMC. Frederick had already bought copies of the pamphlet, giving one to a Presbyterian minister.

8. PATRIOT: CARRICKFERGUS, 1914–1918

1. *CA*, 18 Sept. 1914.

2. Grand Lodge of Free and Accepted Masons of Ireland, *Roll of Honour, 1914–1919* (Dublin, *c.*1920), pp. 22, 107, 133. [JL]

3. LOL 1537, Roll Book (1911–23), in private hands.

4. *Ibid.*, Minutes (1910–14), 2 Aug., 6 Sept. 1915.

5. *CA*, 16 July 1915.

6. *CA*, 1 Jan. 1915.

7. FM, *Carrickfergus*, pp. 79–80, 92–6. 17 women 'who left Home to Serve in Hospitals, Refreshment Huts, etc., etc.' were also named (p. 96). The 625 male servicemen amounted to 45.5% of the parish's male population aged 18–39 in 1911 (1,374): Census of Ireland, County Report for Antrim (1911).

8. *Carrickfergus Parish Magazine*, no. 45 (Aug. 1914): incomplete run (May 1914–Mar. 1916) in FM Papers, Dep. d. 807, BLO.

9. *Ibid.*, no. 46 (Sept. 1914). Later issues also avoided such commentary.

10. *CA*, 11 Sept. 1914.

11. Clerical Society for the Diocese of Down and Connor and Dromore, Minutes of Quarterly Meetings (1914–41), 10 Sept. 1914, MS 659, RCBL.

12. Clerical Society, Minutes, 11 Mar. 1915. He was also twice elected to the committee: Minutes, 14 Mar. 1918, 13 Mar. 1919.

13. *CA*, 2 Oct. 1914.

14. *Ibid.*

15. FM, *Carrickfergus*, p. 76.

16. *CA*, 9 Apr. 1915.

17. *CA*, 18 June 1915. He was not , however, among those elected to office in the Carrickfergus unionist club: *CA*, 26 Feb. 1915.

18. *CA*, 15 Oct. 1915.

19. *CA*, 14 Apr. 1916. The occasion was a tribute to Captain Robert H. McNeill, Royal Naval Reserve, whose name was included 'on our congregational roll of honour' even though he had evidently died of natural causes.

20. *CA*, 5, 12 May 1916.

21. *CA*, 14 July 1916.

22. *CA*, 18 Aug. 1916.

23. Case-Notes, St Patrick's Hospital Archive (kindly transcribed by Andrew Whiteside, consultant archivist).

24. Personal Ledger (1910–17), C/8, f. 148, St Patrick's Hospital Archive.

25. A 'judicial' (controlled) rent of £3 12s. 6d. was payable annually by Thomas McWilliams, less £1 10s. payable to Colonel Frewen as head rent: Administration Papers, 18 Oct. 1915, PRONI. The Register of Burials for Omey Parish (with Ballinakill) records the burial by Hyacinth D'Arcy of Eliza Clesham of Tullawoheen, aged 70, on 21 Mar. 1864: P 742.1.2, RCBL. In 1858, the Primary Valuation returned George McWilliams as the occupant of land in Tullyvoheen valued at £1 10s. annually, with no house or buildings.

26. See ch. 6, note 86.

27. LM, *Strings*, pp. 53–4; [EN], notes on family illnesses, LM Papers, Don. c. 197, f. 24, BLO.

28. *CA*, 15 Jan. 1915; LOL 1537, Minutes, 6 Jan. 1915.

29. *CA*, 9 Apr. 1915.

30. FM to Beatrice Greer, 25–27 Dec. 1915, CMMC; *Our Heroes: Containing the Photographs with Biographical Notes of Officers of Irish Regiments and of Irish Officers of British Regiments who have Fallen in Action, or who have been Mentioned for Distinguished Conduct, from August, 1914, to July, 1916* (Dublin, *Irish Life*, 1916), p. 216. [JL]

31. LM, *Strings*, p. 60.

32. *Ireland's Memorial Records, 1914–1918*, 8 vols (Dublin, Committee of the Irish

National War Memorial, 1923), vol. iii, p. 229; *Our Heroes*, p. 216; Commonwealth (Impe-rial) War Graves Commission (hereafter, CWGC), Register (on-line). [JL]

33. *Our Heroes*, p. 217.

34. *Ireland's Memorial Records*, vol. iii, p. 229; CWGC, Register.

35. Photograph of plaque (dated 1 May 1945) in P.J. Clarke and Michael Feeney, *Mayo Comrades of the Great War, 1914–1919* (Ballina, Padraig Corcoran, 2006), pp. 90, 189. [JL]

36. *Ireland's Memorial Records*, vol. vi, p. 102.

37. *Our Heroes*, pp. 238–9; *Ireland's Memorial Records*, vol. ii, p. 71; CWGC, Register; University of Dublin, Trinity College, *War List, February, 1922* (Dublin, Hodges Figgis, 1922 edn), p. 34. Thomas Henry Clesham (*1883*–1916), BA (1906), took the Divinity entrance examination in Hilary term, 1904, with indifferent success: Divinity School Entrance Examination Book (1888–1915), MUN/V/85/7, TCD.

38. Jane Leonard is my informant on memorials of Clesham's war service.

39. Grand Lodge of Free and Accepted Masons of Ireland, *Roll of Honour, 1914–1919* (no provenance, with printed insertions), p. 11 (insertion). [JL]

40. *CA*, 14 July 1916.

41. *CA*, 29 Sept., 6 Oct. 1916. Frederick again eulogized McAteer at the evening service in Carrickfergus, and took part a few months later in the centenary service for McAteer's lodge at Joymount Presbyterian church: *CA*, 29 June 1917.

42. LM, *Strings*, pp. 56–8.

43. LM to FM, 'Sunday evening', LM Papers, Don. c. 197, ff. 10–11, BLO.

44. FM to LM, 24 Feb. 1936, LM Papers (unsorted, Box 7), BLO.

45. *CIG*, lviii (23 June 1916), 453.

46. *CIG*, lix (27 Apr. 1917), 322. The number of incumbents returned for 1913 was 1142: *ICD* (1913), pp. 49–149.

47. *BNL*, 26 Oct. 1916.

48. The fund had reached almost £24,000 by late 1919: *CIG*, lx (17 May 1918), 330; lxi (14 Nov. 1919), 738. In 1913, the united diocese had 165 incumbents, 70 curates and 9 non-parochial clergy: *ICD* (1913), p. 70.

49. Marriage certificate, FM Papers, Dep. c. 759, BLO. The dominant form of his name remained Frederick John MacNeice until the later 1920s.

50. LM, *Strings*, p. 62.

51. Margaret Greer's personal estate exceeded £54,000; she also had power of attorney over investments worth about £41,000. Some £12,000 went to Eva, £8000 to Helena and £35,000 to Thomas: Will (4 Apr. 1916) and Probate Papers (7 May 1917), NAD.

52. LM, *Strings*, p. 62. The preparatory school for boys was founded in 1899 by the unionist MP, John Kenelm Digby Wingfield-Digby of Sherborne Castle, and his Galwe-gian second wife.

53. LM to John Hilton, 1929, quoted in Stallworthy, *LM*, p. 139.

54. Guthrie Hutton, *The Royal Scottish National Hospital: 140 Years* (Larbert, Forth Valley Primary Care NHS Trust, 2000); Neill Anderson and Arturo Langer (ed. H.

Freeman), 'The Development of Institutional Care for "Idiots and Imbeciles" in Scotland', in *History of Psychiatry*, viii, 30 (1997), 243–66.

55. Royal Commission on the Care and Control of the Feeble-Minded, *Minutes of Evidence*, vol. iii, pp. 72–3 (Q 21,997, 22,055): HCP, 1908 [Cd. 4217], xxxvii.

56. The first adult inmates were admitted in 1927, 3 years after William's departure, and the 'colony' was formally opened in 1935: Anderson and Langer, 'Development', p. 253; Hutton, *140 Years*, p. 24.

57. 3 & 4 Geo. V, cap. 38; General Board of Control for Scotland, *Third Annual Report*, pp. xxviii–xxxi: HCP, 1917/18 [Cd. 8565], xvi.

58. Board of Control, *Twelfth Annual Report*, pp. lxii, lxiii, 44: HCP, 1926 [Cmd. 2737], xiii.

59. *CA*, 6 July 1917.

60. *CA*, 13 July 1917; FM, *A Plea for Unity and Peace in Ireland: Address to Orangemen* (Carrickfergus, pr. James Bell, *1917*).

61. Letter from William Calwell, Ballycarry: *CA*, 20 July 1917.

62. *CA*, 20 July 1917.

63. *CA*, 3 Aug. 1917, 28 June 1918.

64. He came eleventh among the 15 clerical representatives of Connor to the general synod in 1915, and ninth among its 11 delegates on the diocesan council in 1917: *BNL*, 28 Oct. 1915, 1 Nov. 1917. Connor had about 85 incumbents and 41 curates all told: *ICD* (1913), p. 70.

65. His attendance as a non-episcopal member of the synod was recorded annually in GS, *Proceedings* (1916–31). He attended only one of the four sittings, 17–20 Apr. 1917, being married on the 19th. Of Connor's 15 clerical representatives, between 10 and 12 attended every day's sitting in 1916, 1918, 1920, 1922, and 1930.

66. The motion was seconded by William Lee, his old colleague at St Donard's: *BNL*, 26 Oct. 1916.

67. *CA*, 20 July, 5, 26 Oct. 1917.

68. *CA*, 23, 30 Nov. 1917; text issued as a pamphlet and reproduced in FM, *Some Northern Churchmen*, pp. 26–9.

69. *CA*, 4, 18 Jan. 1918.

70. *CA*, 15 Nov. 1918.

9. PEACEMAKER: CARRICKFERGUS, 1918–1926

1. *CA*, 13 June 1919.

2. *CA*, 11 July 1919.

3. *CA*, 9, 30 Aug., 1 Nov. 1918, 30 Jan. 1920.

4. The Roll included 10 who had died in action, 1 while a prisoner-of-war, and 2 when 'drowned by submarine action': *CA*, 26 Mar. 1920.

5. *CA*, 3 Dec. 1920; *BNL*, 29 Nov. 1920. The Roll of Honour was also to include members of the various regiments quartered in the town during the war. I am grateful to

Jane Leonard for alerting me to this rare example of an ecumenical church memorial.

6. FM, *Words for the Times: Christ's Way for His Disciples in Ireland* (Carrickfergus, Bell, 1920).

7. *BNL*, 22 July 1920, *Freeman's Journal*, 23 July 1920: letter to editor signed by FM, Alexander Cuthbert and John Minford (Presbyterian), and James Ritchie (Methodist). When reproduced in FM et al., *The Way to Peace for Ireland* (Carrickfergus, Bell, 1920), the letter was also endorsed by James Lyon (Congregational minister) and John Weatherup (Baptist deacon).

8. FM, *Words for the Times: Christ's Call to His Disciples in Their Work and Sorrow* (Carrickfergus, Bell, 1920).

9. *CA*, 20 Aug. 1920.

10. F. E. L. Hurst to FM, 14 Aug. 1920, CMMC. Hurst stated that 'my dear old father never would preach a "big-drum" sermon on the Sunday before the 12th, so as a lad I was spared some baneful & unchristian teaching'. Frederick Edward Lloyd Hurst, former engineer, deacon (1911), curate, Prestwich (1918–22), vicar, St Peter's, Bury (1922–); son of Francis James Hurst (1834–1906), rector, Clabby (1873–1900), vicar, Donaghmoine (1900–6), archdeacon of Clogher (1903–6).

11. Bolton Charles Waller (1890–1936), son of Queenstown curate, Scholar in Classics, TCD (1911); founder, Irish Christian Fellowship (1915); narrowly failed to secure third seat for Dublin University in Dáil Éireann (June 1927); deacon (1931), curate, Rathmines (1931–6), incumbent, Clondalkin (1936).

12. Irish Christian Fellowship, *Looking at Ireland* (London, SCM Press, 1937), p. 10.

13. The branch proposed excursions to Carrickfergus in May 1921 and June 1925, and Frederick was suggested as a substitute speaker at further meetings in 1923 and 1929: Irish Christian Fellowship, Belfast Branch, Committee Minutes (1920–7, 1928–33), 21 Sept., 5 Nov. 1920, 18 Mar. 1921, 4 June, 11 Sept. 1923, 7 Apr. 1925, 11 Jan. 1929, D/3921/A/1–2; Membership Cards, D/3921/D/1/1, PRONI.

14. *BNL*, 3 Sept. 1920.

15. FM, *Carrickfergus*, pp. 83–5.

16. FM, *Words for the Times: Retaliation or Reconciliation? A Sermon to Orangemen* (Carrickfergus, Bell, 1920); *CA*, 12 Nov. 1920.

17. George McKay, PP, to Patrick Convery, PP (St Paul's, Belfast), *CA*, 10 Dec. 1920 (from *Irish News*).

18. *Freeman's Journal*, 11 Dec. 1920.

19. *CA*, 6 Dec. 1918, 3 Jan., 28 Feb., 7, 14 Mar, 18 Apr., 9, 23 May, 13 June 1919. In Dec. 1918, McCalmont defeated Daniel Dumigan (Sinn Féin) by 15,206 votes to 861; in the by-election of 27 May 1919, George Boyle Hanna (a Ballymena solicitor) defeated Major William Agnew Moore by 8714 votes to 7549, Legg receiving only 1778. Charles McFerran Legg (1858–1934), Presbyterian shipowner and coal merchant; chairman, UDC (1902–3, 1911–20, 1925–8+); bequeathed Legg Park to the public in memory of his only son, 2nd Lieutenant Charles Legg (1893–1918): Rutherford, *Old Families*, p. 160.

20. Both LOL 1537 and Miriam's Daughters Women's LOL 7 were sharply divided between supporters of Hanna and Major Moore: LOL 1537, Minutes (1914–22), 28 Apr. 1919 (in private hands); *CA*, 18 Apr., 9 May 1920.

21. *CA*, 21 Jan. 1921.

22. *CA*, 5 Dec. 1919.

23. *CA*, 9, 23 Jan. 1920. The occupations given upon nomination by successful councillors were gentleman, magistrate, company director, manager (2), accountant, grocer (2), fruiterer, tailor, painter (2), caulker, bricklayer, shipwright, bread-server, carter and retired NCO. Of the 9 unsuccessful candidates, 4 were joiners.

24. John Dermot Campbell (d. 1945), native of Drumsough, Randalstown, Co. Antrim; member of select vestry and protestor; chairman, UDC (1921–4); 1st station commandant, 'B Specials', Carrickfergus; MP, Carrickfergus (1943–5).

25. *CA*, 13 Aug. 1920; FM, *Carrickfergus*, p. 97. In 1921, Campbell's honour was restored by his election as club chairman, this office being separated from the presidency held by Dobbs: *CA*, 25 Feb. 1921.

26. *CA*, 1 Oct. 1920.

27. James Ritchie (1870–1958), Antrim farmer's son; ordained 1898, Methodist minister, Clones (1912–16), Ballyclare (1916–19), Carrickfergus (1919–22), Castlederg (1922–5) and finally Ballinmallard (1936–41); admitted to Masonic Lodge 346, Carrickfergus (1922); DGC, Fermanagh (1938–41).

28. *CA*, 16 July 1920.

29. *CA*, 25 Feb., 18 Mar. 1921. George Hanna (already an MP at Westminster) was the third among 6 unionists elected for Antrim on 24 May 1921, the nationalist Joseph Devlin taking the seventh seat.

30. *CA*, 25 Mar. 1921.

31. *CA*, 1, 8, 22 Apr. 1921; LOL 1537, loose undated resolution in Minutes. Sections of the relevant minutes were erased or torn out, suggesting divisions on the issue within the lodge.

32. *CA*, 14 July 1922; LOL 1537, Minutes, 27 June, 31 July 1922.

33. FM, *Carrickfergus*, pp. 88–91 (reproducing the full text of the King's speech, largely drafted by General Smuts).

34. *CA*, 1, 8 July 1921.

35. FM, *Carrickfergus*, p. 85.

36. *CA*, 25 Nov. 1921.

37. *IT*, 6, 13 Dec. 1921.

38. *BNL*, 4–7 Jan. 1922.

39. James Ernest Davey (1890–1960), fellow, King's College, Cambridge, then professor of Church History (1917–22) and New Testament Greek (1922–30, 1933–60), secretary (1918–20), and president (1942–60), Presbyterian College, Belfast; moderator, General Assembly (1953–4). For his career and the trial for heresy (1927), see Austin Fulton, *J. Ernest Davey* (Belfast, Presbyterian Church in Ireland, 1970); R. F. G. Holmes, *Our Irish Presbyterian Heritage* (Belfast, Presbyterian Church in Ireland, 1985), pp. 153–4; William

Corkey, *Glad Did I Live: Memoirs of a Long Life* (Belfast, BNL, 1963), pp. 268–72.

40. Frederick J. Frizelle (1881–1922), enrolled (1901), sergeant (1 July 1921), 'shot while on duty' (1922), 5′ 11″: RIC General Register, HO 184/31 (59994), NAL (microform copy, NAD).

41. *Irish Independent*, 5, 6 May 1922; *The Times*, 5 May 1922.

42. *CA*, 14 July 1922; FM, *For Peace with Honour between North and South: An Address to Orangemen* (Carrickfergus, Bell, 1922).

43. 'For the present an all-Ireland Parliament was out of the question, possibly in years to come – 10, 20, or 50 years – Ulster might be tempted to join with the South… If he were convinced it were in the interests of the people of Ulster, he would frankly tell them of his views, but should such an eventuality arise, he would not feel justified himself in taking part in an all-Ireland Parliament': Cabinet Conclusions, 26 Jan. 1922, in CAB 4/30/9, PRONI, quoted in Patrick Buckland, *James Craig, Lord Craigavon* (Dublin, Gill and Macmillan, 1980), p. 57.

44. Waller to FM, 22 Aug. 1922, CMMC. Gwynn considered the address by 'Macneill' to be a 'model of Christian thought on Irish affairs. Carrickfergus has been free from outrage and reprisal. Its Rector at least shares the praise.' Cutting from *Observer*, 20 Aug. 1922, in Gwynn, 'Newspaper Cuttings', vol. iii, NLI (IR9410995).[JL]

45. FM to Rosamond Stephen, 2 Oct. 1923, MS 253/3/4/12, RCBL. Rosamond Stephen (1868–1951), daughter of Sir James Fitzjames Stephen and first cousin of Virginia Woolf; confirmed by Archbishop Plunket (1896); founder, (Irish) Guild of Witness (1901), working in Belfast, Dublin, and Dundalk; strong opponent of Carson: *An Englishwoman in Belfast: Rosamond Stephen's Record of the Great War*, ed. Oonagh Walsh (Cork, UP, 2000).

46. *CA*, 16 Nov. 1923.

47. FM, *Words for the Times: Housing Conditions in Carrickfergus: New Year's Address* (Carrickfergus, J. Matthews, 1924): copy in FM Papers, Dep. d. 807, BLO.

48. *CA*, 3 Oct. 1924; *IT*, 23 Sept. 1924. The signatories, in addition to Frederick, Cuthbert, and Minford, were James M. Calder (Congregational) and E. B. Cullen (Methodist: omitted from version in *IT*).

49. *CA*, 10 Oct. 1924.

50. Exercise book entitled 'Hymns' (undated), FM Papers, Dep. c. 757, BLO.

51. *CA*, 2 May 1924, 24 Apr. 1925.

52. *CA*, 1 Feb. 1924.

53. *CA*, 30 Oct. 1925, 26 Nov. 1926.

54. *CA*, 5 Feb. 1926.

55. *CA*, 20 Feb. 1925. The sermon (delivered on 26 Apr. 1925) appeared as a booklet entitled *'Death is Swallowed Up in Victory': Sermon on 'The Resurrection and the Life'* (Carrickfergus, Printing Co., 1925): copies in FM Papers, Dep. d. 807, BLO.

56. *CA*, 18 May 1923.

57. *CA*, 14 Oct. 1921.

58. *CA*, 15 June 1923.

59. Returns of parochial contributions for the 12 months ending in mid year appear

in ICM, *Reports* (1908/9–1919/20) and thereafter in the corresponding reports of the Irish Branch (available for 1919/20 and 1924/5–1938/9). The latter also listed members of the executive committee, Belfast Auxiliary, up to 1912/13, when Frederick's name appeared as it had since 1907/8.

60. *CIG*, lxi (28 Nov. 1919), 764; committee report inserted in GS, *Journal* (1920), at p. 194.

61. Church Reform League (Diocese of Down and Connor and Dromore), Minute Book (1920–2) [hereafter, CRL, Minutes], 3 Feb. 1920, MS 652, RCBL. Frederick and Kerr were among those delegated to give evidence to the Committee on Retrenchment and Reform.

62. George Ashton Chamberlain (1881–1968), deacon (1904), curate in England and Castlerock (1904–13) and St Ann's, Dublin (1913–17); incumbent, Clondalkin (1917–24) and Mariners' Church, Kingstown (1924–59); editor, *CIG* (*1919*–24).

63. CRL, Minutes, 23 Mar. 1920.

64. *Ibid.*, 5 May 1920; *IT*, 10, 19 May 1920; *CIG*, lxiii (21 May 1920), 327.

65. CRL, Minutes, 27 May, 9 Sept. 1920.

66. *CIG*, lxiii (12 Nov. 1920), 696.

67. *BNL*, 10 Nov. 1920.

68. CRL, Minutes, 20 Dec. 1920. The fact that the second encomium was added 5 months after the original discussion, in an addendum signed by Frederick as chairman of a general meeting (2 May 1921), suggests that some members were unhappy with his performance.

69. Hugh W. B. Thompson (League secretary, St Catherine's rectory, Dublin) to R. S. Breene (Down branch secretary, Killinchy rectory), 27 Mar. 1922, in CRL, Minutes.

70. See letters by Crozier, Kerr and several other synodsmen concerning a 'List of [Lay] Representatives to the Synod' circulated by the Church of Ireland Laymen's Association, Belfast, just before the diocesan synod of 1909: *BNL*, 27, 28 Oct. 1909.

71. *CIG*, lxiii (4 June 1920), 364.

72. CRL, Minutes, 21 Oct. 1920.

73. *Ibid.*, 5, 19 Oct. 1921.

74. *Ibid.*, 15 Dec. 1921. Only 4 of the 10 committeemen had been elected a year earlier.

75. *Ibid.*, 5 Jan, 1, 22 Feb. 1922, with newspaper cutting on meeting of 23 Feb. Hugh Davis Murphy (1849–1927), from Co. Antrim; deacon (1874), curate, Ballinderry (1874–5), assistant chaplain, Bethesda, Dublin (1875–8), curate (1878–80), then rector, St George's (1878–1926); chaplain, Actors' Union; Prince Mason.

76. *IT*, 26 Aug. 1922.

77. CRL, Minutes, 6 Dec. 1921, with note, 3 Apr. 1941, signed by R. S. Breene, secretary.

78. The only exceptions were in 1921 (second) and 1929 (third). He came second in the triennial election for the general synod in 1921 and 1924, heading that list also in 1927 and 1930. See reports of diocesan synods and elections, *BNL*.

79. *CIG*, lxiv (26 Mar. 1921), 192.

80. Charles Thornton Primrose Grierson (1857–1935), from Rathfarnham; deacon, 1881, rector, Seapatrick (1888–1911), dean of Belfast (1911–19), bishop of Down and Connor and Dromore (1919–34).

81. *IT*, 15 May 1924.

82. Frederick Chesnutt-Chesney, BA, TCD (1919), deacon (1920), curate, Ballymacarrett (1920–3) and All Souls', South Hampstead (1924–), chaplain to the forces, Territorial Army (1930–). I am grateful to Jane Leonard for information on Chesney's career, and for enabling me to identify the case leading to Murphy's motion in the general synod.

83. John Redmond (1876–1967), from Portadown; deacon (1912), temporary chaplain to the forces (1916–18), incumbent, Ballycarrett (1920–9) and Kilbride (1929–51); DGC, Antrim (1932–67) and Ireland (1955–67). He is remembered for having tended his dying Catholic namesake, Major William Redmond, MP, at Messines in 1917.

84. *BNL, NW, IT*, 2, 12 Oct. 1923. Though regretting Redmond's impetuous humiliation of his curate, Grierson considered that Chesney was 'ethically wrong' in distinguishing between vice and sin, and also in asserting that smoking and dancing were vices (though not sins).

85. *BNL*, 5 Nov. 1924.

86. *BNL*, 4 Nov. 1925.

87. *CIG*, lxviii (13 Nov. 1925), 692.

88. Sealed letter of appointment, 7 Apr. 1926, FM Papers, Dep. c. 759, BLO.

89. Though first elected as a Connor diocesan nominator in Nov. 1927, Frederick (as Connor's first supplemental) had replaced Dean Collins of Belfast upon his elevation to the see of Meath (Mar. 1926).

90. *CA*, 2 Apr. 1926.

91. Robert Cooke Birney (*1880*–1921), Dubliner; deacon (1911), curate, St Michael's, Belfast (1911–15) and Carrickfergus (1915–18), rector, Castlerahan and Ballyjamesduff (1918–21); Thomas Bloomer (1894–1984), from Dungannon; deacon (1918), curate, Carrickfergus (1918–22) and English parishes (1922–7), vicar, Lyncombe (1927–35) and Barking (1935–46), bishop of Carlisle (1946–66); assisting bishop, Johannesburg (1968).

92. LM, *Zoo* (London, Michael Joseph, 1938), p. 71.

93. *CA*, 16 Apr. 1926.

94. William John Parr (*1896*–1954), from Ballysillan, Belfast; deacon (1918), curate, Ballymena (1922–6) and Carrickfergus (1926–30), rector, Lambeg (1930–53); Alfred Weller Mussen Stanley Mann (1898–1968), b. Howth; deacon (1922), curate, TCD Mission, Belfast (1922–4), St Luke's (1924–30), and Carrickfergus (1930–4), dean's vicar, Belfast (1934) and vicar choral (1935), rector, Killyleagh (1935–62), precentor of Down (1954–64), bishop's curate, Kilwarlin (1962–8), dean of Down (1964–8).

95. Elizabeth Nicholson to John Hilton, 30 Aug. 1977: LM, *SL*, p. 715.

96. LM to Hilton [autumn 1929]: LM, *SL*, p. 213.

97. Robert and Edna Wright, 'Carrickfergus Rectory and Louis MacNeice: His Home and Ours', p. 30, in *Carrickfergus and District Historical Journal*, vii (1993), 21–31.

98. 'Autumn Journal', XVI: LM, *CP*, p. 140.

99. 'Landscapes of Childhood and Youth' (*c.*1927), in LM, *Strings*, p. 227.

100. LM to [Fortescue Eric Vesey] Ross, July [1924]: LM, *SL*, pp. 95–6. In late 1925, Frederick returned to the West, visiting Mayo and Galway: *CIG*, lxviii (13 Nov. 1925), 692.

101. LM, *Strings*, pp. 82, 228 ('Landscapes').

102. *Ibid.* p. 235.

103. FM, Diary, 'Holiday, June 1925', FM Papers, Dep. c. 758, BLO.

104. Among his son's lovers was another Miss Hunt, attractive, beautiful, but lacking a lower leg (a fact cruelly lampooned in the poem 'Christina', written in July 1939): Stallworthy, *LM*, pp. 238–40, 255–6; LM, *CP*, pp. 190–1.

10. UNIFIER: CARRICKFERGUS, 1926–1931

1. FM to John Hilton [summer 1926]; FM to Anthony Blunt, 25 Sept., 14 Oct. 1926: LM, *SL*, pp. 116–17, 122, 129.

2. LM, *Strings*, p. 111; see ch. 2, above.

3. FM, Diary of visit to Norway (July 1928), FM Papers, Dep. c. 758, BLO.

4. LM, 'When I Was Twenty-One: 1928' (1961), p. 222, in LM, *Selected Prose*, pp. 230–9; LM, *Strings*, p. 116.

5. Louis had already informed Blunt that 'my father reads the Bible in his Bath'. See LM to Blunt, 31 Dec. 1927, 3 Aug. 1928 (warning repeated, 22 Aug.): LM, *SL*, pp. 181, 193, 194.

6. John Hilton, 'Louis MacNeice at Marlborough and Oxford', p. 255, in LM, *Strings*, pp. 239–84. John Robert Hilton (1908–94), director of antiquities, Cyprus (1934–6), architect for firm manufacturing paper bags (1936–41); captain, Royal Engineers (1941–3), diplomat, twice posted to Istanbul (1943–69); president, National Schizophrenia Fellowship (1985–9).

7. Hilton to his parents, 20 Sept. 1928, in LM, *Strings*, pp. 268–70.

8. John Charles Nicholson (1904–86), 3rd Bt (succ. 1949), BA, Oxon (2nd class, Physiology, 1927), BM, BCh, Oxon (1929), FRCS, England (1936), consulting surgeon at 3 London hospitals (retired 1969), Major, Hon. Lieut.-Col. (1945), RAMC, Territorial Army (1932–45).

9. Caroline Elizabeth MacNeice (1903–81), BA, Oxon (2nd class, Physiology, 1925), BM, BCh, Oxon and LMSSA, London (1932).

10. LM to Hilton [autumn 1928]: LM, *SL*, p. 196; LM to BM, 21 Jan. [1923]: copy kindly supplied by Jonathan Allison.

11. *CA*, 19 Oct., 22 June 1928.

12. *IT*, 24 Nov. 1928; EN to John Hilton, 30 Aug. 1977: LM, *SL*, p. 715.

13. LM, *Strings*, p. 118.

14. BM, Diary (1929), 1, 7, 8 Jan., 10 Feb. 1929, CMMC.

15. *Ibid.*, 16 Feb. 1929; Stallworthy, *LM*, p. 128.

16. Hilton to his parents, 18 Feb. 1929, in LM, *Strings*, pp. 274–8; FM to Hilton [*c*.16] Feb. 1929, quoted in Stallworthy, *LM*, pp. 128–9.

17. Stallworthy, *LM*, pp. 129–30; Hilton to his parents, 22 Feb. 1929, in LM, *Strings*, pp. 278–80.

18. BM, Diary, 19 Feb. 1929.

19. Hilton to his parents, 22 Feb. 1929.

20. This novel was eventually rejected by Heinemann: Stallworthy, *LM*, p. 134.

21. BM, Diary, 20, 21 Feb. 1929.

22. Hilton to his parents, 22 Feb. 1929.

23. BM, Diary, 8, 19, 20, 28, 29 Mar., 3, 6, 7, 20, 24 Apr. 1929, and appointments, 15 Apr.; Stallworthy, *LM*, p. 134.

24. BM, Diary, 10, 11, 16 June 1929.

25. *Ibid.*, 13, 18, 19, 20 July 1929.

26. Evidence of Dr Clarkson (2 Mar. 1906) to Royal Commission on the Care and Control of the Feeble-Minded, *Minutes of Evidence*, vol. iii, p. 70: HCP, 1908 [Cd. 4217], xxxvii, 1. Robert Durward Clarkson, MB, Edinburgh (1890); president, Royal Medical Society (Edinburgh); medical officer, later superintendent, (Royal) Scottish National Institution for the Education of Imbecile Children (*1893–1935*).

27. FM, address to 30th annual meeting, Carrickfergus District Nursing Society, on the social origins of tuberculosis: *CA*, 16 Mar. 1928.

28. BM, Diary, 19, 24 July 1929.

29. Barbara Coulton, *Louis MacNeice in the BBC* (London, Faber, 1980), p. 21.

30. LM, *Strings*, p. 123; BM, Diary, 1, 2, 4, 18, 25, 27 Aug. 1929; see also ch. 16, below.

31. BM, Diary, 22 Nov. 1929. *Oxford Poetry 1929* was jointly edited by Louis and Stephen Spender: Stallworthy, *LM*, p. 134.

32. BM, Diary, 23 Nov. 1929.

33. Rutherford, *Old Families*, p. 113.

34. Stallworthy, *LM*, p. 143.

35. BM to LM, 23 July 1930, LM Papers (uncatalogued), Box 6, BLO.

36. BM, Diary (1931), 4 Feb., 9, 12 Mar. 1931, CMMC.

37. *Ibid.*, 9, 12 Jan. 1931. *The Diary of a Provincial Lady* (London, Macmillan, 1930), by E. M. Delafield (ps. for Edmée Elizabeth Monica Dashwood, née de la Pasture), gives a wry account of tennis, amateur theatricals and the lot of a vicar's wife in a village resembling Kentisbeare, Devon, where the author presided over the Women's Institute and her young family.

38. BM, Diary, 18, 22 Oct. 1929; *CA*, 25 Oct. 1929; *BNL*, 23 Oct. 1929. The 3rd Duke of Abercorn had been elected an Honorary Burgess (Freeman) on 18 July 1927; Sir William and Lady Coates followed suit on 23 Jan. 1931, as did the Duchess on 17 May 1935: City and County Borough of Belfast, *Memoranda ... and General Information for 1935–36* (no imprint), p. 21.

39. BM, Diary, 15 Mar. 1931.

40. *BNL*, 5 Nov. 1925.

41. In the annual diocesan council election, Frederick (with 87 votes) had more than twice the vote gained by the junior successful candidate from the Connor clergy (39). At the triennial election for general synod representatives, he received 91 votes as against 45 for the last elected candidate. The 3 candidates elected to the Connor board of patronage were Frederick (with 164 votes), Dean Dowse of Connor (132), and a layman, W. A. Ferrar (150): *BNL*, 3 Nov. 1927.

42. Heading all three polls, he secured 95 votes for the diocesan council, 90 as a general synod representative, and 128 as a diocesan nominator: *BNL*, 30 Oct. 1930.

43. FM, *Some Northern Churchmen*, p. 46 (sermon, 24 Mar. 1929).

44. BM, Diary, 13, 14, 16 May 1929. Sarah Henrietta Purser (1848–1943) presided over the Co-operative Stained Glass and Mosaic Works, Ltd, at *An Túr Gloine*, 24–5, Upper Pembroke St (1903–40). This is presumably the institution referred to by BM as 'Miss Purser's Art School'. [JL]

45. BM, Diary, 21 Nov. 1929.

46. The honorific prebend of Clonmethan, 1 of 8 canonries in the gift of the dean and chapter, carried an annual stipend of £10.

47. Diocesan Temperance Society Committee (Down and Connor and Dromore), Minute Book (1917–31), 11 June 1926, MS 651/3, RCBL.

48. Charles Campbell Manning (1871–1954), Dubliner; deacon (1896), curate, Carrickfergus (1896–1900), rector, Muckamore (1903–11) and finally Holywood (1920–45), archdeacon of Down (1930–45); temporary chaplain to the forces (1914–18), MC (1918).

49. Diocesan Temperance Society, Minutes, 1 Dec. 1926, 5 Jan. 1927. Grierson's ingenuous declaration of loyalty to Craig was amended to 'fully support the Prime Minister'.

50. Down and Connor and Dromore Quarterly Clerical Society, Minute Book (1914–41), 11 Mar, 9 Dec. 1926, 12 Mar., 11 June 1931, 13 Mar. 1930, MS 659, RCBL. Between 1926 and 1931, he attended no less than 10 quarterly meetings in Belfast.

51. Clerical Society of Ireland, Minutes (1918–29), 21–2 Nov. 1928, MS 142/2, RCBL; *IT*, 28 Nov. 1928.

52. Clerical Society of Ireland, Minutes, 20–1 Nov. 1929; *CIG*, lxxi (15 Nov. 1929), 659.

53. FM, *Reunion: The Open Door. A Call from Ireland* (Belfast, W. Erskine Mayne, 1929), pp. 3, 5, 58–61; *CIG*, lxxi (30 Mar. 1929), 180; *Faith and Order: Proceedings of the World Conference, Lausanne, August 3–21, 1927*, ed. H. N. Bate (London, SCM, 1927).

54. *CIG*, lxxi (10 May 1929), 254–5; *IT*, 17 May 1929.

55. Irish Christian Fellowship, Minute Book of the Committee of the Belfast Branch (1928–33), 3 Nov. 1930, 6 Dec. 1931, D/3921/A/2, PRONI.

56. FM, *Reunion*, pp. 17, 24.

57. George Seaver, *John Allen Fitzgerald Gregg: Archbishop* (London, Faith Press, 1963), p. 163; Charles Frederick D'Arcy, *The Adventures of a Bishop, a Phase of Irish Life: A Personal and Historical Narrative* (London, Hodder and Stoughton, 1934).

58. *CIG*, lxxi (24 May 1929), 291–2.

59. *CIG*, lxxii (23 May 1930), 290.

60. *Ibid.* 286. The motion was defeated by a single vote, being supported by 81 clergy and 70 laymen, and opposed by 62 clergy and 90 laymen.

61. *CIG*, lxxiii (22 May 1931), 285–6; *Statutes of the General Synod*, 1920, cap. 2; 1949, cap. 8; GS, *Journal* (1959), pp. vii–xii.

62. See appendix, Table 9.

63. Statistics for 1926 presented to the diocesan synod by Bishop Grierson indicated

that mean attendance at Sunday services amounted to 21.3% of the estimated 'church population' (19.2% in Belfast and 23.3% elsewhere in the united diocese): *CIG*, lxviii (12, 19 Nov. 1926), 667, 684.

64. FM, *Church of Ireland*, p. 111.

65. *BNL*, 4 Nov. 1925; *IT*, 14 May 1925.

66. LM to BM, 13 May 1926: LM, *SL*, p. 112.

67. *BNL*, 3 Nov. 1926; *IT*, 20 May 1926; *CIG*, lxx (9 Nov. 1928), 649.

68. *BNL*, 29 Oct. 1930. Clarke's amendment, said by Grierson to carry 'an anti-epis-copal taint', was supported by 117 clergy and 76 laymen, being opposed by 66 clergy and 122 laymen. To prevail, the amending motion required a majority in both orders.

69. Division was opposed by 116 of the 173 clergy (67.1%) and 130 of 203 laymen (64.0%): *BNL*, 4 Feb. 1931.

70. FM, *Church of Ireland*, pp. 109–10.

71. In Jan. 1945, Shaw Kerr became bishop of Down and Dromore while Charles King Irwin retained the see of Connor.

72. *Belfast Telegraph*, 28 Mar. 1938: Local Newspaper Cuttings, vol. 25, p. 191, Belfast Central Library.

73. *CIG*, lxix (13 May, 3 June 1927), 271–2, 324.

74. *CIG*, lxx (27 Apr., 11, 18 May 1928), 246, 276–7, 289.

75. The 5 new Belfast churches built between 1927 and 1932 were funded by £40,500 in grants from the general synod, £15,288 in diocesan grants, and £11,758 in liabilities assumed by the parishes: FM, *Church of Ireland*, p. 132.

76. *CIG*, lxx (9 Nov. 1928), 649; *BNL*, 31 Oct. 1928.

77. Richard Best (1869–1939), Irish Bar (1895), KC (1912), unionist MP, Armagh and Attorney-General, NI (1921–5), Lord Justice of Appeal, Supreme Court, NI (1925–39); Member, Grand Committee, GOLI (1923–5); Deputy Grand King, Grand Royal Arch Chapter of Ireland (1915). For the friendship between his son Richard, John Hilton and Louis, and their tennis games in Belfast in Oct. 1928, see LM, *Strings*, pp. 255, 269.

78. The Commission's interim and final reports are reproduced in FM, *Church of Ireland*, pp. 57–8, 112–27.

79. The former church has in fact been reduced to housing the IT unit of the library of 'Inst.' (the Royal Belfast Academical Institution). [JL]

80. *BNL*, 30 Oct. 1929.

81. The Commission's report declared that 'its pew-rents, which seem in conflict with much that the church has stood for, should go': FM, *Church of Ireland*, p. 117. Even after the reform had been accomplished, Frederick remained 'generally hostile' to St George's according to J. R. B. McDonald, his last ordinand and still today a minister in the parish: quoted in Fauske, *'Side by Side'*, p. 22.

82. Henry O'Connor (1871–1951), MBE (1920), formerly general secretary, YMCA, Dublin; deacon (1920), incumbent, Kilmegan, Dundrum (1926–51); DGC, Ireland (1930–50), DGC, Belfast, subsequently Down. During a protracted exchange of letters to the press

prompted by the synod's discussion, O'Connor denounced St George's for 'extravagances – such as "Sung Eucharist," "Altar" cloths of many colours, eastward position, &c., with regular whist drives and dances on week nights': *BNL*, 2 Nov. 1929.

83. *CIG*, lxxi (8 Nov. 1929), 645–6; *BNL*, 30, 31 Oct. 1929.

84. FM, *Church of Ireland*, p. 120.

85. *CA*, 27 Aug. 1926.

86. *CA*, 15 July 1927.

87. *CA*, 21 Dec. 1928.

88. *CA*, 24 Jan. 1929. Bunyan's *The Pilgrim's Progress* was favourite reading for Frederick, Beatrice, William, and even Louis: LM, *Varieties of Parable* (Cambridge, UP, 1965), pp. 43–50.

89. *CA*, 15 Nov. 1929.

90. *CA*, 14 Nov. 1930. The sermon was published as FM, *Mobilize for Peace: Address Given in the Parish Church, Carrickfergus* (no provenance, 1930): copy in FM Papers, Dep. d. 807, BLO.

91. *CA*, 27 Jan.–29 June 1928.

92. *CA*, 27 Apr. 1928.

93. *CA*, 23 Mar., 12 and 26 Oct. 1928 (quoting reviews in *Belfast Telegraph* and *BNL*).

94. FM, *Carrickfergus*, pp. 44–5, 47, 55.

95. *Ibid.* p. 70.

96. *Ibid.* p. 71.

97. *Ibid.* p. 83.

98. The government had grudgingly agreed to fly the flag on the few days appointed for its official buildings, while agreeing to consider displaying it on Sundays 'if it could be shown that there was a pronounced desire on the part of the local residents': report of exchange in Senate of Northern Ireland, *CA*, 20 Dec. 1929.

99. *BNL*, 11, 12 July 1930.

100. BM to LM, 23 July [1930], LM Papers (uncatalogued), Box 6, BLO.

101. FM, *Church of Ireland*, preface (29 Apr. 1931).

II. ANOINTED: WATERFORD, 1931–1934

1. BM, Diary (1931), 29 Apr. 1931: CMMC.

2. FM to EN, 5 Aug. 1931: CMMC.

3. A 'select list' was compiled by inviting synodsmen to vote for as many as 3 candidates. Frederick received 54 out of 245 votes in this preliminary exercise (17 of 88 clerical votes and 37 of 157 lay votes), ahead of Dean John Percy Phair of Ossory (49), Canon Andrew Pike of Thurles (31), Dean Henry Robert Brett of Belfast (30), Dean John Herbert Leslie of Lismore (26), and Archdeacon St John Drelincourt Seymour of Cashel and Emly (23), with scattered support for 11 others including Frederick's old rector, Archdeacon Robert Scott Bradshaw Burkitt of Lismore (3). In the course of three ballots, in which up to 40 clerical and 85 lay synodsmen voted for 1 of 5 candidates, Frederick's vote rose

from 50 (17 clergy and 33 laymen) through 65 (22 and 43) to 94 (29 and 65). Support for Phair, his only serious rival, fell away from 28 (3 and 25) through 26 (4 and 22) to 18 (2 and 16): Waterford and Lismore, Diocesan Synod, Minute Book (1921–34), 29 Apr. 1931 (joint synod), D 9.2.1, RCBL.

4. *BNL*, 30 Apr. 1931.

5. *CIG*, lxxiii (1 May 1931), 238; *BNL*, 30 Apr., 1, 7 May 1931.

6. Newspaper cutting in BM, Diary (1931), 13 June 1931: CMMC.

7. Richard Simmons Breene (1886–1974), Belfast coastguard's son; deacon (1911), rector, Killinchy (1920–6, including Kilmood from 1923) and St Peter's, Belfast (1926–63), chancellor (1941–56) and dean of Connor (1956–63); editor, *Irish Churchman* (from 1920, evidently succeeding Shaw Kerr), Church of Ireland correspondent, *BNL*.

8. *Irish Churchman*, xxi, 31 (7 May 1931), 4, 15.

9. *BNL*, 12 June 1931. The ring may be inspected in the Carrickfergus Museum.

10. Rural Dean's Visitation Returns (1934), D 9.2.3.14 (Waterford and Lismore), D 9.1.3.8 (Cashel and Emly), RCBL; Holy Trinity Parish, Register of Baptisms (1903–19), 25 Mar. 1903–23 Mar. 1904, CR/1/3/1/5, PRONI; Board of Education, Report for year ended 31 Mar. 1934, in RCB, *Report* (for 1934).

11. BM, Diary, 14, 15 May 1931. Bishopsgrove had been purchased by the diocese after Frederick's predecessor had given up the palace, 'on the ground that he could not maintain it out of his income'. Churchmen in Tipperary wished the bishop to vacate Waterford altogether: *Irish Churchman*, xxi, 34 (28 May 1931), 3.

12. BM, Diary, 15 May, 22 June 1931.

13. *BNL*, 25 June 1931.

14. BM, Diary, 24 June 1931.

15. Diocese of Waterford and Lismore, *Reports of the Diocesan Council … for the Year 1930* (Waterford, Diocese, 1931), p. 15; Diocese of Cashel and Emly, *Sixty-Second Report of the Diocesan Council* (Clonmel, Diocese, 1931), p. 8 (synod resolution): set of reports in RCB Office, Dublin.

16. Waterford and Lismore Clerical Society, Minute Book (1927–55), 8 Sept. 1931, 16 June, 12 Oct. 1933, 6 Feb. 1934, 12 Jan., 28 June 1932: MS 716, RCBL. The bishop attended 7 of the society's 10 meetings during his episcopate.

17. *CIG*, lxxvi (20 Nov. 1931), 692.

18. BM, Diary, 9 Aug. 1931. According to Wilfred Baker's letter in *CIG* (7 Sept. 2001), such requests were 'complied with somewhat grudgingly and to the discomfiture of the then Dean Mayers, who was a gentle, mild-mannered man': quoted in Fauske, '*Side by Side*', p. 22.

19. Diocese of Waterford, *Reports* (1932), p. 15; (1933), p. 15; Diocese of Cashel and Emly, *Sixty-Fourth Report* (1933), p. 12.

20. *IT*, 22 June 1932.

21. Bernard Hackett, CSSR (1863–1932), from Dungarvan; priest (1888), professor, St John's College, Waterford (1888–1900); joined Congregation of the Most Holy Redeemer (1904), becoming its rector, Dublin and Limerick; bishop of Waterford and Lismore (1916–32).

22. *IT*, 16 Sept. 1931; *Munster Express*, 18 Sept. 1931. James A. McCoy (*1863–1931*), representative of the greatest local landowners, with 3 sons in the Royal Navy and Indian army, was buried at the Abbey church, Ferrybank.

23. BM, Diary, 24 Oct. 1931.

24. *Irish Independent*, 3 June 1932; *Munster Express*, 10 June 1932.

25. R. B. McDowell, *Land and Learning: Two Irish Clubs* (Dublin, The Lilliput Press, 1993), p. 145.

26. McDowell, *Land and Learning*, pp. 145–7; Dublin University Club, *Rules and Regulations and List of Members* (Dublin, pr. Alex Thom, 1932). Graduates of Dublin University comprised 95% of the club's membership.

27. *IT*, 12 May 1932. Newport John Davis White had preceded Frederick as prebendary of Clonmethan in St Patrick's Cathedral.

28. 'The Supreme Good' (14 May 1934), p. 37, in FM, *Our First Loyalty*, pp. 26–37. This theme was elaborated in 'The Church's Sword' (7 July 1935), pp. 51–8, and previously expounded on 25 July 1920: FM, *Words for the Times: Christ's Call to His Disciples in Their Work and Sorrow* (Carrickfergus, Bell, 1920).

29. *IT*, 18 May 1934.

30. *IT*, 16 May 1934. The conference, planned for Lausanne, was held in Edinburgh in Aug. 1937.

31. *CIG*, lxxix (14 Sept. 1934), 574.

32. *Irish Churchman*, xxi, 30 (30 Apr. 1931), 3.

33. FM, *Spiritual Rebirth or World Revolution: Essays and Addresses* (Dublin, Church of Ireland, 1932), preface (3 Feb. 1932).

34. *CIG*, lxxvii (6 May 1932), after p. 280; FM, *Continuity, Catholicity, Witness* (Dublin, Church of Ireland, 1932).

35. FM, 'War and Peace' (13 Oct. 1932), in *The Church of Ireland, A.D. 432–1932: The Report of the Church of Ireland Conference held in Dublin, 11th.–14th. October 1932*, ed. William Bell and N. D. Emerson (Dublin, Church of Ireland, 1932), pp. 167–77.

36. *IT*, 6 June 1934.

37. *BNL*, 16 May 1931. The review by Richard Breene of St Peter's ('R.S.B.') was virtually identical to that in Breene's journal, the *Irish Churchman*, xxi, 33 (21 May 1931), 3.

38. *IT*, 20 May 1931.

39. 'Interpreting This Time' (17 Oct. 1931), p. 68, in FM, *Spiritual Rebirth*, pp. 59–69.

40. 'Continuity, Catholicity, Witness' (2 Apr. 1932), p. 11, in FM, *Some Northern Churchmen*, pp. 8–15.

41. *CIG*, lxxvii (1 July 1932), 387; *IT*, 17 May 1934. The discussion concerned J. L. Gough Meissner's article on 'The Mission of St Patrick', in the officially commissioned *History of the Church of Ireland*, ed. Walter Allison Phillips, 3 vols (London, Oxford UP, 1933–4), vol. i, pp. 77–103.

42. 'Russian Communism, German Fascism' (3 May 1933), in FM, *Some Northern Churchmen*, pp. 48–59.

43. Fauske, *'Side by Side'*, p. 37 (note 24); *The Times*, 10, 20, 25, 27, 29 Apr., 3 May 1933.

44. Sermon in Christ Church, Belfast (2 July 1933), p. 37, in FM, *Some Northern Churchmen*, pp. 36–42.

45. Introduction (27 Apr. 1934), in FM, *Some Northern Churchmen*; *CIG*, lxxix (11 May 1934), 291–2.

46. Down Clerical Society, Minute Book, 11 Oct. 1934; *CIG*, lxxix (19 Oct. 1934), 655.

47. EN to John Hilton, 30 Aug. 1977: LM, *SL*, p. 712.

48. BM, FM to EN, 5 Aug. 1931: FM Papers, CMMC.

49. BM, Diary, 3 Sept. 1931.

50. *Ibid.*, 9, 12 Sept., 13 Aug. 1931.

51. *Ibid.*, 19, 25, 29, 21, 24, 27 Sept. 1931.

52. LM to Blunt, 8 June 1934: LM, *SL*, p. 242.

53. Frederick received 82 lay votes in the preliminary contest, compared with 96 for Flewett and 106 for Bishop Holmes of Tuam. In the first ballot of the 'select list', he scored only 27 votes, as against 61 for Holmes and 96 for Flewett: *CIG*, lxxviii (13 Oct. 1933), 575–6.

12. SAVIOUR: BELFAST, 1934–1936

1. Letter signed by 6 clergy and 5 lay synodsmen, and supportive leading article, *NW*, 30 Nov. 1934. The clerical signatories included Dean Carmody of Down, Archdeacon Manning of Down, Canon Clarke, Richard Breene of St Peter's, and Archdeacon Shirley of Connor (one of the select list of candidates chosen by the synod); Milne Barbour and Judge Thompson were among the lay signatories.

2. Letter from Frederick Hatch, *NW*, 1 Dec. 1934. Frederick Hatch (1886–1954), from Hillsborough, Co. Down; deacon (1911), curate-in-charge (1927–8) and incumbent, Drumbo (1928–45), dean of Down (1945–54).

3. United Diocese, *Proceedings* (1934), pp. xxiii–xxvi. In the preliminary vote to determine a select list, when electors could support several candidates, MacNeice received 342 votes (164 clerical, 178 lay); Kerr 280 (114, 166); Quinn 187 (63, 124); and Shirley 133 (70, 63).

4. *BNL*, 12 Dec. 1934. In the 3 single-preference ballots for these 4 candidates, MacNeice's support rose from 148 through 170 to 189 clerical voters and from 170 through 191 to 240 lay voters. The total votes for the 4 candidates in these 3 ballots were as follows: MacNeice (318, 361, 429); Kerr (130, 100, 65); Quinn (111, 79, 43); and Shirley (13, 3, 0).

5. The 'correct text' appeared in *CIG*, lxxix (21 Dec. 1934), 829. According to *NW*, 12 Dec. 1934, his charge as bishop was to be 'just' rather than 'gentle'.

6. *CIG*, lxxix (14, 21 Dec. 1934), 809, 833.

7. *BNL*, 12 Dec. 1934. This issue contained 3 separate tributes to the new bishop.

8. *NW*, 12 Dec. 1934. D'Arcy had specified these qualities in his address preceding the election.

9. *Belfast Telegraph*, 12 Dec. 1934.

10. *IT*, 3 Jan. 1935.

11. 'Respice: Prospice' (6 Feb. 1935), pp. 41–2, in FM, *Our First Loyalty*, pp. 38–50; reports of enthronements in Belfast, Downpatrick, Dromore, and Lisburn, in *NW*, 7, 8, 15, 28 Feb. 1935.

12. *BNL*, 12 July 1935.

13. See appendix, Table 9.

14. Down and Connor and Dromore, Diocesan Clerical Society, Minute Book (1914–41), 14 Mar., 10 Oct. 1935, 9 Jan., 9 Mar., 11 June, 8 Oct. 1936, MS 659, RCBL.

15. *BNL*, 9, 12 Feb. 1935. The bishop was absent at the funeral of his brother-in-law, Thomas Cecil Magee, the clergyman whose first wife had been Frederick's sister Alice.

16. *BNL*, 11, 12, 13 Nov. 1935.

17. *CIG*, lxxx (6 Dec. 1935), 780.

18. Kerr to FM, 19 Mar. 1936, CMMC. D— failed to secure this elevation, ending his unspectacular career as a private chaplain to the bishop of Clogher.

19. Robert Moore Morrow (d. 1959), from Raheny, Co. Dublin; deacon (1888), chaplain, Townsend St Mission (1890–3), rector, Billy (1893–1936), curate-in-charge, Duneane (1936), incumbent, Duneane and Ballyscullion, and prebendary of Connor (1936–43).

20. BM, Diary (1936), 19 May 1936, CMMC.

21. Receipts in each calendar year between 1934 and 1941 (in £1000s) were 129 (1934), 120 (1935), 124 (1936), 134 (1937), 127 (1938), 128 (1939), 115 (1940) and 125 (1941): returns of revenue on account with RCB, in United Diocese, *Proceedings* (1935–42).

22. *BNL*, 6 Nov. 1935, 3 Nov. 1937.

23. See appendix, Table 10.

24. Return of 'Residence in Free State' in 3 years ending on 31 March, under 'Expenses', in FM, Diary (1938), FM Papers, Dep. c. 758, BLO.

25. Letter signed by Thomas M. Johnstone, FM, and John A. Walton: *IT*, 12 Jan. 1935.

26. *BNL*, 16 May 1935; *IT*, 16 May 1935; George Seaver, *John Allen Fitzgerald Gregg: Archbishop* (London, Faith Press; Dublin, Allen Figgis, 1963), pp. 176–9. Seaver pronounced that 'Gregg had saved the Church of Ireland from what would have been a perilous lapse into latitudinarianism' (p. 179).

27. *BNL*, 30 May, 5, 6 June 1935.

28. FM to F. W. Christie, 13 June 1935, FM Papers, Dep. c. 759, BLO. Frederick Christie, a bookkeeper in East Belfast, was one of Down's lay representatives to the general synod. As secretary to the Irish Church Union, he urged voters at Easter vestries to support candidates 'of evangelical principles who will make a stand against any innovation in the conduct of public worship or the introduction of objectionable ornaments': *BNL*, 11 Apr. 1936.

29. *BNL*, 6 Nov. 1935.

30. *BNL*, 1 July 1935.

31. *BNL*, 8 July 1935; 'The Church's Sword' (7 July 1935) and 'The Supreme Good' (14 May 1934), in FM, *Our First Loyalty*, pp. 51–8, 26–37.

32. FM, *Our First Loyalty*, p. 57.

33. Herbert Oswald Lindsay (1876–1968), deacon (1908), Canadian appointments

(1908–13), curate, St Thomas's, Belfast (1913–19), rector, St Batholomew's (1919–58), precentor of Connor (1953–8); DGC, Belfast (by 1936), DGC, Ireland (by 1941).

34. *BNL*, 2 July 1935.

35. Percy Marks (1874–1951), from Armagh; deacon (1900), incumbent, Ballymore (1925–47), archdeacon of Armagh (1945–7); DGC, Armagh (by 1931), GC, Armagh (by 1936), DGC, Ireland (by 1936).

36. *BNL*, 8 July 1935; see also Rutherford, 'FM', pp. 41–2.

37. Addressing Orangemen in Derriaghy, Kerr had declared that 'no decent Orangeman or Protestant should descend to disreputable stone-throwing or un-Christian revolver-shooting', Orangeism being 'primarily religious' and not 'a political body'. It seemed 'to be the regular policy of those who desire to discredit our Protestant community to excite outbreaks at times when Ulster is attracting Imperial attention. Whatever the provocation we should refrain from giving way to illegal retaliation': *NW*, 8 July 1935.

38. *BNL*, 9 July 1935.

39. O'Connor to FM, 9 July 1935, FM Papers, Dep. c. 759, BLO.

40. *BNL*, 10 July 1935.

41. *Ibid.* Edward Sullivan Murphy (1880–1945), from Stillorgan, Co. Dublin; called to Irish bar (1903), KC (1918), MP, Londonderry City (1929–39), attorney-general, NI (1937–9), Lord Justice of Appeal, NI (1939–45); Friendly Brother of St Patrick; DGM, Ireland (1934–45: name replaced by asterisks after elevation to bench); initiated, Eldon LOL 7, Belfast (1924).

42. Joseph Davison (1868–1948), Kt. (1921); pawnbroker, jeweller, and fancy goods merchant, Shankill Rd; HS, Belfast (1920–1), DL, alderman, Belfast (to 1924), senator, NI (1935–48); GM, Belfast (1922–48) and Ireland (1941–8), Imperial GM (1937–48).

43. *BNL*, 13 July 1935; see also Rutherford, 'FM', p. 42.

44. Edward Mervyn Archdale (1853–1943), 1st Bt (cr. 1928); landowner, Riversdale, Ballinamallard; Royal Navy (1866–80); HS, Fermanagh (1884), DL; minister for Agriculture and Commerce (1921–5) and Agriculture, NI (1925–33); GM, Ireland (1924–40), Imperial GM (1926–37).

45. *BNL*, 13 July 1935.

46. *Irish Independent*, 8 July 1935.

47. *Irish News*, 8 July 1935.

48. Mackenzie, admittedly a spiteful witness, surmised that Louis was hoping his scornful tone would impress his accompanying lover and illustrator, Nancy Coldstream (née Sharp): Compton Mackenzie, *My Life and Times: Octave Seven, 1931–1938* (London, Chatto and Windus, 1968), p. 206. The exchange is not mentioned in LM, *I Crossed the Minch*, ill. (pseud.) 'Nancy Sharp' (Edinburgh, Polygon, 2007; 1st edn 1938). I am grateful to John Kerrigan for this reference.

49. Terence Trevor Hamilton Verschoyle (1894–1993), MC (1918), PH.D., London University (1926), research chemist, ICI; landowner, Tullycleagh, Ballinamallard; DL (1920), HS, Fermanagh (1929): see *Passion and Prejudice: Nationalist–Unionist Conflict in Ulster in the 1930s and the Origins of the Irish Association*, ed. Paul Bew, Kenneth Darwin, and Gordon

Gillespie (Belfast, Institute of Irish Studies, 1993), p. 124 (n. 41), quoting *BNL*, 7 Jan. 1993. Verschoyle was a member of the Clogher diocesan council and a representative to the general synod in 1938.

50. Brian Barton, *Brookeborough: The Making of a Prime Minister* (Belfast, Institute of Irish Studies, 1988), pp. 78–9.

51. Verschoyle to FM, 8 July 1935, FM Papers, Dep. c. 759, BLO. Verschoyle's maverick views are confirmed by a postscript: 'I am on my way to a Friends of Russian conference.'

52. *Irish News*, 13 July 1935.

53. For an authoritative chronicle and statistical study, which ignores clerical interventions, see A. C. Hepburn, 'The Belfast Riots of 1935', in *Social History*, xv (1990), 75–96.

54. Catholics accounted for 68% of gunshot injuries, 65% of 'trivial' injuries, 86% of houses subjected to arson, and 83% of houses evacuated because of violence or intimidation: report on 'Disturbances in the City of Belfast from 12th July, 1935', with covering letter by Dawson Bates, 1 Aug. 1935, CAB/9B/236/1, PRONI. This file, used by the late Tony Hepburn but subsequently withdrawn, was released at my request in Sept. 2008.

55. Protestants comprised 63% of those arrested before 31 July, including 53% of curfew-breakers, 62% of rioters, and 75% of offenders against property: report on 'Disturbances'. Protestants comprised 68% of those brought to court by mid August, including 50% of those fined, 73% of those imprisoned, 80% of those bailed under the Public Order Act, and 85% of those awaiting trial in higher courts. Though official returns revealed that 83% of both officers and constables were Protestants, Catholics were surprisingly numerous among head constables (36%) and sergeants (29%). See 'Offences Arising out of Disturbances in Belfast – 1935' and 'Religious Composition of the Police Force' at 1 June 1935, CAB/9B/236/1.

56. *BNL*, 18 July 1935. A few days later, Kerr balanced his impassioned denunciation of the murderers of 4 local Episcopalians with a scathing attack on reprisals, attributed to 'some organisation external to Ulster. At any rate the Protestant who retaliated was acting just as the gunman desired in paralysing the city': *BNL*, 22 July 1935.

57. The third signatory was William H. Smyth, president of the Methodist Church in Ireland in 1921 and 1927: *BNL*, 19 July 1935.

58. *BNL*, 19 July 1935. Though not an Orangeman, Moody stated in his autobiography that it was 'quite certain that the Orangemen were not the aggressors': A. F. Moody, *Memories and Musings of a Moderator* (London, James Clarke, 1938), p. 47.

59. James Emmet Kirkwood Haddick (d. 1955), deacon (1911), curate in England (1911–13) and Belfast parishes (1913–17, 1920–1), curate-in-charge, Billy (1918–20), curate, St Anne's (1921–33), on general licence (1933–6), curate in charge, Kilmore (1936–8), bishop's chaplain (1936–42), diocesan curate (1938–51).

60. *BNL*, 19 July 1935.

61. *BNL*, 20 July 1935.

62. 'An Open Letter' (19 July 1935), in FM, *Our First Loyalty*, pp. 58–9.

63. 'The Way to Peace' (21 July 1935), in FM, *Our First Loyalty*, pp. 62–8; *BNL*, 22 July 1935.

64. 'The Way to Peace' and 'The Church's Sword' (7 July 1935) were published simultaneously on 27 July: *BNL*, 17, 24 July 1935.

65. Dedication (27 July 1935), in FM, *Our First Loyalty*, pp. 61–2.

66. *BNL*, 23 July 1935; FM, *Our First Loyalty*, p. 69.

67. *NW*, 20 July 1935.

68. Rutherford, 'FM', p. 44.

69. Nicholas Mansergh, *The Government of Northern Ireland: A Study in Devolution*
(London, Allen & Unwin, 1936), pp. 258–9. [JL]

70. *BNL*, 22 July 1935.

71. Canon E. H. Lewis-Crosby (Stillorgan) to FM, 29 July 1935, CMMC.

72. Montgomery to FM, 25 July 1935, with cuttings, FM Papers, Dep. c. 759, BLO;
Bew, *Passion and Prejudice*, p. 15. Hugh Maude de Fellenberg Montgomery (1870–1954), of
Blessingbourne, Fivemiletown, Co. Tyrone; CB (1918), CMG (1919), DL; retired as Major-
General, Royal Artillery (1925); member, Ulster Unionist Council; first hon. treasurer, Irish
Association (1938).

73. Bew, *Passion and Prejudice*, pp. 13–15. James Edward Geale Caulfield (1880–1954), 8th
Viscount Charlemont (succ. 1913), of Drumcairn, Stewartstown, Co. Tyrone; active in UVF;
minister of Education and leader of Senate, NI (1926–37); president, Irish Association (1939–46).

74. This may refer to an offshoot of the Ulster Protestant League, formed in 1931 to
promote preferential employment for Protestants and often blamed for sectarian violence
in 1935. At least four local so-called 'Protestant (Defence) Associations' were active in 1935:
'Protestant Associations in Belfast', CAB/9B/236/1.

75. Undated anonymous letter to FM, FM Papers, Dep. c. 759, BLO.

76. Letter to FM, 22 July 1935, FM Papers, Dep. c. 759, BLO. Rather surprisingly, the
letter ends with a (misquoted) Latin tag.

77. *BNL*, 23 Oct. 1935.

78. NI Cabinet Conclusions (4, 6 June 1935), CAB/4/343/11 and 344/16, PRONI. 'In
view of the special circumstances' and risk of disclosure during Carson's lifetime, these
minutes were recorded but not circulated. See also Gillian McIntosh, *The Force of Culture:
Unionist Identities in Northern Ireland* (Cork, UP, 1999), pp. 49–50; McIntosh, 'Symbolic
Mirrors: Commemorations of Edward Carson in the 1930s', pp. 108–9, in *Irish Historical
Studies*, xxii, 125 (2000), 93–102.

79. According to the constitution of the Church of Ireland, St Anne's should have
had 2 select vestries, whose lay members were evidently identical to those on the cathedral
board. Clerical representation on the parochial select vestry was restricted to the dean and
his curate, but all members of the cathedral chapter (including several clergy not on the
board) belonged to the cathedral select vestry.

80. Minutes of select vestry, 5 June 1935, and cathedral board, 21 Oct. 1935, in St Anne's
Cathedral Board, Minute Book (1928–42), pp. 120–2, Cathedral Archive. I am grateful to
Dean Houston McKelvey for permission to inspect this volume, and to Norman Weath-
erall for his guidance.

81. *In Memoriam: Last Honours to Ulster's Leader Lord Carson of Duncairn, Enshrined in Cathedral of St. Anne Belfast, Saturday, 26th October, 1935* (Belfast. W. and G. Baird, 1935), p. 29.

82. Louis elegantly concluded that 'it is about time someone kicked that bloody corner of the earth up the arse': LM to Blunt [19 Nov. 1935]: LM, *SL*, pp. 258–9.

83. *In Memoriam*, p. 25.

84. Francis J. McKenna (Delaware St, Belfast) to FM, 28 Oct. 1935, FM Papers, Dep. c. 759, BLO.

85. M. Williams (43, Ballygomartin Rd, Belfast) to FM, 28 Oct. 1935, CMMC. Marrable Williams (1879–1968), son of Dublin wholesale druggist; deacon (1904), curate (1907–15) and rector, St Luke's (1916–52), precentor of Connor (1931–52); 'pure mustard' (so I am informed by Norman Weatherall) when dealing with Sunday School children, whom he would leave shivering or soaking outside the hall until the appointed hour.

86. *Irish News*, 5, 10 Dec. 1935; *Telegraph*, 9 Dec. 1935; *BNL*, 9, 10 Dec. 1935; Stallworthy, *LM*, pp. 173–4. No copies of the *Lower Falls Magazine* for this period have been located.

87. *Telegraph*, 10, 12, 14 Dec. 1935.

88. In response, Williams informed his parishioners (and therefore the *Irish News*) that 'I was so grieved that my article should have been used in the Board's statement as being in some way responsible for the wretched attack on the Bishop that I sent in my resignation of the Canonry to the Bishop', only to have it refused: *Irish News*, 6 Jan. 1936. He remained on the board until 1937.

89. *BNL*, 14 Dec. 1935.

90. *Irish News*, 14 Dec. 1935.

91. Cathedral Board Minutes, 8 Nov. 1935, pp. 125–7.

92. St John Ervine, *Craigavon: Ulsterman* (London, Allen & Unwin, 1949), p. 191. William Moore (1864–1944), 1st Bt (cr. 1932); from Ballymoney, Co. Antrim; MP, N. Antrim (1899–1906), N. Armagh (1906–17); Judge, King's Bench (1917–21), Lord Justice of Appeal, NI (1921–5), Lord Chief Justice, NI (1925–37); chancellor, diocese of Down and Connor and Dromore (1921–44).

93. Cathedral Board Minutes, 13 Dec. 1935, pp. 128–31.

94. I am informed by Norman Weatherall that the erection of any permanent structure in a cathedral required a 'faculty' from the bishop. If withheld, aggrieved parties might petition the diocesan court and ultimately appeal to the general synod.

95. Letters to FM from 11 deans and Somerset Herald, mainly 16–17 Dec. 1935, FM Papers, Dep. c. 759, BLO; Cathedral Board Minutes, 5 Feb. 1936, p. 131.

96. In recent years, the lectern instead displayed 1 of the 8 volumes of *Ireland's Memorial Records, 1914–1918* (Dublin, Committee of the Irish National Memorial War Memorial, 1923). [JL]

97. Cathedral Board Minutes, 5 Feb. 1936, pp. 131–5.

98. *Ibid.*, 21 Feb. 1936, pp. 135–7; *NW*, 22 Feb. 1936.

99. Cathedral Board Minutes, 24 Apr., 29 June, 23 Oct. 1936, 4 Feb. 1937, pp. 138–45, 153.

100. *Ibid.*, 12 Nov. 1936, 4 Feb., 29 July, 21 Oct. 1937, pp. 151, 153, 167, 170.

101. Gerald Valentine Ewart (1884–1936), Major (RASC), OBE (1919), DL; director, William Ewart and Son, Ltd, flax spinners, linen manufacturers, merchants and bleachers of 17 Bedford St, Belfast. Ewart belonged to the Ulster chapter of Prince Masons (no. 6); Barbour to the Ulster and Heredom chapters (nos 6, 15); Kerr and Thompson to the Belfast chapter (no. 8); and Bates to the Province of Down chapter (no. 14): *Irish Freemason's Calendar and Directory* (Dublin, Grand Lodge of Ireland, issues for 1935–7).

102. GB, Diary, 22 Feb. 1936.

103. Judge Thompson, by contrast, had 'stood by me splendidly in all the "flag" business': FM to LM, 24 Feb. 1936, LM Papers (unlisted), Box 7, BLO.

104. FM to Craigavon, 14 Mar. 1936, with memorandum by Craigavon (typed copies), Carmody Papers, MS 529/1/48, RCBL; copy of same letter in FM's hand, CMMC.

105. W. S. Kerr to FM, 19 Mar. 1936, CMMC.

106. FM to D'Arcy, 23 Apr. 1937 (draft), FM Papers, Dep. c. 759, BLO.

107. LM, *Poems* (London, Faber, Sept. 1935) included 'Belfast', 'Valediction', and other expressions of dissatisfaction with Ulster and Ireland. Frederick observed that the poems were 'serious but then life is too. ... You were right in thinking I had not read much modern poetry. Your explanatory note was helpful': FM to LM, 16 Sept. 1935, LM Papers, Box 7, BLO.

108. FM to LM, 16 Sept. 1935. The joint letter has not been traced, but was presumably addressed to Bates as minister of Home Affairs.

109. *BNL*, 16 Sept. 1935.

110. A. F. Moody to Craigavon, 16 Sept. 1935 (with covering letter to Bates, 18 Sept.), CAB/9B/236/1.

111. *BNL*, 23 Sept. 1935.

112. Detention Orders, 24–6 Sept. 1935, HA/32/1/616, PRONI (file released, at my request, in Sept. 2008). Of those detained, no less than 7 were unemployed. On 7 Oct., the attorney-general rejected police applications for the longer-term internment of those detained, and ordered the release of all ten suspects.

113. FM to LM, 16 Sept. 1935.

114. Its second annual general meeting, at the YMCA Minor Hall, called for the application of sanctions against Italy for her invasion of Abyssinia: *BNL*, 23 Sept. 1935.

115. *BNL*, 25 Sept. 1935.

116. *BNL*, 9 Oct. 1935.

117. Moody, *Memories*, pp. 47–8.

118. *BNL*, 8 Nov. 1935.

119. John Reginald McDonald (1885–1966), son of Tyrone magistrate; deacon (1909), rector, St Matthew's (1932–51), archdeacon of Connor (1946–65); DGC, Down (1918–32), DGC, Belfast (1933–*c.*1951), DGC, Ireland (1918–58), GC, Ireland (1959–66).

120. John N. Spence, ordained (1901), Belfast Central Mission (1901–14, 1925–50), Dublin Central Mission (1914–18), chaplain, forces (1918); secretary, Methodist Church in Ireland (1937–40) and president (1941).

121. John Waddell (1878–1949), son of Presbyterian minister, Newington, Belfast;

ordained (1902), minister, Bangor (1902–14), Egremont, Liverpool (1914–20), Fisherwick, Belfast (1920–45); convener, Home Mission (1935–42), moderator (1937), clerk, Belfast presbytery (1945–9).

122. Harry C. Waddell, *John Waddell: By His Brother* (Belfast, BNL, 1949), esp. pp. 43–4.

123. *BNL*, 11 Nov. 1935.

124. Letter from Henry H. Dobbs (Monavert, Cushendall), *BNL*, 14 Nov. 1935.

125. Letters from 'A Believer' and R. D. H. (Belfast), *BNL*, 19, 18 Nov. 1935.

126. *BNL*, 2 Nov. 1935.

127. *BNL*, 6 Nov. 1935.

128. *BNL*, 29 June 1936.

129. *BNL*, 29, 30 June 1936.

130. *BNL*, 3 July 1936.

131. Hepburn maintains that poor weather was the main factor in preventing a recurrence of violence in 1936: 'The Belfast Riots', p. 94.

132. BM, Diary, 13 July 1936.

133. 'Bishop's House', at 603 Antrim Rd (between Fortwilliam Park and Fortwilliam Drive), was occupied by the government for much of the war, having lain vacant for some years after its reported sale by the diocese in 1935.

134. 5, Green Rd, Knock is the address given in FM to F. W. Christie, 13 June 1935; its recorded occupier from 1927 to 1932 was Thomas MacGregor Greer, after which it was returned in directories as 'vacant' for several years. The unflattering description of the Greers' Belfast villa in 1928, following the sale of Sea Park, is by EN to E. R. Dodds, 30 Aug. 1977: LM, *SL*, p. 716.

135. *BNL*, 26 June, 29 Oct. 1935.

136. Paul Larmour, *The Architectural Heritage of Malone and Stranmillis* (Belfast, Ulster Architectural History Society, 1991), p. 103; Denis Johnston, *Orders and Desecrations: The Life of the Playwright Denis Johnston*, ed. Rory Johnston (Dublin, The Lilliput Press, 1992), pp. 11–13. Following division into flats and then conversion into 'Aquinas House' (for Catholic female undergraduates at the Queen's University), no. 77, Malone Rd is now occupied by the Arts Council of Northern Ireland as 'MacNeice House'.

137. LM, 'Snow' (Jan. 1935), *CP*, p. 24. The association between 'Snow' and Dunarnon is asserted in Paul Muldoon's naughty poem 'History', recalling clandestine visits to Aquinas House, and more tentatively in brochures issued by the Arts Council. The true setting, so Jonathan Allison informs me, was in Birmingham.

138. LM to Blunt, 11 June [1935]: LM, *SL*, p. 254.

139. BM, Diary, 11 Jan., 24 Feb., 30 Apr. 1936.

140. *Ibid.*, 10 Feb., 14 Apr. 1936.

141. *Ibid.*, 17, 15, 19 Apr., 16 May 1936.

142. *Ibid.*, 25, 26, 29 Mar., 2 Apr. 1936.

143. Stallworthy, *LM*, pp. 171–7.

144. BM, Diary, 1–4 Feb. 1936.

145. FM to LM, 24 Feb. 1936.

146. LM to FM and BM, 25 Apr. 1936: extract in Stallworthy, *LM*, p. 181.

147. FM to Peter Montgomery, 7 July 1936, Montgomery Papers, D/627/A/2/58, PRONI; BM, Diary, 10 July 1936; Stallworthy, *LM*, p. 124 (proposed visit to Carrickfergus, 1 Aug. 1928). For Blunt's 'first real love affair' (with Montgomery), see Miranda Carter, *Anthony Blunt: His Lives* (London, Macmillan, 2001), pp. 51–2, 278; John Costello, *Mask of Treachery* (London, Collins, 1988), pp. 136, 211, 462–3; Barrie Penrose and Simon Freeman, *Conspiracy of Silence: The Secret Life of Anthony Blunt* (London, Grafton, 1987), pp. 51–2.

148. BM, Diary, 12 July 1936; *BNL*, 15 July 1936.

13. SAGE: BELFAST, 1936–1939

1. BM, Diary (1936), 16 July, 2, 5, 6 Aug. 1936, FM Papers, CMMC.

2. BM, Diary, 17, 19 Sept. 1936; record of breaking of headstone and notification of owner, 21 Jan. 1936, in Register of Perpetuities, Mount Jerome Cemetery (7875/1889): microfilm, Gilbert Library, Pearse St, Dublin; W. H. Thrift (secretary, General Cemetery Co. of Dublin) to FM, 20 Feb. 1936, FM Papers, CMMC.

3. BM, Diary, 20, 21 Sept. 1936.

4. *Ibid.*, 2 Oct., 7 Nov. 1936.

5. Stallworthy, *LM*, pp. 197, 220.

6. LM to Mary MacNeice, 10 Nov. [1936], *bis*: LM, *SL*, pp. 279, 280.

7. BM, Diary, 20, 24 Nov., 20, 26 Dec. 1936. A tabulation of 14 'tips' to 17 recipients, amounting to £2 9s. 4d., appears in the dairy under the cash account for Dec. 1936.

8. LM to Mary MacNeice, 10 Jan. [1937]: LM, *SL*, p. 290.

9. FM to LM, 16 July 1937, LM Papers (unsorted), Box 8, BLO.

10. Addressing a plenary session on 16 July, 'Mr Thomas S. Eliot, London' discussed 'The Oecumenical Nature of the Church and Its Responsibility towards the World': *The Churches Survey Their Task: The Report of the Conference at Oxford, July 1937, on Church, Community, and State*, intr. J. H. Oldham (London, Allen and Unwin, 1937), p. 284.

11. 'Rugby Football Excursion' (1938), in LM, *CP*, pp. 748–9 (recalling match played on 28 Feb. 1938).

12. Stallworthy, *LM*, pp. 220–1, 225. During periods of domestic disruption or travel, Daniel and his nurse circulated among various relatives, especially the Nicholsons in Highgate.

13. LM, *Zoo* (London, Michael Joseph, 1938), pp. 78–84.

14. LM to Eleanor Clark, 2, 8 May [1939]; LM to FM, undated: LM, *SL*, pp. 327, 328, 340–1.

15. LM, *Strings*, pp. 210–13; Stallworthy, *LM*, pp. 258–9.

16. 'The Coming of War', III (Aug.–Sept. 1939): LM, *CP*, p. 682.

17. See appendix, Table 10.

18. Draft letter from 'John F. Down', 10 July 1937, FM Papers, CMMC.

19. *BNL*, 4 Nov. 1936.

20. *BNL*, 3 Nov. 1937,

21. *CIG*, lxxxii (19 Nov., 26 Nov., 3 Dec. 1937), 752, 762, 784–5.

22. *IT*, 13 May 1938; *CIG*, lxxxiii (18 Nov. 1938), 641.

23. RCB, *Report* (for 1939), p. 29. By the end of 1941, central advances amounted to £37,886, parochial contributions to £32,934, and diocesan contributions to £11,089: RCB, *Report* (for 1941), p. 23.

24. LM to Mrs E. R. Dodds, 2 May [1937]: LM, *SL*, p. 300

25. *BNL*, 28, 29 July 1937; green admission cards for Banqueting Hall, 28 July 1937, CMMC.

26. *IT*, 9 July 1937. The event was an 'at home' at 'Cairndhu', Larne, one of the homes of the unionist grandee Sir Thomas Dixon, 2nd Bt.

27. *BNL*, 14 July 1937.

28. FM, Diary (1938), 19 Dec. 1938, FM Papers, Dep. c. 758, BLO.

29. I am grateful to Jane Leonard for this information. See also Stallworthy, *LM*, pp. 258, 267.

30. Clerical Society of Down and Connor and Dromore, Minutes of Quarterly Meetings (1914–41), 13 Jan., 14 July, 13 Oct. 1938, 12 Jan. 1939, MS 659, RCBL. He attended 5 of the 8 meetings in 1937–8, compared with every meeting (Mar. 1935–6) and 5 of 11 meetings (1939–Mar. 1942).

31. *BNL*, 2 Feb. 1938.

32. Charles Frederick D'Arcy, *The Adventures of a Bishop, a Phase of Irish Life: A Personal and Historical Narrative* (London, Hodder & Stoughton, 1934), pp. 237–8.

33. 'An Appeal to Christian Irishmen' (6 Oct. 1933), p. 23, in FM, *Our First Loyalty*, pp. 15–25; FM, *Carrickfergus*, pp. 14–15.

34. His wife's health was also an important factor: George Seaver, *John Allen Fitzgerald Gregg: Archbishop* (London, Faith Press and Dublin, Allen Figgis, 1963), pp. 216–20.

35. *IT*, 13 Apr. 1938. Forde Tichborne (1862–1940), dean of Armagh (1928–38), bishop of Ossory, Ferns, and Leighlin (1938–40), was elected bishop of Armagh *ad interim* on 1 Mar. 1938, being thereby entitled to the see vacated by the bishop subsequently elected to the primacy (or else, if the archbishop of Dublin were so elected, to the see vacated by his successor).

36. *IT*, 2 May, 1 Oct. 1938; *BNL*, 1 Oct. 1938.

37. *BNL*, 16, 17 Nov. 1938. Frederick was 1 of 3 contenders named in the former report, but not on the following day when Gregg's candidacy was reactivated. After 2 bishops elected *ad interim* for Armagh had withdrawn, the office passed to Albert Edward Hughes (1878–1954), incumbent, Christ Church, Leeson Park (1923–39), hon. sec., general synod (1934–9), bishop of Kilmore (1939–50).

38. Seaver, *Gregg*, pp. 220–2.

39. In the preliminary vote for a select list, Bishop Barton of Kilmore received 324 votes (131 clerical, 193 lay); Bishop Harvey of Cashel, 251 (111, 140); Bishop Patton of Killaloe, 64 (21, 43); and Frederick, 52 (22, 30). In the first ballot, Barton scored 255 (83, 172) and Harvey

scored 98 (45, 53), leading to a decisive victory for Barton in the third ballot, when he gained 129 of 152 clerical votes and 193 of 221 lay votes: *IT*, 8 Feb. 1939; *BNL*, 8 Feb. 1939.

40. FM to D'Arcy, 23 Apr. 1937, referring to correspondence of Mar. 1936: FM Papers, Dep. c. 759, BLO. Frederick O'Neill was replaced as moderator in June 1937 by Frederick's ally, John Waddell.

41. *BNL*, 26 Nov. 1940.

42. Diocesan Temperance Committee, Minute Book (1931–45), 5 Jan., 25 Feb. 1938, MS 651/4, RCBL.

43. Oldham, *The Churches Survey Their Task*, esp. pp. 77–86, 242–74, 297–9; *CIG*, lxxxii (23, 30 July 1937), 475–6, 490–1.

44. *The Second World Conference on Faith and Order held at Edinburgh, August 3–18, 1937*, ed. Leonard Hodgson (London, SCM Press, 1938), esp. pp. 198–9, 204, 283–302; *CIG*, lxxxii (13, 27 Aug. 1937), 520, 553.

45. *BNL*, 15 Apr. 1942.

46. Hodgson, *Second World Conference*, pp. 216, 369–72.

47. *IT*, 13 May 1938.

48. *CIG*, lxxxiii (18 Nov. 1938), 640.

49. *CIG*, lxxxvi (19 Dec. 1941), 505–6.

50. Montgomery to McNeill, 21 Dec. 1937, 6, 17 May, 2 June 1938, McNeill (Irish Association) Papers, D/2661/B/2/1, PRONI. I am grateful to the Irish Association and its president, Pauline Murphy, for permission to consult these papers.

51. (Sir) William Keith Hancock (1898–1988), then professor of History at Birmingham University (1934–44), travelled, talked and studied extensively in the Free State (but evidently not in Northern Ireland) while preparing the impressive Irish chapters in his *Survey of British Commonwealth Affairs*, vol. i, *Problems of Nationality, 1918–1936* (London, Oxford UP, 1937), ch. 3, 6 (esp. p. 392). The passage quoted on p. 382 is the opening couplet from 'Belfast' (Sept. 1931): LM, *CP*, p. 25.

52. Hancock to Montgomery, 25 Oct. 1937, 25 Jan., 26 June 1938, Montgomery (Irish Association) Papers, D/2661/C/1/H/2/44, 6, 7.

53. FM to Montgomery, 30 Nov. 1937, Montgomery Papers, D/2661/C/1/D/1/41. The reference may be to Hancock's letter of 25 Oct., concerning economic unity.

54. Montgomery to McNeill, 9 Jan. 1938, McNeill Papers, D/2661/B/2/1. Robert Mitchell Henry (1873–1950), professor of Latin (1907–38) and pro-vice-chancellor (1938–9), Queen's University, author of *The Evolution of Sinn Féin* (Dublin, Talbot Press and London, Unwin, 1920), was lukewarm in his responses to Montgomery's overtures: *Passion and Prejudice: Nationalist-Unionist Conflict in Ulster in the 1930s and the Origins of the Irish Association*, ed. Paul Bew, Kenneth Darwin, and Gordon Gillespie (Belfast, Institute of Irish Studies, 1993), pp. 16–17, 59, 121.

55. Though its creation was announced on 23 Dec. 1938, in response to a press leak, the decision in favour of 'proceeding with the project' was delayed until 3 Feb. 1939, to allow potential members to respond to a preliminary circular: Bew, *Passion and Prejudice*,

pp. 63–4; Mary A. McNeill and William A. Beers (secretaries, Irish Association), circular calling for subscriptions: McNeill Papers, D/2661/B/9/1.

56. The Irish Association, printed *List of Members, 1939* and associated documents: McNeill Papers, D/2661/B/7/1.

57. *IT*, 18 May 1937; *BNL*, 17 May 1937. David Frederick Moore (1905–78), rector, Derrykeighan (1937–76), had become DGC, Antrim by 1941 and remained so throughout his life.

58. FM, Diary, 12 July 1938.

59. *BNL*, 12 Nov. 1936.

60. FM, *Our First Loyalty*, p. 5.

61. Fred Rea, 'Protestantism in the New Ireland', p. 65, in ICF, *Looking at Ireland* (London, SCM Press, 1937), pp. 51–65. Frederick B. Rea, secretary, SCM in Ireland, entered the Methodist ministry in 1931.

62. *BNL*, 3 Nov. 1937.

63. *BNL*, 12 Nov. 1937.

64. FM, Diary, 26, 28 Sept. 1938.

65. *IT*, 1 Oct. 1938.

66. *BNL*, 12 Nov. 1938.

67. FM, Diary, 20, 31 Dec. 1938.

14. APOSTLE: BELFAST, 1939–1942

1. *BNL*, 4 Sept. 1939.

2. *BNL*, 8 Nov. 1939; FM, *On Matters relating to Church and State* (Belfast, United Diocese, 1939).

3. United Diocese, *Proceedings* (1939), p. 16. The reports of the council, though primarily referring to the previous calendar year, in fact covered events up to their completion in October.

4. *BNL*, 8 Nov. 1939. The objector was Robert Charles Ross-Lewin Ellis (b. 1906), from Spanish Point, Miltown Malbay; curate-in-charge (1932–45), then rector, Dunmurry (1945–79); father of Catherine McGuinness, president, Law Reform Commission (Republic of Ireland), retired justice, Supreme Court.

5. *IT*, 8 Nov. 1939 (leading article).

6. United Diocese, *Proceedings* (1939), pp. 15–16.

7. *CIG*, lxxxiv (10 Nov. 1939), 603.

8. *IT*, 2 Jan. 1940.

9. *BNL*, 21 May 1940.

10. *BNL*, 22, 27 May 1940.

11. United Diocese, *Proceedings* (1940), p. 15.

12. *BNL*, 6 Nov. 1940.

13. *BNL*, 8 Nov. 1939.

14. *BNL*, 13 Nov. 1939.

15. United Diocese, *Proceedings* (1940), p. 16.

16. Brian Barton, *The Blitz: Belfast in the Blitz Years* (Belfast, Blackstaff Press, 1989), pp. 150–1, 222, 226–7; Barton, *Northern Ireland in the Second World War* (Belfast, Ulster Historical Foundation, 1995), pp. 44, 49; John W. Blake, *Northern Ireland in the Second World War* (Belfast, HMSO, 1956), pp. 232–3, 238; D. A. Chart, 'Northern Ireland, 1939–1945: A Historical Survey', pp. xxxii–xxxviii, in *The Ulster Year Book: The Official Year Book of Northern Ireland, 1947* (Belfast, HMSO, 1947), pp. xv–xliii. Though most of Barton's statistics are taken from Chart *via* Blake, his estimate of deaths exceeds those previously published by 200 or more.

17. Barton, *The Blitz*, p. 222.

18. RCB, *Proceedings* (for 1940), pp. 26–30. Slightly variant figures appear in United Diocese, *Proceedings* (1942), p. 3, which noted drily that 'the work of the Church Extension Committee is of necessity now greatly limited owing to war conditions'.

19. [S. H. Reid], *The Story of Holy Trinity Church, Belfast: 1843–1941–1956* (Belfast, Howard Publications, 1956), pp. 17–18.

20. *BNL*, 19 Apr. 1941.

21. The MacNeices' contribution of £30 was soon trumped by Bishop Mageean, who (like Craigavon and the Abercorns) subscribed £100: *BNL*, 24, 26 Apr. 1941.

22. *BNL*, 8 May 1941.

23. *BNL*, 21 June 1941.

24. In Nov. 1942, the diocesan synod was told that £3795 had been received for the diocesan War Damage fund: United Diocese, *Proceedings* (1942), p. 5.

25. The amount received in the united diocese was £124,859 in 1941 and £114,978 in 1940 (the lowest return in the period 1934–41). In the diocese of Connor (including most Belfast parishes), receipts increased from £61,721 to £69,852, whereas only small increases were returned for Down and Dromore: United Diocese, *Proceedings* (1935–42).

26. Grants to 5 parishes amounting to £378 were dispersed during 1941 by an RCB committee, acting in consultation with the diocesan War Damage committee, and advances were also made of amounts claimed in properly compiled applications pending under the War Damages Act: RCB, *Report* (for 1941), pp. 26–30.

27. *BNL*, 3 Dec. 1941.

28. *CIG*, lxxxvi (12 Dec. 1941), 498.

29. Barton, *The Blitz*, pp. 147, 150, 312–15.

30. *BNL*, 22 Apr. 1941.

31. Chart, 'Northern Ireland', p. xxxiii; Blake, *Northern Ireland*, p. 233.

32. *BNL*, 22 Apr. 1941.

33. *BNL*, 8 May 1941; *CIG*, lxxxvi (12 Dec. 1941), 498.

34. LM to Eleanor Clark, 24 Sept. 1939; LM to E. R. Dodds, 6, 19, 22 Nov., 8 Dec. [1939]: LM, *SL*, pp. 356, 357, 364, 367, 372.

35. FM to LM, 19 Aug. 1940 (extract); LM to Mary MacNeice, 4 Sept. [1940]: LM, *SL*, p. 407.

36. Stallworthy, *LM*, pp. 259–62, 267, 272, 292–3, 309, 317.

37. BM, Diary (1942), 1, 5 Jan. 1942, FM Papers, Dep. c. 758, BLO.

38. BM to LM, 4 Jan. 1942, LM Papers, Box 9 (unsorted), BLO. Madre remarked that her niece Betty Percival 'must be very anxious about Arthur in Singapore' (the Japanese accepted his surrender 6 weeks later).

39. BM to LM, 25 Jan. 1942, LM Papers, Box 9.

40. BM, Diary, 30 Mar. 1942.

41. *Ibid.*, 26, 27 Jan. 2 Feb. 1942.

42. *Ibid.*, 11, 12, 18, 19 Mar., 8 Apr. 1942.

43. *Ibid.*, 9, 10, 12 Apr. 1942.

44. *Ibid.*, 14 Apr. 1942. The informant of death was William Colquhoun (Green Gables, Dunmurry), a medical graduate of Queen's University (1925).

45. *Ibid.*, 15–17 Apr. 1942.

46. *BNL*, 18 Apr. 1942. Oddly, this service is not mentioned in Beatrice's diary.

47. BM, Diary, 17 Apr. 1942; 'The Kingdom', VII: LM, *CP*, p. 247.

48. *BNL*, *NW*, and *Irish News*, 18 Apr. 1942; Stallworthy, *LM*, p. 309.

49. BM, Diary, 17–24 Apr. 1942.

50. LM to E. R. Dodds, 25 Apr. [1942]: LM, *SL*, p. 443.

51. BM, Diary, 26 May, 1 Oct. 1942.

52. Letters of administration, 22 Sept. 1942, 31 Mar. 1958, PRONI; Fauske, 'Side by Side', p. 23. After correction on 25 Nov. 1942, the net assets amounted to £4350 in Northern Ireland and £445 in Great Britain.

53. LM's personal estate was assessed for probate at £7455 gross, £4588 net: *The Times*, 20 Feb. 1965.

54. LM to Laurence Gilliam (BBC), 17 Apr. 1945: LM, *SL*, p. 454.

55. After payment of duty, BM's net personal estate of £38,000 slightly exceeded the bequest she had received from her mother in 1917. After correction on 23 Jan. 1959, it amounted to £13,358 in Northern Ireland and £24,417 in Great Britain: Probate papers, 27 Nov. 1956 (including will, 20 May 1949), PRONI. £1000 was bequeathed to Eva Greer, with legacies of £200 to 2 cousins.

56. The myocarditis was ascribed to 'Hypertension and Senility'; the informant of death was Elizabeth Nicholson, whose address was returned on the death certificate as Oakfield.

57. *Carrickfergus and Kilroot Parish Magazine* (May 1956), pp. 4, 5: copy in CMMC; same report in *CA*, 13 Apr. 1956.

58. *BNL*, 12 Apr. 1956.

59. In the third and final ballot, Elliott received 261 votes (86 clerical, 175 lay); Kerr, 200 (88, 112); Canon Hodges, 47 (27, 20); Dean King of Derry, 6 (0, 6); and Irwin, 2 (1 clerical, 1 lay): United Diocese, *Proceedings* (1942), p. xxvii; *IT*, 11, 18 June 1942. In accordance with a statute passed by the general synod in 1939, the select list was no longer elected by the diocesan synod but chosen by a board of selectors, including the entire hierarchy and representatives of other dioceses.

60. 'R. R.', possibly Richard Noel Ruttle (d. 1950), incumbent, Jordanstown (1918–50), in *IT*, 16 Apr. 1942. An obituary published in the previous issue recalled 'his great powers of organisation' in Carrickfergus' and 'untiring labours' as bishop of Down.

61. *NW*, 15 Apr. 1942. Three days later, the *NW* apologized for the last error after being chastised by 'Roamer' in *BNL*.

62. *Belfast Telegraph*, 15 Apr. 1942.

63. *Irish Independent*, 15 Apr. 1942. No obituary appeared in the *Irish Catholic*, the *Sunday Independent*, or the *Tablet*, while the *Irish Press* printed only 5 lines under the heading 'Protestant Bishop Dead': 15 Apr. 1942.

64. Gertrude Gaffney, 'I Sketch Your World', in *Irish Independent*, 17 Apr. 1942.

65. *NW* and *BNL*, 18 Apr. 1942.

66. *CIG*, lxxxvii (8 May 1942), 177.

67. GS, *Journal* (1942), p. 313.

68. *CIG*, lxxxvii (17, 24 April 1942), 139, 151. The quoted passage is from 'Auden and MacNeice: Their Last Will and Testament', in W. H. Auden and LM, *Letters from Iceland* (London, Faber, 1967; 1st edn 1937), p. 230.

69. United Diocese, *Proceedings* (1942), p. 3.

70. According to EN, however, her parents in pre-war Carrickfergus 'were on friendly terms with all kinds of people – Roman Catholics and Protestants, gentry and mill-girls': LM, *Strings*, p. 49.

71. 'Russian Communism and German Fascism' (3 May 1933), p. 56, in FM, *Northern Churchmen*, pp. 48–59; Fauske, *'Side by Side'*, p. 37 (note 24); see above, ch. 11.

72. I am grateful to Jane Leonard for her notes on a report, in the *Jewish Chronicle* (11 Nov. 1938), of the prize-giving ceremony and Shachter's speech over lunch at the Belfast Royal Academy.

73. I am again grateful to Jane Leonard for passing on recollections by Robert Sugar, who as a boy in the Millisle refugee settlement got to know Popper after his departure from the MacNeice household. See also LM to E. R. Dodds, 28 Nov. 1939: LM, *SL*, p. 371; LM, *Strings*, p. 215.

74. *CIG*, lxxxvii (24 April 1942), 151.

75. 'The Strand' (1945): LM, *CP*, p. 263.

76. LM, *Strings*, p. 255.

77. Margaret Gardiner, *A Scatter of Memories* (London, 1988), p. 119; see also Fauske, *'Side by Side'*, p. 23; Stallworthy, *LM*, p. 265.

78. *My Mother Wore a Yellow Dress*, ed. Kate Newman (Carrickfergus, Borough Council, 2008), pp. 97–8 (recollections of Maybeth Cameron, recounted by her niece June Thunder). [JL]

79. John Barry, 'The Bishop Remembered', in *Carrickfergus and District Historical Journal*, vii (1993), 47. John Barry (b. 1915), deacon (1938), curate, St Matthew's (1938–41) and St Mark's, Dundela (1941–5), rector, Dunluce (1945–9) and Hillsborough (1949–83); lecturer in Comparative Religion, Queen's University (1974–83).

15. HIS FATHER'S SON

1. Margaret Gardiner, *A Scatter of Memories* (London, Free Association Books, 1988), p. 126.

2. LM to BM [May 1927]; LM to Eleanor Clark, 21 May [1940]; LM to E. R. Dodds, 17 Nov. 1940: LM, *SL*, pp. 169, 396, 415.

3. LM to Daniel MacNeice, 30 Aug. [1952]: LM, *SL*, p. 552.

4. LM to W. H. Auden, 21 Oct. 1937: LM, 'Letters to Eliot and Auden', p. 216, in *Irish Pages* (spring–summer 2005), pp. 210–19 (first published in *New Verse* (Nov. 1937), pp. 11–12).

5. LM, *Modern Poetry: A Personal Essay* (London, Oxford UP, 1938), pp. 1, 4.

6. *Ibid.* p. 35.

7. 9 of the texts for sermons reproduced in 2 of Frederick's books were altered by the revisers. Apart from 3 cases where he adopted a third (unidentified) rendering, Frederick invariably followed the revised version: FM, *Northern Churchmen*; FM, *Our First Loyalty*.

8. LM, *Modern Poetry*, p. 38; LM, *Strings*, p. 37; 'Hymns', including lists for G. B. MacNeice, C. E. MacNeice, and 'No Name' (perhaps FM): FM Papers, Dep. c. 757, BLO.

9. LM, *Varieties of Parable* (Cambridge, UP, 1965), pp. 23, 44–7.

10. LM, *Strings*, pp. 54–5. In 1949, he stated that 'my private reading at about the age of eight was the Book of Revelation but, long before that, biblical imagery had been engrained in me': LM, 'Experiences with Images', p. 18, in *The Honest Ulsterman*, 73 (Sept. 1983), 12–23 (first published in *Orpheus*, ii (1949), ed. John Lehmann).

11. 'Childhood Memories' (2 July 1963), p. 271: LM, *Selected Prose*, pp. 267–73; cf. LM, *Strings*, p. 74.

12. 'Landscapes of Childhood and Youth' (*c*.1957), in *Strings*, p. 217.

13. 'Louis Malone', *Roundabout Way* (London, Putnam, 1932), p. 258.

14. LM, *Strings*, p. 58.

15. LM, *Zoo* (London, Michael Joseph, 1938), p. 80.

16. 'When I Was Twenty-One: 1928' (1961), pp. 223, 228–9: LM, *Selected Prose*, pp. 222–35.

17. LM, *Strings*, pp. 56, 63.

18. 'Landscapes', in LM, *Strings*, pp. 222, 216–17.

19. LM, *Strings*, pp. 111–12.

20. *Ibid.* p. 112; 'Landscapes', in *Strings*, p. 226.

21. LM, *The Poetry of W. B. Yeats* (London, Oxford UP, 1941), p. 45.

22. LM, *CP*, pp. 7–10.

23. LM, 'Under the Sugar Loaf', in *New Statesman*, lxiii (29 June 1962), 948–9.

24. LM to Eliot, 14 Sept. 1939: *Irish Pages* (2005), p. 218.

25. Entry in *Twentieth Century Authors: A Biographical Dictionary of Modern Literature* (1942 edn): LM, *Selected Prose*, pp. 71–3.

26. LM to Ellen Borden Stevenson, 21 Mar. [1953]: LM, *SL*, p. 562.

27. LM, *Zoo*, pp. 20–1.

28. Report from Information Service, London (Ulster) Office, in Cabinet Publicity Committee, Minutes, 11 Apr. 1944, CAB/9F/123/34, PRONI. See also Gillian McIntosh, *The Force of Culture: Unionist Identities in Twentieth-Century Ireland* (Cork, UP, 1999), pp. 203–4. I am grateful to Edna Longley for the latter reference.

29. Ervine to R. Gransden (Cabinet Office, Belfast), 22 Feb. 1944; E. P. Northwood (NI Government Agent, London) to Gransden, 24 Feb. 1944, CAB/9F/123/23A.

30. Northwood to F. M. Adams (Stormont Castle), 17 Aug., 27, 31 Oct., 27 Nov. 1944, CAB/9F/123/23A.

31. 'Northern Ireland and Her People' (*c.*Oct. 1944): LM, *Selected Prose*, pp. 143–53.

32. Correspondence in CAB/9F/123/23A and 34; McIntosh, *Force of Culture*, p. 205.

33. LM, *CP*, pp. 261–2.

34. *Ibid.* pp. 780–1.

35. 'Talking about Rugby', in *New Statesman*, 28 Feb. 1959: LM, *Selected Prose*, pp. 214–16.

36. LM, *CP*, p. 25.

37. 'Landscapes', in LM, *Strings*, p. 213.

38. LM, *Yeats*, pp. 82, 147, 151.

39. Review of *Mind You, I've Said Nothing!*, in *New Statesman*, 7 Nov. 1953: LM, *Selected Prose*, pp. 189–92.

40. Stallworthy, *LM*, pp. 424–5.

41. 'Prologue' (1959): LM, *CP*, p. 779.

42. 'Tree Party' (1962): LM, *CP*, p. 595.

43. This incident occurred in a Soho club in Oct. 1952. After their first meeting four years earlier, Davin divined that 'he had in mind and understanding, if not in sympathy, the uncompromising obstinacy of the I.R.A. gunman as well as that of the Orange Order': Dan Davin, *Closing Times* (London, Oxford UP, 1985; 1st edn 1975), pp. 51, 48.

44. LM, *Strings*, p. 57.

45. 'Town Gossip', in *Carrickfergus Advertiser*, 10 July 1925.

46. LM, *CP*, pp. 732, 138.

47. Frederick Richard Lindsay (1886–1972), a graduate of TCD, succeeded Powys as (joint) headmaster in 1923, serving for half a century before giving way to his son Robin. The MacNeices later became friendly with Lindsay's half-brother James, a Belfast solicitor who eventually became chancellor of the Armagh diocesan court and Chief Probate Registrar. For a sympathetic account of the family, see EN to E. R. Dodds, 30 Aug. 1977: LM, *SL*, pp. 711–12.

48. LM, *Strings*, pp. 65, 78–9.

49. 'Landscapes', in LM, *Strings*, p. 223.

50. LM, *Strings*, p. 71.

51. LM to Eleanor Clark, 20, 27 June, 16 July [1939]: LM, *SL*, pp. 343, 346, 350.

52. 'Northern Ireland and Her People': LM, *Selected Prose*, pp. 148–9.

53. LM, *CP*, p. 196; Edna Longley, *Louis MacNeice: A Study* (London, Faber, 1988), p. 80.

54. John Fellows, *The Mysteries of Freemasonry* (London, Reeves and Turner, 1877; 1st edn New York, author, 1835), p. 300. This edition incorporated British and Irish variants of

American practice. See also Albert G. Mackey, *A Lexicon of Freemasonry* (4th edn, London, Charles Griffin, 1869), another American work (by a leading Freemason) revised for British and Irish readers by Donald Campbell.

55. Rituals of Mark Master Mason and Royal Arch degrees, containing reference to St Mary's Church, Youghal, Co. Cork: undated exercise book (*c.*1930s), in private hands.

56. Fellows, *Mysteries*, p. 302. This episode does not appear in the handwritten Irish ritual.

57. The scriptural sequence of the modern RAP degree does not overlap with that of Royal Arch Masonry, though the 'travel' (travail) endured by the candidate likewise involves episodes from Exodus, notably the flight out of Egypt and return towards the Promised Land. The second part of the ritual relates mainly to the New Testament with no reference to the destruction or rebuilding of the temple: David Cargo, 'The Royal Arch Purple Degree', p. 194, in *History of the Royal Arch Purple Order* (no imprint, 1990), pp. 171–202.

58. *Autumn Journal*, II (1938): LM, *CP*, p. 104.

59. 'Débâcle' (*c.*1941): LM, CP, p. 193.

60. I am grateful to Diane Clements, director of the Library and Museum of Freemasonry, London, for establishing that LM's name was not entered in the registers of the Grand Lodge of England as a member of the Apollo University Lodge 357, Oxford, whose notable recruits included Oscar Wilde.

61. LM, *Varieties of Parable*; LM, *Astrology* (London, Bloomsbury Books, 1989; 1st edn 1964). This tongue-in-cheek pastiche refers only once to Freemasonry, when discussing Karl Anderson's *Astrology of the Old Testament* (1892): 'He also likes a rich, complicated recipe and flavors the soup with the Free Masons, the Great Pyramid, and some odd etymology' (p. 188).

62. 'Auden and MacNeice: Their Last Will and Testament' (1937), section attributed to 'WL' (Wystan and Louis): LM, *CP*, p. 735; LM, *Modern Poetry*, p. 81; LM, *W. B. Yeats*, pp. 118, 123–9.

16. EIGHT POEMS AND COMMENTARY

1. The contextual references to some extent duplicate episodes explored in earlier chapters.

2. *The Oxford Outlook*, x, 52 (May 1930): LM, *CP*, pp. 673–4, 813; Stallworthy, *LM*, p. 143.

3. William T. McKinnon, 'The Rector's Son', p. 39, in *The Honest Ulsterman*, 73 (Sept. 1983), 34–54.

4. Verse dialogue composed in late 1936 and published in *Letters from Iceland* (London, Faber, 1937): LM, *CP*, pp. 731–2.

5. Stallworthy, *LM*, pp. 171, 198–200.

6. Sir Arthur Hezlett, *The 'B' Specials: A History of the Ulster Special Constabulary* (Belfast, Mourne River Press, 1977; 1st edn 1972), p. 122 and photographs. I am grateful to Jane Leonard for identifying these vehicles by a process of deduction.

7. BM, Diary (1931), 12 Mar. 1931, CMMC; Probate Papers, 27 Nov. 1956 (including will, 20 May 1949), PRONI.

8. LM, *CP*, p. 517; Stallworthy, *LM*, pp. 420–1.

9. The *Titanic* left Southampton on 10 April 1912, pausing at Queenstown (Cobh) on 11 April before striking an iceberg off Newfoundland on 14 April: Shan F. Bullock, *Thomas Andrews: Shipbuilder* (Dublin and London, Maunsell, 1912), pp. 60–4. BM's death on 7 April was followed by a funeral service at the Church of St Nicholas and burial in Drumbeg on 11 April: *CA*, 13 Apr. 1956.

10. The programme, by Commander C. H. Lightoller, was first broadcast in 1936: *BNL*, 9 Apr. 1956.

11. Undated MSS notes in EN's hand, clearly referring to a draft of William T. McKinnon, *Apollo's Blended Dream: A Study of the Poetry of Louis MacNeice* (London, Oxford UP, 1971), in notebook entitled 'The World Call', FM Papers, Dep. c. 757, BLO.

12. Stallworthy, *LM*, p. 119; Valuation Revision Books, DED Derrylea, Co. Galway (1857–98), and Ballyasadare West, Co. Sligo (1858–1928), VOD. These record a holding in Killymongaun of 32 acres occupied by William Clisham, valued at only £2 15*s*. for land and 10*s*. for buildings, which passed to Martin Clisham (Lily's father) in 1867 and to Martin Duane in 1898. Anthony Macnice's holding of 30 acres in Lisduff, valued at £11 5*s*. for land and 15*s*. for buildings, passed to his representatives in 1893 and James McNeece in 1896. Until the Great Famine, slightly less than half of this farm had been occupied by William McNeice's father, Ferguson (see above, ch. 2).

13. Published in *The Earth Compels* (London, Faber, Apr. 1938): LM, *CP*, pp. 55–6.

14. Fran Brearton, *The Great War in Irish Poetry: W.B. Yeats to Michael Longley* (Oxford, UP, 2000), p. 127.

15. John Banville, *The Untouchable* (London, Picador, 1998; 1st edn 1997), pp. 144–5.

16. LM, *Strings*, pp. 49–50.

17. See appendix, Table 6.

18. *Ibid.*, Table 3.

19. 'Autumn Journal', XVI (1938) and 'Belfast' (Sept. 1931): LM, *CP*, pp. 138, 25.

20. 'Country Week-End', IV (*c*.1961): LM, *CP*, pp. 547–8.

21. Published in *Plant and Phantom* (London, Faber, Apr. 1941): LM, *CP*, pp. 200–1.

22. LM to Eleanor Clark, 3 Sept. 1940: LM, *SL*, p. 404.

23. LM, *Strings*, pp. 42–6, 53–5; 'Childhood Memories' (recorded 2 July 1963, broadcast 29 Sept. 1963), in LM, *Selected Prose*, pp. 267–73.

24. EN, 'Trees were Green', p. 11, in *Time was Away*, pp. 11–20.

25. Nicholson, 'Trees were Green', pp. 15, 16, 17.

26. 'Miss Craig', whose 'face was sour and die-hard Puritanical', is memorably caricatured in LM, *Strings*, pp. 41 *et seq*. (cf. Elizabeth Nicholson's corrective footnote at p. 42, suggesting of her alleged references to 'hell-fire' that 'Louis may have heard or read these elsewhere and unconsciously projected them on to his memory of her'). In 1949, LM misleadingly referred to 'calvinist alarums from our Presbyterian housekeeper': 'Experiences with Images', p. 18, in *The Honest Ulsterman*, 73 (Sept. 1983), 12–23. She appears in the MacNeices' census return for 1911 as Margaret McCready, Mother's Help, Church of Ireland, able to read and write, aged 34, unmarried, and born in Co. Armagh: microform in

NAD. She was not sufficiently 'die-hard' to sign the Women's Pledge against Home Rule on 28 Sept. 1912: see signature sheets, PRONI (on-line).

27. Published in *Springboard: Poems 1941–1944* (London, Faber, Dec. 1944): LM, *CP*, pp. 247–8.

28. Stallworthy, *LM*, pp. 309–10.

29. As McKinnon observes ('The Rector's Son', p. 53), this is presumably a (somewhat garbled) reference to the passage in which a Shunammite woman, who had recently lost her child, is asked 'Is it well with thee? is it well with thy husband? is it well with the child?' (2 Kgs. 4: 26). Though dutifully answering 'It is well', her soul remains 'vexed within her' until the the child is miraculously restored to life by Elisha.

30. Clarke also participated in a service at the Bishop's House, preceding the removal, but not, it seems, in the memorial service at St Anne's Cathedral: *BNL*, 18 Apr. 1942; BM, Diary (1942), 17 Apr. 1942, FM Papers, Dep. c. 758, BLO.

31. Report of Easter Vestry meeting in *BNL*, 20 Apr. 1903.

32. *BNL*, 25 June 1931.

33. *BNL*, 12 Dec. 1934.

34. E. R. Dodds, *Missing Persons: An Autobiography* (Oxford, Clarendon Press, 1977), p. 34; see above, ch. 5, n. 12.

35. FM, *'Death is Swallowed up in Victory': Sermon on 'The Resurrection and the Life', preached in Parish Church, Carrickfergus on Sunday, 26th April, 1925* (Carrickfergus, Printing Co., 1925), pp. 2, 6 (1 Cor. 15: 35–46).

36. Written in Achill in June or July 1945, 'The Strand' was first published in *Holes in the Sky* (London, Faber, May 1945): LM, *CP*, pp. 263–4; Stallworthy, *LM*, pp. 335–6.

37. FM, Diary of Holiday in West of Ireland in 1930, transcribed by EN, 28 Aug. 1930, CMMC.

38. LM, *CP*, pp. 261–2.

39. BM, Diary (1929), CMMC. Elizabeth and her new husband, John Nicholson, travelled from London with Louis and Mary, arriving on 1 Aug.

40. *Ibid.*, 18, 25 Aug. 1929.

41. *Ibid.*, 3, 4 Aug. 1929. Mary's lobster, unlike Beatrice's macaroni cheese, is commemorated in LM, *Strings*, p. 123.

42. Charles Cunningham Boycott (1832–97), before moving to Lough Mask near Ballinrobe as agent and leaseholder to the Earl of Erne and so earning the notoriety associated with his name, had secured a sub-lease of 2000 acres on Achill from the ICM in 1855: D. J. Hickey and J. E. Doherty, *A New Dictionary of Irish History from 1800* (Dublin, Gill and Macmillan, 2003), p. 40.

43. FM, 'Diary of Holiday', 31 Aug. 1930.

44. *Autumn Sequel* (London, Faber, Dec. 1954), Canto XXII: LM, *CP*, pp. 470–5.

45. Stallworthy, *LM*, pp. 78, 89.

46. 'Woods' (1946): LM, *CP*, pp. 271–2.

47. Published in *Solstices* (London, Faber, Mar. 1961): LM, *CP*, p. 565.

Index